GATHERED COINCIDENCE

A singular history of Sixties' pop

by
Tony Dunsbee

An M-Y Books Production
m-ybooks.co.uk

Take what you have gathered from coincidence

*To my wife Nicky,
with love and thanks for her patience and belief
in my ability to give at least this much semblance
of form and meaning to a lifetime's obsession.*

Contents

Chapter 1

The Intro ...

This may or may not turn out to be the book in my head but I'm still driven, even now in retirement, to write it by my undimmed passion for the music of the Sixties and a desire to set – no pun intended – the record straight. The *one and only* record? Well, all right then, by no means, but informed by my ambition to set down *my* record of the interweaving of the events of those tumultuous years and the impact of the music made in parallel to them, as I lived through the decade then and as I recall it now. Make no mistake, then: this is unashamedly a highly selective rather than a comprehensive account, dictated wholly by my own personal tastes and interests as they were shaped and developed by the consecutive twists and turns of the era. Such omissions as there may be, therefore, are entirely of my choosing and for which, this being so, I am unrepentant.

Yet at first sight, it's a journey not even worth attempting. Can there really be any cultural significance in critically appraising a leap of ten years that, judged by the first and last Number 1 records of the period at least, rewarded musical retrospection rather than evolution? Emile Ford and the Checkmates, in January 1960, did no more than put a rock-and-roll gloss on a vaudevillian song originally recorded in 1917[1], while in December 1969 the then still seemingly respectable Rolf Harris shamelessly plundered the style and content of rousing patriotic ballads from the Edwardian music hall, to rapturous popular acclaim. Did we all blink and miss the in-between bit?

Of course, if you remember the Sixties, so they yawningly keep saying, then you weren't there. But as one who does and was, the sadness for me is that most of the popular myths circulating in Britain today about the Sixties are perpetuated by people who weren't there; not least because many of them weren't even born then. What's worse is to find, as I have done in the course of my researches, that this state of affairs is compounded not just by false conjecture but by errors and omissions of objective fact across a range of supposedly reputable reference works. (To take a simple three at random, see how quickly *you* can find: a) the title of the Hollies' second LP, b) the title of the Merseybeats' third hit single, and c) Spencer Davis's date of birth.)

For those of us who were there as the decade unfolded, the Sixties definitely were memorable but – disappointingly for the scandal-mongers – by no means for the sensational reasons attributed to my generation by the latter-day media. Increasingly irked, therefore, by the general acceptance of the distortions of this false memory as I have grown older, I'm making my own statement about the historical significance of the music of the Sixties by writing this book.

In his intensely personal memoir of how listening to music has enriched his life, Ian Clayton, the northern broadcaster and writer, captures, seemingly effortlessly and succinctly, the essence of the quest thus:

> … we all collect records. The records then become a soundtrack to our lives. Records are about escaping, finding out, searching and planning routes. Of course for most of us the records we gather never bring us anywhere near the people who make them. Records are just 'things' that we end up hoarding. But records can be more than 'things'.[2]

This, then, is the true burden of the mystery. Pop music, as a distinctive strand of entertainment, undeniably came of age in the Sixties, becoming an industry in its own right; and while it brought variable combinations of wealth, artistic fulfilment and hedonistic pleasure to those performing, it also offered enjoyment and escapism to those who became their fans and audiences. It was, however, only for a decadent minority that that escapism was ever transmuted into grosser excesses in the garden of earthly delights.

Dominic Sandbrook rates "teenage affluence" as "the single biggest factor in explaining the spectacular development of popular music between the mid-fifties and the early sixties".[3] Thanks, so he says, to the increasing availability of cheap radios and record-players, "music was more accessible than ever before, not only played in concert halls, pubs and restaurants, but enjoyed in the privacy of the office, the living room and the teenage bedroom".[4] That in itself, though, is implicit testimony to the power of the promoters of pop music in what must now seem almost the steam age of broadcasting media.

Throughout my early childhood in the 1950s, the radio was on all day long in our house. In the week, my mother relied on the BBC's Light Programme as a constant source of mildly entertaining distraction from the tedium of her household chores; the pattern continuing through the weekends, when my father was home from work. This, then, interspersed with interludes selected by my parents from their modest collection of 78s and LPs on the radiogram, provided the musical wallpaper to my home life and from which, for me, as an only child, there was no escape. Looking back on it now, even nostalgia cannot compensate for the reality that this represented for me – as, I suspect, for many others of my post-war generation – a depressingly prematurely middle-aged introduction to so-called 'popular' music.

Although initiated little more than two months after the end of the war in Europe in 1945, as a new beginning in mass-appeal radio broadcasting, the Light Programme remained reliant for what now seems an extraordinary length of time on stalwarts intended to boost production in wartime factories, the clue being in their titles. For example, I can recollect clearly the two daily doses – morning and afternoon – of the light orchestral medley *Music While You Work* (first broadcast in 1940) and the three lunchtime editions a week of the variety show *Workers' Playtime* (first broadcast in 1941).

The theatre organ also featured prominently. There was Sandy MacPherson, resident organist at the Empire Theatre, Leicester Square, who had actually been one of the first performers when the Light Programme was launched on 29th July 1945. His theme tune was "Look For The Silver Lining" and his regular programme *The Chapel in the Valley* always struck me as a piously cheerless mix of requests and homilies, more often than not relating to distressed gentlefolk who had fallen on hard times. For light relief, by contrast, there was Reginald Dixon, resident organist at the Tower Ballroom, Blackpool, with his inescapable theme tune "I Do Like To Be Beside The Seaside".

Then there was music from the bandstand and the ballroom, from the likes of Henry Hall (he of "The Teddy Bears' Picnic"), Jack Payne, Joe Loss, Victor Sylvester and Edmundo Ros, not to mention the multiplicity of the BBC's own resident orchestras. At the coarser end of this spectrum, complete with its opening cry of "Wakey, Wake-eye!" all set to ruin your digestion on Sunday afternoons, came *The Billy Cotton Band Show*, its oompah approach to anything vaguely musical leavened only fleetingly by resident singers Alan Breeze and Kathy Kay.

If this seems grim – and I'm not making any of this up – it's because it was; and as the Fifties tried to accommodate to rock'n'roll, it didn't get much better. The iron grip of 'live' music on the BBC at the time, reinforced through the negotiating strength of the Musicians' Union representing the members of all those bands and orchestras employed directly by the Corporation, meant that air time for records – so-called 'needle time' – was at an absolute premium for years and years and years.

If you only wanted to hear records, you were pretty much restricted to the homely fare of request programmes such as *Housewives' Choice* every weekday morning or *Children's Favourites* (with 'Uncle Mac') every Saturday morning. Whilst the playlist of the former predominantly fell into what we know today as the 'easy listening' category, the latter, under Uncle Mac's custodianship, was stuck in a timewarp of excruciating novelty records from years gone by. "Sparky's Magic Piano", for example, had originally been recorded in 1947, whilst "(How Much Is) That Doggie in the Window?" by Lita Roza and "Christopher Robin At Buckingham Palace" by Petula Clark had both been released in 1953.

Far and away the leader in the field of record requests, however, was *Two-Way Family Favourites* at Sunday lunchtime. Famous for romantically connecting its principal presenters Cliff Michelmore and Jean Metcalfe, its format was a simple exchange of family messages and dedications between the UK and British forces overseas. However, it was:

> … one of the few BBC radio programmes devoted exclusively to records, so its audience was in consequence huge, going far beyond the audience at which it was aimed. It offered the 'real thing', the popular records themselves which by the late 1950s were what people wanted to hear, as against versions of the songs being played live in a studio in London.[5]

Even so, there were two obvious drawbacks to request programmes such as these. Firstly, their musical content was generally conservative, only to be expected given, as John Peel noted, that "there wasn't much popular music at the time that wasn't conservative".[6] Specifically, as he remembered:

> Glenn Miller and his Orchestra featured an awful lot, as did Doris Day, Guy Mitchell, Frankie Laine, Johnnie Ray and Winifred Atwell. Selections from *Oklahoma!*, *Carousel* and other popular musicals were also on pretty heavy rotation … [They] also featured lots of light classical stuff …[7]

And secondly, half the airtime was, of course, taken up with reading out the requests. Hence, for example, what came eventually to be an apparently generous ninety minutes' airtime for *Two-Way Family Favourites* equated to no more than forty-five minutes of actual music.

It was not until the late Fifties that anything seriously resembling a regular programme of contemporary popular music for a target audience below the age of forty struggled onto the Light Programme. *Saturday Club*, hosted by Brian Matthew, began in 1958 as the successor to *Skiffle Club*. It quickly became the listening highlight of the weekend, *the* radio programme on which up-and-coming solo artists and groups would not only perform live in the studio but also be interviewed about their current repertoire and future aspirations. In other words, it began to set the stamp of authority on the critical appreciation of pop music as a genre in its own right and to exercise its own influence on that genre. (It was, for example, the *Saturday Club* producer Jim Grant who had the vision to see the hit potential of the Shadows' "Apache" as an A-side rather than the originally intended B-side and promoted it as such.[8]) In 1959, it was supplemented by its Sunday companion *Easy Beat*, again with Brian Matthew in charge, but this was much less to my taste, since initially it tended to be heavily dependent on trad jazz and standards performed live by resident musicians such as Kenny Ball, Monty Sunshine and George Melly.

The impetus for pop music programmes on television came with the breaking of the BBC's broadcasting monopoly by the establishment of ITV in 1955. This said, however, it has to be acknowledged that from the very outset ITV sought to accommodate and contain a comfortable version of popular music within the variety show format of *Sunday Night at the London Palladium*. Originally running from 1955 to 1967, it very much projected an old-fashioned, establishment view of light entertainment, showcasing musical celebrities as 'star turns'. (It is, therefore, intensely ironic that such a staid programme should inadvertently give rise to the coining of the term 'Beat-lemania' by Fleet Street, following the Beatles' appearance on 13th October 1963 and the behaviour of their "screaming fans who made themselves very audible not only inside but outside the theatre too".[9])

One of the earliest exclusively pop shows, beginning in December 1956 and running until February 1961, was *Cool for Cats*, transmitted by ITV in 3 fifteen-minute evening slots a week and hosted by Kent Walton, who came to the show as an already established DJ on Radio Luxembourg. Kent introduced current rock'n'roll records, augmented by dance routines from the resident Dougie Squires Dancers, a lively young troupe including the still unknown Una Stubbs.

The BBC's first comparable programme was *Six-Five Special*, broadcast on Saturday evenings from February 1957 to December 1958, with the well-established DJ Pete Murray as the main host, supported by Jo Douglas. Its scheduling was not only musically significant but also represented the Saturday component of the ending of the so-called 'toddlers' truce', the hitherto strictly enforced closedown of BBC television between six and seven o'clock every evening so that children could be put to bed before adult viewing began.

Originally conceived as a magazine programme for young people, it was the musical content that came to predominate under the guiding hand of innovative producer Jack Good – a mix of skiffle, trad jazz and rock'n'roll, all performed live before a young jiving audience on the studio floor. Led by trombonist Don Lang, his Frantic Five were the resident 'band' but more colourful performances, in this black-and-white era of broadcasting, came from the likes of Lonnie Donegan, Tommy Steele and Wee Willie Harris.

However, when Jack Good switched allegiance to ITV, he sparked an early ratings war between the two channels that ran for years. Good is best remembered today as the producer of ITV's *Oh Boy!*, which ran from September 1958 to May 1959. Going out live at six on Saturday evenings from the stage of the Hackney Empire, it was "ITV's answer to the *Six-Five Special* on the BBC, and quite revolutionary in its time: non-stop rock'n'roll with a studio audience, most of them girls who screamed solidly for half an hour".[10]

Most notable for promoting Marty Wilde as a British rock star (staunchly supported by the Vernons Girls, the Dallas Boys and resident orchestra Lord

Rockingham's XI, with Cherry Wainer on the organ), amongst its other
no less significant achievements were plugging "Move It" (the "first original British rock and roll classic"[11]) and helping Cliff Richard emerge as a
rock'n'roller in his own right:

> Jack Good … worked really hard in creating an image for me: he
> went through the songs line by line telling me how to stand, how
> to look, where to look, how to curl my lip and what to do with my
> hands. Jack turned me into a front man … He didn't want an Elvis
> impersonator; what he wanted was someone who had the same
> appeal as Elvis and who would have the same impact. I couldn't see
> that I was that someone.[12]

Coming up with *Drumbeat* from April to August 1959, the BBC's mission was
clearly retaliation, as recalled by Adam Faith, who was persuaded to audition
by John Barry and whose own pop career was subsequently nurtured by the
programme:

> *Drumbeat* was going to be an all-new, fast-moving show, based
> around live artists singing the latest hits. Not terribly original – Jack
> Good had done that with *Six-Five Special* years earlier. But … all
> these TV pop shows had really taken off. Every kid in the country
> tuned in to them. If you became a teen favourite now on a show
> like *Drumbeat*, your chances of stardom were extremely good.[13]

As well as Adam Faith, other guest stars included Cliff, Anthony Newley,
Petula Clark, Billy Fury, Dickie Valentine and Paul Anka.

That same June, however, the BBC pulled a masterstroke by launching
Juke Box Jury, which quickly moved to a regular Saturday evening slot where it
ran until December 1967.[14] Masquerading as a panel game whilst shamelessly
plugging the latest pop releases, it was constructed to a very simple formula
and presided over by the urbane David Jacobs. Every week four 'celebrity'
panellists, drawn from the world of music and TV light entertainment, were
asked to comment on the excerpts of records 'played' on the juke box prominently placed on stage and to judge whether they would become 'hits' or
'misses'. As the chairman, Jacobs would acknowledge a majority vote by the
'jury' either for a 'hit' by dinging a bell, of the sort still to be found today on
hotel reception desks, or a 'miss' by sounding a klaxon, the rasp of which
most closely resembled a ratchet mechanism desperately in need of oiling.

In an element of the 'game' transposed directly from *What's My Line?*,
the presence from time to time on the set of the performer of a record under
discussion would be disclosed to the audience but not the panel. Having
delivered its 'hit' or 'miss' verdict, the 'jury' would then either be delighted
or discomfited by the artist being invited to step out on stage. Whatever the
outcome, the revelation was greeted by all concerned with the greatest hilarity

and surprise, such were the simple pleasures of television in those days.

Juke Box Jury was transmitted live before a studio audience, who became a distinguishing feature of the programme in their own right. For instance, as each new record was played, the cameras cut between shots of the panellists looking thoughtful and members of the audience looking vacant, although rowdier elements would do the 'hand jive' to the beatier numbers. There was also a selected 'jury' in the audience, armed with discs marked 'Hit' and 'Miss', to whom Jacobs would turn for a verdict in the event of a tie on the part of the celebrity panel.

In danger of getting ahead of myself here, it is nevertheless worth noting that ITV saw fit to plagiarise *Juke Box Jury* in due course in the 'Spin-a-Disc' section of its competing show *Thank Your Lucky Stars*; out of which emerged the temporary fame of Janice Nicholls from Wednesbury, with her Black Country catchphrase "Oi'll give it foive". That, however, was a development to come in the Sixties. To end the pop ratings battle of the Fifties, in September 1959 ITV brought on *Boy Meets Girls*, another Jack Good production in succession to *Oh Boy!*, with Marty Wilde and the Vernons Girls still the main attractions but now augmented by Joe Brown.

Notwithstanding these various efforts, the fledgling British pop music industry of the late Fifties was still struggling to disentangle itself from the post-war legacy of seemingly all-pervading American culture. "Whereas", says Dominic Sandbrook, "the war had left Britain tired and battered, it had invigorated American capitalism, turning it into a strident, vulgar, commercialised threat to British identity and traditions".[15] Indeed, the musical stranglehold of unadulterated Americana in Britain wasn't effectively broken until the full-scale eruption of the Beatles in 1963. Until then, as noted at the time by Michael Braun, the British press would "patriotically bemoan the fact that the top-selling records have always been made by Americans or by singers such as Cliff Richard and Billy Fury who have studied Elvis, [Frankie] Avalon, and [Paul] Anka and mastered American accent and presentation".[16]

Nevertheless, a British chart of best-selling records, equivalent to the initiative of the American *Billboard* magazine from July 1940 onwards, did not come into being until the publication, on 14th November 1952, of the first "Record Hit Parade" by the *New Musical Express* [*NME*]; an idea, albeit belated, "novel in its day because it recognised records as an important commodity in their own right".[17] Originally only a Top 12, it expanded to a Top 20 in October 1954 and Top 30 in April 1956. (Other charts proliferated over time, causing confusion and inconsistency for music historians and those with long memories alike, but I'll declare my hand here and now as a dedicated *NME* reader and chart-follower for much of the Sixties.)

The weekly revision of the chart was a heaven-sent mechanism for promoting sales of music papers and records alike. It also became a significant and keenly observed ritual for performers themselves, a measure of their worth and prospects. As Adam Faith testified:

> Everyone in the record business lived in a state of suspended animation on the day the charts were announced. The biggest weekly telephone call was the one that came over from *New Musical Express*: if you got that, you'd made it.[18]

Looking back so far, these diverse beginnings now seem fragile, primitive, even quaint – definitely of another age – and yet, against all odds, they do represent the dubious foundations on which the superstructure of the Sixties' music industry came to be built. In the opinion of the music genealogist Pete Frame, December 1959 brought a "pretty grisly" year to an end, leaving fans "waist deep in the soggy middle ground between rock'n'roll and The Beatles".[19] Against this background, then, was it any wonder that the seemingly sunlit uplands of the Sixties beckoned to the likes of me, in the hope that British pop music would finally escape the gloom of Fifties' mediocrity to come of age?

NOTES

1   By Ada Jones and Billy Murray, as cited by Warwick, Kutner & Brown, "The Complete Book of the British Charts" (Omnibus, 3rd edition, 2004), p. 420.

2   Ian Clayton, "Bringing It All Back Home" (Route, 2007), p. 14.

3   Dominic Sandbrook, "White Heat: A History of Britain in the Swinging Sixties" (Abacus, 2007), p. 102.

4   Dominic Sandbrook, op.cit., p. 103.

5   Quoted from the Light Programme pages of www.radiorewind.co.uk.

6   John Peel & Sheila Ravenscroft, "Margrave of the Marshes", (Corgi, 2006), p.66.

7   Ibid.

8   Rob Bradford, CD liner notes to *The Shadows Complete Singles As & Bs 1959-1980* (EMI, 2004).

9   Mark Lewisohn, "The Complete Beatles Chronicle" (Pyramid, 1992), p.124.

10   Cliff Richard, with Penny Junor, "My Life, My Way" (Headline Review, 2009), p.61.

11   Alwyn W. Turner, "Halfway to Paradise: The Birth of British Rock" (V&A, 2008), p.124.

12   Cliff Richard, with Penny Junor, op. cit., pp. 61-62.

13   Adam Faith, "Acts of Faith" (Bantam, 1996), p.50.

14   As testimony to the programme's early popularity, the theme tune to *Juke Box Jury* ("Hit

And Miss", by the John Barry Seven) was one of the first television themes to become a best-selling record in Britain, reaching No.18 in April 1960.

15   Dominic Sandbrook, "Never Had It So Good: A History of Britain from Suez to the Beatles" (Abacus, 2006), p.136.

16   Michael Braun, "Love Me Do: The Beatles' Progress" (Penguin, 1964), p.11.

17   Dafydd Rees, Barry Lazell & Roger Osborne, "40 Years of NME Charts" (Boxtree, 1992), p.1.

18   Adam Faith, op.cit., p.63.

19   Pete Frame, "Rock Family Trees" (Omnibus, 1993), p.57.

Chapter 2

1960

FIRST NO.1 OF THE DECADE –
"What Do You Want To Make Those Eyes At Me For?"
by Emile Ford & The Checkmates

LAST NO.1 OF THE YEAR –
"It's Now Or Never" by Elvis Presley

New Year's Day 1960 dawned on a Friday and, as it did so, in Liverpool the last of the revellers from the Cavern Club in Mathew Street were straggling home. For the cost of a ticket at 4/6d each, they had chosen to celebrate New Year's Eve with a mixture of jazz and skiffle from a line-up that included Micky Ashman's Jazz Band, the Yorkshire Jazz Band, the Dallas Jazz Band, Hank Walters with his Dusty Road Ramblers and the Swinging Blue Genes. Undoubtedly they welcomed the freshness of the early morning air and the chance to stretch their limbs after the noisome heat of the barrel-vaulted cellar, for:

> There was only dancing – the Cavern stomp – when there was
> room to move … Most people smoked and within minutes of
> opening, the Cavern could contain hundreds of sweaty bodies.
> Condensation would cover the walls and drip off the ceilings. There
> was no ventilation.[1]

Recuperating through the day, those possessed of sufficient stamina and enthusiasm could return that same night to see the Swinging Blue Genes again, this time sharing the bill with the Cy Laurie Jazz Band.[2]

By now, the Swinging Blue Genes were in their third incarnation and well-established regulars at the Cavern. Some six months after its opening, they had first played there as the Blue Genes, on 31st July 1957. (Three weeks earlier, one 15-year-old James Paul McCartney had first encountered 16-year-old John Winston Lennon, on 6th July, performing with the Quarry Men at the Woolton Parish Church fete. As it happens, the Quarry Men played the Cavern themselves on 7th August 1957, a week after the Blue Genes' debut, and again on 24th January 1958 – performances reportedly neither accomplished nor popular.[3] But it would be another three years after that until the Beatles took the stage at the Cavern for the first time, on 9th

February 1961; and when they appeared there in their first evening concert, on 21st March 1961, it would be as visiting guest group for the Blue Genes' Guest Night!)[4]

The band mixed skiffle and trad jazz, the mis-spelling of 'Blue Genes' for 'Blue Jeans' owing as much to its members' unwitting illiteracy as to a possibly sub-conscious namecheck of the American rock'n'roller, Gene Vincent – of whom more anon. According to Ray Ennis (guitar and vocals), their original aim was to "combine good quality music with a bit of fun"[5], but they inclined towards rock'n'roll as time went on. Ralph Ellis (guitar and vocals), poached by the Blue Genes in 1958 from his rival eponymous skiffle group after they went head-to-head at the Stanley Dale National Skiffle Contest[6], characterised this as a transition to a "rock'n'roll front line with a trad jazz rhythm section".[7]

It was a popular shift of emphasis with the punters, even with those initially drawn to the Cavern for its jazz. Given the prevailing cultural pref-erence for jazz at the time, however, their approach also attracted hostile reviews in the local press. On 10th January 1960, as part of Liverpool's first-ever jazz festival, they played with Acker Bilk's Paramount Jazz Band. Acker himself reportedly found them too loud and the music critic for the *Liverpool Daily Post*, Derek Jewell, damned them with equally faint praise, describing them as being "unhappily, more in line with contemporary mass-produced and mass-reflected taste – all whining words and jangling guitars".[8]

Despite these knocks, they doggedly defended their often uncomfort-able musical middle ground, whilst simultaneously playing throughout the year with a host of established stars – amongst them, Sister Rosetta Tharpe (the legendary American gospel and blues singer who accompanied herself on amplified electric guitar) and the jazz bands of Humphrey Lyttelton, Acker Bilk (again, despite his earlier reservations), Terry Lightfoot, Nat Gonella and Ray Ellington.

Nonetheless, in the end the honour of formally breaching the Cavern's barricades against acceptance of rock'n'roll fell not to the Swinging Blue Genes but to Rory Storm and the Hurricanes, the group for which a certain Richard Starkey – *aka* Ringo Starr – then played the drums. On the night of Sunday, 17th January 1960, they took on the local 'jazz brigade' by launching unannounced into a set of Jerry Lee Lewis songs. For their pains, they were shouted down by the second number and showered with pennies (then substantially weighty coins and a painful reinforcement of disapproval). To add to their woes, Ray McFall, then owner of the Cavern, docked 10 shillings from their fee as a fine for daring to play rock'n'roll.[9]

By the middle of the year, however, McFall was feeling the pinch from a significant loss on a jazz festival and the stirrings of competition from clubs in suburban Liverpool offering rock'n'roll nights. He therefore opted to promote his first 'Rock Night' at the Cavern, on Wednesday, 25th May 1960, with an entrance fee of 2/6d; the acts being Cass and the Cassanovas (later becoming the Big Three) and who else but Rory Storm and the Hurricanes. Unsurprisingly, for this event the 'jazz brigade' was ousted by a younger age-group; and very soon afterwards Rock Nights had become a runaway success.

By this time, then, the influence of American rock'n'rollers on British pop performers – current successes and hopefuls alike – was pronounced. And nobody could deny they were a mixed bag. The young John Lennon, for example, cited Elvis as supreme in determining from the outset the musical direction he wanted to take himself; but was almost equally in awe of other contemporaries of Presley such as Little Richard, Carl Perkins, Buddy Holly, Eddie Cochran, Gene Vincent, Jerry Lee Lewis and Chuck Berry. Indeed, the day of the Woolton Church fete was no less memorable for him in being the first day he sang Gene Vincent's "Be Bop A Lula" on stage than also happening to be the day he first met Paul – who, in his turn, then more than impressed John by demonstrating how he could play Eddie Cochran's "Twenty Flight Rock".

Sadly, Holly was already dead by 1960, having been killed in a plane crash en route to a tour date in Minnesota on 3rd February 1959, together with fellow performers Ritchie Valens and the Big Bopper. He had, however, toured the UK in March 1958 with the Crickets, including an appearance on *Sunday Night at the London Palladium*, and among those who went to see him live were those destined for varying degrees of imminent prominence them-selves in British pop music; such as Dave Clark, Allan Clarke, Freddy Garrity, Mick Jagger, Graham Nash, Paul McCartney and Brian Poole.[10]

Holly's extraordinary influence in Britain in his lifetime, given that he was only 22 when he died, was multi-faceted and cannot be under-estimated. As Alwyn Turner observes:

> … in his brief career he had changed the course of the music,
> and nowhere more so than in Britain. His simple guitar, bass and
> drums line-up, without sax or piano, became the norm; his Fender
> Stratocaster (a 'strangely shaped guitar', noted the *NME*) and his
> horn-rimmed glasses were passed on through Hank B. Marvin of
> the Shadows to future generations; and his experimental approach
> to writing rock songs influenced the beat boom yet to come.[11]

The body and quality of compositions he left behind him were such that his fame was sustained throughout the Sixties – in common, as we shall see later, with several other artists – by intermittent posthumous releases and re-releases of his records, together with many cover versions, which have continued down the years. In the course of the decade, noteworthy covers were to come from the Rolling Stones ("Not Fade Away"), the Beatles ("Words of Love"), the Searchers ("Listen to Me") and Peter and Gordon ("True Love Ways"). Historically, however, the most celebrated of them all, actually pre-dating Holly's death, must surely be "That'll Be The Day" by the Quarry Men. Regarded today as probably the rarest and most collectable recording of all time[12], it was cut at their own expense – 17/6d – as one side of their first record in 1958, at Phillips Sound Recording Service in Liverpool, by a line-up already including the three guitars of John Lennon, Paul McCartney and George Harrison.

Compared to Buddy Holly, the repertoires of Eddie Cochran and Gene Vincent were slight, yet both established strong reputations in their different ways amongst aspiring British musicians.

Whilst Cochran is best remembered today for three songs – "Summertime Blues" (1958), "C'mon Everybody" (1959) and "Three Steps to Heaven" (1960) – it was his performance of "Twenty Flight Rock" in 1956, in the seminal rock'n'roll film *The Girl Can't Help It*, that first caught the attention of his British fans, Paul McCartney included. Unfortunately, when he eventually came to Britain, in January 1960, he was not destined to survive the year.

After appearing on *Boy Meets Girls* on 16th January, he embarked on a lengthy tour, supported by Gene Vincent and Billy Fury, with a young Brian Bennett (then of Marty Wilde's Wildcats) providing accompaniment on drums. This included a week in March at the Empire Theatre, Liverpool, where he was seen by, amongst others, John Lennon, George Harrison and John Peel (the latter rating it as one of his "Ten Best Gigs of All Time"[13]). With the end of the tour approaching, on 17th April, he was travelling by taxi from Bristol with his girlfriend Sharon Sheeley and Vincent, when the car veered off the road and crashed in Chippenham, Wiltshire. While both Sheeley and Vincent sustained serious injury, Cochran was killed, aged 21; making "Three Steps to Heaven" his painfully apt musical epitaph on its posthumous British release in May.

Gene Vincent, then aged 25 and who broke his collarbone in the crash, was already partially disabled, following a motorcycle accident in 1955 which had permanently damaged his left leg and required him to wear a calliper. The resulting discomfort meant that when singing he had to adopt an awkward stance, with his left leg thrust out behind him at the microphone and unwittingly contributing an air of menace to his stage persona.

As with "Twenty Flight Rock", Vincent's classic hit "Be Bop A Lula" was also showcased in *The Girl Can't Help It*. The first record that Paul McCartney ever bought[14], it reached No. 16 in the *NME* Top 30 when released in Britain in the summer of 1956, its legacy set to endure long beyond its fleeting total of 3 weeks in the charts.

Three years on, "rescued", in Pete Frame's words, "from oblivion"[15] and brought to Britain in December 1959 by Jack Good to headline on *Boy Meets Girls*, Vincent allowed Good, as with Cliff Richard before him, to mould his looks for maximum performing impact, so that "by the time the star reached the television screen, he was dressed in black leather and ostentatiously dragged his damaged leg behind him"; a modern cross, to Good's eyes, between Shakespeare's Richard III and Hamlet.[16] Three months on, when John Peel saw him at the Liverpool Empire, he was firmly established as the archetypal moody rocker, looking "completely out of control … almost completely [ignoring] the audience, staring wild-eyed into the wings as though demons lurked behind the Empire's plush curtains".[17]

Prior to Cochran's death, he and Vincent had been scheduled for another Liverpool concert, at the Stadium, on 3rd May. After the car crash, Vincent flew back to America to recuperate but returned to Britain for the Stadium commitment. In these changed circumstances, the promoter, Allan Williams, decided to augment the support acts with local groups and hence Vincent became the catalyst for what went down in history as the "first ever Merseybeat rock'n'roll show"[18]; featuring Rory Storm and the Hurricanes, Bob Evans and the Five Shillings, Cass and the Cassanovas and Gerry and the Pacemakers.

Yet for the time being, at least, all this activity by over-enthusiastic lads in the north-west of England directed towards forming groups was bucking the trend of the charts nationally. Of all the best-selling singles making the Top 40 in 1960 as a whole, almost 60% were American in origin (in May and again in July the figure was as high as 65%) and well over half were by solo male artists, whereas only 14% were by groups.[19]

This said, it was a British group, Emile Ford and the Checkmates, with their revamp of "What Do You Want to Make Those Eyes at Me For?" (a song first recorded in 1917), who held the No.1 spot from before Christmas 1959 for the first four weeks of 1960. Ford also had the distinction of being the first black British-resident male performer to reach No.1 in the charts and the record, an early success as producer for the quixotic Joe Meek, sold over a million in the UK alone. Nevertheless, for those of us eagerly awaiting some sign of progression musically in the new decade, it was not a promising start, especially given some of the other chart contenders at the turn of the year.

Even allowing for the impact of the just-concluded holiday period, novelty and sentimentality had a worryingly strong foothold in the January charts. For instance, there were the Avons, with "Seven Little Girls Sitting in the Back Seat"; Max Bygraves, with "Jingle Bell Rock"; and the Beverley Sisters, with "Little Donkey"; not to mention piano medleys from Russ Conway and Winifred Atwell.

Then one step beyond even these questionable limits of popular taste, there was Tommy Steele's "Little White Bull", from his musical comedy film *Tommy the Toreador*, showing how rapidly the first hothead flush of British rock'n'roll could dissipate in the face of calculated transition to mainstream showbusiness. (For Steele, of course, this process had already begun several years earlier, with a starring role in pantomime following his chart success with his version of "Singing The Blues". As Barry Miles succinctly put it: "Exit the rock'n'roller, enter the all-round entertainer".[20]) In this frivolous farce, he starred as Tommy Tomkins, a sailor from London who ventures into bullfighting on landfall in Spain, supported by a core of familiar actors from the *Carry On* stable – including Bernard Cribbins, Sid James, Eric Sykes and Kenneth Williams.

On concurrent release was Cliff Richard's second film, *Expresso Bongo*, adapted from the successful 1958 stage musical parodying the discovery of stars like Tommy Steele in the coffee bars of Soho; with Cliff as singer Bert Rudge, manipulated into the pop persona of 'Bongo Herbert' by crooked agent Johnny Jackson (played by Laurence Harvey). Taken from the film soundtrack, both an EP and the single "A Voice in the Wilderness" gave Cliff Top 20 hits by the end of January, an early indicator of the increasingly profitable links to be exploited between the complementary cinema and music industries as the Sixties progressed.

Whilst the likes of Cliff Richard and Adam Faith may have trodden in Steele's footsteps in pursuit of wealth, aspiring to buy smart cars and houses (for "conspicuous consumption was an essential part of the glamour" of stardom [21]), for now, at least, they saw themselves – and were still being projected –as teen idols. Yet if any further proof was needed of how precarious the musical pretensions of younger performers were at this time, it came in spades at the end of March with the direct entry at No. 1 in the charts of Lonnie Donegan's "My Old Man's A Dustman". There could, after all, be no clearer sign of how much the novelty factor in records endeared itself to an older record-buying public. Described variously as a "modernised version of a traditional song sung by World War 1 troops"[22] and an "archetypal music-hall comedy song"[23], sales were boosted on release by its live performance on *Sunday Night at the London Palladium*. Catching "the popular imagination like nothing he had cut previously", on the strength of first-week sales of over a quarter of a million records it went straight to No.1; making Donegan the first British act and only the second in history, after Elvis with "Jailhouse Rock" in January 1958, to achieve this. Staying at No.1 for four weeks, total sales eventually reached over a million.

There was no doubt that the song not only had an obvious, in-your-face humour but also a raucous, irritating catchiness about it. Whilst its runaway success was nothing less than deplorable to those of us craving the emergence of new musical departures, it has to be conceded that, for its time, it proclaimed the light-hearted Donegan king of that particular genre, surpassing his previous achievement of a No.3 chart position in February 1959 with the almost equally insufferable "Does Your Chewing Gum Lose Its Flavour (On The Bedpost Overnight)?" In the long term, history has been kind to Donegan, following his death in 2002, acknowledging his broader-based jazz, skiffle and blues influences on the next generation of popular British musicians; yet it is salutary to reflect that many others would have seen these comedy diversions as his greatest achievements. At this juncture, however, he was not quite done with chart success and in June his return to more melodic roots with the ballad "I Wanna Go Home" reached No.5. Based on the traditional "The Wreck of the John B", this was a very British take on an old song that the Beach Boys were later destined to revisit in their own distinctive way in 1966, as one of the classic suite of songs constituting *Pet Sounds*.

As the year progressed, so the relentless success of best-selling novelty records continued: Tommy Steele with the pseudo-Cockney rant "What A Mouth (What A North And South)", Rolf Harris with "Tie Me Kangaroo Down Sport"[24], Peter Sellers and Sophia Loren with "Goodness Gracious Me!" (a spin-off from the film in which they both starred, *The Millionairess*, and produced by George Martin in his pre-Beatles incarnation), Charlie Drake with "Mr. Custer". Some, like Anthony Newley, even tried to breathe new hip credibility into old English folk songs such as "Strawberry Fair". Nor were American artists who should have known better immune to this money-spinning gimmickry; notably Perry Como with "Delaware", Bobby Darin with "Clementine", a precocious 16-year-old Brian Hyland with "Itsy Bitsy Teeny Weeny Yellow Polka Dot Bikini" (notwithstanding the exotic image it conjured up in the days of the one-piece swimsuit) and, at the very end of the year, even Frank Sinatra with "Ol' Macdonald". Yet stranger in its own way was the converse of these aberrations, the emergent phenomenon of the professional comedian with pretensions to be taken seriously as a balladeer, as exemplified at the height of summer by Ken Dodd with his first hit, "Love Is Like A Violin". As Dr. Johnson once famously observed: "It is not done well; but you are surprised to find it done at all".

As we have already seen, the dominant presence in the charts was that of solo male artists; and of the younger British contingent, the most consistent and successful by far were Cliff Richard and Adam Faith, both with a steady stream of hits throughout the year, including a No.1 each (Faith with "Poor Me" in March, Richard with "Please Don't Tease" in July and August). However, Richard, accompanied by the Shadows, had also taken a significant step towards international recognition, in the vanguard of what, some years later, would become known as the 'British Invasion', by embarking in

January on a six-week tour of Canada and the USA. Performing alongside American pop stars such as Frankie Avalon, Bobby Rydell and the instrumental rock group Johnny and The Hurricanes in the "Biggest Show of Stars 1960 Winter Edition", Richard was so overcome by nerves on the opening night in Montreal that he was physically sick before going on stage. Travelling through a North American midwinter was also hard and relentless:

> We went everywhere by Greyhound bus and for six weeks we spent hours and hours on the move, anything from eight to sixteen hours at a stretch, freezing cold and uncomfortable, trying desperately to sleep in our seats with nothing more than overcoats to keep us warm … a long time to be living like this …[26]

Nevertheless, it represented a landmark in taking the fight for popular music supremacy back across the Atlantic.

Back home, the rivalry between Richard and Faith was intense, to the extent that Faith prided himself on being the contrasting 'bad boy' to Richard's 'good boy' image. Taken to its extreme, he even wanted people to think "that if Cliff Richard and I were walking towards them with cut-throat razors in our hands, they'd expect Cliff to use his for a shave, and for me to use mine to slit their throats".[27]

Of the two, however, Faith was handicapped by a particularly intimidating management regime, in the person of Eve Taylor, whom he later described as a "cruel and destructive woman" who "looked and sounded like Thora Hird, and behaved like Attila the Hun".[28] With the end of the year approaching, against his better judgement Faith allowed her to dragoon him into recording the mawkish "Lonely Pup In A Christmas Shop". As he pointed out, he had had five hit records in a row and "good songs were getting harder to find"[29]; but this, he knew intuitively, was a step too far:

> Despite knowing that the song could be disastrous for me, I let myself be bullied and browbeaten by Eve into recording it.
> The song was a big hit, all right.[30] But for me, it was the beginning of the end and it nearly buried my record career. It attracted universal derision from the critics and the fans alike. It was a ridiculous, stupid thing to do, and it served me right. It was against all my instincts, and was one example of how little control I had over my singing career.[31]

Hence it came home to Faith, as many other singers before and after him, that the key to his survival in the long term was to secure as high a degree of artistic autonomy as possible. Disillusioned by this particularly galling experience and concerned, too, at the distance widening between himself and his erstwhile arranger John Barry, as Barry's own popularity grew, Faith unilaterally determined to take a new direction and set about recruiting a backing group, the Roulettes. Not only was this a move calculated to bring him more personal satisfaction but it also, of course, followed the unmissably impressive precedent set by Cliff Richard and the Shadows; a collaboration through which Richard, working notably with Bruce Welch at that time, was extending his range by actively exploring songwriting as well as performing.

Nevertheless, with the possible exception of Anthony Newley, it appeared there simply were no other young British male singers with the necessary combined strength of personality and material capable of making a consistent impact on the higher reaches of the charts in the course of the year. Artists such as Craig Douglas, Mark Wynter, Billy Fury or Marty Wilde could make only fitful showings in the hit parade, such was the strength of male solo competition from America. Even if a breakthrough could be achieved, it was often only on the back of recording cover versions of American originals and, as such, more likely than not to be short-lived; a classic case in point being that of Ricky Valance (born David Spencer, in April 1939). He has the distinction of being the first Welshman to reach the British No.1 spot, as he eventually did for the first two weeks of October with his cover of Ray Peterson's infamous 'death disc' "Tell Laura I Love Her". Having overcome much initial resistance from broadcasters to the song's morbid theme of Tommy's farewell with his dying breath to his sweetheart Laura, after a fatal crash in a stock-car race, Valance then found himself doomed to be consigned to musical history as a one-hit wonder.

Of all the transatlantic challengers, 1960 marked a watershed for Elvis Presley in particular. On completion, at the age of twenty-five, of his 2 years' service as an Army conscript with a posting in Germany, Presley famously touched down fleetingly on British soil for a refuelling stop at Prestwick Airport, Glasgow (then a US Air Force base), on the evening of 3rd March, en route for home and demob. Once out of the army and back in harness as a full-time entertainer, his manager, 'Colonel' Tom Parker, saw to it that a steady stream of product – films as well as records – ensued, although by now the musical content was increasingly softening towards balladry from the original stripped-down rock'n'roll of his early career. In effect this was the launch of a 'new' Elvis, who, as noted incredulously by rock historian Robert Palmer:

> celebrated his return to civilian life by donning a tux and singing
> a television duet with … Frank Sinatra? Apparently, Elvis (or his
> management) was out to prove that he could be as malleable as
> any of the impeccably coiffed and manicured 'teen idols' being
> manufactured to order by the corporate music business.[32]

Whether through loss of edge or not, in April, with "Stuck On You", not even Elvis could overcome the obstacle of the massive sales of "My Old Man's A Dustman", paradoxically finding himself blocked at No.2 by Lonnie

Donegan, the only other performer until then to have rivalled him with a direct entry to the British charts at No.1. By November, however, a resurgence of his popularity carried him again straight to No.1 with "It's Now Or Never", a modern reworking of the 1901 Italian ballad "O Sole Mio". Advance orders of almost half a million were rapidly followed by sales of over 750,000 in the first week of release and six weeks later it became a million-seller, staying at No.1 for an unbroken nine weeks.

Below Presley, from the late Fifties onwards, there had been a flourishing second order of male North American teen-and-twenty performers, steadily growing in number and regularly scoring hits in Britain. As well as Cliff Richard's erstwhile touring companions Frankie Avalon and Bobby Rydell, they included the likes of Neil Sedaka, Paul Anka, Jimmy Jones, and Sam Cooke. Of these, the late Cooke (killed in a shooting in Los Angeles in December 1964) stands out today as an early exponent of the genre that became soul music. Back in 1960, his British hit of the year was "Chain Gang" (reaching No.8 in October), following the lesser success in July of "Wonderful World" (only making No.27 in the *Record Retailer* chart and subsequently covered to greater effect by Herman's Hermits in April 1965); but he was outdone by Jimmy Jones, whose "Good Timin'" was No.1 for the first three weeks of July.

By way of complete contrast, Neil Sedaka was a brassily precocious singer/songwriter, already successful as a composer of hits for others and readily distinguishable by his strident delivery over his own piano accompaniment. Seeing him perform was like watching Liberace on speed. In collaboration with Howard Greenfield, Sedaka perfected the composition of "songs of neurotic love"[33], their lyrics typically interweaving the emotional insecurity of adolescence with unfulfilled yearnings of desire and sentimental speculation. The turn of the year from 1959 to 1960 brought him notable success with his smash hit "Oh! Carol". Ostensibly written in praise of his high school girlfriend Carole Klein (who later became singer/songwriter Carole King)[34], it first entered the charts in November 1959, making No.3 twice, in December and January. Coasting thereafter, his next release "Stairway To Heaven" nevertheless spent 14 weeks bouncing around the Top 30, from 2nd April to 2nd July, climbing and dipping several times in the process and peaking twice at No.12, in May and June.

For solo female singers, the early Sixties were lean years and 1960 was no exception, when they provided only 8% of Top 40 entries. While the main contenders from America were Connie Francis and Brenda Lee, and even the French *chanteuse* Edith Piaf, at the age of 44, could reach No.22 in May with "Milord", it was the beginning of the end for British artists such as Alma Cogan who had previously enjoyed a long run of chart success in the

Fifties. Against this decline of her predecessors' fortunes, the young Shirley Bassey's career, however, remained in the ascendant, the characteristically passionate intensity of her delivery elevating ballads that in others' hands would have been merely safe and unremarkable to entirely another dimension. For example, with her version of "As Long As He Needs Me" (Nancy's song from Lionel Bart's hit musical of the day *Oliver!*), she gained the No.2 slot in late October, denied the No.1 placing by Roy Orbison's "Only The Lonely".

The time for others ultimately destined to establish themselves in history as British queens of pop in the Sixties was still to come; although, at 21, Mary O'Brien had taken a decisive step nearer fame by ending her year's membership of close-harmony girl trio the Lana Sisters. In the perverse traditions of pop, the three were not sisters, of course, but two friends whom Mary had joined in response to an advertisement in *The Stage*. Despite the fact that the Lana Sisters shared Eve Taylor as their manager with Adam Faith, they have left precious little of a legacy in their own right. Yet their popularity at the time was sufficient to ensure a recording contract with Fontana and at least three television appearances; on *Six-Five Special, Drumbeat* and a Christmas *Tommy Steele Spectacular*. After twelve months of what she acknowledged had been "good tough training"[35], in early 1960 Mary elected to team up instead with her brother Tom and friend Tim Feild to form The Springfields and hence:

> ... with a catchy name and a strong identity, they embarked on a frenetic round of concerts and cabaret appearances. They were booked in at Butlin's holiday camps, and spent sixteen weeks on the road in an old Volkswagen bus. Their trademark was versatility: with folk-harmony accessibility, a collection of instruments that included piano, guitar, bongos and conga drums, and songs composed by Tom that featured words in Hebrew, German, Greek, Czech and Russian, the band could play to any audience.[36]

So it was that through this mix of the mundane and the exotic began to emerge Mary's new persona as Dusty Springfield, with the twin advantages of age and professional experience at this stage over current schoolgirls Helen Shapiro, Marianne Faithfull, Sandra Goodrich and Marie Lawrie. As for Priscilla White, who had turned 17 in May, her musical future beckoned imminently in the Liverpool clubs and coffee bars where she worked part-time as an office assistant, occasional cloakroom attendant and even waitress.

A much larger share of the Top 40 – over 13% – fell to instrumentals. At a time when songwriting in general was unimaginatively formulaic, not that far removed from the 'moon/June' romantic cliché, instrumentals

– at their best – enabled the listener to attach their own imaginative associations to danceable tunes. Where the performers displayed a high degree of technical proficiency into the bargain, admiration, if not a desire for emulation, provoked added enjoyment. In a year in which the American sounds of Duane Eddy and Johnny and The Hurricanes became commonplace, it was the Shadows who eventually prevailed over all other competition and secured the No.1 slot for six consecutive weeks from 20th August with their seminal interpretation of "Apache"; knocking Cliff Richard's "Please Don't Tease" from top place in the process. Composed by Jerry Lordan and actually recorded first by the popular guitar virtuoso Bert Weedon[37], it even included Cliff himself on bongos in the opening bars – which, in retrospect, he argued was the record's unique selling-point, to "ensure [The Shadows] were given the best possible promotion":

> … at the very beginning there is a little drum intro – I think two
> bars. Well, that was me: that was it, my contribution; but they were
> able to go to the press and say, 'Cliff Richard plays the drums in the
> opening of the record', and it had the desired effect.[38]

Be that as it may, there can be no doubting Jim Grant's judgement over Norrie Paramor's as to the merits of "Apache" over "Quatermasster's Stores", the whimsical version of the traditional Scouting and Army refrain originally favoured as the A-side.[39] For the Shadows, the tight structure and pace of "Apache", with its insistent beat, marked a quantum leap away from the tentativeness of their first instrumental release (as the Drifters) a year earlier, "Jet Black" coupled with "Driftin'", and pushed them firmly in a new – and highly profitable – direction, irrespective of their association with Cliff. Eventually selling over a million copies, the arrangement deserves recognition as a genuine departure in style to create the first two-minute wonder of the year truly of the Sixties rather than the Fifties; and it was, of course, only the first of a monumental string of hit records from the Shadows stretching out for years to come.

Leaving the technical impact of the tremelo on the music to be played aside, the physical organisation of the Shadows as a guitar band also has its deserved place in British pop history, the classic line-up of Hank Marvin (lead guitar), Bruce Welch (rhythm guitar), Jet Harris (bass guitar) and Tony Meehan (drums) laying down the blueprint for aspiring groups for the rest of the decade and beyond. This said, British male vocal groups built in this image were still struggling to get into their stride; with the exception, perhaps, of Johnny Kidd and The Pirates, who managed to take "Shakin' All Over" to No.3 in July. On stage they dressed as pirates, reputedly following an accident suffered by Kidd himself (*aka* Fred Heath), when he was forced to wear an eyepatch after being hit in the eye by a broken guitar string[40], but their musical competence was not betrayed by this nod to pantomime. Although the lyrics of "Shakin' All Over" owe as much to the old spiritual "Dem Bones" as they do to contemporary rock'n'roll, earlier songs such as "Shake, Rattle and Roll" and "Whole Lotta Shakin'[Goin' On]" had already imbued any reference to 'shakin" with clear sexual connotations. In addition, the record is an instrumental triumph, with its distinctive pizzicato riff, its hiccupping tempo and its impassioned guitar break all genuine indicators of a shift in style.[41]

Nevertheless, the greatest paradox of the year was that the most significant contribution towards the creation of a new music for the Sixties turned out to be the leaving of the country by a group who had yet to cut a record professionally. On 16th August, under an agreement between Liverpool music promoter Allan Williams and German club-owner Bruno Koschmider, the Beatles (now configured as a five-man line-up of Paul McCartney, John Lennon, George Harrison, Pete Best and Stuart Sutcliffe) left for Hamburg. They were to spend three-and-a-half months as resident band at first the Indra Club, then the Kaiserkeller, both venues in the red-light district of St. Pauli. Here endurance, versatility and inventiveness were the watchwords of their musical apprenticeship, in front of largely unsophisticated and often intimidating audiences just out for a good time – from teenagers in the early evening to over-18s after ten o'clock at night, until from two in the morning onwards they were left with the tail-enders, a rough and ready assortment of drunks and local mobsters, the latter in particular vividly remembered by John:

> All these gangsters would come in – the local Mafia. They'd send a crate of champagne on stage, imitation German champagne, and we had to drink it or they'd kill us. They'd say, 'Drink, and then do "What I'd Say".' We'd have to do this show whatever time of night. If they came in at five in the morning and we'd been playing seven hours, they'd give us a crate of champagne and we were supposed to carry on.[42]

Given the obviously disreputable nature of the club district itself, the opportunity for them to make the acquaintance of any vaguely respectable young German peers was remote – and yet one day, drawn by the music and fate, a young commercial artist called Klaus Voorman ventured into the Kaiserkeller basement and found himself intrigued by this group who "played together so well, so powerful and so funny".[43]

Voorman having conveyed his enthusiasm to friends Astrid Kirchherr and Jurgen Vollmer (both photographers), this unlikely trio of intellectuals quickly became club regulars and the Beatles' drinking companions. The closeness that developed between them was driven in large part by Astrid's infatuation with Stuart Sutcliffe, prompting her to take the earliest professional photographs of the group, at the club and various other locations around Hamburg. (These include the iconic black-and-white picture of the five early Beatles in leather jackets against the backdrop of an open-sided goods truck in a railway siding; and her trademark half-shadow portraits were prophetic precursors of the monochrome images used later for the sleeves of their second and third LPs, *With The Beatles* and *A Hard Day's Night*.) What is more, by the beginning of November Astrid and Stuart were engaged.

From October, the Beatles shared club billings at the Kaiserkeller with fellow Liverpudlians Rory Storm and The Hurricanes, through which a closer association with their drummer, Ringo, began to develop, as he spent "a lot of sitting-out time watching the Beatles and requesting songs from them".[44] Furthermore, along with fellow Hurricane Lou Walters, Ringo was invited to join John, Paul and George on 15th October, when they made another amateur recording at their own expense, of the Gershwin standard "Summertime", at the Akustik studio, the first known occasion on which the future foursome played together.[45]

Little did the Beatles appreciate, however, the peril of association with other visiting British musicians, which was destined to bring their first experience of Hamburg to an untimely end several weeks before Christmas. In a fit of pique at the time they had started, in their breaks at the Kaiserkeller, to spend (and play) with Tony Sheridan and The Jets at a newly-opened rival club, the Top Ten, Bruno Koschmider gave them a month's notice at the end of October for alleged breach of contract. At the same time, coincidentally, it came to the attention of the German police that George was under 18, meaning he could not legally be or work in the clubs after midnight, and on 21st November he was deported; as were Paul and Pete Best soon afterwards, at the end of that month, for alleged arson in respect of a minor fire at the Bambi Kino, a cinema also owned by Koschmider, where he had provided the group with makeshift lodgings. This left John and Stuart to make their own way back to England, which they did separately; John by train in mid-December and Stuart last of all, eventually flying home (with his air fare courtesy of Astrid) in late February 1961.

Despite the ragged disarray of their piecemeal retreat to Liverpool, the Beatles' time abroad had initiated both personal and professional relationships of lasting meaning for the group's future, which they would revisit and consolidate in the months ahead. And, unlikely as it must have seemed to them then, with the core of the group reunited on John's return, the best was yet to come, for they had unexpectedly been booked by Bob Wooler as a late addition to a concert bill on 27th December at the Litherland Town Hall Ballroom; where, if the music on offer was not to the crowd's taste, fighting habitually broke out on the dance floor. Since they were still virtually unknown locally, Wooler had had to press promoter Brian Kelly hard to give them an opening alongside the three existing acts of the Del Renas, the Deltones and the Searchers.[46] In Stuart Sutcliffe's continuing absence in Germany, Pete Best had secured Chas Newby as temporary stand-in on bass guitar and the rest, as Wooler's eye-witness account makes clear, is history:

> The stage at Litherland is quite high, so [the audience] were all
> looking up and I was looking down at the sea of bewildered faces.
> They hadn't seen or heard anything like it. Yet they were familiar
> with the songs because the Beatles were doing songs by Little
> Richard, Chuck Berry, and Carl Perkins. They were all familiar with
> those [songs], but it was that extra something the Beatles always
> gave to their performances and songs. And that was the beginning
> of Beatlemania.[47]

This, then, was the turning-point for the group whose ultimate destiny was to change the style, direction and influence of British pop music forever. Yet their immediate success, as Wooler evidences, lay in the originality not of their material but of their performance, their unique live interpretation of classic rock'n'roll standards which had no parallel in the contemporary commercial record charts. The critical factor was that the music they played then was instantly recognisable as music to dance to but given a new spin. Indeed, this was just as much a requirement of them from the local concert fixers in Liverpool as it had been from Bruno Koschmider in Hamburg, whose constant entreaty to them had been to 'mach shau' – to 'make show', with a view to keeping audiences engaged whilst they drank their way ever deeper into his clubs' profits.

By virtue of their time away, as well as the hard school of knocks they had endured in Germany, the Beatles found themselves out of step, in every sense, with the trend that had blossomed in their absence for aspiring groups at home to ape the Shadows:

> Every group was copying their sober, terribly neat stage dress of
> grey suits, matching ties and highly polished shoes. They did little
> dance steps, three one way and three the other. In their appearance
> as well as in their music, everything was neat, polished and
> restrained.[48]

In contrast, the Beatles "played loud and wild and looked scruffy and disorganised", creating a sound "light years away from the discreet Shadows" – a sound which "you had to run away and hide your ears from, or go as wild and ecstatic as the people producing it".[49] John Lennon, for one, was unrepentantly proud that the Beatles "played what we liked best", whilst robustly contemptuous of the fact that "everyone else was playing Cliff Richard shit".[50]

Notwithstanding the arrogance of Lennon's youth, it could not be denied in general that music of a more temperate persuasion held sway with the mass of the record-buying public throughout the year. Whether the young bloods from Liverpool and elsewhere cared for it or not, for now melodic songs, predominantly on the theme of young love and as singable as they were danceable, continued to be the best sellers. Cliff and the Shadows even pushed beyond the boundaries of the success of their singles with LP sales strong enough to secure the No.7 and No.10 positions amongst the Top Ten albums of the year, with *Cliff Sings* and *Me And My Shadows* respectively.[51] Here was a difficult but potentially lucrative extended market for their talents, in competition not so much with their British and American peers as with the film and show soundtracks beloved of adults rather than teenagers.

Just how wedded older buyers of the period could be to songs from the shows is illustrated most obviously (or painfully, depending on your point of view) by the soundtrack to *South Pacific*. First entering the album charts in November 1958, it was the top-selling LP of 1959 and then again of 1960; falling to No.3 in 1961 and No. 5 in 1962, before its four-year run in the Top Ten came, at long last, to an end.[52] (No-one then, of course, could have foreseen the ominous precedent thus set for *The Sound Of Music*, to which I shall endeavour to make as little reference as possible in the pages to come.)

The longing for escapism implicit in the phenomenally extended success of sales of *South Pacific* is, of course, in itself the clearest statement possible of the total lack of interconnection then between the music business and events in the wider world. No-one then thought to make great assumptions about popular music, to inflate it to an art form or to credit it with any specific insight into the human condition: it was there to be enjoyed at a superficial level and to turn a profit in the process.

The closest pop came to the most marginal of intrusions in current affairs in the course of the year arose from the disingenuous marketing of a now little-remembered record by the pianist Russ Conway. 1960 had begun with a 33-year-old Elizabeth the Second as Queen, in the seventh year of her reign and seven months pregnant with her third child. The new Prince, Andrew, was born on 19th February, coinciding with the release of Conway's "Royal Event". Recorded on 31st January and backed with "Rule Britannia", it had the distinction of being the last 78rpm record to be pressed and issued by EMI – and caused a minor furore when played as a new release on *Juke Box Jury*. Panellist Pete Murray, the disc jockey, was beside himself, denouncing it as being in the "worst possible taste" as a blatant attempt to cash in on the royal birth, and declared that he would refuse to play it.[53] His outrage missed the point, that the tune's crime against taste actually lay in its composition, described even by a lifelong Conway fan as "a sort of cross between 'The Dam Busters' and the *Music While You Work* theme 'Calling All Workers'".[54] In its four-week run in the charts in March, it reached no higher than No.16 and turned out, after all, to have been written originally to publicise the opening of the Theatre Royal, Lowestoft – at best a jingoistic damp squib, never to be taken seriously. And so, while the music played, the world still turned.

Even when, some twenty-five years later, he had finally imbued the record industry with a social conscience, Bob Geldof remained of the view that of itself:

> Pop music should be treated with the disrespect it deserves. If … society chooses to over-compensate some people for having the mediocre talent of being able to think up a few lines worth whistling, fine, take the money, but don't confuse the amount of money with the value of the work.[55]

In inevitable alliance with cinema, radio and television, which between them provided the means of delivery, pop was but one fledgling facet of what would grow, in the course of the Sixties, to be a whole new entertainment industry, affording diversion from the concerns of real life – which, for young people, were on the whole dull, remote and in the hands of another generation entirely.

Political direction, both at home and abroad, came from old men. Harold Macmillan, the fourth post-war Prime Minister, was 65, at the head of a Conservative government for his second term of office following a general election the previous October. Despite the country's efforts throughout the Fifties to maintain its post-imperial supremacy by a succession of protracted military operations overseas – in Malaya, Korea, Kenya, Suez, Cyprus and Oman – by 1960 the law of diminishing returns had eroded Britain's international sphere of influence severely and global attention was sharply focussed elsewhere.

As a result, for many young men, the year ended on a celebratory note of relief, as 31st December marked a critical step in the phasing-out of National Service, with the last-ever issue of call-up papers to 2,049 males aged between 18 and 26. A government review in 1957 had concluded that reliance on nuclear technology, coupled with the strategic use of a professional rapid deployment force, would better serve the nation's defence in future than the continuation of conscription.

In Trevor Royle's view, the social consequences of ending National Service were unexpectedly far-reaching, with "freedom from conscription" being a contributory factor to the "rapidly mushrooming youth culture" of the Sixties.[56] For those who had previously been required to serve, views on the experience inevitably differed. For example, Bill Perks (the future Bill

Wyman), who turned 18 in 1954, had "really enjoyed" his National Service in the Fifties in the RAF, signing on for extra service and being posted to West Germany, where he revelled in exposure to a whole host of unimagined American musical influences.[57] John Peel, just too old to avoid the cut-off birthdate, pre-empted the inevitable and applied for early call-up on leaving school, joining the Royal Artillery and becoming "that rare creature, the ex-public-schoolboy who failed to get a commission".[58] The furthest he went in eighteen months was Anglesey. Jet Harris, on the other hand, faced with the call-up in the summer of 1960, resorted to a variety of ploys to ensure success in failing his medical, including drinking "a bottle of gin the night before, which was supposed to produce similar symptoms to sugar diabetes, and [swallowing] rolled-up balls of chewing gum which would show up on the X-ray as ulcers".[59]

As the decade began, the Cold War between West and East intensified, with the world stage given over to growing confrontation between the super-powers of the USA and USSR (Union of Soviet Socialist Republics). The Soviet Premier, Nikita Kruschev, at 65, was actually two months younger than Macmillan but notoriously combative and unpredictable; while the American President (and ex-Supreme Commander of the Allied Forces in World War II), Dwight Eisenhower, 69, was entering his eighth and final year in office, to be succeeded at year-end by the much younger and more forthright John F. Kennedy.

Chided by Macmillan in his speech to its Parliament in Capetown in February, prophesying a wind of change across the African continent, the South African apartheid regime adopted an increasingly isolationist stance towards the rest of the world. Anti-government demonstrations by the black population were forcibly suppressed by arms, as in the massacre of 56 protesters in April in the black township of Sharpeville, and the African National Congress Party was banned.

In May, Nazi-hunters successfully completed a secret operation to track down and snatch Adolf Eichmann from his hiding place in Argentina, to bring him to trial in Israel for war crimes. Eichmann, responsible in the Second World War as an SS Lieutenant-Colonel for implementing the mass extermination of Jews in the concentration camps, thus came to be immor-talised as the 'man in the glass booth' (with reference to the armoured glass screen erected around the dock), prior to his eventual execution on 31st May 1962.

In the same month, covert American surveillance of Soviet military sites was exposed when Francis Gary Powers was shot down in Russian airspace in his U2 spy plane, bringing in its wake the collapse of an international summit in Paris intended to explore closer ties between East and West. Tried for espionage in July, to which he pleaded guilty, he was subsequently convicted and sentenced to 10 years' imprisonment but repatriated in February 1962, in exchange for a Soviet agent, Rudolph Abel, who had been captured by the Americans in 1957.

At home, in September Penguin Books were charged with obscenity for the proposed paperback publication of D.H. Lawrence's last novel *Lady Chatterley's Lover*, the trial opening on 20th October and concluding on 2nd November. In an age in which, for example, the state still presumed as of right, through the person of the Lord Chamberlain, to censor even the mildest of expletives in respect of stage performances, forensic discussion of the graphic descriptions of the physical encounters between Connie Chatterley and her gamekeeper lover Mellors, including the frequent repetition of explicit sexual language, was bound to excite prudery and hypocrisy on the part of the ruling classes in equal measure. Counsel for the prosecution, Mervyn Griffith-Jones QC, apparently saw nothing extraordinary in famously asking the members of the jury, in all seriousness, if the book was one they would wish their wives or servants to read and the common man finally gave him a definitive answer as to public opinion when, on 10th November, after a 'not guilty' verdict, Penguin sold its initial print run of 200,000 copies on the first day of publication. At 3/6d a time, no book before or since can have seemed such a bargain. The first cracks in the hitherto sure and certain foundations of the Establishment's cultural supremacy were beginning to show; a debunking to which the nouveau riche of pop music would eventually add their own colourful contribution as the decade got into full swing.

NOTES

1   Spencer Leigh, "The Cavern: The Most Famous Club In The World" (SAF, 2008), p.21.

2   See Spencer Leigh, op. cit., p.49.

3   See Spencer Leigh, op. cit., pp. 32 & 37.

4   See Spencer Leigh, op. cit., pp. 61 & 65.

5   Spencer Leigh, op. cit., p.39.

6   See Pete Frame, "The Beatles and Some Other Guys: Rock Family Trees of the Early Sixties" (Omnibus, 1997), p.16.

7   Spencer Leigh, op. cit., p.42.

8   Quoted in Spencer Leigh, op. cit., p.49.

9   See Spencer Leigh, op. cit., p.49.

10   See Alwyn W. Turner, op. cit., p.86.

11   Alwyn W. Turner, op. cit., p.90.

12   One copy of the 78 rpm acetate (to which the B-side was the McCartney/Harrison instrumental composition "In Spite Of All The Danger") is known to be in the possession of Paul McCartney, who purchased it privately in 1981 from John Duff Lowe, one-time pianist with the Quarry Men. The estimated opening price for its purchase today stands at £200,000. [See Ian Shirley, "The Top 200 Rarest Records: The Ultimate Collectables" in *Record Collector* No.408 (December 2012), p.90.]

13   John Peel & Sheila Ravenscroft, op. cit., p.169.

14   See "The Beatles Anthology" (Cassell, 2000), p.22.

15   Pete Frame, "Rock Family Trees" (Omnibus, 1993), p.57.

16   Alwyn W. Turner, op. cit., p.94.

17   John Peel & Sheila Ravenscroft, op. cit., pp.169-170.

18   Quoted in Spencer Leigh, "Twist and Shout: Merseybeat, The Cavern, The Star-Club and The Beatles" (Nirvana, 2004), p.39.

19   All statistics quoted from this point onwards in the text, unless otherwise credited, derive from my own analysis of the monthly Top 40 charts of UK best-selling singles collated and published on the everyHit.com website in 2009.

20   Barry Miles, "The British Invasion: The Music, The Times, The Era" (Sterling, 2009), p.41.

21   Alwyn W. Turner, op. cit., p.134.

22   By Alan Clayson in Heatley et al., "Remember The Sixties" (Green Umbrella, 2008), p.11.

23   Dafydd Rees, Barry Lazell & Roger Osborne, "40 Years of *NME* Charts" (Boxtree, 1992), p. 85.

24   Although peaking at No.7 in the UK in August 1960, it would, eventually and extraordinarily, become an even greater US hit in the summer of 1963, then reaching No.3 in the *Billboard* Top 40.

25   Pete Frame, op. cit., p.59.

26   Cliff Richard, with Penny Junor, op. cit., pp.52-53.

27   Adam Faith, op. cit., p.77.

28   Adam Faith, op. cit., p.76.

29   Adam Faith, op. cit., p.77.

30   It peaked at No.5 for 3 weeks, from 24th December 1960 to 7th January 1961 inclusive.

31   Adam Faith, op. cit., p.77.

32   Robert Palmer, "Dancing in the Street: A Rock and Roll History" (BBC, 1996), p.144.

33   Colin Larkin (ed.) et al., "The Encyclopedia of Popular Music" (Omnibus, 5th Concise Edition, 2007), p.1237.

34   Although Sedaka claimed she'd been his girlfriend, Carole King's view of history was different. To her recollection, she'd never been in a relationship with Sedaka, only on one date with him while at school. See Ken Emerson, "Always Magic in the Air: The Bomp and Brilliance of the Brill Building Era" (Fourth Estate, 2006), pp.84-85.

35   Lucy O'Brien, op. cit., p.24.

36   Lucy O'Brien, op. cit., p.26.

37   Weedon's version is markedly slower than the Shadows', a more stolid attempt to create a portrait in sound, complete with flute accompaniment.

38   Cliff Richard, with Penny Junor, op. cit., p.168.

39   Rob Bradford, op. cit.

40   See Cross, Kendall & Farren, "Encyclopedia of British Beat Groups and Solo Artists of the Sixties" (Omnibus, 1980), p.46.

41   Composition is credited to Kidd himself (*aka* Heath). The Pirates' line-up at this time was: Alan Caddy (lead guitar), Brian Gregg (bass guitar) and Clem Cattini (drums). However, lead guitarist at the recording session at Abbey Road on 13th May 1960 from which "Shakin' All Over" emerged was actually 'guest' player Joe Moretti, his playing enhanced by using his cigarette lighter as a slide. Caddy played rhythm guitar instead. [See www.johnnykidd.co.uk.]

42   John Lennon, "The Beatles Anthology" (Cassell, 2000), p.49.

43   Quoted by Hunter Davies, "The Beatles: The Authorised Biography" (Heinemann, 1968), p.88.

44   Hunter Davies, op. cit., p.86.

45   See Mark Lewisohn, "The Complete Beatles Chronicle" (Pyramid, 1992), p.23.

46   See Pritchard & Lysaght, op. cit., p.53.

47   Quoted in Pritchard & Lysaght, op. cit., pp.54-55.

48   Hunter Davies, op. cit., p.99.

49   Ibid.

50   Quoted in Hunter Davies, op. cit., pp.99-100.

51   See Sharon Mawer, "The Official UK Albums Chart - 1960" (Official UK Charts Company, 2007), at www.theofficialcharts.com.

52   See Sharon Mawer, "The Official UK Albums Chart" (Official UK Charts Company, 2007), at www.theofficialcharts.com.

53   I am indebted for these details to Bill Murden's article at www.russconway.co.uk.

54   Ibid.

55   Bob Geldof, "Is That It?" (Penguin, 1986), p. 159.

56   Trevor Royle, "The Best Years of Their Lives: The National Service Experience 1945-63" (Coronet, 1988), p.274.

57   See Bill Wyman, with Richard Havers, "Rolling With The Stones" (Dorling Kindersley, 2002), p.20.

58   John Peel & Sheila Ravenscroft, op. cit., p.145.

59   Quoted in Mike Read, "The Story of the Shadows" (Elm Tree, 1983), p.78.

Chapter 3

FIRST NO.1 OF THE YEAR –
"Poetry In Motion" by Johnny Tillotson

LAST NO.1 OF THE YEAR –
"Moon River" by Danny Williams

With a No.1 record already to their credit and its follow-up, "Man Of Mystery", still in the Top 30 ten weeks after its entry, the Shadows had suddenly become a headline act in their own right. It was to be expected, therefore, that when they toured, their personal appearances were eagerly awaited by audiences up and down the country. On the evening of Wednesday, 18th January 1961, however, their performance at the Cavern was memorable for all the wrong reasons.

Whereas local acts took the cellar club's unpredictable acoustics in their stride, essentially relying on volume to carry them through, the Shadows made their first mistake by rehearsing to an empty room in the afternoon, crucially failing to compensate for the later damping effect of a full house. Come the evening and time for their performance, some of the regular lads amongst the club's clientele went elsewhere for a drink while the Shadows were on, not finding these sharply dressed southerners at all to their taste, leaving those who stayed to be treated to the unimaginable spectacle of the country's premier group coming to further grief.

They started to play "Shadoogie", a tune that rattles along to a syncopated beat in the then prevalent boogie style as popularised by Bert Weedon but adapted for group purposes to accommodate solos for lead guitar and drums. Unhappily, as they attempted their signature sidestep and stagewalk in the restrictive confines of the Cavern, they found themselves literally wrong-footed. To his chagrin, Hank Marvin described what happened next:

> Going to the Cavern was like going back to the 2 I's[1] with the audience looking up our nostrils. Jet Harris had consumed vast quantities of alcohol and could barely stand up, let alone play. He fell forward at one point, stiff as a board and the front row caught him and pushed him back up again. I made an excuse about Jet not being well and some Scouser shouted, "He's pissed". We were

a four-piece band, and the bass and the drums were our anchor.
When the bass player is out of time and playing wrong notes, it
doesn't make things easy.[2]

In hindsight, Jet's fall from grace was symptomatic not just of personal problems but of tensions slowly building between group members which had
yet to come to a head. Yet it was one of those classic moments of farce that
instantly enter local folklore and as such could always be relied on to strike a
resonance with the Cavern crowd long after the event; even to the extent that
Paul McCartney, when the Beatles became regular performers there, mercilessly incorporated it into his act.

Brushing this momentary loss of dignity aside, in the course of a year
in which they also had to meet extensive touring and filming commitments,
the Shadows went on to rack up four more Top Ten hits: "FBI" (No.4), "The
Frightened City" (No.3), "Kon-Tiki" (No.3) and "The Savage" (No.9). The
last of these, originally titled "Witchdoctor", came from the soundtrack of
the film *The Young Ones*, in which they starred with Cliff Richard – of which
more later. In addition, their eponymous first LP became the first by a British
pop group to reach No.1 in the LP charts, ending up as the fourth best-selling
album of the year even with the opening track being the "Shadoogie" of ill
omen.[3]

It was, however, to be their one and only LP featuring Tony Meehan on
drums, as he was sacked in the autumn, on the eve of a tour with Cliff of
Australia and New Zealand, and replaced by Brian Bennett. Meehan's own
version of events was that he left the Shadows to pursue a new career with
the Decca record company in A&R management; but according to Hank, his
poor timekeeping and arrogant streak had become increasingly irritating and
he was eventually fired for failing to appear on stage at the Blackpool Opera
House, in the course of a joint six-week season there with Cliff.[4] One can see
their point: after all, a four-piece group with an absentee drummer is doomed
to be less than impressive, to say the least, lacking that fundamental bedrock
of substance and conviction at the core of its playing.

Although for the year as a whole, instrumentals only made up 7% of
Top 40 entries, just over half the previous year's figure, and despite the insid-
ious emergence behind the scenes of fault-lines within the group's structure,
still the Shadows' record sales grew impressively. Furthermore, their steadily
expanding repertoire was highly coveted and much imitated by aspiring new
groups all over the country, even including those at the Cavern; where a list
of all the songs performed there by groups in early 1961, compiled by John
Cochrane (drummer with local heroes Wump and the Werbles), contained
44 mentions of Shadows' material.[5] And however outwardly dismissive they
may have been of this style of music, neither were the Beatles immune to this
trend, for at least one fan could remember them playing "Apache" complete

with imitation Shadows' sidestep.

Such gratuitous plagiarism was not only commonplace but wide-ranging in its scope at the time, encompassing outright hero-worship at one extreme to keeping the customers satisfied at the other. As the Beatles became more firmly established in 1961 as Cavern residents, so their closest fans took an almost academic interest in their eclectic repertoire.[6] Trouble was, cover versions – or, more accurately, covers of cover versions – were the stock in trade of all the other local groups as well, so that even digging deeper into obscurity to play generally unheard American B-sides was no guarantee that your playlist would remain sacrosanct.

How, then, to steal a real march on your rivals? The Beatles' brainwave was to write their own songs and incorporate them into their act, on the unflatteringly self-deprecatory premise that no-one else would think them worth copying, a fine piece of reverse logic they soon found rewarded. "The first couple of songs we did of ours were rather laughed off," Paul said, "but a couple of girls in the audience quite liked them and would request them … For you to write it yourself was a bit plonky, and the songs obviously weren't that great, but I felt we really had to break through that barrier because if we never tried our own songs we'd just never have the confidence to continue writing."[7] Here, then, in this unassuming manner, were the first seeds sown of what would eventually flourish into a revolutionary approach to creating, performing and recording pop music in Britain; exemplified by the Beatles, above all others, in the principle of self-composition leading to self-determination of artistic direction.

For the time being, however, imitation and interpretation of others' material remained very much the bedrock of the Beatles' live act; and nowhere more so than in Hamburg, to which they returned at the beginning of April for a 13-week stint at Peter Eckhorn's Top Ten Club, "playing a staggering 503 hours on stage over 92 nights"[8] for the equivalent of £3 a day each plus free lodgings in the club's attic. By now, Stuart Sutcliffe was effectively out of the group, only having returned to Liverpool from their first German escapade for less than a month before once again setting off independently to Hamburg on 15th March, in renewed pursuit of art and love through his continuing relationship with Astrid Kirchherr. As a result, Paul found himself obliged to take over as bass guitarist, in his view the least desirable role in the line-up; and so it was at this point, to overcome the awkwardness of playing a conventional guitar left-handed, that Paul bought what became his trademark Hofner bass, with its symmetrical violin-shape body.

The musical imperatives of the Reeperbahn remained much as before, maximum volume and a pounding beat rather than subtlety or originality, hardly surprising with a majority clientele of merchant seamen aiming to be three sheets to the wind as soon as possible after making landfall. Still, renewing their acquaintance at the Top Ten with Tony Sheridan, now without a band, paid unexpected dividends when the Beatles were seen playing as his backing group in April by Alfred Schacht, director of a German music publisher. His positive feedback on their performance, to popular bandleader and record producer Bert Kaempfert, led to their inclusion in a recording session with Sheridan for the German label Polydor on 22nd June.

This first professional recording opportunity for the group, it has to be said, was less than distinguished, the credits going to 'Tony Sheridan and the Beat Brothers'. Given the year and the relative unsophistication of the intended audience in Germany, the chief issue of concern was, inevitably, the paucity of the material. The five tracks on which Sheridan took the lead, for example, included his own rock'n'roll versions of "My Bonnie Lies Over The Ocean" and "When The Saints Go Marching In" [9] (both subsequently chosen as the respective A- and B-sides of a single released in August). Although the Beatles themselves cut two other tracks, one of them was a somewhat strident and unconvincing version of the standard "Ain't She Sweet", originating from the 1920s but revamped more recently by Gene Vincent, with John on lead vocal. And whilst the second was an original composition, it was uncharacteristically an instrumental, "Cry For A Shadow" (uniquely credited amongst the Beatles' canon to Harrison and Lennon). Little could the Beatles imagine, then, that thanks to their seemingly inauspicious association with Sheridan on "My Bonnie" (reputedly selling 100,000 copies in Germany), they would come to owe a monumental change of fortune to that very record, through the curiosity it was to generate later that year in their fans and significant others back home in Liverpool.

In this year in which the Beatles still craved a favourable recording contract, the Top 40 at home continued to be dominated by solo male artists, the majority (some 60% of them) American; the perennial themes of the songs emanating from the professional composers' collectives being unreconstructed expressions of female beauty, young love, yearning, jealousy and remorse, in pretty equal measure.

January, for example, began with Johnny Tillotson at No.1, with "Poetry In Motion"[10], his ogling hymn in praise of the fluid mechanics of the perfect female body. Drooling at the sight of his girl's "lovely locomotion", her "swaying gracefully" at his side outdoes the "waves out on the ocean", making her nothing less than "a flower of devotion" – what more could an insufferable US teen male want?

This callow immaturity was then succeeded at the end of the month by the maturer but no less smug blandishments of Elvis, whose seductively low-key ballad "Are You Lonesome Tonight?"[11] took the No.1 slot for 5 weeks. Notwithstanding Elvis's international popularity, it was, on reflection, a peculiar success; not least because it was actually a reworking of an Al Jolson number from 1927.[12] With the melody played at waltz tempo, this is a record on which the majority of the lyrics are spoken rather than sung and one so obviously aimed at an older woman, addressed as 'dear' throughout, that if you didn't know better, you'd think he was singing to his mother. After all, it's not teenage angst that would readily find everyday expression through questions such as:

> Do the chairs in your parlor seem empty and bare?
> Do you gaze at your doorstep and picture me there?

The typically measured British response came from 30-year-old ex-London bus driver Terence Parsons. Renamed Matt Monro at the instigation of 'pop' pianist Winifred Atwell, his very correct but utterly passionless delivery, as a crooner in a suit, of "Portrait Of My Love"[13] amazingly still had sufficient charm to reach No.3. Like "Are You Lonesome Tonight?", it is a meringue of a song, its vapid lyrics hardly standing close scrutiny.

Awash with sweeping strings, and declaring in its opening lines that "You will never see a portrait of my love/For nobody could paint a dream", the song is based on a persistently negative image of beauty that cannot be seen, rather than (as presumably intended) an ethereal image of beauty that transcends capture in any form. Does she even exist – and if she does, do we care? Why would we, for there's no depth of feeling, nothing here remotely resembling desire in evidence or on offer? Released on Parlophone, it yet remains noteworthy for marking the start of a collaboration with an in-house record producer for EMI called George Martin, whose earlier credentials had been established in making comedy records with the likes of Peter Sellers.

More intense male emotions, however, were evident in the Everly Brothers' "Walk Right Back"[14], supplanting Elvis as No.1 in March with an altogether different take on what it means to be lonesome, a song pitched uncomfortably between self-righteousness and self-pity. From the petulance of the opening line, classic for its lack of insight, "I want you to tell me why you walked out on me", Don and Phil step briskly to the all-too singable demands of the refrain:

> Walk right back to me this minute,
> Bring your love to me, don't send it,
> I'm so lonesome every day.

Although bereft of that aching public humiliation explicit in their 1960 No.1, "Cathy's Clown"[15], any edge to this song is dissipated by the softness of the Everlys' harmonies, with production values courtesy of Nashville.[16] Those looking for feelings articulated more strongly need to turn instead to the palpable bitterness of Del Shannon's later hits of the summer, fast and furious two-minute thrashes in which he is consumed by rage and jealousy to the point of falsetto torment.

"Runaway"[17] was a phenomenal success, taking the No.1 spot twice (first for a week on 20th May then again for 3 weeks from 24th June) and ending up as the best-selling single of the year in Britain. Initially, the lyrics suggest we are once again in the familiar territory of male bewilderment:

> As I walk along, I wonder
> What went wrong with our love,
> A love that was so strong.

But suddenly the darker side of this failed relationship comes to the fore, as it emerges the girl is on the run; leaving the man wondering "why – why- why – why - why she ran away" and "where she will stay/My little runaway – run – run- run- run - runaway". As the song ends on this repeated refrain, pursuit and retribution are unspoken yet distinct possibilities.

The follow-up, "Hats Off To Larry"[18], reaching No.8 in October, saw Shannon deeper into gratification through revenge. Once he had "a pretty girl/Her name it doesn't matter", who had the audacity to leave him for another, the Larry of the title. But now it's "Hats off to Larry" for casting her aside, playing her at her own game. Magnanimously, she can come back but only on the strict understanding that because she "laughed at me when we were through", first it's her turn to "cry – cry – cry/Now that Larry's said goodbye to you".

With Elvis posturing as a latter-day Valentino with another direct entry at No.1 in May, "Surrender", the image of the domineering male appeared to have a stranglehold on the higher chart positions for much of the year. Yet it did not pass entirely unchallenged. In mid-February, for instance, the Shirelles entered the charts at No.22 with "Will You Love Me Tomorrow?".[19] Written by Gerry Goffin and Carole King, and already distinguished as the first No.1 hit in America achieved by an all-black girl group, it enjoyed a 12-week run in the British Top 30 altogether, with a highest position of No.3 in March.

Even though ironically, to English ears, it contains echoes of the lament of the wronged maiden in the traditional folksong "Early One Morning", the song was way ahead of its time for modern music in its forthright exploration of the terms on which a girl consents to a sexual relationship with her boyfriend; especially given the prevalence then of judgemental morality and remembering that there still remained sufficient popular currency in the scandal of extra-marital sex five years on for Roy C to have a hit with a song about a "Shotgun Wedding". It is not about unconditional surrender, not about being swept away in the heat of the moment, but about facing up to and accepting mutual responsibility:

> Is this a lasting treasure
> Or just a moment's pleasure?
> Can I believe the magic of your sighs?
> Will you still love me tomorrow?

And Gerry Goffin's lyrics came from the heart, since he and Carole King had found themselves marrying young as a consequence of unexpected pregnancy.[20] Hardly surprising, therefore, that the song ends plaintively with a final request for reassurance and commitment:

> So tell me now, and I won't ask again
> Will you still love me tomorrow?

Still very much in the minority, nevertheless individual female singers were also capable of strong sales. Of the more conventional established artists, Petula Clark's success throughout the year was particularly notable. After a lengthy absence from the charts, she returned in January with her version of "Sailor"[21], which reached No.2 for five consecutive weeks in February and March and trounced her rival, wartime Forces sweetheart Anne Shelton, in the course of a total ten weeks in the Top 40. Then in July she embarked upon a further eleven-week run with "Romeo", making its highest position at No.4, and rounded off the year in December with "My Friend The Sea", which reached No.11 over eight weeks ending in late January 1962.

It was, however, more than an extraordinary year for newcomer London schoolgirl Helen Shapiro, who, at the age of 14, made her debut in April with the precociously outspoken "Don't Treat Me Like A Child". In the Top 40 for three months, it peaked at No.5 in May but was then swiftly followed by two No.1 records in succession; "You Don't Know" and "Walking Back To Happiness". As a result, for more than eight months she was never out of the charts. Obviously intended to complement a voice unusually strong and deep for a girl of her age, neither the orchestral nor choral arrangements of these songs could remotely be described as subtle; yet clearly these big, brash, bouncy numbers struck a chord with a particular segment of the record-buying public. The promotion of her youth definitely played a significant part in the equation, too, bringing echoes of the attention lavished a few years earlier, in 1957, on the 13-year-old Laurie London with his first-time hit "He's Got The Whole World In His Hands".[22] Perhaps most closely seen as British competition for an artist like Brenda Lee, Helen Shapiro undoubtedly peaked early but her impact in both the short- and mid-term should not be underestimated, given that by February 1963 she could still be seriously marketed as the headliner for a concert tour introducing the Beatles as a support act.[23]

By contrast, having now thrown her lot in with the Springfields, Dusty's early recording career was following a very different path in 1961, as Tom

Springfield plundered traditional American and continental sources for his composing inspiration. At the end of April, they recorded and issued their first single, "Dear John", a reworking of the American Civil War song "Marching Through Georgia" to accommodate a romantic theme, complete with banjo-picking accompaniment and mid-Atlantic intonation. It disappeared without trace. Their second record, "Breakaway", however, brought them into the charts for five weeks from 16th September and a top position of No.23. To conclude the year, a shorter chart-run of three weeks followed in December, with "Bambino", a modern version of a Neapolitan Christmas carol which, despite its seasonality, got no higher than No.25 (although in composite charts it was credited ultimately with a Top 20 placing at No.16). Yet these two relatively modest successes, taken together with the group's increasingly frequent exposure on radio and television as bankable light entertainers, were enough to secure the Springfields national recognition and prestige in the form of two annual awards from the musical press of the day. Winning Best Vocal Group from *NME* and Top Vocal-Instrumental Group from *Melody Maker*, their efforts to date had surely delivered a triumph of style over content, which Dusty herself summed up as follows: "We were terribly cheerful … We were also very loud and we jumped up and down a lot, and that seemed to impress people!"[24]

Surprising though it might now seem that the popularity of the Springfields' early performances, with Dusty at their core, derived from a hearty intercontinental gusto, for the time their music-making occupied a comforting middle ground between the rock'n'rollers and the balladeers. For all their alleged eclecticism, they were, if anything, reassuringly just out of date, typically blending folk and spirituals with bluegrass and skiffle in a manner reminiscent of Chas McDevitt and Nancy Whiskey, Johnny Duncan or early Lonnie Donegan; and later in the decade, the natural heirs of their musical legacy would turn out to be the Australian group, the Seekers.[25]

"Certainly the worst year ever for rock music!"[26] was Pete Frame's verdict, a year in which "pop music is all controlled, neat and clean; anything vital is suppressed. No sense of rebellion anywhere. NO EXCITEMENT!".[27] By the end of the year, he was in despair:

> *NME* readers declare Bert Weedon Top Instrumental Personality
> and the Highwaymen the World's Second Best Vocal Group!
> Frankie Vaughan and Danny Williams have the best-selling singles!
> We have surely reached nadirsville. What's happening?[28]

In the charts, neither rock'n'roll nor its latter-day derivatives appeared to make any significant headway, baulked – in Frame's view, at least – by the competition from "the trad jazz fad … as the music is progressively commercialised and trivialised for mass consumption: the Temperance Seven join Acker Bilk and Kenny Ball at the head of the movement".[29]

Frame's frustration was completely understandable, not least in the case of the Temperance Seven. Appearing as a faux Twenties' dance band, they virtually fell off the edge of trad jazz into the novelty category, with their annoyingly catchy No.1 from April, "You're Driving Me Crazy" – a record nevertheless still noteworthy today for being the first produced by George Martin to reach No.1. (The follow-up, "Pasadena", in similar vein, came straight into the charts at No.6 but peaked at No.4 in August.) Despite their name, there were in fact nine in the group altogether, all taking pride in a stage presence redolent of English eccentricity, with vocals being delivered in the semi-spoken languor of Received Pronunciation down a megaphone by 'Whispering' Paul McDowell. Their style eventually enjoyed a fleeting revival in 1966, in the form of the New Vaudeville Band's "Winchester Cathedral", which reached No.4 that October.

But all was not quite lost for the future. For instance, when Kenny Ball appeared at the Cavern in June and heard Cilla Black singing with Gerry and the Pacemakers, he asked her to be the vocalist with his Jazz Band: she would not be swayed, opting instead to stick with building up her local following, singing not only with Gerry Marsden but also Kingsize Taylor and the Dominoes and the Big Three.

In Liverpool, the summer also brought with it a new music journalism enterprise, initiated by local art student Bill Harry, with the publication on 6th July of the first edition of *Mersey Beat*. Having originally envisaged a fortnightly magazine for jazz fans, Harry decided instead to cover rock'n'roll, given its steadily growing fanbase in the city. On page 2 of issue 1, he famously printed a piece of whimsy commissioned from John Lennon, "Being A Short Diversion On The Dubious Origins Of Beatles":

> Many people ask what are Beatles? Why Beatles? Uh, Beatles, how did the name arrive? So we will tell you. It came in a vision – a man appeared on a flaming pie and said unto them 'From this day on you are Beatles with an A'. Thank you, Mister Man, they said, thanking him.[30]

Under the byline of 'Beatcomber', Lennon's oddball musings were to become a regular feature; whilst in issue 2, Priscilla (*aka* Cilla Black) contributed fashion notes for girls.[31] With its combination of local reportage and, at the end of the year, the obligatory popularity poll, *Mersey Beat* was destined to be in the vanguard of consolidating and promoting a hitherto unnamed and unrecognised brand of pop music peculiar to the north-west.

It would, however, be some time yet before the charts echoed to anything resembling a regional accent and in September, from his newly set up recording studio at 304 Holloway Road, London, independent record producer Joe Meek demonstrated at last that his idiosyncratic techniques were capable of delivering gold, even with the least promising of vocal talent. A world away from the clinical environment of EMI's Abbey Road, complete with its white-coated recording engineers, Meek's achievement was even more remarkable, given that 'studio' was a very grand term indeed for the inauspicious arrangements forced upon him by the chaotic constraints of a three-floor flat above a leather goods shop. Converting the largest room of all, a former bedroom on the second floor, to a makeshift studio meant gaining access to it by "climbing two flights of steep, narrow stairs – not much fun for musicians with drum-kits and other bulky instruments".[32]

Here, where Meek aspired to turn his recording fantasies into reality, John Leyton, an actor and minor television celebrity with, on his own admission, no singing voice, came in the summer to lay down the track "Johnny Remember Me". Released in July, its success was guaranteed by Leyton performing the song in a cameo role in an episode of the early television soap *Harpers West One*, at the instigation of his manager, Robert Stigwood. At the end of August, it went to No.1, ousting Helen Shapiro's "You Don't Know", and stayed there for five out of the next six weeks, a slip of one week to No.2 due to a temporary surge in sales of Elvis Presley's "Wild In The Country".

Most appropriately for a song depicting the interaction of love, loss and death through high melodrama, the composer, Geoff Goddard, a close collaborator with Meek, was a spiritualist, who claimed direct inspiration and approval for the song from no less than the late Buddy Holly: "he said it was a great song and would be the start of good things for me."[33] Whoever Goddard's muse may have been, Meek's production stopped at nothing to impress, incorporating his twin trademarks of relentless beat and palette of sound effects to create a pre-emptive English equivalent of Phil Spector's 'wall of sound'.[34] The imperfections of Leyton's voice were lost in echo, albeit that less kindly critics of the day likened his singing to that of a man at the bottom of a well, while the song's title was turned into a ghostly refrain in high octave by session singer Lissa Gray, as the voice of poor Johnny's dear departed lover "singing in the sighing of the wind".[35] The end result was undeniably the most distinctive and original No.1 of the year, vindicating Meek's tortured self-belief in his own abilities and far removed from some of his earliest work pre-recording the weekly TV soundtrack for *The Black and White Minstrel Show*.

Elsewhere in the south of England, a very tenuous pattern of geographical connections and chance encounters began to emerge, drawing together a disparate group of five young men, all with an esoteric interest in jazz and rhythm and blues; who, as yet unbeknown to any of them, were destined to become the archetypal anti-heroes of Sixties' pop, the Rolling Stones. Of these five, the two oldest, Bill Wyman and Charlie Watts, were already ambitious semi-professional musicians.

Having set up home with his wife Diane the previous October in a flat in Beckenham, Chuck Berry fan Wyman – then by day a storekeeper in a Penge department store – had bought his first electric guitar and was devoting more and more of his leisure time to playing in local dance-halls, in a five-piece group he had co-founded called the Cliftons. Dissatisfied with the sounds he was getting from his instrument, inspiration came unexpectedly one weekend from seeing the Barron Knights play at a dance in Aylesbury. So, assisted by Tony Chapman, the Cliftons' drummer, Bill tracked down and bought an old Tuxedo bass guitar, for £8, then rebuilt it to his own design.

As for Charlie, working as a commercial artist for a London advertising agency after attending Harrow School of Art, he had pursued his passion for jazz in tandem with becoming an accomplished drummer. By late 1961, he had a regular Saturday night booking playing with a jazz group at The Troubadour, a popular Earls Court coffee bar; and it was here that he was seen and approached by the noted blues musician and broadcaster Alexis Korner to join a new band he and Cyril Davies were putting together, to be called Blues Incorporated.

Meanwhile, one autumn morning at Dartford railway station, two near-contemporaries at Wentworth Primary School and both now commuting from home as students – Keith Richards and Mike Jagger – met again for the first time in years. In the subsequent course of their education, their paths had diverged considerably. Richards, expelled from Dartford Technical School, had since taken up graphic design at Sidcup Art College; whereas Jagger had stayed the course at Dartford Grammar School through to A Levels and was newly enrolled at the London School of Economics, where he was becoming known as Mick rather than Mike.

On the train journey that day, their conversation quickly revealed a common interest in the music of Chuck Berry and his ilk, prompted by Jagger having with him several new rhythm and blues LPs he'd obtained by mail order from America. Follow-up meetings led rapidly to Richards' recruitment to a group of which Jagger, together with mutual friend Dick Taylor[36], was already a member, Little Boy Blue and the Blue Boys. The only catch was that they were strictly a "bedroom group", who "never played a gig, nor attempted to get one".[37]

And at the end of 1961, from left-field, from Cheltenham in the Cotswolds to London, came a 19-year-old would-be bluesman called Brian Jones, whose acknowledged musical versatility already encompassed the piano, saxophone and guitar. His permanent move to the capital could be attributed to mixed motives, to say the least. On the one hand, he was openly abandoning a personal relationship to which he would not commit himself, with his then girlfriend Pat Andrews and their newly-born son Mark; having previously, it should be noted, left school to save face in the wake of the scandal associated with impregnating a 14-year-old girl. On the other, as his various biographers would have it, he was hell-bent on pursuing his all-consuming dream of professional musicianship, having been to date entirely lacking in application to a variety of paid employment found for him through the well-intentioned efforts of friends and family. Whether calculating or obsessive, he quickly ingratiated himself with Alexis Korner after seeing him in concert in Cheltenham and became a regular weekend visitor to Korner's London home, from where, of course, many new musical possibilities now opened up to him.

Little then did any of the five realise that from these hesitant beginnings, within a few months, they would all find themselves being drawn together under Korner's tutelage in early 1962 and starting to put down the roots of their as yet unforeseen success.

In sharp contrast to the endearing amateurism of the Blue Boys, back in the north-west the Beatles were now well into their stride as established regulars at the Cavern and, as the year drew towards its close, were on the brink of unexpectedly reaping the rewards of their imperfect recording session for Polydor in the summer, with an outcome to change not only their lives but also, more significantly, the very evolution of pop music itself.

Legend has it that "at three o'clock on the afternoon of [Saturday] 28 October 1961":

> A youth in a black leather jacket called Raymond Jones walked into the NEMS[38] record store in Whitechapel, Liverpool, and asked for a record called 'My Bonnie' by a group called the Beatles. Brian Epstein, who was behind the counter, said he was terribly sorry. He'd never heard of that record, nor of a group called the Beatles.[39]

Despite the fact that Raymond Jones actually did exist and was a Beatles' fan, down the years the comforting precision of this story has been eroded by the circulation of various conflicting claims of others' involvement.[40] Suffice it to say that local interest in the record had certainly been generated by its inclusion on the playlist of the Cavern's DJ, Bob Wooler, and NEMS store manager Epstein, who prided himself on his policy in records to "look after whatever request was made"[41], soon placed an order for 200 imported copies from Germany, which sold steadily on receipt.

Supposedly in the wake of this arousal of interest in 'My Bonnie' amongst his customers, Epstein was prompted to make further enquiries about the Beatles, leading him and his personal assistant, Alistair Taylor, to see them at a lunchtime concert at the Cavern, on Thursday, 9th November; although by then several months had already passed during which he had apparently been intimating a wish to expand into pop group management to local acquaintances on the music scene.[42]

Irrespective of whether or not this was actually the first time Epstein had seen the Beatles perform, on this occasion, an incongruous figure in the dank, noisy cellar as a 27-year-old suited businessman, he was definitely captivated by them:

> They were rather scruffily dressed – in the nicest possible way or, I should say, in the most attractive way: black leather jackets and jeans, long hair of course … I immediately liked what I heard. They were fresh and they were honest, and they had what I thought was a sort of presence and, this is a terribly vague term, star quality. Whatever that is, they had it, or I sensed that they had it.[43]

And he was nothing if not persistent. Subsequently revisiting the Cavern more than once to see them again, Epstein convened a series of loosely structured 'business' meetings with the Beatles in early December, the third of which (on Sunday, 10th December) culminated in an agreement that he should become their representative. This goal secured at last, albeit only by word of mouth as yet, he immediately threw himself into securing their release from their contractual obligations to Polydor and seeking auditions for them with leading British record companies.

Despite the initial randomness of the correspondence he generated and favours he attempted to call in on their behalf, an early response from Decca was forthcoming; to the extent that Mike Smith, assistant to Dick Rowe, Head of A&R (Artistes and Repertoire), travelled up from London to see the Beatles at the Cavern on Wednesday, 13th December. Although it must be said that Smith's visit was prompted more by deference to Epstein in his established role as a major record retailer in Liverpool than as manager of a quite possibly sensational but largely unknown new group, nevertheless he was sufficiently impressed to invite them to London for a test recording session after Christmas.

While the Beatles were thus tantalised by the prospect of a possible breakthrough into the home recording market, 13th December coincidentally marked a high point for the most successful British artists of the year, with the Leicester Square premiere of the musical film *The Young Ones*, starring Cliff Richard and the Shadows. Casting Cliff as the hero Nicky, the least likely and most thoroughly wholesome youth club leader ever to grace the back streets of Paddington, and vintage actor Robert Morley as an unscrupulous property-developing millionaire (who just happens to be Nicky's father into the bargain), in brief the story revolves around the youth club's efforts to put on a fund-raiser to save their hut and the land on which it stands, with the inevitably happy ending, as follows:

> Nicky immediately goes onto the stage and begins to sing, his singing talent captures the noisy audience and he finishes to tremendous applause. He leaves the stage to find his delighted father offering to build them a big new club! The gang accept the offer and Nicky returns to the clamouring audience for a grand finale.[44]

At the age of 21 and after two years of hit-making, the film was to elevate Cliff (and, by association, the Shadows) once and for all to the British musical Establishment. Typical of most musicals of its day in being heavily subservient to American theatrical tradition[45], the score brashly proclaims its knowing over-enthusiasm for confection and artifice in such numbers as "What D'You Know We've Got A Show & Vaudeville Routine", performed by Cliff, the ensemble and the Associated British Studio Orchestra with the Mike Sammes Singers! We can only be thankful, therefore, that its saving grace lay in the incorporation of "half a dozen pop songs to connect with the teenage audience"[46], including the melodious title track which has long since deservedly achieved iconic status.

Another film, however, from America was to be the source of the last British No.1 of 1961. Released in the autumn, *Breakfast At Tiffany's*, directed by Blake Edwards and starring Audrey Hepburn and George Peppard, boasted an Oscar-winning score by Henry Mancini; who also, in collaboration with Johnny Mercer, clinched an Oscar for Best Song with the film's theme tune "Moon River". Recorded here by a 19-year-old South African singer, Danny Williams, and his only British hit, it entered the Top 30 on 4th November, eventually reaching the No.1 slot in the last week of December, to end a 4-week run for Frankie Vaughan's "Tower Of Strength".[47]

Hollywood fantasies aside, throughout the autumn of 1961 another equally significant but very different musical development for the future direction of American pop was in train elsewhere in California, where a group made up of family members and friends suddenly found themselves projected into a recording career by an imperious patriarch.

At their family home in Hawthorne, some 30 miles outside Los Angeles, the Wilson brothers – Brian, Dennis and Carl – had been dabbling in music for their own amusement with their cousin Mike Love and Brian's friend from high school, Al Jardine, for some time, modelling themselves in particular on the Four Freshmen, the highly successful close-harmony quartet of the Fifties. Head of the Wilson family was the brothers' father, Murry, a self-made man with a forceful personality, a lifelong passion for popular music and long-nurtured dreams of composing a hit song. Like so many parents frustrated in realising their own personal ambitions, eventually he determined to settle for second-best and act them out through his children, with sometimes ferocious consequences, as long remembered and resented by Brian, who attributed deafness in his right ear to a blow to his head administered by his father in a fit of rage.

Taking advantage of their parents' absence on holiday for a few days in early August, the Wilson brothers' group (now christened the Pendletones[48]) took over the house, devoting most of their time to making music and tape-recording their efforts. Despite his initial outrage on his return, when Murry finally calmed himself sufficiently to listen to the tape they'd made, he was fired up into contacting independent record producers and music publishers Hite and Dorinda Morgan, with a view to promoting his boys. Then Al Jardine followed this up, securing them an audition for early September, at which the group sang several contemporary hits, as well as an arrangement of the song "Sloop John B".[49]

From the Morgans' perspective, though, it was an unimpressive performance. However, when Hite showed an interest in hearing more original material, out of the blue Dennis Wilson volunteered the information that they did have a song of their own, called "Surfin'", which turned out to be an inspired bluff. For the simple reason that it wasn't yet completed, they couldn't play it then and there; but Brian Wilson and Mike Love improvised a draft for the Morgans' approval and returned with the Pendletones to cut a demo of the finished article on 15th September. That same day, the Morgans signed Brian and Mike up to a songwriting contract, after which events gathered apace.

With a final take of "Surfin'" laid down at the next recording session on 3rd October, the Morgans then negotiated its release on a local independent label, Candix Records. Issued on Friday 8th December, a further surprise was in store, for executives of the record company, without prior consultation, had decided to ditch 'The Pendletones' and renamed the group 'The Beach Boys'.

Interest and airplay built strongly, first locally and then nationally, so that sales by the end of December had reached over 40,000 copies. (National sales of "Surfin'" finally peaked at the end of March 1962, when it reached No.75 in the *Billboard* Top 100.) Inevitably, this in turn created the necessity for the group to perform live and the Beach Boys' first ever public concert appearance was on 23rd December (at the Rendezvous Ballroom Balboa, Newport Beach), when they sang two songs in the interval at the Dick Dale Christmas Show. (Originally a country-and-western singer, Dick Dale (*aka* Richard Monsour) was responsible for launching the trend of instrumental surf music in the early Sixties. Together with his group the Del-Tones, he was resident at the Rendezvous Ballroom and his favoured guitar, like Buddy Holly before him, was a Fender Stratocaster.)

Feeling awkward in the gold jackets they had elected to wear for the occasion, the Beach Boys were coolly received, which upset Brian but didn't seem to matter much to Dennis, who clearly felt the buzz from being on the same bill as Dick Dale since of the three Wilson brothers he was the only one seriously into surfing as a lifestyle. (Luckily for Brian, this handicap didn't preclude him from seeing the strong commercial potential of writing and performing songs in the surfing idiom.) They closed 1961 with a second live performance on New Year's Eve, at the Municipal Auditorium, Long Beach, following Ike and Tina Turner on stage and being paid $300 this time for playing a three-song set. The promise of greater success seemed to be beckoning.

Though not remotely foreseen at the time, the absolute antithesis to this seductive shimmer of Hollywood and Californian culture lay in the cafes and folk clubs of Greenwich Village, New York, to where Bob Dylan had gravitated after dropping out at 19 from the University of Minnesota in December 1960. Dylan's ultimate influence on the music and musicians of the Sixties, in Britain just as much as in the USA, was to be profound but grew from these inauspicious beginnings, fuelled by an unshakeable self-belief: "I felt like [destiny] was looking right at me and nobody else."[50]

Originally inspired by his all-time hero Woody Guthrie, under the influence and benevolent patronage of those playing on and running the contemporary folk and blues circuit in the Village, Dylan quickly established himself there in his own right as an edgy and idiosyncratic performer. In due course, his eagerness to discover and interpret traditional songs, combined with his ability not only to write and promote his own original material but also to insinuate himself into the charmed circle of those already signed up to record professionally, would pay him handsome dividends.

The real ace card for Dylan, however, came in late September, by catching the eye of influential music critic Robert Shelton when he appeared at Gerde's Folk City, as a secondary act on a bill headed by popular bluegrass musicians the Greenbriar Boys. Published on Friday, 29th September 1961, Shelton's critique portrayed Dylan as a "cross between a choir boy and a beatnik ... bursting at the seams with talent". Whilst accepting that his "highly personalised approach towards folk song is still evolving" and that "at times ... his stylisation threatens to topple over as a mannered excess", Shelton credited Dylan with being "both comedian and tragedian" and his music with wearing "the mask of originality and inspiration, all the more noteworthy for his youth." Wryly noting his affected vagueness "about his antecedents and birthplace", Shelton's ringing conclusion was that "it matters less where he has been than where he is going, and that would seem to be straight up".[51]

Given that Dylan, as he himself was the first to acknowledge, wasn't even headlining on this occasion, the piece was extraordinary, an unprecedented and controversial compliment to this virtual unknown "and it created some jealousy in folk circles" for "the boost [it] gave to Dylan".[52] Shelton, however, was unapologetic for the stir he had created by the robustness of his views, content to live with the fact that "much of the Village music coterie reacted with jealousy, contempt and ridicule".[53] In its wake, Dylan was swiftly approached by John Hammond, a senior and highly respected executive of Columbia Records[54]; and on 25th October 1961, Hammond signed him to a five-year contract. Understandably, Dylan couldn't believe his luck: "It felt like my heart leaped up to the sky, to some intergalactic star ... It seemed too good to be true."[55] Previously, the most he had dared hope for was to record on one of the smaller, cult folk labels, which themselves had gained a high currency in and around the Village at that time and thus far had rejected him; but now, thanks to Hammond's far-sighted generosity, he suddenly found himself at the very heart of the US national record industry, transported to what he termed "the center of the labyrinth".[56]

The following month, Dylan went into the studio to record his eponymous first LP. It is hard to imagine anything further removed – in terms of style, content or delivery – from contemporaneous commercial pop culture. *The Young Ones* might as well have been produced on another planet. Yet Dylan was on the threshold of composing a prodigious catalogue of songs[57] that would rightly come to be revered for the biting vision of their sheer poetry; seeming, in their often absurd and paradoxical blending of introspection with topicality, love with hate, to pour just scorn on a complacent society and expose the raw nerve-endings of personal relationships. Overtly repudiating the values of Tin Pan Alley by daring to say that the Emperor has no clothes, through the power of self-composition his music would eventually expose an unimagined realm of possibilities and at last give pop the serious edge it had hitherto lacked.

All the more ironic, then, that down in the Village Dylan should still be proud to claim past friendship with no less a pop star than Bobby Vee (who had scored a US No.1 in 1961 with "Take Good Care Of My Baby").[58] Indeed, his personal tastes in music were nothing if not catholic. Whilst now absorbed with folk and blues, he still had a pronounced liking for what we would now call 'standards', which he happily bracketed with pop music, and would all too readily admit to being spellbound by Henry Mancini's "Moon River": "I could sing that in my sleep."[59]

So, just as in previous years, romantic escapism still preserved pop's isolation from the pressing concerns of the real world, even for the singer who would soon be acclaimed as nominal leader of the protest movement in music; all this played out against the background of political preoccupation with the tightening grip of the Cold War, as American imperialism confronted Soviet expansionism.

In Britain, espionage and counter-espionage were rife: rumour and counter-rumour abounded. March and May both saw major trials in London of double-agents Gordon Lonsdale and George Blake, who on conviction received sentences of 25 and 42 years' imprisonment respectively. And on Saturday 8th July, at a weekend house party at Cliveden, the Buckinghamshire country seat of the Astor family, the first seeds of the most notorious political scandal of the decade were sown, by the bringing together of John Profumo, Secretary of State for War in Macmillan's government, and a girl of 19 on the make called Christine Keeler, through the machinations of Stephen Ward, a London osteopath, socialite and procurer of young women.

Strolling in the grounds of Cliveden, Profumo and Lord Astor happened upon Keeler shortly after dusk, as she emerged naked from the outdoor swimming pool, and gave chase, only to be stopped in their tracks by Ward mischievously turning on the garden floodlights:

> It is a pity no one photographed the moment: Christine, her hair streaming water, trying to cover herself with a towel that was obviously too small; two out-of-breath husbands looking slightly guilty; a party of men in dinner jackets and women in long gowns standing slightly on one side, spectators at an event the import of which has escaped them; all frozen for a moment in the sudden glare of white light.[60]

Apparently unabashed, Profumo was rapidly to pursue his suddenly aroused interest in Keeler to a full-blown affair; all the while blissfully unaware that on that same weekend of their first encounter, she had also embarked upon a sexual relationship with "thirty-seven-year-old Captain Eugene Ivanov, nominally a Soviet Assistant Naval Attache in London but also an officer in Soviet Military Intelligence, GRU".[61] It was set to be another two years before the full ramifications of Ward's pandaring and Profumo's indiscretions, in all their salacious detail, were to be exposed.

On another plane, the Cold War was already responsible for shrinking the world to the status of what Marshall McLuhan would later term the "global village".[62] At a stroke, on Wednesday 12th April, the horizons of humanity as a whole were simultaneously shortened and extended through the launching into space of the first man to enter orbit and see Earth from beyond our atmosphere; shortened by our new physical ability to contemplate the Earth as a finite entity, extended by taking that first faltering step towards interplanetary travel.[63]

The fact, however, that the man in question was a Russian, Major Yuri Gagarin, rather than an American, was to have profound significance, for the essence of the so-called space race was about military supremacy in the technology of inter-continental ballistic missiles, originating as it did from the German V-2 rocket programme in the closing months of the Second World War. On the fall of Germany in 1945, while the V-2 programme director Wernher von Braun and many of his scientific staff were 'liberated' to America by the US Army, the Russians released Sergei Korolev from long-term political imprisonment, gave him the rank of Lieutenant-Colonel in the Red Army and despatched him to Berlin, to develop a successor to the V-2. Sixteen years later, both von Braun and Korolev were firmly embedded as directors of opposing space programmes. Gagarin's achievement, in a flight of 108 minutes, could therefore equally well be seen as having made the world a more dangerous place, for "the development of missiles and rockets went hand in hand with the struggle to develop the capacity to deliver nuclear weapons, to spy on the enemy and to control space".[63]

Further damage to the USA's standing as a world power was to follow in less than a week, when, on 17th April, America began an abortive attempt to overthrow the Cuban communist leader Fidel Castro, with a seaborne landing at the Bay of Pigs. With the bungled invasion triumphantly crushed within three days, American humiliation at the hands of the Soviet bloc was complete, forcing the new US President, John F. Kennedy, to contemplate a spectacular diversion to regain public confidence. Heralded by the first American sub-orbital spaceflight of pilot Alan Shepard on 5th May (for a mere 15 minutes), Kennedy determined, in an historic speech to Congress on 25th May, that the space race should be the means of restoring US ascendancy in the world, whatever the cost:

> Now is the time to take longer strides, time for a great new
> American enterprise, time for this nation to take a clearly leading
> role in space achievement, which in many ways may hold the key
> to our future on earth … I believe this nation should commit itself
> to achieving the goal, before the decade is out, of landing a man
> on the moon and returning him safely to the earth. No single space
> project in this period will be more impressive to mankind or more
> important for the long range exploration of space; and none will be
> so difficult or expensive to accomplish.[64]

In the immediate short-term, a tit-for-tat competition ensued for the remaining months of the year, with Russia still the victor. Although Virgil 'Gus' Grissom became the second American in space as soon as 21st July, effectively he did no more than replicate Shepard's first space flight in terms of both distance and duration; whereas on 6th August, Russia sent Major

Gherman Titov on a much longer mission than Gagarin's, to complete 17 Earth orbits in just over 25 hours.

Unbeknown to the West, the timing of Titov's flight had been brought forward at the insistence of no less than Premier Kruschev himself as a diversionary tactic, linked as it was to far greater political imperatives. Kruschev gave an uncomprehending Korolev strict instructions to ensure Titov's lift-off before 13th August; the day, as it transpired, on which the USSR embarked upon the physical partitioning of Berlin and thus made an emphatic statement of Soviet supremacy. Within a week, the barbed wire was being replaced with a concrete wall, finally breaking the terms of the post-war agreement between the four occupying Allied powers as to freedom of movement across the city and securing the isolation of the East German sector of Berlin for the next twenty-eight years.

For the United States, however, there were equally pressing foreign policy issues to address in the Far East, as reports reached Kennedy from Vietnam that the stability of the government in the South was increasingly threatened by communist Viet Cong infiltrators from the North. Inescapably committed to a programme of support for South Vietnam inherited from his predecessor Eisenhower, Kennedy, "as a hard-nosed cold warrior … considered Communist victory in South Vietnam an intolerable prospect" and by the end of 1961 raised "the number of US military personnel in Vietnam from eight hundred to three thousand".[65] Supposedly confined to acting only as advisers in non-combatant roles, it was nevertheless reported on 22nd December that one James Davis had become the first American soldier to be killed in action by the Viet Cong.[66]

With a musical vocabulary as yet inadequate to the task of expressing concern at the possible consequences of these and related actions by hostile world powers, in Britain it fell instead to satire to challenge the post-war complacency of the jingoistic upper middle classes, in the form of what became a long-running theatrical revue, *Beyond The Fringe*. Written and performed by a quartet of recent Oxbridge graduates – Alan Bennett, Peter Cook, Jonathan Miller and Dudley Moore – it had originally been commissioned as a quasi-professional alternative to the distinctly amateur humour of the Fringe of the Edinburgh Festival in August 1960, hence its title.

Compared to most productions of the day, costume ("white shirts, dark ties, sensible grey pullovers and grey worsted suits"[67]) and staging were minimalist, wherein lay the most disarming element of the show's destructive force as the quartet launched their satiric onslaught on the Establishment. Exactly as hoped, it was an undeniable hit with Edinburgh audiences, ensuring its subsequent transfer to London's West End, where it opened at the Fortune Theatre on Wednesday, 10th May 1961; and where in July an LP of highlights was recorded for George Martin's latest comedy production on the Parlophone label.[68]

Some of its sharpest barbs were voiced by Peter Cook; for example, impersonating Macmillan in a monologue exactly capturing the self-congratulatory banality of a Prime Ministerial television broadcast on his recent return from a world tour, reflecting on the regard in which other world leaders supposedly held Britain.[69] In the guise of a government spokesman, Cook also had this persuasively practical yet essentially useless advice to offer in the event of a nuclear attack:

> Well, the first golden rule to remember about hydrogen warfare is to be *out* of the area where the attack is about to occur – get *right out* of the area, because that's the danger area, where the bombs are dropping. Get right out of it – get right out of it – if you're out of it you're well out of it, if you're in it you're really in it. If you *are* caught in it when the missile explodes, for goodness sake don't move; stand absolutely stock still – not under a tree, of course, that could be extremely dangerous. Now, what about radiation, I hear a strangled cry. Well, there is a lot you can do about radiation as soon as the dust has settled – the best thing you can do is hold your breath and jump into a brown paper bag. There's nothing like good old brown paper for protecting you.[70]

It was a worryingly authentic echo of the style and content of contemporary government 'public information', which somehow contrived to ridicule the perfectly rational fears of ordinary citizens more than it managed to allay them.

Amid the end-of-year revelry, then, beyond the embrace of the last waltzers to the comforting strains of "Moon River", there was nevertheless more than a hint of foreboding, of trepidation; and on New Year's Eve, instead of performing, the Beatles set off on a miserable overnight journey by road in heavy snow, to be in London the next day for their audition with Decca. 1962 promised to be a very different year indeed for everyone.

NOTES

1   The Soho coffee bar at 59, Old Crompton Street, named after one-time owners the Irani Brothers and renowned as the Fifties' birthplace of British rock'n'roll. A venue thinly fictionalised in *Expresso Bongo,* a young Hank Marvin and Bruce Welch regularly played in the basement there and so it became the first meeting place of Cliff Richard and the would-be Shadows.

2   Spencer Leigh, "The Cavern: The Most Famous Club In The World" (SAF, 2008), p.59.

3   With its composition credited to the four original group members, "Shadoogie" still holds pride of place today in the Marvin/Welch canon and the Shadows opted to play

it as the opening number of their first dedicated instrumental segment on the 50th Anniversary Final Reunion concert tour with Cliff in 2009.

4 See Mike Read, "The Story of the Shadows" (Elm Tree, 1983), p.98.

5 See Spencer Leigh, "Twist and Shout! Merseybeat, The Cavern, The Star-Club and The Beatles" (Nirvana, 2004), p.64.

6 See, for example, Spencer Leigh, op. cit., p.64 for a contemporaneous record of their playlist (compiled by John Cochrane), which typically for the time is almost exclusively American in origin and embraces a broad range of genres, from rock'n'roll and blues to standards and country.

7 Quoted in Barry Miles, "Paul McCartney: Many Years From Now" (Henry Holt, 1997), pp.82-83. "Like Dreamers Do", one of his earliest songs that they performed, would later be gifted to Solihull group the Applejacks (see Ch.6).

8 Mark Lewisohn, op. cit., p.42.

9 The reworking of standards like these was commonplace at the time, representing an all too obvious crossover from traditional jazz to rock'n'roll, and such tunes formed a staple part of most groups' repertoires. Starting life as 'fillers' in live sets, their generally unimpressive quality seems not to have bothered contemporary record executives, who all too readily perpetuated the trend. Even by late 1963, for instance, the Searchers, another well-established Liverpool group who served a Hamburg apprenticeship, were recording a thinly disguised version of "When The Saints Go Marching In" under the title "Saints and Searchers", as the B-side of their second single, "Sugar And Spice".

10 Kaufman/Anthony, © 1960 by Vogue Music Inc. & Warner/Chappell Music Ltd.

11 Turk/Handman, © 1961 by Redwood Music Ltd./BMG Music.

12 Colin Larkin (ed.), "The Encyclopedia of Popular Music" (5th concise edition, Omnibus, 2007), p.1120.

13 Ornadel/West, © 1960 by Edward Kassner Music Co. Ltd.

14 Sonny Curtis, © 1960 by Cricket Music/BMI-Worldwide.

15 The best-selling single in Britain for that year.

16 Where the song was recorded, on 17th September, 1960.

17 Shannon/Crook, © 1961 by Vicki Music (subsequently renewed by Big Top).

18 Shannon, © 1961 by Vicki Music (subsequently renewed by Stylus Music Ltd.).

19 Goffin/King, © 1961 (renewed 1989) by Screen Gems/EMI Music Inc.: a song quickly added to the Beatles' club repertoire. The B-side, "Boys" (composed by Dixon/Farrell), despite so obviously being a song for girl singers, also became an enduring Beatles' staple. Ringo made it a favourite party piece of his at concerts and recorded it as the 'Ringo song' on their first Parlophone LP, *Please Please Me*.

20 "Rock'n'roll led to romance. King became pregnant in the summer of 1959, and the young lovers, only seventeen and twenty, wed on August 30." See Ken Emerson, op. cit., p.87.

21 Composed by Scharfenberger/Busch/West and originally a German hit for Lolita, under the title "Seeman".

22   Not to my taste at all, Laurie London always seemed to be on the radio or the television at the time with this rocked-up spiritual. Amazingly, the record was even more popular in America (where it reached No.2 in April 1958) than in Britain (where, despite the excessive airplay, it only reached No.12, in December 1957).

23   The tour began at the Gaumont Cinema in Bradford, on Saturday, 2nd February 1963. Helen Shapiro topped the bill, which, apart from the Beatles, also included Danny Williams, Kenny Lynch, the Red Price Band, the Honeys and the Kestrels. See Martin Creasy, "Legends on Tour: The Pop Package Tours of the 1960s" (Tempus, 2007), p.9.

24   Quoted in Sharon Davis, "Dusty: An Intimate Portrait of Dusty Springfield" (Sevenoaks, 2008), p.25.

25   A debt they acknowledged in due course by their own sympathetic interpretation of "Island of Dreams" on their 1966 LP *Come The Day*.

26   Pete Frame, "Rock Family Trees" (Omnibus, 1993), p.59.

27   Ibid.

28   Ibid.

29   Pete Frame, op. cit., p.58.

30   Quoted in Hunter Davies, op. cit., p.108. In homage to Lennon, Paul McCartney eventually revisited the cod mythology of Flaming Pie as the title track of his 1997 album.

31   To the effect that "grey was now the colour for evening wear". See Hunter Davies, op. cit., p.109.

32   See John Repsch, "The Legendary Joe Meek: The Telstar Man" (Cherry Red Books, 2008), pp. 89-90.

33   Quoted in John Repsch, op. cit., p.117

34   Over time, as Meek's successes dwindled and the sale of Spector's records began to flood the British charts, Meek grew more and more paranoid about protecting his own production ideas from theft, seeing Spector as little better than an interloper. In early 1964, Spector called Meek up, in the hope of meeting him on a forthcoming trip to England, but it was not to be: "Joe … blew his top. Somewhere amongst the flood of invective he screamed down the telephone was an accusation that Spector had been listening to his records and pinching ideas, and then he slammed the phone down with such force that it broke." See John Repsch, op. cit., p.222.

35   Goddard, © 1961 by Southern Music Publishing Co. Ltd./Peermusic (UK) Ltd. As originally composed, the lyric recalled "the girl I loved who died a year ago", making the song a potential companion to the 1960 No.1 hit for Ricky Valance, "Tell Laura I Love Her" – also, as it happened, recorded unsuccessfully by Leyton. Robert Stigwood was all for a new 'death disc' but other counsels prevailed in the face of possible BBC antipathy and the line was changed, not very convincingly, prior to recording, to "the girl I loved and lost a year ago". See John Repsch, op. cit., pp.107-108.

36   Taylor eventually became a founder member of the Pretty Things, a group deliberately marketed in the beginning as more of a threat to social order and the virtue of young girls than even the Rolling Stones.

37   Pete Frame, "The Beatles and Some Other Guys: Rock Family Trees of the Early Sixties" (Omnibus, 1997), p.27.

38   The acronym for North End Music Stores. "By the time Brian [Epstein] met the Beatles, NEMS had nine record shops in Liverpool, stocking over 500,000 records. They were the biggest record retailers in the north-west." (Barry Miles, op. cit., p.86.) In keeping with the times, NEMS' record departments had blossomed from within a more traditional furniture and music retailing business, with their stock in trade being pianos, televisions, gramophones and radiograms. In such stores, record sales gradually complemented, then eventually outstripped, sales of sheet music for the home. At the time, the Whitechapel store was the newest in the chain, having been officially opened by Anthony Newley in 1959.

39   Hunter Davies, op. cit., p.114.

40   Most conveniently summarised by Spencer Leigh in "Twist and Shout! Merseybeat, The Cavern, The Star-Club and The Beatles" (Nirvana, 2004), pp.69-70.

41   Quoted in "The Beatles Anthology" (Cassell, 2000), p.65.

42   Bill Harry suggests that it might have been as early as July or August 1961 when Epstein first discussed the possible management of the Beatles with him, on the back of which he arranged a visit for Epstein then to the Cavern. (See Pritchard & Lysaght, op. cit., p.82.) Jim Gretty, guitar tutor at Hessey's (a music shop close to NEMS in Whitechapel), also claims that Epstein had already discussed the possibilities of managing a local group with him. On the strength of this, Gretty invited him to a charity concert he had organised for Sunday, 15th October, 1961, at which Epstein saw the Beatles play. (See Pritchard & Lysaght, op. cit., p.77.)

43   Quoted in Mark Lewisohn, op. cit., p.35.

44   Peter Lewry & Nigel Goodall, CD liner notes to *The Young Ones Soundtrack* [EMI, remastered 2005], p.5.

45   With an eye, of course, to potential box-office receipts in the US, where *The Young Ones* was snappily retitled *Wonderful To Be Young* and a new title track correspondingly recorded.

46   Peter Lewry & Nigel Goodall, op. cit.

47   Even without another British hit to his name, in 1963 Williams was still deemed worthy of inclusion in the UK tour headlined by Helen Shapiro and featuring the Beatles. See note 22 above.

48   Brian Wilson thought it would be "real cool" to name the group after the Pendleton plaid wool shirt then popular with surfers. See Keith Badman, "The Beach Boys" (Backbeat, 2004), p.16.

49   The original line-up was as follows: Mike Love – lead vocals & saxophone, Carl Wilson – lead guitar, vocals, bass & percussion, Al Jardine – bass, rhythm guitar & vocals, Dennis Wilson – drums & vocals, and Brian Wilson – keyboards, bass, percussion & vocals.

50   Bob Dylan, "Chronicles (Volume One)" (Pocket Books, 2005), p.22.

51   Reprinted in Robert Shelton, "No Direction Home: The Life & Music of Bob Dylan" (Omnibus, revised/updated edition, 2011), p.86.

52   Anthony Scaduto, "Bob Dylan: An Intimate Biography" (W.H. Allen, 1972), p.97.

53   Robert Shelton, op. cit., p.87.

54　　Then America's largest record label, generally referred to in Britain as CBS (from the title of the parent company, Columbia Broadcasting Systems) to distinguish it from EMI's subsidiary Columbia label.

55　　Bob Dylan, op. cit., p.279.

56　　Ibid.

57　　According to Clinton Heylin, between 1957 and 1973, Dylan composed 300 songs, of which he wrote 207 between 1962 and 1967. See Heylin, "Revolution in the Air {The Songs of Bob Dylan Vol.1: 1957-73}" (Constable, 2009), pp.4-5.

58　　Vee was almost as popular in the UK, where "Take Good Care Of My Baby" got to No.2. His other UK hits included "Rubber Ball" (No.3 in 1961), "Run To Him" (No.8 in 1962) and "The Night Has A Thousand Eyes" (No.3 in 1963).

59　　See Bob Dylan, op. cit., p.81. He included his own interpretation of "Blue Moon" on *Self Portrait* (1970), whilst his song "Beyond The Horizon" (on Modern Times, 2006) owes more than a passing debt to "Red Sails In The Sunset".

60　　Phillip Knightley & Caroline Kennedy, "An Affair of State: The Profumo Case and the Framing of Stephen Ward" (Jonathan Cape, 1987), p.85.

61　　Anthony Summers & Stephen Dorril, "Honeytrap" (Coronet, 1988), p.18.

62　　Marshall McLuhan & Quentin Fiore, "The Medium is the Massage: An Inventory of Effects" (Penguin, 1967), p.63.

63　　Deborah Cadbury, "Space Race" (Fourth Estate, 2005), p.ix.

64　　Quoted in Tom Wolfe, "The Right Stuff" (Bantam, 1981), pp.228-229.

65　　Christian G. Appy, "Vietnam: The Definitive Oral History Told from All Sides" (Ebury Press, 2006), p.61.

66　　See Derrik Mercer (ed.) et al., "Chronicle of the 20th Century" (Longman Chronicle, 1988), p.872.

67　　Harry Thompson, "Peter Cook: A Biography" (Hodder & Stoughton, 1997), p.96.

68　　See Alan Bennett, Peter Cook, Jonathan Miller & Dudley Moore, "The Complete *Beyond The Fringe*" (Methuen, 1987), p.150. Appendix 4 on the history of the revue on record may safely be regarded as definitive, even though Hunter Davies (op. cit., p.166) originally attributed this recording to the pre-West-End run in Cambridge.

69　　Alan Bennett, Peter Cook, Jonathan Miller & Dudley Moore, op. cit., p.54. Cook not only got an opportunity to deliver this piece directly to the target of his anger, when "Macmillan himself plucked up the courage to try and prove what a good sport he was, by turning up to see himself impersonated", but also subsequently to the Queen, who – to the cast's dismay – "openly roared with laughter" at it. See Harry Thompson, op. cit., pp.113-114.

70　　Alan Bennett et al., op. cit., pp.81-82.

Chapter 4

1962

FIRST NO.1 OF THE YEAR –
"Stranger On The Shore" by Mr. Acker Bilk

LAST NO.1 OF THE YEAR –
"The Next Time" by Cliff Richard

When all is said and done, the Beatles ultimately owe their success not to intuitive managers or prescient record producers but to President Kennedy[1]; for while 1962 was the year that brought the pre-Beatles' era of pop music to a close, it would also, without Kennedy's determination to outface Kruschev in the Cuban Missile Crisis, have been the year in which the modern world ended in a war of nuclear attrition – and the rest would have been silence, not history. Hence for my generation, there never was – nor ever has been since – a more ominous year in our collective memory, when we all held our breath to bursting point in mortal dread of "One push of the button/And a shot the world wide"[2] becoming a vengeful reality totally beyond our control.

It is for this reason, then, that I see 1962 as a watershed in the course of this progress through the Sixties, after which our lives and the music of our lives were totally re-energised by the repercussions of that one defining outcome of world history. From that autumn onwards, we sought more keenly, more urgently, the words to capture, express and proclaim our fears and aspirations and found them in the most accessible vocabulary of pop, a modern and occasionally, at its finest, an ultra-radical poetry set to music, "moon and June" worn down and washed away by "hard rain". A quest initially embraced more fervently in America than Britain, nevertheless its universal impact not only on lyrical content but also musical form would become irreversible within the space of the next three years.

The events of October 1962 inescapably provided the chilling historical context in which the Beatles launched their professional recording career proper, for by then Britain had already lost any pretence of strategic military independence to the USA. In 1960, Macmillan had struck a bilateral arms agreement with President Eisenhower, one of its provisions being that:

> ... the US Navy could use the Holy Loch on the Firth of Clyde as
> a Polaris submarine base. However, not only was the Holy Loch
> disturbingly close to major population centres in western Scotland,

but the Americans made no commitment to consult their British counterparts before using their Polaris fleet in anger, an act which would quite probably bring utter devastation to the British Isles.[3]

By 1962, the potentially catastrophic consequences of this subservience were all too clear:

> Britain was, in military terms, little more than a client state. The most important nuclear decisions were made not in Whitehall or Westminster but in Washington DC ... There is no doubt that British forces would have seen action if the crisis had not been peacefully resolved, and little doubt either that the country would itself have been a target.[4]

Specifically, the British commitment would have been to launch the RAF's V-bomber force on retaliatory nuclear strikes, a task for which it stood on high alert throughout the crisis.

Friday, 5th October saw the release of the Beatles' first single for Parlophone, "Love Me Do"; and in the course of the next two weeks, President Kennedy ordered U2 spy planes to overfly Cuba, to secure hard photographic evidence of the suspected installation of Russian missile bases. By Sunday 21st October, that evidence had extended to pictures of airbases housing new Russian warplanes under construction. Thus, against all the imagined odds, the real and imminent danger of a nuclear attack had now manifested itself right in America's backyard. In a Presidential broadcast the next day, Kennedy denounced the Russians' actions and imposed a naval blockade on Cuba. There then followed, in the agonisingly slow diplomatic ritual of the pre-computer revolution, an exchange of hostilities by formal letters passing between Kennedy and Kruschev, embodying threats and counter-threats to resolve their differences. Finally, on Sunday 28th October, came the breakthrough:

> The world took a step back from the brink of nuclear war today when Mr. Kruschev promised that the Russian missiles based in Cuba would be dismantled and shipped back to the Soviet Union. In return, President Kennedy promised that the United States would not invade Cuba and would lift the blockade imposed on Cuba by the US.
>
> The two super-powers have been head-to-head for the past week in their game of nuclear poker while the rest of the world watched, fascinated, but hardly daring to breathe in case one of the players made a fatal mistake.[5]

Knowing now for certain that the space race really was all about developing the capability to blow people to bits all round the world, it was surely the richest of paradoxes that for the whole of the period in question, the No.1 record in Britain was "Telstar", by the Tornados[6], a tune composed and produced by self-confessed space fanatic Joe Meek in praise of the first-ever telecommunications satellite. Indeed, had diplomacy not prevailed over lunacy on this occasion, I am more than certain that he would have been perversely pleased if his greatest hit had turned out at the end to be the theme tune to Armageddon.

Launched from Cape Canaveral in Florida on 10th July 1962, Telstar-1 was the first commercial satellite to be placed in earth orbit, transmitting both transatlantic television and telephone signals at strictly limited inter-vals between America, Britain and France. Originally a television engineer before turning to record production, Meek could not fail to be instantly captivated by this breakthrough and had stayed up after midnight to watch the first transatlantic TV broadcast, which of itself was less than compelling: a 30-second blurred monochrome image of "a man in a dark suit sitting motionless at a desk".[7] Yet strangely this was enough to give Meek a restless night's sleep, from which he emerged next morning with the germ of a tune in his head which he then committed to tape.

Summoning the Tornados on a Sunday from Great Yarmouth (where they were appearing in summer season as Billy Fury's backing group) to his ramshackle Holloway Road studio, Meek set them to work recording his instrumental composition. The session not concluded to his satisfaction by the end of the day, the group returned next morning but had to set off back to Great Yarmouth soon after midday to honour a matinee commitment, leaving Meek to call upon the services of his psychic collaborator Geoff Goddard to finish the track. By nightfall, a combination of Goddard's piano playing, overlaid by the clavioline (a miniature battery-operated keyboard akin to Rolf Harris's stylophone[8]) and further sound effects created by Meek, together with the speeding up of the entire recording by half a tone, saw the job completed. For the time, the result was a masterpiece of ingenuity, with an unrivalled other-worldly quality. No other record so perfectly encapsulates the distinctive Meek sound, for which he had striven so long: "Nothing like it had ever been heard before and, as intended, it conjured up the very image of a television satellite racing through space ... and finally soaring resolutely away on a crescendo of rampant energy and freedom."[9]

"Telstar" was pitched to Dick Rowe, released by Decca and became an unforeseen smash hit internationally. Achieving total sales in excess of five million, not only was it No.1 in Britain but by Christmas it had also become the first record by a British group to take the No.1 slot in the US *Billboard* chart, its popularity subsequently extending around the world. The first million sales were recognised on 15th December by the presentation of a Gold Disc to the Tornados on *Thank Your Lucky Stars*, with the second million clocked up by the first week of January 1963.

In honour of this extraordinary success, in March the Tornados once again returned to *Thank Your Lucky Stars*, but now to present Meek their mentor with a unique special Gold Disc on prime-time television. The following May saw him honoured as the composer of "Telstar" by an Ivor Novello Award. At that very moment of triumph, however, he found the remainder of his life blighted, when a French composer of film scores embarked upon legal action against him (turning out to be protracted over many years) for alleged breach of copyright, a claim Meek strenuously denied.[10] The royalties accruing to him for "Telstar" (which at the onset of the action amounted to some £29,000) were immediately frozen, pending determination of the case, but a final settlement was not to be reached until after Meek's violent and untimely death in 1967, the principal cause of which was his morbid preoccupation with the continuing strain of litigation and his perceived loss of reputation.[11]

For all the joy – and, ultimately, grief – that it brought him, Joe Meek's composition of "Telstar" still stands out as a rare example in British Sixties' pop of art imitating life. As a general rule, throughout the decade the evolution of pop can be seen to be running in parallel with history but at one or two isolated points, such as this one, a surge of creative energy fuels a crossover, when the music finds itself directly inspired by world events. Of the fact that Meek was immediately seized with the idea and ran with it, there can be no doubt. From his seeing the first Telstar-1 transmission on Wednesday, 11th July, both the composition and recording of his tune literally took him only a matter of days, to be rapidly followed by securing deals with his music publisher and a major recording company, the record then being released on 17th August. Within two months of its inception, on 15th September "Telstar" had entered the *NME* Top 30 at No.10. In another three weeks, outselling Elvis Presley, it reached No.1, holding that position for five weeks all told, and continuing sales were so strong as to sustain it in the Top 30 until 26th January 1963.

What makes the Tornados' success with "Telstar" all the more remarkable is that they were taken up by Decca, the company that earlier in the year gained eternal notoriety in pop history by declaring that "guitar groups are on the way out". For this was the supposedly considered basis on which Dick Rowe and Mike Smith denied the Beatles a recording contract, following their audition for Decca on New Year's Day.

In a van driven by road manager Neil Aspinall, the Beatles' overnight journey from Liverpool to London on New Year's Eve was long, cold and uncomfortable. (Brian Epstein travelled separately by train.) Altogether it took them ten hours, with an unwelcome hiatus in Wolverhampton en route when driving snow temporarily caused them to lose their way; hardly surprising, since Aspinall had never actually been to London before. Sadly, as befitted this period long before the present well-lit, well-signed national motorway network was established, little better could be expected of long-distance night-time motoring then. So it was in itself an achievement for them to have made it at all to London in midwinter, in time to attend Decca's West Hampstead studios at 11 o'clock on Monday, 1st January (New Year's Day then still being a working day, not yet a public holiday, in England).

In a session overseen personally by Mike Smith, on this occasion the Beatles recorded fifteen songs of Epstein's choice, intended to demonstrate their breadth and versatility. The result, though not unusual for its time and reflective of their current stage act, was nevertheless a hotch-potch:

> … three Lennon-McCartney compositions ('Like Dreamers Do', 'Hello Little Girl' and 'Love of the Loved'), two eccentric arrangements of old standards, seven cover versions of 1950s material – encompassing rock and roll, R&B and C&W – two soft ballads and a contemporary chart hit.[12]

Still, from that mixed set time has shown that their own compositions alone had hit potential, as proved in due course when they were subsequently passed on to and recorded by other artists[13]; and, of the covers, two became contrasting but strong tracks in their own right when revisited on the 1963 LP *With The Beatles*.[14]

Although they and Epstein left the studios strong in the belief that they had impressed Smith, they were to be unsuccessful. A group from north-east London who auditioned immediately after the Beatles that same day, Brian Poole and the Tremeloes[15], found greater favour with Smith, after further discussion of both groups' merits with Dick Rowe, and turned out to be the ones to be offered a contract with Decca. Rowe himself admitted that geography as much as talent had informed their decision:

> So [Smith] chose Brian Poole, and I can understand that because I heard the auditions. The auditions by Brian Poole were better than the Beatles'. Another reason why Mike made that decision was that the Beatles were resident in Liverpool. Brian Poole lived only a mile away from Mike Smith, so he knew he could spend night and day with Brian Poole at no cost to the company, whereas Liverpool is a long way away. You've got to get on a train. You've got a hotel bill to pay. You don't know how long you're going to be up there. And London is so very strange about the north of England. There's sort of an expression that if you live in London, you don't know anywhere north of Watford. So, you see, Liverpool could have been in Greenland to us then.[16]

To add further insult to this blatant injury of regional prejudice, Rowe and Smith prevaricated for weeks before finally confirming the outcome to Epstein, out of grudging – if not downright patronising – respect for his strong business standing with the record company, eventually withdrawing behind the pretence that the Beatles were weak musically. Even though Smith was clearly equally culpable, it was this disingenuousness on Rowe's part which drew opprobrium to him for all time as 'the man who turned down the Beatles':

> … when I heard the audition tapes and I heard their renditions of
> tunes like 'Money' and 'Twist And Shout'[17], to me, they were the
> same as a number of English artists like Terry Dean [*sic*] and even
> Billy Fury. They were adequate, they were making adequate covers,
> but there was nothing really that startling about them … Eventually
> I told Brian that the people at Decca didn't like the boys' sound
> and that groups with guitars were on the way out. Brian replied,
> "You must be out of your mind. These boys are going to explode.
> I'm completely confident that one day they'll be bigger than
> Elvis Presley." I told Brian, "You have a good record business in
> Liverpool, Mr. Epstein. Stick to that."[18]

Luckily for the Beatles, for all that Smith and Rowe then lacked in originality and foresight[19], it was to the redoubtable Mr. Epstein's eternal credit that he could more than make up for this rebuff through his own dogged determination. Knowing how strong their home fanbase was becoming, it was of no consequence to him that the music industry of the day should decree that the north was another country.[20] After all, on 4th January, only three days after their trip down to London, *Mersey Beat* declared the Beatles the top group in Liverpool in its first-ever popularity poll[21]; and the following day saw at long last the official release by Polydor in Britain of "My Bonnie".

One last throw with Decca proved abortive, when Tony Meehan, the ex-Shadow turned A&R man and producer, was as dismissive as his colleagues of a proposal to cut a single with the Beatles. Nevertheless, now armed with the audition tapes from New Year's Day, Epstein still persisted in travelling to and from London, trying to prise a contract from one of the other major British record companies yet repeatedly drawing a blank.[22] The problem was (as later acknowledged by John Lennon) that whoever he approached on the group's behalf, record executives seemed locked in the past, incapable of spotting a new trend:

> … they were so dumb, when they listened to these audition tapes
> they were listening for The Shadows. So they were not listening to
> it at all – they're listening like they do now – you know how these
> people are – for what's already gone down. They can't hear anything
> new.[23]

But in early February, Epstein accessed technical facilities at HMV's flag-ship store in Oxford Street to convert the precious tapes (on cumbersome reels, it must be remembered, not convenient latter-day cassettes) to more manageable 78 rpm demo discs. As luck would have it, the building also housed the offices of music publishers Ardmore and Beechwood; and at the suggestion of the record-cutting engineer, Jim Foy, Epstein was intro-duced to their general manager, Sid Colman, with a view to pursuing possible publishing rights to Lennon and McCartney's own compositions. In turn, Colman, showing some sympathy towards Epstein in his continuing quest for a recording contract, offered him an introduction to George Martin and so it was that on 13th February they met for the first time at EMI's head offices. From this one fortuitous meeting, all else would flow, rightly earning Epstein the Beatles' respect, including that of John, the arch-sceptic:

> He got us to EMI, it was his walking round. If he hadn't gone
> round London, on foot, with the tapes under his arm, and gone
> from place to place, and place to place, and finally to George
> Martin, we would never have made it.[24]

That the Beatles had readily accepted Epstein's managerial interventions more or less from his first overture to them was not in doubt, although legally their contractual relationship with him still remained tenuous. The previous December's loose discussions of intent between them had become more formalised at a further meeting on 24th January, at which all four Beatles (i.e., John, Paul, George and Pete Best) were presented with and signed a contract, duly witnessed by Epstein's aide, Alistair Taylor. Yet oddly this was still a document which Epstein himself did not sign and two of the signatories (Paul and George) were too young in law to independently make a contract. Epstein's view at this stage, handed down to posterity, was apparently that he considered himself sufficiently bound by a gentleman's agreement to work in their interests.[25]

Despite all Epstein's best endeavours, at last now showing real promise, the Beatles themselves would, however, have a three-month wait before they met and auditioned for Martin in person. In that interim period, while Martin appeared to be in no particular hurry to advance matters, Epstein busied himself by setting up an increasingly widening variety of performing commitments for them; encompassing concert dates, travelling to Manchester (twice) to audition for and then record songs for their first-ever BBC radio broadcast[26] and culminating in their return to Hamburg in April.

As it turned out, this particular trip back to Germany was to mark the beginning of the end of the formative Beatles' era. For a start, it was the first of their Hamburg contracts to be negotiated directly on their behalf by Epstein. Although originally renewed interest in a return gig had been expressed by Peter Eckhorn (for whom they had performed the year before at the Top Ten Club), he failed to meet Epstein's new higher demands for a weekly fee per group member and the prize subsequently went to Manfred Wiessleder, negotiated through his intermediary Horst Fascher, scooping a seven-week contract for the Beatles to play at his brand new Star-Club.

Then on arrival in Germany, they were greeted by Astrid Kirchherr with her devastating news that Stuart Sutcliffe, aesthete and indifferent bass player in their earlier five-man line-up, had died of a brain haemorrhage on 10th April, aged 21. Although no longer associated with the Beatles musically, nevertheless the sudden finality of his death pulled them up short, tearing down as it did a bridge to their past as well as inevitably spooking them with premature intimations of their own mortality. Paul's reflections possibly speak best for the feelings of the group as a whole, painfully mixing sincere loss and ill-at-ease sorrow, in the realisation that what had passed between them all, be it for good or ill, was now beyond remedy:

> Not many of our contemporaries had died; we were all too young.
> It was older people that died, so Stuart's dying was a real shock.
> And for me there was a little guilt tinged with it, because I'd not
> been his best friend at times … Everyone was very sad, though the
> blow was softened by the fact that he'd stayed in Hamburg and we'd
> got used to not being with him.[27]

Still, the Beatles' show had to go on, starting from the Star-Club's opening night on 13th April and continuing until 31st May, this experience different from those before in that for two out of the seven weeks they played in company with their rock'n'roll idol Gene Vincent. Although they retained abiding memories of some of his wilder antics off-stage (he prided himself on being an ex-Marine and being versed in unarmed combat but nevertheless also carried a gun), John, for one, nurtured the impossible dream of his hero forever regenerating the magic of past moments of rock'n'roll frenzy long since frozen on vinyl, feeling that by this time Vincent had lost his performing edge.

In some ways, securing the Beatles their third contract in Hamburg at this pivotal point in their career was a perverse deal for Epstein to have struck. Whilst it did guarantee them an uninterrupted seven weeks' good income, sending them out of the country simultaneously with trying his hardest to promote them to English record companies could be seen at the least as managerial naivety on his part; even though it enabled him to indulge in the hyperbole of describing it as a "European tour" on local handbills.

Then there was the issue of the German club milieu to which Epstein was returning the Beatles, at a point when domestically he had already taken his first resolute steps towards altering their image by insisting, for example, on them wearing sharp new suits for all their engagements; his mission being, in Philip Norman's words, to rearrange "the four, black-leather, drag-gle-headed, swearing, prancing Hamburg rockers to reflect his own idea of what a successful Pop group ought to be".[28] For all that it was the newest on the block, neither was the Star-Club any more sophisticated nor any less 'exotic' than its predecessors on the Grosse Freiheit:

> [Manfred] Weissleder had hired Horst Fascher and his gang of freelance strong-arm waiters to rule the Star-Club's enormous darkness. From 8pm to 4am, as many as 15,000 people could pass through it, staying long enough to hear one favoured group, then moving on to other clubs and returning after midnight for the same group's second 'spot'. After 2am, the club was packed with the Freiheit's own population of whores, pimps, bouncers, strippers and transvestites. There were also the ships' companies – French, American and British – from the port, in consideration of whom Horst Fascher maintained a special bouncer called Ali who could do wrestler's drop kicks and still land on his feet.[29]

Aside from the unpredictable Gene Vincent, this stint at the Star-Club saw the Beatles sharing the stage with local Liverpool rivals Gerry and the Pacemakers. It also reunited them with Tony Sheridan, with whom they returned to a recording studio in late April as his backing group, to honour a final commitment to Bert Kaempfert before he would relinquish his original contract with them in favour of Brian Epstein. It must, however, have been a remarkably undistinguished session, since seemingly no reliable evidence survives as to its content and outcomes, eluding even the professional Beatles' researcher and chronicler, Mark Lewisohn.[30]

The greater recording opportunity, of course, was to await them in England a matter of days after their return home. While they were still rocking through the night from spring into summer in Hamburg, George Martin had reopened communications with Epstein, the two of them meeting again on Wednesday, 9th May, at EMI's Abbey Road studios. The upshot was that Martin offered Epstein a contract for the Beatles; or, more properly, an option to record them subject to satisfactory audition. A jubi-lant yet concise telegram sent by Epstein to Germany straight after this meeting put the group on immediate notice to brace themselves for the biggest break yet in their musical career: **"CONGRATULATIONS BOYS. EMI REQUEST RECORDING SESSION. PLEASE REHEARSE NEW MATERIAL."**[31] At the same time, not allowing his excitement to cloud his eye to consequent publicity, Epstein also telegraphed Bill Harry of *Mersey Beat*: **"HAVE SECURED CONTRACT FOR BEATLES TO RECORDED [sic] FOR EMI ON PARLAPHONE [sic] LABEL. 1ST RECORDING DATE SET FOR JUNE 6TH."**[32]

On the wider British pop scene, the first half of 1962 had continued in a very similar vein to 1961, with vocal groups still in a significant minority, male solo artists predominant and the charts in general leavened from time to time by instrumental highlights; such as Acker Bilk's plaintive interpretation of the theme tune to the BBC TV serial *Stranger On The Shore*, which notably demonstrated (effectively for the first time) the specific power of television in relation to promoting a record to No.1.[33] (Following the same trend, in the spring, though with less spectacular success, came the theme tunes from the BBC's new, down-to-earth police drama *Z Cars*[34], the imported American hospital drama *Dr. Kildare*[35] and the series based on Georges Simenon's pipe-smoking French detective *Maigret*.[36])

Unsurprisingly, the popularity of Cliff Richard and the Shadows received a massive boost from the success on general release of *The Young Ones*. Cliff's single of the title track went straight into the Top 30 at No.1 on 13th January and held that position for 6 weeks in a row, not just becoming a million-seller but also his best-selling record ever. (Additionally, the original film soundtrack became the third best-selling LP of the year.) The edge was somewhat taken off his success, however, by the belated arrival from America of the twist as a dance craze in Britain, meaning that Cliff was pushed out of the No.1 slot at the end of February by an American interloper, Chubby Checker, with "Let's Twist Again".

The next few months then saw an unseemly rush of managers and record producers eagerly (though not always wisely) trying to cash in on Checker's success; with, ironically, Checker's own relentless output becoming the mechanism by which the market was saturated and then exhausted, with simultaneous releases of "The Twist"[37] and "Let's Twist Again" quickly followed by "Slow Twistin'". Although the dance itself was fun, its scope for musical diversity was strictly limited and enough very soon became enough. The best of a generally bad crop amongst Checker's competitors, Joey Dee and The Starliters' one-hit wonder "Peppermint Twist" and Sam Cooke's "Twistin' The Night Away" are today probably the only worthy survivors in twist posterity. Others, who should have known better yet nevertheless still let themselves be persuaded otherwise, included Petula Clark ("Ya Ya Twist"), Frankie Vaughan ("Don't Stop Twist") and Frank Sinatra ("Everybody's Twistin'"). While Petula could be forgiven for having youth on her side, the efforts of the two Franks simply smacked of desperation.

With Checker succeeded (briefly – and somewhat incongruously) by Kenny Ball's jazz version of "The March Of The Siamese Children" (from the musical film *The King And I*), the old firm regained its supremacy after three weeks with the Shadows' lush, pseudo-cinematic epic "Wonderful Land", which stayed at No.1 for 8 weeks. Subjected by producer and arranger

Norrie Paramor to the same drenching in strings that had previously given "The Young Ones" its emotive edge, it marked a high point in the Shadows' recording career. But at the same time the group again found itself subject to internal disharmony, fuelled by Jet Harris's increasing personal unhappiness and dependence on alcohol.

Soured by his young wife Carol's infidelity in the past with Cliff[38], Harris persisted in directing his frustration and anger against Bruce Welch, who in return showed callous disregard for his feelings. In April, the consequences for Jet were disastrous and irrevocable:

> Apart from all the good things that were happening to the group, Bruce was pissing me off more and more – he was like a bloody robot. When Carol left me for Cliff, Bruce came out with a real classic line that really hurt me and has remained imprinted on my brain, 'What are you so worried about, Jet, she's only a bloody woman!' The crunch came at the *NME* poll winners' concert at Wembley. The bar was open all day for the artists, so by the time I met up with the lads, I'd had a few. Bruce just turned on me with six little words. 'We don't really need you, Jet.' By then I'd had a bellyful of him. I walked out and never went back.[39]

The Shadows' swiftly recruited replacement as bass guitarist was Brian 'Licorice' Locking, a long-standing friend and professional colleague of Brian Bennett, the two of them last having played together in Marty Wilde's backing group the Wild Cats. Harris, meanwhile, amazingly fell on his feet within a fortnight of his constructive dismissal. Appearing with the Shadows for the last time at the *NME* concert on April 15th, he quickly turned to Jack Good for management and support and on April 27th signed up to a recording contract with Decca (where, of course, Tony Meehan was by now well ensconced in his A&R role). Two days later, on April 29th he was back in the studio, laying down his first single in his own right, with the (for the time being) uncredited Meehan sitting in on drums.

For all his past popularity with Shadows' fans for his mean and moody looks, as a bass player Jet Harris was not that well placed to strike out on a solo pop career. There were precious few precedents for supporting rather than lead musicians to break through and sustain recording success; the closest musical parallel in this instance possibly being Duane Eddy, who had exploited his signature 'twang' of echoing bass guitar riffs in a long-running sequence of American hits from 1958 onwards.

Though record sales were pulled through by the innate loyalty of his followers, and *NME* readers were later to vote him the Instrumental Personality of the Year, Harris's first solo steps were faltering and his early choice of material ill-advised. "Besame Mucho" was one of the least original compositions anyone could have chosen as a first record – by 1962, a well-hackneyed standard as a *song*, let alone an instrumental – and the production is, frankly, dire; an initial run-through of the tune on the electric bass then followed by the undistinguished vocal of anonymous backing singers. It scraped a Top 30 place at No.28 for one week at the end of May. Returning to the studio in June, his second single was far stronger and more in keeping with the idiom of the day, though still hardly contemporary. Clearly indebted stylistically to "Peter Gunn" (a British Top 10 hit for Duane Eddy in 1959), his version of the main title theme to the Fifties' American *film noir The Man With The Golden Arm*[40] combined thunderous bass lines with raucous attacking brass in best gangster tradition. Achieving chart entry in August, it eventually reached No.15 on 22nd September. It would not, however, be until the end of the year, having formally announced in November a performing reunion with Tony Meehan, when Harris would seriously aspire to stardom again.

Leaving the twist to disappear eventually up its own blind alley, the hits kept coming for both Cliff ("I'm Looking Out The Window", "Do You Want To Dance", "It'll Be Me") and the Shadows ("Guitar Tango", "Dance On"). The year ending with the imminent release of their next big film, *Summer Holiday*, and aided by television exposure on *Sunday Night At The London Palladium*, Cliff's final single of 1962, coupling two songs from the soundtrack ("The Next Time"/"Bachelor Boy"), was assured of double-A-side success. As it turned out, the slower, more sentimental "The Next Time" just had the edge, becoming the last No.1 of the year on 29th December.

Other already well-established artists experienced more mixed fortunes, many of the better performances again being American despite the fact that in percentage terms there was an almost even division between Top 40 records of US and UK origin. This was the year, for example, when Brenda Lee sold well in Britain, "Speak To Me Pretty" and "Here Comes That Feeling" being two of her strongest records ever (although the less said about her novelty best-seller "Rockin' Around The Christmas Tree", from which annually there seems to have been no escape since, the better). Neil Sedaka bounced back too, irrepressible as ever, with "Happy Birthday Sweet Sixteen" and "Breaking Up Is Hard To Do". By comparison, times were temporarily leaner in the British charts for Roy Orbison, yet he still managed to produce at least one classic, in the form of "Dream Baby". But in the first half of 1962, two American singles in particular stand out, in terms of their subsequent legacy: "Crying In The Rain" and "Hey! Baby".

"Crying In The Rain"[41] rightly has a place in the gallery of two-minute wonders for which the early Sixties are renowned. To those more attuned to A-ha's brooding Scandinavian revival of the song in 1990[42], it may come as a shock to find that the Everly Brothers' original version is not simply devoid of all sound effects but only plays for 1 minute 58 seconds. Even so, the combination of lyrics and harmony take it to a higher plane, using the classic literary device of pathetic fallacy to align the state of the weather to human emotions. Hence the falling rain fittingly reflects and masks the tears of the broken-hearted lover/narrator:

> I've got my pride and I know how to hide
> All my sorrow and pain:
> I'll do my crying in the rain.
> If I wait for cloudy skies,
> You won't know the rain from the tears in my eyes.

With the relationship irretrievably at an end, for now the rain provides both temporary comfort and refuge:

> But since we're not together,
> I look for stormy weather
> To hide these tears I hope you'll never see.

And, inevitably, when it comes, recovery will one day be heralded by the rainclouds' passing:

> Someday, when my crying's done,
> I'm gonna wear a smile and walk in the sun.

At this point in their career, as Elvis before them, the Everlys had inconveniently been called up for military service and, having enlisted in the Marine Corps, were having to fit time for new recordings into their short spells of leave. "Crying In The Rain" was written for them by two of the rising Brill Building composers, Howard Greenfield and Carole King, in a one-off pairing they attempted on a whim; the care devoted to the task by King herself painstakingly extending to a demo of the song on which "she had even overdubbed the duo's harmonies" and which the Everlys "followed nearly note for note" in the studio.[43] Their efforts were finally rewarded by a top position of No.6 on 17th February.[44]

In stark contrast, Bruce Channel's "Hey! Baby"[45] falls into an entirely different category. By itself, the lyric is inconsequentially vulgar, little more than the equivalent of a wolf-whistle, a shout across the street to the receding vision of a pretty girl passing by from a precocious boy who won't take 'No' for an answer. While the simple refrain gives Channel's voice ample scope to soar and swoop ("Hey, hey hey baby!/I want to know-ow-ow if you'll be my girl"), the record's true magic lies in Delbert McClinton's bluesy harmonica, drawing on his past experience of accompanying the likes of Sonny Boy Williamson, Howlin' Wolf and Jimmy Reed in bars and clubs around Fort Worth, Texas. Taking the No.2 slot for the whole of April, Channel and McClinton later came to England on tour and found themselves (on 21st June) sharing a bill with the Beatles at the Tower Ballroom, New Brighton, where offstage McClinton was pleased to show an impressionable John Lennon, at his request, some of his harmonica tricks.

As the year went on, the harmonica continued to resonate in the charts as the instrument of choice for distinctive accompaniment. For example, it featured prominently on the Everlys' follow-up to "Crying In The Rain", an altogether weaker and now little-known composition called "How Can I Meet Her?"[46] (again emanating from a temporary Brill Building partnership, this time of Gerry Goffin and Jack Keller) which struggled to No.22 in June. Then in July, a returning Australian émigré, Frank Ifield, who originally hailed from Coventry, entered the Top 30 with "I Remember You"[47], a song in which almost every line was punctuated by the harmonica. A fortnight later, it was at No.1, where it stayed for eight weeks, and ended the year as both a million-seller and Best Single in the annual *NME* Pop Poll.

A plaintive harmonica instrumental break was also a highlight of Brian Hyland's "Sealed With A Kiss"[48], a hit from August through to October that peaked at No. 5 in early September. The song gives a teenage male's perspective on the hiatus in a relationship occasioned by the long American summer vacation, with the promise of constancy maintained by daily love letters:

> Though we've got to say goodbye
> For the summer,
> Darling, I promise you this:
> I'll send you all my love
> Every day in a letter
> Sealed with a kiss.

Although the sun may shine, for the parted lovers it will still be a "cold, lonely summer", to be redeemed only when they are eventually reunited:

> Let us make a pledge
> To meet in September
> And seal it with a kiss.

As Hyland's sales tailed off in early autumn, Carole King pushed herself forward to deliver a more forceful female riposte to the same dilemma of enforced separation, in "It Might As Well Rain Until September"[49] (which reached No.3 in mid-October). Here, in the slow opening bars, is a girl who is truly forlorn:

> What shall I write?
> What can I say?
> How can I tell you how much I miss you?

But a punchy beat kicks in on the first verse and the issue is clear. The weather is immaterial and of no consolation in the long months apart:

> The weather here has been as nice as it can be,
> Although it doesn't really matter much to me.
> For all the fun I'll have while you're so far away,
> It might as well rain until September.

While her friends "look forward to their picnics on the beach", she'll stay at home moping, all through the summer, until the lovers can be together again:

> It doesn't matter whether skies are grey or blue,
> It's raining in my heart 'cause I can't be with you.
> I'm only living for the day you're home to stay,
> So it might as well rain until September,
> September, September, oh
> It might as well rain until September.

On that final reprise of the refrain, the plucking of strings fades up, to echo both the seemingly interminable ticking of the clock and the splashing of the raindrops. A lyrical masterpiece of affected moodiness, the nasal, almost gravelly quality of King's voice gives the song a wholly different dimension from what might have been achieved by its original intended recipient, Bobby Vee.[50] (The record as known to us today was actually King's demo for Vee, whose record company prevaricated over its release.)

A good gauge to the musical flavour of 1962 comes from a look at the last Top 30 for October, immediately prior to the resolution of the Cuban Missile Crisis. If this had turned out to be the point at which the music – together with everything else – died, the No.1 playing us out to the apocalypse, as we have already seen, would have been "Telstar". The chart for 27th October as a whole was divided evenly between records of US and UK origins and 60% of the entries were from solo males. For Britain, the line-up included Mark Wynter, Frank Ifield (with three hits that week), Cliff, Adam Faith, Billy Fury and Ronnie Carroll. The American contingent, by contrast, was made up of Tommy Roe, Nat King Cole, Chris Montez, Ray Charles, Del Shannon, Elvis, Marty Robbins, Johnny Tillotson, Bobby Darin and even Buddy Holly (at No.28 with "Reminiscing", a 'new', previously unreleased posthumous single).

Of the 5 solo female performers, the only two British singers were Shirley Bassey (at No.10 with "What Now My Love") and Susan Maughan (at No. 25 with "Bobby's Girl"). They were competing against Little Eva (at No.2 with "The Loco-motion", another hit from the Goffin/King stable), Carole King herself (as we have seen above) and Brenda Lee (with the lesser-known "It Started All Over Again" at No.21).

A hint of jazz still lingered, from trad stalwarts Acker Bilk and Kenny Ball, but there was a more significant new orchestral entry at No.30 from John

Barry, with "The James Bond Theme" from *Dr. No* initiating the modern genre of blockbuster film scores. As for vocal groups, they were few and far between. As the Beatles achieved their first, fleeting entry at No.27 with "Love Me Do", three weeks after its release, pride of place went (at No.12) to the Four Seasons, with their extraordinary falsetto hymn to "Sherry". The only other contenders were the Everly Brothers, with the now obscure "No One Can Make My Sunshine Smile" entering at No.19.

So when the Beatles took up George Martin's offer and presented themselves at Abbey Road on 6th June (the 18th anniversary, as it happened, of the D-Day landings), the prevailing commercial climate for new groups was distinctly chilly. Although Martin himself made no secret of his personal ambition to emulate Norrie Paramor's success with Cliff and the Shadows, seeing rock'n'roll records as "something easy to make"[51], he was by no means overwhelmed by what he saw and heard that day. That he persisted at all was remarkable enough, given that, aside from his work with Matt Monro, in the course of the year he added three Top 30 hits for Bernard Cribbins[52] to his already long list of highly popular comedy productions.

Their chosen audition pieces, taken from their current stage repertoire, were the habitual mix of self-compositions, other contemporary hits and standards; including (from George Harrison's recollection) "Love Me Do", "PS I Love You", "Ask Me Why", "Besame Mucho" and "Your Feet's Too Big".[53] The session was not directly overseen by Martin but by his assistant producer Ron Richards[54] and recording engineer Norman Smith. Eventually called to the studio at Smith's suggestion to give his opinion, Martin concluded that "their music was rubbish" but John, Paul and George had "wonderful charisma".[55] (There would soon be more than passing significance to the fact that he was not taken with Pete Best, who came across as "very much the background boy", looking "moody and sullen in the corner" with little to say.[56])

In the end, therefore, EMI's decision to take the Beatles forward was critically determined by Martin's assessment of how biddable he might find them to work with, underpinned by the good-humoured rapport they sought to strike up with him on first acquaintance. From their perspective, because his speech palpably lacked any hint of a regional accent, he was 'posh', yet there was no sense of an insurmountable barrier between them: for example, George Harrison found him "friendly, but schoolteacherly: we had to respect him, but at the same time he gave us the impression that he wasn't stiff – that you could joke with him."[57]

Given, then, the largely satisfactory outcome of their first encounter with each other, the way was clear for the draft recording contract submitted in advance to Brian Epstein to be confirmed[58] and time to be devoted in earnest to recording the Beatles' first professional single in Britain; an exercise in the course of which both parties revealed the strength of their respective characters, by laying down important parameters for their future working relationship. The process, however, was by no means instant, not being set in train until September, and in the intervening period two other major events, of differing consequence, occurred.

The first of these was the sacking of Pete Best as the Beatles' drummer, carried out by Brian Epstein in his office on the morning of Thursday, 16th August. Locally, it was controversial, not least because of the standing of the Best family in the wider musical community of Liverpool. The basement of their house, converted by Pete's mother Mona to the Casbah Club, had provided a highly popular venue for many fledgling groups – including the would-be Beatles – and their teenage followers in the earliest days of Merseybeat. Hence Pete was well-known and popular; and in the immediate aftermath, the Beatles were not only verbally abused at concerts but George also sustained a black eye from one enraged fan.

Any number of theories continue to circulate to explain his removal, some musical, some more personal. To the extent that there is any consistency between the various explanations or rationalisations, there does seem to be agreement that as a drummer Best was not proficient enough for professional performance and recording. George Martin himself, as we have seen, was unimpressed by his general demeanour at Abbey Road on 6th June. Furthermore, he had decided, on the evidence of that day, that "Pete Best's drumming wasn't good enough and it wasn't going to make [his] life very easy producing good records"[59], an opinion he conveyed directly to Brian Epstein.

Martin was not to know, of course, that this would add to the growing misgivings entertained by the other Beatles at the same time about Pete's continuing membership of the group. Their thoughts had already turned secretly to poaching Ringo Starr from Rory Storm and the Hurricanes, then playing a summer season at Butlin's holiday camp in Skegness. Surreptitious soundings were taken; first by George calling on Ringo's mother at home, then by John and Paul travelling to Skegness to speak to him in person. With Pete Best sacked and a formal offer confirmed, Ringo decamped to Liverpool and made his first appearance with the Beatles on Saturday, 18th August, at the Hulme Hall, the occasion being the 17th annual dance of the Port Sunlight Horticultural Society. The group's definitive, enduring line-up was in place.

Pete Best's dismissal was followed a week later, on 23rd August, by the surprise marriage of John Lennon to his unexpectedly pregnant girlfriend, fellow art student Cynthia Powell; a measure, if nothing else, of the sexual naivety of those days, given that, according to her, the couple had never used contraception.[60] In a ceremony at Liverpool's Mount Pleasant Registry Office which Cynthia described as an "odd mixture of the comically funny and the downright bizarre"[61], the Registrar's words were drowned out at the critical moment by the din from a workman's pneumatic drill outside the building. Brian Epstein stood in as John's best man. Paul and George were also in attendance, Paul sharing with Cynthia's brother Tony and sister-in-law Marjorie the formal responsibility of witnessing the signing of the register.[62] Departing the registry office to find it pouring with rain, the wedding party hurriedly withdrew to nearby Reece's Café, where they had "to queue for the set lunch of soup, chicken and trifle" and raise the customary toasts with water, since Reece's was unlicensed.[63] John shrugged off any discomfort at finding himself married by saying it was "all a laugh": he likened his embarrassment to "walking about with odd socks on or your flies open".[64] They spent their wedding night apart, John having to play with the Beatles at a prior booking in Chester.

These events aside, the weeks passing after the Beatles' EMI audition continued to be packed for them by Epstein with bookings on a slowly widening concert circuit. (In the first two months alone following their return from Hamburg, they "fulfilled a staggering total of 62 live engagements".[65]) His approach, as meticulous as it was demanding, was specifically intended to raise their professional game, with a weekly issue to the group of statements of account for the previous seven days and his own specific briefing notes for each engagement in the seven days to come, unfailingly emphasising "the need for punctuality and smart appearance".[66]

Star quality – or at least hit potential – was certainly what George Martin craved in his bid to challenge Norrie Paramor's supremacy as producer of Cliff and the Shadows. To that end, he was searching for a surefire hit and was pitched a song by music publisher Dick James[67], composed by Mitch Murray, entitled "How Do You Do It". Thinking it commercial enough to be a possible No.1, Martin sent the Beatles a copy of the demo[68], thereby putting them on notice to prepare it as the main number for their first recording session proper with him on Tuesday, 4th September.

While Martin's intuition as to the future success of the song cannot be faulted [69], he had reckoned without the Beatles' unanimous dislike of it and their determination, notwithstanding their relative inexperience, to secure and retain positive control of their artistic direction. For them, succumbing to "How Do You Do It" would have smacked too much of having a traditional show-business formula imposed upon them, one that in their view was outdated. As Paul put it, with unparalleled foresight: "We didn't want to be like Cliff Richard and everyone else in England, because it was all changing then, too. We felt like we were the generation after Cliff."[70] This said, they were canny enough not to be confrontational about it and humoured Martin by taping unenthusiastic take after take of their own re-arrangement of the song until he finally capitulated.

Much studio time was therefore also devoted to perfecting an acceptable take of one of Paul's earliest compositions, "Love Me Do"[71], a task eventually completed at a further recording session on 11th September. On this occasion, having been dissatisfied with Ringo's first input as drummer the week before, Martin exercised his authority as producer by re-recording the song with session drummer Andy White. This was also the day on which "PS I Love You" and an early version of "Please Please Me" were recorded. The eventual outcome was agreement to release "Love Me Do" (coupled with "PS I Love You" as the B-side) as the Beatles' first single on Parlophone, which happened on Friday, 5th October.[72] Henceforward, all subsequent Beatles' singles were to have the distinction of being songs of their own composing, effectively breaking the mould of the old order of pop stars once and for all.

The musicologist Ian MacDonald characterised "Love Me Do" as "extraordinarily raw by the standards of its time, standing out from the tame fare offered on the Light Programme and Radio Luxembourg like a bare brick wall in a suburban sitting-room".[73] Although today it may seem an insubstantial, almost unworthy overture to what was to become by the end of the decade the highly fantastical scope and orchestration of the Beatles' canon, its unique selling point then was the way in which its steady beat and strident vocal harmonies were illuminated and strengthened by the overlay of John's harmonica playing.[74] Put at its simplest, there was no relevant point of comparison to it in the contemporary Top 30. On its entry to the charts, it transcended the local phenomenon of 'Mersey Beat' by introducing a wider audience to the 'Mersey Sound'; and as such, it signposted a new, invigorating direction in British pop music, from which its relatively modest sales can never detract.

Yet despite the excitement of their new recording career actually taking off, the attendant publicity and their increasing marketability as a home-grown act, Brian Epstein's managerial judgement again wavered as he diverted the Beatles' energies at this critical juncture into two last punishing contracts at the Star-Club in Hamburg. From 1st to 14th November, they shared the bill with Little Richard, with whom they had already appeared twice the previous month in concerts in Liverpool.[75] (Amongst Little Richard's supporting ensemble was a talented 16-year-old organist called Billy Preston, whose acquaintance the Beatles would renew professionally at the end of the decade.) Their final stint in Germany was from 18th to 31st December, by which time playing in Hamburg was for them very much a throwback to a now closed jobbing phase of their lives as performers. The taste of fame in England was strong and being out of the country left them, at the very least, jaded and disgruntled. Although they endured it, their old friend Kingsize Taylor made his own amateur recording of their last-ever set at the Star-Club on New Year's Eve, in which:

> Their playing is ragged and careless; they are evidently drunk, and so tired they can scarcely be bothered to reply to the German hecklers. On two songs, the vocal is not by John or Paul but by Horst Fascher, the bouncer. All that seems to concern them about tomorrow is getting out of Hamburg; getting home.[76]

Left with this grim vignette of dejected rising stars, it is hard to envisage how this rite of passage could have been any more painful or dispiriting for them.

Their disenchantment at the very end was, of course, compounded by the fact that by then, in their heads, they were worlds away from Germany, knowing that the release of their next single in early January was imminent. In the intervening period between their penultimate and final residencies at the Star-Club, on 26th November they had returned to Abbey Road where, under George Martin's guidance, they had rearranged and re-recorded "Please Please Me" and its B-side, "Ask Me Why".

For John, composing "Please Please Me" was his "attempt at writing a Roy Orbison song".[77] Originally presented as a "very slow rocker … rather dreary, to be honest"[78], in its final version (Take 18), now much more up-tempo and with the addition of a harmonica part for John (which, stylistically, had previously lifted "Love Me Do" above the mundane), George Martin famously commended them on having recorded their first No.1.[79] Given all that subsequently flowed from the Beatles' realisation of Martin's faith in them on that day, the completion of that one recording session incontrovertibly marked a turning point in their musicianship, signalling, as it did, the end of the beginning of their working life together as a group.

At a tangent to the Beatles' slow but steady rise out of rock'n'roll obscurity in the north-west in the course of the year, in and around London the very different aspirations of Alexis Korner's young jazz and blues acolytes began to take firmer shape, under the unlikely stewardship of Brian Jones. By now totally immersed in the re-creation of the music of his blues heroes and perfecting his mastery of the slide guitar, in January, in Oxford, Brian met fellow-enthusiast Paul Pond, then a university student performing with the impressively named group Thunder Odin's Big Secret. Pond (later to change his name to Paul Jones and front-up Manfred Mann) and Jones briefly exploited their common bond by making a tape as a duo, initially for their own amusement; but on 17th March, Brian passed it on to Korner, after hitch-hiking from Cheltenham to attend the first public performance of Blues Incorporated at the Ealing Club. Come their next week's engagement, Jones had been invited to sit in with the band and first made the acquaintance of Charlie Watts.

Charlie, at this stage playing drums semi-professionally, rated Blues Incorporated as "an amazing band" but acknowledged that to the unaccustomed ear their output was "a total cacophony of sound ... like a cross between R&B and Charlie Mingus".[80] Still, acquired taste or not, they quickly attracted a growing following and for their third week's performance they further augmented their fluid line-up by bringing in Long John Baldry to share vocals with Cyril Davies.[81] Their fourth gig on 7th April drew a curious Mick Jagger, Dick Taylor and Keith Richards from Dartford to Ealing, on the only occasion, as it happens, of Jones and Pond appearing together in public, filling the interval slot. Brian's accompaniment of Paul in a reworking of the Elmore James classic "Dust My Broom" (as "Dust My Blues") immediately aroused Mick and Keith's attention and respect.

They all met up afterwards, to shoot the breeze about their respective musical interests and hopes for the future. Jagger subsequently chanced his arm by sending a tape of Little Boy Blue and the Blue Boys to Korner, which was returned to him without comment. Nevertheless, Mick persisted and on 28th April took the stage at Ealing at the interval, backed by Keith and Dick Taylor, to give a hesitant rendition of Chuck Berry's "Around And Around" – a song which the club regulars would undoubtedly have viewed as lowbrow, if not downright mainstream.[82] Thus, in Alan Clayson's words, "began the flight of Jagger – and Richards and, to a more qualified degree, Taylor – to the very peaks of pop".[83] By the middle of May, the music press formally announced that now Blues Incorporated had also taken on Mick to sing with them, in Ealing on Saturdays and at the Marquee Jazz Club on Thursdays.

As for Brian, despite gaining an enviable foothold in the London jazz and blues scene, he was not to be deflected from his grand plan of forming a band of his own, which followed a crabwise progress to realisation throughout the remainder of the year. On 2nd May, he advertised in *Jazz News* for musicians to join him in a new R&B (rhythm and blues) group, which he followed up with auditions and rehearsals in a hired room at the White Bear pub in Leicester Square. The first recruits through this process were Ian Stewart (a boogie-woogie piano player), Geoff Bradford (a purist blues guitarist), and Andy Wren (a vocalist-cum-piano-player, soon to be replaced by another vocalist, Brian Knight). Following the discovery of Jones's theft of cigarettes, however, they were no longer welcome at the White Bear and relocated to the Bricklayers Arms in Soho, a move shortly followed by Knight's departure in disagreement with Jones over choice of material. When the remaining trio were joined by Mick, Keith and Dick Taylor, their predilection for numbers by Chuck Berry and Bo Diddley next drove Bradford away. What then began to flourish was a truly remarkable affinity between Brian and Keith.

Still, two virtuoso guitar-players couldn't constitute a group by themselves and Brian's fledgling outfit struggled to achieve cohesion and continuity for several months, being notably deficient in its lack of both a regular drummer and bass player. On 12th July, their first big break as performers came by default, on the back of Blues Incorporated foregoing their Thursday slot at the Marquee in order to play on the BBC Light Programme's *Jazz Club*. Threatened with future withdrawal of the slot by Marquee manager Harold Pendleton if no act was forthcoming, Alexis Korner was forced to call in favours to find substitutes as a stopgap. One was Long John Baldry, backed by a scratch formation (including Geoff Bradford) called the Hoochie Coochie Men. The other was Brian, unexpectedly now driven, as reported in *Jazz News*, to commit himself and his associates to appearing as a proper, named band at last; although not, it seemed, to be publicly credited with its leadership:

> 'Mick Jagger, R&B vocalist, is taking an R&B group into the
> Marquee tomorrow night. Called the Rollin' Stones, the line-up
> is: Mick Jagger (vocals), Keith Richards and Elmo Lewis (guitars),
> Dick Taylor (bass), Ian Stewart (piano) and Mick Avory (drums).'[84]

Whilst their debut performance that night may have helped to save Blues Incorporated's bacon, not only did it spark wildly conflicting audience reactions but, sadly, in the process also antagonised the opinionated Mr. Pendleton, "who ran the Marquee on behalf of the National Jazz League, and manifestly disapproved of their music, their clothes, their attitude and – as it seemed to Ian Stewart – their perversely ill-chosen name".[85] He was a bad enemy to make on the London club circuit and consequently other bookings for the Stones at the Marquee were few and far between. They played most of their gigs at Ealing, interspersed with a weekend round of pubs "in Sutton, Richmond, Putney and Twickenham"[86] with the express aim of creating a peripatetic 'club' following.

Meanwhile, they continued to be frustrated in their quest for a permanent drummer. Unbeknown to Bill Wyman, the Cliftons' drummer Tony Chapman had approached Brian and he was taken on temporarily, although his personal work commitments as a commercial traveller rendered him less than reliable. Nevertheless, he did have the distinction of playing drums on the very first Rollin' Stones record when, on 26th October (at the end of the same week as "Love Me Do" entered the Top 30) they convened at Curly Clayton's Studio in north London – minus Dick Taylor – to cut an acetate at their own expense of three of their favourite R&B numbers.[87]

Then, at the beginning of December, Dick Taylor relinquished his role as bass player to take up a course as an art student and Chapman fortuitously suggested Wyman as a possible replacement. Invited to a rehearsal at the Wetherby Arms, Bill found the others disdainful of him personally but his possession of his own amplifiers quickly gained their respect.

Given Bill's age and steady background as a comfortably married man, this initial awkwardness of demeanour between the existing group members and Wyman was hardly surprising,. Neither should it be forgotten that by this stage Brian, having driven his girlfriend and baby away by his obsession with music-making[88], was reduced to living in relative squalor and poverty with Mick and Keith, in a "two-roomed apartment on the middle floor of a three-storey slum in Edith Grove, near the unfashionable end of Chelsea's King's Road".[89] Yet some vestige of musical empathy had been established between them all and, after being asked back to another rehearsal, Bill opted for an unexpected change of direction. Forsaking the Cliftons and throwing in his hand with the Stones, he made his first appearance with them on 14th December at the Ricky Tick Club in the Star and Garter Hotel, Windsor. With a new bass player on board, it now only remained for the Stones to resolve the outstanding issue of a full-time drummer, to which they were to set their minds early in the New Year.

While the Beatles, through Brian Epstein's intervention, progressed in 1962 to the brink of a promising professional career, and the Rollin' Stones muddled on in their amateur endeavours to become a group successful enough one day even to attract the interest of a manager, in America the respective fortunes of Bob Dylan and the Beach Boys seemed much more advanced and assured.

For Dylan, 1962 saw the release, at the age of 20, of his first, eponymous LP on CBS, on 19th March. Not a strong seller at the time (shifting no more than 5000 copies initially) and almost totally lacking in original compositions, *Bob Dylan* would nevertheless come to be regarded, in British eyes, as a 'sleeper', capable in due course of exerting its influence on groups looking for less familiar yet still commercial new material.[90] Carping critics in the US music industry were unforgiving of respected producer John Hammond, referring scathingly to Dylan himself and the whole venture as 'Hammond's Folly', but the enterprise would, in the fullness of time, warrant attention and repay further study. As Michael Gray admiringly sums it up:

> He signed Dylan, spent less than $500 in the studio and came out
> with an album few people liked and that didn't sell. The record
> company was all for dropping him. This album is, in retrospect,
> terrific. It has such a young Dylan on it that he sounds about 85
> … It is a brilliant debut, a performer's tour de force, and it served
> as a fine corrective for Greenwich Village: it was the opposite of
> effete.[91]

For all that it is superficially no more than a standard folk album of its time, nevertheless today it still remains in its entirety an impressively earnest piece of self-accompanied music-making, with the unexpected aged timbre to his voice accentuating the young Dylan's obvious hunger to be recognised, from this point in, as a serious player in the game. In part, of course, his chosen approach was a necessary aspect of establishing his credentials as a worthy interpreter of the predominantly traditional material on the record (i.e., 10 out of the 12 tracks), drawn in the main from blues and folk "narratives of much older men with a lifetime of hardship behind them and bleak futures in front of them".[92] He had, after all, cast himself as successor to his idol Woody Guthrie, whom he characterised as "the true voice of the American spirit".[93]

Long-term artistic considerations aside, Hammond mercifully found himself exonerated by the unequivocal support of CBS's prime recording artist at the time, Johnny Cash, who "made it known he thought Dylan was a giant".[94] From April onwards, therefore, Hammond and Dylan were able to embark unfettered upon recordings for his iconic second LP, *The Freewheelin' Bob Dylan*, in an extraordinary year which, according to Clinton Heylin, "still remains Dylan's most prolific year as a songwriter – he wrote around fifty songs in this twelve-month period".[95]

At this juncture, Dylan had set his face against recording singles, seeing them as insubstantial, dismissing them as "the kind of songs they played on the radio".[96] Experience, combined with hero-worship, told him that to make your mark you had to record LPs. Nevertheless, come December, he was inveigled by his newly-acquired manager, Albert Grossman, into recording and releasing his first single, against Hammond's advice; a song called "Mixed Up Confusion". The full-on rock'n'roll arrangement (with accompaniment from piano, drums, two guitars and a bass) ran completely counter to any of his other contemporary recordings with Hammond and was judged by CBS to be a mistake, leading to its rapid withdrawal from sale. Not currently available even in Dylan's extensive 'bootleg' back catalogue, for now only an alternate take can be accessed, in the respective 1978 and 1985 compilations *Masterpieces* and *Biograph*; a version that rattles along to a chugging beat highly reminiscent of Johnny Cash and the Tennessee Three (Grossman's original vision apparently having been to include a Dixieland band on the track.)

This temporary glitch aside, Dylan's prodigious output encompassed a total liberation in the style and content of his composition, enabling him at his finest to blur the boundaries of pure poetry and popular idiom in ever-more complex and profound songs, through which a lone voice increasingly came to express universal yearnings. Beginning with "Blowin' In The Wind" in April, by the end of 1962 he had also written "Tomorrow Is A Long Time", "A Hard Rain's A-Gonna Fall" and "Don't Think Twice, It's All Right", each one alone an undisputed masterpiece; and in advance of their availability on record, his new songs became popular not only through his own performances but also their regular publication in *Broadside*, a folk magazine of topical songs established in Greenwich Village in late 1961.

What he failed to foresee was that by virtue of their instant appeal these first outpourings of his prolific talent as both social commentator and wordsmith would paradoxically nurture, for him, his very own long-time curse. His misfortune, quite simply, was to capture the spirit of the hour. He didn't set out to be a prophet or a protest singer: he simply wanted to be as successful as Elvis Presley, "but rock-and-roll was dead in this pre-Beatles era, and the only way to do it was alone, through folk".[97] He had, however, reckoned without the phenomenon of "Blowin' In The Wind" being eagerly taken up by civil rights activists as their anthem and himself noised abroad as "spiritual leader and troubadour of the Movement".[98] Thus without seeking it, Dylan, his thoughts and music were swiftly, and bizarrely, seized upon as precious commodities, to be held in common and jealously guarded by the folk establishment of the day. As we shall see, this would later lead to mutual resentment and hostility, when Dylan eventually gathered a band around him and dared to go 'electric', and he would be haunted for years as the perceived mouthpiece of a generation. Asserting that he was "not a spokesman for anything or anybody … only a musician"[99] would be of little or no avail, only serving to make him more world-weary; and, as he recounts fatalistically in his autobiography, by the turn of the decade he still could not elude the burden of being feted as "the authentic expression of the disturbed and concerned conscience of Young America".[100]

On the West Coast, no such elevated considerations troubled the Beach Boys; where Brian Wilson made a growing success out of writing "about things that turned him on, like girls, cars, high school".[101] Following the initial success of "Surfin'", they had returned to the studio on 8th February to record a follow-up, "Surfin' Safari"; but within days, Al Jardine quit the group, citing differences over their repertoire (specifically, objecting to the inclusion of Chubby Checker numbers in their act) and the meagre income per person generated by their first record. Replacing Al in April by David Marks on rhythm guitar, they were invited by singer/songwriter Gary Usher to Western Recorders Studio in Hollywood; where, over two days on 16th and 19th April, they laid down demos of nine songs. But the next hurdle to present itself was the collapse at the beginning of May of their record company, Candix.

After rejections in rapid succession from Dot, Decca and Liberty, they were ditched by independent producer Hite Morgan, leaving their future management solely in the hands of formidable patriarch Murry Wilson. Against all the odds, he secured a meeting on 10th May with Nick Venet, A&R manager for Capitol Records, to whom he played demos of three Beach Boys' tracks from their April sessions, and Venet immediately saw potential in "Surfin' Safari", with its catchy refrain a simple entreaty to the young to take off for an endless, self-indulgent summer of sea and sand. Venet agreed then and there with Murry to purchase the rights to the songs and "Surfin' Safari" was released as their first single for Capitol on 4th June[102], eventually reaching No.14 in the *Billboard* Top 40. (Although it made no impact whatever on the charts here on its British release in October, in November it gave the Beach Boys their first-ever No.1 – in Sweden.[103])

Just as Brian Epstein and Bob Dylan had done for their own purposes, neither could Murry resist using Elvis as the benchmark to delineate his sons' future potential, particularly Brian's; although Nick Venet was ultimately proved to have the greater foresight in his professional assessment by suggesting that rather than be the next Elvis, Brian would ultimately prefer instead to be acclaimed simply as Brian.

For much of the summer, the Beach Boys divided their time between recording tracks for their first LP (*Surfin' Safari*) and undertaking a lengthy concert tour of the Midwest. While their sessions at Capitol's Hollywood studios were formally overseen by Venet, inevitably Murry was also ever-present and super-critical, fuelling the potential for conflict in his relentless urging of the group on to do better. This constant irritant aside, eventually group members themselves (specifically Mike Love and Brian Wilson) became dissatisfied, not only with having to play second fiddle to other professional claims on Venet's time but also with the studio acoustics. Thus in August the resultant discontent led the 20-year-old perfectionist Brian to make what was, for a newcomer, an audacious proposal to Capitol; namely, that the group should record elsewhere, in locations of his choice, and that he should assume the role of producer. Extraordinarily, subject to some contractual adjustments, the company acceded to his demands, meaning that from September onwards Brian took charge of the control booth, to make his music on his terms – first at Harmony Recorders Studio in Los Angeles, then in the already familiar Hollywood studio of Western Recorders.

On 1st October, four days before the release of the Beatles' "Love Me Do" by Parlophone in Britain, the Beach Boys' *Surfin' Safari* LP was released in America by Capitol. Taking till the end of November to enter the US album charts, it would eventually make No.32; but as before with their title-track single, the LP's subsequent release in Britain (in April 1963) made no headway. Capitol then quickly followed up with the release, on 26th November, of a second single, made up of two more tracks taken off the LP ("Ten Little Indians", backed with "County Fair"), which failed completely to make the US Top 40. Once again, its British release the following January proved abortive.

In absolute contrast to the failure of surf music to gain currency on this side of the Atlantic, there was an unlikely and more successful export in the opposite direction by the Springfields of their peculiarly English approximation to country music. Although sustaining their popularity at home as all-round entertainers, to the extent of being voted Top UK Vocal Group in the *NME*'s annual poll for the second year running in 1962, perversely their record sales in Britain struggled. Yet their single released in April, "Silver Threads And Golden Needles", which bombed here, became a summertime success in America.[104] Not only did it reach No.20 in the *Billboard* charts but also led to an invitation from Shelby Singleton, A&R manager for Mercury Records, to record an album of country standards in Nashville, a trip they undertook in December.[105] For Dusty in particular, a stopover in New York, en route back to England, was to prove an epiphany, since it was here that she first encountered and revelled in the sheer "*attack*" of contemporary American soul music – "the most exciting thing I'd ever heard".[106]

In the second half of the year, change had been forced upon the Springfields through Tim Feild's departure, on the pretext of looking after his wife when she became seriously ill – although in reality, he was exhausted by the steady escalation of artistic differences and resultant arguments between Dusty and her brother Tom. He had been replaced by Mike Longhurst-Pickworth (*aka* Mike Hurst), who, although previously acquainted with Tom, had duly to earn his place through competitive audition. Joining the group near the zenith of their career, he first recorded with them in October when they cut the single for which today they are best remembered, "Island Of Dreams", and made his first public appearance with them on *Thank Your Lucky Stars* on 24th November to promote it (Feild staying on until 1st December to complete their immediate live theatre commitments); but it was to be a bumpy twelve months that lay ahead to the point of the Springfields' final collapse and Dusty going solo.

In the aftermath of the Cuban Missile Crisis, historically the remaining two months of 1962 could only be anti-climactic but the intensification of the Cold War to such an extreme was to cast a long, chilling shadow. As we have seen, it redefined the context of the space race, turning it into a subset of the arms race (after all, the refinement of rocket power to project a man into space ultimately had a direct bearing on the speed, range and location of the superpowers' respective arsenals of intercontinental ballistic missiles); whereas in the preceding months, the continuing rivalry between US and USSR space agencies had evoked nothing but praise and wonder in the free press at their latest technical achievements.

On 20th February, Colonel John Glenn had become the first American to orbit the Earth (three times in the course of his five-hour spaceflight); to be followed on 24th May by Scott Carpenter, and on 3rd October by Walter Schirra (who completed six orbits in nine hours). For their part, on 11th and 12th August, the Russians had launched two Vostok spacecraft on consecutive days (piloted by Andrian Nikolayev and Pavel Popovich), contriving to bring them into near-synchronous orbit within three miles of each other and tempting foremost British astrophysicist Sir Bernard Lovell to speculate that "the Soviets are so far ahead in the technique of rocketry that the possibility of America catching up in the next decade is remote".[107] (In addition, a separate strand of 'pure' space exploration had finally yielded the first empirical data about another planet to be gleaned by a man-made probe, when the American Mariner 2, launched in August, sent signals back to Earth from its flight past Venus.[108])

Overshadowed by the big-screen fantasy of Sean Connery and Ursula Andress in *Dr. No*, the more sordid day-to-day reality of East/West espionage and counter-espionage was, for now, still only skirting the outermost fringes of popular imagination. On the very same day that President Kennedy had publicly denounced the presence of Soviet missile bases in Cuba, 22nd October, the trial in London of ex-Admiralty clerk Gordon Vassall was concluded. Found guilty of having spied for the Russians for six years, after being compromised and blackmailed as a homosexual, Vassall was sentenced to eighteen years' imprisonment. Within a fortnight, on 2nd November, British businessman Greville Wynne had been arrested as a spy by the KGB in Budapest and flown to Moscow for further interrogation; and on 11th December, it was announced that the KGB had also taken into custody a Russian intelligence officer, Oleg Penkovsky, accused of being a high-level contact in Moscow for Western agents including Wynne. (Penkovsky had been recruited by the British Secret Intelligence Service as a double-agent in the summer of 1961 and had provided an 'alternative channel of communication' from 'doves' in Moscow to the West in October 1962, suggesting Kruschev was bluffing over Cuba.[109]) As it turned out, these and related events would prove to be the prelude to political turmoil in Britain for much of the year ahead, an uproar fuelled by salacious scandal and culminating in the collapse of the government.

1962 declared its final hand in the form of atrocious weather. At the beginning of December, London was beset by days of unrelenting smog, causing at least 60 deaths from respiratory complications. (On one day alone, of the "19 men and nine women aged between 37 and 86" who died on 5th December, "20 collapsed indoors, six in the streets and two at work".[110]) And then on Boxing Day, blizzards, moving rapidly from the south of England, swept across the country; the heavy snow settling to depths unprecedented since the winter of 1947 and instigating the 'big freeze' that would last until the following March, thus denoting a cheerless end to a cheerless year. Thank goodness, then, for the restorative powers of the musical revolution about to be visited upon us.

NOTES

1   Notwithstanding, of course, that in reality Kennedy's own taste in music lay in entirely a different direction, as frozen for all time in the highlight act of the Birthday Salute staged for him at Madison Square Garden in New York on 19th May 1962. Following the likes of Ella Fitzgerald, Peggy Lee and Maria Callas, at the suggestion of Ratpack member Peter Lawford and less than three months before her own mysterious death, Marilyn Monroe closed the show with her breathless delivery of "Happy Birthday", turning the simple chant of childhood quite calculatedly into a "seduction serenade". [See Anthony Summers, "Goddess: The Secret Lives of Marilyn Monroe" (Victor Gollancz, 1985), p.270.]

2   Bob Dylan, "With God On Our Side", © 1963 by Warner Bros. Inc.; renewed 1991 by Special Rider Music.

3   Dominic Sandbrook, "Never Had It So Good: A History of Britain from Suez to The Beatles" (Abacus, 2006), p.243.

4   Dominic Sandbrook, op. cit., p.246.

5   Derrik Mercer (ed.) et al., "Chronicle of the 20th Century" (Longman Chronicle, 1988), p.886.

6   As put together by Joe Meek, the Tornados included two fugitives from Johnny Kidd and the Pirates, in the form of Alan Caddy (lead guitar) and Clem Cattini (drums); the other members being George Bellamy (rhythm guitar), Heinz Burt (bass guitar) and Roger Lavern (keyboards).

7   See John Repsch, op. cit., p.145. The image was actually of the chairman of the American Telephone & Telegraph Co., the sponsors and builders of Telstar-1, and was received first in France, where its quality was superior to that belatedly picked up for the final minute of the broadcast in Britain. In response, France beamed back live pictures of the singer Yves Montand, whilst Britain, phlegmatic as ever, "sent a test card and an official greeting". [See Derrik Mercer (ed.) et al., op. cit., p.882.]

8   Meek originally bought his clavioline in October 1959 and first used it in 1960 in his earliest experimental work inspired by space, "I Hear A New World". It was "the primitive forerunner of the synthesizers that are so popular today, having but two octaves and notes that could only be played one at a time; it produced a sound like that of an organ but with a rougher quality. He also detected in it the slight air of mystery one often finds in electronic music, making it well suited to depicting the mystery of outer space". [See John Repsch, op. cit., p.76.]

9   See John Repsch, op. cit., pp.147-148.

10   Jean Ledrut sought damages against Meek for plagiarising his "Le Marche d'Austerlitz", written in 1960 as accompaniment to a film about Napoleon. [See John Repsch, op. cit., pp.182-183.]

11   In a letter of 14th December 1966 to his solicitor, Meek expressed the view that his talents, "the desire and even a form of love that one puts into music", had been "stunted" by the case, reducing him in others' eyes to "a liar and a thief". [See John Repsch, op. cit., p.324.]

12   Mark Lewisohn, op. cit., p.63. Apart from their own compositions, the other 12 songs were: 'Money (That's What I Want)', 'Till There Was You', 'The Sheik Of Araby', 'To Know Her Is To Love Her', 'Take Good Care Of My Baby', 'Memphis, Tennessee', 'Sure To Fall (In Love With You)', 'Three Cool Cats', 'Crying, Waiting, Hoping', 'September In The Rain', 'Besame Mucho' and 'Searchin''.

13   By the Applejacks, the Fourmost and Cilla Black respectively.

14   Namely, Side 1 Track 6 ('Till There Was You' – a ballad from *The Music Man*, sung by Paul) and Side 2 Track 7 ('Money (That's What I Want)' – a staple of many groups' repertoires but here, as the finale, rocked up by John to create the definitive interpretation: "a completely worthy climax to this knockout programme", in the words of publicist Tony Barrow).

15   Brian Poole came from Barking, whilst all four Tremeloes (Rick West – lead guitar; Alan Blakely – rhythm guitar; Alan Howard – bass guitar; and Dave Munden – drums) were from Dagenham.

16   Quoted in David Pritchard & Alan Lysaght, op. cit., pp.88-89.

17   The latter, of course, not actually part of the audition set!

18   Quoted in David Pritchard & Alan Lysaght, op. cit., p.90.

19   Having opted for Brian Poole and the Tremeloes supposedly on the grounds of their greater potential talent, what did Smith and Rowe eventually choose in 1963 for their first single release on Decca? Yet another cover version of "Twist and Shout" – a strange choice and strange timing. On its release, it was immediately in competition with the re-release of the Isley Brothers' original version and even though it reached No.4 in August 1963, it was then totally eclipsed by the Beatles' "Twist and Shout" EP, containing 4 tracks from their first LP *Please Please Me*. And how neat a U-turn did Smith perform in 1964 by which time, of course, the Beatles' music had gained universal currency – by producing one of the three original songs from the rejected audition, "Like Dreamers Do", as the Applejacks' second single?

20   Bizarrely, the music scene in the south-east of England was far more receptive to transatlantic influences than any from the provincial north. Keith Richards, for instance, freely admitted that for a long time he "had no idea about what was going on in Liverpool". [See Alan Clayson, "The Rolling Stones: The Origin of the Species" (Chrome Dreams, 2007), p.125.]

21   Beating Gerry and the Pacemakers into second place. [See Spencer Leigh, "Twist and Shout! Merseybeat, The Cavern, The Star-Club and The Beatles" (Nirvana, 2004), pp. 66-67.]

22   Rejection by letter from EMI's prime labels Columbia and HMV had actually predated the Decca audition, in December 1961. [See Mark Lewisohn, op. cit., p.56.] Epstein later also unsuccessfully approached Pye, Oriole and Philips.

23   John Lennon, "The Beatles Anthology" (Cassell, 2000), p.68.

24   Ibid.

25   See John Blaney, "Beatles For Sale: How Everything They Touched Turned to Gold" (Jawbone, 2008), pp.35-36.

26   The Light Programme's *Teenager's Turn – Here We Go*, broadcast on the afternoon of Thursday, 8th March and for which, it seems, the Beatles were not specifically selected

on the basis of originality. At their audition on 12th February, they sang two of their own songs (the by now reliable staples of "Like Dreamers Do" and "Hello Little Girl") and two covers ("Till There Was You" and "Memphis, Tennessee"). Having been chosen to appear on the programme, they returned to Manchester on 7th March, when they recorded a contribution of 3 cover versions (Roy Orbison's "Dream Baby", Chuck Berry's "Memphis, Tennessee" and the Marvelettes' "Please Mister Postman"). See Mark Lewisohn, op. cit., pp.65 & 67.

27   Paul McCartney, "The Beatles Anthology" (Cassell, 2000), p.69.

28   Philip Norman, "Shout! The True Story of The Beatles" (Elm Tree, 1981), p.137.

29   Philip Norman, op. cit., p.142.

30   "Although it certainly took place between 23 and 27 April, the exact date, and venue, of this one 1962 session ... has proved impossible to research ... Precisely what the Beatles recorded with Sheridan, and when and where, may never be clearly be determined." [See Mark Lewisohn, op. cit., p.70.]

31   Quoted in Mark Lewisohn, op. cit., p.56.

32   Ibid.

33   The first No.1 of the year, "Stranger On The Shore" had entered the Top 30 at No.22 on 2nd December 1961 and remained in the charts until 25th August 1962; that is, for a staggering total of 39 weeks. Subsequently released in America, it also made No.1 there and was in the *Billboard* Top 40 for 15 weeks, from 4th July 1962 onwards.

34   Johnny Keating's original recording reached No.16 on 24th March, whilst Norrie Paramor's rival cover version could get no higher than its entry point of No.21 on 7th April.

35   Johnnie Spence's orchestral version (subtitled "Three Stars Will Shine Tonight") reached No.12 on 21st April. Richard Chamberlain, the actor of the title role, subsequently recorded a vocal version, which reached No.11 on 23rd June.

36   Joe Loss and his Orchestra took this to No.19 on 21st April.

37   Already twice a *Billboard* No.1 in America, in 1960 and 1961.

38   In 1959, at the age of 17, Carol Costa, had married Jet, then embarked on an affair with Cliff which ran its course in 1960. Bruce Welch described her as being like "Brigitte Bardot in image: slim waist, large breasts, pouting lips. She was a 1959 darling. If she wanted somebody, she got them, and she got Cliff. The fact that he was her husband's boss made no difference. You have to remember that Cliff was the most desirable person in pop music at the time. He was like Elvis." [See Steve Turner, "Cliff Richard: The Bachelor Boy" (Carlton, 2009), p.95.]

39   Quoted in Mike Read, op. cit., p.124.

40   Released in 1955 and directed by Otto Preminger, the film had starred Frank Sinatra as a recovering heroin addict, a role for which he received an Oscar nomination as Best Actor.

41   Greenfield/King, ©1961 by Aldon Music Inc./BMI-Worldwide.

42   Based on the premise that imitation is the sincerest form of flattery, A-ha's version is first and foremost a powerful, extended tribute to the Everlys, playing as it does for more than the twice the length of the original at 4 minutes 20 seconds. As Pal

explained: "We had a connection with the Everly Brothers through our manager, who played bass for them in the '60s … We went to see them at the Albert Hall, and that song was our favourite. It was easy to see that it could be done in a different way." [See Kieron Tyler, liner notes to *A-ha: 25* (Warner Brothers/Rhino, 2010).]

43   Ken Emerson, op. cit., p.111. Totally smitten, Emerson describes Carole King's melody in this instance as "eloquent … [rising] like a sob that refuses to be stifled".

44   The same position as the Everlys achieved at home in the *Billboard* Top 40.

45   Channel/Cobb, © 1961 (renewed 1991) by Le Bill Music/EMI Unart Catalog Inc.

46   It was a failed middle-class attempt to occupy the same territory as "Hey! Baby", with the unmelodic refrain: "Where does she live?/What's her number?/And how can I meet her?" (Goffin/Keller, © 1962 by Aldon Music Inc./BMI-Worldwide.)

47   A revival of a song from the American wartime musical film of 1942, *The Fleet's In*, starring Dorothy Lamour and William Holden.

48   Geld/Udell, © 1962 (renewed 1988) by EMI Unart Catalog Inc./Warner Bros. Publications (US) Inc.

49   Goffin/King, © 1962 by Screen Gems/EMI Music Ltd.

50   See Ken Emerson, op. cit.., p.118.

51   George Martin, speaking in the BBC TV *Arena* documentary *Produced By George Martin*, broadcast on BBC2 on 25th April 2011.

52   Namely, "A Hole In The Ground", "Right Said Fred" and "Gossip Calypso".

53   George Harrison, "The Beatles Anthology" (Cassell, 2000), p.70.

54   Later to become record producer for Gerry and the Pacemakers and the Hollies.

55   George Martin, BBC *Arena* documentary, as above.

56   Quoted in David Pritchard & Alan Lysaght, op. cit., p.98.

57   George Harrison, "The Beatles Anthology" (Cassell, 2000), p.70.

58   The agreement formalised with George Martin was for a 4-year recording contract with Parlophone, running to June 1966. [See John Blaney, op. cit., p.43.]

59   Quoted in David Pritchard & Alan Lysaght, op. cit., p.99.

60   See Cynthia Lennon, "John" (Hodder & Stoughton, 2005), p.121.

61   Cynthia Lennon, op. cit., p.125. John's parents, Freddie and Julia, had also married there, in 1938.

62   See Cynthia Lennon, op. cit., pp.128-129.

63   Cynthia Lennon, op. cit., p.129.

64   John Lennon, "The Beatles Anthology" (Cassell, 2000), p.73.

65   See Mark Lewisohn, op. cit., p.57.

66   Ibid.

67   Previously a singer in his own right and performer of the "Robin Hood" theme song to the 1950s' ITV children's series starring Richard Greene.

68 Recorded by jobbing singer/songwriter Barry Mason, backed by the then unknown Dave Clark Five. The original intended recipient was to have been Adam Faith. [See Mark Lewisohn, op. cit., p.78.]

69 It was destined to be a No.1, as a spectacularly successful debut single for Gerry and the Pacemakers – using the Beatles' arrangement of the song - in April 1963. See Ch.5.

70 Quoted in David Pritchard & Alan Lysaght, op. cit., p.104.

71 First roughed out by Paul in 1958. See Ian MacDonald, op. cit., p.51.

72 At the end of a week that had begun with the signing – by all parties concerned – of an updated management contract between the four current Beatles and Brian Epstein.

73 Ian MacDonald, op. cit., p.52. By contrast, he regarded the more conventional ballad "PS I Love You" as sounding "like a hopeful 'standard' to be offered to established performers" [op. cit., p.54].

74 Finessed, as noted above, courtesy of Delbert McClinton.

75 For his part, Little Richard was not blown away by the Beatles: "I thought they were a very good group when they performed with me at the Star-Club in Hamburg, but I never thought they were a hit group." Quoted by David Pritchard & Alan Lysaght, op. cit., p.93.

76 Philip Norman, op. cit., p.164.

77 John Lennon, "The Beatles Anthology" (Cassell, 2000), p.90.

78 George Martin, "The Beatles Anthology" (Cassell, 2000), p.90.

79 "At the end of the session I was knocked out because it really was a great record. I said to them, 'Gentlemen, you've got your first number-one hit.'" [Quoted in David Pritchard & Alan Lysaght, op. cit., p.113.]

80 Quoted in Bill Wyman with Richard Havers, op. cit., p.32.

81 Operating as a "loose collective", other notables invited to pitch in with Blues Incorporated included Art Wood and Steve Marriott. [See Alan Clayson, "The Rolling Stones: The Origin of the Species" (Chrome Dreams, 2007), p.103.]

82 Jagger and Richards knew it as the B-side to Chuck Berry's million-selling 1958 hit "Johnny B. Goode". It remained one of their staple songs once the Stones were established as a group; and as if to complete the circle of homage, they recorded a version of it at Chess Studios in Chicago (on 11th June 1964), which was included on their *Five By Five* EP.

83 Alan Clayson, "The Rolling Stones: The Origin of the Species" (Chrome Dreams, 2007), p.109.

84 Quoted in Bill Wyman with Richard Havers, op. cit., p.37. Mick Avory had occasionally sat in as drummer for Brian before and was later to become famous as a permanent member of the Kinks.

85 Philip Norman, op. cit., p.56. Brian's naming of the group supposedly derived from the title of the Muddy Waters song "Rolling Stone": neither Ian Stewart nor Mick Avory were comfortable with it. [See Philip Norman, op. cit., p.55.]

86 Philip Norman, op. cit., p.59.

87 Namely, "You Can't Judge A Book By Its Cover" (Bo Diddley), "Soon Forgotten"

(Muddy Waters) and "Close Together" (Jimmy Reed). [See Bill Wyman with Richard Havers, op. cit., p.40.]

88   Although Pat Andrews had followed Brian to London with their infant son Mark at Easter 1962, their relationship, beset with money and accommodation difficulties, was not to survive the year. She left him that September, taking Mark with her. [See Laura Jackson, op. cit., Ch.3.]

89   Laura Jackson, op. cit., pp.53-54.

90   Although originally released in the UK in June 1962, it did not become a best-seller in the British LP charts until 1965.

91   Michael Gray, "The Bob Dylan Encyclopedia" (Continuum, 2006), p.70.

92   Sean Egan, "Bob Dylan", in Sean Egan (ed.), "The Mammoth Book of Bob Dylan" (Robinson, 2011), p.6.

93   Bob Dylan, op. cit., p.99.

94   Anthony Scaduto, op. cit., p.111.

95   Clinton Heylin, op. cit., p.63.

96   Bob Dylan, op. cit., p.34.

97   Anthony Scaduto, op. cit., p.121.

98   Anthony Scaduto, op. cit., p.117.

99   Bob Dylan, op. cit., p.119.

100   Quoted by Dylan himself, in a state of shock and disbelief, from the introductory address at a ceremony at Princeton University in 1970 to award him an honorary doctorate. (See Dylan, op. cit., p.133.)

101   David Marks, quoted in Keith Badman, op. cit., p.26.

102   Originally issued as the B-side to a track called "409" (composed by Wilson/Usher), Capitol relented after a few weeks and promoted it as the A-side. [See Keith Badman, op. cit., p.24.]

103   See Keith Badman, op. cit., p.28.

104   And was followed up there in September with an LP of the same title.

105   The result was Folk Songs From The Hills, released in the US in March and the UK in April 1963.

106   Quoted in Lucy O'Brien, op. cit., p.38.

107   Quoted in Deborah Cadbury, op. cit., p.271.

108   See the 'Chronology of Lunar and Planetary Exploration', in David McNab & James Younger, "The Planets" [BBC, 1999], pp.231-232, for a concise summary of the mostly failed attempts up to this point by both the USA and USSR to send probes to the Moon, Mars and Venus.

109   See Phillip Knightley & Caroline Kennedy, op. cit., p.107.

110   Derrik Mercer (ed.) et al., op. cit., p.888.

Chapter 5

> **FIRST NO.1 OF THE YEAR –**
> "Dance On" by The Shadows
>
> **LAST NO.1 OF THE YEAR –**
> "I Want To Hold Your Hand" by The Beatles

Pop music came alive for me in 1963. It was the year in which I became not just a passive listener, a bystander, but an active participant and consumer – a full-blown record-buyer in my own right, no less, with pocket-money to spend, a collection to establish and critical faculties to develop. Coincidentally, it was also the year in which the government implemented a cut in purchase tax on records, consequently reducing their retail price by 10%. This meant that a single now cost 6/3d, an EP 10/1d and a standard (as opposed to 'bargain') LP between 30/11d and 32/2d.[1]

My personal access to the airwaves had already been enhanced, regrettably, on the death of my maternal grandmother, my last surviving grandparent, in late 1962; as a result of which I had inherited her old brown Bakelite Bush radio (now installed on my bedside table, tuned to a very crackly and sometimes elusive Radio Luxembourg each evening) and her black-and-white television in its upright mahogany cabinet (complete with portable aerial, which had been set up for me in our dining room, so that I could now watch *Thank Your Lucky Stars* on a Saturday night on my own). The biggest leap forward, however, came on my fourteenth birthday in May, when my parents gave me a portable Dansette Bermuda record player, together with my first two singles: "Scarlett O'Hara", by Jet Harris and Tony Meehan, on the Decca label, and "Casablanca" (the theme tune to the ITV adventure series *Crane*), by Kenny Ball and his Jazzmen, on Pye Jazz.

Anyone of my generation will tell you that a Dansette record player was the business. The main body of mine was encased in textured red leatherette, with the front elevation covered by a cream mesh flecked with grey, concealing the speaker. External controls were simple, in the form of two knobs; one for on/off and volume, the other to adjust the tone between bass and treble. Lifting the lid, secured on either side by a gilt spring-clip, revealed the BSR (Birmingham Sound Reproducers) turntable and autochanger. The turntable had a four-speed setting, for 16 [3], 33, 45 or 78 rpm (revolutions per minute); and mounted in the playing arm was the sound cartridge, which you rotated through 180 degrees to select the appropriate stylus for either 45s and LPs or 78s with a smart click. In any event, sound quality and durability were critical factors related to your choice of stylus, the more expensive diamond being infinitely preferable to sapphire (which quickly wore down, then sounded rubbish and ruined the groove of your record into the bargain[4]).

Rising from the centre of the turntable was a tall spindle, housing to halfway up its length the gizmo that was the autochanger. Onto this stepped articulated flange, you could load a number of 7" 45s, securing the top of the stack with a retaining arm. When you slid the control switch of the turntable to 'auto', the 'step' of the autochanger was retracted, allowing the first record to slide down the spindle onto the turntable, then instantly flicked back into place to hold the remaining records above. Once the disc landed on the turntable, the playing arm then automatically lifted off its rest and lowered the stylus into the play-in groove. When the stylus reached the end of the run-out groove in the centre of the record, the playing arm would lift and return to its rest, ready for disc no.2 to be dropped into place and the playing cycle repeated.

With highly variable quality control from the record manufacturers of the time, it has to be said that autochanging was not always as straightforward or enjoyable as intended. Any significant weight differences between records could easily cause the record playing to slip on the one below, thus distorting the sound; while some discs were so poorly pressed that they could either be warped on purchase or become warped over time, in the worst cases to the point of becoming unplayable because the undulations were so severe as to throw the stylus out of the groove.[5] Build-ups of dust on the tip of the stylus and in the grooves of the record were inevitable consequences of actually playing your music; so that, for example, a rogue speck of dust in the run-out groove could block the stylus from reaching the end-point of the record and it would just continue to rotate with a tell-tale repeated hiss instead of retracting the playing arm. There was nothing for it then but manual intervention.

The sound was full on, of course, in mono (or monaural) mode, fed through a single speaker, with no 'separation' between instruments or, in the case of a song, between vocals and instrumentation. (Historically, Decca's proud boast on its record sleeves and labels had been its commitment to 'true high fidelity', displaying the symbol of an ear and a guarantee of 'ffrr' – 'full frequency range recording' – although quite what listening advantages their records offered over and above those of their competitors were, frankly, hard to determine.) In the absence in those days of multi-track recording and any effective ability to layer or separate the various sound sources, this explains why many digitally remastered CDs of artists from the early and mid-Sixties, particularly of self-accompanied solo singers, can sound so disappointingly flat and lifeless to what has now become, by increments over time, a much more demanding and sophisticated ear. Modern technology dictates, in fact, that you can no longer hear or experience these performances as you originally did.

To achieve anything approaching depth or subtlety, apart from adjusting the volume, you could only resort to adjusting the sound balance between bass and treble. While more bass accentuated the underlying beat, it also had the negative effects of dampening the lead guitar and making the vocals muddy; so my personal preference was to turn up the treble, for greater overall clarity. Stereo records did not become commonplace until much later in the decade, starting as an alternative option to mono LPs and extending only slowly into the singles market. Given the initial expense of full-blown stereo systems with left and right speakers, thankfully for young record-buyers the complete demise of the mono format was protracted; cushioned for several years by the development of compatible cartridges for mono record players and thus enabling you to play the new generation of records that had 'stereo playable mono' stamped on the label.

There still remained one final element of unpredictability, beyond the buyer's control, in the physical quality of manufacture. A faulty pressing of a record could result in, say, the grooves of a track being in too close proximity to one another, causing the stylus to jump, or might leave a microscopic blockage in a groove sufficient to prevent the forward movement of the stylus and throwing it into an endless loop (the 'stuck record' syndrome). If, sadly, you were unlucky enough to find yourself faced with such problems, taking the record back to the shop to exchange it was usually the only remedy but could, all too often, be fraught with difficulty, trying to persuade unscrupulous or uncaring traders to do the decent thing and replace it.[6] That, in itself, was a corollary of the multiplicity of outlets, the majority of which were not specialist.

For example, where I lived, in Knowle in Warwickshire, I started off buying records from Curtis's, our local electrical shop in the village high street, which to its eternal credit could be relied upon for several years to stock the Top 30 and some obscurer new releases besides. For a wider choice, especially once my interest spread beyond singles to LPs, I had to cycle the three miles to Solihull, where redevelopment of the town centre meant that within twelve months or so I would have the considerably extended choice of at least three other electrical retailers, together with the record departments of Boots, W.H. Smith[7], the Co-op, Woolworths and Beatties (an independent department store, where the principal record assistant was a girl of high disdain, who could never forgive me for the affront of having been at primary school with her).

In extremis, a further two miles or so on my bike could take me to Studio Musica, a combined musical instrument and record shop on the Stratford Road in Shirley (where, for example, on one hot summer afternoon in 1965 I finally found and bought my copy of the Beatles' *Help!* LP, a virtual sell-out locally on its release). At the final remove, eight or nine miles away (by bus, train or – through occasional parental goodwill – the family car) was Birmingham city centre, where both Boots (in its 'Big Top' flagship store in New Street, opposite the Odeon) and W.H. Smith (in its original premises round the corner in Corporation Street, opposite C&A) had large record departments (on the first floor and in the basement respectively) that I regularly trawled; and further down Corporation Street was Crane's, a piano retailer that had somewhat reluctantly diversified beyond sheet music and where, with patience, you could sometimes pick up a bargain in a box of remainders (in my case, such as "Everybody's Gonna Be Happy" by the Kinks or "Run" by Sandie Shaw). Besides the records themselves, of course, a good range of record shops at your disposal was also vital for the purchase of essential accessories to maintain your collection in good order – namely, record cleaning cloths, record racks and replacement styli.

For some reason best known to myself, which now even I have forgotten, I had originally intended to collect only instrumentals; so to my first two records, I soon added singles by the Spotnicks ("Just Listen To My Heart"), the Shadows ("Atlantis"), the Surfaris ("Wipe Out") and the Dakotas ("The Cruel Sea").[8] The cause was quickly lost, however, when my parents offered to stump up for an EP. Without hesitation, I chose the Beatles' *Twist And Shout*, with its four tracks taken from their first LP; and from that moment on, I was committed, like so many of my contemporaries, to following the burgeoning of the British pop scene as the old musical order fell into decline and was sidelined.

This said, my initial taste for instrumentals had not been so desperately unfashionable, since the first two No.1 singles of the year were the Shadows' "Dance On", followed by Jet Harris and Tony Meehan with "Diamonds". But by the end of February, the Beatles had changed the pop landscape forever by taking "Please Please Me" to No.1, securing the charts as their own stronghold for the foreseeable future as well as blazing a trail that countless other new and rising vocal groups would seek to follow.

Although the release of Cliff's new film *Summer Holiday* held out the promise of continuing success for him and the Shadows, the auguries were inauspicious. Not only did the day of its premiere – Friday, 11th January – also turn out to be the release date of the Beatles' new single, but Cliff himself, the star of the film, had to endure the ignominy of being refused admission to the gala screening:

> Leicester Square was jammed solid. Thousands of people stood outside the cinema, many of them holding placards saying 'Cliff We Love You'. My limo edged slowly towards the entrance but as the driver pulled up and I started to open the door a policeman said, 'On your way, on your way!'
>
> I said, 'I'm Cliff Richard, it's my film, it's my première.'
>
> He wasn't interested. 'You can't stop here,' he said, and so we didn't. I missed it. I watched the première from my manager's apartment in Maida Vale.[9]

While the film's soundtrack album became the third best-selling LP of the year, the single version of the title track, which dethroned "Please Please Me", was to be Cliff's last No.1 until the spring of 1968, more than five years later. Succeeded at the top of the charts at the end of March by "Foot Tapper", yet another spin-off from the film, even so for the Shadows this would prove to be their last-ever No.1. As recalled by Cliff, a social encounter with their new rivals at around this time only served to confirm to them that they were, at last, outdone:

> It was a party that Bruce [Welch] had thrown and the Beatles were there. This was the first time that we had any inkling that we were in trouble, that these guys were really on the ball when it came to commercial hits. John [Lennon] picked up one of Bruce's guitars and played "From Me To You" in the kitchen. We all just looked at each other. We all knew. In our estimation it could not fail. Of course, we never met them again because they became so huge.[10]

Two days after its release, the Beatles recorded a promotional slot for "Please Please Me" at the Alpha Television studios in Birmingham, to be broadcast the following Saturday, 19th January, on *Thank Your Lucky Stars*. It was to be their first appearance on this popular weekend programme, which scored more highly than the BBC's *Juke Box Jury* by showing 'live' performances of both current hits and new releases. It was of no particular consequence to eager viewers like me that 'live' habitually meant 'mimed' as well as 'pre-recorded'. What mattered most was getting that one significant step beyond the radio, to hear the songs *and* to see the singers.

Yet hitherto radio had always exerted the dominant influence on record sales. So on 21st and 22nd January, the Beatles taped sets first for Radio Luxembourg's *The Friday Spectacular* and then the Light Programme's *Saturday Club*, both sessions including "Please Please Me" and being broadcast on 25th and 26th January respectively. It was the beginning of BBC radio's specific courtship of the group, in the course of which they moved swiftly from being contributing guest artists on compilation programmes like *Saturday Club* to becoming stars of their own regular series, such as *Pop Go The Beatles* or *From Us To You*. Indeed, radio eagerly offered them an unprecedented national platform from which to consolidate their public exposure; to the extent that altogether (i.e., up to and including June 1965) they made 275 recordings exclusively for the BBC.[11]

By the week ending 23rd February, they were at No.1; the news (having been disclosed in advance at the Cavern where the Beatles were appearing on 19th February) receiving an unexpectedly disconsolate reaction from their loyal home following:

> The queue for the show had formed the night before and … Bob Wooler read out a telegram sent c/o The Cavern Club just as the Beatles were going on stage. It was from Brian Epstein and it confirmed that "Please Please Me" had climbed to Number One on the *New Musical Express'* chart. The audience went quiet: they sensed the Beatles no longer belonged to them.[12]

Elsewhere, however, their runaway success soon had a very different and direct impact on the dynamics of the concert tours in which they were then also engaged, as audiences increasingly clamoured to see and hear them. As noted earlier in Chapter 3, the headline act for the first package tour in which the Beatles participated was Helen Shapiro, now aged 16.[13] When it began, in Bradford on 2nd February, they were the show-openers, at the bottom of the bill; but by its end, in Hanley in the Potteries on 3rd March, they had moved up the running order to first-half closers. Much of the rest of March was taken up by a second tour, this time jointly headed by the American singers Chris Montez and Tommy Roe. Arriving at the Liverpool Empire on 24th March, Montez magnanimously conceded the top-of-the-bill slot to them; which they then retained for the remaining six dates. From the outset of their third tour, beginning on 18th May with the much greater American star Roy Orbison, audience demand for the Beatles was so high that posters and programmes were rapidly reprinted to give the group equal billing with him.

As if all this was not enough, the Beatles were simultaneously maintaining a prodigious output of recording and songwriting, not only of benefit to themselves but also to a new wave of artists, emerging in the first instance from Brian Epstein's own expanding management stable. On 11th February, taking a break from the Helen Shapiro tour, they spent all day at Abbey Road (from 10.00 in the morning to 10.45 at night), recording ten new songs to complete the tracklist of their first LP, *Please Please Me*.[14] It was, on George Martin's admission, an unashamed attempt to replicate in the studio their current stage act as the only instantly available source of material for the intended album's rush-release. To Norman Smith, the recording engineer, it was important "to create their live sound as it happened"; so to this end, he "laid down the backing tracks first, then laid on the vocals" and, to his ear, caught them "exactly the way they performed on stage".[15] The result (with eight Lennon/McCartney songs and six others) was a concert performance in all but name, kicked off by Paul exuberantly counting the band into the opening number, "I Saw Her Standing There", and concluding some thirty-one minutes later with his elated shout of "Hey!" as John reached his last gasp at the end of a lacerating interpretation of the Isley Brothers' "Twist And Shout".

Five of the six non-original songs are noteworthy in their exposure of an eclectic mix of musical influences the Beatles had gleaned from black American artists. While "Twist And Shout", of course, stands head and shoulders above the others, with all the stops pulled out as a quintessential early Beatles' rocker, both "Boys" (a Shirelles' B-side) and "Chains" (first recorded by the Cookies) gave Ringo and George respectively much-appreciated solo spots. John had taken "Anna (Go To Him)" from Arthur Alexander. "Baby It's You", another Shirelles' song, was an early Bacarach/David number. The cuckoo in the nest was the British "A Taste Of Honey", with lyrics added to the theme tune of the 1961 film of Shelagh Delaney's play, starring Rita Tushingham.[16] For the period, though, the novelty of the LP undoubtedly lay in the majority of its tracks being original compositions, itself groundbreaking but compounded by the masterstroke of also passing some of them on to other artists; a trend which, as it continued, would not only enhance the group's standing but also help to enrich the growing diversity of the charts.

The first-ever Beatles song to be recorded by somebody else was the album's second track, "Misery". When it missed John and Paul's original target of Helen Shapiro (having been composed, with her in mind, on the tour bus in late January)[17], it was taken up by fellow tour-member Kenny Lynch; and although it failed to become a hit, in succession to his cover of "Up On The Roof"[18], it did achieve popularity through regular airplay.

It was closely followed by an alternative recording of "I Saw Her Standing There", sung by Duffy Power and produced by Ron Richards. Power, a London-based singer then in his early twenties, was one of the less marketable signings of pop manager Larry Parnes (whose biggest stars of the era were Marty Wilde and Billy Fury). Turning away from his roots in skiffle, he gravitated more and more towards the growing rhythm and blues scene in the south-east and on this occasion was backed by the newly-assembled Graham Bond Quartet; which, in addition to Bond on organ, was made up of Ginger Baker (drums), Jack Bruce (bass guitar) and John McLaughlin (lead guitar) – all very recent deserters from Alexis Korner's Blues Incorporated. With such a line-up, a striking reinterpretation should have been the expected outcome but, as is all too often the case in the history of pop, distance only lends unwarranted enchantment to this track. Bewilderingly described by musicologists variously as "vibrant"[19] and "pulsating"[20], it is, in reality, a plodding, pedestrian version of the song, totally lacking any semblance of the brightness, clamour or sheer joy of the Beatles' original track. Released in May, it was – deservedly – lost in the wilderness.

With the third song from the LP, however, "Do You Want To Know A Secret?", they struck gold, helping to launch the recording career of new Epstein signings Billy J. Kramer and the Dakotas in unexpectedly spectacular fashion. Originally, Epstein had offered the song to Shane Fenton (later to become Alvin Stardust) and the Fentones, seemingly oblivious to the fact that there was no business relationship between them and thus predictably inviting Fenton's rejection. Kramer then received the demo tape while he was fulfilling a contract in Hamburg: "It was just John on acoustic guitar and he'd recorded it in the loo because it was the only place where he could get peace and quiet. We did it every night at the Star-Club and it didn't do anything."[21] Despite Kramer's personal misgivings about the commercial appeal of the song (and overlooking the fact that he had not been Epstein's first choice to record it), it was produced by George Martin as their debut single, sold strongly and took them to No.1 in June. To capitalise on this instant popularity, his next two follow-ups were also Beatle compositions (although neither of these had previously been recorded): "Bad To Me" (a second No.1, in August) and "I'll Keep You Satisfied" (making No.4 in November).

So it was groups from the north-west, led by the Beatles, who were to the fore in breaking the old, tired light entertainment monopoly of the British charts and taking mainstream pop music in a new direction, aimed head-on at young people. At the start of 1963, established acts like Cliff Richard and the Shadows, the Springfields or the Bachelors were heavily reliant on having followed the traditional route of broadening their appeal, through film and television variety shows, to sell records to a wide, ill-defined yet intrinsically respectable family market. There were precious few other vocal groups around to pose any serious competition until the emergence of the Beatles. Staunch survivors from the first flush of skiffle and rock'n'roll, like Mike Berry and the Outlaws or Joe Brown and the Bruvvers, had all but had their day, even though ironically both groups registered the highest chart positions of their respective recording careers as the interminable winter showed no signs of relenting. "Don't You Think It's Time"[22] took Mike Berry to No.6 in the week ending 2nd February, while Joe Brown's "That's What Love Will Do" reached No.3 in the week ending 9th March (to be blocked by the Beatles' "Please Please Me" at No.2 and Cliff Richard's "Summer Holiday" at No.1). The incursion of the new groups began in earnest in mid-March, when Gerry and the Pacemakers followed the Beatles into the Top 30 and within a fortnight their version of "How Do You Do It?" (employing the

Beatles' arrangement of the song they had declined to record themselves) had stolen the No.1 spot from the Shadows' "Foot Tapper".

Although, as noted in the previous chapter, Gerry and the Pacemakers had been runners-up in the first *Mersey Beat* popularity poll, in reality they were just as highly regarded as the Beatles, having been their long-standing rivals around the clubs of both Liverpool and Hamburg.[23] Having first founded a skiffle group in 1958, Gerry Marsden (lead guitar and vocals) had been backed from 1959 onwards by the Pacemakers (an alternative name for the group which Gerry picked up from an athletics commentary on television, after the sweet manufacturers withheld their permission to call them the Mars Bars); who now consisted of his brother Freddie (drums), Les Chadwick (bass guitar) and Les McGuire (piano and backing vocals). After the Beatles, they were the next group to sign a management contract with Brian Epstein, in June 1962, but had a longer wait to secure a recording contract, which finally materialised with EMI's subsidiary Columbia in January 1963. Epstein admitted in his autobiography that he "had stalled [in promoting Gerry] because I wanted 'Love Me Do' and the Beatles to get away"[24] but eventually persuaded George Martin to come and see his act, at the Majestic Ballroom in Birkenhead on 12th December 1962; which fortuitously included a performance of "How Do You Do It?" and was soon followed by a successful audition for Martin at Abbey Road.

By the end of the year, Gerry and the Pacemakers had gone on to achieve the distinction of being the first artists ever to reach No.1 with their first three releases. After their debut with "How Do You Do It?", which was No.1 for three weeks in April, their follow-up was another Mitch Murray composition in a similarly bouncy vein, "I Like It". Entering the Top 30 at No.9, it sustained four weeks at No.1, through June into July. The third single, however, represented a defiant departure on Gerry's part from the expectations of those around him, including Brian Epstein, when he recorded what has come to be an iconic version of "You'll Never Walk Alone", from the 1945 Rodgers and Hammerstein musical *Carousel*. Taking the risk of mangling a classic song for the sake of demonstrating his versatility, in the end he confidently delivered an inescapably modern, untutored interpretation of this standard. Entering the charts in October at No.7, a fortnight later it was No.1, where it stayed for four weeks. To the extent that it was subsequently adopted by Liverpool City FC fans and is now almost universally regarded as the ultimate expression of the indomitable Liverpudlian spirit, Gerry's recording can properly be credited as being the first pop anthem of modern times, years in advance of any conscious efforts to contrive anthems as a new musical genre.[25]

Although Liverpool took the lead in the incursion of new northern groups into the charts, two notable exceptions from Manchester also made their Top 30 debuts in 1963, the first of these being Freddie and the Dreamers. Formed in 1959, they were not inclined to take themselves seriously (despite the considerable range of their repertoire, from rock'n'roll through ballads to comedy numbers) and were, visually, the unlikeliest of stars: "Gnomelike Freddie Garrity (vocals), balding Roy Crewson (rhythm guitar), sunglasses-toting Derek Quinn (lead guitar), fat Pete Birrell (bass) and gormless Bernie Dwyer (drums) were undoubtedly one of the most motley-looking aggregations ever to become 'pop idols'."[26]

Freddie, with his heavy-rimmed glasses and shock of black curly hair, had once been a milkman and had originally got into music, like so many others, as an enthusiastic part-timer in a skiffle group (in his case, the Red Sox). Now fronting the Dreamers, he habitually played to the gallery for comic effect with fey prancing across the stage and slapstick trouser-dropping gags, indicative of the frantic efforts needed to engage the majority of audiences they could expect to encounter on the Manchester club circuit. That these routines had undeniable crowd-appeal is confirmed, for example, by Sam Hardie, who remembered seeing them play regularly at the Cavern (where they first appeared on 3rd July 1962):

> I loved seeing Freddie and the Dreamers … as he gave people their money's worth. One day Freddie had a top hat and he turned his back on the audience and pretended to pee into it. Then he turned round and threw the contents over the front row. It was just bits of paper that he had in the hat.[27]

Fun to watch in strictly limited doses, nevertheless it inevitably meant in the longer term that their standing suffered by comparison with their contemporaries, even though they must be given credit for later (in 1965) being one of the quirkier successes in the 'British Invasion' of America. As noted wryly by Terry Rawlings, whereas the "cabaret graveyard" eventually became the only option for most Sixties' groups trying to keep going beyond their sell-by date, Freddie and the Dreamers "started out as cabaret!"[28] Signed to EMI's Columbia subsidiary, in May they scored their first chart entry with "If You Gotta Make A Fool Of Somebody" (a song 'borrowed' from the Beatles' Cavern set[29]), which by the week ending 22nd June reached No.2. Their follow-up, released in August, was "I'm Telling You Now", which made it to no.3 for a three-week stint from the week ending 24th August; and their third and final hit of the year, "You Were Made For Me", also reached No.3, at the end of November.

The second set of newcomers from Manchester, the Hollies, rapidly established themselves as being in an altogether different league and, after the Beatles, became one of the most consistently successful groups of the decade. Old school-friends and founder-members Allan Clarke and Graham

Nash, having sung semi-professionally as a duo for some years in emulation of their heroes the Everly Brothers, took bass-player Eric Haydock on board to form the Deltas; which they then expanded by the further addition of Don Rathbone (drums) and Tony Hicks (guitar and vocals), renaming the group in honour of Buddy Holly. Frequent performers over in Liverpool from 1962 onwards, the Hollies became a regular turn at the Cavern in 1963, where they were billed, to Graham Nash's discomfort, as 'Manchester's answer to the Beatles'; but having been ridiculed initially by Liverpool concert-goers as pale imitators of the Beatles for wearing leather, they soon opted for something more eye-catching, as recalled by Eric Haydock: "We wore white suits and that was aimed at the women. Club owners would tell us that if we got the women in, we would get the men and they would book us again."[30] Yet Freddie Garrity was of the opinion that there was no 'Manchester sound', only a "spin-off of the Liverpool sound", and he felt the Hollies were "very like a Liverpool group with their incessant drumbeat and raucous chords".[31]

Be that as it may, on 27th March, they were seen at the Cavern by EMI A&R man Ron Richards, on the strength of which they were offered a recording contract with Parlophone, and within a week were in London, recording their first single. This was a club-standard, popular with many groups at the time, a cover of the Coasters' "(Ain't That) Just Like Me", a belting rock'n'roll parody of children's nursery rhymes (including "Mary Had A Little Lamb", "Humpty Dumpty" and "Hey-Diddle-Diddle, The Cat And The Fiddle") compressed into less than two minutes.[32] Released in mid-May, it made no impact on the *NME* Top 30 but in mid-September their second single – another Coasters' cover, this time of the Leiber/Stoller composition "Searchin'"[33] – took them into the charts at No.27 and up to No.10 by the week ending 19th October.

In the intervening period between recording sessions in July and October, there was a change of line-up, with Don Rathbone replaced as drummer by Bobby Elliott (from Shane Fenton's backing group the Fentones, having previously played with Tony Hicks in Ricky Shaw and the Dolphins). If by now there was an emerging, embryonic Hollies' sound, then it showed itself in the prominence of harmonies and falsetto swoops traded between Clarke, Hicks and Nash, which were employed most strikingly to date in their third single, "Stay". Again a cover of an American original (this time by Maurice Williams and the Zodiacs[34]) and released in mid-November, it entered a highly competitive Top 30 at the beginning of December at No.21, eventually reaching No.8 the following month as well as becoming the title track of their first LP.

In spite of a reliance on cover versions for A-sides, there was nascent songwriting talent within the group, in the form of the core Clarke/Hicks/Nash trio, as Graham Nash explained:

In the beginning it was mainly Allan and I because we'd been doing that from when we were much younger. We'd have an idea and run it off each other. Then Tony Hicks became a part of that after he joined. He added the third harmony – plus he was a great guitarist, so Tony drifted into writing with us. It was pretty much a three way thing for a long while. It was all done everywhere, anywhere we could find the time – in dressing rooms, TV studios, or waiting backstage for the first act to finish. There was never any time put aside purely to write songs.[35]

For recording purposes, however, for most of the decade their own compositions would be largely confined to B-sides and LP tracks, initially credited to 'L. Ransford' (from Graham's grandfather, L. Ransford Nash). Eventually, though, as their popularity grew, they would overcome this self-consciousness and claim composing credits in their own right.

Reverting to the steady progress of the Liverpool contingent into the charts, next in the course of the year to make the breakthrough were the Searchers; who were not managed by Brian Epstein but initially by Les Ackerley, manager of local club The Iron Door.[36] At this juncture, the group comprised: Tony Jackson (lead vocals & bass guitar), John McNally (rhythm guitar & vocals), Mike Pender (lead guitar & vocals) and Chris Curtis (drums & vocals).

'Discovered' by record producer Tony Hatch after Ackerley's submission of an unsolicited demo tape and signed to the Pye label in April, their first single "Sweets For My Sweet" entered the Top 30 at No.24 in the week ending 6th July and within a month was No.1. A regular feature of their stage act, it was a cover of a US No.16 hit for the Drifters in the autumn of 1961 (which, as Mike Pender recalled, they had first come across the following year in a record shop in Hamburg).

Having originally come together in 1959 to play skiffle, founder-members Pender and McNally had juggled with various line-ups before bringing first Jackson, then Curtis into the group; and from late 1960 to early 1962, this quartet made up the backing group for singer Johnny Sandon. Like many others, they were temporarily knocked sideways by the Beatles' performances in Liverpool after their return from their first stint in Hamburg at the end of 1960. Nevertheless, persevering as Johnny Sandon and the Searchers, they built up a strong following in residence at the Iron Door, although Sandon's last appearance with them (before he left to join the Remo Four) was actually at the Cavern, on 28th February 1962. Now reduced to simply the Searchers, that July they followed their contemporaries on the profitable trail to

Hamburg, where they secured a gruelling 128-day contract at the Star-Club.

Just as those who preceded them had found, the Hamburg experience was to represent an eye-opening apprenticeship and at first just being there was an end in itself. The months they spent there, however, soon became profitable, in terms of the opportunities it offered to expand their repertoire, as they utilised the small hours to try out the latest numbers they had found or heard, when no-one still conscious in the audience cared what they were playing. On their return to Liverpool, they took up where they had left off at the Iron Door but were straight back out to Hamburg immediately after their first recording session with Tony Hatch, only then to be forced to buy themselves out of their club contract and return hurriedly again to England to capitalise on the unexpected chart success of their single.

As "Sweets For My Sweet" eventually left the Top 30 in September, having been No.1 for the first 3 weeks of August, it was succeeded the following week not by another single but by an EP, *Ain't Gonna Kiss Ya*, the title track and other songs being taken from their first LP, *Meet The Searchers*. This reached No.12 and then, as its sales in turn began to subside, it was followed by the issue of a second single, "Sugar And Spice"; a song specially written for them by Tony Hatch, under the pseudonym of 'Fred Nightingale'. Entering the Top 30 strongly at the end of October at No.13, its route to the top was blocked by the domination of the No.1 slot to the end of the year by first Gerry and the Pacemakers and then the Beatles; meaning that the highest position it achieved was No.3, in the week beginning 16th November.

In the same week in early July that "Sweets For My Sweet" had broken into the Top 30, another Liverpool group also made their chart debut. This was the Swinging Blue Jeans, at No.30 – for one week only – with "It's Too Late Now". As noted in earlier chapters, the Swinging Blue Genes (as were) had been amongst the most popular long-term residents at the Cavern from its beginnings as a jazz club and, as such, through their 'guest nights' had hosted the earliest performances there of the Beatles. Their final conversion from their trad jazz origins to beat group had been arrived at via a baptism of fire in Hamburg, at the start of a month's stint at the Star-Club in early September 1962. "Our first night at the Star-Club was terrible," said Ray Ennis:

> We had done about 15 minutes and the audience was whistling at us, which is an insult in Germany. They shut the curtains on us and the owner of the Star-Club, Manfred Weissleder, said, 'You must change your music. They only like rock'n'roll.' We rehearsed a new act the next day and Paul Moss, our banjo player, went on the organ. Les Braid borrowed Jackie Lomax's bass guitar, and we've never looked back.[37]

Perversely, on their return to the Cavern, with a name-change and trad standards like "Down By The Riverside" now forsaken in favour of songs by the likes of Chuck Berry and Buddy Holly, they initially met hostility on their home turf but stuck to their guns. Their original musical leanings had resulted in a management deal with owner of the Mardi Gras Jazz Club, Jim Ireland. First efforts to audition for record deals with the Oriole label and then independent record producer Joe Meek bore no fruit but on 18th February 1963 they completed a successful commercial sound test at Abbey Road, playing three numbers to EMI producer Walter J. (Wally) Ridley. Returning to the studio on 13th May – now minus Paul Moss, their erstwhile banjo player – they cut their first single for EMI's HMV label; the group now consisting of Ray Ennis (lead guitar & vocals), Ralph Ellis (rhythm guitar & vocals), Les Braid (bass guitar) and Norman Kuhlke (drums). Both sides were original compositions by group members ("It's Too Late Now", the A-side, by Ennis and the B-side, "Think Of Me", by Ellis and Kuhlke) and the record was released on 7th June.

Their next single, "Do You Know", again written by Ennis, failed to chart following its release at the end of September; but in November, they turned to full-blooded rock'n'roll for their salvation, by recording "Hippy Hippy Shake". Originally written and recorded in 1959 by US singer Robert Lee 'Chan' Romero, this was an old favourite on the set list of many Merseyside groups, including the Beatles.[38] Nevertheless, it was the Swinging Blue Jeans who laid down what remains the all-time definitive version, in one of those frenetic sub-two-minute takes typical of the early Sixties. Released on 6th December at their insistence, against Wally Ridley's judgement that it was not hit material, it caught the Christmas market just in time to enter the Top 30 at No.18 in the last week of the year and by mid-January 1964 had reached No.2.

Although neither the Searchers nor the Swinging Blue Jeans were part of Brian Epstein's empire, his management could not always guarantee runaway success and this was certainly true in the case of the Big Three, the next Liverpool group to achieve chart entry. Long popular and, indeed, much respected as a live act in the clubs, they found themselves both ill at ease and ill-served when it came to making the transition to successful recording artists.

The trio's origins lay with Cass and the Casanovas, the four-piece group who, together with Rory Storm and the Hurricanes, had played the first official rock'n'roll gig at the Cavern in May 1960. After touring Scotland as backing group for Duffy Power, founder and leader Brian Casser[39] split from the group, leaving them to re-form as the Big Three in January 1961; the line-up thus reducing to Adrian Barber (guitar), Johnny Gustafson (bass guitar & vocals) and Johnny 'Hutch' Hutchinson (drums & vocals).

The name-change, an inspired nod to the grandiose, was Barber's idea, referencing the 'Big Three' Allied wartime leaders Churchill, Roosevelt and Stalin. Through Barber's electronic skills in constructing huge amplifiers, five feet high by two feet wide and thus nicknamed 'coffins', they quickly established a reputation as the loudest of the Liverpool groups, playing with "violence and attack", "much bashing of cymbals" and all combined with "obscure R&B material".[40]

They also earned themselves a footnote in pop history as the first group to give then 17-year-old Priscilla White her first professional booking as a singer, at the Zodiac Club where she already worked as a part-time waitress to supplement her weekly wage of £3 11s as a typist. Offered the gig by 'Hutch' and billed by him in the *Liverpool Echo* as 'Swinging Priscilla', one Saturday night she fronted the group in the small space that passed for a stage and, for a fee of £1 10s, sang two numbers with them; "I'll Be Loving You, Always" ("Dinah Washington-style") and "Autumn Leaves" ("in a rock style").[41] Although turning down an offer to sing with them full-time, she still appeared with them occasionally but was relieved to be promoted subsequently as 'Swinging Cilla' by Kingsize Taylor and the Dominoes, with whom she went on to sing most often.[42]

In the summer of 1962, following the lead of the Beatles (with whom they were close friends), they signed up with Brian Epstein but their relationship with him was fraught from the outset. Epstein's over-directive approach to issues such as the clothes they wore on stage and the range of music they played was a constant source of irritation but even more contentious was his insistence that they should expand to become a quartet again, in order to meet a specific stipulation of a contract he had negotiated for them in Hamburg. To overcome this difficulty, Barber recruited another guitarist, Brian Griffiths (late of Howie Casey and the Seniors), who, mercifully, professed it "a privilege to play with Johnny Hutch and Johnny Gus ... the best rock bass player and drummer in Liverpool from that era".[43]

They then spent the whole of July playing the Star-Club, at the end of which Barber opted to leave the group and stay on for the time being in Hamburg, having been engaged by Manfred Weissleder as his stage manager and recording engineer. So it was Griffiths, Hutchinson and Gustafson who returned to the familiar circuit of Liverpool clubs and concert halls as the reconstituted Big Three; and on 19th December, end-on from completing another brief trip to Hamburg, it was this trio who auditioned in London for Decca, an experience unhappily generating a host of problems.

The entire episode of that sound test is indicative of the low regard in which many fledgling groups of the period were held not only by their own management but also record executives. It was an inauspicious start to proceedings to find on arrival at the studio that they were not even expected. Apparently, Epstein had substituted them at short notice for Gerry and the Pacemakers but neglected to inform either them or staff at Decca of the change. Yet the producer tasked with overseeing the day's session, Noel Walker, was seemingly prepared to take it in his stride and immediately pressed on with making a recording of "Some Other Guy". The Big Three themselves, however, felt very different about being given only one rushed shot at performing the song, a Leiber/Stoller rocker with which they were closely associated back home. Exhausted from travelling, they were highly dissatisfied with their first take but then further infuriated to be denied an opportunity to re-record it. They also had another issue with Walker's indifference to their complaints; in that while he too was from Merseyside, his previous musical background had not been rock'n'roll but jazz, as former leader of Noel Walker's Stompers. Insult was then finally added to injury when Decca decided, in March 1963, to release the unedited test recording as the Big Three's first single.

As one of their fans recalled, the record simply did not reflect the group's potential as demonstrated by their habitual live performance of the song:

> The Big Three did the definitive version of "Some Other Guy",
> even better than the Beatles. In concert, it was totally different
> to the record. Just multiply their record by five to imagine the
> excitement of it live. It had a very long 12 bar intro before the
> vocal came in whereas it comes straight in on the record. They were
> doing it like "What I'd Say" and there was a very long guitar solo in
> the middle. The whole thing was about five minutes long and very
> exciting.[44]

In response to the single's notable lack of success (it failed to make the Top 30), the group found themselves forced down a by now familiar (albeit, to them, unacceptable) path, as Epstein and Decca opted to play safe by requiring them to record a Mitch Murray composition next, the Latin-tinged "By The Way". It was backed by a B-side, "Cavern Stomp" (credited to the three group members and Noel Walker), which Epstein fondly hoped would attract local sales but on first hearing, Bob Wooler, the Cavern's DJ, had the temerity to disillusion him. Paradoxically, "By The Way", released at the end of June and which the group loathed, gave them their only hit. With a total of five weeks in the Top 30, it peaked at no.22 in the week ending 3rd August; but even before then, on 20th July, their management contract with Epstein had already been terminated.

Artistically, the Big Three found themselves completely at odds with their record company, victims of its innate conservatism as succinctly encapsulated by Brian Griffiths:

Decca couldn't grasp the notion that many of the Liverpool bands
didn't want to sound like the British rock'n'rollers of the 50s.
We were playing songs by American R&B singers unknown to
most people in England. Being a trio, we played the music more
aggressively and this was not accepted in the studio.[45]

And temperamentally they could not submit to Brian Epstein's mannered
image of perfection. Griffiths again:

He tried to establish dress codes and polite, non-threatening
behaviour when speaking in public or to the press. We were a rowdy
band on and off stage, so at times these rules were hard to comply
with. We had run-ins with Epstein all the time. Looking back, it was
like we self-destructed. The Big Three was at its best playing two
o'clock in the morning in sweat drenched clothes, with a case of
beer at the side of the stage, and Johnny Gus bellowing out "Good
Golly Miss Molly".[46]

Thus despite all that must have initially seemed to be going in their
favour, including a recording contract and TV exposure on the then prestigious *Thank Your Lucky Stars*, the Big Three crashed and burned. Of all his
signings, it clearly rankled with Epstein that they had been the most awkward
and their reward for not playing the game his way was a tart, unforgiving
postscript in his autobiography, replete with the whiff of sour grapes:

This group, when I took them on, had a very good sound and I was
most optimistic, but there was a lack of discipline and this cannot
be tolerated because it is bad for business, awful for reputation and
extremely bad for morale.[47]

In the long gallery of pop history, however, it is only fitting that they should
be more kindly and deservedly remembered by fellow artists, like Allan
Clarke, for their enduring influence as musicians' musicians:

[The Hollies] played at the Cavern on a bill with the Beatles, but the
Big Three were the stars for me. I idolized that group. Griff played
a Guyatone guitar with rusty strings and he made it sing. Johnny
Gus was a marvellous bass player. They did songs that nobody had
ever heard before and it used to make my back tingle.[48]

On the other hand, the last of the Liverpool groups to break into the
charts in 1963 were firm favourites with manager Epstein from the outset
and he obviously regarded them as something of a catch, at last lending an
air of intellectual respectability to NEMS Enterprises:

With the Fourmost – in contrast – I have had an increasingly happy
relationship and they are now one of the country's leading groups,

full of fun and brain with a lot of the reckless charm of the Beatles.
They, more than any of the others, were the most difficult to secure
for a contract for though they were old hands at the Cavern and
enjoyed playing, they were firmly involved in apprenticeships or at
college and they didn't wish to know about management or full-
time professionalism ... Between them they have twenty-seven
GCE passes – I remember being impressed by this since I had none
...[49]

The Fourmost had evolved from long-term Cavern favourites the
Four Jays, first appearing under their new name on 19th October 1962 to
avoid conflict with Joe Loss, who had then just registered the Four Jays
as the name of his band's vocalists. At this juncture, the group members
were: Brian O'Hara (lead guitar & vocals), Mike Millward (rhythm guitar &
vocals), Billy Hatton (bass guitar & vocals) and Dave Lovelady (drums &
vocals). Content to combine playing semi-professionally with their respective
studies for respectable full-time occupations, they resisted a series of offers
of management from Epstein until, once the 'Mersey Sound' had broken
through nationally, they had to concede that they had almost let a golden
opportunity pass them by. Hitherto known as a group only too ready to mix
comedy with pop (including impressions of Jerry Lewis, Gracie Fields, Chic
Murray and send-ups of songs such as "Happy Talk" from *South Pacific*[50]),
a first encounter with George Martin on a visit to the Cavern in December
1962 had favourably attracted his attention but a subsequent sound test at his
invitation had not gone well. Although they were pleased with their efforts,
auditioning with "Happy Talk", they found themselves criticised by Martin
for playing the wrong chords.[51]

Luckily, this did not constitute an obstacle the following summer, when
they eventually succumbed to Epstein's powers of persuasion and agreed to
turn professional. The first recording they then undertook with Martin for
the Parlophone label turned out to be a Lennon/McCartney song, rejected
at the time by Gerry and the Pacemakers in favour of Mitch Murray's "I Like
It" as the follow-up to "How Do You Do It?". This was "Hello Little Girl",
one of the songs originally included by the Beatles in their unproductive
Decca audition for Dick Rowe. Since they were unfamiliar with the number,
Billy Hatton remembers John Lennon and George Harrison running through
it for them at Lennon's house before making them a demo tape:

We received the tape at 4 o'clock on Monday morning ... As we
had to record on the following Wednesday, we had two days in
which to make an arrangement good enough to put on disc. As a
matter of fact, when we were recording, we were just learning the

song as we went along and were tremendously encouraged by A&R man George Martin.[52]

Breaking into the chart at No.30 in the week ending 21st September (the same week as the Hollies first charted with "Searchin'"), the Fourmost took "Hello Little Girl" to No.10 a month later, the high point of an impressive nine-week debut in the Top 30. Because of the timing of recording sessions and release dates, it was, however, to be their only hit of the year. Their second single, "I'm In Love" (another Lennon/McCartney composition but this time written specifically for them and unrecorded by the Beatles themselves), was released in December, thus ending the year awaiting chart entry. Meanwhile, as we shall see later in this chapter, they were to be included by Epstein as a supporting act in a Christmas stage show, giving them a new platform and new audiences for their well-tried comedy routines.

Whilst this cluster of groups from north-west England spearheaded the diversification of the UK charts in the course of the year, broadening choice and establishing new allegiances, competition from rivals in London and the south-east slowly began to develop and be exploited in parallel. To the fore in this were Brian Poole and the Tremeloes, Dick Rowe's preferred choice to the Beatles at the beginning of 1962 and (according to Alan Clayson) regarded proudly by him as a "benchmark of pop group professionalism"[53]; comfortably compliant in their allotted role as "purveyors of popular songs that people would hum, whistle and partly sing over a few chart weeks before the forces behind them prepared another harmless ditty for easy consumption".[54] But it was not until early July 1963 that they actually had a hit, with their fifth single for Decca[55], their version of "Twist And Shout", which entered the Top 30 at No.19. Immediately in competition with the Isley Brothers' original recording, which had charted the week before and hovered in the lower reaches of the Top 30 for a month, the main battle for sales was engaged with the Beatles, whose *Twist And Shout* EP[56] broke into the singles chart at No.13 a fortnight later and by mid-August had sold (for an EP) a record-breaking 250,000 copies. In terms of highest chart position, honours were ultimately even, with both records having reached No.4; but in terms of chart run, Poole and the Tremeloes had the edge over the Beatles by eleven weeks to ten.

With their next single, which gave them an autumnal No.1 hit, they all too easily saw off their rivals, who this time were another group from London, the Dave Clark Five. The song, "Do You Love Me"[57], was a cover of a 1962 US hit for the Contours[58], written by Berry Gordy Jr., the founder of Tamla Motown Records. A year on, it was, irrespective of its composer's standing, an already sadly dated number, all too typical of the early Sixties, in which the singer boastfully reclaims his lost love through his prowess at dancing:

I can mash potato,
I can do the twist.
Well now, tell me, baby,
Do you like it like this?

His exhibitionism completed to perfection, the inescapable punchline of the chorus is: "Do you love me/Now that I can dance?" What it lacked in imagination, this banal song admittedly made up for in pace, although it remains a mystery how, in the enlivened pop context of the second half of 1963, Poole's anglicised version could ever have caught on to the extent of taking the charts by storm and supplanting the Beatles at No.1.

Dave Clark's version, of course, had all the hallmarks of his group's later hits (principally a walloping drumbeat, laid down by Clark himself, and lyrics filtered through the iron lungs of lead vocalist Mike Smith, exemplifying what came to be dubbed the 'Tottenham Sound'[59]) but could get no higher than No.24. Nevertheless, it had at last brought Clark and the band much-needed commercial success, with their fifth single to date and their second release on EMI's Columbia label. Any lingering doubts that they might not make the big time were finally dispelled at the end of November, when they returned to the charts with a new self-composition, "Glad All Over"[60], which was destined to become No.1 early in the New Year.

In the same week that the Beatles' *Twist And Shout* EP entered the Top 30 (the week ending 20th July), an unexpected revival of interest brought London rockers Johnny Kidd and the Pirates back into the charts, after an absence of almost three years since September 1960, with "I'll Never Get Over You". Where had they been all this time? As recording artists, there could be no doubt that they had been languishing in the doldrums, recording five unsuccessful singles in the intervening period since "Shakin' All Over"; a period which had ominously included a complete absence of recording for some ten months, between December 1961 and September 1962, as well as a wholesale reconstruction of the Pirates.[61] In such circumstances, they were extremely fortunate to have retained the faith of their producer Wally Ridley and their contract with EMI's HMV label, an outcome increasingly less likely for acts on the wane as the decade progressed and recording executives became more ruthless. Equally amazingly, they had remained a hard-working band on the road, touring at various times with Joe Brown, Jerry Lee Lewis and Bruce Channel; and had been totally reinvigorated by a month spent, in July 1962, playing the Star-Club in Hamburg, as drummer Frank Farley explained: "We were a typical beat group and then we heard all these scouse bands playing rave stuff like 'Castin' My Spell' and 'A Shot Of Rhythm And Blues'. When we came back to England we were a different band entirely."[62]

Composed by Gordon Mills, "I'll Never Get Over You" dramatically restored Kidd's credibility with a chart-run lasting thirteen weeks, of which the high point was two weeks at No.5 in September. His next release, "Hungry For Love", was another Mills composition, with the potential to be even more memorable[63]; but disappointingly getting no higher than No.24 over three weeks from the end of November to mid-December, in the face of massive pre-Christmas competition from newer artists, it turned out instead to be his swan-song in the UK charts.

Of the London contingent of the time, one group in particular, with a chaotic 1962 behind them, had yet to make a breakthrough in recording as professional musicians. For the Rolling Stones, 1963 was to be the year in which outstanding issues of group membership were resolved, a new manager acquired and a record deal with Decca secured. As a consequence, they appeared for the first time in the *NME* chart for the week ending 3rd August, at No.26 with their version of Chuck Berry's "Come On"; in so doing, officially embarking upon one of the longest continuous careers of any rock band.[64]

Who was to be their permanent drummer was dealt with peremptorily in mid-January. On the 11th, after a gig at the Ricky Tick Club in Windsor, Tony Chapman was fired and finally replaced, for the following night's gig at the Ealing Jazz Club, by Charlie Watts; who, even so, had justifiable initial doubts about his future financial security. Pete Frame credits "meticulous" Charlie, following his recruitment, with becoming a driving force for change, turning the group, musically speaking, "from a rabble to a band".[65] Socially, they were self-confessed misfits; particularly Mick, Brian and Keith, who since the summer of 1962 had revelled in living in collective squalor on the middle floor of a dingy three-storey house at 102 Edith Grove, Fulham, now rendered even more uncomfortable by the relentless extremes of winter weather. According to Keith, they spent their first year together as the Rolling Stones "hanging places, stealing food and rehearsing"[66], with the ultimate goal of turning themselves into not only a proficient but, far and away more importantly, an authentic blues band: "We went for a Chicago blues sound, as close as we could get it – two guitars, bass and drums and a piano – and sat around and listened to every Chess record ever made. Chicago blues hit us right between the eyes."[67]

Still striving from the outset of the New Year to further develop the club following they had already begun to establish, their first flush of success in attracting ever larger crowds to the Marquee and Flamingo Jazz Clubs – between 600 to 1,000 strong – temporarily became their undoing. By daring to play, in deference to their fans, what a precious minority saw as the wrong kind of music, they perpetuated the offence they had earlier given to reactionary club managers like Harold Pendleton, as well as further alienating jazz sophisticates such as Chris Barber, who deemed the music of Bo Diddley and Chuck Berry to be not "authentic enough" and decidedly "too commercial".[68] Compounding these transgressions by having the nerve to ask for more money, by the end of January their growing popularity had paradoxically cost them both residencies; and so the hunt for more profitable gigs elsewhere began, which, as it progressed, brought with it a number of significant new encounters.

For example, at the Red Lion in Sutton, where they played for the first time on 23rd January, they linked up with Glyn Johns, musician and recording engineer at the IBC (Independent Broadcasting Company) Recording Studios in Portland Place; owned at that time by George Clouston and Eric Robinson, whose light orchestral BBC TV series *Music For You* was a long-running favourite with the middle-aged. IBC was where Joe Meek had worked when he first moved to London from Gloucestershire and housed the biggest independent recording facilities outside the major record labels' own studios. Johns, who had access to IBC in his free time (on the understanding that any recordings he made would then belong to the studios), offered the Stones an opportunity to make a demo tape under his supervision; which they took up on Monday, 11th March. In three hours that day, they recorded five songs: two by Bo Diddley ("Diddley Daddy" and "Road Runner"), two by Jimmy Reed ("Honey What's Wrong" and "Bright Lights, Big City") and Muddy Waters' "I Wanna Be Loved". Unfortunately for them, on completion, of course, the material reverted, under a six-month option, to the control of Clouston and Robinson, who, both having a disposition towards classical music, could inevitably do no more than make ill-informed, abortive attempts to pitch the Stones to record companies.

On 6th February, at Brian's invitation, Giorgio Gomelsky came to the Red Lion to see the Rolling Stones play. From a chance meeting at the Marquee, Brian had cultivated Gomelsky's acquaintance, for he was not only a fanatical jazz and blues enthusiast but also, amongst his other interests, an impresario and music club manager. Having previously run the now defunct Piccadilly Jazz Club (where some, at least, of the Stones had apparently played one poorly-attended concert on Boxing Day and failed to impress him[69]), he had just set up a new Sunday-night music club at the Station Hotel, Richmond, for where Brian pressed him for a booking. Their chance came when Gomelsky's regulars, the Dave Hunt Rhythm and Blues Band[70], made a no-show and he called the Stones in as replacements on 24th February, after which he retained them to play there every Sunday night. Through his contacts, he then helped them to secure a Sunday-afternoon slot at Studio 51, Ken Colyer's Jazz Club in Soho; so from March onwards, every Sunday they would play consecutive sets at Studio 51 and the Station Hotel (the latter being renamed the Crawdaddy Club from 7th April) and Gomelsky became their *de facto* first manager. Unfortunately for him, Gomelsky's promotion of the band derived more from a touching but misplaced sense of altruism than from any profit motive, with nothing formalised between them, leaving him vulnerable within no more than two months to being outmanoeuvred by an opportunistic 19-year-old on the make: Andrew Loog Oldham.

In the preceding two or three years, Loog Oldham had insinuated his way into the mainstream pop music business in and around London, a wheeler-dealer with grand delusions of becoming an agent or promoter. Moving from role to role as a junior press officer and general factotum with popular artists like Kenny Lynch and Mark Wynter, it just so happened that on 13th January 1963 he was with Wynter at the ABC-TV Studios in Birmingham for a recording of *Thank Your Lucky Stars*, where the Beatles were also in attendance to record their performance of "Please Please Me". Seizing the moment, he engaged Brian Epstein in conversation, managing to persuade him that he would be the very person to represent the Beatles' press interests in London. Having thus inveigled his way into NEMS Enterprises and following through by renting himself office space for £4 a week at the Regent Street booking agency of Eric Easton, he then set about perfecting "a new role – that of an independent, self-employed publicist"[71]; although ultimately his destiny was to become possibly the greatest self-publicist of the era.

Meanwhile, Giorgio Gomelsky had developed the notion of making a documentary film about the contemporary music scene and had himself approached the Beatles at a subsequent *Thank Your Lucky Stars* recording session in London, this time on Sunday, 14th April. He had also invited them to see the Rolling Stones perform that evening, at what had by now become the Crawdaddy Club; which they did, afterwards spending time in small talk with the Stones at Edith Grove into the early hours of the next morning before returning to their hotel in Russell Square.[72] When the Beatles turned down his filming proposal, Gomelsky came up with the alternative of shooting a short film in Richmond, featuring the Stones, and sought to drum up publicity for the revised project by contacting the editor of *Record Mirror*, Peter Jones; who came to the Station Hotel to see work in progress – somewhat chaotically, under Gomelsky's direction – on the afternoon of 21st April and stayed to catch the group's regular Sunday-evening performance. He liked what he saw and, conscious that interest in rhythm and blues would surely grow, he passed the word to Loog Oldham.

So, on the following Sunday evening, at the end of a week in which the Stones had played their first gig at Eel Pie Island, Twickenham – yet another venue secured for them directly through Gomelsky's good offices – Loog Oldham was the latest new member of their audience at the Crawdaddy and for him it was an epiphany:

> I'd never seen anything like it. They came on to me. All my
> preparations, ambitions and desires had just met their purpose …

I was in love. I heard the anthem of a national sound, I heard the
sound of a national anthem. I heard what I always wanted to hear.
I wanted it; it already belonged to me. Everything I'd done up until
now was a preparation for this moment. I saw and heard what my
life, thus far, had been for.[73]

This was all very well but now he had to move quickly to devise a strat-
agem whereby somehow he could take control of the Rolling Stones, since,
at under twenty-one, he was legally too young to be licensed as an agent
by London County Council. By his own account, in the course of a week
after seeing them for the first time ever, he completed all the key moves.
Firstly, he extracted himself from his obligations to NEMS, although taking
great care in the process of a personal telephone call to diplomatically offer
Brian Epstein the opportunity to come in with him – an offer which Epstein
politely declined. Then he took soundings of Peter Jones, with particular
interest in what he might know of Gomelsky's relationship with the group.
Jones reassured him with his understanding that there was "nothing official
or signed" between them.[74] Finally, he determined to persuade Eric Easton,
as a *bona fide* agent, to become his partner in the deal he was planning, for
without him he lacked specific means to legitimise or finance the operation.
He prevailed upon Easton to accompany him to Richmond the next Sunday,
to see the Stones for himself; and with Easton satisfied after that night's
performance at a packed Crawdaddy, in an atmosphere he likened to a "free
Turkish bath"[75], before they left the two of them approached the group with
an offer to discuss terms.

In the subsequent negotiations, Brian Jones naturally assumed the role
of spokesman for the group, a position to which the other Stones deferred.
Although accounts vary as to the extent of Mick and Keith's participation
with Brian in these preliminary meetings with Loog Oldham and Easton,
Bill, Charlie and Ian were all excluded by default, by virtue of their respective
daytime work commitments. The outcome was that Brian agreed to sign a
three-year contract on behalf of the Stones with the newly-formed management company Loog Oldham had christened Impact Sound[76], only then
disclosing that he was precluded by the existing IBC option from signing
up to an associated record deal. At the behest of Loog Oldham and Easton,
Brian retrieved this awkward situation by contacting George Clouston
and buying back the rights to the demo tape cut with Glyn Johns, recom-
pensing IBC to the tune of £90 (the notional cost of the Stones' studio
time). This then conveniently cleared the way for Easton and Dick Rowe
to conclude a two-year recording contract for them with Decca[77]; with the
proviso that Decca would only be responsible for the manufacture and distribution of discs from master tapes which were to be independently sourced
and produced by Loog Oldham. (This leasing arrangement allegedly drew

its inspiration from conversations between Loog Oldham and a contemporary idol of his, the extraordinary American record producer Phil Spector, at the tail end of 1962: "That way, Spector explained, you keep control and you earn much more money."[78] Although not unique in the UK, it was relatively unprecedented, Joe Meek being the only other prominent independent producer of the early Sixties.)

For the Stones themselves, one almost immediate negative consequence of their new management contract was that Loog Oldham demanded Ian Stewart's withdrawal from live performances with the group: he personally disliked Stewart's physical appearance and felt that even five on stage was pushing it in terms of the public's capacity to identify with individuals and form an attachment to the group. It fell to Brian to convey this decision to Stu, who took it badly – as a personal rebuff from Brian, for which he never forgave him – but yet loyally agreed to remain the sixth group member behind the scenes and take on the role of road manager.

On Friday, 10th May, Loog Oldham accompanied the Stones to the Olympic Sound Studios in London to make their first record together, where they were assisted by recording engineer Roger Savage. The track they chose for the A-side was "Come On", a Chuck Berry song, running in their version to just 1 minute 45 seconds; while for the B-side, they revisited Muddy Waters' "I Want To Be Loved", one of the set originally recorded at IBC with Glyn Johns two months earlier. Although Loog Oldham was nominally the producer, on his own admission he was then totally ignorant of the mechanics of recording or mixing, which irksome technicalities he was content, on this occasion, to leave to Savage. (His principal input appears to have been to instruct Savage to cut the microphone to Ian Stewart on piano, so that Stu was completely absent from the master tape.) As a result, Dick Rowe was less than satisfied with the quality of what was presented to Decca for pressing, insisting that the Stones re-record the single at the company's own studio, under the supervision of an in-house producer; but to Loog Oldham's relief, Mick reported back that "It didn't go well, in fact it's worse than the Olympic session".[79] In the end, therefore, the Impact Sound production, for all its faults, was the preferred choice and was released on 7th June.

It was never a record the Stones particularly liked or were even willing to own. They didn't include the song in their club sets and by all accounts only ever played it at Loog Oldham's insistence. It was very much a means to an end and therefore tolerated pragmatically, as described by Keith:

> I quite cold-bloodedly saw this song as just a way to get in. To get into the studio and to come up with something very commercial. It's very different from Chuck Berry's version; it's very Beatle-ized, in fact. The way you could record in England, you couldn't get fussy, you went in and did it. I think everybody thought it stood a

good shot. The band itself were like "We're making a record, can you believe this shit?" There was also a sense of doom. Oh my God, if the single makes it, we've got two years and that's it. Then what are we going to do? Because nobody lasted.[80]

Notwithstanding their disaffection, in the week ending 3rd August it broke into the Top 30 at No.26 and was in the charts for a total of 7 weeks, reaching the highest position of No.20. For their television debut to promote "Come On", a recording made on 7th July for *Thank Your Lucky Stars*, Loog Oldham had the group kitted out uniformly in collars and ties, houndstooth jackets with black velvet collars, black trousers and Cuban-heel boots; a conservative move, akin to Brian Epstein's remodelling of the Beatles from their origins as leather-clad rockers as one dimension of his assertion of management control. He quickly appreciated, however, that the Stones' innate tendency to scruffiness, born for the three principal players out of the studied disorder of Edith Grove, was his free wild card to generate publicity; and even despite his early attempts to impose a 'uniform' on them, their early exposure on television prompted plenty of antagonistic comment and correspondence from older viewers, outraged by their then unfashionably long hair. Indeed, Bill Wyman recalls Pete Murray, co-host of *Thank Your Lucky Stars* on their first appearance, making "some unfunny remarks about a delegation from the Hairdressers' Union wanting to see the Stones because they hadn't had a haircut since last year".[81]

As if it mattered – but it was a gift for Loog Oldham, stirring up, as it did, the interest of the popular – never mind the musical – press in his new act. Thus were the seeds sown of the myth of the Stones as anti-Establishment, although not everyone was duped. Keith Altham of the *NME*, for one, understood perfectly how calculated a strategy this was from the outset, to exaggerate their non-conformity so that they came to be seen as "working class heroes"; whereas, as yet, they were no more than "middle-class kids rebelling against a middle-class background".[82] The rest fell into place in due course, given the inanity of the media of the day. After all, there were 'expectations' still of performers on television, radio and in the press, which were outmoded to the point of inflexibility and inconsequence. The Beatles were the first act to suffer this inquisition of fools in depth, choosing to meet it head-on with an ironic wit which went unrecognised as 'cheeky humour' and paradoxically only endeared them more to their self-appointed, self-righteous commentators. As time passed, it was only to be expected that the Beatles' patience with this state of affairs would grow thinner, in inverse proportion to the disrespect increasingly shown towards them; and as for the Stones and – most pronouncedly – Bob Dylan, it would be entirely predictable that it would become second nature for them not to give a damn. For the moment, however, the Stones were the fortuitous recipients of a backlash from an older middle-class generation, teenagers' parents now in their early forties and whose fathers, like my own, had fought in the Second World War; for whom the passing of National Service had denoted a decline in the moral fibre of modern youth and the curling of hair over the male collar, in defiance of the obligatory short-back-and-sides, unmistakably represented incipient rebellion against the established order of things.

Once the record was out, irrespective of its modest success and its almost total non-alignment with the music the Stones had been playing in the clubs, there was no going back. Much to Keith's surprise, "in a matter of a week or so, we'd been transformed into pop stars ... propelled into show business".[83] Their lives were taken in completely new directions, by the demands of touring, television and – of course – the *sine qua non*, having to find and record new material.

For the remainder of the year, they found themselves hooked into a seemingly relentless round of live performances. In addition to fulfilling their existing commitments on the club circuit in and around London (i.e., at Studio 51, the Crawdaddy[84], Eel Pie Island and the Ricky Tick Club), they began by touring widely across England and Wales for three months; playing, by Bill Wyman's reckoning, from "13 July to 28 September ... 78 shows in 76 days".[85] With Eric Easton responsible for the group's accounts from mid-August onwards, each member was paid a weekly wage of £18 and Bill was finally forced to turn professional, "unable any longer to hold down a job and play with the band".[86] From 29th September onwards, Easton had booked them on a package tour headlined by the Everly Brothers and Bo Diddley, to which Little Richard was added after the first five concerts.[87] The tour ran until 3rd November, taking them again all over England as well as this time to Cardiff and Glasgow, 30 dates altogether in 36 days; then was followed immediately by another national tour of clubs, ballrooms and concert halls, which lasted until 5th January 1964 and entailed a further 58 shows in 62 days.

Somewhere between engagements, however, it was imperative to find time to make new recordings and then undertake the associated promotional appearances on television. At first it proved hard to summon up collective inspiration as to how to follow "Come On". In the course of July, two sessions at Decca's studios resulted in recordings of existing popular rock'n'roll standards "Fortune Teller" and "Poison Ivy"; the former produced by Loog Oldham, the latter by Decca's own Michael Barclay. Although the Stones were seemingly enthused by neither of these, they were provisionally slated as the two sides of their next single. With "Poison Ivy" intended as the A-side, a release date of 26th August was scheduled. In the interim, returning to the West Hampstead studios on 8th August and now looking even further ahead, Loog Oldham produced three of the four tracks for a proposed EP; two of the cuts from that session being issued on the final version (Chuck

Berry's "Bye Bye Johnny" and Arthur Alexander's "You'd Better Move On").

The release of "Poison Ivy" as a single was eventually shelved by Decca as "Come On" continued to enjoy relatively robust sales throughout August and the Stones were obliged to make two more television appearances to promote it. The first of these was on 23rd August, on only the third edition of a new ITV music programme broadcast on Friday evenings, *Ready Steady Go!* (habitually shortened to its acronym *RSG!*). Stars of the first edition, on 9th August, had been Billy Fury and Brian Poole and the Tremeloes. Originally using the Surfaris' instrumental "Wipe Out" as its theme tune and promising its teenage target audience that "The weekend starts here", it was the first serious attempt in the Sixties to recreate a beat club atmosphere in a television studio. (Not since *Six-Five Special* had a live audience on the studio floor been featured dancing to songs on camera, for its successors, from *Oh Boy!* onwards, had all effectively been televised stage shows.) It also broke new ground in its division of hosting between practised professional Keith Fordyce, then in his mid-thirties and a Radio Luxembourg DJ to boot, and complete newcomer 19-year-old Cathy McGowan, specifically recruited for her youth and sense of style. Together with her obvious enthusiasms for new music and new fashions, McGowan's exuberant, unaffected approach to interviewing performers rapidly transformed *RSG!* into a highly-respected institution of the pop scene. By comparison, the programme's older brother, *Thank Your Lucky Stars*, began to look a little staid; although in the short term it was still to retain its premier ranking as an important and popular showcase, thus seeing its reprise of "Come On" on 23rd August.

With "Poison Ivy" now out of the frame, Loog Oldham was growing ever more anxious in his quest for another song for the Stones' second single. The story of how that song fell into his lap through a chance encounter is apocryphal, varying from one teller to another, but it unequivocally demonstrates the power of the Beatles' patronage by this point in 1963. What can be corroborated from more than one source is that on the afternoon of 10th September, while the Stones were in fraught rehearsal at Studio 51 in Soho, Loog Oldham took a walk outside to clear his head, only to meet John Lennon and Paul McCartney; who, having attended a formal lunch to receive an award from the Variety Club, had just alighted from a taxi in the Charing Cross Road outside Leicester Square tube station. At Loog Oldham's entreaty, they returned with him to Studio 51 in Great Newport Street, where they offered the Stones a new song they were still in the process of composing, "I Wanna Be Your Man". Roughed out in their heads as a proposed track for Ringo to sing on their forthcoming second LP, John later recalled that:

> Paul and I just went off in the corner of the room and finished the song while they were all still there, talking. We came back and that's how Mick and Keith got inspired to write: 'Jesus, look at that. They

just went in the corner and wrote it and came back!' Right in front
of their eyes we did it.[88]

Described by Ian MacDonald as "palaeolithically simple" in its structure[89],
as subsequently recorded by the Beatles the song nevertheless caused them
an inordinate amount of effort and some sixteen takes, spread over several
weeks, to perfect (the first being laid down on 11th September, the very next
day after John and Paul's impromptu meeting with the Stones). It ended up,
in Tony Barrow's words, as a "real raver" of a song for their "fierce-voiced
drumming man"[90], with backing on the Hammond organ provided by John.

In absolute contrast, the Stones went to De Lane Lea Studios on 7th
October and, under Eric Easton's supervision this time as producer, rattled
through their version to create their next single. With Brian playing bottle-
neck guitar and Mick virtually shouting the lyrics, Keith proudly regarded the
outcome as unmistakably their own. (The B-side, a bluesy instrumental in the
style of Booker T and the MGs called "Stoned", gave the group their first
composing credit, under the pseudonym 'Nanker/Phelge'; 'Nanker' being "a
revolting face that band members, and Brian in particular, would pull" and
'Phelge' from Jimmy Phelge, a notorious Edith Grove flatmate.[91]) Released
on 1st November, it took a month to enter the Top 30 but by the week ending
18th January 1964 had climbed to No.9.

It is impossible to underestimate the socio-cultural impact of the Beatles
on the Britain of 1963. According to Brian Epstein, as their name became "a
household word", it was "impossible to enter a discussion without the Beatles
being mentioned", a problem readily encountered by "men, and women and
children of all ages, all classes, all shades of belief and intelligence".[92] Aside
from the halo effect they created, in the light of which, as we have seen
so far in this chapter, others' careers unexpectedly blossomed, in their own
right suddenly they became unstoppable, going from strength to strength in
popular esteem, from success to success. Even in stark summary, the evidence
speaks for itself. In the course of this one year, they had four consecutive
No.1 singles, two best-selling LPs and three hit EPs. They completed four
UK tours, as well as a week-long tour of Sweden, concluding with their own
Christmas show at the Finsbury Park Astoria. Although not winners themselves (because voting had taken place the previous year), an additional slot
was created specially for them at the *NME*'s Annual Poll-Winners' Concert,
held at the Empire Pool, Wembley. Their exposure on radio and television
rose to unprecedented levels, including, as already noted above, playing the
Albert Hall and appearing on *Sunday Night At The London Palladium*, with the
crowning glory being their participation in the Royal Variety Performance.
And, diverting momentarily from this heady path to becoming national

treasures, they also took their final leave of the Cavern.

Behind all this, there was – up to a point – a plan, of Brian Epstein's devising. As stated in his autobiography:

> The Beatles have always been happy to leave timings, plots, plans, schemes and the development of their career to me because they were good enough to trust me and because they knew that if there was some important decision to make I would consult them to sound their remarkable instincts and to gauge their reactions.[93]

But even he had not foreseen the signal shift in the level of adulation that occurred that autumn: "Beatlemania descended on the British Isles in October, 1963. It happened suddenly and dramatically and we weren't prepared for it."[94]

With hindsight, he attributed it to his master-stroke of having engineered the Beatles' inclusion in the Royal Variety show and the resultant surge of press interest following its public announcement; whereas the Beatles themselves were particularly taken aback by the mass hysteria of the throngs of fans who turned out to greet them at London Airport on their return from Sweden, attracting wide press and television coverage only two weeks after the bewildered reporting of the chaos those same fans had caused outside the London Palladium.

Following the release of *Please Please Me* on 22nd March, Parlophone issued their next single, "From Me To You", on 11th April. Written by John and Paul on 28th February, then on the road nearing the end of the Helen Shapiro tour, it had been recorded at Abbey Road on 5th March, together with what became the B-side, "Thank You Girl".[95] Entering the Top 30 at No.6 in its first week on sale, boosted by advance orders, the next week it was No.1, pushing aside the rejected "How Do You Do It?" and staying put for five weeks to the end of May, until finally overtaken by that other Lennon/McCartney composition let out on licence, "Do You Want To Know A Secret?"

If truth be told, only one specific event was the real catalyst of Beatlemania, the release on 23rd August of their fourth single. Of them all, "She Loves You" [96] still endures today as *the* song marking the unreserved admission of the Beatles to the Hall of Fame that is the wider public consciousness; being held up to critical admiration as nothing less than "an authentic distillation of the atmosphere of that time, and one of the most explosive pop records ever made".[97] To me, it was, quite simply, the most exciting record of the year so far. It was the first vocal single I bought to add to my collection and I was not alone in my enthusiasm, for in the coming months accumulated sales reached 1.89 million, making it the top-selling Beatles' single of all time.[98]

In my mind's eye, if there is any one song that most perfectly captures the very essence of Beatledom in its performance, aurally and visually, then this is it. It's inescapably loud. It starts with an impressive drumroll and then you're straight into the chorus, with its compulsive repetition of 'Yeah-yeah-yeah!' Suited and booted, the Fab Four are there before you. John stands apart from the others, eyes narrowed in his short-sightedness, weighed down in the earnestness of his delivery of the lead vocal, a little crouched in his stance, a little bow-legged, as if his guitar was just that much too big for him. Singing in harmony, Paul and George are leaning in towards each other at the microphone and shaking their heads as they add their falsetto embellishments from the end of the second verse onwards.[99] Behind the drums, Ringo bounces and sways on his stool with a big grin on his face as he keeps up the pounding beat. This is the iconic image of the most famous group in the world, doing what they do best – and, unbelievably, they've written this song as well, and there are more and more and more still to come, as yet undreamed of. Two minutes twenty seconds of pure magic.

Within a week, "She Loves You" vaulted straight into the Top 30 at No.2 and then was No.1 for the whole of September, having sold half a million copies by the 3rd of that month. Deposed from the top slot for the next three weeks by Brian Poole and the Tremeloes, and then for another month by Gerry and the Pacemakers, it never fell below No.4 during this hiatus, at the end of which it returned to No.1 for the last two weeks of November and had by then sold a million; only to be replaced by the Beatles' own next single, "I Want To Hold Your Hand" (which, having been released on 29th November, immediately entered the charts at No.1). Altogether, "She Loves You" was to enjoy a Top 30 stint lasting 24 weeks.

In addition, already with an eye to promoting the back catalogue of only a few months' standing, Parlophone issued two Beatles' EPs during the autumn. The Beatles' Hits came out on 6th September, including their first three singles and the B-side "Thank You Girl"; followed on 1st November by The Beatles (No.1), featuring four tracks from Please Please Me.[100] Then, with impeccable timing for Christmas, on 22nd November this marketing exercise was converted from possible madness to pure genius by an impressive display of new material in the form of their second LP With The Beatles. Along with their two latest singles and given renewed sales of the Twist And Shout EP from earlier in the year, all three of these records entered the Top 30 and, unbelievably, the whole six all had places in the chart for the week ending 14th December.

The sleeve for With The Beatles, with Robert Freeman's distinctive monochrome shot of their four heads part-lit and part in shadow (harking back to some of the art photographic studies Astrid Kircherr had made of the group in Hamburg), broke new ground in product packaging in this long-pre-digital age; in absolute contrast to other LP covers of the period and, specifically, that of *Please Please Me*, with Angus McBean's safe but uninspiring stock shot of the four group members looking down into the stairwell of EMI's head offices.[101] In unspoken pursuit of Marshall McLuhan's principle that the medium is the message, the cover alone signified the inter-relatedness of art and pop; an image, in Jon Savage's words, taking "the group, and pop, out of early sixties parochialism into a new era".[102]

For an LP, the speed and strength of its sales were extraordinary by any standards. Released only six weeks before year-end, with a quarter of a million advance orders, sales in that period alone were sufficient to make it the best-selling LP of 1963, ahead of *Please Please Me*, as well as projecting it into the singles' Top 30 (where it stayed for seven weeks, with a highest position of No.11). *With The Beatles* remained the no.1 LP until the end of April 1964, by which time the group's first two albums had racked up between them 51 consecutive weeks at the top of the LP charts.

In terms of its content, it was, like *Please Please Me*, another eclectic mix, though this time not bulked out by hit singles; and that, in itself, denoted a greater confidence in its reception on the part of both group and producer. While it followed the broad structure of its predecessor, with both sides beginning and ending with faster numbers, this time there was more discernible evidence of a diversity of approach and taste between group members. Of the seven Lennon/McCartney compositions, the most enduringly popular turned out to be "All My Loving", on which Paul was the lead singer, a faster-paced reworking of the sentiment underlying "PS I Love You" which would easily have made a strong single.[103] There was also a first solo composing credit for George, with "Don't Bother Me"; for me, a personal favourite, but a song about which Harrison himself seemed to be unnecessarily defensive and dismissive throughout his recording career.

Of the remaining six tracks, five were covers of songs originally recorded by black American artists, two of them by girl groups; "Please Mr. Postman" (by the Marvelettes), as reinterpreted by John, and "Devil In Her Heart" (by the Donays), on which George sang the lead. John was also the lead singer on Smokey Robinson's "You Really Got A Hold On Me"; daringly, and passionately, at the very dawn of the permissive era, playing up every sigh and innuendo to tease and tantalise the disbelieving listener into the realisation that, yes, at its core this was indeed a song in celebration of sexual intercourse. In deference to precedent from their stage act, George more happily took the lead in Chuck Berry's "Roll Over Beethoven"; leaving John to close Side Two with his definitive blistering rendition of "Money".[104] This left a cuckoo in the nest, in the form of Paul's silky-smooth take on the standard "Till There Was You", from the 1957 musical *The Music Man*.[105] A beautiful love song beautifully sung, it put down a marker for Paul to claim ever-more distinctive solo spots on their future LPs.

From February onwards, all the Beatles' recording sessions were undertaken in brief intervals between extensive touring and broadcasting commitments. As noted above, the ever-upward surge in their record sales combined with a frenzy of public acclaim to shift them rapidly on tour from support act to headlining stars; a position confirmed from the outset of their third tour in May, with Roy Orbison and Gerry and the Pacemakers. Although originally booked as the main attraction, by the time Orbison arrived from America to go on the road the Beatles were riding high on the success of "From Me To You". Programmes were hurriedly reprinted to put their name above his and he was content to take the penultimate slot on the bill. The contrast in the audiences' reception of the two acts could not, however, have been starker. Those who attended recalled Orbison's solo performances with the affection and respect his international status properly demanded. Standing alone in the spotlight centre stage, he ran through a string of hits with seeming effortlessness (including "Only The Lonely", "Running Scared", "Crying", "Dream Baby" and "In Dreams"), to which the audience listened in appreciative silence with applause after each one; "but when the Beatles took the stage, girls who had sat patiently in their seats now rose to their feet and the din of the screaming was almost enough to drown out the band."[106]

By the time of their fourth tour in November, the Beatles had indisputably become the star attraction and the support acts – some with minor hits by then well in the past, others with none at all – all but irrelevant. To my everlasting envy, my cousin, who is eighteen months older than me, badgered her parents into buying her Beatles' concert tickets as a special birthday present and went, with an old school friend, to see them on her sixteenth birthday on 10th November at the Birmingham Hippodrome. Because they had the last of the tickets on sale, they found themselves up in the gods:

> The 2 seats we had were behind one another in the very back rows and as we climbed up to them it got steeper and steeper. When we finally reached the seats we were so high up the seats had to slope forwards for you to be at the right angle to see the stage. But we could see it, even if rather a long way away. I can remember it being quite difficult to stay seated, as the seats were tipping you forward so much.[107]

As to the concert itself, the support acts were "unimportant to [them] (and probably the rest of the audience)" and "you could feel the tension building and building as the show progressed" to the top of the bill:

> The curtains were certainly drawn as they set up all the equipment and when they started to rise, before they had gone more than a couple of inches, the screaming started. I should imagine every

single one of us in that 2000-strong audience screamed throughout the whole of the Beatles' performance. I have absolutely no idea what they played, all you could hear was the screaming, but I thought it was absolutely fantastic.[108]

On that fourth tour alone, the Beatles played thirty-six different venues, replicating my cousin's experience thousands of times over in display after display of pure, unadulterated pop idolatry. For girls then, at any rate, the music itself counted for far, far less than the collective act of worship implicit in just being there with them under the same roof and seeing them: after all, "there was no way we could tell what they were singing and we were too far from the stage to lip-read."[109] And herein lies the supreme paradox of the Beatles' career, that in these naïve, spontaneous outpourings of pubescent adulation were sown the very seeds of their ultimate demise as performers.

No such problems, however, attended their participation in the Royal Variety Performance, recorded live from the Prince of Wales Theatre on Monday, 4th November and televised by ITV the following Sunday; when I watched the broadcast at home with delight, while that same evening, less than ten miles away at the Hippodrome, my cousin was embroiled in seeing the Beatles in the flesh yet not hearing a word of anything they sang. Appearing seventh on a bill that also included Harry Secombe, Tommy Steele and Marlene Dietrich, they played a short set of four numbers: "From Me To You", "She Loves You", "Till There Was You" and "Twist And Shout". It was in his introduction to the last of these that John Lennon extended his famously barbed invitation to that privileged audience basking smugly in the presence of the Queen Mother, Princess Margaret and Lord Snowdon:

For our last number I'd like to ask your help … Would the people in the cheaper seats clap your hands? And the rest of you, if you'd just rattle your jewellery.[110]

It drew laughs, for the sheer audacity of its juvenile disrespect, but in the dress circle the response was certainly also one of discomfort and embarrassment. The Beatles and sycophancy towards the Establishment were the strangest of bedfellows, despite, no doubt, Epstein's every fervent wish to the contrary: little wonder, therefore that "What the public never discovered was that, every year after 1963, the Beatles were invited back and always said no".[111]

On Saturday, 7th December, they pulled off another television coup by making up the entire panel of a special edition of *Juke Box Jury*, recorded live before a not unexpectedly overwrought audience at the Empire Theatre, Liverpool. (John had already been a panel member earlier in the year, in an edition broadcast on 29th June, causing more than a little discomfort when he breached the programme's cosy unwritten etiquette by slating every record played.) On this occasion, they collectively voted for the majority of the records played to be hits; but when televised, despite its novelty celebrity value, technically the programme was a disaster, since the fans' constant screaming played havoc with the sound levels as well as the overall management of the production.

The Beatles concluded their year with their Christmas Show at the Finsbury Park Astoria, a pantomime in all but name specially devised by the erstwhile failed drama student Brian Epstein, playing to two full houses per night for 16 nights in total over the Christmas and New Year period until 11th January 1964. Apart from the Fourmost, other NEMS acts drafted in to take part were Tommy Quickly, Cilla Black, and Billy J. Kramer and the Dakotas; augmented by the Barron Knights and with Rolf Harris as compère completing this melange of performing talents and styles.

By now the simple spontaneity of gigs at the Cavern was already well behind them; their final appearance there having been on 3rd August, playing to a capacity crowd generating so much sweat and condensation in the packed cellar that their farewell performance was temporarily interrupted by blown fuses shutting off the power. (Billy Kinsley recalls John and Paul busking their way through an early rendition of "When I'm 64" while they waited for the electricity to be restored.)[112] In Epstein's Christmas extravaganza, as well as closing the show with the obligatory set of their most popular songs, no expense was spared to exploit the Beatles' natural talents for clowning around and sending themselves up to the full:

> After the curtain rose, the Beatles were first seen jumping out of a giant Christmas cracker and then descending from a cardboard helicopter (The S.S. Beatle) on to the stage as compère Rolf Harris introduced each performer on the bill to take their bow. The Beatles popped up in further skits between the acts … For the pantomime in the first half, entitled 'What A Night' in which Fearless Paul the Signalman rescued Ermyntrude Our Heroine (George) from the villainous Sir John Jasper (John) off the railway track, while Ringo ran across the stage sprinkling paper snow, the Beatles often mimed to a pre-recorded tape over the antiquated PA system as the fans made the group's own voices inaudible. The dialogue was also presented on a screen behind them as they spoke.[113]

This was probably as perilously close as they were ever driven by Epstein to selling out to the commercial imperatives of traditional entertainment in Britain, in the manner of earlier pop stars who had gone before them; although the so-called 'dramatic' elements of the show perhaps have their natural antecedents in the indulgence temporarily afforded by a kindly-disposed schoolmaster to giddy sixth-formers letting off steam in an end-of-term revue.

Interestingly, the Beatles faced no theatrical competition over this festive period from their nearest chart-rivals, Cliff Richard and the Shadows, who had flown out to the Canary Islands at the beginning of December for a ten-week stint on location for their new film *Wonderful Life*. Despite any personal anxiety about the market shift towards groups, Cliff's position as premier British male solo singer was as yet unchallenged and his own record sales remained buoyant, with six consecutive Top Ten singles in 1963; namely, "The Next Time", "Bachelor Boy", "Summer Holiday", "Lucky Lips", "It's All In The Game" and "Don't Talk To Him".

For the Shadows, however, as noted earlier above, it was a different matter, as vocal groups began their onslaught on the charts in earnest and started to push instrumentalists to the margins. After "Foot Tapper", admittedly they did achieve two more Top Ten hits, with "Atlantis" and "Shindig"; but in December, "Geronimo" missed the cut and peaked at No.11. To add to the pressure they now found themselves under, and despite much higher record sales than the duo formed by their ex-members, they then had to endure the gall of Jet Harris being voted Instrumental Personality for the second year running in the *NME* Pop Winners' Poll for 1963.

Their Christmas expedition abroad with Cliff followed another turbulent period in the collective life of the Shadows during the autumn, when both Bruce Welch and Brian 'Licorice' Locking had announced they were leaving. In Welch's case, his notorious obsession with perfection had brought him, at the age of twenty-one, to the edge of collapse. The threat to the group's future was then made all the more serious by Locking's firm decision in October, after eighteen months with the Shadows, to forsake pop music for evangelical work in the service of the Jehovah's Witnesses. After a brief search for a replacement bass guitarist, at Bruce's suggestion John Rostill was recruited to the role (having previously played with the Interns and an early line-up led by Zoot Money). At this point, Welch fortuitously overcame his own personal crisis and determined to stay with the band after all, turning Rostill's arrival to his advantage in the process by paying him ten pounds a week to tune his guitar for him before each performance.[114]

Although the Shadows' glory days threatened to be over, at least they were still managing, notably with Cliff's patronage, to continue in business; unlike the Springfields, for whom the Beatles, in their unforeseen role as catalysts for change, sounded their death knell. Faced with both external commercial pressures (emanating from the runaway success of the new wave of groups) and internal tensions (between Dusty and brother Tom), the Springfields' habitual derivative jollity suddenly became jarringly out of fashion. After an uncertain start in December 1962, a resurgence in sales of "Island Of Dreams" had taken it to No.7 in February 1963, to be followed in April by another Top Ten hit, "Say I Won't Be There"; an anachronistic adaptation by Tom of "Au Claire De La Lune", which amazingly made it to No.5 in the long Merseybeat shadows cast by "How Do You Do It" and "From Me To You". But in late July, when what turned out to be their last single, "Come On Home"[115], scraped only one week at no.30, the game was up, for Tom had sadly been blind to the weakness of his new composition:

> A lot of people say it's not us. But it is. I wrote it myself and because I was a bit frightened the group would get stuck in a groove after our last two hits I decided to go for a rhythm and blues number. Not out and out, because nothing out and out is commercial, but the kind of number which I consider to be nicely adapted for British disc buyers.[116]

Whatever the song was, in the context of the contemporary London club scene calling it 'rhythm and blues' was less naïve than simply delusional. If the record had any merit at all, it lay solely in Dusty's valiant struggle to carry off a poor song in spite of the other group members and Johnny Franz's hopelessly muddled production; but nevertheless the strain in her voice is all too evident. You just know she wanted to be somewhere else.

The formal parting of the ways came at the first weekend of October. On the evening of Friday the 4th, Dusty appeared on her own as a celebrity co-host of *Ready, Steady/Go!* [117], only a week after the Springfields themselves had been on the show. As a promotional opportunity for her, a better one was inconceivable, since this edition included the Beatles' first appearance on the programme and Dusty was unwittingly drawn on camera into a scurrilous conversation with John about her complexion. Two nights later, on the 6th, *Sunday Night At The London Palladium* provided the platform from which the Springfields made their official farewell to their public; performing as their last song together – at Dusty's insistence – "So Long, It's Been Good To Know You". (The following week, in stark contrast, that same show was to become the vehicle through which the Beatles irrevocably enhanced their appeal to a mass UK audience.) After the break-up, Tom pursued his interests in orchestral arranging, composing and producing, eventually finding success again in these capacities with the Seekers; and Mike Hurst, after failing to make it as a solo folk artist, would also turn to record production, working initially on the early hits of Cat Stevens.

As for Dusty herself, staying with the Springfields' producer Johnny Franz and musical director Ivor Raymonde, on 25th October she embarked upon the third phase of her professional career in music by returning to the Olympic Sound Studios to record her first solo single, "I Only Want To Be

With You". The song was Raymonde's own composition, written in collaboration with lyricist Mike Hawker (although originally she had thought of
recording either "Money" or Bacharach and David's "Wishin' And Hopin'").
She was consciously striving to capture the American beat and sound that
had so fired her imagination previously in New York and the final production, though orchestrally top-heavy, owed much to the style of Phil Spector,
whose records with girl groups the Crystals ("He's A Rebel", "Da Doo Ron
Ron", "Then He Kissed Me") and Ronettes ("Be My Baby") had already
been big UK hits in the course of the year.

Released on the Philips label on 8th November, Dusty's record faced
its strongest competition, in a relatively barren period for female soloists,
from established artists Shirley Bassey and Kathy Kirby, whose respective
songs ("I (Who Have Nothing)" and "Secret Love") were in the Top Ten
when "I Only Want To Be With You" charted a fortnight later at No.17.
Nevertheless, it brought her instant success, rising to No.4 by the first week
of January 1964 and thus overtaking the Singing Nun's "Dominique", on
the way down from its exalted position of No.3 at the end of December;
an irony doubtless not lost on the ex-convent schoolgirl Mary O'Brien. Its
promotion at home had been aided not only by another appearance (this time
as performer) on *Ready Steady Go!*, but also by her inclusion as a special guest
in a mid-November concert tour of England, in the company of Brian Poole
and the Tremeloes, the Searchers and Freddie and the Dreamers. Eventually
total sales were to earn her not only a silver disc in the UK but a gold disc
internationally[118], with the added satisfaction of having reached No.12 in the
US *Billboard* chart; and even with just this one solo hit to her name, she came
second in the British Female Singer category of the *NME* Poll Winners for
the year, as runner-up to Kathy Kirby.

More than anything else, it was the scale of Dusty's breakthrough, at the
age of twenty-four, that at last gave much-needed impetus to the emergence
of other modern British female singers. Despite having toured with the
Beatles in February and March, Helen Shapiro's hitmaking career had already
stalled well before then, with her last Top 30 record in the summer of 1962.
Other contenders from the early Sixties, like Susan Maughan and Maureen
Evans, had similarly disappeared from view; whilst their would-be successors struggled – and failed – to gain a consistent following. Billie Davis, for
example, having provided the female half of a comedy duet with Mike Sarne
on "Will I What" the preceding autumn, achieved her only Top 30 solo hit
in spring 1963, making it to No.12 in March with her cover of the Exciters'
"Tell Him" (one of the contemporary American hits enjoying regular airplay
when Dusty had been in New York and thus informing her change of musical
direction). Julie Grant likewise had one fleeting success, taking "Count On
Me" to No.23 in early May; although both Davis and Grant would feature in

later years as supporting artists on some of the Rolling Stones' many concert tours.

For the time being, Petula Clark was out of favour in Britain, although sustained by her continuing popularity in France. Kathy Kirby's two hits of 1963 were almost her last and both bereft of originality; "Dance On" having grafted lyrics onto the melody of the Shadows' No.1 instrumental, and "Secret Love" reviving in big-band style Doris Day's song from the 1953 musical film *Calamity Jane*.[119] Her immediate future lay in television variety, principally as a singer on ITV's *Stars And Garters* and later – in 1965 – as Britain's representative in the Eurovision Song Contest (when she came second, singing "I Belong"). Last but not least of the old guard, Shirley Bassey had consolidated her position as undisputed queen of pathos and melodrama, an unassailable role which she would further extend in the coming years through her uniquely brooding interpretation of theme songs for the James Bond films. The only other serious female competition around came, as noted above, from American girl groups, such as those in Phil Spector's stable and the Chiffons, who had scored two Top 30 successes with "He's So Fine" and "One Fine Day". Sadly, English duo the Caravelles could hardly be rated as rivals, turning out to be no more than one-hit wonders after taking "You Don't Have To Be A Baby To Cry" to No.6 in September.

In those same closing months of the year, a matter of weeks ahead of Dusty, Cilla Black had also made her chart debut – though without the benefit of either Dusty's prior professional exposure or her spectacular initial volume of sales – having finally been signed up that September, at the age of twenty, by Brian Epstein. Mercifully well behind her was the embarrassment of her first failed audition for him the year before at the Majestic Ballroom in Birkenhead when, backed by the Beatles unwittingly playing in the wrong key, she had mangled an unrehearsed rendition of "Summertime", then one of her favourite songs. She had eventually redeemed herself in his eyes in the late summer of 1963, after Epstein, unbeknown to her, had seen her again, this time "at the Blue Angel coffee club in Seel Street, doing a spot with John Reuben's modern jazz group ... [singing] mainly non-rock'n'roll numbers like Della Reece's 'Bye Bye Blackbird'".[120] Speaking to her after that performance (by which he was much impressed), he invited her to his office to talk terms the next day and a contract soon followed; signed grudgingly on Cilla's behalf by her father, who objected to the substitution of Black for the family surname of White. Next came a trip to London and a recording test for George Martin at Abbey Road, for whom she sang "Get A Shot Of Rhythm'N'Blues". The first A-side chosen for her, recorded on 28th August and released on Parlophone on 27th September, was the early Lennon/McCartney song, "Love Of The Loved", now revitalised from the doldrums of the Beatles' Decca audition by a punchy arrangement with a prominent brass section. Already knowing the number well from the Beatles' gigs at the Cavern, she had been expecting to sing it with a group but:

> I was ever so disappointed when I got to the studio and there was brass and everything. Les Reed did the arrangement. He was playing piano and Peter Lee Stirling was on lead guitar. I thought it was very jazzy and I didn't think it would be a hit.[121]

Bearing in mind all the subsequent hits Cilla would rack up by the end of the decade, "Love Of The Loved" still stands out today from the rest as essentially a rock record, and the one most typifying the full-on style with which she originally made her name around Liverpool. Despite her misgivings, it secured her the No.30 slot for one week in mid-October and remains one of my own personal favourites from amongst her Sixties' repertoire.

Habitually referring to her as "my lovely Cilla" [122], she was the only girl for whom Epstein acted as manager, apparently believing that the "disc charts cannot stand very many girls, however gorgeous they may look on stage"[123], and *Mersey Beat* editor Bill Harry, for one, was disdainful of the changes he would impose on her: "He put her in pretty dresses and had her sing … ballads. Before Brian Epstein took her over, I had imagined her becoming a rock singer and she became a modern Gracie Fields."[124] In truth, Epstein himself laboured under the somewhat more flattering delusion that he could turn Cilla into the next Judy Garland.

With her first record out, she was thrust onto the customary promotional treadmill of radio, TV and concert appearances. Beginning straight away on 28th September with a seat on *Juke Box Jury*, tour engagements followed on smartly – first with Gerry and the Pacemakers and then Billy J. Kramer and the Dakotas – before she concluded the year in London in December with a gallery of fellow NEMS artists in the cast of the Beatles' Christmas Show. Having effectively been accepted as an honorary lad amongst the Merseybeat groups with whom she had been comfortable singing semi-professionally, she still harboured throughout this early formative period the notion that she should be a lead singer fronting her own band, but even momentary reflection would have highlighted for her the absence of any commercially viable precedent. For now, in due deference to Epstein's judgement, she "just went along with the solo singer idea and accepted Sounds Incorporated as [her] backing group".[125] The die would, however, be cast firmly in another direction to her expectations on her return to the recording studio in the New Year.

In America, the Beach Boys went from strength to strength in their favoured role as *the* group on the rise, combining punishing rounds of touring with a prolific output of self-composed recorded material. For a group still relatively inexperienced at the start of the year, their touring schedule was both ambitious and demanding. It took a particular toll of Brian Wilson, who increasingly sought to opt out of the hard travelling beyond California from the end of April onwards in preference for asserting and developing his role as principal songwriter and producer and whose absence from the concert stage was then covered by the recall of Al Jardine. This withdrawal was one of the earliest indications of Brian's extreme fragility as a creative artist. One of his supposed objections was the volume of the music they played live; which literally brought the house down at the University of Arizona in Tucson, where the vibrations from their amplifiers caused the ceiling of the auditorium to collapse, mercifully without injury. At the end of August, however, he was forced to rejoin the group on the road and reunite the original five-man line-up, after David Marks (still only fifteen at the time) had one too many arguments with Murry Wilson while en route from Wisconsin to Chicago and quit the band.

Prominence was nevertheless still given to recording and in the course of the year, as Brian insisted on ever more responsibility for arrangements and production, the Beach Boys released four new singles and three LPs. The earlier records still pursued the surfing theme. From recording sessions interspersed throughout January and February, Capitol issued "Surfin' USA" as a single on 4th March (following it three weeks later with the complete LP of the same title); the song being an unashamed adaptation by Brian of Chuck Berry's "Sweet Little Sixteen". It would eventually reach No.3 in the *Billboard* Top 40; and also become, on its subsequent release in Britain, the first Beach Boys' single to enter the UK Top 30 (which it did in the week ending 24th August, at No.28). The LP was a massive hit, entering the American album charts on 4th May for what grew to be an uninterrupted run of 78 weeks.

Their next single, "Surfer Girl" (for which Brian was supposedly inspired by "When You Wish Upon A Star" from Walt Disney's *Pinocchio*), came out on 22nd June, two days after Brian's twenty-first birthday. As on past precedent, it provided the title track of their second LP of the year, released on 16th September; the first album for which Brian was officially credited as producer, following Nick Venet's departure from Capitol in August. (In any event, Venet had not effectively carried out this role since March, at Murry Wilson's request on Brian's behalf, who had been increasingly distressed by Venet's apparent indifference to the integrity of the Beach Boys' sound.)

By this point, however, in his capacity as composer, Brian was growing weary of the surfing motif and was looking to expand his talent in other directions. For example, the *Surfer Girl* album track "In My Room" is a classic exposition of Brian's pronounced tendency to introversion, extolling the virtues of withdrawing from the world to your own personal secure haven decades before it would be legitimised by an entirely different generation of internet surfers and computer game addicts. He had also begun to explore a new theme of hot rod and drag car racing, hence the B-side to "Surfer Girl" being "Little Deuce Coupe". In turn, this latter song gave its title to a third LP, extraordinarily released only three weeks after its predecessor on 7th October and for which Capitol felt it necessary to provide DJs and retailers with additional promotional guidance on the argot of drag racing. Another three weeks later saw the release of the third single of the year, coupling a re-recorded version of "Be True To Your School" (originally a track from the *Little Deuce Coupe* LP) with "In My Room". It trounced the previous success of their "Surfer Girl" single by one chart placing, eventually peaking at No.6 in the US Top 40. Their fourth and final single of 1963, issued on 9th December, was an unapologetically seasonal combination of the Christmas novelty song "Little Saint Nick" and an acapella version of "The Lord's Prayer".

As well as all the time and effort he devoted to the Beach Boys' recording career, it was a tribute to Brian that his considerable skills should also be called upon – much to Murry's displeasure – by rival Californian duo Jan and Dean. Already a well-established act, Jan Berry and Dean Torrence had been recording together since their late teens in 1958. First meeting and befriending the Beach Boys on a concert bill together on Valentine's Day 1963, by that spring they had had four US Top 40 hits. Not only co-writing both sides of their May single "Surf City"/"She's My Summer Girl", Brian took part in the recording too, contributing to both lead vocals with Jan and background harmonies. When it made it to No.1 (on Brian's birthday, into the bargain), Murry was unsurprisingly furious but Brian was determined to withstand his father's rebukes, "proud of the fact that another group had had a number 1 song with a track that I had written and that this would give me, a young songwriter, just that much more credibility".[126]

For their LP *Jan And Dean Take Linda Surfin'*, they further extended this promising collaboration by recording more of Brian's songs and using Brian and the Beach Boys as their backing group; although since Jan and Dean were not Capitol artists but recorded for the Liberty label, these joint ventures were not well received commercially. When they returned to the studio in November, to record their next single 'Drag City' (as they too just happened to switch their musical focus from surfing to cars), Brian had to give Murry the slip to join them and once more add his vocals to the track. In addition, he used such escapades to accumulate an invaluable breadth of knowledge about record production techniques. Dean noted that Brian was a quick and eager learner and was particularly taken with Jan's reliance on professional session musicians.[127]

Another direct influence on Brian in his capacity as producer was Phil Spector. In mid-June, at the outset of laying down possible tracks for the *Surfer Girl* LP, the Beach Boys had for the first time used the Gold Star

Studios in Los Angeles, a venue much favoured by Spector from August 1962 onwards[128], and were to return there for later sessions in August and November. On 26th September, however, Brian accepted a personal invitation from Spector to participate in the recording at Gold Star of his new album *A Christmas Gift For You*; in the course of which he was asked to play piano on "Santa Claus Is Coming To Town". Less than a month later, Brian would emulate Spector's example by marshalling the Beach Boys at the Western Recorders Studio in Hollywood to record his own new Christmas compo- sition, "Little Saint Nick", in an arrangement embellished by glockenspiels and sleigh bells. The following summer, still obviously in thrall to Spector, he took the group a step further by embarking upon the recording of a complete Christmas LP, for which "Little Saint Nick" was then significantly reworked. Whilst not uncommon, diversions such as these from the main thrust of developing a new popular music on the West Coast were, at best, ill-considered, a temporary suspension of good taste and sound judgement in the lucrative, yet strictly limited interests of seasonal sentimentality.

Shifting focus to the eastern seaboard, here Bob Dylan's popularity also continued to grow, although paradoxically by the end of 1963 it was to bring him to the edge of despair. The adulation generated by his peculiar talents weighed heavily upon him, posing for him an almost tangible threat to his sense of autonomy. In a qualitatively different way to the Beatles in England, he too became hot property, to the extent that his songs, performances and other public appearances were all regarded by others – though not seem- ingly by him – as highly charged with socio-political significance; a phenom- enon not only opening doors for him but also causing serious obstacles to be strewn in his path. All this as yet without any of the visible trappings of a pop or rock star.

CBS Records finally released his second LP, *The Freewheelin' Bob Dylan*, at the end of May, following unease on the company's part about its proposed contents and the substitution of four tracks. There had been particular concern about the original inclusion of "Talkin' John Birch Society Blues"[129], a sideswipe at an active faction of hard-line American right-wingers which Dylan had composed in January 1962, had published in the first issue of *Broadside* and then recorded in April 1962 in one of the earliest prepara- tory sessions for the album. Throughout the rest of the year, it remained a popular and witty choice of his in live concert, well-received by his regular audiences of hip young intellectuals.[130] Equating membership of the Society to endorsement of Hitler's treatment of the Jews ("It don't matter too much that he was a Fascist/At least you can't say he was a Communist!"[131]), the whole point of the lyric was its satirical controversiality and its notoriety was further assured by Dylan being prevented from performing the song on

The Ed Sullivan Show (the US equivalent of *Sunday Night At The London Palladium*) on 12th May 1963. According to John Bauldie, the objection to it was lodged not, as one might have expected, by Sullivan himself (an archetypal American stuffed shirt) but "one Stowe Phelps, editor of CBS-TV program practices"[132], who caught wind of it in rehearsals and feared it was potentially libellous. Even though an appearance on the show would have given him massive nationwide TV exposure, Dylan refused to compromise and walked away from the opportunity rather than sing any other song. It then became something of an in-joke on his part to perform it everywhere else as "the song they wouldn't let me sing on TV".[133]

The LP is as renowned for its cover as its contents, the front sleeve shot being a colour photograph of Dylan and his one-time girlfriend Suze Rotolo arm-in-arm walking in the winter's slush of the New York city streets. It was just one of many images taken by CBS staff photographer Don Hunstein in the course of an impromptu photoshoot that began in the apartment they shared on West Fourth Street in Greenwich Village and ended up outside, not "planned or produced in any way".[134] Suze's account gives a fine sense of how the banal pseudo-spontaneity of that walk nevertheless still managed to play convincingly into the pictorial reinforcement of Dylan's presence as an up-and-coming musician:

> Bob stuck his hands in the pockets of his jeans and leaned into me. We walked the length of Jones Street facing West Fourth with Bleecker Street at our backs. The snow on the streets was slushy and filthy from the traffic. The sidewalks were icy and slippery, but at least there wasn't much of a wind blowing. To keep warm we started horsing around. Don kept clicking away. A delivery van pulled up and parked, so we turned onto West Fourth Street. In some of the outtakes it is obvious that by then we were freezing; certainly Bob was, in that thin jacket. But image was all.[135]

Suze credits the album cover, deservedly, as marking a turning-point in pop iconography "precisely because of its casual, down-home spontaneity and sensibility … The album spoke the time-honoured language of youth and rebellion against the status quo, and the cover embodied the image".[136] Although they appeared carefree in the picture, by the time of the record's release their affair was on the rocks, the rupture of their relationship forever commemorated – some might say callously – in one of the finest tracks of the set, "Don't Think Twice, It's All Right". And, as they drifted apart, Suze became all too conscious of Dylan's wider discomfort at how the success of his second LP was altering others' perceptions of, and attitudes towards, him:

> After *The Freewheelin' Bob Dylan* had been out a while, at parties I noticed that people would approach him with reverence and tell

him involved stories about their lives and then wait for him to speak. They wanted him to suggest solutions for them, to enlighten them in some way.

It made him uneasy. He wanted to make music, not address a congregation.[137]

The sea-change from the content of *Bob Dylan* was all too obvious in the predominance and enlarged scope now of his own compositions; of which the most powerful and poetically substantial on this record were arguably "Blowin' In The Wind" and "A Hard Rain's A-Gonna Fall", both of which completely transcend any mundane contemporary allusions. There is more explicit anti-war polemic, in the form of both "Masters Of War" and, albeit in an entirely different genre, "Talkin' World War III Blues", an absurdist vision of the nuclear apocalypse. In the latter song's opening lines, Dylan as narrator is driven to seek medical advice about the dreams that have been troubling him about the future:

Some time ago a crazy dream came to me
I dreamt I was walkin' into World War Three
I went to the doctor the very next day
To see what kinda words he could say
He said it was a bad dream
I wouldn't worry 'bout it none, though
They were my own dreams and they're only in my head.
I said, "Hold it, Doc, a World War passed through my brain"
He said, "Nurse, get your pad, this boy's insane."[138]

Here, it seems to me, is subconscious mimicry of the behaviour of another doctor charged with the defence of the indefensible, Joseph Heller's Doc Daneeka, the ultimate guardian of Catch-22, the impossible get-out clause simultaneously activated and negated by madness born of war: "There was only one catch and that was Catch-22, which specified that a concern for one's own safety in the face of dangers that were real and immediate was the process of a rational mind."[139]

There was a belated measure of topicality, too, in "Oxford Town", Dylan's commentary on the race riots triggered at the end of September 1962 by the efforts of James Meredith to seek enrolment as the first black student at the University of Mississippi. Little wonder, then, on the strength of all this challenging material, that he should begin to be regarded, rightly or misguidedly, as a man with answers to deep and serious questions.

Strong sales in America swiftly took the edge off the previous carping at 'Hammond's Folly' (and, in Britain the following summer, would take Dylan to the top of the UK album charts[140]). Through a clever ploy by his manager, Albert Grossman, Dylan's popularity was further inflated in the summer of

1963, by the release in June on a single of an alternative version of "Blowin' In The Wind", recorded by Peter, Paul and Mary. The trio, also managed by Grossman, were already past masters of pitching a blander, more commercial interpretation of folk music to the mass market. Their take on the song was instrumental in introducing Dylan's music by default to a wider audience not only in America (where it gave them their second consecutive No.2 of the year, after "Puff (The Magic Dragon)") but also in the UK (where it got to No.16 in November) and went on to sell a million copies. They pressed home their advantage with their next US single, a cover of "Don't Think Twice, It's All Right", not as successful but still a very respectable No.9 hit.

As well as artist management, Grossman's interests extended to being the promoter and co-founder (with George Wein, in 1959) of the prestigious Newport Folk Festival, an offshoot of the annual Jazz Festival Wein had initiated in 1954. For three years, from 1963 to 1965 inclusive, Dylan performed there, increasingly attended by controversy on each successive appearance but the first occasion (26th - 28th July, 1963) was historic in that, as noted by Robert Shelton, Dylan arrived as "an underground conversation piece, and left a national star"[141].

Over the three days, Dylan took to the stage five times but, as befitted "the prized and private discovery of the extended family of folk music enthusiasts"[142], this was often in the company of others; notably Joan Baez (with whom by this time he was in a relationship), Pete Seeger and Peter, Paul and Mary, who all behaved towards him as if his was a rare, hothouse talent to be shielded from the potential ravages of over-exposure. It was his more explicit songs of social conscience and political revisionism, such as "Blowin' In The Wind" and "With God On Our Side", that this new-found 'family' of his fellow artists were keenest to parade and commandeer; their condescension only heightened by his inclusion in an ensemble concert finale, singing "We Shall Overcome".

It has to be said that Dylan's stance towards the contemporary American civil rights movement, especially in 1963, was always equivocal. The Newport festival was not the only place that year where he was both encouraged and apparently content to be seen sharing a platform with other singers and prominent activists, or where specific songs of his were construed as important contributions to the organised cause of protest. Indeed, "Only A Pawn In Their Game", later to be a track on his next LP, was composed by Dylan within a matter of days after the racist murder of black political activist Medgar Evers[143] on 12th June in Jackson, Mississippi; and first publicly performed by him on 6th July, at a modest rally of about 300 in support of black suffrage near Greenwood, Mississippi, to which he – together with other folk worthies such as Pete Seeger and Theodore Bikel – had been invited by the Student Non-Violent Co-ordinating Committee.

This modest event would soon pale into insignificance, however, in the face of the civil rights march on Washington undertaken by over 200,000 people on 28th August, culminating in the rally at the Lincoln Memorial where Martin Luther King delivered his historic "I have a dream" speech. As part of the entourage of entertainers also present that day:

> Dylan sang "[Only A] Pawn In Their Game", Baez sang "We Shall Overcome", and Peter, Paul and Mary did "[Blowin' In The] Wind" … but even then, as the speeches and the songs filled the seat of national government, even before assassinations would lead so many to abandon the dream, Dylan was questioning the reality of it all.
>
> "Think they're listening?" he asked, glancing towards the Capitol. "No, they ain't listening at all."[144]

Three months later, on Friday 22nd November, at 12.30 p.m., the course of American history was irrevocably changed, not by social discord but by the assassination of President Kennedy as his motorcade crossed Dealey Plaza in Dallas, Texas.

Only six days earlier, the President had fulfilled what would be one of his last public engagements by making a personal visit to Cape Canaveral in Florida, to review the progress made by the US Air Force in constructing the launch centre from which the new giant Saturn V rocket would take Americans to the moon. It was deemed to be a necessary distraction from the severely negative impact of continuing Russian successes. One of his guides on this occasion was the only American astronaut to have been on a space mission in the course of 1963, Gordon Cooper. His orbital flight of one and a half days (beginning on 15th May) had been the longest to that point but at the end had been marred by instrument failure, requiring him to manually navigate his own re-entry into the Earth's atmosphere in his Mercury capsule. On 14th June, his achievement was demonstrably outshone by the Russians; who sent up Valery Bykovsky in Vostok 5 on a solo flight that would last five days, and capped even this on 16th June, by also launching in Vostok 6 the first woman in space, Valentina Tereshkova, into a near-synchronous orbit with him for three days. The counter-balancing injection of optimism into the US space industry engendered by the euphoria of Kennedy's visit was to be cruelly short-lived. With his sudden death, "the space programme had lost its most powerful ally"[145] and hence, on the intervention of fate, "by the end of 1963, a shroud of uncertainty seemed draped over American space projects".[146]

Although not the only holder of his office to meet a violent end, Kennedy's shooting did mark the first assassination of a figurehead of Western civilisation in the modern post-war era; an event that by virtue of its rapid transmission throughout the global village brutally forced the barely adequate broadcasting media to come of age.

Everyone of a certain generation supposedly knows where they were and what they were doing when they learnt of Kennedy's death. For myself, I got home in the early evening, having been to my weekly Scouts' meeting after school, to find all normal television programmes suspended in deference to the enormity of the news; and on the wireless, Radio Luxembourg had replaced its usual quickfire succession of pop programmes and sponsors' adverts with unmitigated solemn organ music. The disturbing sensation of being flung into instantaneous mourning, of time standing still in horror, was inescapable, overwhelming and novel. Even the professionally disrespectful television satirists of BBC's *That Was The Week That Was* were moved, the next evening, to ditch their typically irreverent take on the week's scandals and instead present a totally serious tribute of their own, which David Frost introduced thus:

> The reason why the shock was so great, why when one heard the news last night one felt so suddenly empty, was because it was the most unexpected piece of news one could possibly imagine. It was the least likely thing to happen in the world. If anyone else had died – Sir Winston Churchill, De Gaulle, Kruschev – it would have been something we could understand and even perhaps accept. But that Kennedy should go – well, we just didn't believe in assassination any more. Not in the civilised world anyway.[147]

Little immediate attention would be given to Kennedy's successor, his Vice-President, Lyndon Baines Johnson (LBJ); although, as we shall see in the next chapter, his first year in office would come to be delineated by a hawkish stance on foreign policy, as he channelled more and more military resources into the escalating war in Vietnam.

As for the influential American musicians whose progress I have followed so far, their responses were not altogether what one might conceivably have hoped or expected. The Beach Boys had been booked to play a concert in Marysville, California that Friday night but it appeared to be in jeopardy as news of Kennedy's death spread across the United States and Murry Wilson, in shock and out of respect, was unwilling to commit the group to travelling. (News broadcasts had already made him aware, for example, that the theatres on Broadway were abandoning their productions for the night and closing.) Their hustling young promoter, Fred Vail, still only nineteen, chanced his arm by persuading him that continuing with the concert would, in effect, be doing a public service for young people. So the concert proceeded but not without some further improvisation from Vail when, after a local band had opened the show and there had been an interval, the Beach Boys still needed more time to set up:

> They asked for a few more minutes so I went out front and told the crowd we should have a moment of silence for our fallen president, John Kennedy. I said, 'It was a tragedy in America today. We lost our president and before we bring out the Beach Boys, I think we should have a moment of silence in honour of the president.' So everybody was quiet. It was dead quiet. The whole audience. I didn't know how long was a suitable silence. A minute? Half a minute? So after about 30 seconds, out of the corner of my eye, I could see the curtain open a little bit and Mike Love threw out a towel. It hit me and I knew it was time to bring out the boys.[148]

When they finally played, it was to a capacity audience of at least two thousand, from whom Vail contentedly collected takings of around $6,000. To round off what Brian would later recall as "a spiritual night"[149], he and Mike Love were moved to compose their own tribute to JFK, "The Warmth Of The Sun" (which they subsequently recorded the following January for inclusion on the Beach Boys' first LP of 1964).

By contrast, the stance Dylan adopted was in part reflective but more just plain bewildered. Having seen the breaking news from Dallas on television in manager Albert Grossman's office:

> The next night, Saturday, I had a concert upstate, in Ithaca or Buffalo. There was a really down feeling in the air. I had to go on stage, I couldn't cancel. I went to the hall and to my amazement the hall was filled. Everybody turned out for the concert. The song I was opening with was "The Times They Are A-Changin'" and I thought, 'Wow, how can I open with that song? I'll get rocks thrown at me.' That song was just too much for the day after the assassination. But I had to sing it, my whole concert takes off from there.
>
> I know I had no understanding of anything. Something had just gone haywire in the country and they were applauding that song. And I couldn't understand why they were clapping or why I wrote that song, even. I couldn't understand anything. For me, it was just insane.[150]

Close acquaintances of his at that time believe that Dylan was more profoundly affected by what had happened than he was willing to admit. Now acutely aware "that there were a lot of maniacs out there"[151], his future attitude to political involvement would, so his friends claimed, be tempered by fears for his own safety; although he himself would deny this:

> It didn't knock the wind out of me. Of course, I felt as rotten as everyone else. But if I was more sensitive about it than anyone else, I would have written a song about it, wouldn't I? The whole thing about my reactions to the assassination is overplayed.[152]

For someone who at this stage of his career was frequently moved to write topical songs elevating to national significance what he first stumbled across as news items of strictly local interest, the absence of a Dylan tribute to Kennedy is perhaps surprising, though hardly blameworthy. (He was, nevertheless, already familiar with and had regularly performed a traditional song which another up-and-coming folk musician, Jim McGuinn, adapted and later recorded – with the Byrds – as his tribute to the late President, "He Was A Friend Of Mine".[153])

Dylan's libertarian credentials were, however, soon to be severely tested and called into question by the adverse reactions to a speech he made as guest of honour at a fund-raising dinner for the Emergency Civil Liberties Committee on 13th December; an annual event notable for the presentation of the Tom Paine Award. Worse the wear for drink and totally unprepared, Dylan's impromptu comments on receipt of this award were rambling and ill-advised. Beginning with some inept observations on the relatively high age and therefore presumed lack of commitment of his audience, he touched on the inspiration of Woody Guthrie, the civil rights march on Washington and the isolationism being shown towards Cuba, before committing the final *faux pas* of appearing to condone the actions of Kennedy's assassin:

> … I have to be honest, I just got to be, as I got to admit that the man who shot President Kennedy, Lee Oswald, I don't know exactly where – what he thought he was doing , but I got to admit honestly that I, too – I saw some of myself in him. I don't think it would have gone – I don't think it could go that far. But I got to stand up and say I saw things that he felt in me – not to go that far and shoot. [Boos and hisses.] You can boo, but booing's got nothing to do with it.[154]

Bearing in mind that Oswald had rapidly and publicly been consigned to history himself, having been shot dead by Jack Ruby at Dallas police head-quarters on 24th November, any possibility of definitively establishing his motivation was already evaporating, in the face of manifold conspiracy theories. Ignoring the golden rule that once you find yourself in a hole you should stop digging, after the event Dylan made concerted efforts to explain and atone for the controversial line he had taken, but these singularly neither aided clarification nor repaired his damaged credibility. Ruefully acknowledging his inexperience as an orator, the episode was an object lesson in the perils of confusing popular acclaim with popular influence. He would not come to fully appreciate until much later in the decade, however, that he "had never intended to be on the road of heavy consequences ... and didn't like it."[155]

Though nowhere near as catastrophic as the violent death of a head of state, Great Britain had also had to endure political upheaval, including a change of Prime Minister, in the wake of the exposure and resignation of the Minister for War, John Profumo. It was, for its time, a sensational and yet typically British scandal, with its murky intertwinings of sexual misbehaviour within the Establishment, espionage and gangsterism, the final truth lost sight of forever between, on the one hand, the suicide of a principal player and, on the other, the obfuscation of a government-commissioned judicial inquiry. The associated publicity revived the exquisitely prurient discomfort of the trial of *Lady Chatterley* three years earlier, as Mervyn Griffiths-Jones QC again assumed the role of anguished prosecutor and parents at the breakfast table once more were driven to wonder if the daily newspaper really constituted suitable reading matter for younger members of the family. Exposure of the *affaire* not only engendered an opportunistic single, "Christine" by Miss X – then considered too risqué for public broadcasting[156] – but also a better known belated musical response in the form of Pete Brown's song "Politician" (co-written with Jack Bruce), as recorded by Cream on their 1968 double-LP *Wheels Of Fire*[157]; its introductory lines suitably blending cynicism with menace:

> Hey now baby, get into my big black car
> Hey now baby, get into my big black car
> I wanna just show you what my politics are.
> I'm a political man and I practise what I preach
> I'm a political man and I practise what I preach
> So don't deny me baby, not while you're in my reach.

On 22nd March, political intrigue on the part of the Labour opposition had trapped Profumo into making a statement to the House of Commons about the nature of his past relationship with Christine Keeler, in which he resolutely denied any "impropriety" with her. Although he had severed contact with her at the end of 1961, she was now seriously out of control, running scared after seeking cheap thrills in the clubs of Notting Hill's West Indian gangland in the course of 1962 had brought her nothing but violent encounters. Since December of that year in particular (when she and her partner in crime Mandy Rice-Davies had survived an attack by former lover Johnny Edgecombe – armed with a gun he had stolen from her – at the Wimpole Mews home of Stephen Ward), Keeler had good reason to fear for her future safety. In desperation, therefore, she had tried to buy herself protection by attempting to sell her story to the then *Sunday Pictorial* (which later became the *Sunday Mirror*), implicating both Profumo and Ward in alleged threats to national security. Too hot to handle, the story was never printed but inevitably came to the attention of the government, via the police and intelligence service. By the time Edgecombe's case came to trial at the Old Bailey on 14th March, Keeler – who should have been a prosecution witness – had temporarily fled the country to Spain, arousing even greater publicity and suspicion as to her past history and present motives.

Tracked down in Madrid by a posse of reporters, the *Daily Express* arranged for her to be flown back to England as part of a deal for the rights to her story. On her return, however, she was subjected to a series of lengthy interviews by the police and MI5; not only about her relationship with Profumo but also about her dealings with Stephen Ward, on the basis that she was his accomplice in espionage. The upshot was that on 4th June Profumo was forced to retract his earlier statement to Parliament and tender his resignation to Harold Macmillan:

> In my statement I said that there had been no impropriety in this
> association. To my very deep regret I have to admit that this was
> not true, and that I misled you, and my colleagues, and the House
> … I have come to realise that, by this deception, I have been guilty
> of a grave misdemeanour, and … I cannot remain a member of
> your Administration, nor of the House of Commons.[158]

Determined not to be forced out of office himself, on 21st June Macmillan commissioned the Master of the Rolls, Lord Denning, to carry out an inquiry into the circumstances leading up to Profumo's resignation. His report would not be completed and published until September.

In the interim, on 22nd July Stephen Ward was called to the Old Bailey, to answer five charges relating to living off immoral earnings and the procuring of girls under the age of twenty-one to have sexual intercourse with a third party.[159] According to Christine Keeler, this was an elaborate government subterfuge to neutralise Ward without having to disclose the political embarrassment of his treasonable activities. Be that as it may, the trial proceeded to 30th July, when it was adjourned for the day partway through the judge's summing up. That evening, while out on bail Ward took an overdose from which he would not recover, dying in hospital while his trial resumed and the jury found him guilty *in absentia* on two charges of living off the immoral earnings of Keeler and Rice-Davies: "The judge postponed sentence until Ward could appear. Had he survived, he faced a possible seven years in prison. He did not survive … At 3.45 on the afternoon of 3 August, after seventy-nine hours in a coma, Ward died."[160]

With Ward's death the Profumo scandal also died, "as if one moment the newspapers had been full of only that and the next moment there was nothing."[161] (The vacuum would quickly be filled by a new outrage, at the audacity of the Great Train Robbery in Buckinghamshire on 8th August and the theft of £2.5 million.) Nevertheless, when finally published on 26th September, the Denning Report occasioned a temporary revival of sensationalism, as queues for copies formed at Her Majesty's Stationery Office and it became an instant best-seller. Breaches of national security were conveniently sidestepped in a wholesale but not unexpected condemnation of Ward's all-pervading immorality, which had led Profumo into temptation and thus to his downfall, and the Prime Minister, to his great relief, was effectively exonerated of any blame. Macmillan had, however, been brought to near exhaustion by the sustained political intrigue of the year, succumbed to a painful affliction of the kidneys and, from his hospital bed, resigned on 18th October, to be succeeded by the cadaverous Sir Alec Douglas-Home.

Once the news coverage of the Denning Report had subsided, the entirely inappropriate excitement occasioned by the Profumo affair finally evaporated, much to my disappointment. By chance, the whiff of scandal lingered for a fraction longer in our neighbourhood, because the family home of Mandy Rice-Davies happened to be in Shirley, literally just round the corner from where my best friend at school lived. (Setting aside her own notoriety, it was a matter of local disapproving comment that her father was a policeman.) As two gauche adolescents, it was only natural that we should take a casual stroll, at his suggestion, from my friend's house to see the suburban semi where Mandy had lived, staring hopefully up at the front bedroom window but sadly having to come away unrewarded by any sign of life.

Denied our guilty pleasure as the dust settled, we eventually had to content ourselves with walking in the opposite direction to the Shirley Odeon, to see the new James Bond film, *From Russia With Love*. On general release from 11th October, this offered a more acceptable form of fantasy, as Rosa Klebb (played by veteran actress Lotte Lenya) sought to ensnare Bond (Sean Connery) through the feminine wiles of Tatiana Romanova (Daniela Bianchi, an Italian former Miss World) in a variety of exotic locations: Istanbul, Trieste, Venice. It was the first of the Bond films to have a theme song, performed somewhat incongruously to accompany the closing credits by the stodgy Matt Monro, whose stilted lack of emotion was a woeful mismatch to the excitement of the preceding storyline. Indeed, the lyrics, as conceived by composer Lionel Bart, bore no direct relation to the film's content at all, other than through the repetition of its title. Arranged by John Barry, George Martin's production was a throwback to the conservative values of his pre-Beatles days in the studio. Although it came across well enough in the dark of the cinema when amplified by the Odeon's primitive sound system, it was hardly the stuff of hit records and only flirted intermittently with the lowest third of the Top 30 during November and December, never going higher than No.23.

Taken as a whole, though, 1963 was the year in which British pop music had been rescued from the doldrums of the early Sixties and revitalised; a sea-change squarely attributed by Pete Frame to the irresistible "three prong attack" of "Merseybeat … London R&B … [and] a nationwide beat boom inspired by both".[162] After despair at the stranglehold on the charts of "wimp smoothies" in previous years had come at last:

> Rejuvenation! All the great records are no longer coming from
> America, where less classics originate than ever before. Practically
> everything exciting, vital and raw is coming out of England. Some
> of it may not be particularly musical and innovative – and nearly all
> of it is American inspired – but at least it's REAL. It's not dummies
> being manipulated by old farts.[163]

And the next two years in particular would be better still, representing a truly golden age in which the influence and ingenuity of new British artists would be pushed to even greater heights.

NOTES

1   The price of LPs varied considerably from one record label to another but one unforeseen impact of this tax cut for Pye Records was to detract from the purposeful branding of its 'Golden Guinea' series of LPs, by reducing their hitherto bargain price of 1 guinea (or 21/-) to below £1, to 19/-. [See Kingsley Abbott, "Lost Gems of the Sixties" (Ovolo, 2008), p.65.]

2   *Crane* starred Patrick Allen as the lantern-jawed eponymous hero, an ex-pat English adventurer running a bar in Morocco, wheeling and dealing with the assistance of ex-Legionnaire Sam Kydd and love-interest Laya Raki to outsmart Colonel Mahmoud, the Chief of Police (played, in those long-lost days before both colour television broadcasts and the invention of political correctness, by the English actor Gerald Flood).

3   16 rpm represented a never-to-be realised format commercially, supposedly to be developed for long-playing records of the spoken word.

4   The first time it happened to me, I thought my precious copy of "Needles And Pins" by the Searchers was a goner! When I realised what had happened, my worst fears were, thankfully, allayed by replacing the stylus.

5   The worst offender in my own collection was the Poets' 1965 single on Decca, "I Am So Blue", b/w "I Love Her Still". It took me over 40 years to obtain this on a 2011-issue CD and hear it again at last.

6   Sometimes you could overcome the problem yourself, by putting the record on to play and delicately applying additional pressure to the head of the playing arm, thereby using the tip of the stylus to cut a new path to track. Of course, it was a risk and by no means foolproof. Although it didn't work for my faulty copy of the Kinks' "Tired Of Waiting For You", it did on "Dear Eloise", the first track of the Hollies' LP *Butterfly*. The only time I chanced my arm with a direct complaint to the record company, about the appalling gravelly sound quality of Fleetwood Mac's "Albatross", the CBS subsidiary Blue Horizon not only sent me a replacement single but also a letter of apology!

7   In the late Sixties, one of the regular assistants in Smith's was a serious young man with horn-rimmed glasses, with a passing resemblance to Peter Asher (of Peter and Gordon), who always had the air of suspecting that customers might be trying to put one over on him. It was, therefore, one of my greatest moments when I went in and asked him, in all seriousness, for a copy of "The Great Banana Hoax" by the Electric Prunes – which, no doubt to his surprise, was in stock and he was able to sell it to me!

8   The Spotnicks, a Swedish instrumental group, had adopted a space theme as their gimmick, incongruously performing in mock space-suits complete with helmets! The Surfaris, as hinted in their name, were from California. The Dakotas, like the Shadows, lived a double musical life: although originally from Manchester, they first came to fame on record as Billy J. Kramer's backing group after being paired up with the Liverpool singer by Brian Epstein

9   Cliff Richard with Penny Junor, op. cit., pp.105-106.

10   Quoted in Steve Turner, op. cit., p.105.

11   They included 36 songs recorded nowhere other than at the BBC: see Mark Lewisohn, op. cit., pp.356-357. In 1994, George Martin remastered some 56 songs recorded in these sessions, which, together with a miscellany of studio conversations, were issued by Apple/EMI as a 2-CD compilation, *The Beatles: 'Live At The BBC'*. In 2013, a second 2-CD compilation of a further 40 songs and 23 speech recordings was issued, as *The Beatles: 'On Air – Live At The BBC Volume 2'* [Universal/BBC].

12   Spencer Leigh, "The Cavern: The Most Famous Club in the World" (SAF, 2008), p.110.

13   And already voted Best Female Singer UK for two years running (1961 & 1962) in *NME*'s annual Pop Poll.

14   Four, of course, were already in the can, from their first two singles. However, the sessions on this day also included 13 takes of "Hold Me Tight", a song which didn't make the cut and was eventually relegated to their *second* LP, *With The Beatles*.

15   Quoted in David Pritchard & Alan Lysaght, op. cit., p.118.

16   Composed by Scott/Marlow. Acker Bilk's instrumental version had already made the UK Top 30 in early 1963, climbing to No.18 at the beginning of February, but the tune is best-known internationally through its later recording by Herb Alpert and the Tijuana Brass on the LP *Whipped Cream And Other Delights*, a track, released as a single in the autumn of 1965, which reached No.7 in the *Billboard* Top 40.

17   The offer of the song to Helen Shapiro was received and rejected, without her

knowledge, by Norrie Paramor. She only heard about it, after the event, from Paul: "I was a bit upset that nobody had told me. Of course, the Beatles hadn't made their name as songwriters yet, but I was disappointed." [See Martin Creasy, op. cit., p.19.]

18   Which had enjoyed 9 weeks in the Top 30, outselling the Drifters' version by a mile and reaching No.11 on 19th January 1963.

19   Brian Hogg, in his CD liner notes to *Rhythm & Blues At Abbey Road 1963 to 1967* [EMI, 1998].

20   Colin Larkin, "The Virgin Encyclopedia of Sixties Music" (Virgin, 1997), p.352.

21   Quoted in Spencer Leigh, "Twist and Shout! Merseybeat, The Cavern, The Star-Club and The Beatles" (Nirvana, 2004), pp.130-131.

22   Another Joe Meek/Geoff Goddard collaboration, like his 1961 hit "Tribute To Buddy Holly". Bass player for the Outlaws was Chas Hodges, later to become the piano-playing half of Chas and Dave.

23   "That they were a bigger Liverpool name than the Beatles … is proved by the fact that [Allan] Williams booked them on the Liverpool Stadium bill with Gene Vincent on Tuesday 3rd May 1960." [Liner notes by Bill Harry, "Gerry and the Pacemakers Scrapbook" (*British Invasion, Reeling In The Years* DVD), p.6.]

24   Brian Epstein, "A Cellarful of Noise" (Four Square, 1965), p.70.

25   For all its success, it was, nevertheless, a one-off. Gerry's later attempt to revive another classic ballad of similar sentiment, "Walk Hand In Hand" (originally a UK hit in the summer of 1956 for Ronnie Carroll, amongst others), met with no Top 30 placing when released in October 1965.

26   Cross, Kendall & Farren, "Encyclopedia of British Beat Groups & Solo Artists of The Sixties" (Omnibus, 1980), p.32.

27   Quoted in Spencer Leigh, "The Cavern: The Most Famous Club in the World" (SAF, 2008), p.95.

28   Terry Rawlings, "British Beat 1960-1969: Then, Now and Rare" (Omnibus, 2002), p.84.

29   On 12th September 1962, "Freddie and the Dreamers heard the Beatles perform James Ray's 'If You Gotta Make A Fool Of Somebody' and stuck it in their own repertoire." [See Spencer Leigh, "The Cavern: The Most Famous Club in the World" (SAF, 2008), p.102.]

30   Quoted in Spencer Leigh, "The Cavern: The Most Famous Club in the World" (SAF, 2008), p.110.

31   Quoted in Spencer Leigh, "Twist and Shout! Merseybeat, The Cavern, The Star-Club and The Beatles" (Nirvana, 2004), p.126.

32   Composed by Carroll/Guy. For the Searchers, for example, Chris Curtis would regularly sing it as the group's 'drummer's song' (the equivalent, if you like, of "Boys" as sung first by Pete Best, then Ringo, with the Beatles) and their recorded version (on their second LP, *Sugar And Spice*) is, frankly, far gutsier.

33   A US No.3 hit in the summer of 1957.

34   Written by Maurice Williams himself, it was originally a US No.1 in November 1960.

35   Graham Nash, interviewed by Mick Houghton, CD liner notes for *The Hollies – Clarke,*

Hicks & Nash Years (The Complete Hollies April 1963-October 1968) [EMI, 2011].

36 Which was opened at 13, Temple Street on 9th April 1960 by founders Geoff Hogarth and Harry Ormesher.

37 Quoted in Spencer Leigh, "The Cavern: The Most Famous Club in the World" (SAF, 2008), p.101.

38 The CD compilation *The Beatles Live At The BBC* [EMI, 1994] includes their previously unreleased version, recorded for radio on 10th July 1963 and broadcast on *Pop Go The Beatles* on 30th July.

39 In 1957, at RAF Oldenburg in West Germany, Casser had played in a skiffle group with Bill Wyman, then approaching the end of his National Service. [See Bill Wyman with Richard Havers, op. cit., p.26.] After leaving Liverpool for London, with spells as manager of what was to become the notorious Blue Gardenia Club and as a stuntman, he formed Casey Jones and the Engineers in early 1963, a line-up that included Tom McGuinness and Eric Clapton. [See John Reed, CD liner notes to *The Big Three: Cavern Stomp – The Complete Recordings* (RPM, 2009).]

40 Johnny Gustafson, quoted in Spencer Leigh, "Twist and Shout! Merseybeat, The Cavern, The Star-Club and The Beatles" (Nirvana, 2004), p.76. The 'obscure' songs they introduced included "Some Other Guy" and "Money", both eagerly taken up by many other groups to the point of quickly becoming rock'n'roll standards.

41 Cilla Black, "What's It All About?" (Ebury, 2003), pp.60-61.

42 See Cilla Black, op. cit., p.62.

43 Quoted in John Reed, CD liner notes to *The Big Three: Cavern Stomp – The Complete Recordings* (RPM, 2009).

44 David Crosby, quoted in Spencer Leigh, "The Cavern: The Most Famous Club in the World" (SAF, 2008), p.107. The CD compilation *The Beatles Live At The BBC* [EMI, 1994] includes their previously unreleased version, recorded for radio on 19th June 1963 and broadcast on *Easy Beat* on 23rd June; and the Searchers recorded a particularly robust interpretation on their second LP *Sugar And Spice*.

45 Quoted in John Reed, CD liner notes to *The Big Three: Cavern Stomp – The Complete Recordings* (RPM, 2009).

46 Ibid.

47 Brian Epstein, op. cit., p.74.

48 Quoted in Spencer Leigh, "Twist and Shout! Merseybeat, The Cavern, The Star-Club and The Beatles" (Nirvana, 2004), p.76.

49 Brian Epstein, op. cit., p.74.

50 This latter number anticipating Captain Sensible's deadpan version by years [as originally noted by Alan Clayson, "Call Up The Groups" (Blandford, 1985), p.90].

51 See Dave Lovelady, as quoted by Spencer Leigh, "The Cavern: The Most Famous Club in the World" (SAF, 2008), p.106.

52 Quoted in Bill Harry, CD liner notes to *The Best Of The Fourmost* (EMI Gold, 2005).

53 Alan Clayson, "The Rolling Stones: The Origin of the Species" (Chrome Dreams, 2007), p.163.

54   Ibid.

55   Aside from recording what turned out to be a series of unsuccessful releases in their own right, they had been used extensively by Decca as session musicians; perhaps most bizarrely as the backing group to Radio Luxembourg DJ Jimmy Savile on his 1962 single "Ahab The Arab".

56   The first spin-off from the *Please Please Me* LP, the four tracks on the EP were: "Twist And Shout", "A Taste Of Honey", "Do You Want To Know A Secret?" and "There's A Place".

57   Gordy, © 1963 by Jobete Music Co. Inc./Jobete Music (UK) Ltd.

58   Entering the *Billboard* Top 40 on 22nd September 1962, it eventually reached No.3.

59   The Five's full line-up was: Dave Clark (drums & vocals), Mike Smith (lead vocals & keyboards), Lenny Davidson (lead guitar & vocals), Rick Huxley (bass guitar & vocals) and Denis Payton (saxophone, harmonica & vocals).

60   Written by Clark/Smith. Not to be confused with the song of the same title written and recorded by Carl Perkins at the Sun Studios in the 1950s.

61   Disillusioned by the drought of successful singles, in the summer of 1961 Alan Caddy (lead guitar), Brian Gregg (bass guitar) and Clem Cattini (drums) left Kidd, to join Colin Hicks and his Cabin Boys on what turned out to be a short-lived concert tour in Italy; Caddy and Cattini being subsequently recruited by Joe Meek to the Tornados. They were replaced by Johnny Patto (lead guitar), Johnny Spence (bass guitar) and Frank Farley (drums); but in January 1962, Patto, whose health was dogged by stomach ulcers, was replaced as lead guitarist by Mick Green. Kidd first recorded with this revised line-up on 26th September 1962. [See www.johnnykidd.co.uk.]

62   Quoted by Adrian Barrett on www.johnnykidd.co.uk.

63   The Searchers would include a cover version on their second LP *Sugar And Spice*.

64   Longevity and continuity are the key concepts here. Given the 2009 reunion tour of Cliff Richard and the Shadows, with original members Hank Marvin and Bruce Welch as well as Brian Bennett, they perhaps have the edge in being the first to publicly celebrate a fiftieth anniversary of performing together since they had their first hit with "Move It".

65   Pete Frame, "The Beatles and Some Other Guys: Rock Family Trees of the Early Sixties" (Omnibus, 1997), p.27.

66   Keith Richards with James Fox, "Life" (Weidenfeld & Nicholson, 2010), p.99.

67   Keith Richards with James Fox, op. cit., p.103.

68   Quoted in Laura Jackson, op. cit., p.61.

69   While both Philip Norman and Laura Jackson refer to this gig in their respective accounts of the period, Bill Wyman does not include it in his list of their engagements in late 1962, showing none taking place between 22nd and 29th December. He may not, therefore, have been present, although he only records gigs on the 18th and 19th December as definitely having been without him. [See Bill Wyman with Richard Havers, op. cit., p.41.]

70   With whom, at Alexis Korner's suggestion, Ray Davies played guitar three nights a week in early 1963, whilst still ostensibly a student at Hornsey College of Art.

71   Andrew Loog Oldham, op. cit., p.185.

72   The Beatles reciprocated by inviting the Stones to see them 'in concert' at the Albert Hall, contributing to a live BBC Light Programme pop concert, entitled *Swinging Sound 63*, on 18th April. This event was otherwise notable for the first meeting between Paul McCartney and Jane Asher. [See Mark Lewisohn, op. cit., pp.107-108.]

73   Andrew Loog Oldham, op. cit., p.190.

74   Quoted in Andrew Loog Oldham, op. cit., 194.

75   Quoted in Bill Wyman with Richard Havers, op. cit., p.57.

76   Also protecting his own interests, according to Laura Jackson, by secretly signing a separate contract with Easton to guarantee him £5.00 more per week than the other group members. [See Laura Jackson, op. cit., p.73.]

77   Prior to striking the deal, Dick Rowe, accompanied by his wife, had also been to see the Stones play live at the Crawdaddy, on 5th May. This was on the recommendation of George Harrison, with whom he had co-judged a Liverpool talent contest in the intervening period since the Beatles' own visit to the Crawdaddy on 14th April.

78   Andrew Loog Oldham, op. cit., p.183.

79   Quoted in Andrew Loog Oldham, op. cit., p.213.

80   Keith Richards with James Fox, op. cit., p.130.

81   Bill Wyman with Richard Havers, op. cit., p.64.

82   Quoted in Andrew Loog Oldham, op. cit., p.219.

83   Keith Richards with James Fox, op. cit., p.130.

84   It closed down at the Station Hotel in mid-June, amid concerns from the brewery about health and safety, and was relocated by Giorgio Gomelsky at the clubhouse of Richmond's athletics track.

85   Bill Wyman with Richard Havers, op. cit., p.74.

86   Bill Wyman with Richard Havers, op. cit., p.69.

87   Apart from the Rolling Stones, the other support acts were the Flintstones, Mickie Most and Julie Grant.

88   John Lennon, "The Beatles Anthology" (Cassell, 2000), p.101.

89   Ian MacDonald, op. cit., p.85.

90   Tony Barrow, sleevenotes to *With The Beatles* (Parlophone, 1963).

91   See Bill Wyman with Richard Havers, op. cit., p.85.

92   Brian Epstein, op. cit., p.80.

93   Brian Epstein, op. cit., p.15.

94   Brian Epstein, op. cit., p.77.

95   "Thank You Girl" was originally to have been the A-side. At the same session, the Beatles also recorded two other songs not revisited until years later, "The One After 909" and "What Goes On". [See Mark Lewisohn, op. cit., p.102.]

96   Like "From Me To You", written on tour, this time in Newcastle on 26th June after a concert at the Top Rank Majestic Ballroom. It was recorded, together with the B-side "I'll Get You", at Abbey Road on 1st July. [See Mark Lewisohn, op. cit., pp.114-115.]

97   Ian MacDonald, op. cit., p.74.

98   And it remained the UK's top-selling single for the next 14 years, until displaced in 1977 by Paul McCartney & Wings with "Mull of Kintyre".

99   "When the Beatles first showed this to their colleagues on tour, it was greeted with hilarity. Lennon, though, insisted that it would work, and was proved correct. Whenever the head-shaking 'ooo's came round, the level of the audiences' delirium would leap." [See Ian MacDonald, op. cit., p.75.]

100   Namely: "I Saw Her Standing There", "Misery", "Anna (Go to Him)" and "Chains". The EP's title, however, was a misnomer, since it was, of course, the *second* EP (after *Twist And Shout*) on which tracks from *Please Please Me* were repackaged and reissued.

101   And recycled for the cover of *The Beatles (No.1)* EP. McBean also took the formally posed group photograph, cropped to sit on a completely white background, on the cover of *The Beatles' Hits* EP.

102   Terence Pepper & Jon Savage, "Beatles to Bowie: The 60s Exposed" (National Portrait Gallery, 2009), p.15.

103   "The Beatles' rivals looked on amazed as songs of this commercial appeal were casually thrown away on LPs." [Ian MacDonald, op. cit., p.84.] It was later released separately as the title track of an EP, on 7th February 1964.

104   Composed by Bradford/Gordy and originally a hit in America for Barrett Strong.

105   Composed by Meredith Willson.

106   Martin Creasy, "Beatlemania! The Real Story of The Beatles UK Tours 1963-1965" (Omnibus, 2010), p.96.

107   Private correspondence with the author, November 2011.

108   Ibid.

109   Ibid.

110   Quoted in Mark Lewisohn, op. cit., p.93. John admitted that he was "fantastically nervous, but I wanted to say something to rebel a bit, and that was the best I could do". [Quoted in "The Beatles Anthology" (Cassell, 2000), p.105.]

111   Mark Lewisohn, op. cit., p.92. John's view of it was: "That show's a bad gig, anyway. Everybody's very nervous and uptight and nobody performs well." [Quoted in "The Beatles Anthology" (Cassell, 2000), p.105.]

112   See Spencer Leigh, "It's Love That Really Counts: The Billy Kinsley Story" (Cavern City Tours, 2010), p.63.

113   Andy Neill, "The Beatles Across The Universe: John, Paul, George & Ringo On Tour and On Stage" (Haynes, 2009), p.81.

114   See Mike Read, op. cit., p.144.

115   Not to be confused with the Jackie Edwards song of the same title, which was a Top 20 hit for Wayne Fontana in June 1966.

116 Quoted in Paul Howes, "The Complete Dusty Springfield" (Reynolds & Hearn, revised edn., 2007), p.27.

117 In fact, this was her second solo TV appearance of the year, having already been a guest panel member on *Juke Box Jury* in March.

118 The qualifying thresholds then were 250,000 sales for a silver and 500,000 for a gold disc.

119 Which, in its original form, had been the UK No.1 for eight weeks in the early summer of 1954.

120 Cilla Black, op. cit., p.69.

121 Quoted in Spencer Leigh, "Twist And Shout! Merseybeat, The Cavern, The Star-Club and The Beatles" (Nirvana, 2004), p.138.

122 Brian Epstein, op. cit., p.71.

123 Ibid.

124 Quoted in Spencer Leigh, "Twist And Shout! Merseybeat, The Cavern, The Star-Club and The Beatles" (Nirvana, 2004), p.152.

125 Cilla Black, op. cit., p.86.

126 Quoted in Keith Badman, op. cit., p.39.

127 Among those regularly called upon by Jan were Hal Blaine (drums), Earl Palmer (drums) and Glen Campbell (guitar). [See Keith Badman, op. cit., p.43.] All three achieved fame in their own right as prominent members of the self-styled Wrecking Crew (a title coined by Blaine), a sophisticated extended group of West Coast session musicians who first helped Phil Spector create his 'wall of sound' and later contributed to recordings by a wide variety of artists, the Beach Boys included.

128 In alternation with Mira Sound Studios, New York. Spector habitually worked at Gold Star with recording engineer Larry Levine and musical arranger Jack Nitzsche.

129 It appears in published collections of Dylan's lyrics as "Talkin' John Birch Paranoid Blues".

130 Extant live recordings of the song can be found on *Bob Dylan: The Bootleg Series Vol.1*, *Bob Dylan: The Bootleg Series Vol.6* and *Bob Dylan In Concert: Brandeis University 1963*.

131 Bob Dylan, "Lyrics 1962-2001" (Simon & Schuster, 2004), p.17 (© 1970 by Special Rider Music; renewed 1988 by Special Rider Music).

132 John Bauldie, CD liner notes to *Bob Dylan: The Bootleg Series Volumes 1-3/ (rare and unreleased) 1961-1991* [Columbia/Sony, 1991]. Robert Shelton dismissed Phelps' job title as "a fancy title for a censor". [See Robert Shelton, "No Direction Home: The Life and Music of Bob Dylan" (Omnibus, 2011 revised edn.), p.127.]

133 Ibid.

134 Suze Rotolo, "A Freewheelin' Time" (Aurum, 2008), p.214.

135 Suze Rotolo, op. cit., p.216.

136 Suze Rotolo, op. cit., pp.216-217.

137 Suze Rotolo, op. cit., p.274.

138   Bob Dylan, "Lyrics 1962-2001" (Simon & Schuster, 2004), p.64 (© 1963, 1966 by Warner Bros. Inc.; renewed 1991, 1994 by Special Rider Music).

139   Joseph Heller, "Catch-22" (Corgi reprint, 1967), p.54. This, his most famous novel, was first published in 1961, so was equally reflective of American paranoia at the time in question.

140   Historically, it remains the best-seller of all Dylan's original albums in the UK (outdone only by the 1967 *Greatest Hits* compilation), with a 49-week run in the LP charts. [See Martin Roach (ed.), "The Virgin Book of British Hit Albums" (Virgin, 2009), p.97.]

141   Robert Shelton, op. cit., p.130.

142   Tom Piazza, DVD liner notes to *The Other Side Of The Mirror: Bob Dylan Live At The Newport Folk Festival 1963-1965* [Columbia Performance, 2007], p.5.

143   He had held the position of Field Secretary for the National Association for the Advancement of Coloured People.

144   Anthony Scaduto, op. cit., p.151.

145   Deborah Cadbury, op. cit., p.279.

146   Alan Shepard & Deke Slayton, "Moon Shot: The Inside Story of America's Race to the Moon" (Virgin, 1994), p.167.

147   David Frost, "An Autobiography: Part One – From Congregations to Audiences" (Harper Collins, 1993), p.105.

148   Quoted in Keith Badman, op. cit., pp.44-45.

149   Ibid.

150   Quoted in Anthony Scaduto, op. cit., p.160.

151   Ibid.

152   Anthony Scaduto, op. cit., p.161.

153   Finally recorded on 1st November 1965, it closed Side 1 of the Byrds' second LP of that year, *Turn! Turn! Turn!* Dylan's own recording of the original song, on 20th November 1961, was made for but eventually not included on *Bob Dylan*, and can be found on *Bob Dylan: The Bootleg Series Vol.1*.

154   Quoted in Robert Shelton, op. cit., p.143.

155   Bob Dylan, op. cit., p.121.

156   With composing credited to Count Jaine-de-Mora y Aragon/Leslie Bricusse, it was released on the Ember label in the summer of 1963 and entered the Top 40 for one week only at No.37 in the week ending 15th August. 'Miss X' was reputedly the pseudonym of Joyce Blair (sister of the dancer Lionel), who speaks in short, mildly suggestive snatches over a hotel-lounge Latin American arrangement for piano and bongos; but Jane Birkin and Serge Gainsbourg it is not!

157   Jack Bruce/Pete Brown, © 1968 by Dratleaf Ltd. Brown explicitly acknowledged the inspiration for the song in the BBC4 TV documentary *Blues Britannia: Can Blue Men Sing The Whites?*, first broadcast on 1st May 2009.

158   Quoted in Phillip Knightley & Caroline Kennedy, op. cit., p.187.

159   "Two other charges, that Ward had helped procure an abortion, were on a separate

indictment which meant that they would not be heard until this case was over." [See Phillip Knightley & Caroline Kennedy, op. cit., p.216.]

160   Anthony Summers & Stephen Dorril, "Honeytrap" (Coronet, 1988), p.304.

161   Phillip Knightley & Caroline Kennedy, op. cit., p.248.

162   Pete Frame, "Rock Family Trees" (Omnibus, 1993), p.59.

163   Ibid.

Chapter 6

1964

FIRST NO.1 OF THE YEAR –
"I Want To Hold Your Hand" by The Beatles

LAST NO.1 OF THE YEAR –
"I Feel Fine" by The Beatles

In the former Wesleyan church on Dickenson Road, Rusholme, Manchester, at around 6.00 p.m. on the evening of Wednesday, 1st January 1964, tensions were running high in what passed for dressing rooms in these premises now converted to a television studio by the BBC, in anticipation of the launch of a new programme dedicated to the charts but as yet only scheduled for an initial six-week trial run, *Top Of The Pops*.

Its inaugural host was to be its original proponent, the as then unsuspected disc-jockey Jimmy Savile[1], whose vision had been for television to build on the already successful format of his Friday-night Radio Luxembourg show *Teen And Twenty Disc Club*. Unlike its ITV predecessor, *Ready Steady Go!*, the editorial policy of *Top Of The Pops* was to be neither style-conscious nor trend-setting. Whereas for Vicki Wickham (editor of *RSG!*), the guiding principle was to book "artists on our show from our heart and not from any commercial expectations", it then being a matter of luck that "the ones we liked were the hit acts of the day"[2], the BBC's line from the outset of *Top Of The Pops* was that its content would be strictly governed by record sales, in that "every show would end with the week's #1 single, no record would be played two weeks in succession unless it was at #1, and no record would feature if it was dropping down the charts".[3]

At a time when there was still no consistency across the musical press in determining either the volume of record sales or resultant chart placings, the BBC would opt to follow a chart of its own, which had earlier been devised for its radio programme *Pick Of The Pops*; namely, a composite derived from the charts published by the four main music papers of the day – *New Musical Express*, *Melody Maker*, *Disc* and *Record Retailer*. This was in marked contrast to ITV's *Thank Your Lucky Stars* and *RSG!*, both of which were content to rely on the *NME* chart as their point of reference.[4]

The dressing of the set beneath the giant illuminated wall-mounted listing of the BBC's current Top 20 was intended to enhance the illusion of a club, with the host standing by a turntable on which a 'dolly bird' [5] supposedly played each new record, to which the successive acts would mime on the adjacent stage in front of a studio audience of random teenagers who danced or shrugged more or less in time to the music – usually, it has to be said, with little obvious outward display of enthusiasm or enjoyment. Treated more as props than a malleable adornment of extras, those hapless individuals not on their guard could easily find themselves unceremoniously shunted aside as cumbersome camera 'dollies' were manoeuvred across the studio floor without warning into position for new shots.

Where budgetary constraints or touring commitments precluded 'live' appearances, a troupe of dancing girls (originally a trio led by Jo Cook called the Go-Jos) would perform a demure routine to a selected record, in deference to the time-honoured BBC tradition of wholesome light entertainment. Alternatively, specially prepared film clips of performers might be shown instead, primitive black-and-white forebears of the modern music video; an innovation implemented from the outset for this first edition, with film clips of Cliff Richard and the Shadows (who were out of the country at the time, on location in the Canary Islands for their next film *Wonderful Life*), Freddie and the Dreamers, Gene Pitney and newsreel footage of the Beatles as visual accompaniment to their New Year's No.1.

Of the five remaining acts gathered together in Manchester to perform 'live' on the first programme, there was only one soloist – Dusty Springfield. The remaining four groups exemplified the north/south split that was already threatening to polarise the opinions and tastes of fans as the initial euphoria of Merseybeat slowly dissipated. From Manchester, the Hollies. From London, the Dave Clark Five. So far, so good. But a fracas erupted when, taking their lead from sarcastic digs by Brian Jones, new London upstarts the Rolling Stones traded insults, if not blows, before the show with old hands from Liverpool the Swinging Blue Jeans; and before the evening was out, Jones's disagreeable behaviour had also extended to pitching into Harry Goodwin, the professional photographer engaged by the BBC to provide still shots of the acts for captions to the weekly chart run-down.

With some semblance of order eventually prevailing, the programme went on air from 6.36 p.m. and in the space of the next twenty-five minutes the first nine records ever broadcast on *Top Of The Pops* were, therefore, as follows:

"Stay", by the Hollies,
"Don't Talk To Him", by Cliff Richard and the Shadows,
"I Wanna Be Your Man", by the Rolling Stones,
"Hippy Hippy Shake", by the Swinging Blue Jeans,
"You Were Made For Me", by Freddie and the Dreamers,

"Twenty-Four Hours From Tulsa", by Gene Pitney,
"I Only Want To Be With You", by Dusty Springfield,
"Glad All Over", by the Dave Clark Five, and
"I Want To Hold Your Hand", by the Beatles.[6]

Given the limited screen-time available, it was an undeniably coherent cross-section of the best sellers of the day, reflecting as it did the contemporary predominance of the new groups and making the programme's launch an instant success. Those artists whose records were omitted failed almost without exception to meet the BBC's stipulated criteria for inclusion, thus sparing viewers on this occasion the likes of the Singing Nun ("Dominique"), Kathy Kirby ("Secret Love") and Big Dee Irwin ("Swinging On A Star"); although Elvis Presley's latest single, "Kiss Me Quick", was on the rise. As a genre, instrumentals were no longer finding the favour they had once enjoyed with younger record-buyers, "Geronimo" by the Shadows having been eclipsed by the middle-aged Latin American lilt of "Maria Elena", as performed by Brazilian brothers Los Indios Tabajaras; and of the remainder, continuing sales over the preceding Christmas period of "She Loves You", together with the Beatles' EPs and LP, meant that a significant number of chart places were still blocked to other artists for the time being.

While the arrival of *Top Of The Pops* provided a welcome additional vehicle for record companies to promote both their headliners and potential new acts at home, subject, of course, to the weekly vagaries of sales, prominent managers like Brian Epstein and Andrew Loog Oldham were steeling themselves to exploit the rich pickings to be found internationally. Taking its lead from Epstein and the Beatles, the British music industry was now about to enter a truly audacious period of cultural cross-fertilisation around the world but most notably with the USA, which initially would leave the Americans reeling.

As Mark Lewisohn observed: "If 1963 had been the year in which the Beatles conquered Britain, then in 1964 they conquered the world."[7] The standard sociological interpretation of the so-called 'British Invasion' of America is that it happened in 1964 as a concession by default to the traumatisation of that country following President Kennedy's assassination. According to Barry Miles, for example, "The Beatles, lacking the guilt complex that overshadowed the nation and hung there for months after the event, were allowed to perform with a palpable sense of joy that seemed crass for American singers at the time".[8]

What is not accounted for here, however, is the irresistible commercial urge of British managers to find and develop new markets abroad; bluntly, to make more money elsewhere and, in the process, guard against the possible saturation of the home market. Irrespective, therefore, of the death of a

President, it is perfectly reasonable to suppose that the outward expansion of British pop music would have happened anyway, in the course of natural progression. Indeed, by November 1963 Epstein had already judged that the time was right to launch what he styled 'Operation USA' and had taken his protégé Billy J. Kramer on a reconnaissance mission to New York; "first of all to promote him and secondly – and more importantly as it turned out – to find out why the Beatles, who were the biggest thing the British pop world had ever known, hadn't 'happened' in America."[9] In undertaking this trip, Epstein was not only making what he saw as a significant investment in the future but also taking a massive gamble, given that he "didn't know anybody over there beyond three contacts whose names were in my pocketbook".[10]

In a flurry of meetings with television and record executives, he quickly encountered an innate prejudice, a "view ... that whatever the British did at their best, an American at his best would do very much better".[11] (Hitherto, the minor US record companies contracted to handle earlier Beatles' records, Vee-Jay and Swan, had largely shown indifference and achieved correspondingly low sales.) Nevertheless, far from feeling rebuffed, Epstein was determined to persevere in proving that the Beatles were capable of matching the clear preference for "an American 'sound' on disc which appealed to the American public" and was confident, moreover, that "I Want To Hold Your Hand" was *the* song to deliver that "certain American *feeling*".[12] His ultimate coup was the successful conclusion of negotiating appearances for the Beatles on *The Ed Sullivan Show*, which he achieved after four days of face-to-face wrangling with the irascible host (whom he found "a most genial fellow"[13]), in the face of entrenched opposition to his demands. In its turn, this unprecedented television deal then proved the catalyst to persuading Capitol Records to get behind the new single (on which "I Saw Her Standing There" would be the American B-side) and invest seriously in pre-tour marketing.

Even before reaching America, however, the Beatles began 1964 by flying to France on 14th January for a three-week season of concerts at the Paris Olympia, staying at the prestigious Georges V Hotel[14] from where George Harrison supposedly penned daily articles on their adventures for the *Daily Express* (but which were, in reality, ghosted for him by NEMS press officer Derek Taylor, Epstein already being wise to the need to sustain interest in his artists wherever they might be at any given time). Sharing the bill with US recording star Trini Lopez and French *chanteuse* Sylvie Vartan, the Beatles found Parisian concertgoers distinctly lukewarm compared to their previous German or British experience, covering a broader age spectrum than they had become used to and with the added novelty that for once they could actually hear themselves playing as the habitual "female screams of adoration were replaced by roars of approval from a mainly male audience".[15]

It was here that Paul acquired a copy of *The Freewheelin' Bob Dylan*. John said that "for the rest of our three weeks in Paris we didn't stop playing it. We went potty on Dylan."[16] George went even further in his admiration: "The day Bob Dylan *really* turned us on was the day we heard his album *The Freewheelin' Bob Dylan*. Right from that moment we recognised some vital energy, a voice crying out somewhere, toiling in the darkness."[17] This clearly marks the starting-point of Dylan's subsequent strand of influence on the group's attitudes to composition and performance, as later evident in songs by both John and George in particular and publicly acknowledged in 1967 by the inclusion – at George's suggestion – of his photograph on Peter Blake's cover for the *Sgt. Pepper* LP.

It was also in Paris that they received the news from America that, within three weeks of its release there on 26th December, "I Want To Hold Your Hand" had reached No.1 on the *Billboard* chart; "becoming the fastest-rising disc by any British artiste in the States, with sales surpassing a million, 10,000 copies a day selling in New York alone".[18] Returning to London on 5th February, they had the briefest of respites before 'Operation USA' proper got under way with their departure from Heathrow on 7th February for New York.

For a relatively unknown group on the far side of the Atlantic, the Beatles received a tumultuous welcome on arrival that afternoon at Kennedy Airport from a screaming crowd of up to 5,000 teenagers, some of whom had been waiting to see them since long before daybreak. Not yet out of the airport buildings, they then had to face an estimated throng of some 200 reporters and photographers at an impromptu news conference (where, as George said, "They started asking us funny questions, so we just started answering them with stupid answers"[19]), before at last being chauffeur-driven in a motorcade of Cadillacs to their suite at the Plaza Hotel.

There could be no question as to the effectiveness of Capitol's sustained publicity campaign, which had ensured widespread circulation in advance of Beatle badges, Beatle wigs and fly-posters declaring "THE BEATLES ARE COMING". "Put them up anywhere and everywhere," Capitol's marketing team had been instructed:

> It may sound funny but we literally want your salesmen to be
> plastering these stickers on any friendly surface as they walk down
> the street ... Make arrangements with local high school students
> to spread the stickers around town. Involve your friends and
> relatives ... It's going to be "BEATLES ARE COMING" stickers
> everywhere you look.[20]

Before they had even disembarked, the melee visible from the aircraft on touchdown had instantly struck Cynthia Lennon, accompanying John for once, as being "Beatlemania all over again, but bigger, louder and wilder"[21];

the incredulity of it all only growing on her on their drive into the heart of New York:

> In the streets around the hotel, madness had descended: thousands of singing, shrieking teenage girls in bobby-sox were waiting for us, waving Beatles wigs, banners, photos and T-shirts. Lines of police, red-faced with exertion, were holding back the crowds as our car inched towards the hotel entrance.[22]

This, then, was the true beginning of the siege mentality characteristic of this and all future Beatles' engagements, the paradox of their extreme popularity that ultimately drove them to abandon live performances out of their own fear and loathing.

Although this initial tour was a conglomeration of record promotion, TV and radio broadcasts and some concerts for good measure, hyperbole was attendant upon almost everything they did. In advance of their first appearance on *The Ed Sullivan Show*, on 9th February, more than 50,000 people had applied for the 728 seats in the CBS Television Theatre (Studio 50) in Manhattan and the estimated total viewing audience was 73 million; Sullivan himself saying that he had "never seen any scenes to compare with the bedlam that was occasioned by their debut".[23] The next day, they were feted at their hotel by the President of Capitol Records, at a specially-convened press conference to present them with gold discs for sales of "I Want To Hold Your Hand" and their first Capitol LP *Meet The Beatles* (which had only been released on 20th January).

The logistics of the three live concerts they compressed into little more than twenty-four hours were tortuous. On 11th February, snow – and their fear of flying in snow – dictated that they should take the train from New York to Washington, where they played their first ever US concert that evening at the Coliseum. Here the makeshift stage had been accommodated within a boxing arena, so they interrupted their playing at intervals to turn and face a different section of the 8,000-strong audience seated on all four sides of them. A post-concert reception for them at the British Embassy, where a charity ball had been in progress, was marred by one of the 'Hooray Henrys' present – described by John as "some bloody animal" – cutting off a lock of Ringo's hair as a souvenir; a "stupid incident" at a "miserable event", according to the usually mild-mannered drummer.[24]

Returning to New York by train the following day, on the night of 12th February they played to two houses in succession at Carnegie Hall. The capacity for each house only normally being 2,900, an additional 50 seats for both these concerts was put in place on stage, to either side of and behind the Beatles as they played. To the surprise and delight of promoter Sid Bernstein, tickets had sold out within the first day of going on sale: "There had never been a one-day sellout in the history of concerts up to that time."[25] (Bizarrely, given that the overt objective of the trip was to garner publicity, Epstein turned down Bernstein's offer for a third New York concert at Madison Square Garden, for fear of overexposure.)

Flying out to Miami Beach on 13th February for a supposedly extended holiday before their return home, much of the next two days were actually taken up in rehearsal for a second *Ed Sullivan Show* on the evening of 16th February, for which their performance was televised in front of an audience of 3,500 at the Deauville Hotel. Viewing figures, though down from the week before, were nevertheless still estimated at around 70 million. Their remaining five days in Miami were devoted to an intensely public period of 'rest', mixing recreation on the beach and messing about in boats with interviews and photo-opportunities (including a visit to the gym where heavyweight boxer Cassius Clay – *aka* Muhammad Ali – was in training for his fight with Sonny Liston [26]).

From beginning to end, the trip had been a masterpiece of media manipulation, attention and sales boosted by the peculiar advantage conferred by the unregulated, commercial approach to radio broadcasting in the US compared to the tight restrictions of 'needle time' imposed in Britain on the BBC as the sole state broadcaster and the Beatles, in their bemused naivety, gave unprecedented access to all manner of interviewers who approached them on their travels. Not only were the Beatles 'adopted' by brash New York DJ Murray the K almost from the moment of their arrival, but they were also intrigued by the multiplicity of radio stations to which they could tune in Stateside, to hear their records being played over and over again as well as those of their own personal favourites of the moment (like the Ronettes, Marvin Gaye, the Miracles and the Shirelles). As for their television audiences on *The Ed Sullivan Show*, the estimated figures on both occasions were way in excess of the entire population of the UK at that time.[27]

In the end, this first phase of 'Operation USA' had exceeded all expectations by encapsulating their greatest achievement to date; namely, that of absorbing key elements of American rock'n'roll into their act, refashioning and Anglicising them through their own previous live performances and compositions, and replaying them to the new youth of America in what was now uniquely and winningly their own style. The instantaneous nature of their success there can be attributed as much to the virtual lack of any competition as to the product of their own talent. Ed Sullivan's producer, who had originally urged caution upon the host in embracing the Beatles by virtue of them being nothing more than another pop group, had nevertheless been right to draw attention to the long-standing absence then in America of a thriving group scene.

There really had been no precedent in the USA since the demise of

Buddy Holly and the Crickets for what we have since come to regard as the traditional pop group of vocalist(-s), assorted guitars and drums. Whereas in Britain, that had been the model seized upon by Cliff Richard and the Shadows, adding vocals to a strong instrumental line-up, which was then imitated and built upon by an army of successors, American groups – including the Beach Boys – had remained in the minority of performers, opting themselves by and large to pursue the elusive perfection of vocal harmonies. The likes of the Everly Brothers, the Four Seasons, the Motown crooners, the girl groups in Phil Spector's stable – all were typically big on harmony to the virtual exclusion of instrumental versatility.

Brian Wilson in particular was ultra-sensitive to the threat posed to his ambitions by the Beatles from the very outset of their visit: "I just couldn't handle the fact that there were these four guys from England coming over here to America to invade our territory. When we saw how everybody was screaming for the Beatles, it was like, 'Whooa!' We couldn't believe it. I was shook up as hell."[28] Little surprise, then, that the British press and TV should sit up and take notice when, on their homecoming on 22nd February, Heathrow Airport was mobbed by thousands of screaming fans and even the ritual Saturday coverage of sport on BBC's *Grandstand* was interrupted for almost a quarter of an hour to carry an interview with the Beatles by David Coleman.

For the next two months, however, the Beatles' time would principally be devoted to their next big project; making their first film, *A Hard Day's Night*, together with completing the associated composing and recording of new songs (the latter having already begun back in January in Paris with initial work on "Can't Buy Me Love") *before* the scheduled start of filming on 2nd March. Liverpool playwright Alun Owen had been commissioned to write the script and Richard Lester[29] was the director, with comic acting stalwarts Wilfrid Brambell, John Junkin and Norman Rossington leading the supporting cast. Unlike the colourful fantasy adventures starring Cliff Richard and the Shadows, this film was shot in black and white, with its storyline firmly rooted in comically documenting the experience of Beatlemania, depicting "something like 48 consecutive hours of activity in the bustling lives of four beat group boys".[30]

In fact, in the brief period he had spent with the Beatles in the interests of preliminary research, Alun Owen had been shocked by the constraints imposed upon them by their popularity, seeing them as "prisoners of their own success, trapped by fame, free only when actually performing"[31], the theme he then sought to develop through his screenplay. Although based at Twickenham Film Studios, shooting actually commenced at Paddington Station, followed by several days spent travelling by chartered train through Somerset and Devon. Before its completion on 24th April, the list of other locations, mostly in and around London, grew to include Marylebone Station, the Dorchester Hotel, the Scala Theatre and even Gatwick Airport.

With UK advance orders of 1 million copies, 20th March saw the release of "Can't Buy Me Love" as the Beatles' next single (four days after its release in America, with advance orders there in excess of 2 million and a gold disc guaranteed on the strength of sales on the first day alone). Backed with "You Can't Do That", incorporating John's first solo outing on lead guitar, first-week sales of more than 1.2 million took it straight to No.1, for four consecutive weeks.

In Ian MacDonald's view, "Can't Buy Me Love" marked the end of the fully collaborative phase of Lennon/McCartney composition and he also notes it as "the first Beatles single to feature only one singer"[32]; i.e., Paul. From here onwards, a pronounced divergence of musical taste between John and Paul would become more apparent, each taking the lead responsibility for writing songs best matched to their respective styles and inclinations. Hence we find "You Can't Do That" dominated by John, with his customary lyrical themes of insecurity, blame and retribution:

> I've got something to say that might cause you pain.
> If I catch you talking to that boy again,
> I'm gonna let you down
> And leave you flat,
> Because I told you before, oh,
> You can't do that.[33]

Paul, on the other hand, was in the first full flush of romantic commitment to Jane Asher, with whose family he had been living (in the attic of their London home at 57, Wimpole Street) since November 1963.[34] Wearing his heart on his sleeve, his own newest compositions such as "And I Love Her" and "Things We Said Today" were patently dedicated to her in all but name.

There were other early signs of fragmentation at this time, with the publication on 23rd March of John's collection of whimsical fragments, *In His Own Write*, about which he was interviewed that evening by Kenneth Allsop, on the BBC's popular magazine programme *Tonight*. Of the book, he said himself disparagingly: "It's about nothing. If you like it, you like it; if you don't, you don't. That's all there is to it. There's nothing deep in it, it's just meant to be funny."[35] It became a best-seller, of course, and led later in the year (in November) to an invitation from Peter Cook and Dudley Moore to participate in the filming of the first episode of their new comedy series for the BBC, *Not Only … But Also*. However, when honoured as principal guest at a literary lunch, organised by the famous London booksellers Foyles at the Dorchester Hotel, John, for all his pride at his achievement, found himself overcome by stage-fright and "couldn't think of anything to say – I was scared stiff, that's why I didn't."[36]

Although an intense few days at Abbey Road immediately after the Beatles' return from America had ensured the recording of the majority of the songs for their film, the title *A Hard Day's Night* reputedly did not emerge until mid-March; attributable to a chance remark made by Ringo about the pressure of work they found themselves under. The title song was therefore the last of the set of seven to be written and not recorded until 16th April but this still left the second side of the prospective LP to be completed. This was finally accomplished in an intensive three days of recording from 1st to 3rd June, in the course of which they also laid down (after an interval of two months) two outstanding tracks for an unrelated EP.

On 19th June, this EP, *Long Tall Sally*, became their next UK release after "Can't Buy Me Love". In style and content, it was a blast, a hard-rocking throwback to much earlier days in the clubs of Liverpool, or even Hamburg, given extra emphasis on the cover of its sleeve by Robert Freeman's cool, cropped image of the Beatles standing in line in reefer jackets (with George in a leather coat), silhouetted against a bare white ground.[37] The title track was Paul's outstanding reinterpretation of Little Richard's classic – "a wild, hoarse, screaming thing"[38] – on Side 2 John sang "Slow Down" by Larry Williams and Ringo pitched in with his version of Carl Perkins's "Matchbox".[39] The only original composition of the four was the remaining track on Side 1, "I Call Your Name" (a song already donated to Billy J. Kramer and the Dakotas in August 1963, as the B-side to "Bad To Me").

Derek Taylor's exhortation to buyers in his sleevenotes was: "Dip it in gold and give it to your grandchildren. Or just simply wear it out."[40] He omitted, however, to mention the strongest selling point of all, which was that this was their first – and, until 1967, only – EP of newly released material and thus represented particular value for money; every other Beatles' EP being a retrospective compilation of either LP tracks or hit singles. Given the songs' relative lack of airplay in this format, their appeal to fans like me lay in their representing, in common with the B-sides and the majority of LP tracks, an essentially private, otherwise unheard performance straight to the individual listener. Punchy, even decidedly rough in places, running entirely counter to the grain of contemporary pop as now dictated by the Beatles themselves, *Long Tall Sally* nevertheless enjoyed six weeks in the Top 30, entering at No.13 in the week ending 4th July and peaking at No.11.

Good as it was, nevertheless it offered only the briefest of stopgaps before the simultaneous release, on Friday 10th July, of the single "A Hard Day's Night" (b/w "Things We Said Today") and the complete LP. If you discounted the four tracks already released as A- and B-sides, the LP *A Hard Day's Night* only offered you nine new songs, yet it still retained the distinction of being "the first-ever album release to be made up entirely of self-composed and self-performed Beatle compositions"[41] (an achievement they would not emulate again until the end of 1965, with *Rubber Soul*). Of the thirteen tracks in total, although John and Paul shared the double-tracked vocal of the title song, otherwise John was predominant as lead vocalist on eight of them (most plaintively in the minor-key ballad "If I Fell" and the concluding track on Side 2, "I'll Be Back"), while Paul led on just three ("And I Love Her", "Can't Buy Me Love" and "Things We Said Today"). George sang "I'm Happy Just To Dance With You" but on this third LP there was to be no solo spot for Ringo.

Just as *With The Beatles* before it, the front cover of the LP sleeve was a work of art in its own right, again incorporating a series of striking black-and-white head-and-shoulder portraits by Robert Freeman but this time set out in four rows of five pictures per Beatle, parodying the Polyfoto set of multiple miniature square images popularised by child photographers in the Fifties; with the borders between and around each picture delineated by a latticework of contrastingly bold inky blue. It was inescapably eye-catching, another stylish addition to the otherwise humdrum record racks and shop windows of retailers across the country.

Both record releases had been timed to coincide with the two premieres the film enjoyed in the week beginning Monday, 6th July. On that day, the Royal gala premiere was held at the London Pavilion, near Piccadilly Circus, attended by Princess Margaret and Lord Snowdon; but for the Beatles, it was the second, northern premiere on 10th July back in Liverpool that they regarded as the far more testing occasion, where – as John admitted – they were far less sure of their welcome:

> We had all been keyed up for days, wondering what reception we
> would get. We never expected so many people would turn out. We
> thought there would only be a few people standing on the odd
> street corner. We heard we were finished in Liverpool, you see.[42]

To Paul's relief, however, their anxieties proved to be unfounded, although the obvious warmth of feeling extended towards them still lent an unfamiliar air of novelty to their homecoming:

> We landed at the airport and found there were crowds everywhere,
> like a royal do. It was incredible, because people were lining the
> streets that we'd known as children, that we'd taken the bus down,
> or walked down. We'd been to the cinema with girls down these
> streets. And here we were now with thousands of people – for us.
> There was a lot of, 'Hello, how are you? All right?' It was strange
> because they were our own people, but it was *brilliant*.[43]

What makes Paul's heartfelt response all the more remarkable is that it came hard on the heels of a 27-day 'world' tour that had occupied the Beatles for the whole of June[44] (taking them to Denmark, Holland, Hong Kong,

Australia and New Zealand); in the course of which they had been greeted – in Adelaide – by over 300,000 people, "the biggest crowd ever assembled to see the Beatles at any time in their careers".[45]

Despite their monumental record sales nationally and internationally, the Beatles had all but starved the British public of live performances in the first half of 1964; with the notable exception of their appearance at the *NME*'s Poll-Winners' Concert, on 26th April. (After being added to the bill as a post-voting special attraction the previous year, this time they were there as of right, with awards for Best Vocal Group, Best Vocal Group (UK) and Best Single of 1963 for "She Loves You".) On 29th April, they had flown to Scotland for two nights of concerts, playing first in Edinburgh – specifically in response to a petition from more than 10,000 fans – before transferring the next day to Glasgow. For most of May, however, they had sought seclusion for themselves in their own respective private holidays abroad; John and Cynthia in Tahiti with George and Pattie Boyd, Paul and Jane Asher in the Virgin Islands with Ringo and Maureen Cox. At a time when world travel remained unfamiliar and inaccessible to most British holidaymakers, these destinations were decidedly exotic, serving to underline the Beatles' new-found status as the first truly international rock celebrities.

A short season of five Sunday concerts in English seaside resorts began in Brighton on 12th July, followed by ones in Blackpool, Bournemouth and Scarborough before a concluding return to Blackpool on 16th August (an all too welcome sequence of performances to home audiences but interrupted nevertheless by a two-day flying visit to Sweden at the end of July for four concerts staged at an ice-hockey arena in Stockholm). With these commitments all but completed, they were required to set aside 11th and 14th August for two days of recording at Abbey Road (in preparation for their fourth LP, to be released for Christmas) before departing again, on 18th August, for a major tour of America. Marvelling at the logistical challenge of managing their punishing itinerary, the *Daily Mail* heralded it as the "most arduous, intensive and improbable adventure this side of science fiction".[46]

Over a month later, by the tour's end on 20th September the Beatles had given "32 shows at 26 concerts in 24 cities in 34 days"[47], covering 18 US States (not to mention three diversions along the way to Vancouver, Toronto and Montreal in Canada); and on their return to Heathrow the next day, all told the trip was calculated to have entailed them spending "over 63 hours travelling 22,621 miles … (22,441 in the air, 180 on the road)".[48]

Wherever they went, they encountered unprecedented levels of mass hysteria but this time the adulation acquired an edge of menace. From the outset, George admitted to feeling "all the time, constantly … frightened by things"[49] and was highly sensitive to the seeming generality of political unrest throughout North America. But as lunatics issued direct death threats to group members, genuine concern arose for their individual safety, meaning, for example, that Brian Epstein and George Martin, who were accompanying them, began to make their own apprehensive assessments of possible angles of sniper fire from in and around each new venue visited. These, then, were the earliest indications of the Beatles' dreams of fame and fortune turning sour, as the act of live performance itself was rendered meaningless not only by barely articulated fear but also the rampant, undiscerning throngs of fans and goodness knows who else filling one vast arena after another. At this juncture, while John remained equivocal in his response to the mayhem, for George, however, wearied by a combination of exhaustion and frustration, the constant clamour induced profound disenchantment with being a Beatle: "The only place we ever got any peace was when we got in the suite and locked ourselves in the bathroom. The bathroom was about the only place you could have any peace."[50]

It had been hoped to make a live recording of the show when they played the Hollywood Bowl on 23rd August but, as George Martin explained, the primitive nature of the recording equipment then at his disposal – on loan from Capitol Records – was completely inadequate to the task:

> Frankly, I was not in favour of recording their performance. I knew the quality of recording could not equal what we could do in the studio, but we thought we would try anyhow. Technically, the results were disappointing; the conditions for the engineers were arduous in the extreme. The chaos, I might almost say panic, that reigned at these concerts was unbelievable unless you were there. Only three-track recording was possible; the Beatles had no 'fold back' speakers, so they could not hear what they were singing, and the eternal shriek from 17,000 healthy, young lungs made even a jet plane inaudible.[51]

(Another attempt would be made when the Beatles revisited the venue a year later but neither recording became commercially available until 1977, when Martin and sound engineer Geoff Emerick were commissioned to produce a remastered edit. Released that May as *The Beatles At The Hollywood Bowl*, the overall sound quality was still appalling but, following the group's demise, the tracks had since gained considerable nostalgic value as the only official live concert recordings of the Beatles and the LP went to No.1 in the album charts, going gold in the process.)

Five days on from Hollywood, with concerts to play on two consecutive nights at the Forest Hills Tennis Stadium, the Beatles had touched down in New York; and it was here, during their temporary respite at the Delmonico Hotel, that they and Brian Epstein were famously – or should that be infamously? –visited on the evening of 28th August by Bob Dylan and at his instigation they smoked marijuana together. (Indeed, pop mythology has it that Dylan was the first to turn the Beatles on to pot, as apparently confirmed by Paul; yet this conflicts, for one, with George's recollections of an earlier episode back home in Southport. Be that as it may, Dylan was an openly avowed admirer of the Beatles, who had mistakenly assumed that they were already regular users after mishearing the line "I can't hide" from "I Want To Hold Your Hand" as "I get high".) Dylan also later attended the final concert of the tour on 20th September, when the Beatles revisited New York to play a charity fund-raiser at the Paramount Theatre; then (according to biographer Howard Sounes) remarking "with satisfaction that the show was the opposite of his concerts, where audiences listened to every word in silence, applauding at the end".[52]

After completing this American marathon, it may seem extraordinary that within another three weeks the Beatles would be on the road again; kicking off in Bradford on 9th October and this time racking up "54 shows at 27 concerts in 25 cities in 34 days"[53] on their only British tour of the year. Yet they still saw it as a matter of pride on their part to fulfil these commitments, irrespective of their new-found international status. (Contrastingly, long-suffering road manager Neil Aspinall attributed the group's work ethic less to altruism than to lack of guile.)

On 27th November, Parlophone released the third Beatles' single of the year; "I Feel Fine" (b/w "She's A Woman"). Notable for the distortion of John's opening guitar chords by feedback (originally unintentional but consciously retained in subsequent takes), as with its two predecessors it went straight into the Top 30 at No.1. It was followed a week later by the release of their fourth LP, *Beatles For Sale*, which, under the constraints of time on both songwriting and recording, finally emerged as a mixture of their own compositions and old favourites from their stage act.

For me, irrespective of its musical content, *Beatles For Sale* was aesthetically a handsome Christmas gift in its own right. In its overall design, it was the first pop LP to bear witness to what today we would recognise as corporate rebranding; and, packaged in an innovative gatefold sleeve (lying on the table beside me as I write these paragraphs), it more than amply testifies to the superior pictorial quality of a 12" album cover over the later miniaturised inadequacies and atrocities of tape cassette inlays or CD inserts.

On the front cover, squeezed into the top left-hand corner the Parlophone logo of the pound sign is shown to the left of a new EMI logo, of a globe compressed into an ellipse, carrying beneath it the slogan "The greatest recording organisation in the world"; and to the immediate right of these two symbols, in modest capitals, appears the title BEATLES FOR SALE. The remaining 90% of the picture space is given over to a grainy colour portrait of the Beatles by Robert Freeman, seemingly suspended between both blurred foreground and background of hazy greens, pinks and russets in an indeterminate autumnal setting. The back cover bears no text at all, only another colour photograph of the group, this time shot from above against a backdrop of fallen leaves. (Freeman actually took both pictures near the Albert Memorial, in and around Kensington Gardens and Hyde Park.)

The inner contents of the gatefold are printed in black and white. The track listings for Sides 1 and 2 take up the top half of the inside left-hand page, bracketing Derek Taylor's sleevenotes (the last, as it happened, to be written for any Beatles' LP[54]), with the bottom half given over to a photo-graph of the Beatles on stage at the Washington Coliseum during their first US concert in February. The picture fully occupying the inside right-hand page is of the Beatles at Twickenham Film Studios, standing in front of a photo-montage of old movie stars.

Taylor exuberantly describes the fourteen tracks as "… eight new titles wrought by the incomparable John Lennon and Paul McCartney, and, mingling with the new, … six numbers culled from the rhythmic wealth of the past extraordinary decade …"[55] The oldies provide a showcase for each group member's individual talents, with an eclectic mix of barnstorming rock'n'roll (while John delivers a blast of Chuck Berry's "Rock And Roll Music", Paul gives Little Richard's "Kansas City/Hey-Hey-Hey" medley a gutsy revival), rockabilly (Ringo sings "Honey Don't" and George sings "Everybody's Trying To Be My Baby", both Carl Perkins numbers) and unashamed sentimentality (John reprising "Mr. Moonlight", a well-worn standard in the Liverpool clubs of the period, then later joining Paul in a duet for Buddy Holly's "Words Of Love"). Of their own compositions, the first three tracks on Side 1 form a melancholy trio on which John's is the prominent voice: "No Reply", "I'm A Loser" (a precursor of the introspection that later characterises "Help!") and "Baby's In Black". "I Don't Want To Spoil The Party" on Side 2 is in similar vein. The nearest Paul comes to a romantic ballad in this collection is "I'll Follow The Sun", a reworking of one of the earliest songs he had written in Hamburg in 1960 in an arrangement now bearing faint country-and-western overtones (in common with much of the rest of the album).

The opening track on Side 2, "Eight Days A Week", rings the changes with a fade-up intro and was subsequently released the following February as a single in America, giving them their seventh US No.1 and thus easily making it the most memorable song from the whole LP. (In Ian MacDon-ald's opinion, it captured the "soaring sunshine optimism of the mid-Sixties", together with "I Want To Hold Your Hand" and "Penny Lane".[56]) This leaves "Every Little Thing" and "What You're Doing", not just very closely related to each other in their sound and feel but both belated companion pieces musically to one of the minor tracks on *With The Beatles*, namely "Not A Second Time". (And yet, for those in the know, "Every Little Thing" still retains the power to surprise and delight; as, for example, when resurrected in 2004 by Jon Anderson and Yes as an encore at their 35th anniversary concert.)

Probably now the most under-rated and/or overlooked of all their LPs, the original impact of *Beatles For Sale* was phenomenal. Despite not being released until December and with the end of the year therefore only weeks away, its sales were such as to instantly render it the best-selling LP of 1964, spectacularly outstripping the cumulative sales of both *A Hard Day's Night* and *With The Beatles* (which ended up as Nos. 2 and 5 respectively of the year's Top Ten albums); and would eventually grow to secure it the No.6 slot in the Top Ten LPs of the entire decade, above other Beatles' albums more highly regarded in posterity.

The Beatles ended their year in London, in *Another Beatles' Christmas Show*, staged at the Hammersmith Odeon from 24th December onwards; their second – and last – seasonal show and not this time an extravaganza of NEMS talent. With Jimmy Savile as compère, Freddie and the Dreamers headed a list of otherwise minor support acts of the day that included the utterly dependable instrumental stalwarts Sounds Incorporated, an unknown 18-year-old girl singer from Salford called Elkie Brooks and an up-and-coming rhythm-and-blues group from Surrey, the Yardbirds.

The fact that the Yardbirds had incongruously found their way onto the Beatles' Christmas bill was indicative not just of the extent to which the scope of British pop music had expanded and developed in the preceding twelve months but, more particularly, of the growing regional divergence of taste in that same period from the previously frantic predominance of Merseybeat. In a breakthrough led by the Rolling Stones and principally, though not exclusively, rooted in a fanbase in London and the south-east, a variety of groups labouring within the broad church of rhythm-and-blues had at last achieved commercial success.

Hard on the heels of their appearance on the inaugural *Top Of The Pops*, with "I Wanna Be Your Man" still in the Top 10, in the week ending 18th January, the Rolling Stones had another entry to the Top 30 with their eponymous first E.P.[57] Manager Loog Oldham's sleevenotes in praise of the Stones, though typically overblown, concealed a nugget of truth:

> Their approach to their music is far closer to the brash, hard-driving Chicago style rhythm and blues than the majority of the groups currently riding the beat wagon, and it is probably this refusal to compromise their music to match the 'current sound' that has gained them their legions of fans. Their performances have an honesty and power about them that make those of their contemporaries look insipid.[58]

Although all his commercial instincts were against continuing to give them their head in the direction of the blues, Loog Oldham was forced to equivocate in the face of the reality of the EP outselling the group's first two singles. As he put it himself: "For a second time, the collision between my pop opportunism and the Stones' R'n'B purity had ended amicably in a hit."[59]

Recording of their next single on 10th January was a calculated inter-ruption to yet another national tour (this time with the Ronettes), which had started on 6th January and from which every night they were required to travel back to the Regent Sound studios in London. Now desperate to record "an out-and-out smash", Loog Oldham had stumbled across the next hit by accident, chancing one day upon Keith:

> … fag in mouth, guitar on knee, singing bits of Buddy Holly's "Not Fade Away". He was injecting an acoustic Bo Diddley riff into one of our favourite songs. I heard our next record. I could actually hear the record in the room. The way he played it – you could hear the whole record. It was less pop and more rock. It was a magical moment for me.[60]

Initially the recording session was an ill-tempered affair, the exhaustion of touring fuelling a fractious atmosphere in the studio that Loog Oldham finally dispelled by inviting Gene Pitney and Phil Spector to sit in. With the connivance of their unexpected guests and lubricated by measures of brandy doled out by Pitney, the mood suddenly lifted and the take was completed within twenty-five minutes. When originally recorded by Buddy Holly and the Crickets in 1957, it was put out as the B-side to "Oh, Boy!" and played for 2 minutes 20 seconds. In the hands of the Rolling Stones, however, it acquired a faster tempo, inventive bursts of harmonica from Brian Jones and lost half a minute in the process even with a fadeout. Where Holly's version vocally exuded the teasing charm of the boy next door, in this new interpretation Mick Jagger seized the opportunity from the start to load the lyrics with overtones of what would soon become his distinctive brand of cocksure chauvinism:

> I'm gonna tell you how it's gonna be:
> You're gonna give your love to me …[61]

Released on 21st February, "Not Fade Away" was the biggest hit yet for the Stones, with 12 weeks in the Top 30 and a highest position of No.3. (Its other claim to fame lies in being the first record to which a group mimed on *Top Of The Pops* in a purpose-made promotional film clip, shot on 22nd February on a freezing cold beach near Weymouth, before that evening's concert performance in Bournemouth. When it was televised, I particularly remember enjoying its punning highlight, an opening sequence of stones rolling down the cliff face onto the sand. This briefest of shorts in black and white was thus the unassuming forebear of the pop video.) Building on the momentum of its success, Loog Oldham proceeded with a press campaign deliberately aimed at portraying the Stones as "dangerous, dirty and degenerate"[62] and his proudest moment came in persuading music journalist Ray Coleman to write a feature article for *Melody Maker*, which appeared on 14th March under the (for the day) sensational headline "Would you let your sister go with a Rolling Stone?"[63]

In other equally brief intervals at Regent Studios, snatched from the touring commitments that stretched incessantly all the way from January through to May, Loog Oldham worked with the Stones on the twelve tracks that would make up their first LP. Chiefly a collection of American rhythm-and-blues standards, the most enduring have turned out to be their takes on "Route 66", "Carol" and the risqué "I Just Wanna Make Love To You"; although it did contain one Jagger/Richard original, "Tell Me". In a further push of their image, on the premise that by now everyone knew who they were, Loog Oldham determined, in the face of Decca's opposition, that for the finished article the sleeve would bear neither a title nor the group's name. And in the opening sentence of his sleeve notes, he boasted that: "The ROLLING STONES are more than just a group – they are a way of life."[64] Released on 17th April and propelled by advance orders of more than 100,000, it rapidly became the No.1 LP, as well as emulating the earlier achievement of the Beatles by entering the singles' Top 30 (reaching No.23 in a three-week run).

In June, while the Beatles had flown east for their 'world tour', the Rolling Stones had headed out west from London Airport – on BOAC Flight 505 – for a more modest tour of America, hurriedly arranged by Eric Easton, playing twelve concerts in eight venues from 5th to 20th June. Unfortunately for them, as they all too quickly discovered, Beatlemania was not yet a readily transferable commodity. Keith put their problem in a nutshell: "Back in England we had a number one album, but out in the middle of America nobody knew who we were."[65] Furthermore, their general appearance being deliberately far less groomed than the Beatles, they found themselves subject to ridicule and prejudice from ultra-conservative white Americans; including Dean Martin, who as host of the *Hollywood Palace* TV show, gave his special guests a gratuitously insulting introduction:

> [He] introduced us as something like "these long-haired wonders from England, the Rolling Stones ... They're backstage picking the fleas off each other." A lot of sarcasm and eyeball rolling. Then he said, "Don't leave me alone with *this*," gesturing in our direction.[66]

Immersing themselves in the vibrant culture of US music, however, just as Dusty Springfield and the Beatles had before them, they were in Wonderland, delighting in the diversity available at the touch of a button from the plethora of radio stations. The undisputed highlight of the tour was the two days they spent on what was for them the "hallowed ground"[67] of Chess Records at 2120, South Michigan Avenue, Chicago; conceived by Loog Oldham as a necessary diversion from the dismal reality of their concert engagements and fixed at short notice through intercession on their behalf by Phil Spector. Here, on 10th and 11th June, in the studios that had nurtured the likes of Howlin' Wolf, Muddy Waters, Chuck Berry and Bo Diddley, they recorded fourteen new tracks. These included their next UK single, "It's All Over Now", and the five tracks that went to make up their *Five By Five* EP.

For all his deeply-held reservations about the wisdom in the longer term of the Stones' over-dependence on the blues as their main source of inspiration, Loog Oldham was generously philosophical in acknowledging that they were "to South Michigan Avenue born, and the session was a joy to record".[68] There can be no question that for Loog Oldham and the group these two days in June marked an epiphany; the change the experience wrought being immediately evident on their return to England, where "they were now rhythm kings, champions of stress and groove who knew what it was all about".[69]

Barely a fortnight after it had been recorded, Decca released "It's All Over Now" in the UK on 26th June, giving the Rolling Stones another massive hit. Composed by Bobby Womack and sister-in-law Shirley, the song had not even previously been in their repertoire but had been brought to their attention on their arrival in New York at the beginning of the month by the ubiquitous Murray the K, as performed on record there by the Valentinos (*aka* the Womack Brothers). In its thirteen weeks in the Top 30 – of which the first nine were in the Top 10 – it reached No.2, fended off the No.1 spot by the Beatles with "A Hard Day's Night"; despite the fact that on its release, the unsophisticated British music press were completely thrown by it, hack journalists bizarrely categorising the Stones' uncompromising arrangement of a song written by former gospel-singing black musicians as 'country-and-western'.

This was the song that not only audibly put a sneer into Mick Jagger's voice, together with a transatlantic drawl, but also visibly energised his physical performance as he writhed and gyrated to the beat laid down by his fellow group members. If Del Shannon had thought he was a hard man when he sang about loss and retribution, Jagger showed him up as a wimp. In the Stones' world, for which Mick was now the mouthpiece, relationships were cut and dried, standing or falling by the willingness of the woman to be compliant and submissive. The only tears he shed were bitter. One false move on her part and she was out – for good:

I used to wake up in the morning, get my breakfast in bed.
When I got worried, she would ease my aching head.
But now she's here and there, with every man in town,
Still trying to take me for that same old clown:

Because I used to love her, but it's all over now.
Because I used to love her, but it's all over now ...[70]

A month later, with sales of "It's All Over Now" exceeding half a million, 180,000 advance orders had already been placed for *Five By Five*. A week after its release on 14th August, this new EP jumped straight up into the Top 20 at No.13 and eventually reached No.7, thereby firmly setting the stamp on the group's new 'Chicago' sound. Following the precedent of their LP and completely against the grain for EPs of the day, the front cover bore no group name, overall title or song titles, only a striking colour photograph of the five Stones in line, in varying degrees of casual dress, against a totally blank sky-blue backdrop, with Bill and Mick on the left both standing with half-smoked cigarettes between their fingers. In further breaking the mould of convention by containing five tracks rather than the customary four, none of which had previously been released, it also offered record-buyers better value for money than its many competitors. The 'extra track' (included, according to Loog Oldham's sleevenotes, "by way of saying 'thank you' to you, their friends and fans") was an instrumental but by no means a make-weight. The second of two original compositions in the set (the first being "Empty Heart"), "2120 South Michigan Avenue" brings Side 1 to a cracking close, driving along at a furious pace to a tempo firmly set by Ian Stewart on organ and Stu also plays on "If You Need Me"; although nowhere is he credited as having been the sixth Stone at the party. Side 2 is given over to two classic Chuck Berry numbers: "Confessin' The Blues", followed by the definitive English take on "Around And Around". The whole package could not be faulted as yet another unapologetically assured piece of marketing on Loog Oldham's part.

Once back from America, the Stones had resumed touring in the UK with hardly a pause for breath, meaning that subsequent recording sessions had again to be accommodated somehow within their rigorous schedule of concerts. After flying through the night to land at London Airport at 7.30 a.m. on 22nd June, they had individually snatched the briefest of downtime before reconvening in Oxford to play two sets that same evening as top billing at Magdalen College's Commemoration Ball. Their next tour, occupying them for much of July and August, included gigs in Northern Ireland, the Channel Islands and even a one-off trip to Holland; as well as bringing them further notoriety in the form of a riot on 24th July at the Empress Ballroom, Blackpool, when Keith decided to take on a crowd of drunken abusive Glaswegians. The upshot was instant pandemonium, as the popular press gleefully reported the next day, with the Stones having to flee the stage in the face of rampaging youths who, before being brought under control by the police, smashed up their instruments and amplifiers.

Between that tour ending in Bournemouth on 30th August and the next one beginning in London a week later, on 2nd September they went back into Regent Studios to record their next single, still determined to push the boundaries of rendering the blues more commercial in Britain. Their unlikely choice of number, certainly in terms of pop potential, was "Little Red Rooster", written by Willie Dixon and recorded by Howlin' Wolf at the Chess studios in 1961; the seemingly innocuous first-person reflections of a lethargic cockerel yet heavily invested with double meaning, the highlight of their arrangement being Brian's languid slide guitar.

The session left Loog Oldham full of admiration, yet afterwards he procrastinated about the wisdom of proceeding with the record's release. When eventually he climbed down off the fence, he decided to back the Stones' hunch. Released on Friday, 13th November, the following week "Little Red Rooster" had gone straight into the charts at No.1; leaving Loog Oldham's latest business associate, Tony Calder, for one, completely taken aback:

> I'd just thought it was the greatest mistake ever – you couldn't
> dance to it, Decca hated it and Eric Easton thought Andrew was
> nuts. It *made* the Stones. That they were able to take a blues thing
> to no.1 took the game to a whole new level. Andrew was able to
> show the business the band's popularity and translate it into record
> success. I was staggered; I hated the record.[71]

Being uncomfortably close to Christmas, however, it only stayed at No.1 for the first two of its nine weeks in the Top 30 before being deposed by the Beatles' new seasonal offering, "I Feel Fine" (coincidentally – as already noted – also entering the Top 30 at No.1 and then commanding that position all through December into the New Year). Impressive as this *coup de main*, for all its brevity, may nevertheless have been, the hyperbole of Loog Oldham and Calder glosses over the inconvenient truth that the Stones were actually the *second* British group to strike lucky with a blues-based No.1 in 1964; the original honour having already fallen in July to the Animals with "House Of The Rising Sun".

All hailing from Tyneside, by the mid-Sixties the Animals had formulated their own distinctive north-eastern interpretation of rhythm and blues, although the group's roots lay in an enthusiasm for jazz shared by founder-members Eric Burdon and John Steel from the time of their first meeting in 1956, as fellow students at the Newcastle College of Art and Industrial Design. Working their way through a variety of short-lived jazz bands, such as the Pagan Jazzmen and the Kansas City Five, their random encounters with other local musicians finally coalesced in September 1963, in a five-man line-up then catchily known as The Alan Price Rhythm and Blues Combo:

Eric Burdon (vocals), Alan Price (keyboards), Hilton Valentine (lead guitar), Bryan 'Chas' Chandler (bass guitar) and John Steel (drums).

Playing in Newcastle clubs owned by local hustler Mike Jeffery, like the Club A'Gogo or the Downbeat, the Combo's very earliest performances together were random and unrehearsed, drawing on what common ground they could find between their disparate musical tastes to pull together a repertoire; an amalgam of jazz, rock'n'roll and rhythm and blues that turned out to be surprisingly popular. On 15th September, a week after coming together, the Combo bought session time at the Graphic Sound Studios in Newcastle, where they recorded a four-track EP, with the intention of touting it round promoters in London and the major record companies as a demo disc.[72] (In the interim, however, they recovered the costs of their initial outlay by selling some 500 copies to their local club followers.) Soon afterwards, they came to the attention of Graham Bond, when he brought his Organisation out on the road to Newcastle, and Bond enthused about them on his return to London. As a result, suddenly Mike Jeffery was being approached on their behalf to take them down south and seized the opportunity to formalise his position as the group's manager.

Jeffery rapidly negotiated with London club-owners Giorgio Gomelsky and Ronan O'Rahilly for the Combo to join the Yardbirds in taking over those slots at their venues which had newly been vacated by the Rolling Stones; but somewhere in the course of this process, unilaterally he determined that henceforth the group should be known as the Animals. (The origin of the name-change is disputed but perhaps most reliably attributed by John Steel to a suggestion made by Graham Bond.) With the exception of Alan Price, who at Jeffrey's whim had just lost his musical identity, the group were acquiescent and so it was now the Animals who travelled down to London in December to fulfil their new commitments.

Well received in the capital over a ten-night stint despite the prevalence of what was to them the unfamiliar Mod culture, the Animals ended the year back on home turf at the Club A'Gogo, performing on 30th December with Sonny Boy Williamson (in a session astutely recorded by Giorgio Gomelsky for his own future disposal). In January 1964, however, they took the decision to relocate permanently to London, in pursuit of a recording contract; quickly followed by signings with both concert promoter Don Arden and independent record producer Mickie Most. With an initial offer from Arden of a concert tour with Chuck Berry in the bag, it was – according to John Steel – on 12th February when Most started working with them at the De Lane Lea Studios; the outcome being their first single, "Baby Let Me Take You Home". Suggested by Most himself (as his part of a deal in which he would choose the singles but allow the group leeway in the choice of LP tracks), this was a rearrangement of a traditional song recorded by a variety of black American artists but probably best known to the Animals under the title "Baby Let Me Follow You Down", as recorded by Bob Dylan on his eponymous first LP. Most then secured a contract for them with EMI's Columbia label, on which the single was released on 27th March. Promoted by pre-release appearances on *Top Of The Pops* and *Ready Steady Go!*, it afforded them a respectable five-week debut in the Top 30, reaching its highest position of No.15 at the beginning of May, a week before they went on the road with Chuck Berry.

Kicking off on 9th May, the tour with Berry (which also included Carl Perkins and an as yet unknown new group from Surrey, the Nashville Teens) exposed the Animals to their largest live audiences yet. For their part, they opted to include in their set their own arrangement of another number from the *Bob Dylan* LP, an electric version of the traditional American ballad "House Of The Rising Sun", taken to another level entirely by the striking guitar work of Hilton Valentine and the Vox Continental organ solo of Alan Price. Whilst the "House" of the title was in Dylan's version one of ill repute in New Orleans and the song the lament of a world-weary whore, Eric Burdon reworked it to become the tale of a "poor boy" degraded and criminalised by frequenting a notorious gambling den:

> There is a house in New Orleans
> They call the Rising Sun,
> And it's been the ruin of many a poor boy
> And God I know I'm one.[73]

In their hands it went down a storm.

So successful a piece was it for them on stage that they immediately saw its potential as their next single but Mickie Most was not so easily persuaded; having already lined up the Ray Charles song "Talkin' 'Bout You" as the new A-side, in anticipation of its possible consideration as the new theme tune for *Ready Steady Go!*[74] In an early morning session before dawn at De Lane Lea on 18th May, to which the Animals had travelled from Liverpool in a 'break' snatched en route to the next tour date in Southampton, they prevailed upon Most to let them record it, albeit reluctantly on his part as no more than a possible B-side. John Steel noted Most's reaction when he listened to the playback after just one take:

> He played it back and said, "Yep, that'll do." One take. The whole bloody process took about ten minutes. He played it back and that was the moment when he realised it was a single. That was the first time he accepted what we were saying. *That's* when he said, "How long is it?" And Mickie said, "Oh what the fuck, we'll still go with it, you can't take anything out of that." That was a tremendous decision.[75]

At four minutes twenty seven seconds, in length the track was effectively the equivalent of one whole side of a conventional EP; and in the
days when the two-minute single was the norm, the record company's prime
concern was that broadcasters might be resistant to playing it with 'needle
time' still at a premium, rather than the alternative consideration of offering
fans significant value for money. Yet at Most's insistence, Columbia capitulated, releasing "House Of The Rising Sun" as the A-side (b/w "Talkin'
'Bout You") in mid-June. Selling strongly from the outset (a quarter of a
million in the first three days), it entered the Top 30 in the week ending 27th
June at No.10, then went straight up to No.1 for the next fortnight, only to
be pushed aside by the instantaneous success of the Beatles' "A Hard Day's
Night". With total sales of over five million, it subsequently also reached
No.1 in America (albeit in a crudely edited, much shorter version).

Unquestionably a true Sixties' masterpiece in its own right, "House
Of The Rising Sun" thus took the blues to the top of the charts some
four months before "Little Red Rooster" made its appearance; proving in
the process that the attention and imagination of young people could be
captured by a longer than average single if its content and production were
sufficiently dynamic. Its longest lasting legacy, however, is reputedly to have
inspired Dylan to take a new musical direction out of the folk mould, which
shortly would bemuse and incense the most blinkered of his followers. Eric
Burdon gleefully recounts the implausible tale:

> that Dylan and Joan Baez were driving across America in a fishtail
> convertible Cadillac, and somewhere in Kansas they heard the
> Animals on the radio. Bob yelled to Joan to stop the car. He got out
> and banged on the front fender, "Electric!" he yelled, "Electric!"[76]

Unlikely though it seems that Dylan's response would in reality be so extreme,
when the Animals met him in New York that September on their first American tour he confirmed it to them in person.

Sadly for the Animals, this, their greatest record, also turned out to be
the source of the bitterest rift between the five original group members.
Keen to maximise royalties from the total sale of records and sheet music as
well as airplay, Mike Jeffery knew it was vital to be able to credit the arrangement of a traditional song in some way to the group. Hence in their naivety
the Animals accepted without question his proposal that he would nominate
one person as arranger, to whom royalty payments would then be channelled
on behalf of the band for equitable redistribution between them all. This is
how "House Of The Rising Sun" came to be credited on release as "Trad.
– arr. Price". Given that there was already a history of mistrust between
Price on the one hand and Burdon and Steel on the other, when his past
failure to honour a commitment to the earlier Kansas City Five had led to

that group's demise, it is all the more extraordinary that this deal should have gone unchallenged. Unfortunately, when the payments eventually came through several months later, Alan Price retained them for himself, denying his four colleagues any reward for their collaborative endeavour and spurring his departure from the group in April 1965.

Whilst acrimony and recriminations lay in the future, the Animals capitalised on the phenomenal success of "House Of The Rising Sun" by following the Beatles and the Rolling Stones to America. As noted above, their first visit at the beginning of September took them to New York, where they were not only to meet Bob Dylan but also fulfil a ten-day concert booking at the Paramount Theatre, now with Chuck Berry and Little Richard as supporting acts to them: in Eric Burdon's words, nothing less than "a carnival of madness".[77] Back again at the end of the month for a wider US tour, on 18th October they were given star billing on *The Ed Sullivan Show*, an experience they found less than enjoyable as they went through endless rehearsals in fear and trepidation of its intimidating host, Eric later likening Sullivan to Richard Nixon as: "an old man with uplifted shoulders, a long, shallow jaw, dark eyes and gangly arms that would flap around like a traffic cop's. We soon found it was best to keep out of his way."[78]

They had all agreed they should aim for an original composition as their third A-side. The result was "I'm Crying", with music by Price and lyrics by Burdon; in an arrangement which, taken at a gallop compared to "House Of The Rising Sun", highlighted the hard edge of Valentine's lead guitar. Released in early September, it was their last UK single of the year, making it to No.6 in the week ending 10th October. Insisting on playing it as an additional number on *The Ed Sullivan Show*, however, as grudgingly agreed to by Sullivan after his initial refusal to allow it at all, turned out to be a disaster for them. To the Animals' disbelief, the taping of its performance was interrupted by the shouts of an anti-war protester in the audience and therefore excised from the final broadcast in its entirety by CBS-TV.

In addition to the Animals and the Stones, the influence of rhythm and blues on the charts of 1964 was further extended by the admittedly lesser successes of early singles by groups such as the Yardbirds ("I Wish You Would"), the Downliners Sect ("Baby What's Wrong") and the Pretty Things ("Don't Bring Me Down"), all of which crept into the lower reaches of the Top 30 between May and October. While all three outfits benefited from hard-core followings sustained through residencies at London venues like the Marquee, Studio 51 and Eel Pie Island, it was the Yardbirds who were destined to achieve the most commercially in the short- to mid-term until the group finally disintegrated in 1968, leaving their rivals behind on the wilder shores of R&B. Although the Sect, originating from Twickenham and signed to EMI's Columbia label, and the Pretty Things, with a Fontana recording contract and hailing from Sidcup, had much in common musically, it was the latter who courted the greater publicity by turning an appearance even more uncouth than that of the Rolling Stones into their unique selling point – to the horror of mid-Sixties' parents; the group, of whom ex-Blue Boy Dick Taylor was a founder member, boasting in lead singer Phil May a more extreme combination of long hair, stage aggression and downright unattractiveness than even Mick Jagger or Keith Richards could ever hope to emulate.

The Surrey-based Yardbirds, however, had had the good fortune to be courted and nurtured by Giorgio Gomelsky as replacements for the Rolling Stones at the Crawdaddy, sealing the deal with him contractually as their manager in October 1963. Formed only in June of that year through the consolidation of two embryonic groups, the Metropolitan Blues Quartet[79] and the Country Gentlemen, its original five-man line-up had been: Keith Relf (vocals & harmonica), Anthony 'Top' Topham (lead guitar), Chris Dreja (rhythm guitar), Paul Samwell-Smith (bass guitar) and Jim McCarty (drums). Only being sixteen, Topham very soon succumbed to parental pressure to leave the Yardbirds for the sake of furthering his education; to be replaced, at Relf's suggestion, on lead guitar by a promising eighteen-year-old newcomer, Eric Clapton (formerly of the Roosters, and latterly Casey and the Engineers).

Like so many of his contemporaries, Clapton prided himself on being a pure blues aficionado, hence: "What I immediately liked about the Yardbirds was that our entire reason for existence was to honour the tradition of the blues."[80] Yet Giorgio Gomelsky's burning ambition, after his loss of the Rolling Stones to Andrew Loog Oldham, was to secure the Yardbirds a recording contract; which, after what proved to be an abortive approach to Decca in December, he achieved in early 1964 with a signing to EMI Columbia. The company released their cover of Billy Boy Arnold's "I Wish You Would" on 1st May, forcing Clapton, on his own admission, in an uncomfortable direction, because "it wasn't just me, and as exciting as it was to be actually making a record, when we listened back and compared it to the stuff we were supposedly modelling ourselves on, it sounded pretty lame. We just sounded young and white …"[81] Indeed, even though it would be through his membership of the Yardbirds that Clapton would first establish his reputation as a virtuoso guitarist and earn the nickname 'Slowhand', artistic and social differences between him and nominal group leader Paul Samwell-Smith in particular meant that he remained ill at ease in his role.

Still, if there was any recording with the group of which Clapton unreservedly approved, it must surely have been the seminal LP *Five Live Yardbirds*, which captured them in performance on 13th March 1964 at the reopening of the Marquee Club in its new Soho premises on Wardour Street. At the time – and for some time yet to come – while most new groups blithely regarded their live sets as representing their best performances, in general that vital spark eluded capture by the poor quality of sound recording equipment robust enough for use in the field rather than in the studio; a fear, as already noted above, legitimately expressed on the Beatles' behalf by George Martin. (One of the worst examples in due course would be the Stones' *Got Live If You Want It!* EP, cynically promoted by Loog Oldham despite his open acknowledgement of its inferiority as a product.) In his original sleevenotes, Giorgio Gomelsky captures the endearing amateurism of the lead-up to the gig:

> All through the afternoon 'people' were wandering about the red and white stripes of the empty MARQUEE CLUB muttering singularly private things to themselves. From a detached distance it all looked like some abstract ballet about people supposed to be at work but in fact doing all they can to avoid it … All is vague, with just that little touch of nervous tension so that everybody knows that *something* is supposed to happen sooner or later.[82]

What came out at the other end, edited down to around forty minutes on the final LP, was a rough and ready encapsulation of the early Yardbirds at their most excitable. It's a dirty, scruffy recording of a typical club set of R&B standards, the sound is poorly balanced and often distorted (particularly the vocals), yet for all its technical shortcomings it remains highly listenable, still managing to exude enthusiasm and atmosphere aplenty. As Chris Dreja admitted afterwards:

> Apart from doing a sound check in the afternoon there was no pandering to the fact that we were recording. It was a huge laugh. None of us took it seriously except Bill Relf [Keith's father], standing on the stage with a contraption like a fishing rod, with a mike on the end for recording the audience noise.[83]

Nevertheless, he went on to say: "The audience loved it. We played twice as loud and fast as normal. It was a great night."[84]

And there would have been more to it, had Paul Samwell-Smith not been so eager to play the completed tape back at the end that he fast-forwarded it by mistake and thereby accidentally erased part of the concert, including a live take of "I Wish You Would" – to which the rest of the group generously responded by "falling about laughing".[85] The highlight of what remains is Track 3 of Side 1, Clapton's favourite, "Smokestack Lightnin'", when they really get into their stride (Clapton trading guitar with Relf's harmonica) and hold it together for more than five and a half minutes.

The LP stayed in the can for months, finally seeing its release on 31st December, by which time the Yardbirds were in their Christmas run in support of the Beatles, and was put out essentially as a stopgap pending suitable material for a new, third single. ("Good Morning Little Schoolgirl", another song favoured by Clapton and included in their March set at the Marquee, had been released on 30th October as the belated follow-up to "I Wish You Would" but met with no chart success.) As we shall see in the next chapter, the eventual choice of song for single no.3 would prove to be both a step too far for Clapton and herald a sea-change in the Yardbirds' fortunes.

From north of the Thames – Muswell Hill, to be precise – emerged in August another new group grounded in an eclectic mix of jazz, blues, swing and rock'n'roll, who would contribute their own rough spontaneity to the Top 30 with a startlingly original composition, the sound of which had been enhanced by the lead guitarist's wilfully deliberate damage to his amplifier:

> The crowning glory of my simple yet effective experiment was to slash the speaker cone of the Elpico [10-watt amplifier] with a razor blade so that the material, although now shredded, still remained intact with the outer side of the cone. As it vibrated it produced a distorted and jagged roar. In fact, the original set-up was so crude that the main amp's hum was almost as loud as the sound I had created. A sound was born, but I didn't know it at the time.[86]

The vandal in question, Dave Davies, finally realised his ambition to inflict that raw guitar sound publicly on the teenagers of 1964, first on tour and then on record, with a group of which he had been a founder-member and had struggled through various changes of name and line-up to now end up as the Kinks. He laid it down as the prominent, distinguishing feature of a composition by his older brother Ray, "You Really Got Me", in a five-chord riff reverberating throughout the song as well as in a manic solo guitar-break. Ray thought of it as a love song, about total possession:

> Girl, you really got me going,
> You got me so I don't know what I'm doing.
> Yeah, you really got me now,
> You got me so I can't sleep at night.[87]

But it was like no other love song that had shouldered its way into the charts to date. Even more extraordinarily, the inspired version that actually only made it to No.1 for one week – in the week ending 12th September – was the one in Ray's head, re-recorded in defiance of the original take overseen by a professional record producer.

The previous chapter provided an early fleeting glimpse of Ray, as an occasional member of the Dave Hunt Rhythm and Blues Band (who lost their slot at the Station Hotel, Richmond to the Rolling Stones); and in his pseudo-autobiography, X-Ray, Ray records his admiration for the early Stones' hunger to forge their own musical identity, in contrast to Hunt's dismissal of their efforts: "Dave Hunt had described the Stones as a skiffle group ... [whereas] I felt that the Stones were actually turning the Chuck Berry-Muddy Waters standards they were playing into their own music."[88] As well as playing with Hunt, Ray had also been playing for some time in a group with brother Dave, together with school friends Pete Quaife and John Start. Originally billed as the Ray Davies Quartet, in spring 1963 they decided to call themselves the Ramrods, only to change again that September to the Boll-Weevils, when Micky Willett replaced John Start on drums. Through Willett's upward social connections, the Boll-Weevils found themselves hired by self-styled 'manager' Grenville Collins as backing group to would-be pop singer Robert Wace and thus moving on into the hitherto unfamiliar realms of "lucrative society dances" and "debutante balls"[89]; the incongruity of which was not lost on Ray.

Kitted out at Grenville's expense in "pink tab-collar shirts and dark blue corduroy trousers from John Steven"[90], the Boll-Weevils themselves joined the growing ranks of the "Carnabetian army", whose antics in pursuit of fashion in the boutiques of London Ray would later elect to satirise in song. Unfortunately, Ray's misgivings about upper-crust Robert Wace's popular appeal proved to be only too well-founded and his short-lived career as a singer came abruptly to a halt in early October. Memories are clouded as to when and where the penny finally dropped, but of all the surviving accounts Dave's is the most entertaining and lends greatest weight to the group's emergence in its own right:

> During one set at the Casanova Club in London, Robert came
> on stage and started to sing "Rave On". As we reached the first
> chorus, he accidentally smashed the mike into his mouth, removing
> both his top front teeth. He promptly left the stage and Ray took
> over singing. This was probably the first time Ray fronted as a
> singer. I remember that it felt so natural and so right. After the
> show Grenville told Robert that he thought Robert's singing was
> atrocious and that the band sounded a lot better without him
> and with Ray singing. It was Grenville's enthusiasm that gave Ray
> the confidence to sing. Robert was forced to accept the idea of
> managing and not performing.[91]

So it was that Wace and Collins took on the mantle of pop management together and set about the arduous task of marketing their new-found talent, who in November plumped for another name-change, now calling themselves the Ravens. By the end of the month, however, Micky Willett had decided that he could no longer work with the Wace/Collins partnership and left, to be replaced as drummer by "a northerner called Johnny Green".[92]

From these unpromising, faltering beginnings, as if transmuted through a strangely unforetold process of alchemy, by the end of January 1964 Dave and his fellow band-members were amazed to find that "we had managers, an agent, a publisher and a record contract".[93] The earliest demos cut by the Ravens had been touted round the record companies without success: Dave specifically identifies Decca and Philips as being amongst those who turned them down. Through a chapter of happy accidents, the offer of a recording contract was nevertheless eventually forthcoming from Pye, the critical mass having been toppled in the Ravens' favour by the active interest shown in their potential by experienced manager Larry Page and visiting American record producer Shel Talmy. Prior to this deal being concluded, they had already entered into a song publishing agreement with Kassner Music, optimistically assuming that in due course Ray and/or Dave might show some promise as songwriters, and attracted the attention of booking agent Arthur Howes into the bargain. Self-evidently, all they lacked now was a record – and a permanent drummer, since 'Johnny Green' had taken his leave of them when the other three had committed to turning professional.

Howes was reputedly responsible for nominating the song for their first single, a cover of Little Richard's "Long Tall Sally", enthusing over its performance by the Beatles at their opening concert at the Paris Olympia yet seemingly oblivious to the fact that for a group with no established credentials in rock'n'roll it would have been better disregarded as a well-intentioned suggestion coming out of left-field. For its recording as one of a number of tracks at Pye's Marble Arch studios on 20th January, session drummer Bobby Graham played with them; but within a week, satisfactory auditions had resulted in the permanent addition to the group of Mick Avory on drums, who thus unsuspectingly secured his place in what all too soon would grow into a dysfunctional quartet of malcontents. To set the seal on this welter of activity, a final name-change had also been implemented, turning the Ravens into the Kinks. While Dave attributes the inspiration for this to Howes, Ray more firmly gives the credit to Page, who had "concluded that, because of the kinky clothes we wore, and the fact that the new drummer looked a little like a police identikit version of a pervert, we might as well call ourselves the Kinks".[94]

Released on 7th February, even with the obligatory TV promotion on *Ready Steady Go!* that same evening, "Long Tall Sally" in the hands of the Kinks was not destined to be a hit: as seen earlier in this chapter, its time as a best-seller would eventually come with the Beatles' much more assured interpretation in the summer. So while they waited for that elusive break, they went on the road playing one-nighters, kicking off in Oxford on 1st February (on that occasion supporting the Downliners Sect) before taking in a variety of venues chiefly across the north-west (including a lunchtime session at the Cavern on 21st February, supporting Billy J. Kramer in Wigan on 2nd March and even playing on a bill headlined by Gene Vincent in Manchester on 22nd

March). From 29th March to 14th May, they cast their net more widely, since Howes had assigned them to an extended tour headed up by the Dave Clark Five and the Hollies; on which they embarked, in Ray's euphemistic words, "a little under-prepared and disorganised".[95] It was while they were on this tour, on 17th April, that Pye released their second unsuccessful single, "You Still Want Me"; one of Ray's early compositions, recorded in the same January session as "Long Tall Sally".

As the tour continued, Howes became increasingly unsettled by reports of the Kinks' lack of stagecraft and despatched a man called Hal Carter to inject some life into their act, who on his arrival was at great pains to berate them for their unprofessionalism. Formerly an adviser to Billy Fury, his suggested blocking-in of choreographed stage moves for the group fell largely on deaf ears, with Dave the least tolerant of all towards him, writing him off as being a "sweet, well-meaning bloke but his ideas were rather passé".[96] In the end, their salvation lay in Graham Nash of the Hollies, who told Carter forthrightly to stop trying to turn a blues group into a cabaret act. Any smartening-up of the Kinks was therefore eventually restricted to sartorial matters, with a decision to adopt "new stage clothes … red hunting jackets [matched] with white frilly shirts … black riding trousers and Chelsea boots, and, lo and behold, we looked like us"[97]; a move of which, to Ray's pleasure, both Nash and subsequent audiences instantly approved.

In the course of the tour, the Kinks intermittently featured "You Really Got Me" in their set, finding it well received. Ray had composed it on the piano at the family home in early March, with Dave taking the keynote riff and transposing it for guitar, but it was not until mid-June that Pye conceded an attempt to record it commercially as their third single. The outcome, to the extreme disappointment of the Davies brothers, was a version ruined by what they felt was Shel Talmy's over-production. At the risk of losing Pye's goodwill and patronage altogether, Ray pronounced himself totally opposed to the release of the record in its current state, lobbying Talmy and the managerial triumvirate of Wace, Collins and Page to ditch it. With the threat of legal action in the air, Larry Page contrived to tie the record company's hands on a technicality, by persuading the song's publishers Kassner to deny Pye a mechanical licence – without which they could not proceed to press or distribute any records of the song – and at last it was agreed that "You Really Got Me" should be re-recorded, albeit at the Kinks' own expense.

So it was that a second session was booked in mid-July, this time at the IBC Studios rather than Pye's own, at which Talmy (assisted here by recording engineer Glyn Johns) long-sufferingly indulged Ray in realising his vision. By the time it came for Ray to lay down his vocal track, he was transported by the sure and certain knowledge that success was within his grasp second time around. Six weeks after its release on 4th August, "You Really

Got Me" was No.1 and Ray's truculent stance had been vindicated.

Seeking to capitalise urgently on their sudden fame, Pye set the Kinks to work throughout August and September in recording tracks for an LP, a task which they fitted around an ever-expanding list of live gigs and television appearances. Released on 2nd October under the plain title of *Kinks*, the fourteen tracks included "You Really Got Me" and five other compositions by Ray (one of which, "Revenge", was an instrumental); with the others being a medley of R&B standards and older blues and folk numbers, little more than the predictable bare bones of their stage repertoire to date.[98] Three weeks later, after completing a concert tour on which they joined the Yardbirds as supporting acts to Billy J.Kramer, their fourth single was issued, another new song by Ray, "All Day And All Of The Night", uncompromisingly extending the lyrical theme and Dave's thrashings on lead guitar exactly where "You Really Got Me" had left off:

> I'm not content to be with you in the daytime.
> Girl, I want to be with you all of the time.
> The only time I feel all right is by your side.
> Girl, I want to be with you all of the time,
> All day and all of the night,
> All day and all of the night,
> All day and all of the night.[99]

Recorded "simply and quickly" this time at Pye Studios in late September, Dave noted the occasion with pride as a turning point in their hitherto uphill struggle to gain due respect for the band's potential: "All of a sudden it seemed that engineers, musicians, etc. had become very interested in my distorted and raunchy little sound. The frowns of derision and sarcastic scowls had now turned to smiles of approval and looks of admiration."[100] Although it only reached No.3 (in late November), it still equalled the achievement of its predecessor by similarly holding a place in the Top 30 for a total of ten weeks and thus saw the Kinks comfortably into the New Year.

Out of all the blues-inspired groups emerging from the London club scene of the period and insinuating themselves into the pop mainstream of the mid-Sixties, arguably the most versatile instrumentalists were Manfred Mann. When the Manfreds made their debut in the Top 30 in January 1964 with "5-4-3-2-1" – a rocket of a record at under two minutes long, commissioned from them as the new theme tune for *Ready Steady Go!* to replace the Surfaris' "Wipe Out" – they were a newly reconfigured five-piece band: Manfred Mann (organ & vocals), Paul Jones (vocals & harmonica), Mike Vickers (guitar), Tom McGuinness (bass guitar) and Mike Hugg (drums).

This classic line-up, which went on to clock up three more hits by Christmas, represented a distillation of diverse talents, built around the core of the original Mann-Hugg Blues Combo, an ad-hoc assemblage of jobbing musicians (which had also included Graham Bond for a while) playing jazz for the entertainment of holidaymakers enjoying the 1962 summer season at Butlin's Clacton. (Mann – real name Lubowitz – who had opted for self-imposed exile from his native South Africa in 1961, was an accomplished pianist, in his dress and appearance the archetypal beatnik. Hugg, by contrast, was a virtuoso on the vibraphone.) Further recruitment that autumn saw the Combo expand into a more ambitious octet with a brass section, becoming the Mann-Hugg Blues Brothers yet still retaining pronounced jazz leanings; with Hugg now taking on the drums. Jones (introduced in Chapter 4 as Paul Pond, in the most temporary of partnerships with Brian Jones) had come on board as harmonica player and vocalist, while Vickers had been brought in to double up on saxophone and guitar.

A chance encounter outside EMI's London offices between the Brothers' manager Ken Pitt and his old acquaintance John Burgess, by now a record producer for the HMV label, led fortuitously to an audition and then a contract, in March 1963; with the proviso that the group must change its name, hence Manfred Mann (after the briefest of transition periods as Manfred Mann and the Manfreds). From May onwards, when they started recording, they had reduced to a quintet: Mann, Jones, Vickers and Hugg, together with Brothers' bass player Dave Richmond. Their first single – released in July – was an undeniably stylish, cool instrumental, a hip arrangement of a jazz waltz composed by Mann in which both the saxophone of Vickers and the harmonica of Jones were prominent, entitled "Why Should We Not"; but nonetheless utterly hopeless from a commercial point of view. This was followed in November by a second flop, "Cock-A-Hoop", although Jones's spirited performance of his own song, in which he included a whimsical reference to the Manfreds, offered greater promise of success in the future.

Come 1964, and formidably underpinned by the popularity of *Ready Steady Go!* with which, by definition, it immediately became associated, "5-4-3-2-1" went straight into the Top 30 the week after its release on 10th January and by mid-February had climbed to No.4. In a composition credited to Jones, Hugg and Mann, the nonsense lyric juxtaposed historical assumptions about the Charge of the Light Brigade and the Trojan Horse with the supposed mischief-making of the Manfreds, the whole driven along at breakneck speed by Jones's powerfully impressive harmonica-playing. In the interval between recording and release, however, the group had parted company with Dave Richmond, who had been "something of an incongruence for some time: older, balder, jazzier, and considerably less commercially-orientated than the rest of Manfred's Menn, he neither looked nor played like potential teen idol fodder".[101] His replacement was guitarist – though not at that point with any experience as a bass player – Tom McGuinness (a friend of Paul Jones and ex-colleague of Eric Clapton in both the Roosters and Casey and the Engineers), whose performing debut with the band actually came at the Ealing Club on 21st December 1963.

After the excitement engendered by "5-4-3-2-1", their fourth single, "Hubble Bubble (Toil And Trouble)" came as something of an anti-climax in April. The song, a group effort projecting the sentiments of the witches from *Macbeth* onto a troublesome modern miss ("I never knew a girl who was so hubbly-bubbly"[102]), had the shortest Top 30 run of all their 1964 hits (only 5 weeks) and could get no higher than No.11 at the beginning of May; although I do also remember its life being extended by a soft drinks company using it as the theme tune to the weekly *Hubbly Bubbly Show* on Radio Luxembourg. Henceforward, producer John Burgess, in spite of the steadily mounting evidence to the contrary from Lennon and McCartney, would hold "to the accepted wisdom of the day, 'Groups don't write their own material, leave that to professional composers'. So, after "Hubble Bubble", we looked elsewhere for inspiration …"[103]

According to Tom McGuinness, that alternative source was forthcoming from Paul Jones's personal record collection; taking the group down what rapidly turned out to be the very profitable route of recording cover versions for A-sides. (From here on in, their more esoteric exploration of jazz and blues, including their own compositions, would be reserved for B-sides, LP tracks and a particularly impressive set of original EP releases.) With their next single, "Do Wah Diddy Diddy", which came out in July, their fortunes changed dramatically and before they knew it they had a No.1 hit on their hands, as they displaced the Beatles' "A Hard Day's Night" in mid-August. A classic Brill Building blend of a love theme with a nonsensical hook from the pens of Jeff Barry and Ellie Greenwich, the song in its first incarnation by the Exciters in 1963 had struggled to get above the low 70s of the US Hot 100; whereas now the Manfreds breathed new life into it, eventually adding insult to injury by taking it to No.1 in America as well as in the UK. Following on in October, in a similar vein, came "Sha La La", their last single of the year. No more than a minor US hit a few months earlier for the Shirelles, nevertheless Manfred Mann succeeded in taking it not only to No.4 in Britain but also subsequently to No.12 in America. (Unusually for the time, however, they chose only to undertake one brief US tour, for three weeks in December, preferring in due course to seek wider recognition internationally.)

Inevitably, as the blossoming alternative genre of rhythm and blues came into its own, it threatened more and more the privileged position of Merseyside chart domination inherited from 1963; with, of course, the notable exception of the Beatles, now exalted as national treasures. Hence although the wider Liverpool brand remained relatively strong, at least for the time being, it was now increasingly subject to a more selective – and therefore potentially more fickle – market, meaning variable fortunes across the board for yesterday's favourites.

Of all those Mersey groups who were not the Beatles, in terms of their overall popularity it turned out to be the Searchers who fared the best throughout 1964, although at the same time they were also faced with and had to overcome some difficulties in interpersonal relationships. They were subject to new, experienced professional management, on the part of Tito Burns, who had now supplanted Les Ackerley; in the spring Pye renewed their contract for another twelve months; and in early April, they flew to New York to appear on *The Ed Sullivan Show*. As well as regular concert engagements at home, in the remainder of the year they completed two tours of America and one of New Zealand and Australia. Most importantly for them, however, the year kicked off with two consecutive No.1 hits, the first of which – "Needles And Pins" – remains today as being way and above the most memorable of all their recordings.

Composed by two of Phil Spector's regular musical associates in California, Jack Nitzsche and Sonny Bono, "Needles And Pins" is a study in the sheer anguish of failed love, in complete contrast to the previous bouncy optimism of either "Sweets For My Sweet" or "Sugar And Spice". Originally a minor US hit in 1963 for Jackie DeShannon, it came to the Searchers' attention through seeing it performed in Hamburg with an alternative male slant by fellow English musicians Cliff Bennett and the Rebel Rousers. Documenting the extreme discomfort of a chance encounter between estranged lovers, the "needles and pins" of the title are the physical manifestation of the protagonist's pain at his loss:

> I saw her today, I saw her face,
> It was the face I loved and I knew
> I had to run away and get down on my knees and pray
> That they'd go away.
> But still they begin,
> Needles and pins,
> Because of all my pride,
> The tears I gotta hide.[104]

On reflection, however, he takes bitter comfort (reminiscent of Del Shannon in "Hats Off To Larry") from the thought that she too may yet suffer at the hands of her new love:

> Hey, I thought I was smart, I wanted her,
> Didn't think I'd do, but now I see
> She's worse to him than me.
> Let her go ahead, take his love instead,

And one day she will see
Just how to say 'Please'
And get down on her knees.
Yeah, that's how it begins.
She'll feel those needles and pins …[105]

Strangely, it was the perfect song for the Searchers, who made it their own for all time with their combination of jangling guitars and high-register harmonies; and who, in so doing, would unknowingly complement the Beatles in their joint influence on the earliest work of the Byrds in America.[106]

It also turned out to be the catalyst for precipitating the departure from the group of bass guitarist Tony Jackson, who had hitherto been lead vocalist but was usurped on this occasion by Mike Pender; at the insistence of drummer Chris Curtis, who was convinced Jackson's voice was totally unsuited to the song. Curtis's judgement call was spot-on, the distinctiveness of Pender's delivery being enhanced by the artifice of adding emphasis to the end of every line; in particular, by elongating the final vowel sound '-ay' in words like 'pray' ('pra-yee-ay') and 'away' ('awa-yee-ay'), and by pronouncing 'pins' as 'pinz-er'. It was these flourishes that contrived to turn the record into a classic, giving the Searchers their second No.1 from their first three singles for Pye and a hold on the top of the charts for three consecutive weeks in February.

The B-side (on which Jackson did take the lead) was a catchy oddity called "Saturday Night Out".[107] This was the title song from an X-Certificate B-movie, a sleazy comedy about the night-time exploits of a group of seamen on shore leave in London, in which the Searchers appeared as themselves playing a gig in a backstreet pub. (Committed Searchers fanatics proudly point to the fact that when *Saturday Night Out* went on general release from 1st April, it predated the Beatles' film debut in *A Hard Day's Night* by some three months.)

The harmonies of Pender and Curtis prominently remained in place as the distinguishing feature of the next single, "Don't Throw Your Love Away" (which Curtis had ferreted out from the B-side of an obscure US 45 by the even obscurer Orlons). In the week ending 9th May – but this time round, only for that week, as well as, so it transpired, for the last time ever – it took them back again to No.1. April, the month of its release, had been busy in other ways too; for not only had it included their US TV performance for Ed Sullivan, but it had also seen the start of informal soundings being taken by Curtis to find a replacement for Jackson:

It was with Tony Jackson that the other three were not getting on
at all well and it had come to an impasse. They were arguing all
the time. He wasn't performing well. He was getting drunk before
shows and not tuning up properly, they claimed … And there was

a clash of personalities, not just with Chris with whom he had never bonded but with John and Mike too. It had even come to fisticuffs.[108]

The object of his interest was Frank Allen, then bass guitarist with Cliff Bennett and the Rebel Rousers and a long-standing acquaintance from the time together shared by both groups in Hamburg. At first, although flattered, Allen was taken aback and optimistically professed his continuing loyalty to the Rebel Rousers, who had just been signed up by Brian Epstein. When he later confided in fellow band member Moss Groves, however, Groves pulled him up short with a reality check and urged him to take the offer. A telephone call to Curtis then secured the deal in principle, pending his necessary further discussions with Pender and McNally and the final playing out of the long game in respect of Jackson. In the end, in the wake of growing rumours about discontent within the Searchers, it fell to manager Tito Burns to propose a face-saving opt-out, namely to retain and promote Jackson as a solo artist with his own backing group.

Notwithstanding this outstanding show of diplomacy, Tony Jackson bitterly resented what he saw as his betrayal by Chris Curtis and his severance from the group was acrimonious. The last single on which he could be heard playing with the Searchers was their June release of "Some Day We're Gonna Love Again", which eventually reached No.11. His last public appearance with them was at Great Yarmouth on Sunday, 2nd August; and Frank Allen took over his role on bass guitar the following day, in Coventry at the start of a new UK tour. Jackson's solo career never seriously took off, even though Burns, true to his word, got him a separate record deal with Pye and he did recruit his own backing group, the Vibrations. Only his debut single in September, "Bye Bye Baby", scratched the surface of the charts, with one week in October at No.30 (and I suspect I was not the only one to 'discover' it a little later as a makeweight track on Pye's compilation LP *The Hit Makers*); after which he was effectively lost to sight.

So readily was Frank Allen assimilated into the Searchers that he would find himself sharing the vocals with Mike Pender on their next single, the Jackie DeShannon composition "When You Walk In The Room" (the recording of which was brought forward to 31st August, to forestall any possible competition from Tony Jackson). The outcome, a No.6 hit by mid-October, was what many now regard as the "ultimate Searchers 45", with its "majestic 12-string intro ... fulsome harmonies, galloping finale and a *de rigeur* lyric of love and pride being trampled underfoot".[109] For their fifth and final single of the year, however, they gambled on a change of approach, to a slower modern American folk song they had included in their set on their autumn tour of the UK with Dionne Warwick and the Isley Brothers. This was "What Have They Done To The Rain", originally composed and performed in 1962 by Malvina

Reynolds[110] in protest against the atmospheric testing of nuclear weapons, but here softened to the point of obscure understatement by the addition of strings in Tony Hatch's arrangement. Released at the beginning of December in an effort to capitalise on pre-Christmas sales, in Frank Allen's words it "raced up the charts like a dog with no legs"[111], yet even so it managed to carry them into 1965 with a hit record in the Top 20. This disappointment was mitigated in part by sales of an EP released in parallel, *The Searchers Play The System*; the title track being the theme song of yet another X-rated sex comedy (this time directed by Michael Winner and starring Oliver Reed as a predatory male seeking to seduce as many girls as possible on their summer holidays in Torbay).

Third in line in terms of chart success in 1964 for the already established Liverpool acts, after the Beatles and the Searchers, came Gerry and the Pacemakers. Having conclusively proved his point about artistic independence with "You'll Never Walk Alone", Gerry Marsden next reverted to up-beat pop, initiating a string of releases of his own compositions with "I'm The One", a characteristically breezy song with a catchy piano riff from Les McGuire. Although another best-seller, it was destined to be held down at No.2 in mid-February by the Searchers, with "Needles And Pins". A sentimental ballad followed in April, "Don't Let The Sun Catch You Crying", which, while only reaching No.6 in the UK in May, went on to reward Gerry and the Pacemakers with their first US hit, a No.4 in the *Billboard* Top 40. The alternation between beat and ballad continued with their remaining two singles of the year, both taken from the soundtrack of *Ferry Cross The Mersey* – in which Gerry was to star at the suggestion of Brian Epstein, following the success of *A Hard Day's Night*. The first and least successful of these releases, in August, was "It's Gonna Be Alright". Bouncing around in the lower reaches of the Top 30, it could only manage No.24; but it was followed at the very end of the year by the film's title track, entering the *NME* chart the week before Christmas and heading for the Top 10 in the New Year.

Others, unhappily, such as the Fourmost, did less well overall. Their second single, "I'm In Love", broke into the Top 30 in the week ending 11th January but, disappointingly for them, could ultimately get no higher than No.12, thus demonstrating that not every Lennon/McCartney song was a surefire Top 10 certainty. Recovering their equilibrium for a time with "A Little Loving", which gave them their biggest hit of all with two weeks at No.6 in May, they then found themselves on a downward spiral, as their popular appeal evaporated. In mid-August, "How Can I Tell Her" made a solitary appearance at No.30; to be followed in mid-December by a similar showing for their cover of the Four Tops' first US hit, "Baby I Need Your Loving". (Sadly, in parallel with this fall from grace in the charts came the devastating news that rhythm guitarist Mike Millward had contracted leukaemia, forcing his withdrawal from performing for a prolonged period of treatment prior to his untimely death in March 1966.)

In late February, having initially profited like the Fourmost from their reliance on Lennon/McCartney songs, Billy J. Kramer and the Dakotas resurfaced, this time with a composition from American writers Mort Shuman and John McFarland. "Little Children" was a song pitched directly to Kramer by its publishers and one in which he personally had great faith, but breaking away from the successful formula of the past necessitated his uncharacteristic persistence in the face of Brian Epstein's opposition.

In her autobiography, Cilla Black describes Kramer as "one of the most insecure guys I've ever met" and has an account of him visiting her family home to play her and her mother a preview copy of "Little Children", to seek their reassurance. It genuinely moved them both to tears and they "knew at once that it would be a big hit for him".[112] With a lyric teetering on the edge of 'novelty', with its bitter-sweet depiction of a shy, frustrated boy trying to get time alone with his girlfriend away from her younger siblings, one can readily understand Epstein's nervousness. Earlier in the decade, there is little doubt that it would have had the potential to be translated straight into a comedy record without a moment's thought. Ultimately, however, Kramer prevailed – another interesting example, in the process, of George Martin as producer allowing an artist their head – and before March was out the record had given him his third No.1. Despite the fact that two months later, it broke into the *Billboard* Top 40, climbing to No.6 in America, leaner times were fast approaching. After "Little Children", Billy J. Kramer and the Dakotas had only one more hit left in them for the year: the Lennon/McCartney song "From A Window", which went no higher than No.13 in August.

After all their years of hard graft at the Mersey rock-face, the Swinging Blue Jeans too would ultimately encounter disappointment. Having followed up "Hippy Hippy Shake" with a remake in the same mould of Little Richard's frenetic "Good Golly Miss Molly" (reaching No.11 in April), they then took a more reflective turn with the much slower "You're No Good". Originally recorded by US soul singer Betty Everett, their version, distinguished by a strong bass line and an echoing guitar break, still stands as one of their strongest performances on disc and rose to No.5 in July; yet subsequently they would find themselves cast out of the Top 30 until their swansong in 1966.

In the circumstances, it was hardly surprising that precious few new Liverpool groups were now able to sustain a worthwhile professional career. Take the five-piece band the Mojos, for example. On the back of a speculative signing to Decca in late 1963, they briefly enjoyed the limelight of the Top 20 when they took their rocking "Everything's Alright" up to No.13 at the end of April; only to find fame already eluding them by July, when the follow-up "Why Not Tonight" failed to get beyond No.30, after which every other release bombed.

Of all the other hopefuls, it was really only the Merseybeats who looked as though they might have the potential to stay the course. Originally formed as the Mavericks in September 1961, they were a Liverpool quartet built around founding members Billy Kinsley and Tony Crane, taking on their new group name in early 1962 at the suggestion of Bob Wooler – in part to promote Bill Harry's *Mersey Beat*. From April 1962 onwards, they became Cavern regulars and were briefly managed by Brian Epstein (who signed them up after the Beatles and the Big Three) until that September, when they lost favour with him through a change to the line-up, which nevertheless subsequently brought them recording success: Billy Kinsley (bass guitar & vocals), Tony Crane (lead guitar & vocals), James (*aka* Aaron) Williams (rhythm guitar & vocals) and John Banks (drums).

As later catalogued in meticulous detail by Kinsley, their repertoire at this juncture closely resembled that of the Beatles and their contemporaries: an eclectic mix of numbers by Elvis, the Everly Brothers, Little Richard, Larry Williams, Buddy Holly and the Crickets, Chuck Berry, the Shirelles and Arthur Alexander.[113] Their recording debut was in early 1963, for the minor independent record label Oriole, whose A&R manager, John Schroeder, auditioned a variety of Liverpool groups (including, as it happened, the Nomads, as the Mojos were originally known) for two compilation LPs, *This Is Mersey Beat Vols.1 & 2*. The Merseybeats' contribution was a cover of the US hit "Our Day Will Come", by Ruby and the Romantics.

Schroeder was soon followed to Liverpool by Jack Baverstock of Philips Records, to hold auditions at the Cavern. After hearing the end of one of their lunchtime sessions there, he offered the Merseybeats a contract with Fontana Records, the new subsidiary of Philips, and in June 1963 they went to London to record their first single. Allowed a free rein by Baverstock, who was not a pop aficionado himself, they opted to lay down a Shirelles' cover, "It's Love That Really Counts", and "Fortune Teller" (as recorded in America by Benny Spellman). According to Billy Kinsley, however, they only reached agreement on which was to be the A-side by putting both songs to the vote before the audience at the Cavern; when "It's Love That Really Counts", one of Bacharach and David's lesser-known compositions, won the day. Good, melodic soft-rock number that it is, it made no showing at all in the *NME*'s Top 30 following its release in August; although it did enter the lower reaches of *Record Retailer*'s Top 40, where it stayed for 10 weeks (with a highest position of No.24 at the beginning of November). Artistic licence was therefore later to be stretched to the maximum by promotional material for the American market which described the record, from these "leaders of the 'Mersey

Sound'", as "an overnight sensation, zooming straight into the English music charts where it stayed on top for sixteen consecutive weeks".[114]

The song for their next single, "I Think Of You" (a new composition by British session musician Peter Lee Stirling), was strongly urged upon them by Baverstock, despite their own misgivings that it was "too simple and too lovey-dovey".[115] Released in January 1964 and entering the Top 30 in the same week as "I'm The One" and "Needles And Pins", it was to give the Merseybeats the biggest hit of their short chart career when it eventually reached No.4 at the beginning of March. Between its recording and release, however, Billy Kinsley had left the group, following a disagreement with their then manager, Alan Cheetham, to be replaced by Johnny Gustafson (late of the Big Three). It was this revised line-up that went on to record their last two hits, the first of which was another Peter Lee Stirling song (written this time in collaboration with Barry Mason), "Don't Turn Around". Although habitually overshadowed by its successor or even completely overlooked in many standard pop reference works, this third Merseybeats single, with an arrangement much enhanced by the inclusion of Tony Crane playing a 12-string acoustic guitar, has always been a personal favourite of mine since I originally bought it in the early summer of '64. It deserved much better than the No.14 position in the Top 30 that it finally achieved in mid-May.

Their last hit – not just of the year but forever – followed in the height of summer, their interpretation of Bacharach and David's "Wishin' And Hopin'", which eventually made it to No.12 in early August. Historically, however, there can be no question that it has lost hands down in collective musical memory to Dusty Springfield's version; although there was no contest between them at the time, since Dusty's recording was consigned to be no more than an LP track in the UK and only released as a single in the US (where, as such, it became, of course, a spectacular success).

As Tony Crane asserted, the Merseybeats were convinced they had a sound strategy to inform their choice of headline material:

> Every band that came after the Beatles was in their shadow. We tried to get our own style by recording ballads for our A-sides and thereby keeping away from what the Beatles were doing. In those days, they never recorded ballads for A-sides.[116]

Unfortunately for them, 1964 had turned so rapidly into a year of unparalleled choice of groups and musical genres all clamouring for the attention of the young record-buying public. The Merseybeats were also unquestionably overshadowed by the Searchers in their similar reliance on a softer style, so that by the autumn their last lingering appeal as balladeers was gone and for want of originality their hits dried up. As Andrew Loog Oldham pithily expressed it (out of concern for his own charges), a "band without songs" was "akin to an aeroplane without parachutes".[117]

While the broader sweep of Mersey groups thus experienced mixed fortunes from early 1964 onwards, as a soloist Cilla Black suddenly found herself projected to the heights of stardom, with the release on 31st January of her second single, "Anyone Who Had A Heart". Entering the Top 30 at No.18 in the week ending 8th February, a fortnight later it was No.1, a position it held for a month. Composed by Bacharach and David, it had originally been recorded in America by Dionne Warwick (as yet generally unknown in the UK), where the song had taken the fancy of Brian Epstein on his initial visit to New York. Bringing a copy back to England with him, he had played it to George Martin, whose first reaction had been to regard it as the perfect song for Shirley Bassey. Epstein persuaded him, seemingly against his better judgement, that it would be right for Cilla and her version (with lavish orchestral arrangement by Johnny Pearson) was recorded at Abbey Road in two sessions, on 10th and 15th January.

As far as Cilla was concerned, this choice of song was a happy accident, because she obviously had her own import copy and was "already playing 'Anyone Who Had A Heart' back home unbeknown to [Epstein] before he had picked it up in America".[118] Yet she freely acknowledged that the speed of its success, earning her a silver disc in March for more than a quarter of a million sales, was to her mind "amazing ... [given] that the UK was still in the grip of Beatlemania, and that the pop scene was dominated by groups, almost to the total exclusion of solo singers like me".[119]

Even though it was the first serious indication of Cilla's true virtuosity as a singer, her performance left Dionne Warwick, for one, bitterly resentful, particularly in the wake of a switch of distributors in the UK which denied British audiences at large access to her early recordings; to the extent that she felt she had been reduced to making "very expensive demonstration records ... for European artists to enjoy and reap success from".[120] (This expression of ingratitude, it should be noted, is notwithstanding the fact that in America her own version of the song eventually reached No.8 in the *Billboard* Top 40, hardly denoting a lack of support from within her own home market.) And forty years on, Bacharach's biographer, Michael Brocken, could not refrain (somewhat perversely, given his role as a university lecturer in Liverpool in popular music studies!) from making the sour observation that what he terms "*the Cilla Black saga* [my emphasis] ... illustrates perfectly the way in which British covers pre-empted the American originals and continued to frustrate the commercial progress of US artists in the UK".[121]

Nevertheless, the fact remains that in Britain Cilla's performance was rightly seen as a *tour de force* from a virtually unknown singer, her interpretation sensitively bringing light and shade to the plaintive lyric. At the beginning, the unfamiliar softness of her voice sets exactly the right tone of pained apprehension:

> Anyone who ever loved could look at me
> And know that I love you.
> Anyone who ever dreamed could look at me
> And know I dream of you,
> Knowing I love you, so ...[122]

On the upbeat taking us into the second verse, however, she makes a more forthright declaration of her fear that the relationship is going wrong, before spiralling back down again to the quiet expression of despair in the rhetorical question of its last line:

> Anyone who had a heart
> Would take me in his arms and love me too.
> You couldn't be another heart that hurt me,
> Like you hurt me and be so untrue.
> What am I to do?[123]

And so the cycle is renewed and builds to the song's finale, an overwhelming litany of denunciation carried through into the fadeout:

> Anyone who had a heart would simply take me
> In his arms and always love me.
> Why won't you? (Yeah!)
> Anyone who had a heart would love me too.
> Anyone who had a heart would simply take me
> In his arms and always love me.
> Why won't you?[124]

The overall impression is that of a singer coming of age, confidently exhibiting power and control to bring a new depth to her material. Cilla thus emerged as the first – but only the first – serious contender against Dusty Springfield, at the start of a year which witnessed the blossoming in full of the British pop diva, not only through the emergence of other new talent but also the revival of past good fortunes for some.

Of the newcomers, the next to arrive was the youngest of the class of '64, 15-year-old Marie Lawrie, who had only just left school the preceding Christmas. She may have been diminutive in stature but on stage in the concert halls and clubs in and around her home city of Glasgow, originally as lead singer with local group the Bellrocks and latterly with the Gleneagles, she was full of energetic self-belief and her voice was raw and loud. Quite fortuitously, in autumn 1963, on the back of a search for new pop acts north of the Border mounted by the *Scottish Daily Express*, she found herself recommended by the paper's show business correspondent, Gordon Reed, to a talent scout from EMI's Columbia label. Accompanied by her band yet still only fourteen at the time, she auditioned unsuccessfully in West Hampstead for Ron Richards, who then referred her on to rival producer Peter Sullivan at Decca.

Her song of preference in both instances was one she had been performing regularly for more than a year, "Shout"; a cover of a cover, in fact, because she had first picked up on this Isley Brothers' number from a clandestine visit to a Glasgow club where she had seen it performed by the rock singer Alex Harvey: "It was an absolute revelation for me. No other music had ever resonated with me in quite the same way. I was in awe. I knew I had to do that song."[125] She had, nevertheless, hedged her bets by also rehearsing Gene Pitney's "Twenty-Four Hours From Tulsa", because "I wanted to sing a ballad and not just something fast and loud, to show my versatility".[126]

Unlike Richards, Sullivan succumbed to her youthful charms and offered her a recording contract, but met his match when she refused to be signed purely as a solo artist, insisting that the Gleneagles be included in the deal (to which Decca reluctantly agreed). At this juncture, taking on the group as well must have struck Sullivan as a deeply unattractive business proposition, since it was a sextet, as follows: Alec Bell (vocals/keyboards), Jim Dewar (rhythm guitar), David Miller (drums), Ross Nelson (lead guitar), Jimmy Smith (saxophone) and Tony Tierney (bass guitar). Several months passed from their signing until they were recalled to London to make their first record; which, to Marie's surprise – given that she had naively harboured hopes of being offered a Lennon/McCartney song – was to be her old faithful, "Shout". Their rebranding as Lulu and the Luvvers came at the suggestion of new manager Marian Massey and her brother Tony Gordon (the original source of their recommendation to Gordon Reed, in the course of his own developing interest in club management in Glasgow) and Decca finally released the single under this new performing credit on 15th April 1964.

Entering the *NME* chart at No.30 in mid-May, "Shout" enjoyed nine weeks in the Top 30 through early summer, with a highest position of No.9 in the week ending 20th June. Not a record to be easily ignored by dint of Lulu's sheer volume and enthusiasm, it was nevertheless highly derivative[127] and finding a follow-up to generate equivalent sales or better was to prove elusive for another twelve months. In the interim, both Lulu and the Luvvers relocated to London (the group slimming down to a quintet on the departure of saxophonist Jimmy Smith) and the inevitable touring and television appearances would maintain Lulu's popularity, while she rode out the frustration of her second and third singles ("Can't Hear You No More" and "Here Comes The Night") missing the charts altogether. Whilst the former was (and remains today) totally unmemorable and deservedly a miss, the latter, which she interpreted sensitively as a ballad, should have afforded her success had it not been (as we shall see in Chapter 7) for Decca's crassness in diverting its resources into promoting another artist's alternative version on the same label.

Lulu's debut was followed in summer by that of a singer completely her opposite in every way imaginable, not least in background, demeanour and musical ambition. Marianne Faithfull was the daughter of an Austro-Hungarian Baroness displaced by the Second World War and a former British Army officer, whose tempestuous marriage ended in their separation when she was six. Moving then from Oxfordshire to a new home with her mother in Reading, she was sent away to board at a girls' convent school and by the mid-Sixties had grown into a well-read but highly impressionable and directionless 17-year-old; with social connections through her boyfriend, Cambridge undergraduate John Dunbar, to the charmed circle of the new glitterati of pop culture in central London.

She had already dabbled vaguely herself with amateur acting and with folk music, in thrall to the perceived pure simplicity of Joan Baez, but as yet had no substantial history as a performer. After the lightning strike of an entirely unforeseen social encounter, her life would never be the same again. In her own words, firmly tongue in cheek:

> According to Pop mythology, my life proper began at Adrienne Posta's 'launch party' in March 1964, for it was there that I first met Mick Jagger. Mick fell in love with me on the spot (or so the story goes), decided I was fit to be his consort, and wrote "As Tears Go By". I, on the other hand, immediately began taking drugs and having a lot of sex.[128]

The critical meeting that Good Friday was not, however, with Jagger but with Andrew Loog Oldham, who had just produced Adrienne Posta's second single (the long-lost non-hit "Shang A Doo Lang", successor to the equally unknown "Only Fifteen") as a favour to her father. The party, held at the Postas' flat, was nominally intended to promote the record, although Tony Calder, now Loog Oldham's new partner in a pop publicity agency, had a more cynical take on the enterprise: "Sid Posta, this wealthy guy in the furniture business, wanted his daughter to be a star. We saw the chance to earn a few bob, maybe a grand, and we made this dreadful record. No one fancied her, so we threw a party."[129] History, it has to be said, has been equally unkind to Adrienne's thwarted musical ambitions[130] but the party retains its notoriety for bringing Marianne to the attention of Loog Oldham. (She and Dunbar were there at the invitation of Peter Asher[131]; whilst other guests included Paul McCartney and Jane Asher, Mick Jagger and Chrissie Shrimpton, as well as Keith Richards and Brian Jones.)

Marianne's arrival not only turned Loog Oldham's head but also registered her in his consciousness as an object of fantasy. In his account of events, his motives in wanting to know more about her were – allegedly – purely professional: "The moment I caught sight of Marianne I recognised my next adventure, a true star. In another century you'd have set sail for her; in 1964 you'd record her."[132] In contrast, Calder's recollections dwell on the baser, carnal desires that he and others entertained from that first glimpse of the attractive, well-endowed sixth-former whose entrance silenced the room and the "stunning sight" of whom set them drooling.[133]

A week later, a telegram from Loog Oldham summoned Marianne to Olympic Studios for her first recording session (to which she was accompanied by her school friend Sally Oldfield). His original intention had been for her to record a song by Lionel Bart, "I Don't Know How (To Tell You)", but after several abortive takes – Loog Oldham likening "poor Marianne" to "sounding like an inbred hyena"[134] – this was abandoned in favour of the proposed B-side, the earliest Jagger/Richards composition "As Tears Go By", as now arranged for orchestra by Mike Leander. By comparison she recorded this in indecent haste, at last bringing a painfully long three hours to a satisfactory conclusion.

Although "never that crazy" about the song herself, she has always acknowledged the achievement it represented, "an absolutely astonishing thing for a boy of twenty [i.e., Mick Jagger] to have written, a song about a woman looking back nostalgically on her life".[135] However, not only was it a hit (nine weeks in the Top 30, peaking at No.9 in mid-September) but also it became, to Marianne's eventual regret, an inextricable part of that defining image as a performer encapsulated by Loog Oldham's extraordinarily distorted vision:

> "As Tears Go By" was not, contrary to popular folklore, written
> for me, but it fitted me so perfectly it might as well have been. It's
> a marketable portrait of me and as such is an extremely ingenious
> creation, a commercial fantasy that pushes all the right buttons.
> It did such a good job of imprinting that it was to become, alas,
> an indelible part of my media-conjured self for the next fifteen
> years.[136]

As the record entered the charts, Marianne chanced her arm by leaving school and leaving home, little knowing that these would be irrevocable first steps for her on a tortuous, corrupting journey of self-destruction. Thus committing herself prematurely to a voyage into the unknown, by the end of the decade she was fated to become a spectacular casualty of the decadence now beginning to shape the preferred lifestyle of the new generation of rock stars.

On the back of her first hit, while waiting an agonisingly long time for the second, Marianne – like Lulu – was unceremoniously pitched into TV and touring; but in her case, it turned out to be a damaging experience for which she found herself totally unprepared and unsupported. The first package tour to which she was attached in the autumn was overwhelmingly the province of northern male groups: the Hollies, Freddie and the Dreamers, Gerry and the Pacemakers, the Four Pennies, all flung together to make up a typically random caravan of performers. In most places, as a raw newcomer she was received badly and, being barracked by hostile audiences only interested in seeing the groups, "soon learned to make paralysis part of my performance"; not making "the slightest movement for the very good reason that I was quite unable to budge", being "glued to the spot by sheer terror".[137] Yet against all the odds, amazingly she still managed to force herself to sing:

> I simply stood there in front of the microphone, completely still, my hands dangling by my side and sang from some place deep inside me and out came this clear, ethereal voice. People loved it, it wasn't the least sexy or hip, it was about as far as you could get from sexy.[138]

Her new career – if it can properly be called that, in this earliest phase of Marianne's fragility – took an unfortunate backward step when Loog Oldham agreed to let her draw on what politely passed for her folk roots and record a cover of "Blowin' In The Wind" as her second single. In doing so, even she was forced to admit that it was a "total disaster"[139], notwithstanding an accompaniment on acoustic guitar from Keith Richards. Released on 23rd October, it never troubled the charts and on the back of its failure Marianne decided to forsake Loog Oldham (by whom she had found herself completely overawed) as her manager in favour of his partner Tony Calder. The truth of the matter was that Loog Oldham had rapidly lost interest in her after proving to himself that he could make her a star, conveniently rationalising his lack of ongoing concern for her by blaming it on depression. At least to Calder's credit, he did make an initial effort to find more commercial material for her and in December took her back into the studio to record her next single, resulting in what was to be her biggest hit of all in early 1965 before her business relationship with him would also rapidly founder in recrimination.

Two months younger than Marianne, at the age of 16 schoolgirl Sandra Goodrich originally sought to follow a more conventional route into the music business in 1963 by entering a talent contest at the Ilford Palais, in which she came second. On the back of this near-success, however, she was offered an audition by music publisher Terry Oates and Radio Luxembourg DJ Jimmy Henny, who then added her to the bill of a charity concert in Hammersmith with headline acts the Hollies and Adam Faith and the Roulettes. Enthused by her performance, Roulettes guitarist Russ Ballard insisted on ushering her then and there into Adam Faith's dressing room, where he accompanied her in an impromptu rendition of "Everybody Loves A Lover". Faith was equally enamoured by her and called his tyrannical manager Eve Taylor in to listen as well, who "tugged on a cigarette and tapped her foot impatiently":

> Eve nodded to Adam and I started nervously to sing again.
> Eve listened to one line, glared at me, then at Adam, whispered something in his ear, then turned on her teetering high heels and tapped briskly out ... Adam reached up and patted my shoulder. 'Don't worry, luv. I'll fix it for ya. You're gonna be a star,' he pronounced.[140]

Faith was true to his word and, by bestowing his patronage upon her in what was by her account an entirely selfless manner, would ensure that gawky Sandra from Dagenham did indeed become a star, even though with his connections it took some time for her to get established.

While she waited for success to beckon her on, the irksome issue facing all teenagers sooner or later – what to do when she left school – remained to be settled. She had previously applied for a place on a foundation course at art college and been shortlisted for interview (which she went to with her mother), only to find that it would mean embarking on a possible course of study for up to five years:

> This seemed an extraordinarily long time to someone just turned sixteen. When we arrived home I informed [my mum] that I would not be going to art college because it interfered with my plans to become a singing star. As I had never mentioned these plans before, they came as a bit of a surprise.[141]

As a temporary fallback position, at least to Sandra's way of thinking, and "to shut her mum up" who "was nagging her to get a proper job"[142], she took an office post with the largest local employer at Ford's Dagenham factory. Here, in an early, primitive phase of workplace computerisation, she was nominally employed to process punch cards of individual employees' details in preparation for the weekly pay run; but in reality she was miles away, "sitting at my idle punch card machine sketching away dreamily, wishing for the day to end. I must have stretched everyone's patience to the limit."[143]

Her first audition for Tony Hatch at Pye Records went badly. Eve Taylor, "who liked showbizzy Fifties female artists in sparkly frocks like Connie Francis and Lena Horne", had primed Sandra to sing what she thought of as "stuffy Tin Pan Alley songs" (such as "Secret Love" and "Bobby's Girl"), whereas her own preference was for "songs full of strident teen drama, like the Crystals' "He's A Rebel" or the Shirelles' "Will You Still Love Me Tomorrow?" ... the kinds of songs I could relate to, the songs I had been singing with local guitar-based bands in dance halls".[144]

Hardly surprising, therefore, that despite her best efforts in front of

Hatch, who played piano for her, she left without having secured a deal. Yet Adam Faith, to his credit, still remained loyal to her and persisted on her behalf in the face of this setback:

> In an enterprising leap of the imagination, Adam suggested that
> Eve finance the recordings herself and lease them to the record
> company to manufacture and distribute. This would enable us
> to make the kind of records he felt I was capable of. He also
> suggested that Eve team me up with the writer of his latest hits,
> Chris Andrews, who also happened to come from Dagenham.[145]

Relieved of the initial risk of having to pay an unknown new artist in advance for potentially abortive recording sessions, as well as obfuscating in the small print the issue of the future ownership and retention of any master tapes, Pye were much more interested second time around. As Eve Taylor incautiously allowed herself to be taken down the path of licensing previously trodden by the likes of the more savvy Joe Meek and Andrew Loog Oldham, so at last Sandra secured a recording contract.

From the start, she enjoyed a close affinity with Chris Andrews, who was to write the majority of her hits (although, as it turned out, only one of her three No.1s). To her delight, she found they shared a passion for "West Indian ska, blue beat and black American artists, which seems to surprise everyone, considering the pure pop we produced".[146]

Andrews had originally come to Adam Faith's attention in the bleak midwinter of 1962/63, at a time when Faith's own career was seriously threatened by the unstoppable swell of interest in the Beatles. In Faith's words, Andrews, "gums bleeding with hunger", had "walked into Eve Taylor's office with a fistful of wonderful songs that he'd written. Eve, never backward in taking advantage of a starving man, signed him up for thousands of years and I was the beneficiary."[147]

The pay-off from this new association took some time to come to fruition but on 23rd June 1963 Faith, now backed in the studio as well as on stage by the Roulettes, had recorded his first Andrews composition – coincidentally entitled "The First Time". Released as a single on 13th September, it was to re-establish Faith as a Top 10 artist after a year-long absence when it reached No.5 in the week ending 12th October.[148]

Although he undoubtedly restored Faith's waning fortunes, Andrews's songs on the whole did lend a retro flavour to much of his subsequent output. There was a real sense in which Faith and the Roulettes had left it fractionally too late to capitalise on the group phase already well advanced in British Sixties' music at this point; and this was compounded, even in his better-sounding efforts for them, by a simplistic streak of sentimentality in Andrews's lyrics that was becoming increasingly outmoded.

However, his collaboration with his 17-year-old Dagenham soulmate eventually turned out to be far more effective overall, in terms of the closeness of fit between composer, artist and audience to deliver consistent chart success, although it was by no means instantaneous. The first commercial recording she embarked upon was of his song "As Long As You're Happy Baby"[149], at a session in Pye's Marble Arch studios where for comfort she opted to sing barefoot; an idiosyncrasy in its turn prompting Eve Taylor's husband, Moishe, to come up with the feeble play on words that conferred upon her the stage name Sandie Shaw. Released in July 1964 as her first single, even its promotion on *Ready Steady Go!* could not make this shrill, rather forced rendition a hit, yet at least it pleased Sandie to find that "it had succeeded in getting me 'in' with the 'in crowd'".[150]

For her second single in September, Andrews was passed over in favour of a Bacharach and David composition reputedly heard by Eve Taylor on a visit to America, "(There's) Always Something There To Remind Me", where it had been a minor hit for soul singer Lou Johnson. Opening to a shuffling bossa nova beat emphasised by muted brass and underscored by echoing guitars, this song definitively launched Sandie on the road to success, enabling her as it did to demonstrate a greater control of her vocal range and inject true pathos into her performance. Breaking into the Top 30 at No.12 in the week ending 10th October, three weeks later it was No.1 and her dream of being a star, which she had cherished intently from classroom to workplace, was finally realised. From this point on, her association with Andrews belatedly began to flourish, even though for her next hit in December, it may have been temporarily disappointing to find that record-buyers were more attracted to the originally intended B-side, "Girl Don't Come", as a traditional, play-safe follow-up with sound and tempo highly reminiscent of its predecessor.[151]

While Lulu, Marianne Faithfull and Sandie Shaw may all have been welcome new arrivals with future potential, none of them could offer serious competition to either Dusty Springfield or Cilla Black as the predominant female solo artists of the year.

For her part, Dusty would be voted Best British Female Singer of 1964 in the *NME*'s annual Pop Poll[152] – an accolade signally denied to Cilla for the rest of the decade – after amassing another three hit singles in a row; the first being "Stay Awhile", released at the beginning of February (when "I Only Want To Be With You" was still in the Top 30) but proving to be the least successful of the three by only reaching No.13 in early March. With a best-selling debut LP, *A Girl Called Dusty*, released in the intervening period[153], her second new single of the year was in an entirely different league. Coming out at the end of June and making it to No.3 within a month, this Bacharach/David composition, "I Just Don't Know What To Do With Myself", earnt her a second UK silver disc. A melancholy, introspective reflection on the sense of loss attendant upon the end of a relationship, it remains to this day forever associated with her name as one of her most distinctive classic recordings. Finally, in mid-October, she publicly signified an easing of tension between herself and brother Tom with the release of "Losing You" (a song co-written by Tom with Clive Westlake), which resulted in a No.10 hit by the end of November.

Away from the recording studio, Dusty's year was filled with television appearances and touring commitments at home and abroad, which from time to time understandably took their toll of her voice and constitution in general. Within the UK, she undertook three principal tours which occupied her from 29th February to 29th March[154], for most of August[155] and from 14th November to 6th December.[156] Her international commitments, however, were even more demanding. On the day after completing her British spring tour, she flew out to Australia and New Zealand, for a 12-day tour with Gerry and the Pacemakers, Brian Poole and the Tremeloes and Gene Pitney. With a short break for a holiday in Honolulu, this was then followed from 26th April to 15th May by a promotional tour of America, combining concerts on the West Coast with slots on nationally networked television shows, including a live appearance on *The Ed Sullivan Show* on 10th May. By the time she touched down again in London, she had travelled an estimated 50,000 miles.

She returned again to America on 1st September, in advance of ten days in concert (with an average six shows per day) in Brooklyn's Fox Theatre, promoted by Murray the K. Far from having to keep up with or outdo the laddish behaviour of British male groups to which she had otherwise been subjected, here, after overcoming an initial bout of chronic insecurity coupled with homesickness[157], she eased herself into her element with the biggest names in contemporary black American music: such as the Miracles, the Temptations, the Ronettes, Martha and the Vandellas and the Supremes. Just as Martha Reeves and the Vandellas would back her performance of "Wishin' And Hopin'", so she would repay the compliment by singing accompaniments for them from the side of the stage: "I never actually got to go on stage with them but I knew all the routines and knew exactly how to sound like a Vandella. And since they were singing back-ups for Marvin Gaye from the wings, I used to do that as well."[158]

Enriched and enlivened by this experience, she left New York on 14th September, to commence what had been scheduled as an eight-day concert tour in the company of the Searchers and Eden Kane, but failed to make it beyond the first venue in Tulsa, Oklahoma where – according to her biographers – she collapsed through exhaustion and had to submit to doctor's orders to rest. A more sceptical Frank Allen (by then into his second month as a Searcher) was nevertheless convinced that it was a purely tactical withdrawal on her part, to remove herself from the drudgery of "trekking from anon-ymous town to anonymous town performing in unsuitable halls along with all the bad sound and lighting that came with the territory".[159] While Dusty jetted off to an extended convalescence in the Virgin Islands, rounded off by another stay in New York, the tour proceeded in her absence. She eventually flew back to London on 14th October, to begin promoting "Losing You".

Her last foreign trip of 1964, however, brought her year to a controver-sial end. Her manager Vic Billings had negotiated a concert tour of South Africa, on the basis of what was for the time a radical condition in the contract stating that Dusty and her backing group the Echoes would only perform to non-racially segregated audiences. (All being members of the UK Musicians' Union, they were openly abiding by that union's embargo on playing in South Africa to segregated audiences, which had been in place from 1962 onwards, having been given to understand that live shows staged in cinemas were exempt from the requirement for segregation.) Prior to her departure on 9th December, Dusty had been quoted in defiant mood by the NME:

> I've got a special clause written into the contract which stipulates that I shall play only to non-segregated audiences. That's my little bit to help the coloured people there. I think I'm the first British artist to do this. Brian Poole and the Tremeloes were supposed to do the same, but I believe that in the end they had to play some segregated concerts. If they force me into anything like that I'll be on the first plane home.[160]

Although she did manage to complete two shows in Johannesburg and two more in Wittebome (near Cape Town) without interference, after her fifth concert in Cape Town itself the South African police intervened and her whole party was served with deportation notices for their flagrant breach of race laws. Dusty's premature return to London on 17th December was met by a frenzy of press and political interest which continued for several weeks, a confused mix of praise for her stance counterbalanced by overt hostility and vilification from those (including some prominent contempo-rary performers, such as Max Bygraves and actor Derek Nimmo) who saw her action as no more than an ill-conceived publicity stunt.

Shocked to the point of disgust by the adverse reactions she had provoked, Dusty held firm to her principles by relinquishing her £2,000 fee for the tour, donating the money instead to South African charities for black orphans. Like Bob Dylan a year earlier, she would eventually be obliged to admit: "Whatever your personal political feelings are, if you become involved in them publicly you're bound to come out the loser. I wasn't making any statement, I just felt better about it that way, being the naïve person I was."[161]

Back in the Fifties, British politicians and aesthetes alike had been quick to criticise the emergence of rock'n'roll as nothing more than an incitement to violence and depravity, which teenagers in the UK had rightly scorned and ignored; but here was a new and ugly reminder of the fact that elsewhere in the world seeking equal access to the simple pleasure of listening to popular music could be construed first and foremost as an act of political rebellion. (In this context, it should also be remembered that only six months earlier the black political activist Nelson Mandela had been found guilty of treason and sentenced to life imprisonment in the Robben Island penal colony.) Before December was out, hard on Dusty's heels into South Africa went an unsuspecting Adam Faith, rapidly finding himself embroiled in the backlash from her curtailed visit and being treated even more threateningly by the authorities. Placed under house arrest in his Johannesburg hotel, he was only freed to come home on the strength of a payment into court of £20,000 by his record company (which EMI subsequently reclaimed off him by deductions from his royalties).

By comparison, Cilla Black's professional life was easily kept within more conventional bounds by Brian Epstein's conservative style of management. After her breakthrough with "Anyone Who Had A Heart", she was apprehensive for her future. As she well knew: "No British girl had ever had two successive number one hits."[162] Yet she was set to achieve "the unthinkable"[163] with an English version of an Italian ballad, "You're My World" as the follow-up. Released on 1st May and entering the Top 20 a week later at No.18, to her delight it enjoyed three weeks at No.1 from May into June. For her next single, however, she reverted to a Lennon/McCartney composition, "It's For You", arranged by Johnny Spence as a "sort of jazz waltz".[164] In this instance, despite highly gratifying "advance orders of 200,000 copies"[165] prior to its release at the end of July, its best chart position was No.8, in the week ending 29th August.

Although there were to be no more chart entries for the rest of the year, Epstein had ensured she would remain in the public eye by booking her into what turned out to be an extended season at the London Palladium, in a show called *Startime* in which the headline acts were Frankie Vaughan and Tommy Cooper. From May to December, Cilla did "thirteen shows a week … a total of over four hundred performances".[166] In addition, she appeared at the Royal Variety Performance (singing "You're My World") and was given a cameo role in *Ferry Cross The Mersey*, which (as noted earlier) had been conceived primarily as a film showcase for Gerry and the Pacemakers. Interspersed between these commitments from July to December were recording sessions at Abbey Road with George Martin, largely devoted to laying down tracks for her first LP.

This clutch of young pretenders were not, however, destined to have it all their own way. In the autumn, two veterans of the charts made their respective comebacks; the first being the 27-year-old Shirley Bassey, returning to the Top 30 after almost a year's absence in mid-October with the menacing theme song from the third James Bond film *Goldfinger*, a collaborative composition by Anthony Newley, Leslie Bricusse and John Barry. An inspired pairing of artist and material, it dispelled at last the flabby disconnection that Matt Monro had brought to its disastrous predecessor, *From Russia With Love*, and initiated the trend of classic Bond themes that would be set to continue, with one or two admitted wobbles, for many years to come. Considering at this distance the long-standing, even affectionate association in popular collective memory between singer and song, surprisingly it was not an immediate best-seller, only reaching No.21, but it was nevertheless sufficiently strong to bring her back to public prominence.

As for the second, it was as unexpected as the Spanish Inquisition, beginning quietly and unassumingly enough with a gentle piano intro:

> When you're alone and life is making you lonely,
> You can always go
> Downtown.
> When you've got worries, all the noise and the hurry
> Seems to help, I know,
> Downtown.[167]

Then suddenly both tempo and volume were cranked up and a blast of brass lifted the song into the stratosphere:

> The lights are much brighter there.
> You can forget all your troubles, forget all your cares and go
> Downtown!
> Things'll be great when you're
> Downtown!
> No finer place for sure.
> Downtown!
> Everything's waiting for you.
> (Downtown!)[168]

"Downtown", a new song by her producer Tony Hatch, was the means by which, in mid-November, at the age of 32, Petula Clark set about reinventing herself and breathed new life into a British recording career that effectively had been moribund since the summer of 1962 (whereas a parallel career in France since 1959, recording in French on the Vogue label, had brought her great prestige and a massive following across the Channel).

Deceptively simple, with a strong beat and a catchy hook, "Downtown" deserves due recognition as one of Hatch's cleverest compositions from his most prolific period of songwriting. Its universal appeal lies in its pretence of the singer's direct address to the listener as an individual – rather than forcing that audience to identify tangentially with an absent third party (most commonly a spurned or deceitful lover). Just as importantly, this is no novice speaking: Petula is a mature singer, who can *swing*. In particular, it is the quintessential pop song of entreaty for wallflowers everywhere, offering the perfect antidote of sheer escapism to the dreariness of enforced isolation in bedsit-land: three minutes of unadulterated, uplifting fun is yours for the taking if only you will abandon yourself, albeit in your head, to be seduced by "the music of the traffic in the city".[169]

For this reason alone, its release in the dark days of autumn descending into winter was unintentionally inspired on the part of Pye and it proved to be a triumph. Not only did it enjoy a thirteen-week run in the UK Top 30 from its entry at No.21, only kept off the No.1 spot at year-end by the Beatles, but it also inaugurated a new string of English-language hits for Petula for the next three years, as we shall see in later chapters. Furthermore, with worldwide sales eventually topping three million, it enabled her to break into the American market, giving her a US No.1 in February 1965 and gaining her a Grammy Award into the bargain.

Other, fleeting home-based competition came from the likes of Julie Rogers (in August, with "The Wedding"), Julie Grant (in September, with "Come To Me") and, in November, Twinkle (*aka* Lynn Ripley) with her self-composed saga of death by motorcycle misadventure, "Terry". From further afield, courtesy of her winning entry in the Eurovision Song Contest, came the Italian singer Gigliola Cinquetti, with the wistful but unfathomable "Non Ho L'Eta Per Amarti", still making No.14 in May even though hardly anyone could understand it.

The most striking new element in terms of female performers in the British charts of 1964 was, however, represented by a pronounced influx from afar of black girl soloists and vocal groups. With the exception of Jamaican Millicent Small – who as Millie had a No.2 hit in May with "My Boy Lollipop" – it was black American artists who consistently racked up successes throughout the year.

Dionne Warwick and Mary Wells came in the vanguard, with "Walk On By" and "My Guy" in April and May respectively, to be followed in the summer and autumn by groups previously unknown in the UK. In July the Dixie Cups reached No.20 with "Chapel Of Love" and in September the Supremes shot to No.2 with "Where Did Our Love Go". While Dusty's heroines Martha and the Vandellas flirted with the lower reaches of the Top 30 intermittently from October to December with "Dancing In The Street", the Supremes' next single "Baby Love" went all the way to No.1 in November. (Cuckoos in the nest were the Shangri-Las who, although stable mates of the Dixie Cups on the Red Bird label, were four white girls with attitude from the Queens district of New York. In October, half-speaking, half-crying, they nudged into the Top 30 at No.27 with "Remember (Walkin' In The Sand)", the agonised intensity of their recollection of lost love on the beach embellished by sound effects of crying seagulls wheeling above waves crashing on the foreshore.)

However intriguing these developments may have been, there is no escaping the fact that the major battle for pop supremacy was waged between the ever-growing multiplicity of white male British groups. By definition, this was a world in which girl instrumentalists had no place, save for the novelty value of those very few daring enough to stake out an equal footing on stage alongside the boys; and in 1964, only two such performers came to the public's attention, Honey Lantree of the Honeycombs and Megan Davies of the Applejacks.

The Honeycombs, for whom Anne 'Honey' Lantree played the drums, are famous for one record, and one record only – their No.1 hit of the late summer of '64, "Have I The Right" – which also represents the last true commercial success of its independent producer, Joe Meek, who by this stage in his life was paranoid about being shunned by the record industry and thus increasingly descending into despair. The group, hailing from north London, had originally been formed as the Sheratons by Honey's hairdressing colleague Martin Murray (rhythm guitar), with her brother John (bass guitar), Alan Ward (lead guitar) and Dennis D'Ell (vocals). After fortuitously seeing them play one evening at the Mildmay Tavern on the Balls Pond Road, song-writing duo Ken Howard and Alan Blaikley approached them with the offer of several numbers, "Have I The Right" being the one they then opted to audition for Meek.

The song was recorded at Meek's chaotic Holloway Road studio in his typically eccentric fashion, as recalled by D'Ell:

> It was all over and done with in no time. We did about four takes of it and I did about two or three vocal tracks … Joe was trying for a bass drum sound and couldn't get what he wanted and came in saying, 'Stop, stop, stop', and lined us up on the stairs; Anne stayed on the bass drum. We had about four mikes to cover the length of the staircase, with bicycle pump clips under the stairs and he just clipped the mikes into them. For about an hour we all stood about stomping in time with the music. His cleaner had actually been cleaning the stairs and was waiting at the bottom for us to finish. I don't think she understood what was going on.[170]

Apart from the bottoming-out of the drums with the multi-layered stamping of feet (a trick used to equally familiar effect by the Dave Clark Five), the finished product bore the typical Meek trademark of echo-laden guitars, with an accentuation of the treble register further enhanced by distortion achieved through speeding up the relevant instrumental track on the master tape. Yet it cost Meek some effort to place the record with a major company, until Louis Benjamin of Pye Records finally agreed to press and distribute it, subject to his proposed name-change for the group. Even then, initially it was a slow seller, the boost in its sales principally attributable – in the opinion of Howard and Blaikley – to frequent plugs by DJ Tony Blackburn on the newly-launched pirate station Radio Caroline (a view with which he concurred himself in his autobiography). Although the resultant UK No.1 would later be complemented by a No.5 hit in America, making it an international million-seller, and Pye were suitably emboldened to commission an LP on the back of its success, the Honeycombs subsequently struggled for serious attention and, try as he may, Meek's magic touch now repeatedly eluded him. In stark contrast, their second single, "Is It Because", could get no higher than No.30 in October. Simply squeezed out by the constant churn of other exceptional talent, they would only resurface much later with two more minor Top 30 hits in the course of 1965, a cover of Ray Davies's song "Something Better Beginning", followed by Honey herself being brought forward as vocalist on "That's The Way"; by which time, unfortunately, any lingering novelty element to their act had long since dissipated.

As for the Applejacks, they were a six-piece band from my own immediate neighbourhood of Solihull and as such were amongst the forerunners of the regional flowering of pop in the West Midlands eventually recognised in its own right as 'Brum Beat'. (My father, who usually only ever betrayed a cynical passing interest in pop music, nevertheless boasted of having his hair cut by lead singer Al Jackson, who had started working life as an apprentice hairdresser at Greatorex's the Barbers in Burlington Passage in the centre of Birmingham.) The original members – rhythm guitarist Phil Cash, lead guitarist Martin Baggott and drummer Gerry Freeman – had formed themselves into a skiffle group, the Crestas, in 1961 while they were all Scouts together in the Olton district of Solihull, and had then drawn in Megan Davies, an Assistant Cub Mistress in the same Scout Group, as an additional guitarist. Moving on quickly from the homely delights of Gang Shows to the guiltier pleasures of playing at dances in the wider locality, Phil and Martin upgraded to electric guitars for themselves, railroaded Megan into taking on electric bass and brought in Don Gould on keyboards. This quintet now became the Jaguars, predictably playing instrumentals under the all-pervading influence of the Shadows and the Tornados; until deciding in mid-1962 to recruit Al Jackson as a vocalist and subsequently become the Applejacks. It was from their weekly residency at Solihull Civic Hall, with what had by then grown into a versatile repertoire of rock'n'roll and R&B covers, that they attracted the attention of Decca's Mike Smith in 1963 and were offered a recording contract.

Recorded in January 1964 and released on Valentine's Day, their first single, "Tell Me When", was a smash hit, breaking into the Top 10 and tucking itself in at No.5 (immediately below Billy J. Kramer's "Little Children") in the week ending 18th April; its sparkling jollity attributable in large part to the bouncy piano part contributed by producer and arranger Mike Leander (and redolent of Gerry and the Pacemakers' Les McGuire). Unfortunately, its runaway success prematurely marked the high point of the Applejacks' pop career. Although for a while the press maintained a chauvinistic curiosity as to Megan's role as bass player, and perked up still further when it was made known that Lennon and McCartney had personally given the group leave to record one of their songs, as a follow-up "Like Dreamers Do" was a disappointment in the summer, peaking at No.23 in July. A third single, "Three Little Words", fared even less well, only making No.24 in October; and despite Decca's additional investment in releasing an LP that month (which included as one of its tracks the by now universally obligatory cover of "Too Much Monkey Business"), in the space of barely a year the Applejacks found time called on their fifteen minutes of fame.

If the Applejacks had parted company with the charts earlier than expected, there still remained other groups from the Birmingham area to show future promise, the first of these being the Rockin' Berries. Originally related most closely to the Fourmost in style and repertoire, they too started out as more musical entertainers than a pop group, combining Fifties' rock'n'roll with comic songs and impressions. Founded as the Bobcats in 1959 by lead guitarist Brian 'Chuck' Botfield, they served a lengthy apprenticeship in Hamburg in the early Sixties, including a residency at the Star-Club, before defections and the necessary recruitment of replacements in mid-1962 forced their reconfiguration as the five-piece Rockin' Berries. With Botfield still on lead guitar, the other members of the new line-up were: Clive Lea (vocals), Geoff Turton (vocals & rhythm guitar), Roy Austin (bass guitar) and Terry Bond (drums). And it was now that Turton unexpectedly disclosed a hidden asset:

> It was at this point that I found out I could sing. I'd never really
> sung before, just played the guitar. But we were doing these long,
> six-hour sets in Germany, and needed more than one singer. Clive
> was doing all the lead vocals at that time, I was singing back-ups,
> and so I tried a few things out. We suddenly found that I could
> sing falsetto. The first thing I ever did on stage was Frank Ifield's "I
> Remember You"![171]

Returning to Birmingham from Germany in 1963, they blagged their way into a record deal with Decca but were released from their contract after two consecutive singles failed to chart. Persevering in maintaining a full diary of engagements as a popular live band in local clubs, in the summer of 1964 they were next seen by John Schroeder, late of Oriole Records and now recruited by Pye to develop Piccadilly as a new subsidiary label. Suitably impressed to sign them up, Schroeder had immediately identified the group's "*real* commercial strength" as vested in Turton's "truly exciting vocals", whilst simultaneously acknowledging the associated difficulties that might yet lie ahead in utilising his undoubted talent to greatest effect:

> He was blessed with a very high, projected voice, capable of a wonderful falsetto – something similar to Frankie Valli. It was an extremely powerful and commercial sound – but material-wise, it was very hard to know what to do with it. The Rockin' Berries were great copyists, and could easily emulate the sounds of most of the chart records at that time. They were particularly adept at covering American discs. But unfortunately they didn't write their own material, and finding something original would be a recurring problem ...[172]

For their first release on Piccadilly in September, Schroeder had pulled out a song from the Rockin' Berries' live setlist, their cover of a Shirelles' B-side, "I Didn't Mean To Hurt You". A workmanlike recording that featured the precious Turton falsetto, it nevertheless failed to make a quick enough impression on the singles charts; although its popular appeal would later be broadened as the title track of their first retrospective EP. In any event, efforts to promote it further were hastily abandoned as a second single, "He's In Town", was rush-released within a matter of weeks. While out on the road on tour with Texan solo singer P.J. Proby, his companion, record producer Kim Fowley, had played the Berries a demo of this song by US group the Tokens, urging them to cover it as a surefire hit for themselves. Backing Fowley's judgement, Schroeder recorded the track with the group without delay, only then to discover that an imminent UK release from RCA Victor of the Tokens' original was in the pipeline, hence the hitherto unexpected rival issue from Piccadilly. Breaking into the charts at No.19 in late October, it rose to its highest position of No.4 in the week ending 21st November – the same week in which the Rolling Stones blasted straight to No.1 with "Little Red Rooster". By then, the Berries had moved on to tour with Manfred Mann and Bill Haley and the Comets when, for the first time, they experienced the novelty of their live act being drowned out by the screams of their own new contingent of teenage fans; a high point to savour while they had the chance.

Following the Rockin' Berries into the Top 30 by Christmas came another Birmingham group of an entirely different musical persuasion, the Moody Blues, although there were very close similarities in the earlier experiences of their founding members. The Moody Blues of 1964 represented an amalgamation of talents from, on the one hand, the defunct El Riot and the Rebels (Ray Thomas and Mike Pinder) and, on the other, Denny Laine and the Diplomats (Denny Laine himself); augmented by Graeme Edge (from Gerry Levene and the Avengers) and Clint Warwick (from Gerry Day and the Dukes). When El Riot – whose first love was early rock'n'roll – failed to pass muster for a recording contract with EMI in early 1963, the group folded; leaving Pinder and Thomas free to take up R&B as the Krew Cats and venture abroad to the German beat clubs of Hanover and Hamburg. Returning to England broke and busted that November, in Ray Thomas's words:

> We got back to Birmingham to find the scene in total chaos. There were about 250 groups: half thought they were Cliff Richard & the Shadows and the other half thought they were the Beatles! There was so much competition that the only way to get any gigs was to put together a local supergroup – so that's what we did.[173]

Thomas exactly dates the formation of this supposed 'supergroup' to 4th May 1964. Originally calling themselves the Moody Blues 5 (shortened to the M&B 5 for pub gigs, in a forlorn attempt to attract sponsorship from local brewery Mitchells & Butlers), they eventually settled for the Moody Blues, as indicative of their preferred genre, with the following line-up: Laine (vocals & guitar), Thomas (vocals, flute & harmonica), Pinder (keyboards), Warwick (bass guitar) and Edge (drums).

Jointly managed at the outset by Alex Wharton (former singing partner of Mickie Most and erstwhile A&R manager with Decca) and London-based hustler Tony Secunda, the group were quick to relocate to the capital themselves. Having obtained a recording contract with Decca and much enhanced their reputation as a live blues band by succeeding Manfred Mann in residency at the Marquee Club, after a failed debut single in August ("Steal Your Heart Away") they struck gold in December with a song by US soul singer Bessie Banks, "Go Now".

Wharton had received Banks's original version in a consignment of records sent to him from America to consider; and when the Moody Blues incorporated it into their live act, it was an instant crowd-pleaser. To save money on professional fees, Wharton took advantage of a makeshift studio under construction at the Marquee ("simply a garage with a home-made 12 channel mixer"[174]) to record and produce the Moodies' cover of the song; which is somewhat speeded up from the original tempo, although Laine still pretty faithfully reproduces the pattern of Banks's phrasing. Characterised by the dominance of Pinder's thumping piano and Laine's edgy vocal, Wharton laboured for several days to arrive eventually at a satisfying final take, sounding as if "it had been recorded in a public lavatory, dirty and full of ambience which was what I was after".[175] Its appeal lay precisely in its raw imperfections: Wharton admitted, for example, that the inescapable abruptness of the concluding fade-out was simply due to the fact that by then Laine's voice was shot and had cracked trying to hold the final note of the last chorus. Entering the Top 30 the week before Christmas, five weeks later it had become the third No.1 of 1965.

If Birmingham still had some way yet to go by the end of 1964 to establish its credentials firmly in the national consciousness as a worthwhile source of hits, this was not, of course, true of Manchester and the greater north-west; as the Hollies and Freddie and the Dreamers had already proved. Of these two acts, however, while the Hollies continued to grow and prosper, Freddie Garrity's fortunes took a downwards turn.

For the Hollies, 1964 was unquestionably a good year, taking them well on their way to consolidating their position as the fourth most popular British group (that is to say, after the Beatles, the Stones and the Searchers) despite not yet having a No.1 to their name; and, like the Beatles before them, without being winners themselves, they were nevertheless invited to Wembley to perform at the annual *NME* Poll-Winners' Concert in April. All three of their single releases were Top 10 hits: "Just One Look" reached No.3 in March, "Here I Go Again" made No.4 in June and "We're Through", the first of their own compositions to be credited as an A-side, got to No.7 in October. They also released two LPs: *Stay With The Hollies* in January and *In The Hollies Style* in November (the latter – though surprisingly unplaced in the LP charts – including, for me, the definitive cover of the year of "Too Much Monkey Business", as well as seven self-compositions out of the twelve tracks, concluding with the cracking *tour de force* "Set Me Free").

By contrast, Freddie and the Dreamers could no longer sustain themselves through zaniness alone and were gradually brought down by inferior material in the face of ever-more formidable – and, it has to be said, better promoted – competition. Of their respective four singles, "Over You" reached No.10 in March; only to be followed, disappointingly, by a No.17 hit in May with "I Love You Baby" and then, even more disappointingly, in July by "Just For You", which failed to make the Top 30 at all. Although they returned to the Top 10 with a No.6 hit in December, "I Understand" would never have sold in such quantities were it not for the tune's seasonal associations with "Auld Lang Syne" on which it was so excruciatingly based. Some writers euphemistically describe "I Understand" as 'sentimental' but in reality it was a cheap, maudlin shot at a Christmas hit, which miraculously just managed to pay off. If you like that kind of thing, then you might be inclined to say it couldn't be bettered; but the brutal truth was, no-one could have made it sound good, and it marked the beginning of the group's end in the UK.

There were, however, other new acts coming forward to swell the ranks of the northern contingent in terms of pop talent; including two more from Manchester, the first of these being Wayne Fontana and the Mindbenders. Seeking an alternative to his day job as a telephone engineer, Glyn Ellis had been playing the Manchester clubs with his group the Jets since 1961. In 1963, the Merseybeats' mentor, Jack Baverstock of Fontana Records, ever widening his search for talent, lighted upon him and offered him an audition at the Oasis; but when two-thirds of the Jets failed to show up, Ellis had to hastily commandeer the services of two local session musicians, guitarist Eric Stewart and drummer Ric Rothwell, to make up the numbers with his existing bass guitarist Bob Lang. After this impromptu quartet succeeded in securing a contract from Baverstock, Ellis, in grandiose style, decided to call himself Wayne Fontana for recording purposes (the Fontana in this instance not referring to his record company but chosen in homage to D.J. Fontana, drummer to Elvis Presley on all his greatest hits) and his new backing group, in a joking reference to a contemporary horror film, became the Mindbenders. A hard road lay ahead of them. Beginning with a cover of the rock'n'roll standard "Hello Josephine" in July 1963, it took another four attempts before at last they made the Top 30 in October 1964 with the curiously-titled but gently melodic "Um, Um, Um, Um, Um, Um"; a cover of a song by US performer Major Lance that in the week ending 21st November tied with the Rockin' Berries' "He's In Town" for the No.4 slot. Impressive though this was, they would now have to wait until the New Year for their biggest break.

More appealing initially to record-buyers were their local rivals, Herman's Hermits, who in the spring of 1964 were seen in concert in Bolton by Mickie Most and signed to EMI's Columbia label. Their lead singer was Peter Noone, already with a TV acting credit to his name as Len Fairclough's son in the early years of *Coronation Street*, backed by a standard four-piece line-up of three guitars and drums. Starting out as Pete Novac and the Heartbeats, they had originally presented themselves as a Buddy Holly tribute band, Noone even wearing glasses to strengthen the likeness; but as Herman and the Hermits, before eventually shortening the band's name, their repertoire broadened out into what had by now become the traditional club mix of rock'n'roll, R&B and comedy numbers. Consistently unsuccessful throughout 1963 in auditions for all the major record companies, Most's decision was ultimately more to do with the look of the group rather than their sound:

> Their managers [Harvey Lisberg and Charlie Silverman] had sent
> me a photograph of Herman's Hermits at Piccadilly Station in
> Manchester, and Peter Noone looked like a young Kennedy. I
> thought this face is saleable, especially in the United States. All I
> need to do is find cute songs to go with it.[176]

The song he opted to produce with them as their first single was by US songwriters Goffin and King, "I'm Into Something Good", which he had come across in its original American version by Ethel McCrea (under the pseudonym 'Earl-Jean'). Even after having augmented the Hermits' own indifferent instrumentation with session pianist Roger Webb, Most's production remains lightweight, carried almost entirely by Noone's cheeky lilting voice, yet somehow it still manages to be one of the most memorable hits of the Sixties. Released in August, it quickly climbed to No.1, following on in the starkest contrast from "You Really Got Me" by the Kinks for three weeks from mid-September into early October. At their managers' insistence, they recorded another Goffin and King composition, "Show Me Girl", as the follow-up but in the intense pre-Christmas market it was crowded out to no better than a lowly No.21 at the end of November; leaving Herman's Hermits too awaiting the realisation of their full potential in the year ahead.

Together with Decca's Mike Smith, Most was also responsible for signing up Dave Berry, a very different act from Sheffield, although he soon afterwards relinquished his role as Berry's producer to Smith. Starting out on the northern club circuit in his late teens as one half of a semi-professional duo performing songs by Buddy Holly and the Everly Brothers, in 1960 Berry broadened his musical tastes into rock'n'roll and R&B by falling in with a group originally known as the Frantic Four, who subsequently re-formed as Dave Berry and the Cruisers. The offer to record followed Most and Smith seeing the group in concert in Doncaster in 1963; but once in the studio, Smith effectively converted it from a group to a solo undertaking. Disenchanted with the Cruisers' unaided musical abilities, he deemed them surplus to his requirements, replacing them with regular session musicians such as Big Jim Sullivan, Jimmy Page and John Paul Jones.

In the autumn of '63, Decca put Dave Berry head to head with his idol Chuck Berry by issuing his cover version of "Memphis Tennessee"; a bizarre marketing decision, completely ignoring the confusion many potential purchasers would face in trying to choose between two records with the same title by two artists with the same surname. Although Dave did beat Chuck into the Top 30 by one week, in the end his first hit lost out to the original. Whereas Chuck reached No.8, Dave could only manage No.16. When he eventually returned to the charts in May 1964, it was for one week only at No.30 with another cover, the by then outdated Shirelles' song "Baby It's You" (already well known in the UK, of course, as an early Beatles' LP track). Fortunately, his next release, the haunting Geoff Stephens ballad "The Crying Game", was more auspicious, taking him to No.6 in early September and, on this occasion at least, vindicating Smith's judgement as producer; Berry's soft voice with its hint of a lisp perfectly balanced by the atmospheric arrangement featuring not only a zither but also the pioneering use by Big Jim

Sullivan of a volume swell-pedal to distort his guitar, thus creating what Alan Clayson described as "an unprecedented electric cello effect".[177] And it was this song above all others that was fundamental to establishing his distinctive identity as a tantalising, if not downright eccentric performer on TV. Dressed completely in black and claiming to draw upon the poses struck by Gene Vincent as the model for his own stage presence, Berry was most memorably described by music historian Colin Cross as "resembling a gay vampire as he slithered about, peeping round trees and rocks, sliding his microphone down his back, and hiding his face behind the collar of his leather jacket".[178]

Altogether more endearing were a quartet from Blackburn, the Four Pennies, who for two weeks in May had a No.1 hit with their second single, a romantic ballad of their own composition, "Juliet", that was resonant with sweet harmonies – as befitted the choirboy past of lead vocalist and rhythm guitarist Lionel Morton. It had been written by Morton together with fellow vocalists Fritz Fryer (lead guitar) and Mike Wilsh (bass guitar); Alan Buck (drums) being the fourth member of the group. Although not their first release, they had originally performed the song the year before as their winning entry in a talent competition, the prizes for which were a TV appearance (on *Scene At 6.30*, ITV's northern regional news magazine) and a recording test for Philips Records. When it saw the light of day again, however, in March 1964, it was issued by Philips as the B-side to another of the group's own efforts, "Tell Me Girl (What Are You Gonna Do)", before beginning to attract airplay in its own right and then becoming the best-selling track. While Fryer wrote their next release, "I Found Out The Hard Way" (which made a more modest showing at No.14 in August), they turned to a melodic Anglicised rendition of the Leadbelly song "Black Girl" for their fourth and final single of the year (another Top 20 hit but this time only reaching No.18 at the beginning of December).[179]

The fortunes of the mainstream pop contenders in the south were equally varied. As "Juliet" began its slide down the charts in June, for example, Brian Poole and the Tremeloes passed it on their way up to No.2 at the end of that month with their own biggest hit, the equally sentimental ballad "Someone, Someone", yet they were never again to command such interest.

Far cannier and more robust were the Dave Clark Five, who in the full span of their career contrived to make their no-nonsense, undemanding brand of rock more popular in the USA than here at home. As noted by Barry Miles:

> Though only 20 years old, Dave Clark was tremendously savvy. He was not only the drummer – with his kit placed at the front of the stage – and the songwriter, but he managed the group, produced the records, and kept all the rights. He paid for the sessions and

paid the band a weekly wage. As he succinctly put it: "We're all in it to try and make money."[180]

In the course of 1964, they enjoyed five Top 30 hits in the UK, some admittedly more successful than others. "Glad All Over", the second UK No.1 of the year, was followed by the foot-stomping extravaganza that was "Bits And Pieces" (No.2 in March), then the sax- and keyboard-driven "Can't You See That She's Mine" (No.11 in June); with the less well-remembered "Thinking Of You Baby" (No.23 in August) and "Any Way You Want It" (No.24 in November) bringing up the rear. To arouse initial interest in America, however, Clark traded mercilessly on the fact that sales of "Glad All Over" had eventually overtaken those of "I Want To Hold Your Hand", unseating it from the No.1 spot. When, therefore, he took his group to New York in March (hard on the heels of the Beatles' own American debut the preceding month), their success was assured by promoting "Glad All Over" to its potential new audience as the record that had 'defeated' the Beatles. As a consequence, the Dave Clark Five achieved instant popularity in a huge transatlantic teenage market now with a seemingly insatiable appetite for British music and, in the space of nine months to the end of the year, racked up no less than seven US hits in the *Billboard* Top 40 (of which four made the Top 10 and the remaining three the Top 20). According to Dave McAleer, whereas in Britain their singles sales placed them tenth in the list of best-selling artists for the year, in the USA they came second only to the Beatles.[181]

A group similarly reliant on dynamic vocals and a thumping beat, although in this instance heftily augmented by piano rather than electric keyboard, were the Nashville Teens. Formed in Weybridge in 1962 and with a traditional Hamburg apprenticeship at the Star-Club in 1963 behind them (during which they had backed and recorded with Jerry Lee Lewis), they were signed up as a sextet by manager Don Arden in March 1964, their most distinctive feature being the powerful punch delivered by paired lead vocalists Arthur 'Art' Sharp and Ray Phillips. Set on by Arden to tour Britain with American greats of the stature of Carl Perkins and Chuck Berry, they were eventually discovered by Mickie Most while playing in support of Bo Diddley and a recording deal with Decca negotiated. The resultant single ensued from Most supporting Sharp's choice of a strident cover of John D.Loudermilk's song about poverty in the Deep South of the USA, "Tobacco Road". Released in July, by the end of August it had climbed to No.5 and in the autumn it made its own modest contribution to the British invasion by reaching No.14 in America. Following up with another Loudermilk composition, "Google Eye", was a less successful move. There were, after all, fewer British fans genuinely looking for more of the same in the guise of this saga of a giant catfish and it stalled at No.13 in November, thus curtailing the Teens' occupancy of the Top 30.[182]

Illustrative of the diversity now fuelling the expansion of mid-Sixties' pop, in the same week in August that the full-on thrash of "Tobacco Road" hit its peak, an entirely different song from an entirely different group (albeit housemates on the same record label) entered the charts at No.20: "She's Not There", by the Zombies. A five-piece band from St. Albans in Hertfordshire, its greatest strengths lay in the subtle combination of the fragile vocals of Colin Blunstone and the keyboard and compositional skills of Rod Argent; and, like the Four Pennies, their route to a recording contract came through winning first prize in a local talent contest, in their case for their interpretation of the Gershwin standard "Summertime".

In June 1964, having passed their audition for Decca, they turned professional, striking a management deal with impresario Tito Burns; but "Summertime" was bypassed as their intended debut single in favour of Argent's own composition, "She's Not There", a story of lost love and missed opportunity which in-house producer Kenneth Jones turned into a jewel of minor-key melancholy. In its eight-week British chart run, its highest position was No.13, yet to this day it stands out as a classic Sixties' recording. It was far better received in America, reaching No.2 over there, the middle-class backgrounds and impeccable Received Pronunciation of the group members only serving to cement the Zombies' appeal to the wildly intrigued US record-buyers; and in an unlikely pairing, they would find themselves thrown together in due course with the Nashville Teens to play concerts in New York.[183]

For purity of enunciation, however, there were few to rival ex-public schoolboys Peter and Gordon. Notwithstanding Ray Davies's scorn for the upper-crust Robert Wace's efforts to rock with conviction, these two set out to emulate the Everly Brothers and, with a little help from their friends, carved out a profitable niche for themselves into the bargain. Since Peter had the good fortune to be Jane Asher's older brother, his family association with celebrity lodger Paul McCartney was critical to raising the pair's profile and they were signed to EMI's Columbia label by A&R executive Norman Newell after he had seen them playing in fashionable West End venue the Pickwick Club. Paul reworked one of his earlier songs, "World Without Love", for them to record as their first single and by the end of April they had made it a No.1 hit (even though Newell as producer may have had to live down a grating bum note on the electric organ in the middle instrumental break of the original mono mix). Inevitably, it also featured as the highlight track of their first LP, issued by Columbia in June, the contents of which showed their relative ease in the traditional folk idiom of songs like "Five Hundred Miles" and "All My Trials" compared to the tameness of their desperately buttoned-up interpretation of Little Richard's "Lucille"[184] (so perhaps Ray Davies did have a point after all). Two more McCartney songs were to follow, of which only the first, "Nobody I Know", succeeded, returning them to the

Top 10 at No.9 in late June and early July: their third single, "I Don't Want To See You Again", was released in September but failed to chart. (All three, however, were US Top 20 hits, with "World Without Love" reaching No.1 on both sides of the Atlantic, and Peter and Gordon registered strongly with American audiences from their first US trip in June onwards.)[185]

The high level of activity by so many British artists threatened to develop into a tidal wave that would overwhelm the American home market. As noted earlier in this chapter, the arrival of the Beatles in New York in February, in the vanguard of the 'British invasion', filled Brian Wilson as much with dread as with envy; and even allowing for his habitually low self-esteem, he had good cause to be afraid. Irrespective of the quality of music produced by either group, at the most basic of levels the Beach Boys' supremacy as America's top act on Capitol Records was suddenly at serious risk of being undermined by the emergence of the Beatles as a rival group on the same label, turning the heads of the company's promotional and marketing executives and diverting their energies in hitherto undreamed of directions, beyond the wildest dreams of avarice.

Furthermore, there was precious little reciprocity, as yet, in the attitude of British record-buyers towards new releases by American groups, such as they were. While veteran performers like Elvis and Roy Orbison were still assured of high sales in Britain in 1964 – Presley racked up five Top 20 hits and Orbison four (including two UK No.1 hits with "It's Over" and "Oh, Pretty Woman") – their natural successors were the next generation of soloists, such as Gene Pitney or P.J. Proby. The Everly Brothers' popularity in this country was tailing off, leaving only the novelty of falsetto harmony groups the Four Seasons or the Newbeats to fill the vacuum intermittently, with "Rag Doll" and "Bread And Butter" respectively.

Eager to establish an international following of their own, the Beach Boys (including the increasingly reticent performer Brian Wilson) flew out on 13th January for the first leg of the 'Surfside 64' tour of Australia and New Zealand; in support of headline act Roy Orbison, together with fellow Americans the Surfaris and Paul & Paula, the entourage being joined on arrival by Sydney group the Joy Boys. The tour was well received by young people still enthused by their native geography with a taste for surfing music (whereas back home the craze was by then virtually outmoded) but the group found Murry Wilson's constant presence stifling and overbearing, driving them to reflect seriously on the long-term viability of their professional association with him.

Already beaten to the punch by the Beatles' audacity in starting the New Year with "I Want To Hold Your Hand" as a US No.1, the Beach Boys returned to Los Angeles on 2nd February, just in time for the release next day of their first new single of the year, "Fun, Fun, Fun", four days ahead of the Beatles' arrival in New York. In due course it reached No.5; but its UK release a month later was meaningless, making no impression whatsoever on the British charts. The logical explanation for this is surely that the content of its lyric – celebrating the audacity of a California girl who gets her kicks by defying her father and neglecting her studies in favour of madcap driving exploits in a souped-up Thunderbird – could not be slotted by English record-buyers into any meaningful cultural frame of reference. Yet strangely it was with another song about the love of hot rods, "I Get Around"[186], that the Beach Boys belatedly broke into the UK Top 30 in July and the Top 10 (at No.9) in August. This followed its phenomenal success as their first US No.1 and million-seller, rightfully restoring Americans to the top of their own *Billboard* chart after many months by displacing Peter and Gordon's "World Without Love". Whether or not British teenagers ever fully understood what the song was actually about is, I believe, open to question. True, there are some clues, as in:

> I'm gettin' bugged driving up and down the same old strip,
> I gotta find a new place where the kids are hip.

And:

> We always take my car 'cause it's never been beat
> And we've never missed yet with the girls we meet.

But personally I always struggled to disentangle all the words from the soaring harmonies, even though the chorus did lend itself remarkably well to chanting with like-minded schoolmates; leaving the significance of being "a real cool head" and "making real good bread" indecipherably lost forever in the highest registers.

Recording material for singles and LPs consumed what would be considered today as a disproportionate amount of the Beach Boys' time for the remainder of the year; and it was in the studio, in early April, in the course of recording "I Get Around", that the Wilson brothers finally lost all patience with their father's acerbic running commentary on their musical capabilities and sacked him as the group's manager. In hindsight, it was a Pyrrhic victory, for Brian could never be free of the psychological damage inflicted on him in particular by Murry and he little realised how much pressure would fall upon him in the short term not just as group leader but also principal songwriter, arranger and producer. Nevertheless, under his stewardship, by Christmas the Beach Boys had completed and released four LPs: *Shut Down Vol.2* in March, *All Summer Long* in July, *Beach Boys Concert* in October (which went to No.1 in the US album charts) and *The Beach Boys' Christmas Album* in November. Increasingly – and perhaps unhealthily – the context for this almost obsessive activity was a desire to outdo the external competition posed predominantly by the Beatles and other British acts such as the Rolling Stones. Consider, for example, that against the Beach Boys' own four, the Beatles had no less than seven LPs released in America in 1964 (four of which became No.1 albums).[187] While the Rolling Stones only brought out two that year, their second US LP *12 x 5* was released on Decca's American label London the same week as *Beach Boys Concert* – to coincide with their second US tour in late October/early November – and made it to No.3.

Cashing in on the success of "I Get Around" as a No.1 single and in anticipation of the release of *All Summer Long*, the Beach Boys spent the height of summer on a tour of Western States, under the banner of 'Summer Safari'; starting in Honolulu on 3rd July and closing in San Diego on 8th August. On 21st August, they embarked on a complementary six-week tour of Eastern States (beginning in Cleveland, Ohio), playing thirty more concerts and interrupted on 27th September in New York to make their first appearance on *The Ed Sullivan Show*. This tour ended in pandemonium on 30th September, in Worcester, Massachusetts, the final concert brought to a premature halt by the police after only fourteen minutes in the face of a total breakdown in crowd control in and around the auditorium. Then, on 1st November, they embarked on their second foreign tour of the year, taking the fight back to the UK and Europe on an 18-day series of concerts and promotional appearances.

In advance of their arrival in England, their next single "When I Grow Up (To Be A Man)" was released here on 23rd October, having already been released two months earlier back home and given them a No.9 hit in September. Although the Beach Boys spent eight days in Britain altogether, they played no live concerts as such, concentrating instead on radio and TV broadcasts; which included live appearances on *Ready Steady Go!* and *Thank Your Lucky Stars*. The trip was also noteworthy for their encounters along the way with leading UK managers Brian Epstein, at an enforced stopover at Shannon Airport, and Andrew Loog Oldham, who suffered a punch in the face from Dennis Wilson when he met the group in London for his pains in declaring his respect for Murry. Of greater overall significance from the visit, however, was the clearest indication yet from Brian – at a press conference convened by EMI on 2nd November – that he felt the time for the group to be seen as having moved on musically was overdue:

> We don't play surfing music. We're tired of being labelled as the originators of the surfing sound. We just produce a sound that the teens dig, and that can be applied to any theme. The surfing theme has run its course. Cars are finished now, too … We're just gonna stay on the life of the social teenager.[188]

Despite their efforts, Britain did not take to "When I Grow Up (To Be A Man)", which sold in considerably lower numbers than "I Get Around", only managing to lurch to No.28 by the end of November. Beginning in Dublin, the whistle-stop European leg of the tour was, by contrast, primarily concert-based, taking in venues in seven countries[189] and concluding in Paris on 18th November; after which they flew home to promote their current US single "Dance, Dance, Dance" (which Capitol had released the week before their departure).

December should have been the happiest of months for Brian, committing himself as he did on the 7th to marriage with his 16-year-old girlfriend Marilyn Rovell. Unwittingly, however, in that same month he fell under the perverse influence of a circle of twenty-something Hollywood socialites, through whom he was introduced to marijuana and thus set on a downward spiral of regular drug-taking, much to the growing concern of his new bride. And while he had been an active participant earlier in the year in both international and domestic tours with the Beach Boys, on 23rd December he suffered a catastrophic panic attack in mid-flight from Los Angeles to Houston, at the outset of their latest two-week scheduled tour of Southern and Mid-Western States:

> The plane had been in the air only five minutes when I told Al Jardine I was going to crack up at any minute. He told me to cool it. Then I started crying. I put a pillow over my face and began screaming and yelling.[190]

After the shock of which, things went from bad to worse:

> I told the stewardesses, 'I don't want any food. Get away from me.' Then I started telling people that I'm not getting off the plane. I was getting far out, coming undone, having a breakdown, and I just let myself go completely. I dumped myself out of the seat and all over the plane. I let myself go emotionally. They took care of me well. They were as understanding as they could be. They knew what was happening and I was coming apart. The rubber band had stretched as far as it would go.[191]

In spite of his mounting anxiety and obvious distress, Brian was persuaded to disembark on arrival in Houston and recovered himself sufficiently to play that night's concert; only to wake up next morning "with the biggest knot in my stomach" and feeling "like I was going out of my mind".[192] Accompanied by their road manager, he flew back that day to Los Angeles and Glen Campbell was hurriedly drafted in to take his place for the rest of the tour. Brian would not perform live with the Beach Boys again for the remainder of the Sixties and beyond. From here on in, he would increasingly be beset by a bewildering combination of his own internal demons and external pressures, transformed by such unmitigated turmoil into the first of the celebrity rock casualties of the decade.

Untroubled by self-induced fears of competition and observing the phenomenon of the new imported culture of pop music approvingly from the sidelines, Bob Dylan continued meanwhile to plough his lone furrow somewhere in that indeterminate hinterland between blues, folk and rock. As he openly confided to *New Yorker* feature-writer Nat Hentoff:

> I have no work to do. I have no job. I'm not committed to anything except making a few records and playing a few concerts. I'm weird that way. Most people, when they get up in the morning, have to do what they *have* to do. I could pretend there were all sorts of things I *had* to do every day. But why? So I do whatever I feel like.[193]

Far from feeling threatened by the Beatles, he positively dug them, instinctively understanding that "they were pointing the direction of where music had to go".[194] As we saw earlier in this chapter, he had actively sought out their company at his earliest opportunity; and as for the Animals, he had readily acknowledged how their innovative treatment of the traditional song he had initially helped to popularise, "House Of The Rising Sun", had blown him away.[195] His own recorded output for the year spanned just two LPs, very different in character (production responsibilities now having passed from John Hammond to Tom Wilson) but containing within their tracks some of his most powerful and enduring songs.

First to be released, on 13th January, was *The Times They Are A-Changin'*, its sombre black-and-white cover portrait of a morose Dylan in a denim work-shirt in part reflective of the sombre content within. Aside from the iconoclastic title track, there were two other songs with a similar breadth of prophetic vision: "With God On Our Side" and "When The Ship Comes In". There was a trio of more didactic songs, exploring topical issues of equality, justice and human dignity: "The Lonesome Death Of Hattie Carroll", "Only A Pawn In Their Game" and "Ballad of Hollis Brown". (With the exception of the contemporaneous "Who Killed Davey Moore?", captured only in live performance, he would write and record no other songs of overt protest until his largely ignored December 1971 single release, "George Jackson".) However, the remaining four held particular significance in signalling the onset of a transition in Dylan's songwriting to more intensely personal themes. "North Country Blues", although it adopted the accepted folk convention of narration by someone of the opposite sex to the singer, was a doleful story of decline and decay in an iron mining community closely resembling that familiar to him through his own upbringing in Minnesota. "Boots Of Spanish Leather", "Restless Farewell" and "One Too Many Mornings" were all explorations of different aspects of the protracted, painful fracturing of his relationship with Suze Rotolo (which finally came to grief in March 1964).

This shift in his stance was confirmed in the summer by the contents of *Another Side Of Bob Dylan*, released on 8th August but probably the least well regarded of all his Sixties' albums. All eleven tracks were recorded in a single night in the studio, on 9th June, the end-product representing an uneasy truce between quality (as much of sentiment as performance) and spontaneity: Dylan himself was known not to have cared for Tom Wilson's choice of album title. Opening with the almost throwaway "All I Really Want To Do", semi-humorously advocating realism above commitment in personal relationships, it concludes with a dark trilogy of songs about love and fidelity; of which the most infamous is "Ballad In Plain D", his bitter epitaph to his break-up with Suze in which he castigates "her parasite sister" Carla for interfering:

> Beneath a bare lightbulb the plaster did pound
> Her sister and I in a screaming battleground
> And she in between, the victim of sound
> Soon shattered as a child 'neath her shadows.[196]

This is sandwiched between the heavy sarcasm of "I Don't Believe You (She Acts Like We Never Have Met)", commemorating a girl's ingratitude after a one-night stand, and the stunning resignation to the inevitability of transience in human affairs that is the final track, "It Ain't Me Babe":

> Go lightly from the ledge, babe
> Go lightly on the ground
> I'm not the one you want, babe
> I will only let you down.[197]

Elsewhere there are more promising hints of an impressive new poetry evolving. In "Chimes Of Freedom", a violent electrical storm becomes the dramatic context in which Dylan expresses concern for all those denied a voice of their own:

> Far between sundown's finish an' midnight's broken toll
> We ducked inside the doorway, thunder crashing
> As majestic bells of bolts struck shadows in the sounds
> Seeming to be the chimes of freedom flashing.[198]

As the storm unleashes its fury, its "blowin' rain" and "wild ripping hail" accompanied by "bells of lightning", the catalogue of the dispossessed continues and is not yet exhausted when it at last shows signs of abating:

> Even though a cloud's white curtain in a far-off corner flashed
> An' the hypnotic splattered mist was slowly lifting
> Electric light still struck like arrows, fired but for the ones
> Condemned to drift or else be kept from drifting.

Finally passing over, the dying splendour of the decaying storm still has the power to hold the attention of Dylan the narrator and his companions, to concentrate their minds to the very end:

> As we listened one last time an' we watched with one last look
> Spellbound and swallowed 'til the tolling ended
> Tolling for the aching ones whose wounds cannot be nursed
> For the countless confused, accused, misused, strung-out ones an' worse
> An' for every hung-up person in the whole wide universe
> An' we gazed upon the chimes of freedom flashing.

And in the profundity of contradictions that is "My Back Pages", he grapples with the artist's dilemma of breaking free from the dead weight of past expectations laid upon him, which has prematurely aged him, so as to be able to travel on new roads without fear of being called to account as a hypocrite:

> Yes, my guard stood hard when abstract threats
> Too noble to neglect
> Deceived me into thinking
> I had something to protect
> Good and bad, I define these terms
> Quite clear, no doubt, somehow
> Ah, but I was so much older then
> I'm younger than that now.[199]

This paradox of becoming younger and wiser would eventually be celebrated more widely by the Byrds in 1967 making the song the centrepiece of their immaculate fourth LP *Younger Than Yesterday* (as explored in more depth in Chapter 9). For the immediate future, however, it would stand as Dylan's own resolute statement of intent, at the age of 23, in rebuttal of sustained efforts by America's self-appointed grandees of folk to rein him in. Indeed, he saw the whole album collectively as representative of a new personal agenda, as he explained to Nat Hentoff on the very evening of its inception:

> There aren't any finger-pointing songs in here, either. Those records
> I've already made, I'll stand behind them; but some of that was
> jumping into the scene to be heard and a lot of it was because
> I didn't see anybody else doing that kind of thing. Now a lot of
> people are doing finger-pointing songs. You know – pointing to
> all the things that are wrong. Me, I don't write *for* people anymore.
> You know – be a spokesman ... From now on, I want to write
> from inside me, and to do that I'm going to have to get back to
> writing like I used to when I was ten – having everything come out
> naturally. The way I like to write is for it to come out the way I walk
> or talk.[200]

In late July, at the 1964 Newport Folk Festival, his reception had lacked the universal acclaim of the year before, given, as noted by Tom Piazza, his tangible departure from performing "burning, uncompromising songs of social indictment" in preference for "ironic love songs and imagistic poetry".[201] With hindsight, Dylan himself reasoned that from the outset he should have been more alert to the tensions of the occasion:

> Ronnie Gilbert, one of The Weavers, introduced me ... saying, "And here he is ... take him, you know him, he's yours." I had failed to sense the ominous forebodings in the introduction. Elvis had never even been introduced like that. "Take him, he's yours!" What a crazy thing to say! Screw that. As far as I knew, I didn't belong to anybody then or now.[202]

What followed over that weekend were performances drawing primarily upon his new repertoire that flew full in the face of the festival's overtly political appetite for 'finger-pointing songs'. As his critical friend, Robert Shelton, noted sardonically: "On Friday afternoon [24th July] at the topical-song workshop, he sang "It Ain't Me, Babe" and "Tambourine Man." No one seemed to mind that Dylan's two new songs were topical only to the singer."[203]

This time round, he appeared to distance himself, musically at least, from any indebtedness to Joan Baez for her patronage, a tell-tale sign of his growing ambivalence towards her in public, particularly in such highly charged surroundings. Initially, he duetted with her in a reprise of "It Ain't Me, Babe" at the end of her Friday evening set. Then, at the conclusion of his own ragged, uneven performance on Sunday night – which, to the consternation of the festival organisers, had nonetheless left his audience clamouring for more after he had closed with "Chimes Of Freedom" – he paid her the reverse compliment by bringing her on stage to join him in "With God On Our Side" as an encore, which served only to further delay and disrupt the running order of the festival's finale.

Critical conservative voices were raised against him after the event, reproaching him for departing from the presumed Newport ethos and, at their most hostile, accusing him of "innocuousness ... utter disregard for the tastes of the audience ...[and] selfconscious egotism".[204] If it worried him at all, he proved his resilience by giving what Robert Shelton ranked as one of his greatest performances at the New York Philharmonic Hall on 31st October, the 'Halloween Concert' in which he skilfully combined songs from his once and future catalogue. The occasion was characterised throughout by good-tempered interaction between Dylan and his audience, as he catered to all tastes. There were old favourites, like "A Hard Rain's A-Gonna Fall", "Talkin' World War III Blues" and "Don't Think Twice, It's All Right"; and current tracks from *Another Side* ..., including "Spanish Harlem Incident", "I

Don't Believe You (She Acts Like We Never Have Met)" and "All I Really Want To Do"; liberally interspersed with even newer, as yet unrecorded titles such as "Gates Of Eden", "It's Alright, Ma (I'm Only Bleeding)" and "Mr. Tambourine Man". A particular highlight in this third category was his rare performance of "If You Gotta Go, Go Now", emphasising the latent humour of this anti-love song (described by Shelton in his laudatory review of the evening as a "droll, infectious song of seduction"[205]). In addition, he showed true generosity of spirit towards Joan Baez, who joined him, as a previously unannounced guest, for three duets in the second half of the show. Having thus firmly distanced himself from the carping post-Newport recriminations, the final paragraph of Shelton's critique was now once again fulsome in its unreserved praise of his talents:

> After a half year of detours, Mr. Dylan seems to have returned
> his enormous musical and literary gifts to a forward course.
> His developing control of those gifts and his ability to shape a
> meaningful program added up to a frequently spell-binding evening
> by the brilliant singing poet laureate of young America.[206]

All in all, it was more than a fitting rehearsal for his next unexpectedly ambitious leap of faith. As he would shortly declare enigmatically to a widening international audience:

> i am about t sketch You a picture of what goes on around here
> sometimes. tho i don't understand too well myself what's really
> happening.[207]

The year had witnessed an unprecedented influx of British popular culture into the USA as one opportunistic consequence of the vacuum created by the assassination of President Kennedy. This is not to say, however, that America was incapable of recovering its equilibrium from this unforeseen political calamity in due course and in early July President Johnson made a significant contribution to the cause of social justice by enacting new civil rights legislation, aimed at ending racial discrimination. Unfortunately, a month later, his attention was forcibly diverted from domestic concerns to those of foreign military policy in South-East Asia. On 2nd August, the USS *Maddox*, a destroyer engaged in covert intelligence-gathering operations in the Gulf of Tonkin, off the coast of North Vietnam, was attacked by North Vietnamese torpedo boats; an attack that was renewed on 4th August, following the deployment of a second destroyer in the area, the USS *C. Turner Joy*. The President, in responding by ordering a retaliatory bombing raid, made an irrevocable, historic decision:

> In the first bombing of North Vietnam, sixty-four naval aircraft

struck the oil storage and port facilities at Vinh just north of the Partition line. The Pentagon estimated that ten per cent of the North's oil supply had been destroyed. It had taken ten minutes. The United States had directly entered the Vietnam War without declaration at 11 a.m., 5 August 1964.[208]

Johnson was also known to be as openly committed as his predecessor to boosting national prestige by investment in the space race. Yet 1964 saw no US manned space flights at all, attention having turned instead to intensive consolidation, research and development in preparation for launching the new Gemini spacecraft with a pair of astronauts aboard, as the next stepping-stone towards the Apollo moon-landing. Not to be outdone, Kruschev demanded in February that the Soviet Union should seize the propaganda initiative by sending up a three-man space vehicle as soon as possible; although the necessary diversion of resources and modification of the existing Vostok capsule meant this actually took many more months to achieve. Eventually, on 12th October, the Voskhod mission was launched, carrying a crew of three – Vladimir Komarov, Boris Yegorov and Konstantin Feoktistov – on a successful sixteen-orbit flight around the Earth; a belated triumph in which Kruschev could no longer glory, for it coincided with a political coup in the Kremlin removing him from power. On 15th October, it was announced that he had been replaced by Leonid Brezhnev and Alexei Kosygin, who would henceforth work in tandem as Communist Party leader and Prime Minister respectively. By contrast, in November Lyndon Johnson retained his office for a new term by trouncing his challenger, the hawkish reactionary Senator Barry Goldwater, in the US Presidential election.

Whereas the hitherto unelected President Johnson ultimately gained the confidence of American voters, unfortunately for Britain's unelected Prime Minister, Sir Alec Douglas-Home, that situation was not to be replicated here. In September, he called a general election, which took place on 15th October. Hence at exactly the same moment as Kruschev was brought down by the secretive machinations of the Soviet Politburo, the British electorate democratically decided they had had enough of Sir Alec, three days short of his completing a year in office. Labour had won by the slenderest of margins (only four seats), bringing to an end what they disparagingly dismissed as 'thirteen years of Tory misrule' and ushering in Harold Wilson as the new Prime Minister. Wilson, who was born in Huddersfield and chose to portray himself as a homely, pipe-smoking common man despite his intellectual credentials as a first-class honours graduate of Oxford University, was the first post-war Prime Minister to recognise the potential of the popular arts to enhance his own reputation. Despite soon becoming an easy target himself for television satirists (notably John Bird), he appeared to retain a cheerful indifference to public ridicule when, for example, he blatantly exploited the halo effect of endorsing the Beatles' contribution to international awareness of the UK in general and England in particular.

The year in which the third James Bond film *Goldfinger* was one of the most successful new screen releases was also the year in which 007's creator, Ian Fleming, died, in August at the age of 56. The British influence was all-pervasive in the cinema, as even best-selling US productions were dependent on the major contributions of UK actors: Rex Harrison as Professor Higgins in the film version of the musical *My Fair Lady* – for which he won the Best Actor Oscar; Julie Andrews (passed over as a possible Eliza Doolittle, despite her outstanding success in the role on stage, in favour of Audrey Hepburn, whose singing parts had to be dubbed) taking the title role in *Mary Poppins* – for which she won the Best Actress Oscar; and Peter Sellers dominating the anti-nuclear war satire *Dr. Strangelove Or: How I Learned To Stop Worrying And Love The Bomb* in the three roles of Group Captain Lionel Mandrake, US President Merkin Muffley and the President's scientific adviser Dr. Strangelove – for which he received a Best Actor Oscar nomination. Another hit film of the year, *Zulu*, saw the debut in a starring role of Michael Caine, son of a Billingsgate fish porter, as the quintessentially English Army officer, Lieutenant Gonville Bromhead, at the Battle of Rorke's Drift.

On 20th January, the trial of the thirteen Great Train Robbers apprehended to that date opened in Aylesbury (where the chamber of the new Rural District Council offices had been converted into a courtroom specifically for the purpose), presided over by Mr. Justice Edmund Davies. It was to occupy the next three months. Only one of the defendants, Roger Cordrey, pleaded guilty upon arraignment, leaving twelve to persuade the jury of their innocence. On 6th February, however, in the course of giving his evidence for the prosecution, a Detective Inspector Morris unwittingly disclosed that Ronnie Biggs had previously served a custodial sentence. On the grounds that this was inadmissible evidence, Biggs's QC successfully argued that he should be discharged forthwith and thus he was retried separately in April. When all the cases had finally been heard, all twelve defendants had duly been found guilty on various counts of their involvement in the robbery.

Sentencing took place on 15th April, the exemplary ferocity of which being clearly indicated by the judge in his prefatory remarks to Cordrey, whose guilty plea had been accepted at the outset:

> Let us clear out of the way any romantic notions of daredevilry.
> This is nothing less than a sordid crime of violence inspired by
> vast greed … As the higher the price the greater the temptation,
> potential criminals who may be dazzled by the enormity of
> the price must be taught that the punishment they risk will be
> proportionately greater.

I therefore find myself faced with the unenviable duty of

pronouncing grave sentences.[209]

He was as good as his word, sentencing Cordrey to concurrent terms of twenty years' imprisonment on four counts – one of conspiracy to rob the mail and three of receiving stolen money – in spite of the mitigating circumstances of his guilty plea and assistance to the police in recovering at least some of the proceeds of the robbery. Those who had been tried and found guilty fared even worse. Ronnie Biggs, for example, was one of six defendants given concurrent sentences of twenty-five years for conspiracy and thirty years for armed robbery. Altogether, the prison sentences passed that day amounted to a total of 307 years; although four of the gang, including Cordrey, then lodged appeals, which were heard in July. Two of the twenty-five year convictions for conspiracy were quashed, as was one other conviction for robbery. In Cordrey's case, his robbery conviction was also quashed and his sentence for receiving reduced to fourteen years. The vexing issue of the overall harshness of the original sentences in this case and how far such sentencing might or might not have a deterrent effect on other potentially violent criminals nevertheless continued to play on the minds of the judiciary and legislature alike; and was cited by several concerned participants in the course of the historic Commons debate on 21st December of Sydney Silverman's Private Member's Bill to totally abolish the death penalty for murder.

And there were other obvious instances of repressive tendencies on the part of the courts. In February, for example, more than three years after the publication of *Lady Chatterley's Lover* had been vindicated, the issue of obscenity in literature was again put to the test by a London magistrate's ruling banning from sale an expurgated paperback edition of *Fanny Hill*, the erotic epistolary novel by John Cleland first published in the eighteenth century as *Memoirs of a Woman of Pleasure*. (Opting not to appeal against the ban, the publishers, Mayflower Books, let the matter lie until 1970, by which time they were then able to reissue the same text unrevised and unchallenged.)

The police and courts also found themselves sorely tested by successive outbreaks of juvenile delinquency on the promenades and beaches of seaside resorts. Beginning at Easter in Clacton and erupting elsewhere over the Whitsun and summer holidays, violent confrontations between gangs of Mods and Rockers shattered the peace of several southern seaside towns; notably Bournemouth, Brighton, Margate and Hastings. The unsettling spectacle of these running fights could not fail to provoke a conservative backlash when those who had been arrested and charged in significant numbers were brought before the magistrates; and they, for their part, did not disappoint, duly imposing heavy fines and custodial sentences. In Margate in May, the forty-four who came before Dr. George Simpson, for instance, had no prospect of expecting leniency from the bench, after first being soundly harangued by him as "long-haired, mentally unstable, petty little hoodlums" and "sawdust Caesars who can only find courage like rats, in hunting in packs".[210]

Thanks, of course, chiefly to the Beatles and now, latterly, to the Rolling Stones, through widespread coverage of their growing international popularity, by late 1964 the revitalised music industry had shown itself to be legitimately newsworthy, as one new British act after another followed the trail blazed so spectacularly from February onwards to America. Compared to the situation in the domestic market twelve months earlier, the range of artists and, more importantly, the choice and quality of their records had expanded out of all recognition; leading in turn to a broadening and greater sophistication of taste on the part of record-buyers. To take one unequivocal example, who then could possibly have foreseen the making of a disc like the Animals' "House Of The Rising Sun" or, furthermore, that readers of the *NME* would end up voting it Best Single of the year?

Those artists who had followed the Beatles' lead by persuading A&R managers to back their songwriting as well as performing capabilities found themselves doubly blessed, although sustaining that dual effort rapidly proved too hard for some. The dissemination of pop music had undeniably been enhanced by the advent of the commercial pirate radio stations, punching above their weight in record promotion as they created their own offshore playlists, free of both the restrictive practices governing the much diluted fare offered by the BBC's Light Programme and the nightly reception vagaries of Radio Luxembourg. And with the inauguration of a third terrestrial TV channel, BBC 2, in April, further but as yet remote possibilities for alternative approaches to the redefinition of popular culture, including music, might one day present themselves.

In its way, "I Feel Fine" could hardly have been a more appropriate No.1 with which to close what Pete Frame rapturously dubbed an "Ace year!"[211], summing up as it did the rightful jubilation of the British pop fraternity in having succeeded, against all expectations, in refashioning the traditional idioms of American music and selling them back around the world in dizzying quantities. Yet in reality it also carried with it a faint air of self-satisfaction at the culmination of one quite specific set of endeavours, with roots going back even beyond the start of the decade, and as such held no portent of the sea-change next to come.

NOTES

1　He would go on to appear in rotation with the well-established BBC DJs David Jacobs, Alan Freeman and Pete Murray.

2　Quoted in Andrew Loog Oldham, op. cit., p.341.

3　Alwyn W. Turner, "My Generation: The Glory Days of British Rock" (V&A, 2010), p.48.

4　I am indebted to Alan Smith's article "50's and 60's UK Charts: A History", posted on www.davemcaleer.com, for this information.

5　Originally Denise Sampey, then Diane Hefforan, to be followed by the best-known of all, Samantha Juste (who would later marry Micky Dolenz of the Monkees).

6　Listed here in ascending order of the relevant *NME* chart.

7　Mark Lewisohn, op. cit., p.137.

8　Barry Miles, op. cit., p.50.

9　Brian Epstein, op. cit., p.15.

10　Ibid.

11　Brian Epstein, op. cit., p.16.

12　Ibid.

13　Brian Epstein, op. cit., p.17. In the end, his final tally was three shows for the Beatles, plus two for Gerry and the Pacemakers.

14　Where John and Cynthia had stayed in August 1963 for a belated three-day honeymoon.

15　Andy Neill, "The Beatles Across The Universe: John, Paul, George and Ringo On Tour and On Stage" (Haynes, 2009), p.96.

16　Quoted in "The Beatles Anthology" (Cassell, 2000), p.114.

17　Quoted in Derek Taylor, "It Was Twenty Years Ago Today" (Bantam, 1987), p.92.

18　Ibid.

19　Quoted in David Pritchard & Alan Lysaght, op. cit., p.147.

20　Quoted in Barry Miles, op. cit., p.73.

21　Cynthia Lennon, op. cit., p.179.

22　Ibid.

23　Quoted in David Pritchard & Alan Lysaght, op. cit., p.151.

24　Quoted in "The Beatles Anthology" (Cassell, 2000), p.120.

25　Quoted in David Pritchard & Alan Lysaght, op. cit., p.147.

26　Who, like Dylan, would also be given a place on the cover of Sgt. Pepper.

27　At the time of the 1961 census, the UK population had been 52.8 million; and by 1964 was estimated to have reached 53.9 million. [See "A Century of Change: Trends in UK Statistics since 1900" on www.parliament.uk and www.nationmaster.com.]

28   Quoted in Keith Badman, op. cit., p.52.

29   Born in Philadelphia in 1932 but resident in England since 1953, Lester, like George Martin before him, had the Beatles' respect (particularly John Lennon's) for his earliest TV and film work with Peter Sellers and Spike Milligan. He had also previously directed *It's Trad, Dad!* in 1962, a more conventional 'showcase' musical film starring Craig Douglas, Helen Shapiro and Acker Bilk, with cameo performances from US stars like Chubby Checker, Del Shannon and Gene Vincent.

30   Tony Barrow, LP sleeve notes to *A Hard Day's Night* (Parlophone, 1964).

31   Barry Miles, "Paul McCartney: Many Years From Now" (Henry Holt, 1997), p.160.

32   Ian Macdonald, op. cit., p.95.

33   Lennon/McCartney, © 1969 & 1971 by Northern Songs Ltd.

34   "It was quite an extraordinary household: an eminent doctor [Jane's father, Dr. Richard Asher], a music professor [Jane's mother, Margaret Asher], an actress in a daily radio soap opera [Jane's sister, Claire], an accomplished young stage and screen actress [Jane herself] and two world-famous pop singers [Paul and Jane's brother, Peter], all sharing a Peter Pan town house in the centre of London and behaving as if this was perfectly normal, which, for them, it was." [See Barry Miles, "Paul McCartney: Many Years From Now" (Henry Holt, 1997), p.105.]

35   John Lennon, quoted in "The Beatles Anthology" (Cassell, 2000), p.134.

36   Ibid. In fact, he made only one brief quip. According to Brian Epstein: "In answer to the toast, John stood, held the microphone and said, 'Thank you all very much, you've got a lucky face.' John was behaving like a Beatle. He was not prepared to do something which was not only unnatural to him, but also something he might have done badly. He was not going to fail." [Ibid.] According to Cynthia Lennon, however, both she and John were still badly hungover from the night before: "He managed eight words, 'Thank you very much, it's been a pleasure', then promptly sat down again. There was a stunned silence, followed by a few muted boos and a spatter of applause." [Cynthia Lennon, op. cit., p.190.]

37   The picture actually dates from late October 1963, from the Beatles' first foreign tour (to Sweden), and shows them standing on a wall beside Stockholm Town Hall. [See www.silvergallery.com.au.]

38   As Paul himself described his Little Richard party-piece, "like an out-of-body experience". [See Barry Miles, op. cit., p.201.]

39   A recording, as it turned out, witnessed by Perkins himself on 1st June. [See Mark Lewisohn, op. cit., p.160.]

40   Derek Taylor, sleevenotes to *Long Tall Sally* EP (Parlophone, 1964).

41   Tony Barrow, LP sleevenotes to *A Hard Day's Night* (Parlophone, 1964).

42   Quoted in "The Beatles Anthology" (Cassell, 2000), p.144.

43   Ibid.

44   A tour notable for Ringo's absence, through severe tonsillitis, from the first five dates and his temporary replacement by session musician Jimmy Nicol.

45   Andy Neill, op. cit., p.154. The crowds in Liverpool on 10th June were estimated to have been 200,000 strong.

46 Daily Mail 18th August 1964, quoted in Tim Hill, "The Beatles: Then There Was Music" (Transatlantic Press, 2010), p. 162.

47 Mark Lewisohn, op. cit., p.139.

48 Mark Lewisohn, op. cit., p.140.

49 Quoted in "The Beatles Anthology" (Cassell, 2000), p.153.

50 Quoted in "The Beatles Anthology" (Cassell, 2000), p.155.

51 George Martin, LP sleevenotes to *The Beatles At The Hollywood Bowl* (EMI, 1977).

52 Howard Sounes, "Down The Highway: The Life of Bob Dylan" (Black Swan, 2002), p.199.

53 Mark Lewisohn, op. cit., p. 140.

54 Taylor had resigned from his position as the Beatles' publicity manager at the end of their US tour in September, in the face of constant disagreements and misunderstandings with Brian Epstein, but was compelled by Epstein to work out three months' notice. [See "The Beatles Anthology" (Cassell, 2000), p.157.]

55 LP sleevenotes to *Beatles For Sale* (Parlophone, 1964).

56 Ian MacDonald, op. cit., p.119.

57 Released on 10th January, the four tracks were: "You Better Move On", "Poison Ivy", "Bye Bye Johnny" and "Money".

58 Sleevenotes to *The Rolling Stones* EP (Decca, 1964).

59 Andrew Loog Oldham, op. cit., p.269.

60 Andrew Loog Oldham, op. cit., p.281.

61 Hardin/Petty, © 1964 by MPL Communications Inc.

62 Andrew Loog Oldham, op. cit., p.294.

63 Transmuted editorially from Loog Oldham's original suggestion to Coleman of "Would you let your daughter go with a Rolling Stone?"

64 Sleevenotes to *The Rolling Stones* LP (Decca, 1964).

65 Keith Richards with James Fox, op. cit., p.155.

66 Keith Richards with James Fox, op. cit., p.151.

67 Keith Richards with James Fox, op. cit., p.157.

68 Andrew Loog Oldham, "2Stoned" (Vintage, 2003), p.11.

69 Andrew Loog Oldham, op. cit., p.35.

70 Bobby & Shirley Womack, © 1964 by Kags Music (now Abkco Music Inc.).

71 Quoted in Andrew Loog Oldham, op. cit., p.70.

72 The tracks being: "I Just Wanna Make Love To You" (Willie Dixon), "Boom Boom" (John Lee Hooker), "Big Boss Man" (Jimmy Reed) and "Pretty Thing" (Bo Diddley).

73 Trad. – arr. Price, © 1964 by Keith Prowse Music/EMI.

74 In the end, it wasn't taken up by RSG!

75   Quoted in Sean Egan, "Animal Tracks – The Story of The Animals: Newcastle's Rising Sons" (Askill, revised & expanded edn., 2012), pp.59-60.

76   Eric Burdon with J. Marshall Craig, "Don't Let Me Be Misunderstood" (Thunder's Mouth Press, 2001), p.22.

77   Eric Burdon with J. Marshall Craig, op. cit., p.23.

78   Eric Burdon with J. Marshall Craig, op. cit., p.27.

79   Alternatively known as the Metropolis Blues Quartet: there is no agreement across a wide range of reference sources as to this group's favoured title.

80   Eric Clapton with Christopher Simon Sykes, "Eric Clapton: The Autobiography" (Century, 2007), p.48.

81   Eric Clapton with Christopher Simon Sykes, op. cit., p.49.

82   LP sleevenotes to *Five Live Yardbirds* (Columbia, 1964).

83   Quoted by Chris Welch in liner notes to CD reissue of *Five Live Yardbirds* (Repertoire, 1999).

84   Ibid.

85   Ibid.

86   Dave Davies, "Kink: An Autobiography" (Boxtree, 1996), p.2.

87   Ray Davies, © 1964 by Edward Kassner Co. Ltd.

88   Ray Davies, "X-Ray" (Viking, 1994), p.76.

89   Ray Davies, op. cit., p.88.

90   Ibid.

91   Dave Davies, op. cit., pp.29-30.

92   Ray Davies, op. cit., p.91; although Kinks chronicler Doug Hinman is sceptical of this, believing it to be a pseudonym. [See Doug Hinman, "The Kinks: All Day And All Of The Night" (Backbeat, 2004), p.16.]

93   Dave Davies, op. cit., p.32.

94   Ray Davies, op. cit., p.103.

95   Ray Davies, op. cit., p.112.

96   Dave Davies, op. cit., p.40.

97   Ray Davies, op. cit., p.120.

98   Even though they didn't end up occupying the same musical territory, their earliest efforts exhibit some commonality of interest with the Yardbirds: both *Kinks* and *Five Live Yardbirds* include versions of Chuck Berry's "Too Much Monkey Business" and James Moore's "Got Love If You Want It". From touring with them, Dave concluded that "they were a lot like us, heavy blues-based music" but "rougher and more aggressive". [See Dave Davies, op. cit., p.50.]

99   Ray Davies, © 1964 by Edward Kassner Co. Ltd.

100   Dave Davies, op. cit., p.49.

101 Roger Dopson, CD liner notes to *Manfred Mann: The EP Collection* (See For Miles, 1989).

102 Hugg/Jones/Mann/McGuinness/Vickers, © 1964 by EMI Music Publishing Ltd.

103 Tom McGuinness, CD liner notes to *Manfred Mann At Abbey Road 1963 to 1966* (EMI, 1997).

104 Nitzsche/Bono, © 1964 by Metric Music (now EMI United Partnership Ltd.).

105 Ibid.

106 Evident, for example, in songs like "I Knew I'd Want You" and "Feel A Whole Lot Better".

107 Richards/Anthony, © 1964 by Toby Music Ltd.; Marc Anthony being another pseudonym for Tony Hatch.

108 Frank Allen, "The Searchers And Me: A History of the Legendary Sixties Hitmakers" (Aureus, 2009), p.141.

109 Bob Stanley, CD liner notes to *The Searchers: Hearts In Their Eyes* (Universal, 2012).

110 Also, more famously, the composer of "Little Boxes"; as well as "Morningtown Ride".

111 Frank Allen, op. cit., p.174.

112 See Cilla Black, op. cit., pp.84-85.

113 See Spencer Leigh, "It's Love That Really Counts: The Billy Kinsley Story" (Cavern City Tours, 2010), pp.47-55.

114 Reproduced in Barry Miles, "The British Invasion: The Music, The Times, The Era" (Sterling, 2009), p.66.

115 Spencer Leigh, "It's Love That Really Counts: The Billy Kinsley Story" (Cavern City Tours, 2010), p.65.

116 Quoted in Spencer Leigh, op. cit., p.74.

117 Andrew Loog Oldham, op. cit., p.231.

118 Cilla Black, in CD liner notes to *Cilla Black – Completely Cilla: 1963-1973* [EMI, 2012].

119 Cilla Black, op. cit., p.89.

120 Quoted in Michael Brocken, "Bacharach: Maestro! The Life of a Pop Genius" (Chrome Dreams, 2003), p. 146.

121 Michael Brocken, op. cit., p.147.

122 Bacharach/David, © 1963 (renewed 1991) by New Hidden Valley Music/Casa David.

123 Ibid.

124 Ibid.

125 Lulu, "I Don't Want to Fight" (Time Warner, 2003), p.50. When she saw him, Harvey was already in his late twenties. Born in February 1935, he belatedly achieved wider fame in the Seventies as leader of the Sensational Alex Harvey Band, with summertime hits in 1976 (a remake of Tom Jones's "Delilah") and 1977 ("The Boston Tea Party"). He died a day short of his 45th birthday in February 1982.

126 Lulu, op. cit., p.55.

127   The call-and-response section in the second half of the record is virtually identical to that to be found in Joey Dee and the Starliters' "Peppermint Twist".

128   Marianne Faithfull with David Dalton, "Faithfull" (Penguin, 1995), p.27.

129   Quoted in Andrew Loog Oldham, op. cit., p.309.

130   She never did make it as a singer, despite repeated failed attempts to make a hit record, but eventually broke into films in the late Sixties as one of the many minor British starlets of the day, with her trademark 'panda eyes' delineated by heavy eye-shadow and mascara.

131   Not only a friend to Dunbar but also a financial backer of his joint venture with Barry Miles, helping the pair open the Indica gallery and bookshop.

132   Andrew Loog Oldham, op. cit., p.311.

133   See, for example, Calder quoted in Andrew Loog Oldham, op. cit., pp.311 & 319.

134   Andrew Loog Oldham, op. cit., p.320.

135   Marianne Faithfull with David Dalton, op. cit., p.33. Keith's more grounded take on it was as follows: "With 'As Tears Go By', we weren't trying to write a commercial pop song. It was just what came out. I knew what Andrew wanted: don't come out with a blues, don't do some parody or copy, come out with something of your own." [See Keith Richards with James Fox, op. cit., p.143.]

136   Ibid.

137   Marianne Faithfull with David Dalton, op. cit., p.41.

138   Ibid.

139   Marianne Faithfull with David Dalton, op. cit., p.44.

140   Sandie Shaw, "The World at My Feet: A Personal Adventure" (Fontana, 1992), p. 54.

141   Sandie Shaw, op. cit., p.63.

142   Quoted in Damian Whitworth's interview with Sandie Shaw for *The Times*, 25th September 2010, "Proud to be a Dagenham girl".

143   Sandie Shaw, op. cit., p.64.

144   Sandie Shaw, op. cit., p.137.

145   Ibid.

146   Sandie Shaw, op. cit., p.140.

147   Adam Faith, op. cit., p.107.

148   He had last been in the Top 10 with "Don't That Beat All", at No.9 in the week ending 22nd September 1962. In the interim until the success of "The First Time", the highest chart placings of his next three singles had proved disappointing, viz.: "Baby Take A Bow" (No.17, w/e 22nd December 1962), "What Now" (No.29, w/e 9th February 1963) and "Walkin' Tall" (No.23, w/e 20th July 1963).

149   It had originally been intended as the first solo vehicle for ex-Vernons Girl Samantha Jones.

150   Sandie Shaw, op. cit., p.114.

151 On its release, this third single initially had "I'd Be Far Better Off Without You" as its A-side.

152 And runner-up in the World category to Brenda Lee.

153 Its highest position in its 23 weeks in the LP charts from 25th April onwards was No.6.

154 With the Searchers, Big Dee Irwin, Bobby Vee and her own backing group the Echoes.

155 Including week-long concert engagements in Coventry, Southend and Bournemouth.

156 With Brian Poole & the Tremeloes, Herman's Hermits, Dave Berry and the Echoes.

157 Relieved here and elsewhere, as noted by Frank Allen, by "her weird habit of purchasing stacks of cheap crockery with the sole purpose of smashing it up in an attempt to smash her frustrations away at the same time." [See Frank Allen, "The Searchers and Me: A History of the Legendary Sixties Hitmakers" (Aureus, 2009), p.163.]

158 Quoted in Sharon Davis, op. cit., p.52.

159 Frank Allen, "The Searchers and Me: A History of the Legendary Sixties Hitmakers" (Aureus, 2009), p.165.

160 Quoted in Lucy O'Brien, op. cit., p.68.

161 Quoted in Lucy O'Brien, op. cit., p.73.

162 Cilla Black, op. cit., p.95.

163 Ibid.

164 Cilla Black, op. cit., p.113.

165 Ibid.

166 Cilla Black, op. cit., p.97.

167 Tony Hatch, © 1964 by ATV Music Ltd.

168 Ibid.

169 Ibid. The lyric has a universality transcending Hatch's original inspiration of New York.

170 Quoted in John Repsch, op. cit., pp.232-233.

171 Quoted by Roger Dopson, in CD liner notes to The Rockin' Berries: They're In Town [Sequel, 1998].

172 Ibid.

173 Quoted in Pete Frame, "Rock Family Trees" (Omnibus, 1993), p.13.

174 Quoted from article by Alex Wharton on www.brumbeat.net.

175 Ibid.

176 Quoted by Spencer Leigh, in CD liner notes to Herman's Hermits & Peter Noone: Into Something Good – The Mickie Most Years 1964-1972 [EMI, 2008].

177 Alan Clayson, "Call Up The Groups!" (Blandford, 1985), p.95.

178 Colin Cross et al., op. cit., p.10.

179 After the euphoria of 1964 had dissipated, the Four Pennies had little of interest left

to offer, only achieving one more chart entry in November 1965 (a lowly No.28) with "Until It's Time For You To Go".

180 Barry Miles, "The British Invasion" (Sterling, 2009), pp.82-83.

181 See Dave McAleer, "Beatboom! Pop Goes The Sixties" (Hamlyn, 1994), pp.55 & 63.

182 Although their next two singles received regular airplay, only the first, "Find My Way Back Home", took the Nashville Teens fleetingly back into the Top 30, to No.27 in the week ending 27th March 1965. The second (yet another John D.Loudermilk composition), "This Little Bird", went suicidally head-to-head with Marianne Faithfull's version, both inexplicably released in competition by the same record company; and despite being retained by Decca until 1968, their hit-making days were well and truly over.

183 After "She's Not There", the Zombies never recaptured the British record buyers' imagination. Of a string of singles issued by Decca up to and including 1967, only the third, "Tell Her No", achieved another UK chart entry, at No.30 for just the week ending 6th February 1965. They changed labels to join CBS in 1967, recording their final celebrated LP, *Odessey And Oracle*, that December before breaking up.

184 Although in fairness their take on "Lucille" is closely modelled on that of the Everly Brothers.

185 After beginning 1965 with another non-charting single, "I Go To Pieces", Peter and Gordon bounced back into the UK Top Ten temporarily with two successive cover versions of old hits: Buddy Holly's "True Love Ways" (No.4 in May), followed by "To Know You Is To Love You", a revival of the Teddy Bears' "To Know Him Is To Love Him" (No.6 in July). The overall trend was, however, downwards. "Baby I'm Yours" only reached No.21 in November and in March 1966 "Woman" got no higher than No.22, even though it was a new Paul McCartney song (published under the pseudonym of Bernard Webb). The parlous state of the charts in the latter half of the decade is clearly reflected in the fact that when they resorted to the desperation of the novelty number "Lady Godiva", it went to No.18 in October 1966. The duo parted professionally in February 1967.

186 Brian Wilson/Mike Love, © 1964 by Irving Music Inc.

187 For contractual reasons, these were spread across three different labels – Vee Jay (with whom Brian Epstein had struck the original US record deal for the Beatles), Capitol and United Artists (who owned the US rights to the soundtrack of *A Hard Day's Night*). From mid-1964 onwards, however, all their American releases were on Capitol.

188 Quoted in Keith Badman, op. cit., p.71.

189 Namely: Ireland, Italy, West Germany, Denmark, Norway, Sweden and France.

190 Quoted in Keith Badman, op. cit., p.75.

191 Ibid.

192 Ibid.

193 Nat Hentoff, "The Crackin', Shakin', Breakin' Sounds", published in the *New Yorker* on 24th October 1964: reprinted in Jonathan Cott (ed.), "Dylan on Dylan:The Essential Interviews" (Hodder, 2007), pp.23-24.

194 Quoted in Anthony Scaduto, op. cit., p.175.

195 As it turned out, this was not the first time, however, that "House Of The Rising Sun" had proved inspirational across musical genres. In 1999, Lonnie Donegan gave due credit to an earlier recording of the song, made in the early Fifties by black American folk-singer Josh White, as having been "the first American folk song I heard, and the experience kicked off my career, started me singing American blues and folk. I believe Josh started the British rock scene." [Quoted in Mick Houghton, "Becoming Elektra: The True Story of Jac Holzman's Visionary Record Label" (Jawbone, 2010), p.71.]

196 Bob Dylan, © 1964 by Warner Bros. Music; renewed 1992 by Special Rider Music.

197 Bob Dylan, © 1964 by Warner Bros. Music; renewed 1992 by Special Rider Music.

198 Bob Dylan, © 1964 by Warner Bros. Music; renewed 1992 by Special Rider Music.

199 Bob Dylan, © 1964 by Warner Bros. Music; renewed 1992 by Special Rider Music.

200 Nat Hentoff, op. cit., pp.15-16.

201 Tom Piazza, DVD liner notes to *The Other Side Of The Mirror: Bob Dylan Live At The Newport Folk Festival 1963-1965* (Sony/BMG, 2007), p.9.

202 Bob Dylan, op. cit., p.115.

203 Robert Shelton, op. cit., p.181.

204 Paul Wolfe, quoted in Robert Shelton, op. cit., p.182.

205 Robert Shelton's New York Times review, reproduced in CD liner notes to *The Bootleg Series Vol.6/Bob Dylan Live 1964: The Halloween Concert* (Columbia Legacy, 2004).

206 Ibid.

207 Bob Dylan, LP sleevenotes to *Bringing It All Back Home* (CBS, 1965).

208 Michael Maclear, "Vietnam: The Ten Thousand Day War (Thames Methuen, 1981), p.153.

209 Quoted in Piers Paul Read, "The Train Robbers" (Coronet, 1979), pp.195-196.

210 Quoted in Dominic Sandbrook, "White Heat: A History of Britain in the Swinging Sixties" (Abacus, 2007), p.208.

211 Pete Frame, "Rock Family Trees" (Omnibus, 1993), p.59

Chapter 7

FIRST NO.1 OF THE YEAR –
"I Feel Fine" by The Beatles

LAST NO.1 OF THE YEAR –
"Day Tripper/We Can Work It Out" by The Beatles

1965 was the year in which pop music finally grew up, a bold awakening of maturity bringing with it a corresponding recognition that everything that had gone before had merely been febrile and pubescent. Over the course of the next twelve months, it became clear that the most trusted of the old hands – the Beatles, the Stones, Dylan – had suddenly shifted up a gear, combining new sounds with a previously unimagined lyrical depth, at the same time jump-starting the music industry as a whole into an unprecedented era of internationalism, expansion and diversification to the benefit of a host of new acts.

Impatience with the status quo was to manifest itself in hitherto uncharacteristic candour, as demonstrated here by John Lennon, for example, in an extraordinarily blunt reassessment of the relationship between performer and potential audience:

> People think of us as machines. They pay 6s 8d for a record and we have to do what they say – like a jack-in-the-box. I don't like that side of it much. Some people have got it all wrong. We produce something, a record, and if they like it, they get it. The onus isn't on us to produce something great every time. The onus is on the public to decide whether they like it or not. It's annoying when people turn round and say, 'But we *made* you, you ungrateful swines.' I know they did, in a way, but there's a limit to what we're bound to live up to, as if it's a duty.
>
> I don't want to sound as if we don't like being liked. We appreciate it. But we can't spend our lives being dictated to. We make a record, and if you like it you buy it. If you don't, you don't buy it. It's up to the public to decide.[1]

And, as a consequence, a sudden, healthy injection of social realism from the already established professionals, radically augmented by the efforts of several outstanding new signings, turned 1965 into the pivotal year of the decade musically; although not so much for the Beach Boys who, as Brian Wilson's biographer Peter Ames Carlin explains, were to remain out of the loop for a while longer:

> ... the Beach Boys' public image hadn't matured along with [Brian's] music. So even as Bob Dylan infused rock with a seething political consciousness and literary sensibility, as the Beatles expanded their musical and intellectual horizons in every conceivable direction, and as the Rolling Stones revelled in their own subversive decadence – and all three blazed trails for the politically/socially/intellectually aware groups that would soon transform youth culture entirely – the Beach Boys kept their hair barbered and their striped shirts neatly pressed ... And when the summer sales season neared, everyone still expected Brian to crank out another batch of ready-made tunes set on the beaches, highways, and backseats he'd long since lost interest in describing.[2]

Still, as we shall see later in this chapter, before the year was out Brian too would find the inspiration to embark upon a ground-breaking project of his own, one which in its eventual fulfilment would come to epitomise the Beach Boys at their finest.

Following the predictable twin Christmas successes of "I Feel Fine" and *Beatles For Sale*, UK fans had a four-month wait until the release of a new Beatles record on 9th April, their next single "Ticket To Ride" (b/w "Yes It Is"). Once they had concluded their second – and last – Christmas show in mid-January, the Beatles' time from February through to May was almost exclusively consumed by the demanding efforts of composing for and acting in their second film; which, as it emerged in April, was to be titled *Help!* On 11th February, four days before recording started in earnest at Abbey Road, Ringo, with the ever-discreet Brian Epstein as his best man, married Maureen Cox, in a ceremony at Caxton Hall in London exceptionally brought forward to 8.00 a.m. in an attempt to minimise publicity (since the wedding had been prompted, like that of John and Cynthia before them, by the 18-year-old Maureen finding herself pregnant).[3]

"Ticket To Ride" was the first of seven songs to be recorded for the film, its early release intended as a taster of the eagerly awaited new soundtrack, and it was inevitably straight into the charts at No.1, in the week ending 17th April. Running to over three minutes, it was their longest single to date, John in particular taking satisfaction in the emphatic counterbalance of guitars and drums that he thought made it a "heavy record" for its time.[4] In sharp contrast, the B-side, "Yes It Is" (a stand-alone song not destined for either film or related LP) was a ballad very much in the style of "This Boy" both vocally and structurally, the sombreness of the mood embellished this time around by the application of a volume swell-pedal to the strummed guitars.

Composing and recording the film's title track, however, were necessarily delayed until director Richard Lester had announced his final decision on that title (in preference to both the original but banal *Beatles 2* and the subsequent pun on the frantic storyline, *Eight Arms To Hold You*). As an outcome, the song "Help!" completely transcends its functional origins to rank as one of the Beatles' strongest; marking as it does the realisation of John's ability to fully articulate a depth of personal feeling, by comparison with his fledgling effort on *Beatles For Sale*, "I'm A Loser". Indeed, "Help!" has no worth or meaning if simply taken at face-value as illustrative of the comic pursuit of Ringo halfway round the world by fanatical devotees of the goddess Kali. "Help!" is so much more, a *cri de coeur* from the outset, as John himself belatedly admitted: "I didn't realise it at the time – I just wrote the song because I was commissioned to write it for the movie – but later I knew, really I was crying out for help. "Help!" was about me, although it was a bit poetic."[5]

John's lyric encapsulates the heightened self-consciousness he experienced during filming, especially his concern at his body image in what he subsequently described mockingly as the 'Fat Elvis' period of his life. Yet in its direct plea for compassionate acceptance, it goes far beyond this, to capture a universal, timeless yearning in a few short and simple words:

> When I was younger, so much younger than today,
> I never needed anybody's help in any way,
> But now these days are gone I'm not so self-assured.
> Now I find I've changed my mind, I've opened up the doors.
> Help me if you can, I'm feeling down,
> And I do appreciate you being around.
> Help me get my feet back on the ground.
> Won't you please, please help me?[6]

Had they chosen at this moment to look back over their shoulders, the Beatles would surely have been hard pressed to discern in the far distance the naïve charm of a song like "Love Me Do", the starting point of their long journey. Yet in some respects they were already aware that not all the changes in their lives had been for the better. Despite its greater variety of locations (which included the Bahamas, the Austrian Alps and Salisbury Plain), making *Help!* certainly proved to be far more of a chore than they had found *A Hard Day's Night*, the very strength of its professional supporting cast (eminently bankable actors of the calibre of Leo McKern, Eleanor Bron, Victor Spinetti, Roy Kinnear and Patrick Cargill) seeming to drain the experience of its predecessor's good-natured spontaneity and leading Paul to deride the

Beatles' involvement as being no more than "guest stars in our own movie".[7]

Having started on the Bahamian island of New Providence on 23rd February, the protracted filming finally came to an end on 11th May, after the second of two days spent on location at Lord Astor's country seat, Cliveden, even then still enjoying its notoriety as the venue of that first fateful encounter between John Profumo and Christine Keeler. As with *A Hard Day's Night*, Piccadilly's London Pavilion Cinema hosted the premiere, again attended by Princess Margaret and Lord Snowdon, on 29th July; before *Help!* went on general release during the long school holidays, when I got to see it one midsummer morning at the New Street Odeon in Birmingham. For me, as I suspect for most other fans of my age then, the combination of music and colour cinematography was more than sufficient compensation for the deficiencies of script and plot.

While the single of "Help!" (b/w "I'm Down") was released a week before the film, on 23rd July, the LP came out afterwards, on 6th August, and was, as I have already described at the beginning of Chapter 5, an immediate sell-out. In fact, it was the first album ever to go straight to the top of the British LP charts, although it failed to sustain its initial promise and only stayed at No.1 for nine weeks (whereas *Please Please Me* had remained there for thirty). It did nevertheless end up as the fourth best-selling LP of the year.

The sleeve before me now remains as sharp and instantly recognisable as on that summer afternoon I finally tracked a copy down and bought it. The figures of the four Beatles in royal blue hats and capes, supposedly in semaphore signalling stances, occupy the centre of a stark white ground as a line of cut-outs. Across the top, to the right of the Parlophone and EMI logo boxes, bold black capitals pronounce **THE BEATLES.** In the same font, in the top left-hand corner, immediately below the logos, HELP! is printed in red capitals with a white in-fill. After the muted naturalism of the cover shots for *Beatles For Sale*, Robert Freeman had opted this time for artifice. Far from being on the Alpine ski-slopes of the film, the group shot was actually posed on a platform in front of a white cyclorama in the car park of Twickenham Film Studios. Neither, as you would fondly think, do their semaphore arms from left to right spell out 'Help': if the shapes resemble any letters at all, they are apparently the random but – to Freeman, at least – more aesthetically pleasing 'N, U, J, V'.

Like *Beatles For Sale*, *Help!* is not a complete collection of Beatle compositions; although as with *A Hard Day's Night*, all seven songs from the film's soundtrack on Side 1 are originals – 6 from Lennon and McCartney (including "Help!" and "Ticket To Ride"), plus George's "I Need You". Side 2 includes another Harrison song, "You Like Me Too Much", as well as two covers: the Buck Owens comic country number, "Act Naturally", by means of which Ringo gets to enjoy sending himself up, and a concluding Larry Williams rocker from John, "Dizzy Miss Lizzy". Of the remainder, Side 2 is distinguished by one contribution above all others from Paul: "Yesterday".

Before attempting to record it, on 14th June, Paul had been carrying the germ of the tune in his head for some time, repeatedly revisiting it in the hope someday of completing a full-blown song. He attributed its origin to a melody that came to him in a dream but writing suitable matching lyrics proved an elusive task. For a while, it went under the nonsense title of "Scrambled Eggs", a phrase that just happened to neatly fit the opening bars, but the song unexpectedly came together on 27th May, when Paul and Jane Asher arrived in Portugal for a short private holiday at the villa of Shadow Bruce Welch. On the long drive from Lisbon Airport down to the Algarve, as Jane slept, Paul was "mulling over the tune 'Yesterday', and suddenly getting these little one-word openings to the verse ... so I gradually pieced it together from that journey".[8]

Even so, it still took him another two weeks to complete to his satisfaction. Atypically for him to date, the outcome was an understated ballad, not this time a song of adoration (in the earlier muted style, say, of "And I Love Her") but instead a bittersweet refrain of contemplative remorse:

> Why she had to go, I don't know, she wouldn't say.
> I said something wrong, now I long for yesterday.
> Yesterday, love was such an easy game to play.
> Now I need a place to hide away.
> Oh, I believe in yesterday.[9]

In a busy schedule on 14th June he had other songs to record beforehand: the quirky, pseudo-folk/rockabilly number "I've Just Seen A Face", sung and played at breakneck speed (Side 2, Track 5 of *Help!*), followed by the raver in the rip-roaring style of Little Richard, "I'm Down" (the B-side of the "Help!" single). So it was not until that evening that Paul at last attempted two solo takes of "Yesterday", accompanying himself on acoustic guitar by amicable agreement with his fellow Beatles: "I looked at all the others: 'Oops. You mean a solo record?' They said, 'Yeah, it doesn't matter, there's nothing we can add to it – do it.'"[10]

As a long day in the studio drew to a close, at around 10.30 p.m., George Martin had some final advice to offer Paul:

> Then I said, 'Well, what can we do with it? The only thing I can
> think of is adding strings, but I know what you think about that.'
> And Paul said, 'I don't want Mantovani.' I said, 'What about a
> very small number of string players, a quartet?' He thought that
> was interesting, and I went and worked on it with him and made
> suggestions for the score. He had ideas too, and we booked a string
> quartet and overdubbed the strings – and that was the record.[11]

Thus recording was duly concluded, in a two-hour session on the afternoon of 17ᵗʰ June, leaving "Yesterday" in the form in which it was to become known at home; as Track 6 on Side 2 of *Help!*, to be reassuringly lodged within the latest collection of Beatles' songs despite the fact that had not escaped Martin, that "No other Beatle was on that recording and no other Beatle heard it until we played it back".[12] For other commercial reasons, however, it had not been included amongst the album tracks of the US variant of *Help!* and Capitol decided instead to issue it in America on 13ᵗʰ September as the A-side of a new Beatles single (b/w Ringo's "Act Naturally"), making it a No.1 hit in the *Billboard* chart for a month and a gold disc into the bargain.

The string quartet was not the only flourish on *Help!* indicative of a broadening of the Beatles' musical palette. John's "You've Got To Hide Your Love Away", recorded during a much earlier session on 18ᵗʰ February, had benefitted from the addition of flutes; and between them, John and Paul had played electric piano on three other tracks: "The Night Before", "You Like Me Too Much" and "Tell Me What You See". Less respectfully, John had also contributed a manic Hammond organ solo to "I'm Down"; the B-side, as Ian MacDonald notes chidingly, "rated a rock-and-roll classic in the USA" but "actually a genre prank pushed home at high energy ... conceived mainly as a joke".[13] When they returned to Abbey Road in October, there would be yet more distinctive touches added to the arrangements of their next clutch of songs.

With so much work related in one form or another to *Help!*, it was not until early summer that the Beatles could return to the core business of live music-making for profit, with a brief tour of Europe that, beginning in Paris on 20ᵗʰ June, also took them to Italy and Spain before ending in Barcelona on 3ʳᵈ July. It followed hard on the heels of the announcement on 12ᵗʰ June that they had all been awarded MBEs in the Queen's Birthday Honours List, reputedly on the specific recommendation of the Prime Minister, Harold Wilson, MP for the Liverpool constituency of Huyton. The ambivalence all four of them felt about this was probably best summed up by Paul: "There are two ways to look at it: either it's a great honour that's being bestowed on you – and I think to some degree we did believe that – or (if you want to be cynical) it's a very cheap way to reward people."[14] In the wider, stuffy world of 1965, it was seen by many as an extraordinary departure from past priv-ileged practice, whilst an exceptional minority took it as a personal affront, returning their own decorations in protest and accruing negative publicity for the Beatles into the process.

While they were on the Italian leg of their tour, John's second book of random musings and illustrations, *A Spaniard in the Works*, was published by Jonathan Cape on 24ᵗʰ June. Specifically commissioned to cash in on the previous success of *In His Own Write*, but not as popular, nonetheless it gave him "another personal boost": "The plain unvarnished fact is that I like writing, and I'd go on writing even if there wasn't any publisher daft enough to publish them."[15]

On Friday, 13th August, the Beatles embarked upon their second full concert tour of America by flying off to New York. After spending much of the following day in CBS Television's Studio 50, working alongside Cilla Black to rehearse, then record, their respective performances for *The Ed Sullivan Show* (which were eventually broadcast on 12th September and included Paul singing "Yesterday" solo), the tour proper opened on Sunday, 15th August, with an evening concert at the newly built Shea Stadium – ordinarily home to baseball team the New York Mets. Setting new world records in the history of pop for both attendance (a capacity crowd of 55,600) and gross ticket receipts ($304,000), just getting the Beatles there proved a logistical nightmare, as Mark Lewisohn explains:

> A planned spectacular entry into the stadium by helicopter, landing on the baseball playing area, was vetoed by the New York City authorities. Instead the group travelled by limousine from the Warwick Hotel to a waterfront heliport, flew from there over New York City to the roof of the World's Fair building and made the final 100-yard journey into Shea Stadium in a Wells Fargo armoured truck. They sprinted through a tunnel, out into a deafening wall of screams and onto the stage (positioned at second base) at 9.16 p.m.[16]

Amidst the throngs of people present that night were Mick Jagger and Keith Richards, as well as future Beatle wives Barbara Bach and Linda Eastman, although whether anyone heard anything meaningful in the course of their 12-song, 28-minute set – beginning with "Twist And Shout" and ending with "I'm Down" – is debatable. John's reaction to the experience was full of superlatives: "marvellous … the biggest crowd we ever played to, anywhere in the world … the biggest live show anybody's ever done, they told us."[17] But for Ringo, any impulse to celebrate their achievement was heavily outweighed by an acutely personal sense of regret:

> What I remember most about the concert was that we were so far away from the audience. They were all across the field, all wired in. When I tour now, I like the audience right in my face. I like to have some reaction, something going on between me and them. It was just very distant at Shea. Sure, we were big-time, and it was the first time we'd played to thousands and thousands of people, and we were the first band to do it; but it was totally against what we had started out to achieve, which was to entertain right *there*, up close. And screaming had just become the thing to do. We didn't say, 'OK,

don't forget, at this concert – everybody scream!' Everybody just screamed.[18]

Here then was one of the earliest indicators that in reality the Shea Stadium gig marked the beginning of the end for the Beatles as a live act; although as yet no-one could predict that in another fifty-four weeks' time, their touring days would be over for good.

Their itinerary took them on to Toronto, Atlanta, Houston, Chicago, Minneapolis and Portland, Oregon before they finally caught their breath on a five-day break in California, in the comparative seclusion of a rented Hollywood mansion. On this tour in particular, the Beatles found themselves courted as the leading lights of an exclusive, international mutual appreciation society, the other principal members of which were drawn from the new American aristocracy of music and film. Along the way, therefore, they were visited in New York by Bob Dylan and the Supremes; in Portland, by Beach Boys Carl Wilson and Mike Love; and in Hollywood – where recreational drug-taking assumed a greater importance in their socialising – by Joan Baez, Peter Fonda, and Jim McGuinn and David Crosby, members of the hottest new American group the Byrds (who had themselves only just returned from their own three-week tour of England). Shared musical interests even took George and Paul to sit in on the Byrds' latest recording session, on 25th August.

The Hollywood stopover also afforded the Beatles and Brian Epstein a long-awaited opportunity for a symbolic get-together with Elvis Presley and 'Colonel' Parker. The meeting, which Epstein had stipulated must be "entirely private and unpublicised"[19], took place on 27th August, at Elvis's mansion in Bel Air, but was, by all accounts, a resounding anti-climax. Although all four Beatles afterwards went politely on the record to say what a privilege it had been, circumstantial evidence suggests the occasion was characterised by a high degree of awkwardness between the parties. John said of it, matter-of-factly: "It was nice meeting Elvis. He was just Elvis, you know? ... We never talked about anything – we just played music. He wasn't bigger than us, but he was 'the thing'. He just wasn't articulate, that's all."[20] Much to Ringo's anger, however, it would later emerge that in fact Elvis had harboured deep-seated resentment towards them: "The saddest part is that, years and years later, we found out that he tried to have us banished from America, because he was very big with the FBI ... This is Mr Hips, *the man*, and he felt *we* were a danger. I think that the danger was mainly to him and his career."[21]

In retrospect, Ringo's assessment was undoubtedly close to the mark. In any case, it was largely wishful thinking that any common ground could have existed between them. While the Beatles were paying homage to Elvis as one of their all-time idols, there was nothing to suggest that their adulation of him was remotely reciprocated, and they self-evidently belonged not just to different musical genres but, much more significantly, different eras. The Beatles were clearly most at their ease with their contemporaries or near-contemporaries: Bob Dylan, for example, had not long turned 24.[22] At the time of their meeting, Elvis was 30, some three months younger than Brian Epstein but five years older than the oldest of the Beatles, Ringo, and eight years older than the youngest, George. Incredibly, it had been more than eleven years since he had made his first recordings for Sam Phillips at Sun Studios in Memphis and more than nine since he had recorded "Heartbreak Hotel" for RCA Victor, the hit that had launched his professional career and brought him under the wing of 'Colonel' Tom Parker; who had micro-managed his every move ever since and who, at the age of 56, considerably outstripped everyone else in years.

By 1965, Elvis's popularity at home and abroad was definitely on the wane, although it had received a temporary boost from the unexpected success of "Crying In The Chapel", a gospel ballad released that Easter which had reached No.3 in the US and – amazingly – No.1 in the UK in June. Itself an old song (originally a US hit in 1953 for Darrell Glenn, son of its composer), Elvis's version had lain in RCA's vaults for almost five years, as an out-take from recordings he had made for a gospel album in the autumn of 1960. Bizarrely, it was to be his biggest hit until the belated revival of his fortunes in 1968 with secular songs more obviously of the moment, like "In The Ghetto" and "Suspicious Minds". The eventual verdict of history, however, was to be that of the 25 top-selling No.1 singles in the US in the Sixties, only two were by Elvis, whereas four (including the top-seller of all) were by the Beatles.[23]

Rest days expended, the Beatles remained in California for the last four days of August and the concluding concerts of the tour: in San Diego, at the Hollywood Bowl, and finally at the Cow Palace in San Francisco. Arriving back in London on 2nd September, they then took several weeks off, before reconvening at Abbey Road on 12th October to start work afresh on recording. From now onwards, however, their professional relationship with producer George Martin entered a new realm; for, having resigned in August, he was no longer a salaried employee of EMI.

Understandably, Martin had long been disgruntled with being denied a share of royalties from the steadily growing catalogue of hit records he had produced and had finally determined to go freelance by setting up his own company, Associated Independent Recordings Ltd. (AIR), together with fellow ex-EMI producers John Burgess and Ron Richards[24], and Peter Sullivan from Decca. Their bargaining strength within the industry lay, of course, in the impressive portfolio of top-line acts associated collectively with them and, having announced the creation of AIR to the music press in September, their plan in the longer term was to fund the establishment of their own studios from future royalty earnings – a project they would eventually initiate in 1967.

With Martin's assistance in his new freelance capacity, for the next month the Beatles worked their way through ever-lengthening studio sessions – several taking them up to midnight or even beyond – to meet Parlophone's deadline for the simultaneous release on 3rd December of their next single and LP (with one notable exception on 26th October, when they attended Buckingham Palace to receive their MBEs from the Queen). For Paul, the prolonged pressure of this activity coincided with a difficult period in his relationship with Jane Asher, as her obligation to fulfil repertory acting engagements took her away from home, enforcing a temporary separation, and the tension this engendered on his part was plainly reflected in the lyrical content of some of his latest songs: "We Can Work It Out", "You Won't See Me" and "I'm Looking Through You".

"We Can Work It Out" was destined to be coupled with "Day Tripper" as the group's first double-A-side single, in an arrangement that incorporated John playing the harmonium. (When he saw them performing it on television in due course, my father, who was himself musically untalented, was memorably moved to remark that John "played the organ [sic] like a man with no hands.") As they made progress with the LP tracks, other instrumental innovations emerged, the most notable of which was the addition of George's double-tracked sitar accompaniment to John's cynical short story in song of a flawed affair, "Norwegian Wood (This Bird Has Flown)"; marking the beginning of a newly overt susceptibility in Western pop music to Asian influences.

According to Ian MacDonald, the inspiration for its use may have originated in discussions George and John had had in Hollywood with Jim McGuinn and David Crosby about Indian phrasing in music and the work of renowned sitar player Ravi Shankar.[25] George, however, attributed his interest in Shankar to an un-named 'friend' who had persuaded him to buy one of his records, shortly after which he bought a sitar of his own:

> from a little shop at the top of Oxford Street called Indiacraft – it stocked little carvings and incense. It was a real crummy-quality one, actually, but I bought it and mucked about with it a bit. Anyway, we were at the point where we'd recorded the 'Norwegian Wood' backing track (twelve-string and six-string acoustic, bass and drums) and it needed something. We would usually start looking through the cupboard to see if we could come up with something, a new sound, and I picked the sitar up – it was just lying around, I hadn't really figured out what to do with it. It was quite spontaneous: I found the notes that played the lick. It fitted and it worked.[26]

Ringo was profoundly impressed: "It was such a mind-blower that we had this strange instrument on a record. We were all open to anything when George introduced the sitar: you could walk in with an elephant, as long as it was going to make a musical note."[27]

Other distinctive touches included the addition of a fuzz box to Paul's bass guitar on George's song "Think For Yourself"; and what sounded remarkably like a harpsichord on John's "In My Life", although in reality it was unassuming artifice on the part of George Martin (who improvised a piano solo, taped it at half-speed and then speeded it up again when he played it back into the mix). Of all his compositions of this period, John took "In My Life" the most seriously, regarding it as "my first real, major piece of work … the first song that was really, consciously, about my life".[28] Originally conceived as a chronicle of the bus journey he used to make from the house in Menlove Avenue where he lived with and was brought up by his Aunt Mimi into Liverpool city centre (and thus anticipating the later local referencing of "Strawberry Fields Forever" and "Penny Lane"), "it became … a remembrance of friends and lovers of the past"[29], giving the present an added poignancy:

> Though I know I'll never lose affection
> For people and things that went before,
> I know I'll often stop and think about them,
> In my life I'll love you more.[30]

And in "The Word" – where the harmonium reappeared in the mix, this time courtesy of George Martin – John was striving to express his realisation of a concept for now just beyond his grasp, "like the underlying theme to the universe … the struggle to love, to be loved and express that (just *something* about love) that's fantastic".[31]

The resultant LP, *Rubber Soul*, was completed to order by 15th November; only the second of the Beatles' albums, after *A Hard Day's Night*, to be completely made up of original compositions but from here onwards that became the norm. The fourteen tracks offered the greatest variety of their work to date, even including a joint composing credit for Ringo in respect of "What Goes On" and the notable concession of two songs from George: "Think For Yourself" and "If I Needed Someone". Deservedly popular in its own right as *the* Christmas present of 1965, it was the UK's third best-selling LP of the year, above *Help!* but below *Beatles For Sale*.

In a throwback to an approach to pop music as a mere commodity, largely outdated since the start of the decade, it also hastily spawned a remarkable – but, in many ways, totally pointless – number of cover versions in a scattergun attack on the singles charts: *two* competing recordings of "Michelle" by the Overlanders and David & Jonathan, "If I Needed Someone" by the

Hollies, "Girl" by St. Louis Union, and a complete miss for Frankie Vaughan with "Wait". To my mind, this welter of imitation threatened to impugn the artistic integrity of *Rubber Soul* itself; for there is a very real sense in which the act of playing an LP constitutes a private performance directed towards an exclusive audience of one. While discovering over time that others may – or in some cases, may decidedly not – share your enthusiasm can enhance that experience, being subjected to repeated airplay of inferior copies of tracks in which you personally delight has precisely the opposite effect for me. As for the companion single "Day Tripper"/"We Can Work It Out", that went straight to No.1 for five weeks; but as competition increased and tastes changed, it would be another two years before a Beatles single occupied that position for so long.

On the same day as their new records were released, the Beatles embarked upon what would be their last home concert tour, accompanied by the Moody Blues as their principal support act. Opening in Glasgow on 3rd December and concluding in Cardiff on 12th December, en route, on 5th December, they played their last-ever concerts in Liverpool, to two consecutive 'houses' at the Empire Theatre (where 40,000 fans had applied for the 5,000 tickets on offer). When the tour ended, it was more with relief than regret on the Beatles' part, as expressed here by Paul, reflecting too on the intensity of the effort they had just devoted to creating *Rubber Soul*:

> It's as if we were painters who had never *really* been allowed to paint – we'd just had to go on selling our paintings up and down the country. Then, suddenly, we had somebody telling us, 'You can have a studio and you can paint and you can take your time.' So, obviously, being in a recording studio became much more attractive to us than going on the road again.[32]

But John admitted to other motives for coming to regard touring as a drag, fuelled largely by their unfortunate experiences in America of being expected to pander to the whims of officials and local dignitaries rather than engage with their fans:

> I couldn't take it, it was awful, all that business was awful. One has to completely humiliate oneself to be what the Beatles were, and that's what I resent. I mean, I did it, I didn't know, I didn't foresee, it just happens bit by bit, gradually, until this complete craziness is surrounding you and you're doing exactly what you don't want to do with people you can't stand, the people you hated when you were ten.[33]

On this point, then, they were all agreed and were looking forward to a new common purpose, although even at this juncture Ringo, for one, was conscious of a growing personal "resentment for the studio" as recording now threatened to consume more of their lives. As he said wistfully: "We would go in there and it would be a beautiful day, and we'd come out and days had gone by."[34]

Of all the successful and rising groups of the period, so far it was only the Beatles who, after being subjected to such a sustained onslaught of popular acclaim, scrutiny and criticism for the past three years, found themselves sufficiently troubled by it to have arrived at this crossroads. For everyone else, juggling the competing pressures of touring and recording, as will be explored later in this chapter, remained the norm. For newcomers, it was simply a given – how else were they to get themselves known and build up a following? – while some older hands appeared to thrive on it. Despite it still being comparatively early in their career, the Rolling Stones in particular had already become *the* touring band above all others, playing a huge number of engagements year on year and taking international travel in their stride, almost to the extent, in 1965, of being virtual expatriates. Although, given their blues roots, it feels counter-intuitive to say so, through their many tours the Stones were also actually responsible for promoting the cause of mainstream pop far and wide, by virtue of the huge caravan of support acts that followed and shared a stage with them. (Whereas, for instance, the Beatles only played with 35 other acts in the entirety of their six UK tours between 1963 and 1965, the Stones had already played with 50 by the end of their third UK tour at the beginning of 1964; and by the time they had completed another five UK tours, in October 1964, that total had reached in excess of 180.[35])

As they criss-crossed the world in transit, the Stones increasingly found it just as convenient to record in America as back home in England, so it was little wonder that for their second LP, *The Rolling Stones No.2*, they had laid down the majority of tracks in the States, at the Chess and RCA Hollywood Studios, rather than at their original London stamping-ground of Regent Studios. Graced this time with a shot of the group by rising photographer David Bailey, yet still defiantly devoid of any identifying text on its front cover, it was released on 15th January; courting minor controversy, to Andrew Loog Oldham's delight as usual, by adverse reaction to his tongue-in-cheek sleevenotes, which appeared in one paragraph to condone violence:

(This is the Stones' new disc within. Cast deep in your pockets for loot to buy this disc of groovies and fancy words. If you don't have bread, see that blind man, knock him on the head, steal his wallet and lo and behold you have the loot, if you put in the boot, good, another one sold!)[36]

As before, the musical content was largely derivative. Nine of the twelve tracks were reinterpretations of American blues and soul numbers: the best-known today being Solomon Burke's "Everybody Needs Somebody To Love", Irma Thomas's "Time Is On My Side" and the Drifters' "Under The Boardwalk". Of the three remaining original compositions, "Off The Hook" was already familiar as the B-side to "Little Red Rooster", leaving "What A Shame" as the strongest new contribution. Although sales were good, guaranteeing it the No.1 slot in the LP charts and eventual ranking as the year's sixth best-selling album, it was not ultimately as well-received as its predecessor, the fourth best-selling LP of 1964.

The Stones had cheerfully opened another year's touring with a brief three-day trip to Ireland from 5th to 7th January (playing concerts in Belfast, Dublin and Cork). This was then followed by intermittent efforts, first in London then Hollywood, to record a new single, before leaving Los Angeles on 19th January to undertake a tour of Australia and New Zealand, on which the main support acts would be American stars Roy Orbison and falsetto harmony group the Newbeats. By its conclusion in Perth on 13th February, Bill Wyman calculated that in the course of 34 performances they had played to over 100,000 people.

Both sides of the single in the pipeline were new Jagger/Richards compositions but further work at RCA Studios was still required to complete them satisfactorily, which Mick and Keith addressed under Andrew Loog Oldham's supervision in a Hollywood stopover on 18th February, en route back to England. The outcome was one of their strongest and most distinctive singles so far, "The Last Time" (b/w "Play With Fire").

"The Last Time", despite the admitted plagiarism in the chorus from the Staple Singers' gospel number "This May Be The Last Time", was the first Jagger/Richards song to make it onto an A-side and was one of which its composers were rightly proud, in that at last it broke away from their previous disposition to come up with largely ineffectual ballads. Keith has since described it as "the first one that we felt we could give to the rest of the guys without being sent out the room", as well as underlining that it included "the first recognisable Stones riff or guitar figure on it":

> It had a Stones twist to it, one that maybe couldn't have been
> written earlier – a song about going on the road and dumping
> some chick. "You don't try very hard to please me." Not the usual
> serenade to the unattainable object of desire. That was when
> it really clicked, with that song, when Mick and I felt confident
> enough to actually lay it in front of Brian and Charlie and Ian
> Stewart, especially, arbiter of events.[37]

The B-side, "Play With Fire", succeeds in an entirely different way, as an understated song of menace built around a contemporary English theme of high society intrigue in the fashionable quarters of London (with namechecks for St. John's Wood and Knightsbridge):

Well you've got your diamonds
And you've got your pretty clothes
And the chauffeur drives your car
You let ev'rybody know
But don't play with me
'Cause you're playing with fire.[38]

Although officially credited on the label to the Rolling Stones, it was actually – as explained by Keith – the product of an exclusive one-off performance:

After we finished "The Last Time", the only Stones left standing were me and Mick. Phil Spector was there – Andrew had asked him to come down and listen to the track – and so was Jack Nitzsche. A janitor had come to clean up, this silent sweeping in the corner of this huge studio, while this remaining group picked up instruments. Spector picked up Bill Wyman's bass, Nitzsche went to the harpsichord, and the B-side, "Play With Fire", was cut with half the Rolling Stones and this unique line-up.[39]

Only eight days later, on 26th February, when the record was released in the UK, the Stones were all back together in London, miming to both sides on that evening's edition of *Ready Steady Go!* Entering the Top 10 at No.8 in the week ending 6th March, in its second week in the charts "The Last Time" gave them their second No.1, staying at the top for four weeks in contrast to the two they had previously achieved with "Little Red Rooster".

Impressive as this was, a lengthy interval now followed until their next release for the home market on 11th June, *Got Live If You Want It!* – a seriously flawed EP in terms of its poor sound quality, an issue which Loog Oldham sought to sidestep with a customary burst of hyperbole for the benefit of the music press: "One must remember that one is not selling, in most cases, a melody that will go down in history, one is selling a ball of sound which attempts to hit the audience on first or second impact, because if it does not you can forget it."[40] In addition to the briefest of opening tracks, an audience chanting "We Want The Stones" (outrageously claimed as a composing credit for the group, to maximise royalties), the five songs it contained had all been culled from the opening concerts of their 14-day UK tour in early March[41]; recorded live by engineer Glyn Johns in London, Liverpool and Manchester. There were, it seemed, sufficient numbers of undiscriminating fans to take it straight into the Top 30 at No.13, from whence it rose to its peak of No.7 in the week ending 3rd July. The next release of a new original composition - and a welcome return to the expected higher standard of product – would not take place until late August; by which time the record in question would already have been available in America for the past two months, giving the Stones both their first US No.1 and a gold disc, but also meaning, of course, that for British fans it would prove well worth the wait (as a quarter of a million advance orders demonstrated).

Unmistakeable from the second its buzz-saw snarl of a riff kicks in, "(I Can't Get No) Satisfaction" is one of the truly outstanding singles of the Sixties, let alone one of the greatest singles the Stones ever made. In its style, sound and content, its UK release on 20th August marked an historic moment in British pop. A clean break for the Stones from their previous work within the broad conventions of rhythm and blues, it simply defied comparison with any other contemporary hit or chart-contender and, as such, it polarised opinion: you either loved it or hated it. This said, any further debate on the matter was firmly stifled in due course by NME readers voting it Best Single of 1965 in the music paper's annual poll.

Although the song was initially conceived in England, the end result is to all intents and purposes an American construct, as declared by the howling ungrammaticalness of its full title and its having been recorded almost on the run in the States amidst one of the Stones' most hectic tours of the year. For such a legendary record, it is bizarre, therefore, that Keith should attribute its origin to a happy accident, while unusually he had time on his hands at home in London. Circumstantial evidence fixes the event in question as occurring at some point between the end of a 6-day Scandinavian tour, which had finished on 2nd April, and the group's departure on 15th April for three days in Paris, to play the Olympia:

> I wrote "Satisfaction" in my sleep. I had no idea I'd written it, it's only thank God for the little Philips cassette player. The miracle being that I looked at the cassette player that morning and I knew I'd put a brand-new tape in the previous night, and I saw it was at the end. Then I pushed rewind and there was "Satisfaction". It was just a rough idea. There was just the bare bones of the song, and it didn't have that noise, of course, because I was on acoustic. And forty minutes of me snoring. But the bare bones is all you need.[42]

Shortly after returning from Paris, the Stones were off again, this time to Montreal to begin their third tour of North America. Keith credits Mick with completing the song by writing the lyrics in Florida in early May, while resting between concert dates, and their first efforts to record it followed four days later, in Chicago on 10th May, when they laid down an acoustic version at Chess Studios. Then flying on to Hollywood, they immediately reconvened at RCA Studios where, after two more intensive days, the track was completed on 13th May, Keith's guitar work now distinctively embellished by the addition of a fuzz box (although in his head he had imagined this further flourish ultimately being replaced by a horn section). Even at the end of all this, Mick and Keith, as composers, remained unpersuaded that it was good enough to put out as an A-side, only to find themselves heavily outvoted by their fellow group members plus Ian Stewart, recording engineer Dave Hassinger and producer Andrew Loog Oldham.

"Satisfaction" is a petulant song, an impatient song, possibly just a downright nasty song – all of which also made it, for its time, a controversial song. Performed by Jagger at his most belligerent, it turns out, for all that it was composed by twenty-somethings, to be three verses of highly charged adolescent rant, topped and tailed by an aggressive, shouted chorus. The targets of his frustration are the mindlessness of both the radio ("tellin' me more and more/About some useless information/Supposed to fire my imagination") and television ("But he can't be a man/'Cause he doesn't smoke/The same cigarettes as me"), topped only by his lack of "girl reaction", when a possible pick-up turns out not to be sexually receptive: "baby/Better come back maybe next week/'Cos you see I'm on a losing streak."[43] Its deliberately contrived roughness suddenly made the melodious approach of Lennon and McCartney look tame; and therein, for many, lay its immediate appeal.

For its American release, it was coupled with "The Under Assistant West Coast Promotion Man", a barely-disguised satiric misrepresentation of George Sherlock, known to the Stones as the man who handled their promotions for London Records, and a track laid down during the first "Satisfaction" sessions at Chess. In Britain, however, the B-side was the altogether different "The Spider And The Fly". A product of the subsequent sessions at RCA, this is a mocking, downbeat tale of rockstar sexual infidelity, illuminated by sly innuendo ("She said she liked the way I held the microphone"), in which Jagger boasts of ensnaring an older woman he meets in a bar (a "rinsed out blonde … common, flirty/She looked about thirty") just because he knows he can without his "girl at home" ever finding out: "I said My! My! My! like a spider to a fly!/Jump right ahead in my web!"[44] Irrespective of their varying merits, all three numbers were undeniably indicative of the sudden gelling of the Jagger/Richards songwriting partnership, which from this point on would not only be crucial to carrying the Stones forward into the future but would also herald the increasing marginalisation of Brian Jones within the group.

Those of us bold enough and young enough to declare a commitment to the Stones by buying "Satisfaction" should have known perfectly well that there would be a price to pay in the form of a backlash from the older generation. (After all, a month earlier, hadn't the uncouth trio of Mick, Brian and Bill been brought before East Ham Magistrates' Court, convicted of insulting behaviour and fined for publicly urinating on a service station forecourt in Forest Gate?[45]) Smashing into the charts at No.3 the week after its British release, it went to No.1 for a three-week stint, only to be supplanted in the week ending 25th September by comedian-turned-singer Ken Dodd. It had been two years since we had had to endure "Happiness" breaking into the lower Top 30, but now we faced a prolonged attack of cloying sentimentality from the middle-aged by proxy, who bought his latest ballad "Tears" in such quantities as to keep him at No.1 for an unbroken six weeks. Since the advent of the Beatles, there had never been a clearer generational divide in the purchase of top-selling singles; and "Tears" became only the ninth record since the start of the decade to remain at No.1 for six or more consecutive weeks (one of an elite group headed by the Everly Brothers and Elvis Presley who in 1960 had taken "Cathy's Clown" and "It's Now Or Never" respectively to the top of the charts for nine weeks apiece).[46]

The only saving grace was that in the end the Stones had the last laugh, kicking Dodd off his perch at the beginning of November with their next single, "Get Off Of My Cloud"; the wording of its title alone reiterating the depth to which they had absorbed Americanisms into their thought processes, while its lyric renewed their denunciation of what irked them about modern city living:

> I live in an apartment on the ninety-ninth floor of my block
> And I sit at home lookin' out my window, imaginin' the world has
>   stopped.
> Then in flies a guy all dressed up just like a Union Jack,
> He says I've won five pounds if I have this kind of detergent pack.
> I said, hey you get off of my cloud, hey you get off of my cloud,
> Hey you get off of my cloud, don't hang around
> 'Cause two's a crowd on my cloud, baby.[47]

In spite of being a busier, muddier production, that all but rendered Mick's vocals incomprehensible, it nevertheless repeated the success of "Satisfaction" by reaching No.1 in both the USA and Britain. A week after its UK release on 22nd October, it exactly mirrored its predecessor's progress by first entering the Top 30 at No.3, then going to No.1 for three weeks.

"Get Off Of My Cloud" was the most noteworthy outcome of sessions crowded into two days, 5th and 6th September, at RCA Hollywood, to which the Stones had flown directly after concluding their second short Irish tour of the year (its highlights captured in a long-unseen black-and-white documentary film directed by Peter Whitehead, *Charlie Is My Darling*, finally televised at the end of 2012 as part of the group's fiftieth anniversary celebrations). Several of the other tracks laid down in the course of those forty-eight hours, plus ones from May and the previous November, eventually went to making up the next LP, *Out Of Our Heads*, to be released in the UK on 24th September.[48] Indicative not just of the ever-tighter time constraints under which they were now working but equally the international lifestyle they now actively embraced, recording over, they flew straight back from Los Angeles to London, then on to the Isle of Man, to honour a booking in Douglas on the evening of 8th September regardless of jet-lag.

Having to cram so much into so short a space of time was also primarily a reflection of the greater commercial pressures to which the Stones had become subject. As Keith put it: "One hit requires another, very quickly, or you fast start to lose altitude."[49] He also recognised that resting on their laurels, by offering up a pale imitation of the last record, was not the key to survival:

> If we'd come along with another fuzz riff after "Satisfaction", we'd have been dead in the water, repeating with the law of diminishing returns. Many a band has faltered on that rock. "Get Off Of My Cloud" was a reaction to the record companies' demands for more – leave me alone – and it was an attack from another direction. And it flew as well.[50]

The group's affairs took on a keener edge in the summer with the replacement of their original business manager Eric Easton by notorious New York accountant and 'fixer' Allen Klein, whose showy ruthlessness was immediately appealing to the unscrupulous side of Andrew Loog Oldham's character. Klein's first act to win the confidence of the Stones was to rene-gotiate their recording contract with Decca, which was up for renewal, on the premise that he would secure for them a much improved future share of royalties; and to this end, he staged a confrontational meeting with Sir Edward Lewis, Decca's chairman, attended by the Stones under strict instruc-tions to offer an intimidating presence by wearing dark glasses and saying nothing. Lewis capitulated and a new nine-year contract, starting from 30th July, was agreed, resulting in a much welcomed initial advance payment of £2,500 to each group member for the first year of the deal.

It was only after the event that Bill, for one, discovered to his dismay that prior to these negotiations supposedly in their best interests, "Andrew had already signed Letters of Agreement that Klein had prepared for him" and that consequently the Stones were "committed without ever having a chance to discuss it or verify anything that was agreed".[51] As a result, they had been cunningly and "effectively locked into arrangements that [they] did not fully comprehend"[52] and that were, in the long term, not specifically designed to work in their favour, since any monies nominally due to them had first to be channelled through a holding company under Klein's control.

Like most of their contemporaries and many others soon to follow them into the pop industry in the remainder of the Sixties, the Stones had made themselves vulnerable by unwittingly concentrating on making music to the exclusion of even questioning the action of third parties as custodians of their finances. With the dual benefit of hindsight and history, it is not unreasonable to ask, as Christopher Sandford since has:

Why did the LSE-trained Jagger and the rest of the band allow so much power to be concentrated in the hands of one man? No one at the time grasped the extent of Klein's ambition or thought of his accumulation of duties in those terms; there were jobs to be done which no one else particularly wanted, and which he was willing to take on. Mick, Brian and Charlie seem to have been happy to go along with what struck them as no more than a bit of in-house administrative tinkering. Keith in turn thought Klein (with whom he shared a birthday) 'fantastic', the Stones' ticket 'out of cheapo-dom', while only Bill worried that 'Fatso' might, on the contrary, end up costing them. As it turned out, both men would be proved right.[53]

And there was another straw in the wind. At the same time as Loog Oldham was apparently loosening some of the managerial ties currently binding him to the group he had helped to create in his own maverick image, he was actively diverting his efforts, together with those of Tony Calder, towards another project entirely, which they officially unveiled on 20th August: the founding of a new independent label, Immediate Records, of which more anon.

Notwithstanding this less than transparent mid-year reconfiguration of their management, and with a seemingly more favourable new recording contract under their belts, the Stones threw themselves back into touring with renewed vigour. Six nights of concerts in West Germany and Austria in mid-September were swiftly followed at the end of the month by a UK tour of twenty-four venues in as many days, with leading Birmingham acts the Moody Blues and the Spencer Davis Group providing support and concluding on 17th October in Tooting. Twelve days later, on 29th October, they were in Montreal, opening their second North American tour of the year and their biggest to date, playing "37 venues in 38 days": "There were concerts in 20 different states, along with appearances in Washington, DC, and Canada. The band played matinees and evening shows on six different days and had only seven days off in almost eight weeks away from home."[54] A conservative estimate of the combined total of their audiences was in excess of 250,000.

Having as a group already narrowly survived the crushing of their car by a monstrous scrum of fans in Long Beach, California, in May on their last US tour, this time it was Keith's turn to face a near-death experience of his own unintentional making. On 3rd December, they were back in California, playing Sacramento, when:

> Towards the end of the show [in the first verse of "The Last
> Time"], Keith touched the microphone stand with his guitar. There

was a blinding blue flash and he ended up flat on his back, out cold … Keith came round within a few minutes and seemed none the worse for wear. All his guitar strings were severed and the ends were curled up, melted like fuse wire. Keith was taken to hospital, where doctors claimed that it was the thick rubber soles of his Hush Puppy shoes that had saved his life. Mr Indestructible had survived an early scare.[55]

Mercifully, the tour ended without further mishap two days later, to be followed, after a brief respite, by a return to the RCA studios in Hollywood for three days of new recording sessions, from 8th to 10th December; encompassing not only their next single but also several tracks for their next LP, the first to be made up entirely of original compositions. The effort involved and the burden of commitment now placed upon the shoulders of each group member only served to intensify the ominous rift developing between Mick and Keith on the one hand and Brian on the other. Faced with the reality of having been displaced as the *de facto* leader of the group he had founded, Brian proved to be less and less co-operative musically and sought solace and distraction elsewhere, first in a turbulent new sexual relationship with German model Anita Pallenberg and then in the latest recreational drug of choice on the California scene, LSD (*aka* acid). Keith has remained unsympathetic and unforgiving to the present day. In his 2010 autobiography, in a flurry of epithets worthy of Coleridge's Ancient Mariner, he scathingly refers to Brian as becoming "a pain in the neck, a kind of rotting attachment … a dead weight"[56], attributable in his view to a self-destructive combination of inferiority and jealousy:

> What probably really stuck in Brian's craw was when Mick and I started writing the songs. He lost his status and then lost interest. Having to come to the studio and learn to play a song Mick and I had written would bring him down. It was like Brian's open wound.[57]

And for Keith, once effectively left in the lurch by Brian, it meant having to invest more time and energy in overdubbing, to try to recapture that lost earlier magic of the duelling guitars:

> He barely ever played guitar in the last few years with us. Our whole thing was two guitars and everything else wove around that. And when the other guitar ain't there half the time or has lost interest in it, you start getting overdubbing. A lot of those records is me four times.[58]

Henceforward, at least on record, Brian's contribution would be less and less discernible, offering the occasional lighter touch from time to time on unusual or exotic instruments as they might take his fancy. On stage, it became the norm for his fellow Stones to play on in spite of the liability he represented, trying to ignore him as far as possible even when he was moved to be provocative: Christopher Sandford notes, for example, that when they played "Satisfaction", Brian would often, out of something more than sheer devilment, wilfully launch into the theme tune from "Popeye The Sailorman".[59] Considering the high esteem in which the others had once held him for his virtuosity as a guitarist and the lead he had originally taken in pulling the group together, his self-inflicted fall from grace from here onwards was all the more regrettable.

Sadly, the airing of personal and/or 'artistic' differences was not the sole prerogative of the Rolling Stones (although in their case they were not made public at the time) and they surfaced more and more as the decade wore on. Amongst the earliest casualties of a head-on clash of personalities were the Yardbirds, who lost lead guitarist Eric Clapton in March 1965 in response to Paul Samwell-Smith steering the group in a new musical direction with the recording of their third – and, as it turned out, most successful – single, "For Your Love".

The song, written by aspiring composer Graham Gouldman, was just about as far removed from the Yardbirds' staple diet of blues as imaginable, but it lent itself, in Samwell-Smith's hands as producer, to a brilliantly imaginative and indisputably commercial arrangement. The first of a string of hit singles to fully realise the asset that lay in Keith Relf's quavering intonation, it was decked out with bongos, bowed double-bass and harpsichord; and Clapton hated it:

> When the Yardbirds decided to record 'For Your Love', I knew it was the beginning of the end for me; I didn't see how we could make a record like that and stay as we were. It felt to me that we had completely sold out. I played on it, though my contribution was limited to a very short blues riff in the middle-eight section ...[60]

Having become, on his own admission, "constantly argumentative and dogmatic about everything that came up"[61], Clapton could not be appeased even by being given the B-side, "Got To Hurry", as effectively a solo blues instrumental showcase; and so, by mutual agreement with Giorgio Gomelsky, he left the group, his last public performance with the Yardbirds being in Bristol on 3rd March. Yet it was chiefly on the strength of his appreciation of Clapton's technical skill as denoted by "Got To Hurry" that in April John Mayall invited him to join his Bluesbreakers, an opportunity Clapton gratefully seized, content in the knowledge that Mayall and his band offered him "a frame that I could fit into".[62]

This said, Clapton had every intention of making that frame bend to his will sooner rather than later and joined the group with a fervent desire to convert Mayall from "jazz blues" to "Chicago blues"[63]; while for his part, Mayall had consciously recruited Clapton as a replacement for previous lead guitarist, Roger Dean, in the search for a change of style. The deal was further cemented by Clapton moving in to live with Mayall and his family in their east London home. The line-up thus now became: John Mayall (vocals/keyboards/harmonica), Eric Clapton (vocals/lead guitar), John McVie (bass guitar) and Hughie Flint (drums).

At the time of Dean's departure, the Bluesbreakers were contracted to Decca, who released their second single, "Crocodile Walk", on 2nd April. However, its lack of chart success meant that Decca declined to take up the option of renewing their contract and that consequently Clapton, having officially joined them on 6th April, had only the immediate prospect of performing live on a tortuous club and concert circuit, for a fixed weekly wage of £35, which he later described as "a working schedule the likes of which I had never experienced".[64]

After being with the Yardbirds, whose fortunes were suddenly on the rise, this might well have been seen as a retrograde step but, for the time being at least, Clapton seemed content to be nominally out of the limelight. In a candid interview published in *Rave* magazine in June, he explained that he had experienced "the worst form of loneliness" with the Yardbirds, the feeling of "being alone within a crowd": "I lived as part of the Yardbirds unit yet I was completely out of touch with it. I couldn't speak and be understood. And they couldn't speak to me either. We just couldn't communicate."[65]

By contrast, he now found himself totally at ease: "With John Mayall," he said, "I can play how I like."[66] Indeed, his formidable reputation as a guitar hero grew incrementally during his fifteen months with the Bluesbreakers – this being the period during which a fan was inspired to adorn the walls of Islington Underground with the celebratory slogan 'Clapton is God'[67] – but he would have little chance to record with them until they laid down the tracks for the iconic 'Beano album' in the early summer of 1966 (as discussed in detail in Chapter 8), by which time his departure was imminent.

The only single they recorded in the remainder of 1965 on which he was to play was "I'm Your Witch Doctor", one of Mayall's own compositions (with half an eye to Screamin' Jay Hawkins's "I Put A Spell On You"), to which Clapton contributed some brief but powerful touches of echoing guitar. Produced in August by prolific session musician Jimmy Page for the newly launched Immediate label and released on 22nd October, it was, disappointingly though not surprisingly, the group's third single to meet with no success.

As for the Yardbirds, they had wasted no time in finding Clapton's replacement. After unsuccessfully trying to tempt Jimmy Page out of the recording studio, Page had offered them an alternative suggestion, to check out Jeff Beck, then playing with London R&B group the Tridents. Beck was flattered: "The Tridents had built a great following. But there was no way I could exist – they weren't paying me anything. And I got a free suit when I joined The Yardbirds ..."[68] It was therefore heavily ironic that when he took the stage for the first time as their new lead guitarist, at the Fairfield Hall, Croydon, on 5th March, it should be on the very day that the single so detested by Clapton was released. In another five weeks, "For Your Love" would be No.1 – albeit for one week only, neatly sandwiched between the Rolling Stones' "The Last Time" and the Beatles' "Ticket To Ride", and jointly sharing that honour into the bargain with the least likely of bedfellows, Cliff Richard's "The Minute You're Gone".

Only a matter of days after his joining the Yardbirds, Beck was in the studio with them as they resumed recording. From these sessions spanning March and April emerged their next single, "Heart Full Of Soul", another Graham Gouldman song, released on 4th June and reaching No.2 in mid-July; as well as the three tracks for their *Five Yardbirds* EP, released on 6th August. Side 1 was given over entirely to an ill-considered and largely improvisatory cover of the Vibrations' 1964 US hit "My Girl Sloopy", running to 5 mins. 36 secs. long. Later reworked as "Hang On Sloopy" by American group the McCoys, in that version it became Immediate's first single issued in the UK, making it to No.4 in October, so there was no denying the song's potential popularity; but for the Yardbirds, it was so far removed from their accustomed repertoire that they laboured in vain to bring it to life. However, the EP is redeemed by the two blues tracks on Side 2, "I'm Not Talking" and "I Ain't Done Wrong", both prominently featuring the raw verve and fluidity of Beck's playing.

Towards the end of a summer when they had been almost constantly on the road touring, first in support of the Kinks and then latterly in their own right, they returned to the studio in late July and early August, this time to record the tracks that would be paired on their next double-A-side single: yet another Gouldman song, "Evil Hearted You", and an original composition (from Paul Samwell-Smith and Jim McCarty), "Still I'm Sad". The former was a perfectly logical follow-on to "Heart Full Of Soul", with a stunningly sharp guitar break from Jeff Beck; whereas the latter – my favourite of the two – was a highly melodramatic Gothic fantasy, Keith Relf intoning the lyric against a backing populated by a guttural choir (supposedly inspired by Gregorian chants), echoing percussive effects from cymbals and triangle, and a minimal guitar figure rendered unearthly by volume-swell pedal. Following the single's release on 1st October, chart honours were divided. Although "Evil Hearted You" entered the Top 30 first, getting as high as No.10, "Still

I'm Sad" nevertheless turned out to be the stronger seller of the pair, beating its companion to No.9.

Capitalising on their British breakthrough, Giorgio Gomelsky had also made efforts to promote the Yardbirds in America, where both "For Your Love" and "Heart Full Of Soul" became Top 10 hits. It was inevitable, therefore, that before long they should attempt an American tour and this finally got under way on 2nd September, when they departed for New York, although US employment restrictions seriously curtailed the number of concerts they could play or TV appearances they could make in the scope of an initial three-week visit.

Like the Rolling Stones before them, however, they were able to take advantage of their trip to record new material in illustrious surroundings: first at Sun Studios in Memphis, under the guidance of founder Sam Phillips (where they recorded "The Train Kept A-Rollin'" and "You're A Better Man Than I", on 12th September), then at Chess Studios in Chicago, where on 19th September they laid down the first takes of a reworking of Bo Diddley's "I'm A Man", to be completed on 21st September at Columbia Studios, New York. The latter (b/w "Still I'm Sad") became their third US single release of the year but this time failed to make the Top 10, only reaching No.17.[69] (The Chess version of "I'm A Man", with Beck on lead, never was released in the UK in what remained of the group's life-span, only surfacing here in the Nineties when retrospective anthologies of their work started to be issued on CD, although the song had been a staple of their live act from the beginning with Clapton on board and as such already known to British fans as one of the tracks on *Five Live Yardbirds*.) In December, on the first leg of a longer second US tour, they would spend two more days at Chess Studios (21st and 22nd), this time recording a new original composition, "Shapes Of Things".

Having survived the fracture with Clapton, the Yardbirds had quickly regained their equilibrium and moved on into the most productive phase of their career. By contrast, other groups appeared to nurture and thrive on barely concealed tensions, that would erupt every so often into violent physical confrontation, the Kinks being the classic example of "four separate identities and four conflicting personalities".[70] Quite apart from the constant, nagging sibling rivalry between Ray and Dave Davies, their UK tour in the early summer (on which they had been accompanied by the Yardbirds) was brought to an abrupt and premature end in Cardiff on 19th May by a stand-up fight on stage between Dave and drummer Mick Avory, as a result of which Dave was hospitalised with sixteen stitches to his head. However, in his autobiography, Dave freely admits to having been the instigator, following a disagreement between them the night before, when Mick had blacked both his eyes:

By the following night, after we'd both had time to stew, our feelings were running very high as we took to the stage. A couple of songs into the show I looked at Mick and shouted at him … I sneered at him and kicked his drums all over the stage, then moved over to the mike and acted nonchalant. The next thing I knew I was lying flat on my back in the dressing-room with blood trickling down the back of my neck. Turns out Mick had lost it and hit me over the head with one of his cymbal stands.[71]

Press coverage of the incident was to furnish the phrase taken up later in the year as a new LP title, *The Kink Kontroversy*, although for the sake of avoiding prosecution Mick was subsequently obliged to tell reporters it had been no more than a pre-planned piece of stage 'business' that had unexpectedly gone wrong.

Personal differences aside, 1965 proved to be a punishing year for the Kinks in terms both of their recorded output and a gruelling schedule of touring, such unrelenting pressures making it nigh on impossible for the group to achieve any lasting semblance of compatibility. In the UK alone, Pye released an incredible five singles, one EP and two LPs, the totality of which represented a massively increasing burden on Ray's shoulders as principal songwriter. Depressingly, most of the singles fared badly, only serving to add to Ray's growing sense of disillusionment at a time when he was also despairing of the group's loss of confidence in their management or ever reaping a fair financial reward for his compositions.

Seen collectively, the diversity and spread of singles throughout the year bring into sharp focus Ray's continuing struggle to balance Pye's commercial imperatives with his own search for a unique style of writing that, as yet, still eluded him. The year started well enough, when "Tired Of Waiting For You", released on 15th January, gave the Kinks their second No.1. A much slower, more reflective song than either of its two immediate predecessors, it was delivered by Ray in an idiosyncratic languid drawl. Then in March came "Everybody's Gonna Be Happy", conceived by Ray as "our tribute to the Motown bands we had worked with on various tours"[72] but sounding neither like Motown nor the Kinks to the average British fan, who found its jerky tempo decidedly unsettling. In only three weeks in the Top 30, it made little headway: having entered the charts at No.21, it could get no higher than No.19.

To counter what Dave politely described as "any negative effects" of this "lukewarm reaction"[73], Ray was urgently tasked by agent Arthur Howes to "come up with a great record", to bring "that magic Kinks sound back".[74] He reluctantly got the message, that he had to "acquire the special art of what is described as Hackmanship: to contrive and target an audience rather than write from an inward, subconscious flow".[75] The result was "Set Me

Free", the recording of which made Ray "feel like a whore; our managers, agents, record producers and publishers considered it to be one of the most commercial things I'd written to date."[76] Talents prostituted or not, following its release in May, it did achieve the desired end of restoring the Kinks to the Top 10 when it reached No.9 in the week ending 19th June.

But inconsistency, it seemed, still held sway when their next single, "See My Friends", took them in an entirely different musical direction in July. According to Ray, it owed its inspiration to an episode in January in Bombay (after an overnight stopover en route to Australia), when he had heard "the chanting of native fishermen as they carried their nets to work" early in the morning.[77] Dave credited it as "one of the most beautiful songs Ray ever wrote … a song about tragic loss of a deep friendship that transcends words and defies explanation".[78] Instrumentally, they set out to embody the sound of the sitar without actually using one, a revolutionary development in pop as here summarised by Kinks' biographer Nick Hasted:

> Feedback from one guitar alternated behind a droning second in
> a hypnotic rhythm resembling a sitar, months before the Beatles
> or Byrds recorded one ('Norwegian Wood' was taped in October).
> Heavy bass and drums thickened this into a raga-rock template
> which fully bloomed in the Beatles' 'Tomorrow Never Knows' the
> following spring. Tape hiss from the layers of work to get it right
> added to the hazy feel … Ray's lyrics' repeated mantra of loss,
> abandonment and transformation completed a sense of spiritual
> dislocation.[79]

Despite Ray and Dave's obvious pride in the end result, its release on 30th July as the follow-up to "Set Me Free" was preceded by a rancorous dispute between producer Shel Talmy and manager Larry Page (the latter having unilaterally announced that another of Ray's songs, "Ring The Bells", was to be their next single[80]). In the event, sales were modest; and in a chart run of only four weeks (one week longer than the ill-fated "Everybody's Gonna Be Happy"), "See My Friends" peaked at No.15 in August.

Undaunted, Ray finally found his niche with his next major composition, "A Well Respected Man". "Looking back," he would say, "there are landmarks":

> The beginning of the lyrical stuff was 'A Well Respected Man',
> which was a song that nobody asked me to write. It was something
> that I'd observed on holiday[81], and the first time I actually stood
> back from what I was. Before that everything came from boy-girl
> teenage angst. 'Well Respected Man', that's a watershed because I
> started singing about other people. Something is turning, evolving.[82]

Although Ray viewed it hopefully as a possible new single, Pye's executives were unconvinced of the Top 30 potential of a song ridiculing the epitome of the comfortable middle classes, the "well respected man about town/ Doing the best things so conservatively".[83] So they opted instead to play safe, releasing it on 17th September as one of four original tracks on a new EP, *Kwyet Kinks*, which nevertheless sold in sufficient numbers to become No.1 in the rarely-disturbed backwater of the EP charts.[84]

Thus the Kinks' last single release of the year was deferred until November, in the form of a song Ray knocked out as a pot-boiler that was a reversion to an earlier type. In feel and lyric, "Till The End Of The Day" was recognisably a close relative of both "You Really Got Me" and "All Day And All Of The Night" and as such was well received, sales either side of Christmas eventually pushing it to No.8 in January 1966.

Yet it was the second of Ray's songs within a matter of months to be subject to legal challenge, inadvertently triggered this time by Ray himself when he signed up to a new five-year publishing deal with Belinda Music, in seeming contravention of the existing agreement with Edward Kassner but carefully considered beforehand with manager Robert Wace and legal adviser Michael Simkins.[85] Both publishers went to war over the copyright of "Till The End Of The Day", a threatened injunction on Kassner's behalf circumvented by Pye bringing the record's release forward by a week, and protracted legal action ensued that would not be resolved until October 1970. With the payment of all composing royalties from record sales to Ray frozen in the interim, what he had readily embraced as a beneficial deal proved to be the exact and costly opposite, leaving him for the next five years with songwriting income only from TV and radio performing rights dues.

As far as the Kinks' two LPs of 1965 were concerned, in both instances minimal studio time was dedicated to them by Pye, with sessions shoehorned in between touring commitments and pre-determined release dates for the albums stoking up the pressure to complete them in short order. For *Kinda Kinks*, the majority of tracks were hurriedly recorded between 15th and 17th February, barely in time for its release on 5th March; and it shows in the ragged outcome, from which the hit single "Tired Of Waiting For You" and its B-side "Come On Now" shine out like beacons. It captures a group in a state of awkward imperfection, still trying to find their true musical direction, the low point being an appalling cover of "Dancing In The Street" in which Ray struggles not only to remember all the words but also to keep time. "Naggin' Woman" could be mistaken on first hearing for an early Rolling Stones' track, while "Don't Ever Change" borrows both tempo and melodic structure from the Drifters' "Save The Last Dance For Me." Of the remainder, only "Something Better Beginning" shows genuine signs of being a song consciously crafted by Ray. Despite its many shortcomings, it enjoyed some success, eventually making No.3 in the LP charts.

As for *The Kink Kontroversy*, even though a whole week had provisionally been set aside at the end of October for its recording, this was cut to two days (Monday 25th and Tuesday 26th) in the face of a succession of UK concert dates from Wednesday to Sunday inclusive, with two more days then being crammed in on 3rd and 4th November to allow the LP to come out as planned on 26th November. Again a current hit single, "Till The End Of The Day", and its B-side, "Where Have All The Good Times Gone", were included and again these are undoubtedly the two strongest tracks of the collection, although overall producer Shel Talmy appears to have made serious efforts to give the album a heavier edge with augmentation of the group by seasoned session players Nicky Hopkins on piano and Clem Cattini on drums. However, the opening track, Dave's raucous interpretation of Sleepy John Estes' "Milk Cow Blues", is an anachronism here and would have been far better suited to the naive assortment of styles and influences that populated their debut album. Although a lot louder than *Kinda Kinks*, it is hard to see *The Kink Kontroversy* as representing the next step in a logical musical progression: perhaps only "The World Keeps Going Round" and "I'm On An Island" (on which Ray is to be found in jovial mood) offer any clear pointers to the future. Of their three album releases to date, it would be the least popular so far, spending no more than twelve weeks in the LP charts with a peak position of No.9.[86]

Looking beyond the recording to the touring, Dave characterised 1965 in that regard as having been "even crazier" than 1964: "We toured France, Australia, New Zealand, Hong Kong, Singapore, the USA, Scotland, Scandinavia, Ireland, Holland, Switzerland, Germany, and embarked on our first UK tour as headliners, which ended in near disaster in Cardiff."[87]

Whereas Dave, wherever they went, carried on regardless, in headstrong pursuit of those debauched pleasures he now saw as neither more nor less than a rock star's entitlement, Ray had begun the year as a newly-married man and suffered agonies of separation from his wife Rasa.[88] The trip to Australia in late January and early February – on which the Kinks were accompanied by Manfred Mann and the Honeycombs and their paths repeatedly crossed with the Rolling Stones – was made more bearable by the opportunity it afforded the Davies brothers for a reunion with their older sister Rosie, who had emigrated to Adelaide with husband Arthur and son Terry.[89] But by the end of May, Ray had also become a father and the wrench of having to leave his new baby daughter Louisa so soon after her birth on the 23rd added to his anxieties about the Kinks' first US tour, beginning on 18th June.

Ray's misgivings sadly proved to be well-founded. All told, America was a nightmare for the Kinks. Because the Moody Blues were unable to travel with them as originally billed, due to unresolved visa and work permit issues, their itinerary was subject to last-minute changes. This meant that as the tour progressed into the Mid-West in particular, in several instances they pitched up unsuspectingly to play in ill-prepared and poorly publicised venues, as well as encountering outright hostility from ultra-conservative local promoters who clearly resented them, not just for their appearance but primarily for being British. In Reno and Sacramento, they found themselves in open dispute with booking agent Betty Kaye over payment for their concerts, their disagreements with her finally coming to a head at the Cow Palace in San Francisco on 4th July. Here, starved of ready cash by poor ticket sales, she was only prepared to offer them a cheque, which they declined and then refused to play. Thus rebuffed, Ms. Kaye was a sore loser and a bad enemy, lodging a complaint with the American Federation of Musicians against the Kinks that contributed substantially to them being blacklisted in the USA for the next three years. (Neither had it aided their cause that two days earlier in Hollywood Ray had punched a union official from the American Federation of Television and Radio Artists, who had blatantly riled him with anti-British invective.)

If there were highlights, they were few and far between. Even performing on the same bill as the Beach Boys, as they did on 3rd July at the Hollywood Bowl, lost its edge when both Ray and Dave were upset by the "apparent lack of grace" shown towards them by their heroes backstage.[90] To fend off his homesickness, Ray had demanded of Larry Page that Rasa be brought out to join him; but just as she flew in to California, together with Pete Quaife's girlfriend Nicola, Page had decided after the Cow Palace fiasco that his further presence on the tour was unnecessary and he flew out back to London without explanation, leaving the Kinks behind with another week of the tour still remaining. Although the last concerts in Hawaii and Washington State passed off without further incident, Ray narrowly avoided arrest in transit at Spokane Airport for the alleged 'indecency' of kissing Rasa in public, one final reactionary sideswipe at the upstart long-haired Britishers.

Ray's disquiet at the group's unsatisfactory experience of America, together with his growing unease at the unsupportiveness of the Kinks' divided management, continued to gnaw away at him for months. When not on the road around Britain or abroad, he was at his most contented in the family home he had bought in Fortis Green in north London, making "unfashionable efforts to be a responsible husband and father" and "putting food on the table by writing songs"[91]; finding some semblance of security in the realisation that "suburbia was and would always be a major influence in my writing".[92]

Yet even Dave's acknowledgement of Ray's emerging strengths as a composer at this time could never dispel the enduring tension between the two brothers, as Dave most profoundly illustrates in his autobiography. After first citing his appreciation of the depth of feeling informing Ray's composition of "Where Have All The Good Times Gone", Dave goes on tellingly to say this:

> It's such a weird paradox that Ray, who wrote that lovely song,
> would later become so abusive to me, so cruel and creatively
> draining. When I look back, many times I've become so exasperated
> by his contradictory nature, his unyielding and unreasonable
> behaviour. On the one hand, he's sensitive enough to understand
> even the slightest emotion, to feel for the plight and frustration
> of the underdog, able to offer great insight and compassion. Yet
> at the same time he displays an almost resentful and sometimes
> condescending loathing for his past, his family. He is at times
> venomous, spiteful, and completely self-involved. A puzzling
> dichotomy.[93]

Little wonder, then, that on the threshold of 1966 Ray should consider from his own perspective that an "age of blind, reckless innocence was coming to an end and an era fraught with litigation, emotional turmoil and paranoia was about to begin".[94]

There were other newcomers arriving on the scene in 1965 to whom conflict would equally be no stranger. One of the most single-minded amongst that number was Pete Townshend, who saw the principal *raison d'etre* of being in a group as a means to his own ends: "… a band isn't a unified fellowship, it's an uneasy, sometimes competitive merger of young men with divergent ambitions who've agreed to play music together."[95]

From an early age, Townshend had harboured idealistic notions of capturing and re-creating nothing less than what Elizabethan cosmologists would have called the music of the spheres, to which he fervently believed only he was attuned, thus communicating his own unique vision of the world through the music he himself would strive to make. They were mystically crystallised for him at the age of eleven, as a potential recruit to the Sea Scouts, on a boat trip on the Thames:

> As we swept past the Old Boathouse at Isleworth once again I
> began to hear the most extraordinary music, sparked by the whine
> of the outboard motor and the burbling sound of water against the
> hull. I heard violins, cellos, horns, harps and voices, which increased
> in number until I could hear countless threads of an angelic choir; it
> was a sublime experience. I have never heard such music since, and
> my personal musical ambition has always been to rediscover that
> sound and relive its effect on me.[96]

The intensity of the event, once it had ended, left him weeping and bewildered: "I kept asking the other boys if they had heard the angels singing, but none of them even responded."[97]

Six years later, in early 1962 he was making his first serious, if fitful, efforts to realise such high-flown musical aspirations by playing rudimentary guitar in a group called the Detours, in the company amongst others of his close friend John Entwistle (with whom he had attended Acton County Grammar School) and group leader Roger Daltrey (their senior by a year, who had been expelled from the same school as a persistent troublemaker). The Detours were hard-working semi-professionals who modelled themselves on Johnny Kidd and the Pirates, steadily building up regular bookings on a tight local circuit "where London bleeds into Middlesex and Surrey with side-trips for a while to a palais on Kent's Isle of Thanet"[98] until by the end of 1962 they were "playing up to six nights a week at pubs, halls, parties, weddings, barmitzvahs and clubs"[99], with a repertoire that was a "wide-ranging mix of instrumentals, several trad jazz numbers, some Johnny Cash and American country songs and a smattering of popular ballads".[100] By 1964, they had shifted their musical ground to rely "as heavily on 'uncommercial' R&B as classic rock and the occasional tossing in of a current hit like Johnny Kidd's 'I'll Never Get Over You'".[101]

Along the way, the group had slimmed down to a quartet: Daltrey relinquishing guitar to become lead vocalist, Townshend and Entwistle playing guitar and bass guitar respectively, with the significantly older Doug Sandom on drums. As Townshend explained, they were an ill-assorted bunch:

> Doug was a bricklayer and a father. Roger worked in a factory that
> cut tinplate for specialist equipment boxes and recording studio
> racks. John worked at the local tax office. I was an art student – and
> I was also becoming a recreational drug user, smoking several times
> a week.[102]

Although music superficially gave them a common bond, this alone could not suppress the volatile chemistry that existed between them, fuelled by an increasingly bitter tussle between Daltrey and Townshend for ultimate supremacy:

> Roger had a notoriously quick temper and he argued constantly
> with the guitarist. But while Pete would aggressively state his
> case with verbal dexterity, Roger preferred to use his fists to win
> the argument and demonstrate that he was the one running the
> show. 'He'd punctuate his decisions with punches,' was how John
> Entwistle described it. Doug Sandom was more direct: 'Roger and
> Pete were always at each other's throats. It was nothing to see Roger
> smack him in the nose at rehearsals.'[103]

On Valentine's Day 1964, the Detours decided to change the group's name to the Who, to avoid any possible confusion with Johnny Devlin and the Detours, an Irish group who had appeared on *Thank Your Lucky Stars* on 1st February. Then in April, having endured constant jibes from Townshend about his age for long enough, Sandom (who was in his mid-twenties) finally snapped and quit, forcing Daltrey to hire session drummers to fill the gap in the short term. Soon afterwards, during the interval at a gig at the Oldfield Hotel in Greenford, the Who were treated to an impressively frenzied demonstration of drumming – in response to a friend's drunken bragging – by a seventeen-year-old plasterer from Wembley called Keith Moon; and he was hired as Sandom's official replacement, playing with them for the first time on 2nd May. Moon's personal passion hitherto had been for surfing music, previously indulging this as drummer for another local group, Clyde Burns and the Beachcombers, yet he was to fit in with the Who from very first acquaintance and Townshend was quick to acknowledge how his presence re-energised them: "From the point we found Keith, it was a complete turning point ... He was so assertive and confident. Before then, we had just been fooling about."[104]

The changeover from Sandom to Moon coincided with a serious expression of managerial interest in the Who from Helmut Gorden, a businessman seeking a new profitable investment, and Peter Meaden, already experienced in the PR of pop by virtue of being the Pretty Things' press officer. After the pair had gained the Who's agreement to turn professional, Meaden then sought to capitalise on the stylistic pretensions of the Mods by renaming them the High Numbers and urging them to take on the cultural trappings of a Mod group, a move of especial appeal to art student Townshend. Moulding the High Numbers into the Mod image with suitably hip new clothes and haircuts, Meaden secured a one-off deal with Fontana and wrote the songs for both sides of a single they recorded in early June, "Zoot Suit" and "I'm The Face". Sadly this gave Fontana no good reason to retain them, since of the 1,000 copies pressed and released on 3rd July, no more than half were sold.

Later that month, however, their fortunes were to change, when their paths crossed with the unlikely partnership of Christopher 'Kit' Lambert (son of Constant Lambert, musical director of the Royal Ballet) and Chris Stamp (younger brother of actor Terence). Stamp explains:

> During the summer of 1964 Kit Lambert and I were two young filmmakers looking for a rock group for our first independent film. Our idea was to find a group that somehow represented the emerging ideas of our time. They would be rebellious, anarchistic, and uniquely different from the established English pop scene. We would then manage them to success, all the while filming, cinema verité-style, all that happened.[105]

Having both been impressed by seeing the High Numbers playing live, Lambert and Stamp auditioned them on 19th July and signed them up to take part in their proposed documentary, quickly following this up by supplanting Gorden and Meaden as managers, with new contracts for the group drawn up and signed in August. Soon after an unsuccessful test session for EMI in October, overseen by producer John Burgess at Abbey Road[106], they reverted to being known as the Who and this time the name would stick.

Burgess, by way of letting the group down lightly while still offering them some constructive criticism, had suggested they needed to develop more original material (strikingly ignoring the fact, of course, that earlier in the year his advice to Manfred Mann had strongly been to the contrary). Taking this to heart, Townshend's response was to come up with three songs that were to give the Who a trio of consecutive hits in the course of 1965 and set them on the road to fame.

The first of these was "I Can't Explain", originally written to express Townshend's feelings about music but then reworked as a song about the perplexities of love; and it proved to be the bait by which Lambert and Stamp attracted the interest of the Kinks' record producer Shel Talmy. At a session at Pye's Marble Arch studios in early November, Talmy worked with the Who (and, as a precautionary measure, a host of respected session musicians[107]) to record "I Can't Explain"; subsequently managing to secure its placement with the American arm of Decca, trading in the UK on the Brunswick label. November would also be of significance for the Who as the month in which, from the 24th onwards, they took up a weekly residency at the Marquee Club, the booking for which Lambert coined the iconic slogan "Maximum R&B". For Townshend, it meant a dream come true:

> It was a great adventure, and I was full of ideas. In my notebooks I
> was designing Pop Art T-shirts, using medals and chevrons and the
> Union Flag to decorate jackets I intended to wear. At the Marquee
> I felt, like many in our audience, that Mod had become more than a
> look. It had become a voice, and the Who was its main outlet.[108]

Coinciding with the release of the Kinks' "Tired Of Waiting For You", "I Can't Explain" also went on sale on 15th January 1965 but its progress up the charts was tortuously slow. It took more than a month to enter the Top 30 at No.28, peaking eventually at No.10 in the week ending 10th April, its popularity boosted at long last by the group's growing exposure on *Ready Steady Go!*, *Top Of The Pops* and pirate broadcasters Radios London and Caroline. Then, in a three-day session at IBC Studios starting on 12th April, the Who worked again with Talmy on tracks intended for a debut LP, as well as laying down another Townshend composition as the next single.

"Anyway Anyhow Anywhere" represented an explicit effort on the

Who's part to make an artistic statement their fans could instantly recognise as another facet of those anarchic elements now typical of their live performances: the rough swagger of Daltrey's vocals, the distortion of notes through feedback, the smashing of amps and guitars by Townshend, the destruction of drum kits by Moon. Amongst the Who's extensive catalogue of hits, it is unique in being the only Daltrey/Townshend collaboration, as the latter explained:

> I wrote the first verse and Roger helped with the rest. I was inspired
> by listening to Charlie Parker, feeling that this was really a free spirit,
> and whatever he'd done with drugs and booze and everything else,
> that his playing released him and freed his spirit, and I wanted us
> to be like that, and I wanted to write a song about that, a spiritual
> song.[109]

Not recognisably a 'spiritual' in anyone else's vocabulary, nevertheless, as the title implies, the song is explicitly about breaking with tradition, celebrating the young's right to do as they please:

> I can go anyway, way I choose;
> I can live anyhow, win or lose;
> I can go anywhere, for something new;
> Anyway, anyhow, anywhere I choose.[110]

With the addition of technical gimmickry, "reflected in Townshend's rhythmic flipping of the guitar's toggle switch to produce the solo's morse code bleeps and machine gun fire"[111], Kit Lambert was happy to promote it as "a pop art record, containing pop art music. The sounds of war and chaos and frustration expressed musically without the use of sound effects."[112] Looking back now, this specific example of 'pop art music' – a term that never really caught on – may in fact be better understood as one of the earliest manifestations of that most idiosyncratic and creative genre of Sixties pop, psychedelia, in which the music sets out to mimic and explore that higher plane of awareness supposedly attained through meditation and/or the use of mind-altering substances.

Whatever its artistic heritage or legacy, its release, on 21st May, was once again simultaneous with a single from the Kinks (this time, it was "Set Me Free"). Unlike "I Can't Explain", however, its progress into and up the charts was far quicker, although ultimately not quite as successful despite being honoured for a time as the theme tune to *Ready Steady Go!* The week after release, it had made No.30 and in the course of the next month, by the week ending 26th June, it had reached its highest position of No.13.

But the best was yet to come. Where frustrated young intellectuals had previously turned to drama as the obvious means of exposing and undermining the self-satisfaction of their elders – John Osborne with *Look Back*

In Anger, Peter Cook et al with *Beyond The Fringe*, Joan Littlewood's Theatre Workshop with *Oh What A Lovely War* – now Pete Townshend used the even more fashionable medium of pop, with the Who as his mouthpiece, as the means of delivering his own ultimate anthem of arrogant youth, "My Generation".

Although by mid-1965 Townshend himself was already enjoying the high life in a flat owned by Lambert and Stamp in Belgravia, adjoining their managerial offices in Eaton Place, it was this very experience of living in "a rich neighbourhood where women in fur coats shoved me out of line as if I didn't exist"[113] that somehow he found unsettling and provided him with the inspiration for the song, on which he worked intermittently throughout the summer. As he gave shape and form to his composition, he came to realise that the fundamental concern he was striving to express was:

> … more a matter of class than of age. Most of the young people
> around me in this affluent area of London were working on
> transforming themselves into the ruling class, the Establishment
> of the future. I felt that the trappings of their aged customs and
> assumptions were like a death, whereas I felt alive, not solely
> because I was young, but really alive, unencumbered by tradition,
> property and responsibility.[114]

Recorded and re-recorded at several sessions from mid-August onwards, work on the final version of "My Generation" was completed at IBC Studios on 14th October, prior to its release on the 29th. The outcome was a *tour de force*, an instrumental and vocal showcase for the respective talents of all four members of the group yet one that gained notoriety first and foremost for Roger Daltrey's affected stuttering of key words in each verse: principally the line "Why don't you all f-fade away?", when that moment's hesitation on the 'f' sound, shockingly for its day, set you up to expect nothing less next than the F-word. Its appeal to its intended audience was instant and irresistible. After all, what young person could fail to be enticed by the cool, overstated pomposity of its opening lines?

> People try to put us d-down
> (Talkin' 'bout my generation)
> Just because we get around
> (Talkin' 'bout my generation).
> Things they do look awful c-c-cold
> (Talkin' 'bout my generation).
> I hope I die before I get old
> (Talkin' 'bout my generation).[115]

The Who never managed to achieve a No.1 single but "My Generation" remains their greatest hit of the Sixties, even though it stalled at No.3 from late November into December, fended off the top spot by Len Barry and the Seekers exchanging places at Nos.1 and 2 before the Beatles thrust everyone else aside with "Day Tripper/We Can Work It Out". In addition, it provided the title track of the group's first album, released on 3rd December to reach No.5 in the LP charts in due course. Its success, however, was so very nearly marred by an outburst from Daltrey that temporarily cost him his job with the band he had founded.

At the end of September, the Who had flown to Amsterdam for the filming of a television spectacular, followed by a brief series of concerts in Denmark; where at Helsingor (*aka* Elsinore), Keith Moon and Roger Daltrey came to blows.[116] Trying to stem what Daltrey saw as the detrimental tide of drug-taking by his fellow group members, he had provocatively taken it upon himself to flush Moon's personal hoard of amphetamines down the toilet. However good Daltrey's intent may have been, on this occasion he woefully overestimated the respect he believed his action should rightfully have commanded from the others:

> The drummer went berserk and flew at Roger, who erupted into a rage and decked him. 'I got so violent about it that I almost killed Keith Moon,' Roger confessed. 'It took about five people to hold me off him. It wasn't just because I hated him, it was just because I loved the band so much and thought it was being destroyed by those pills.' For the other three, this was a Daltrey punch-up too far. They were not prepared to take any more beatings from Roger and summarily sacked him from the band. Roger was devastated, and disgusted with Pete, Keith and John.[117]

After a three-day cooling-off period, Kit Lambert brought the group together to resolve their differences, with the others prepared to accept Daltrey's reinstatement, "on condition that he go along with whatever the band wanted to do" and that "there would be no more violent tantrums, no more outbursts and no more use of aggression to get his point across".[118] A suitably penitent Daltrey was left with no option but to capitulate and was taken back into the fold, to be suppressed and patronised henceforward as 'Peaceful Perce'. With the break-up of the group thus narrowly averted, the subsequent photograph for the front cover of the *My Generation* LP was charged with hidden meaning; the "explosive nature of the four personalities that made up the Who" symbolised by the dockside shot that showed them "standing next to four oil drums containing propane".[119]

Setting the Beatles to one side, the muscular ascendancy of groups from in and around London was a major factor in sounding the virtual death knell of the Merseybeat era in 1965, leaving only the tiniest pocket of stragglers behind to bid a final farewell within the following twelve months. As the spotlight moved away from the earlier hitmakers, so they lost their edge and record companies correspondingly began to lose faith. Gerry and the Pacemakers had managed to prolong the pre-Christmas success of "Ferry Cross The Mersey" into the New Year but in the week ending 16th January it peaked at No.8, marking it as their last Top Ten hit. Thereafter, only one more Top 30 entry remained, when Gerry's revival of Bobby Darin's ballad "I'll Be There" got to No.16 in April. Billy J. Kramer and the Dakotas had also come to the end of the road, their final hit that summer being a cover of Burt Bacharach's "Trains And Boats And Planes", which unfortunately for them lost out in a head-to-head with the composer's own version; reaching No.10 in June, whereas Bacharach's own sales were always stronger, taking him all the way up to No.5.

The Fourmost showed up for one week in January at No.29 with "Baby I Need Your Loving", then were gone. A similar fate awaited the Merseybeats, who could shift "I Love You, Yes I Do" no higher than No.30 in October, after their unsuccessful release in May of an arguably stronger song with a prophetic sting in its title, "Don't Let It Happen To Us".[120] Though by no means deserving to be written off yet as a recording act, the Swinging Blue Jeans fared even worse, with a consistent string of misses after "You're No Good" painfully extending over some eighteen months; well-made singles that could easily have been hits for them before, at the height of the good times, like "It Isn't There" or "Crazy 'Bout My Baby", no longer thought different enough to pass muster.

In fact, the only Mersey survivors to ride out the year's turbulence tolerably well were the Searchers. At the end of February, they released "Goodbye My Love", a poignant ballad originally recorded by American singer Jimmy Hughes[121] and now further imbued with atmosphere by producer Tony Hatch through the double-tracking of voices and drums, together with a distinctive 'swishing' sound on rhythm guitar from John McNally and the addition of echo. By the end of March, with the Stones sitting at No.1 with "The Last Time", it had reached No.5.[122] Next came *Bumble Bee*, a collection of four tracks lifted from their current LP, *Sounds Like Searchers*, that went to the top of the EP charts in May.[123] So far, so good – but, armed "with the benefit of hindsight", Frank Allen ruefully maintains that "the slide began for us with the release of 'He's Got No Love' in the first week of July 1965":

> It might sound odd to suggest that a disc that reached a more
> than respectable high of a number ten placing in the *NME* can be
> classed a failure but it has become noticeable through the passing
> decades that the tune, catchy and as well made as it was, has only
> ever been requested a handful of times [in live concert]. I have
> known records that barely entered the top thirty which have made a

significantly greater impression on people's memory banks.[124]

His less than generous assessment of "He's Got No Love" is possibly tainted to some extent by wounded pride, considering that the song was the group's first original composition to be endorsed as an A-side. At the time, its sound was quite distinct from that of "Goodbye My Love", an unusual instrumental combination making it probably the most strikingly jangly of all their singles:

> On top of Mike's arpeggios [played on a Rickenbacker twelve-string semi-acoustic guitar] John's Telecaster overlaid a six-string figure enhanced by putting it through a tremolo effect and taking the chord down a tone and up again in a constantly repeating and almost hypnotic pattern.[125]

Even so, it was the Searchers' last Top Ten hit and for this Allen may be forgiven for bearing it a long-time grudge. It was followed in October by a Bobby Darin song, "When I Get Home", recorded at drummer Chris Curtis's urging as he began to find his own feet in production but which utterly failed to make the Top 30. Although honour was narrowly retrieved in December by a one-week appearance at No.30 of "Take Me For What I'm Worth", a song by the American singer/songwriter then much in vogue, P. F. Sloan, it was to go down in the group's history as their penultimate chart entry.

It was a mixed year too for other northern survivors, particularly the Manchester contingent. Putting their earlier autumnal wobble with "Show Me Girl" firmly behind them, Herman's Hermits quickly regained the confidence of their home market and recovered their hit-making capacity in the UK with four consecutive Top Ten singles. "Silhouettes" reached No.2 at the end of March (three places above the Searchers' "Goodbye My Love"), to be followed by a revival of Sam Cooke's "Wonderful World", a No.7 in May. Then August's release of "Just A Little Bit Better" went to No.10 at the beginning of October; with the year rounded off by the release in November of another P. F. Sloan composition, "A Must To Avoid", which entered the Top 30 the week before Christmas and by mid-January 1966 had climbed to No.7. This was as nothing, however, compared to their phenomenal popularity in parallel in America. "Given the choice," said Peter Noone:

> I would rather play Sheffield City Hall or the Liverpool Empire as they were wonderful places. However, England is a very small market and it's only people in England who think it is a big deal. In America, everything is five times bigger and so the buildings and the audiences are five times bigger.[126]

Despite all four of Herman's 1965 UK single releases also becoming

Top Ten hits in their own right in America, producer Mickie Most shrewdly adopted an alternative strategy to appeal specifically to US fans, by capitalising on the group's 'Britishness' with recordings of two novelty songs in traditional music-hall style. Even by the standards of the day, both records were excruciatingly corny and simplistic but nevertheless they racked up two No.1 hits on the *Billboard* chart, literally selling in their millions from April and October onwards respectively: "Mrs. Brown, You've Got A Lovely Daughter" (which, though it was old-fashioned in feel, had actually been written for a contemporary television play by English actor Trevor Peacock) and "I'm Henry VIII, I Am" (a genuine oldie from 1911, adopted as his signature tune by music-hall star Harry Champion, but later resurrected by Joe Brown and his Bruvvers).

Wayne Fontana and the Mindbenders were also to enjoy a one-off breakthrough in America with the most successful of their UK singles, "The Game Of Love". At home, in the week ending 27th February, it made No.3 (before being pushed out of that slot the following week by Herman's Hermits' "Silhouettes"); but following its US release in March, it spent ten weeks in the *Billboard* Top 40, including a week at No.1. For them it was to be the zenith of their short-lived career together. After two lesser UK hits in June ("It's Just A Little Bit Too Late") and October ("She Needs Love"), neither of which could get higher than No.30, Fontana contrived his unannounced, melodramatic split from the Mindbenders by walking out on them partway through a concert:

> The three Mindbenders … were nearly as shocked as the audience
> when the group's lead singer and front man, Wayne Fontana,
> bounded off the stage with a curt "Right, that's it, it's all yours, I'm
> going," during an October 1965 live performance. "We had already
> suspected that Wayne wanted to pursue a solo career before he
> left," remembers Eric Stewart. "On the night it happened, we were
> playing a gig in Wembley, London, and Ric Rothwell was having
> a joke at Wayne's expense on stage, eventually causing Wayne to
> walk off the stage! Our reaction was, do we leave the stage too and
> cancel the gig, or do we carry on? So we carried on by ourselves,
> and the audience went wild."[127]

Despite the rift, Jack Baverstock of Fontana Records generously retained both Wayne and the Mindbenders as separate acts in their own right; the former then gaining a premature five-week chart advantage over the latter with his first solo offering in December, "It Was Easier To Hurt Her", sharing the No.30 slot in the week before Christmas with the Searchers' "Take Me For What I'm Worth". In the longer term, however, his was not the act record buyers would most favour.

By contrast, Manchester's other big-name group, the Hollies, found they could make little or no headway in America. Despite two visits to the States, in April and September, combining concerts with TV exposure on the nationally networked music show *Hullabaloo*, they were frustrated by the poor promotional efforts made on their behalf by their American record label Imperial[128]; meaning that no transatlantic hit would be forthcoming for them until 1966.

In the UK, however, it was a different story, where, in common with Herman's Hermits, they released four consecutive hit singles in the course of 1965. The first of these, recorded and released in January, was "Yes I Will", although its journey to its eventual high point of No.10 by late March had been faltering and uncertain, having included a worrying three weeks stalled at No.16 in February, immediately followed by two weeks stuck at No.11. Next came the highlight of their year, in the shape of the more upbeat song "I'm Alive", outselling Elvis's "Crying In The Chapel" to take the No.1 slot for the first two weeks of July. After these two American compositions, they turned to British songwriters for new material, beginning with "Look Through Any Window" (co-written by Graham Gouldman), which spent two weeks at No.4 as September faded into October. Finally, and least successfully, they chose – allegedly at George Martin's suggestion – to record one of George Harrison's songs from *Rubber Soul*, "If I Needed Someone", one of the pointless rash of covers at that time of tracks from the Beatles' latest album. Reportedly failing to find favour with Harrison himself, it struggled to make No.28 for one week only in December before resurfacing again for two weeks in January 1966 but not getting above No.24. As the content of their September-released third LP, unimaginatively titled simply *Hollies*, also demonstrated, it seemed that at this stage of their career they were still precariously over-dependent on other people's compositions.[129]

Although potentially facing the same predicament, the Animals' luck was still holding, even surviving a springtime change of line-up, as Mickie Most unerringly found them another four Top Ten hits in a row. First in at No.4 in February was "Don't Let Me Be Misunderstood", a song already appropriated in a slower version by the black American R&B singer Nina Simone as if her own. Much to their annoyance, Simone let her objections to the Animals' gutsier arrangement be publicly known, before backing down, as John Steel explained, when confronted by them in person:

> We were outraged by that. We were the ones who had a hit record. She didn't write it, so I don't know what she was getting her knickers in a twist about. Eric [Burdon] told her so to her face when we met her in the States and had a right shouting match with her and she eventually said, 'Okay, maybe you aren't so bad for white boys.'[130]

Most then raided Sam Cooke's back catalogue for "Bring It On Home To Me", the last Animals' single to feature Alan Price. In the interval between its release and its reaching No.4 in early May, on 28th April – the day the group were due to embark upon a tour of Scandinavia – Price unexpectedly walked out on them, leaving the others to speculate that his long-awaited receipt of royalties for "House Of The Rising Sun" had prompted his departure. Going public soon afterwards, his own statements to the music press variously cited a growing fear of flying, nervous exhaustion and disenchantment with being an Animal as being behind his move but by the summer he had taken up the reins again with an impromptu Alan Price Combo, playing jazz and blues back where it had all started at the Club A'Gogo in Newcastle. Through connections with arranger Ivor Raymonde, he then undertook session work in London, before forming a new band, the Alan Price Set (which included future BBC radio producer John Walters on trumpet), and signing to Decca, who issued an unsuccessful debut single, "Any Day Now", in late August.

With the Animals drafting in Newcastle musician Mickey Gallagher purely as a temporary stand-in to enable them to tour Scandinavia as planned, Price's permanent replacement was Dave Rowberry, previously a member of the Mike Cotton Sound. Given the irrevocable disruption of the original dynamic, opinion within the group about him was divided. Welcomed and accepted by Steel and Valentine, Burdon was less charitable, damning him with faint praise as a "good keyboard player, but with the air of a jazz snob about him … a solid musician but [he] lacked the fire on stage".[131] Even so, Rowberry survived his initial baptism of fire in tours of America and Japan unscathed.

While Price left his legacy to the group in his contributions to their second LP, *Animal Tracks*, released in May, Rowberry's first participation in an Animals' recording was in the making of their next single, the Barry Mann and Cynthia Weil composition "We've Gotta Get Out Of This Place". Once written, the Brill Building couple had apparently envisaged it as a possible number for the Righteous Brothers, which shows in the sub-Spector production values of Mann's own recorded version bemoaning downtown Brooklyn[132]; but in the hands of Most and the Animals – and with some judicious editing of the lyrics to boot – the song's character was changed forever. Infused with a mesmerising combination of despair and anger in the face of grinding poverty, Eric Burdon's vocals deliver, in Sean Egan's words, "a brilliantly gritty evocation of the working class experience".[133] One of the truly outstanding British records of that summer, it went to No.3 in August, much later to take on an entirely new significance as an all-time favourite of disenchanted US troops in Vietnam through its poignant refrain:

We've gotta get out of this place
If it's the last thing we ever do.

We've gotta get out of this place
'Cos, girl, there's a better life for me and you.[134]

Another American composition (this time by Roger Atkins and Carl D'Errico), "It's My Life", not only gave the Animals their last hit of the year (a No.5 in November) but also their last hit with Mickie Most as producer, followed as it was by the expiry of their contract with him. Whereas Chas Chandler would subsequently dismiss Most as "shallow", Burdon was at least prepared to acknowledge his talent as "a great picker of songs", a sentiment more resoundingly endorsed by John Steel:

> Mickie really had a good commercial ear. He could predict that
> a record would be a hit and he was usually right. We had to give
> him credit for that when he presented us with material, but at the
> same time we wouldn't do *anything* that he said. At the time, when
> you compare what we were playing live, things like 'It's My Life'
> and 'We've Gotta Get Out Of This Place' weren't typical Animals
> songs, but by God they were anthems and they were hits. Mickie
> knew that and recognised that. We went along with it because we
> agreed with him. They were real grown up songs – and they still are
> today.[135]

Leaving Most and the Columbia label behind them, the Animals now signed to Decca, in eager anticipation of a change of musical direction.

As noted earlier in Chapter 6, the Dave Clark Five had seen that for them the greater commercial advantage lay in exploiting the US rather than their home market. Nevertheless, during 1965 Columbia kept up a steady stream of their singles here in the UK. Of these five releases, the first ("Everybody Knows", in January[136]) and last ("Over And Over", in October) both failed to chart; yet despite the latter's almost total lack of lyrical merit, it nevertheless still rewarded them with an American Christmas No.1! After they had taken their cover of Chuck Berry's "Reelin' And Rockin'" to No.22 in April, they opted next for a complete change of pace with the self-composed ballad "Come Home", reaching No.15 in June. However, their most popular UK record of the year was "Catch Us If You Can", a No.4 hit in August and the title song from their feature film (which also inevitably generated a 'soundtrack' LP). The picaresque storyline of the film, a cinema directing debut for John Boorman[137], revolved around the relationship between handsome stuntman Steve (played by Clark) and photogenic actress/model Dinah (played by Barbara Ferris)[138], as they sought to escape from the evil designs of London-based advertising executives by running away together to Burgh Island on the South Devon coast.

Manfred Mann also found themselves drawn to the periphery of film-making when in April they were invited to record the song "My Little Red Book" for inclusion on the soundtrack of the comedy film *What's New Pussycat?*, starring Peter Sellers and Peter O'Toole, with screenplay by Woody Allen and score by Burt Bacharach and Hal David. Being in London at the time, the composers attended the recording session, bringing, as Tom McGuinness recalled, a pronounced tension to the proceedings:

> Burt Bacharach arrived to teach us the song, accompanied by his partner, the film star Angie Dickinson. Hal David was also there but sat quietly in the corner. It took us a while to pick up the chord changes and Angie became increasingly snappy. "Why can't you guys get it right? Burt's really tired. He's been up all night recording with the orchestra. They got it right. Why can't you?" But Burt stayed cool. So cool that he tactfully finessed Manfred off the piano stool by asking him to go into the control room to listen to a take with Burt at the keyboard. "Manfred, maybe you can tell me what's wrong with the piano part." When we all went into the control room to listen to that take, Manfred had to admit that the piano was fine.[139]

Whereas the film's title song provided Tom Jones with a No.10 hit single in September, after all their painstaking efforts Manfred Mann's contribution was released unsuccessfully as a single in America and at home remained buried on the soundtrack LP, only to be plundered by the seminal Californian group Love in 1966 in the form of an irreverently aggressive remake of "My Little Red Book" that warrants its own niche in US pop history.

In other respects, however, 1965 was to be a significant year for Manfred Mann. Initially their single releases followed the pattern established the year before, with two more covers of American records in Paul Jones's personal collection. As a slow song, "Come Tomorrow" (originally by Marie Knight), reaching No.4 in January, was quite distinct from previous hits like "Do Wah Diddy Diddy" or "Sha La La" and could just as well have been credited to Jones as a solo performance; the more unified group sound then being restored by their revival of Maxine Brown's "Oh No, Not My Baby", a No.9 hit in May. But after these came a striking success with a new EP, *The One In The Middle*, not only topping the EP charts for weeks but also beating stiff competition in the singles' charts by climbing in July to No.6, one place above the Stones' *Got Live If You Want It*.

Revisiting the earlier self-parodying inventiveness of songs like "Cock-A-Hoop" and "5-4-3-2-1", Paul Jones had originally thought the title track would appeal to Keith Relf and the Yardbirds; but when they declined it, he rewrote it to spotlight the individual members of Manfred Mann:

> Let me tell you 'bout the Manfreds,
> The music that they're putting down.

They started to play one rainy day
And the people came from miles around.[140]

Tongue firmly in cheek, the 'one in the middle' of the title was, of course, Jones himself, the main attraction, "a geezer called Paul/Who's so thin and so tall/And sure wants to be a star":

They didn't come for the rhythm,
They didn't come for the beat.
The people of the town
Came just to stand around
And see the singer looking sweet.[141]

With the group's habitual ease and sophistication, the remaining three tracks covered a broad spectrum, from the jazz standard "Watermelon Man" through the mainstream pop of "What Am I To Do" (originally a possible follow-up to "Come Tomorrow") to the modern folk of Dylan's "With God On Our Side". It remains as hard today as it did then to think of any of their contemporaries capable of carrying off such a diverse repertoire to such a high standard of musicianship.

Their admiration for Dylan extended to their next single, a populist interpretation of his more obscure – and as then unrecorded – "If You Gotta Go, Go Now", which he had witheld for occasional performances in concert, including one televised by the BBC that June which opportunistically had captured Manfred's imagination:

Dylan did it in a concert. And what staggered me was the whole
of Britain was interested in Bob Dylan; he was a great songwriter
everybody knew. He did this song and *nobody* followed it up! I
think it was Tom [McGuinness] and I who discussed it and we
then contacted the publishers and said 'Can we have a copy?' and
then we did it. And you would have thought with all those people
looking for songs to record, there it is on television and nobody is
paying attention! So we did it. Lovely, lovely song.[142]

The path to obtaining a demo of the song was considerably smoothed by Manfred Mann's manager Ken Pitt, who also conveniently had the role of Dylan's UK publicist. Despite concern in some broadcasting quarters about its underlying innuendo, it raced up the charts to No.2 in the week ending 9th October, only to be blocked from the No.1 spot by Ken Dodd's seemingly interminable "Tears".

Although the sleeves of their second LP *Mann Made* (released in October) and another EP *No Living Without Loving* (released in November) both bore photographs of the original Manfred Mann, by that autumn the line-up was subject both to actual and threatened change. Handing in his notice in September, Mike Vickers left a month later to pursue an alternative career in composing and arranging, an expression on his part of the frustration shared at the time by Mann himself that "we never managed … to somehow get the better of our stuff to be also the successful stuff"[143] – that being, in their opinion, the bulk of the less obviously commercial material hived off by producer John Burgess to EPs and LPs. After temporary stopgaps, Vickers was replaced in December, on Graham Bond's recommendation, by Jack Bruce. Following his stint with John Mayall's Bluesbreakers, Bruce joined the group as bass guitarist, thus freeing up Tom McGuinness to return to playing lead. In an obvious effort to recapture the higher ground of jazz as well as fully cover the loss of Vickers' multi-instrumentalism, the reconfiguration was completed by the recruitment of Lyn Dobson on tenor saxophone and Henry Lowther on trumpet. At the same time Ken Pitt was replaced as manager of the group by Gerry Bron.

As if all this upheaval were not enough, Vickers' departure had also swiftly been followed by an announcement by Paul Jones of his intention to leave, which he was persuaded to postpone – for what turned out to be almost another year – until a permanent replacement could be found. In Jones's case, his concerns arose from a different quarter, no longer being prepared to endure what he saw as a loss of identity: "here I was having all these hit records, and one by one they were being gradually notched up to someone called Manfred Mann, and I was not Manfred Mann!"[144] Almost inevitably, his decision signalled a cooling of relations with Mann, leaving the ever-diplomatic McGuinness "in the role of a child of a broken marriage, ferrying questions and answers between the two of them".[145]

Reverting now to those groups with Birmingham roots, the Rockin' Berries had followed "He's In Town" into the Top 30 in January with another song in which Geoff Turton's falsetto predominated, "What In The World's Come Over You", but it failed to break into the Top Twenty, peaking at No.21. For them, this was a doubly disappointing outcome, since it had been a late substitute for a single they had already recorded, "Funny How Love Can Be", unexpectedly shelved when composers – and fellow Brummies – John Carter and Ken Lewis formed the Ivy League with Perry Ford and Pye (Piccadilly's parent company) opted to release their version instead. While the Ivy League were rewarded with a No.6 hit by the end of February, the Rockin' Berries' sidelined version was lost to posterity as a track on their first LP, *The Rockin' Berries In Town*.

Mercifully, it was a different story with their next single, "Poor Man's Son". In a move even more outrageous than Joe Meek's summoning the Tornados to London on a round trip from Great Yarmouth to record "Telstar" (as described in Chapter 4), A&R man John Schroeder was suitably

inspired by the Reflections' original US version of the song to call the Rockin'
Berries all the way back down from Newcastle, their latest destination on
a concert tour with Roy Orbison, to Pye's London studios. Having driven
south overnight to reach Marble Arch for an early morning session, they then
spent three hours making the record before setting off smartly back up to the
north-east to rejoin the tour for that night's gig. Their efforts were rewarded
in due course when it spent nine weeks in the Top 30, with a highest position
of No.6 at the end of May, but subsequent events dictated it was an experience not to be repeated.

Booked to play a summer season themselves in Great Yarmouth with
famously middle-of-the-road Irish close-harmony trio the Bachelors – whose
stagecraft they openly professed to admire – the Rockin' Berries, in Roger
Dopson's words:

> were already beginning to show strong signs of the schizophrenia
> which would ultimately erode their teenage fanbase. Urged by
> management and agents alike, they'd already started taking a wrong
> turn: building on both Clive Lea's "whacky" impersonations and the
> group's natural flair for comedy, they were gradually evolving into
> slick, 'all-round family entertainers'.[146]

Faced with "a lead singer who wanted to be a stand-up comic"[147], a change
of direction of this magnitude made it even harder than before for Schroeder
and Piccadilly to promote them as a pop group to be taken seriously for their
musical ability, which nevertheless still remained in evidence for those few
loyal fans like myself who took the trouble to search it out. Although it may
have impacted adversely on the sales of their August single, "You're My Girl"
(which enjoyed only one week in September at No.28), the virtually simultaneous release of an original EP, *New From The Berries*, captured the group
arguably at the height of their game, both instrumentally and vocally – as
evidenced by the finely balanced strength and subtlety of the stand-out track
"From One Who Knows".

Then in November came the single that sent them into oblivion, "The
Water Is Over My Head", non-charting yet strong enough to be commended
to the discerning by Kingsley Abbott as one of his *500 Lost Gems of The
Sixties*[148]; and with a blistering rockabilly instrumental break that positively
races against the clock on the teasingly short B-side, "Doesn't Time Fly", it
simply reeked of wasted talent. Their second LP, *Life Is Just A Bowl Of Berries*,
effectively forestalled any further hope of chart success when it was released
in December, with its poor-quality mix of second-rate covers and painfully
outdated 'comedy' songs including "When I'm Cleaning Windows" and
"The Laughing Policeman"! Retreating to variety and cabaret performances
for their bread and butter, none of the group's later singles were successful

and Geoff Turton left to go solo in 1968, only to rejoin them in obscurity in the Seventies.

As for the Moody Blues, as noted in the last chapter, their Christmas hit "Go Now" kept on climbing in the New Year. Spending a total of eleven weeks in the Top 30, it captured the No.1 slot for the last two weeks of January, before going on to deliver a debut No.10 hit in America. However, its very success then proved an uncomfortably hard act to follow, leading eventually to the group's complete collapse. Two lesser singles, both woefully lacking the punch of their predecessor, reached the Top 20 in late spring and early summer: the slow ballad "I Don't Want To Go On Without You"[149], making hesitant progress through March into April to No.17, and "From The Bottom Of My Heart", peaking at No.15 in June, to be followed in July by the only LP recorded by this original line-up, *The Magnificent Moodies*. Subsequent singles failed to make any impression on the charts, a situation that could not even be salvaged by the exposure the Moody Blues gained latterly either in September supporting the Rolling Stones on tour or as the top support act on the Beatles' final UK tour in December, and by the summer of 1966 they were on the skids. Clint Warwick left that June, then Denny Laine in August; and when Warwick's replacement on bass, Rod Clark, left in his turn in October, the group folded. Its resurrection a month later, with new members John Lodge and Justin Hayward, was the precursor to the Moody Blues' exploration of a radically different musical genre, a story to be resumed in due course in Chapter 9.

Destined ultimately to be more popular than the original Moodies were their local arch-rivals, the Spencer Davis Group, whose persistence finally paid off in the week ending 11th December with the chart entry of their fifth single release, "Keep On Running", at No.20. Hailing from Swansea, Davis himself had moved to the Midlands in 1960 as an undergraduate student of German at Birmingham University, after which he stayed on to become a modern foreign languages teacher. His personal musical interests in folk and jazz led him into performing with his guitar in pubs in and around Birmingham city centre, accompanied first by fellow student and drummer Pete York and then joining forces in 1963 with the Winwood brothers from Great Barr, previously playing together as the core of their own Muff-Woody Jazz Band. In an amalgamation now called the Rhythm and Blues Quartet, Davis and York thus teamed up with Mervyn (*aka* Muff) Winwood on bass guitar and his younger brother Steve, who, despite only turning fifteen that May, could not only play guitar, piano and Hammond organ but was also possessed of an extraordinarily mature and soulful singing voice, ideally suited to rhythm and blues and far and away the group's strongest asset.

Visiting Birmingham in early 1964 with his protégé Millie Small, Chris Blackwell, owner of the then little-known Island Records, saw the Quartet's

act and offered to become their manager, to which they informally agreed.
Muff:

> We never signed a piece of paper but developed a working
> relationship with him. After he took us under his wing, we decided
> to change our name. It was my brilliant idea to call it The Spencer
> Davis Group. Every group was THE Beatles, THE Rolling Stones,
> THE Mindbenders. Blackwell had a list of names, like The Crawling
> Snakes. And I said, well, Spencer Davis – that's an amazingly
> original name. And Spencer was the only one who enjoyed
> interviews. He'd volunteer; we hated them! I said, if we choose
> 'The Spencer Davis Group', we can stay in bed and he can do the
> interviews![150]

Under Blackwell's direction, after turning down a recording offer from
Decca's Mike Vernon, the newly renamed group signed a contract with the
Philips subsidiary Fontana; a label, it has to be said, that showed compelling
faith in them in the face of their protracted failure to achieve a hit.

Trading on Steve Winwood's distinctive vocal style, their first single,
released in April 1964, was a cover of John Lee Hooker's song "Dimples";
badly timed, in the event, because it soon came into competition with Hooker's own recording (which captured the bulk of the available sales, reaching
No.21 at the end of June). This was followed by three consecutive singles
that attracted greater airplay, collectively enhanced their growing reputation
as musicians' musicians yet were still cursed by insufficient sales to make
the Top 30: "I Can't Stand It" (November 1964), "Every Little Bit Hurts"
(February 1965) and "Strong Love" (June 1965). By now, most other record
companies would have cut their losses, so Fontana's unaccustomed tenacity
with the Spencer Davis Group is to be admired, especially since it extended
in July 1965 to the release of the non-hitmakers' first LP (self-evidently entitled *Their First LP*), even if six of its tracks did just happen to be made up of
the recycled A- and B-sides of their first three singles.

Waiting for that elusive hit finally paid off in the autumn, when the
group was introduced by Blackwell to Jamaican musician Jackie Edwards.
Muff again:

> Jackie had written this song, 'Keep On Running'. There was a piano
> in the corner [of Blackwell's office] so he sat down and played it,
> quite differently to the way we recorded it. It had more of a Ska
> sound. We quickly wrote down the chords so we wouldn't forget it,
> and Steve picked up how Jackie played it on the piano. We had our
> acoustic guitars with us so we learnt the song on the spot and then
> went away to work it out for ourselves. We liked the song, made all
> the arrangements and cut it. In those days, you needed a riff to get

a hit so we came up with an interesting riff and, sure enough, the single became a massive hit.[151]

On this occasion, the thumping bass line of that 'interesting riff' was famously enhanced by Muff Winwood's use of his newest toy, a fuzzbox; and very soon after its chart breakthrough at the end of the year, "Keep On Running" would deliver the first new No.1 single of 1966.

Apart from the Spencer Davis Group, other new disparate strands of jazz, blues and soul threaded their way through the charts of 1965; starting with Georgie Fame and the Blue Flames, whose uneven run of hits on the Columbia label finally began, after three false starts, with a nod to the mainstream with their January No.1 record "Yeh Yeh". Already firmly established as the darlings of the London R&B scene in residence at Soho's Flamingo Club (an act immortalised on the now highly regarded 1964 live LP *Rhythm And Blues At The Flamingo*, which sold only modestly on its release), Fame led from the front on Hammond organ, doubling as vocalist.[152] Sadly, successive follow-up singles struggled by comparison. "In The Meantime" could only make No.16 in March, the downward trend continuing with "Like We Used To Be", peaking at No.22 in August, and "Something", which could get no higher than No.26 in November. Indeed, it would not be until the height of the following summer that Fame would regain the spotlight in style with another memorable Top 10 hit.

Out on the wilder side of the blues was a five-piece group from Belfast, Them, whose reputation today rests on the considerable impact of their only two hit singles and of the formidable character of their lead singer, Van Morrison. Named after a classic American sci-fi film of the Fifties about mutant giant ants, Them represented the joining of forces in April 1964 between Morrison, already a well-seasoned and well-travelled showband singer, and local group the Gamblers, their initial following in Northern Ireland's capital city being built on the foundations of their residency as an R&B band at the Maritime Hotel.[153] Soon signed up by Decca's Dick Rowe and having moved to England in consequence, their first professional recording session in July 1964 included Morrison's own composition "Gloria", in over-excitable praise of the girl who would freely dispense her sexual favours "just around midnight"[154], and the song released that September as their unsuccessful debut single, "Don't Start Crying Now". It was, however, from a later studio session in October, also involving Jimmy Page as sit-in rhythm guitarist, that their first hit, "Baby Please Don't Go", emerged, to which the raunchy "Gloria" was coupled as the B-side for its November release. A dazzling electric reinterpretation of a blues standard that they had discovered as a John Lee Hooker LP track, resounding with echo, reverb and Morrison's harmonica, "Baby Please Don't Go" entered the charts at No.23 in the week ending 9th January 1965 and by the end of the month had risen to its high point of No.10, helped on its way by its temporary adoption as a theme tune by *Ready Steady Go!*.

Visiting American producer and songwriter Bert Berns was then responsible for overseeing Them's subsequent recording of one of his own compositions, "Here Comes The Night", which in mid-April reached No.3 (below Cliff Richard at No.2 with "The Minute You're Gone" and the Beatles at No.1 with "Ticket To Ride"). Where Lulu had failed with the song in its original ballad form as her third single release the previous November, bemusingly an earlier Bert Berns production on the same record label but under-promoted by Decca, Van Morrison utterly stole her thunder with his very particular take on it. Upping the beat almost to a skip in places and sounding like the Ulster equivalent of Eric Burdon, with his throaty Irish-to-American inflections he teasingly injected light and dark into the lyrics that had been transposed to a male perspective. (In her autobiography, although Lulu admits her annoyance at Berns' decision to re-record the song, she nevertheless concedes she felt Morrison's version was the better of the two.[155])

But in spite of having thus consolidated their grip on the UK charts with two impressive hit records, neither any of the individual members of Them nor their manager Phil Solomon now appeared to venture any coherent strategy to take the group forward into the future. They almost literally drove themselves into the ground with incessant, ill-planned touring: "Edinburgh one night, Barnstaple the next, back in Scotland the next – sometimes twice a night".[156] And life on the interminable road more often than not led to violent arguments, notably (though by no means exclusively) between Van Morrison and lead guitarist Billy Harrison. Morrison could, if he chose, also take withdrawal to the extreme: on one occasion, he "never said one word for three days … and we were with him 24 hours a day!"[157] Unsurprisingly, this constant friction prompted frequent changes of personnel, eventually culminating in July 1966 in Morrison's own departure at the end of an eight-week US tour. After "Here Comes The Night", Decca released another five singles – as well as two LPs, *Them* and *Them Again* – by the various manifestations of Them while Morrison was still on board but none of them could recapture the interest of the British record-buyer, not even the semi-impromptu lost gem "Mystic Eyes" (resurrected from the first album and issued as single number six). In the end, Them's true legacy to Sixties' R&B lay after all in their roots as house band and crowd-pleasers at the Maritime Hotel where, as yet undiscovered, they had revelled in the freedom of simply being, in Morrison's own words, "Wild, sweaty, crude, ugly and mad/And sometimes just a little bit sad".[158]

Although viewed in its entirety Decca's promotion of Them was indifferent, as a record company it had finally hit its stride after the embarrassment of rejecting the Beatles and by the mid-Sixties, second only in Britain to the EMI family of labels (i.e., Parlophone, Columbia and HMV), was responsible for a broad church of groups. By 1965, the Rolling Stones had undeniably become the jewel in Decca's crown but, as already noted elsewhere, their acts also included the Nashville Teens, the Moody Blues, John Mayall's Blues-breakers and, by proxy through their distribution of Brunswick Records, the Who, to which cluster by the end of the year they had added the Alan Price Set and the Animals. In other realms of pop, in what was effectively the aftermath of Merseybeat, they now struck if not quite gold then highly promising paydirt with a new influx of artists such as: Unit 4+2, who had a No.2 hit in April with "Concrete And Clay"; one-hit wonders Hedgehoppers Anonymous, the band of ex-RAF servicemen who took "It's Good News Week" to No.4 in October; and the Fortunes, who followed a debut No.2 hit in July, "You've Got Your Troubles", with "Here It Comes Again", a No.4 hit in November.

Most promising and dynamic of Decca's newer acquisitions, however, was a group of four Mods with attitude from London's East End, the Small Faces. A band formed, in Paolo Hewitt's words, "amidst smiles and mayhem"[159], its four original members were: Steve Marriott (vocals & lead guitar), Ronnie 'Plonk' Lane (bass guitar), Kenney Jones (drums) and Jimmy Winston (keyboards). Uniting in the spring of 1965, they started out "with little more in mind than fun and the avoidance of the factory line to which so many of their class were doomed":

> Prior to their formation, three of the band had played skiffle
> music, two had already appeared on records. They had all been in
> unsuccessful groups and, when they finally came together, they had
> lost the initial illusion of instant pop stardom that was the preserve
> of hungry young musicians. All they wanted was a giggle and a
> smile and that, their leader Steve Marriott once explained, was the
> reason they were so successful.[160]

Calling themselves the Small Faces at the enthusiastic suggestion of a girl-friend of Marriott's, combining an apt descriptor of their collective physique with a pride in their status as prominent Mods (or 'faces'), they played their first public gig on 6th May at the Kensington Youth Centre in East Ham. Soon afterwards, still raw and inexperienced, they talked the manager of the Cavern Club, Leicester Square into booking them for four consecutive Saturday nights and it was here that they impressed Pat Meehan and Ron King, two key staff members of Contemporary Music, a management and production company run by the notorious Don Arden.

On his subordinates' recommendation, Arden went to see them for himself, on this occasion finding them still hammering away at their limited set of R&B and soul numbers despite Marriott and Lane literally bearing the scars from a beating delivered by a gang of Tottenham toughs the night before. Liking what he saw and heard, without further delay Arden made his move, cannily structuring a management deal (reckoned by Kenney Jones to amount to "twenty pounds a week [each], plus a percentage of the records and a shopping account in every clothes shop in Carnaby Street"[161]) to which the Small Faces formally agreed on 10th June. Rapidly followed by their first recording session in July at IBC Studios, supervised by the ubiquitous Glyn Johns in the control booth, and Arden's brokering of a licensing and distribution agreement with Decca, their first single, "Whatcha Gonna Do About It", was released on 6th August. With a prominent riff on organ from Jimmy Winston and a sit-up-and-take-notice dose of feedback in Steve Marriott's guitar solo that made it sound more like a vacuum cleaner than a musical instrument, it duly clocked up an encouraging nine weeks in the Top 30, all the way through September and October, with a highest position of No.15.[162] Its progress up and down the charts that autumn tracked the transition at No.1 from the Rolling Stones' "Satisfaction" to Ken Dodd's "Tears" and made the Small Faces first-time chart contemporaries of EMI mainstays the Hollies (with "Look Through Any Window"), Herman's Hermits (with "Just A Little Bit Better"), Manfred Mann (with "If You Gotta Go, Go Now") and the Yardbirds (with "Evil Hearted You"/"Still I'm Sad").

Unfortunately for Winston, the group's exposure on television in the pursuit of their debut hit only served to exacerbate personal differences between him and Marriott, who increasingly resented the organist's intrusion into a multiplicity of camera shots. Furthermore, Winston had fatally incurred Arden's distrust by virtue of the intermediary role he played as collector of the group's dues after every gig, which involved him in passing on 10% of the takings to his brother as a wage for being their road manager. Matters came to a head at a booking in Stockport on 31st October. Deliberately ignoring him throughout the gig, that evening his fellow band members ditched him in a conspiratorial telephone call to Arden, so that on their return to London the next day Winston was summoned to Arden's office and sacked; and that same afternoon, again by prior agreement, he was replaced, on an initial month's trial, by Ian McLagan, former keyboard player with lesser known Boz's People.[163]

Knowing only of his reputation through the music press, on first meeting him in person Marriott, Lane and Jones were taken aback to find that McLagan perfectly complemented them both in temperament and physical stature. Arden's invitation to come and see him had given the new recruit no prior indication of the group he might be joining. Now, unnervingly, from McLagan's own viewpoint, "it was like looking at a mirror of myself ... We all looked alike"[164], while Marriott said: "I couldn't believe that there was a guy standing in front of us who was already one of us … and all I could do was hug him because it was just like he'd been missing."[165] And as soon as he was on board, drummer Jones, for one, was quick to acknowledge the reshaping influence of his unassuming musical expertise: "I didn't realise until that point what I'd been missing out on until we got a proper keyboard player in. Suddenly, this big hole filled up sound wise. I started playing a little differently, much better, and it was great. We all loved Mac."[166]

Yet Winston's legacy initially bedevilled McLagan's integration into his new role. The original line-up had already recorded the follow-up to "Whatcha Gonna Do About It", a Marriott/Lane song called "I've Got Mine" that they had showcased in a supposedly forthcoming comedy thriller film, *Dateline Diamonds*.[167] Slated for release by Decca on 5th November, it atypically featured Winston on guitar, meaning that for promotional purposes his part now had to be mimed – albeit unconvincingly – on guitar by McLagan. The only saving grace was that despite enthusiastic reviews the record bombed, in part-compensation for which Arden rented a four-storey house in Pimlico for the group to live in, all expenses paid plus the services of housekeeper and chauffeur. Thus Marriott, Lane and McLagan moved into 22, Westmoreland Terrace on Boxing Day, while Jones opted for the quieter life by remaining in the parental home. By then, their third single was in the can, promising them their biggest hit yet in the New Year with a song none of them actually liked.

With groups obviously to the fore, by 1965 Decca could justifiably boast of an impressive constellation of artists across the pop spectrum. Commanding the middle ground of easy listening for an older generation with the Irish talents of the Bachelors and Val Doonican, as well as retaining Billy Fury the label was now also home to new Welsh male soloist Tom Jones. Groomed in the style of his eighteenth-century literary namesake with a beribboned ponytail and with a failed debut single already behind him, he shot into the limelight in March with a No.1 hit, "It's Not Unusual", a beat ballad composed by his manager Gordon Mills in collaboration with Les Reed, arranged for maximum impact with stinging brass. As this slid down the charts, it was promptly succeeded in May by "Once Upon A Time", although its meagre three-week tenure of the Top 30 could achieve no higher than No.21; and then by a No.10 hit in August, "With These Hands", before Jones clawed his way back into the Top Ten again in September, as noted above, with "What's New Pussycat?".

Dave Berry, meanwhile, after failing the previous autumn to follow his earlier success of "The Crying Game" with the sound-alike "One Heart Between Two", struck lucky again with the release in March of "Little Things". Readily identifiable by its catchy opening riff on twelve-string guitar (courtesy of Jimmy Page), this cover of an American original by Bobby

Goldsboro took Berry to No.8 in the week ending 1ˢᵗ May; and for many, the record's all-round entertainment value was further enhanced by the concurrence of the B-side, "I've Got A Tiger By The Tail", with the Esso advertising slogan of the day, "I've Got A Tiger In My Tank" (reinforced by its garages giving out free furry tigers' tails for drivers to attach to their petrol filler caps).[168] Whilst Decca may have seen a Top 10 hit as vindication of their marketing of Berry, it has to be said that both sides are essentially frivolous, if not on the borders of being downright twee, and the production values old hat: on "Little Things", for example, Berry is all but singing a duet with the uncredited lead vocalist of his girl backing group. In line with this emasculation of his talent that threatened to strand him in the middle of the road, it became ever clearer that his British audience was increasingly fickle and unforgiving, not knowing what to expect from him, and consequently did not take to his next single, "This Strange Effect", even though this minor-key Ray Davies composition was tailor-made for his idiosyncratic stage moves and Dutch fans were so enthused by it that it went all the way to No.1 in the Netherlands.

Other Decca notables of 1965 included the now discredited Jonathan King, then a first-year Cambridge undergraduate, whose self-composed nonsense poem "Everyone's Gone To The Moon" was one of that summer's unavoidably hummable theme tunes, reaching No.3 in August[169]; Chris Andrews, Sandie Shaw's right-hand man and songwriter, who had two simultaneous hits in mid-December, "Yesterday Man" going down (from No.5) meeting "To Whom It Concerns" on its way up (to No.12); and the beautifully groomed Paul and Barry Ryan, twin sons of Fifties' minor league singing star Marion Ryan, whose "Don't Bring Me Your Heartaches" was a pre-Christmas No.14.

As a company, Decca was, however, disinclined to invest in the more exclusive field of female vocalists. Beryl Marsden, a highly regarded near-contemporary of Cilla Black's in Liverpool, was a case in point. Signed up when still only fifteen, after two failed single releases in August 1963 and January 1964, which she attributed jointly to indifference as to choice of material on the part of A&R and poor promotion on Decca's part, her contract was allowed to lapse (leading eventually, after a new contract in 1965 with EMI's Columbia label, to a solitary solo hit for two weeks with "Who You Gonna Hurt" in November – in at No.29, out at No.30).[170] But even with its more established artists, Decca was barely able to hold its own against the competition. After the motorcycle melodrama of "Terry" had fully run its course, Twinkle returned fleetingly to the lower charts in February with "Golden Lights" before being totally eclipsed, thus leaving the label with only her forerunners, Lulu and Marianne Faithfull, as its flag carriers in this genre. Their experiences, however, would be markedly contrasting.

After the debacle of "Here Comes The Night", in recording terms at least Lulu found herself in limbo, at a loss without the right material. An attempt in April to marry her up with a Jagger/Richards composition, "Surprise, Surprise", could have been a new way forward but ended in failure when it was issued as the B-side to "Satisfied", yet another addition to her growing catalogue of misses. Twelve months after her breakthrough with "Shout", it was with a ballad rather than a rock number that she eventually regained a foothold in the Top Ten, "Leave A Little Love" going to No.9 in July, but its successor in broadly similar vein, "Try To Understand", could only secure one week at No.26 in September. Not even the issue that same month of her LP *Something To Shout About* could compensate for the fact that although she consistently remained in demand as a touring artist, her association with Decca would bring her no more chart entries. So it was that in late 1966, after formally announcing her split from the Luvvers, she switched to EMI's Columbia label, in anticipation of the future rescue of her recording career by Mickie Most.

For Marianne Faithfull, though she was thankful to be free of Andrew Loog Oldham's manipulation, Tony Calder's new management regime was decidedly a mixed blessing, for "in the end Tony had no more idea of what I should be doing than Andrew did. He just gave me more attention!"[171] From a recording perspective, her year began well, with "Come And Stay With Me" becoming her biggest hit when it made No.4 at the end of March. And it was followed by her version of John D. Loudermilk's "This Little Bird", which by the end of May she had taken to No.5, laying waste in the process the senseless in-house competition from Decca stablemates the Nashville Teens.

It was at this point, however, that she had a major disagreement with Calder, when he turned down a flattering approach from the Royal Court Theatre for Marianne to appear in a production of John Osborne's latest play, *Inadmissible Evidence*. Thwarted by his veto on what she had fondly hoped might represent "a way out of my pop nightmare"[172], she left him for a new, third manager, Gerry Bron, another decision that ultimately she came to regret. In the late summer that had brought us both "Help!" and "Satisfaction", she scored her third hit in a row with the stunningly over-produced "Summer Nights", her breathless, fragile voice nearly drowned out by an overwhelming accumulation of woodwind, percussion and harpsichord, a record deserving better than its final August placing of No.12. Then after three consecutive successes, it came as something of a surprise that her last single of 1965, her cover of "Yesterday", should make no showing whatsoever in the Top 30 on its release in October, gallingly trounced by an alternative version from Matt Monro which reached No.6; although by this juncture, as events in her personal life took precedence over everything else, she is unlikely to have cared.

Touring remained an agony to her. In spring, she was on the road with "the typical collection of pop oddities currently in the charts: Gerry and the Pacemakers, the Kinks, Gene Pitney ..."[173] Whilst seeking refuge in a torrid fling with Pitney (whom she nevertheless came to regard as "a complete arsehole"[174]), she found to her alarm that the Kinks too had their own demons. She thought they were "very gothic – creepy and silent ... uptight and fearful of everyone. Terrified. Underneath which there was all this dysfunctional family stuff going on – they hated each other".[175]

After this madness came what was to be her last tour in this phase of her life, this time with Roy Orbison who, with much greater dignity and detachment than Gene Pitney, made his own sexual assumptions, appearing at the door of her hotel room, seeming to her to be "curiously removed, as if he'd left himself at home and sent a cardboard cut-out on the road":

> There were no preliminaries, this wasn't just Roy trying to pull me. He was a real southern gentleman, it was just good old road tour tradition. He was top dog and any women on the tour were his by *droit de seigneur*. It still goes on, but in those days it was expected. I liked Roy but I was afraid. I don't think people realised how scared I was, they all terrified me.[176]

Still several months off her nineteenth birthday as the Orbison tour drew to a close, she was happy to clutch at the escape offered by boyfriend John Dunbar when he proposed to her, additionally discovering that April that she was pregnant by him.[177] Yet there remained one more bruising encounter with pop nobility to overcome before she reached the temporary sanctuary of marrying Dunbar in May, and that was as a hanger-on at the court of Bob Dylan, when he arrived in England for a short concert tour and took up temporary residence at the Savoy Hotel (*see below*). The fatal flaw in this unexpected connection was that because she was intellectually besotted with Dylan as her musical hero, she failed to appreciate that sooner or later there would be a price to pay for being admitted into his circle of intimates.

Slowly, it dawned on her that she was "the chosen one, the sacrificial virgin".[178] However, when Dylan did finally make his move and she rebuffed him, citing her pregnancy and her imminent marriage in her defence, it provoked his rage – exhibited, as she described it, in "a little tantrum of genius"[179] – and he threw her out of his hotel suite forthwith. A week later, she was married and in November, still only eighteen, she gave birth to a son, Nicholas. The following year, her life would undergo yet another juddering change of direction as she joined the "dissolute 'Night Watch' of mid-sixties swinging London"[180], forsaking her now scorned husband in exchange for immersing herself in the decadent exclusivity of the Rolling Stones' coterie.

For all the haphazardness of her career, Marianne Faithfull could still, had she been so minded, take pride in the fact that her record sales on the home market throughout 1965 had made her the second most popular British female singer of the year. Based on a weighted analysis of the movement week by week of entries to the singles charts (counting 30 points for a No.1, down to 1 point for a No.30) and with a total of 22 weeks in the Top 30, she was runner-up only to Sandie Shaw and significantly outperformed all other serious rivals, including Dusty Springfield and Cilla Black. Such statistical considerations ultimately counted for nothing, of course, in the public's perception as measured by the results of the *NME*'s annual poll of its readers, who not only resolutely voted Dusty top UK female singer for the second year running but also this time round proclaimed her top international female singer, thus dethroning Brenda Lee after three generous years of affording her that accolade.

It was a rare compliment that the *NME* readership should pay Dusty after what had been for her, all things considered, a lean year, given her comparatively indifferent showing in the charts and her frequent absences from England. The February release of her follow-up to "Losing You", "Your Hurtin' Kinda Love", had been little short of disastrous, despite its initial prime-time promotion on *Sunday Night At The London Palladium*. Deeming it herself to be "a bad record"[181], it sold poorly, only achieving one week in the Top 30 at No.26 and badly denting her self-confidence in the process. Her response was, literally, to take flight with Martha Reeves to carnival time in Rio, where they partied hard but she sustained a serious cut to her foot from broken glass and was then obliged to cancel planned engagements on her return home; although by the end of March she had recovered sufficiently to go on tour with the Searchers and the Zombies.

Even though her next release in June, "In The Middle Of Nowhere", would restore her to her rightful place in the Top Ten (eventually reaching No.5), this again was a record in which Dusty personally took little pleasure, despite having bolstered herself in its making with backing vocals from Madeline Bell and Doris Troy, together with additional support from Alan Price on piano. As noted by Sharon Davis: "The song was loud and noisy, and once more the singer grew to loathe it, claiming it made no contribution whatsoever to her career."[182] Mercifully, her fans felt differently about it but in July, just as her latest single was realising its deserved hit potential, she succumbed to a combination of strained vocal chords and exhaustion and was ordered by her doctor to take immediate rest. So, cancelling her scheduled summer season in Bournemouth, she flew out to the sanctuary of the Virgin Islands before moving on to America, ending her extended recuperation in her favourite New York; where, on an earlier visit, Gerry Goffin and Carole King had presented her with a demo of a new composition, 'Some Of Your Lovin''.

Here, at last, was the unexpected gift of a song about which Dusty could be genuinely enthusiastic: she described it as "the most comfortable of songs to sing and it was the only record I've ever made that I brought home and played 14 times in a row … I was so ecstatically proud of it and it was, in hindsight, it truly was, light years ahead of its time as a recording."[183] Although originally intended as no more than a track for her forthcoming second LP, *Ev'rything's Coming Up Dusty*, at her insistence Philips released it as a single in September; yet seemingly it lacked the more popular appeal of "In The Middle Of Nowhere", for it fell just short of the Top Ten at No.11. Thus denied the scale of recognition she felt it deserved, Dusty had to console herself with appearing before the Queen at the Royal Variety Performance in November as a more fitting celebration of her talents – from which dizzy heights, improbably she descended to the Northern club circuit to see out December.

By comparison, front-runner Sandie Shaw (almost twelve years Dusty's junior) failed, for now at least, to capture the hearts of the public in quite the same way. Nevertheless, she continued to enjoy success with a string of hits and a best-selling debut LP to boot, thanks largely to the strength of her mutually supportive relationship with songwriter Chris Andrews, with whom she engaged in what she described as a "gawky creative process":

> We drew on our shared urban angst, purging our pain in song, laughing so much we usually spilt the tea over our notes and had to write the whole thing over again.
>
> I was very sure of my likes and dislikes and I directed him … I was ruthless and totally primitive in my taste.[184]

Taking their inspiration from the raw material of "Chris's unhappy first marriage, my fumbling attempts at romance, our successes and tragedies", as Sandie neatly expressed it: "We relived our lives in verse, chorus, verse, chorus, middle eight and out."[185] And the results were impressive, starting off with "I'll Stop At Nothing", a No.5 hit in March. Then came her second No.1, "Long Live Love", a celebratory anthem that heralded the onset of summer by topping the charts for two weeks from May into June, unseating in the process the only other female soloist to have a No.1 in 1965, Jackie Trent with "Where Are You Now". Next up was "Message Understood", sharing its entry to the Top 30 with Dusty's "Some Of Your Lovin'" in the week ending 25th September, albeit at No.30 compared to her rival's No.24: ultimately, however, it would be the bigger hit of the two, climbing to No.6. Finally, there was "How Can You Tell", bringing up the rear with a more modest No.20 by the beginning of December.

With "Downtown" already at No.2 in the last chart of 1964, Petula Clark had begun 1965 with a distinct advantage over her rivals, despite the facts that by this time she was a long-established French resident and that England featured less and less frequently on her international itinerary. Continuing at No.2 into the New Year, it managed to retain a place in the Top 30 until the week ending 6th February, finally bowing out after a thirteen-week chart run. Its successor, "I Know A Place", was, on composer Tony Hatch's own admission, unashamedly a variation on the theme of "Downtown", its further exploration of the healing power of the after-dark club scene for the lost and lonely even referencing "a cellarful of noise"[186] in homage to the title of Brian Epstein's autobiography. With only four weeks of chart placement this time round, its highest position was a worthy though nonetheless disappointing No.16 in March. (Its release in America, however, had quite the opposite effect, consolidating the earlier success there of "Downtown" as a million-selling No.1 with a follow-up No.3 hit and paving the way for Petula to be signed to appear for a short season at New York's legendary Copacabana in November, where every night she was fêted with flowers and a standing ovation.) Two misses then followed, both strong songs in their own right but sadly misjudged in their possible impact on a rapidly expanding and fluctuating UK singles market: "You'd Better Come Home" in August, and "Round Every Corner" in October – the lyric of the latter grandiosely equating the quest for love with the boldness of the space race, asserting as it did that "Man will soon be standing on the moon above".[187] Petula would only briefly recover her chart form in November – by which time, of course, she had conflicting live commitments in New York – with "You're The One", a song she jointly composed with Hatch that rose no higher than its entry slot of No.22.

And what, then, of Cilla Black? Solely in recording terms, 1965 was an even leaner year for her than it was for Dusty Springfield, with only ten weeks in the Top 30 accrued from two single releases, as Brian Epstein persisted in shifting the balance in her professional life still further towards performing live. On 8th January, Parlophone simultaneously released her first, eponymous LP (which would ultimately rise to a more than respectable No.5 in the album charts) and her latest single, "You've Lost That Lovin' Feelin'", which was immediately in contention with the overpowering American version on the London label, as recorded by the Righteous Brothers (*aka* Bill Medley and Bobby Hatfield) and produced by Phil Spector. Both records entered the Top 30 in the week ending 16th January. Initially well ahead, at No.16, of the previously unknown Americans at No.24, Cilla could only retain her lead for another week before they overtook her, leaving her behind at No.5 while they moved through to score the year's first UK No.1 by US artists.

Her second single, released on 15th April, was one about which she harboured personal doubts as to its commerciality, instincts that would subsequently be proved well-founded although she had allowed others, Epstein included, to persuade her of the merits of this Randy Newman composition. In George Martin's hands, "I've Been Wrong Before", with its rising and falling piano glissando accompaniment, was distinctively different from any of Cilla's other singles to date but it lacked the drive to propel it any higher up the charts than No.22 and she would have to wait another eight months before she was able to improve upon that placing. Her time otherwise was largely taken up with touring, both at home and abroad. In March, for example, she travelled to New Zealand then Australia, with Freddie and the Dreamers as principal support act, followed in April by promotional visits to New York and Hollywood for TV appearances on *The Ed Sullivan Show* and *Shindig!* respectively. The former left an indelible impression upon her, when the preceding act, a troupe of unruly performing chimpanzees, rapidly descended into chaos. Sullivan, himself covered in confusion, demanded an unforeseen cut straight to Cilla, but was so disconcerted that he botched her introduction:

> As I came on for my big moment on American TV, the
> chimpanzees were still at it. Ed Sullivan was very embarrassed,
> but, dimly recalling that I had said that my grandfather was Welsh,
> introduced me by saying: 'And now we have a great Welsh singer,
> from Wales in England – Cilla Black!'[188]

To add insult to injury, she then had to be rescued from the amorous attentions of a chimp, which had grabbed her leg, whilst endeavouring not to be overcome by the absurdity of her situation and still trying to make a professional fist of singing "Dancing In The Street". A return visit to New York in July was, mercifully, far less fraught, as she fulfilled a three-week engagement in cabaret at the Plaza Hotel's Persian Room. By absolute contrast, her year ended back in London in pantomime, as the lead in *Little Red Riding Hood*.

Following the shock of the 'British Invasion' of 1964, Cilla's experience of losing out to the Righteous Brothers with "You've Lost That Lovin' Feelin'" was an early indicator that in 1965 American artists would be opening up a retaliatory second front in the UK. So it was that throughout the year a whole host of newcomers were steadily added to an already impressive list of familiar names in the British charts, their collective impact being responsible for a cultural shift every bit as significant as Mersey Beat had represented before it; and in this, of course, lay the irony that many of the new wave of US performers openly acknowledged how their recent exposure to British influences had changed their perceptions of pop music.

With such a sustained influx of these American acts, inevitably the quality of their resultant hit singles was every bit as variable as that originating from Britain's own home market. However, unlike the pre-Beatles era of the late Fifties and early Sixties, when the predominant high-school angst of American teens had imposed an increasingly dull uniformity on original performers and pale British imitators alike, this time round variety was decidedly the keynote, yet still leaving room for some of the older stars to enjoy a temporary renaissance. For example, joining the Righteous Brothers as US interlopers at No.1 were the Everly Brothers, back from the wilderness in June with "The Price Of Love" – to be followed immediately by Elvis (as noted earlier) with "Crying In The Chapel" – and they were still good for another Top 20 hit in the autumn, with "Love Is Strange". The perpetually troubled Del Shannon too returned for an encore, his "Keep Searchin' (We'll Follow The Sun)" making a two-week stand at No.4 in February. Even more noteworthy was the thirteen-week chart run of the Four Seasons' "Let's Hang On", beginning in late November and continuing all the way through to the following February, after reaching a high point of No.5 in January.

With no direct competition over here, the American girl groups were particularly well placed to build on their successes of the year before. The New Year saw the reappearance of the Shangri-Las, to show the less worldly Twinkle just how the right blend of attitude as well as sound effects could enhance a tragic motorcycle death-disc, in the form of "Leader Of The Pack", their iconic No.15 hit of February. The Supremes, though unable to pull off another No.1 in Britain as a follow-up to "Baby Love", nevertheless bagged themselves two more hits here with singles that both reached No.1 back home. Of these, the first, "Come See About Me", made the least promising start, only reaching No.28 in February, but was soon surpassed by a No.7 hit in April with "Stop! In The Name Of Love". This was the song, the highlight of their act on the ground-breaking Motortown Revue tour of England in March and April, for which domineering firebrand Diana Ross now demanded attention-grabbing choreography – and thus was devised:

> … what would become the Supremes' signature gesticulation: right hand straight out, palm forward, left hand on hip as they jointly and dramatically emoted "Stop," then slowly lowering the right arm, with fingers snapping in a cool, circular motion – a freeze-frame of precious, adorable haught …[189]

On the arrival of the Revue's entourage in the UK (which also included Martha and the Vandellas, Stevie Wonder, the Temptations and Smokey Robinson and the Miracles), a television spectacular had been recorded as an additional means of promoting Berry Gordy's newly-founded Tamla-Motown record label. Hosted by Dusty Springfield under the final title of *The Sound of Motown*[190], it was not transmitted by ITV's Rediffusion until 28th April, after the tour had ended, yet the concept proved to be highly influential: "Not only was it the first of its kind to be screened on British television, but it was also the only show devoted to a particular style of music or record company."[191]

Although principally of immediate benefit to the Supremes, the attendant publicity gave an additional boost in April to Martha and the Vandellas, who returned to the lower Top 30 with "Nowhere To Run". Yet the fickleness of British record-buyers meant that they were now through with the Supremes for the time being, affecting disinterest in their later "I Hear A Symphony"; admittedly yet another US No.1 but composed in haste by Motown's classic Holland/Dozier/Holland team and released specifically as a spoiler for a hot rival recording, the Toys' "A Lover's Concerto", a deft marriage of soul to a classical theme derived from a Bach minuet, which had been released in the UK on the rival Stateside label and was in our Top 30 for ten weeks, with a high spot at the beginning of December of No.6.

Other black American artists breaking through in Britain included another Motown group not part of the spring tour, the Four Tops (entering the lower third of the Top 30 in July with "I Can't Help Myself" and "It's The Same Old Song" in September), James Brown (similarly in September, with "Papa's Got A Brand New Bag" – the cultural significance of which was mercilessly parodied by Peter Cook and Dudley Moore in their TV sketch show *Not Only … But Also*), Wilson Pickett (whose "In The Midnight Hour" made No.14 in October) and Fontella Bass (who took her Chess label classic "Rescue Me" up to No.7 in December and again the following January).

As we saw in Chapter 6, Brian Wilson had felt particularly threatened by the Beatles' runaway success in America but in the course of 1965 the Beach Boys slowly but surely stepped up the pace in their own efforts to launch a punishing counter-attack. Still finding it hard going, they could at least now be credited with having edged marginally closer to that goal with three UK Top 30 entries, at least two of which in retrospect should have deserved higher placings. Having succumbed at the close of 1964 to a personal crisis of life-changing proportions, Brian had recovered sufficiently in early January to resume work on recording the part-completed LP *The Beach Boys Today!* Five days into this new round of studio sessions, however, he caught his fellow group-members unawares on 13th January by announcing his irrevocable intention to withdraw from live performances: "I wanted to sit at the piano and write songs while they were out touring … I told them I foresee a beautiful future for the Beach Boys group but the only way we could achieve it was if they did their job and I did mine."[192]

According to Brian's own retrospective account, the overwhelming reaction from the others was one of angered disbelief (although his younger brother Carl appeared unmoved by his decision). So when the band went back on the road at the end of the month for a four-week tour of North

America, they called again on Glen Campbell to stand in as Brian's replacement (although for one week in February, when Campbell had to honour prior commitments elsewhere, Brian was briefly forced to return to the stage in person). By April, however, immediately before the next tour – this time of the Southern and Eastern States – was scheduled to start, Campbell had already signed up to support the Righteous Brothers, meaning that Mike Love had to act hastily to fill this unexpected gap for the first concert in New Orleans. Well-known to Mike as both a fellow musician and manager with CBS Records, Bruce Johnston at first tried on Love's behalf to find a substitute; but then, with none forthcoming, as a last resort volunteered his own services. Flying out from Los Angeles to join them, Johnston had barely a day to run through the Beach Boys' set list before taking to the stage with them for the first time on 9th April, his arrival at such short notice obliging him temporarily to don "a spare set of Al Jardine's trousers, which [were] three sizes and four inches too small".[193] To Brian's great relief, however, "Bruce ended up making the Beach Boys his living ... He came just at the right time when we were against the wall."[194]

True to his word, despite endangering his marriage and his precarious mental health through his increasing use of recreational drugs (now including the new, allegedly mind-expanding LSD *aka* acid), freed from the yoke of live performance Brian immersed himself in composing, recording and production. Even so, things did not always go smoothly. For example, the recording of "Help Me Rhonda" as a single (reworking an earlier version of the song as laid down as a track on *The Beach Boys Today!*) became particularly fraught on 24th February, when unhappily Murry Wilson was in attendance and characteristically behaving badly, repeatedly usurping Brian's authority as producer throughout the session with barbed criticisms of the group's performance. Inevitably, the ensuing tension erupted in a heated exchange between father and son, in the course of which – before he finally walked out – Murry accused the Beach Boys collectively of having got "so big that you can't sing from your hearts" and Brian of getting "a big success and he thinks he owns the business." Brian was only too glad to see him go, having insisted for his part that "We would like to record in an atmosphere of calmness".[195]

Eventually issued in America on 5th April as the Beach Boys' second single of 1965 (following their remake of "Do You Wanna Dance" in February), Brian's efforts were vindicated by "Help Me Rhonda" giving them another US No.1. Released a month later in Britain, the reaction here was far less enthusiastic. It took until mid-June to show up in the Top 30, by which time it was dancing attendance on other, more favoured – though less readily fathomable – US imports, such as "Wooly Bully" by Sam The Sham & The Pharaohs, or "She's About A Mover" by the Sir Douglas Quintet. Unquestionably to be regarded from an historical perspective as one of the Beach

Boys' greatest hits, nevertheless it could get no higher in the UK than No.26, only marginally better than the No.28 they had managed in February with "Dance, Dance, Dance" but so much better than their total miss in March with "All Summer Long".

It was with the recording of the other song eventually to be released as a UK single, "California Girls", that Bruce Johnston made his studio debut with the Beach Boys, in a session on 4th June as one of a sequence dedicated to their next US LP *Summer Days (And Summer Nights!!)*. Taking advantage of the superior technology available to him at the CBS Studio in Los Angeles, this session was also noteworthy for being the first occasion on which Brian experimented with multi-track recording of the Beach Boys' vocals. (Nonetheless, commenting on an earlier related session, Brian was of the opinion that "The intro to this song is the greatest piece of music that I've ever written."[196]) Issued in July as a single in America a week after the release of the new album on which it was featured, "California Girls" climbed to No.3 in the *Billboard* chart; whereas in Britain, following an August release, by early October it had achieved no better than a one-week entry in the Top 30 at No.28. Were it not for the fact that by this point of the year the British charts had already happily accommodated a surfeit of American talent, this exquisitely crafted hymn to the beauties of the West Coast might simply have been regarded as yet another casualty of the transatlantic cultural divide. As it is, poor timing – after all, it is quintessentially a song of the summer – and/or less than adequate promotion are more likely reasons for its initial failure here; although, of course, as the Beach Boys' stature later grew in the UK, so would that of this song as one amongst many – warranting, not least, in tribute an oblique reverse referencing in Paul McCartney's gutsy lyrics to "Back In The USSR".[197]

On 12th July, the day when "California Girls" saw its original US release, Brian had spent the small hours at his favourite Western Recorders Studio with session musicians, laying down a new instrumental arrangement of "Sloop John B", the traditional song the Pendletones had used as an audition piece way back in 1961. Although then left in the can until December, this was the *de facto* origin of the extended project that would bring to realisation the most rounded Beach Boys' LP ever, *Pet Sounds*. In the interim, Brian, under pressure from Capitol for a follow-up album to *Summer Days (And Summer Nights!!)*, brought the group together in September with old friends Jan and Dean to record a pot-boiler supposedly eavesdropping on an impromptu beach party but in fact completely studio-bound. The resultant four sessions delivered *(Recorded "Live" At A) Beach Boys' Party*, largely a mishmash of covers with no new original material at all, to the record company as demanded, spawning in the process, as the album's finale, the 'live' track "Barbara Ann", on which non-Beach Boy Dean Torrence sang lead vocal.[198]

Job done, three weeks later Brian was engaged in leading the far more sophisticated recording and production of one of his latest compositions, "The Little Girl I Once Knew"; but by the time it was released as a single in America, in late November, to Brian's frustration it suffered by comparison with the tracks on the *Party* album, which had come out at the beginning of the month, and would get no higher than No.20.

In order to recover what Capitol saw as lost ground, without prior consultation they formulated and rush-released a longer edit of "Barbara Ann" as yet another single on 20th December, for this to peak at No.2 by the end of the following January. Despite its success, Brian was driven to make his feelings clear:

> But that's not the Beach Boys. It's not where we're at, at all.
> Personally, I think the group has evolved another 800 percent in
> the last year. We have a more conscious, arty production now that's
> more polished. It's all been like an explosion for us.[199]

Indeed, by now he had been inspired to take the Beach Boys to another level entirely, having set himself the daunting task of upstaging the Beatles, whose *Rubber Soul* had seen its release in its American format on 6th December. Even allowing for the notable differences between this US version and its original British counterpart[200], Brian said that it "blew my mind because it was a whole album with all good stuff. It was definitely a challenge for me. I saw that every cut was very artistically interesting and stimulating."[201] More than this, he openly admitted that the experience of hearing *Rubber Soul* for the first time had been an epiphany for him:

> I suddenly realised that the recording industry was getting so free
> and intelligent. We could go into new things – string quartets, auto-
> harps, and instruments from another culture. I decided right then:
> I'm gonna try that, where a whole album becomes a gas. I'm gonna
> make the greatest rock'n'roll album ever made![202]

As a result, after Christmas he brought the rest of the group back into the studio to add vocals to his July instrumentation of "Sloop John B", thus marking the beginning conceptually of their long march towards *Pet Sounds*.

If British record-buyers were still finding it a struggle to get on the Beach Boys' wavelength, nothing could have been further from the truth as far as Bob Dylan was concerned – as noted, with more than a hint of respect, by Robert Shelton: "At this time, most pop excitement emanated from England and Dylan's shock waves flashed back to America."[203] In a year that developmentally was pivotal for him as an artist, he notched up five hit singles in the UK Top 30 (as against three in the *Billboard* Top 40 over the same period) whilst simultaneously maintaining an impressive grasp of the LP charts. In addition, he appeared here in person on a seven-venue concert tour of England, as documented in D. A. Pennebaker's film *Dont Look Back*, beginning in Sheffield on 30th April and ending at the Royal Albert Hall with two consecutive performances on 9th and 10th May. Two months before his controversial reincarnation as an electric musician at the Newport Folk Festival, this would be the last wholly acoustic tour he would undertake.

By the time it broke into the Top 30 at No.21 in the week ending 27th March, in Dylan's terms "The Times They Are A-Changin'" had already been discarded as an elegant anachronism, one of his many songs from "another time, another dimension".[204] Yet even in the spring of 1965 the British market remained largely virgin territory for his output and the single continued to climb, reaching No.9 a matter of weeks before he arrived to commence his tour. Without the benefit of that sense of progression to be presumed of his longer-term US fans, therefore, it was surely a leap of faith to make the sudden, jarring transition to the raucous chant of "Subterranean Homesick Blues", the sales of which in May were spurred on by the continuing tour from a chart entry at No.20 to a high point of No.6. For its opening sequence, *Dont Look Back* employs the iconic short film accompaniment to "Subterranean Homesick Blues" shot by Pennebaker in an alleyway to the rear of the Savoy Hotel (where tour headquarters had been established), in which Dylan, facing the camera and watched from the sidelines by Allen Ginsberg, keeps pace with the progress of the song by sequentially discarding one placard after another displaying crudely daubed key words and phrases from the lyrics.

First tentatively recorded acoustically on 13th January as work began on his fifth LP, then converted into and completed as an electric romp next day, the rapid-fire dictation of nuggets of street wisdom that was "Subterranean Homesick Blues" eventually became the opening track of *Bringing It All Back Home*, the album rectifying the missed step of *Another Side Of Bob Dylan* at a stroke with a title declaring the reclamation of American popular music by its rightful owners from its temporary British commandeers. Although the remainder of Side 1 also relied on electric accompaniment, the fact that all four tracks making up Side 2 were acoustic by no means denoted a continuing acceptance of traditionalism. As Robert Shelton saw it, Dylan had made an irrevocable decision "to leap back into rock, taking with him folk song's storytelling and comment" and thereby create "a new *kind* of expression, more sophisticated than that of his previous three years".[205]

Of the seven tracks on Side 1, the critical mass recognisably resides in the first four, in the sharpness of their alternation between rock'n'roll with a hard edge and bitter-sweet tenderness: "Subterranean Homesick Blues", "She Belongs To Me", "Maggie's Farm", "Love Minus Zero/No Limit". Stripped of amplification, Side 2 in its totality nevertheless displays a more than comparable power in the visionary lyrics of four of Dylan's most compelling songs to date: "Mr. Tambourine Man", "Gates Of Eden", "It's Alright, Ma (I'm Only Bleeding)", "It's All Over Now, Baby Blue".[206] Furthermore, producer Tom Wilson had ensured that Side 2 tore free from the straitjacket of convention by committing to a running order in which all four consecutive tracks each played for far longer than the industry-imposed standard three minutes.

Even the LP cover itself had its own tantalising story to tell, a crisp white rectangular border framing a glossy colour photograph by Daniel Kramer of Dylan to the fore, posing at one end of a chaise longue in a tasteful living room amidst a variety of artefacts each loaded with their own symbolic meaning, but the eye drawn inevitably to the reclining figure behind him of Sally Grossman (wife of manager Albert), in languid repose in a striking red trouser suit; all this to adorn a master work laid down in its entirety within two days. Already out in the USA from 22nd March, its British release in May was timed to coincide with Dylan's tour, the impetus of which soon propelled it to No.1 in the UK LP charts (satisfyingly higher than its American peak of No.6); to be rapidly followed here in June by the single release of "Maggie's Farm" (which achieved no higher than No.26 by the end of that month – when, by the most ludicrous of contrasts, Elvis was at No.1 with "Crying In The Chapel").

Dylan was as bemused by the England he experienced in 1965 as were those unwary reporters who tried to comprehend him and his music by insisting on asking him irrelevant, facile questions from the very moment of his arrival at London Airport onwards. Never renowned for suffering fools gladly, Dylan easily ran rings round them without them even knowing it. If, as they all dimly suspected, there was a deep, underlying secret to his peculiar talents, he certainly felt no compulsion to disclose it. In a good mood, he might use surrealistic props to deflect his pursuers, such as the giant lightbulb he sported at his initial press conference in the airport lounge:

REPORTER: What's the lightbulb for?

Dylan holds up an enormous industrial lightbulb.

DYLAN: What's the lightbulb for? I thought you would ask me that. No, I usually carry a lightbulb. Somebody gave it to me, you know.

REPORTER: Sorry, I didn't quite catch the answer.

DYLAN: Someone gave it to me … a very affectionate friend.

REPORTER: Oh, I see …

3rd REPORTER: What is your real message?

DYLAN: My real message? Keep a good head and always carry a lightbulb.

REPORTER: Have you tried it?

DYLAN: Well, I plugged it into my socket and the house exploded.[207]

If, however, he was in a bad mood, then woe betide the hapless interrogator; such as the science student turned amateur music journalist in Newcastle, whom Dylan lacerated for presuming that he should be expected to explain his attitude to life in two minutes flat; or the *Time* reporter who, after being subjected to a lengthy diatribe from Dylan about the magazine's superficial representation of news, still had the audacity to ask him, in all apparent seriousness, if he cared about what he sang. Despite these temporary setbacks, however, Dylan's reputation had already been significantly safeguarded beforehand in some sectors at least of the British music press; notably by Ray Coleman's article of 9th January for *Melody Maker* entitled "Beatles Say – Dylan Shows The Way."

In retrospect, Dylan expressed himself positively in respect of his new-found English fanbase: "… the kids [in England] are a whole other thing. Great. They're just more free."[208] Nevertheless, he was equally clear that for him the tour had represented the end of an era in his attitude to and content of his live performances, after which he had determined to turn his back on predictability, as shown by his forthright reply to being asked if he had changed his 'program' for English consumption:

No, no, I finished it there. That was the end of my older program. I didn't change it, it was developed and by the time we got there it was all, it was more or less, I knew what was going to happen all the time, y'know. I knew how many encores there was, y'know, which songs they were going to clap loudest and all this kind of things.[209]

The tour brought other important matters to a head, not least the issue, both personally and professionally, of the inter-dependency between Dylan and Joan Baez. After accompanying him to England confident in the expectation that he must surely repay the past compliment of Newport, her constant presence, certainly as coldly captured by Pennebaker's camera, appeared to become increasingly intrusive and irritating to Dylan, so that not once did he invite her to perform with him:

I never sang with him. He wouldn't let me sing, to put it bluntly. I should never have gone on that tour. It was sick. You see, originally I was going to go to England and have a concert tour, and in the middle of that Bobby's rise to fame came so fast that a few months later, we thought we'd go together and do split concerts. By the time it got around to England, Bobby was much more famous there than I was, and so Bobby just took England. I mean I didn't even bother with a tour. But, you see, I thought he would do what I had done with him, would introduce me, and it would be very nice for me because I'd never sung in England before. That's what I had in my mind. And by the time we got to England, whatever had happened in Bobby's mind – I'd never seen him less healthy than he was in England – he was a wreck and he wouldn't ask me on the stage to sing. And I was really surprised. I was very, very hurt. I was miserable.[210]

In truth, unbeknown to Joan she had already been supplanted in Dylan's affections by Sara Lownds, whom he would marry in November. When Sara arrived to join Dylan partway through the tour, therefore, Baez pointedly withdrew from the entourage, choosing instead to stay with her parents, then living in France; but not before diverting her patronage to up-and-coming Scottish folk singer Donovan, who had unwittingly become the butt of a running joke between Dylan and his road manager Bobby Neuwirth.

A particularly painful sequence in *Dont Look Back* shows Donovan naively eager to entertain Dylan and his retinue in his hotel suite by trading a rendition of his own, simplistic "To Sing For You" in exchange for hearing Dylan sing two verses of "It's All Over Now, Baby Blue". Recalling the event years afterwards in his autobiography, Donovan to this day still appears blissfully unaware of the undercurrents in the room; yet for the viewer, who earlier has been privy to Dylan and Neuwirth's sarcastic delight in pronouncing him "our next target ... our target for tomorrow"[211], they are all but palpable. His only misfortune at the time was to have had a massive hit with his first single "Catch The Wind", which had risen to No.6 in mid-April but remained in the Top 30 for the duration of Dylan's tour. He had thus become the subject of prominent articles in the British music papers attempting to draw ill-conceived comparisons between the two artists, compounded by publicity for his own separate tour engagements, inevitably making him the focus of Dylan's attention and dyspeptic wit. (Dylan would eventually concede that while Donovan might not necessarily be a good poet, "He's a nice guy, though."[212]) Despite her inept introductory effort to seduce him in the Savoy Hotel, all things considered he was to fare much better in the company of Joan Baez, who invited him to America, took him as her guest to that year's Newport Festival and included a cover of his song "Colours" on her next LP.

Before Dylan himself showed up at Newport at the end of July, he had returned to the studio in June, to commence the recording of new tracks for his forthcoming sixth LP, *Highway 61 Revisited*. With the bulk of a long session on 15th June having already been devoted to trying to perfect takes of a song then called "Phantom Engineer" (the origin of "It Takes A Lot To Laugh, It Takes A Train To Cry"), he belatedly turned his attention to another song entirely: "Like A Rolling Stone".

Consistently regarded as one of the greatest pop singles ever (to the study of which a multitude of articles, citations in works of reference – even an entire book – have been devoted), "Like A Rolling Stone" was definitively nailed once and for all the next day at its fourth take, driven along by the almost accidental addition of guitarist Al Kooper now playing electric organ: "The confluence of important words, that frat-rock melody, its steady rhythm of hatred, a happenstance of masterful musicians, and the hippest producer on the block fused together and stayed together, for the six solid minutes it took to break all the rules. For all time."[213]

A monumental outpouring of spleen hitherto unparalleled in popular song, it is simultaneously a denunciation of vanity and a celebration of its downfall, cataloguing the descent from the heights of fashion to the depths of despair in strains so virulent from the outset that it makes the old blues standard "Nobody Knows You When You're Down And Out" seem positively benign in its intentions:

Once upon a time you dressed so fine
You threw the bums a dime in your prime, didn't you?
People'd call, say, "Beware doll, you're bound to fall"
You thought they were all kiddin' you
You used to laugh about
Everybody that was hangin' out
Now you don't talk so loud
Now you don't seem so proud
About having to be scrounging your next meal

How does it feel
How does it feel
To be without a home
Like a complete unknown
Like a rolling stone?[214]

As the terror of dislocation, of dispossession increases, in the company successively of "the mystery tramp", "the jugglers and the clowns", the "diplomat/Who carried on his shoulder a Siamese cat" and "Napoleon in rags", so the wording and emphasis of the song's chorus [my italics] transmute to an infinitely more threatening variant:

How does it feel
How does it feel

To be on your own
With no direction home
Like a complete unknown
Like a rolling stone?[215]

Reduced at last to a cipher, the lowest of the low, all that is left is to slide imperceptibly over that final threshold of indignity into a disturbingly new dimension of reality:

When you got nothing, you got nothing to lose
You're invisible now, you got no secrets to conceal.[216]

When Dylan was asked, somewhat superfluously, to what end he was directing the anger of both this song and its near contemporary, "Positively 4th Street", against their intended targets, he simply replied: "I want to needle them."[217] More helpfully, in an interview in early 1966 with Canadian broadcaster Marvin Bronstein and quoted at length by Greil Marcus, he categorically identified "Like A Rolling Stone" as *the* song he felt represented a breakthrough for him:

I wrote that after I had *quit*. I'd literally quit, singing and playing – I found myself writing this song, this story, this long piece of vomit, twenty pages long, and out of it I took "Like A Rolling Stone" and made it as a single. And I'd never written anything like that before and it suddenly came to me that this is what I should do.

Nobody had ever done that before. A lot of people – Anybody can write … a lot of the things I used to write, I just wrote 'em first because nobody else could think of writing them. But that's only because I was hungry. But I've never met anybody, or heard anything – I hear a lot – I'm not saying it's *better* than anything else, I'm saying that I think – I think "Like A Rolling Stone" is definitely the thing which I do. After writing that I wasn't interested in writing a novel, or a play. I just had too much, I want to write *songs*. Because it was a whole new category. I mean, nobody's ever really written *songs* before.[218]

That Dylan saw it as the vehicle through which he felt most able to redefine the descriptor 'song' to his personal satisfaction, just past the mid-point of a decade in which popular music had already undergone a series of seismic shifts, may leave those of us in the wider generality open-mouthed in admiration yet struggling at the same time to grasp his elusive meaning. How far should a song go beyond mere entertainment to be a song on Dylan's terms? What additional elements make it more than just a story set to music? What, indeed, dictates the optimal – or, for that matter, the perfect – relationship between words and music?[219] Should a song always embody some form of critical vision? Should it have a moral purpose?

Questions such as these have no easy answers and serve initially to drive us backwards, rather than forwards, to the rich veins of traditional folk-song and ballads that Dylan himself mined in his apprentice years and continued to hold in awe irrespective of his newly proclaimed self-awareness:

> Certainly I haven't turned my back on it or anything like that. There is – and I'm sure nobody realises this, all the authorities who write about what it is and what it should be, when they say keep things simple, they should be easily understood – folk music is the only music where it isn't simple. It's never been simple. It's weird, man, full of legend, myth, Bible, and ghosts. I've never written anything hard to understand, not in my head anyway, and nothing as far out as some of the old songs. They were out of sight.[220]

"Like A Rolling Stone" was released as a single in America by CBS on Tuesday, 20th July, ahead of Dylan's attendance at Newport from Saturday the 24th, and entered the *Billboard* Hot 100 on that self-same third day of the festival, finally reaching No.2 on 4th September. (Released a month later in the UK, it entered the *NME* Top 30 at No.7 in the week ending 28th August and peaked a fortnight later at No.3, making it the best-selling of all his singles here.) By the time, therefore, of its live premiere at Newport, strong radio plugs had already firmly embedded it in the national consciousness within a week, with DJs thereafter steadily acceding to listeners' demands for them to play it for its full six minutes (the song having been split into two three-minute segments across the A- and B-sides, to be playable within the usual parameters of US commercial broadcasting).

On the occasion of this third and final Newport Folk Festival at which Dylan would appear, his straightforward opening performance on the afternoon of 24th July gave no hint of the controversy that was soon to follow; an acoustic set including "If You Gotta Go, Go Now", "Love Minus Zero/No Limit" and "All I Really Want To Do". But by the time Sunday came, Dylan had decided to do "this very crazy thing"[221] to which there was no certain outcome; that is, to play an electric set, accompanied by a scratch group that just happened to include both Mike Bloomfield and Al Kooper from his June recording sessions.

Neither the fact that the Paul Butterfield Blues Band were electric musicians nor that they had been legitimately booked to perform at Newport in their own right could be in any doubt. Nevertheless, when their turn to play also came on the 24th, the folk traditionalist and archivist Alan Lomax gave them a churlish introduction that provoked an unseemly fist-fight with Albert Grossman. Whether or not this negativity specifically spurred Dylan into action to pay Lomax and the rest of the Newport old guard back for their patronising insults is uncertain. What is known, though, is that through Mike Bloomfield auditions were hurriedly organised to assemble a makeshift band to accompany Dylan, who then led them in an overnight rehearsal off site of three of his latest songs.[222]

The slot allocated to Dylan on the night of 25th July, as part of the festival's finale, was inauspicious, to say the least, for his purposes; shoehorned in as he was between two ultra-traditional folk acts, Cousin Emmy and the Sea Island Singers. Add into the mix the idealistically overblown dedication by Pete Seeger of this closing concert, paraphrased by Robert Shelton as "a message from today's folk musicians to a newborn baby about the world we live in"[223], and the controls were locked on a collision course. Bedevilled by all the problems to be expected of an inadequate, let alone improperly balanced sound system, Dylan and his band kicked off with "Maggie's Farm", followed it with "Like A Rolling Stone" and concluded with "Phantom Engineer". As a gesture of revolt, time and place could hardly have been bettered; but sadly as a performance, it teetered between ragged and shambolic. Precious few of those present then shared the view of Murray Lerner (who had devotedly filmed Dylan's successive appearances at Newport over three years) that "Electricity adds to the thrill of [his] music in its own right".[224] If the festival organisers were outraged and confused, a large part of the audience felt themselves insulted and responded accordingly. For his part, Dylan "didn't know what was going to happen, but they certainly booed, I'll tell you that. You could hear it all over the place. I don't know who they were though, and I'm certain whoever it was did it twice as loud as they normally would."[225]

Silence descended after he and his band had vacated the stage, leaving compère for the evening Peter Yarrow (of Peter, Paul and Mary) thoroughly bewildered. In an effort to appease the angry crowd, he assured them that Dylan would return to sing something else for them if that was what they wanted and tried to coax him back onstage. Anxious to ride out the storm, Dylan was shortly persuaded to play what was, in the circumstances, a bizarre solo encore of "Mr. Tambourine Man" and "It's All Over Now, Baby Blue"; his last ever at Newport, a farewell which the audience now perversely received with a good grace. Yet even after departing Newport and taking on semi-permanently in his support a group of like-minded musicians, booing was a sound to which, extraordinarily, Dylan and those accompanying him would have to grow accustomed; seemingly signifying for the foreseeable future a yawning discrepancy between his phenomenal success as a recording artist and his battered credibility as a live performer.

Having recorded "Like A Rolling Stone" immediately before Newport, the week after the festival Dylan was back in the studio, working from 29th July onwards well into August principally on the remainder of the tracks to be assembled as the album *Highway 61 Revisited*; still drawing heavily on the services of Mike Bloomfield, Al Kooper and drummer Bobby Gregg as the core of a backing group but now forsaking Tom Wilson for the stewardship of a new producer, Bob Johnston. With "Like A Rolling Stone" firmly embedded as the LP's opening track, all those involved were committed to putting together an all-electric set, a principle faithfully adhered to until the final track on Side 2, "Desolation Row", for which Dylan and Johnston forsook an original electric take in favour of a later, much-edited composite acoustic version.

The title song superficially references the US National Highway 61 as recalled by Dylan from his youth, taking its elongated course from the Canadian border in the north right past his childhood home in Duluth, Minnesota all the way down south, skirting Memphis to finally reach New Orleans and the Gulf of Mexico; and in the front cover shot of the LP sleeve (posed once again by Daniel Kramer), he signifies his readiness to be on the road and away, sunglasses in hand, prominently displaying a Triumph motorcycle logo across the tee-shirt he sports as a vest beneath his casual coloured silk shirt. Interwoven throughout the complete suite of songs are the themes of alienation and escape, their imagery embellished with and enhanced by a fantastical cast of characters drawn from history, scripture, fairy tale and popular culture.

In "Tombstone Blues", for example, American outlaw Belle Starr rubs shoulders with – amongst others – Jack the Ripper, John the Baptist, Galileo, Cecil B. DeMille and Beethoven. The "graveyard woman" in "From A Buick 6" "walks like Bo Diddley".[226] The opening verse of "Highway 61 Revisited" reprises the Old Testament wrath of God in a modern context:

Oh God said to Abraham, "Kill me a son"
Abe says, "Man, you must be puttin' me on"
God say, "No." Abe say, "What?"
God say, "You can do what you want Abe, but
The next time you see me comin' you better run"
Well Abe says, "Where do you want this killin' done?"
God says, "Out on Highway 61."[227]

And for a grand finale, the ten verses of "Desolation Row" are peopled by a cavalcade of benighted souls: Cinderella, Romeo, Cain and Abel, the Hunchback of Notre Dame, the Good Samaritan, Ophelia, Einstein, Dr. Filth, the Phantom of the Opera, Casanova, Ezra Pound and T. S. Eliot.

Alienation is personified in "Ballad Of A Thin Man" by the "very well read" yet distracted, disconcerted, uncomprehending Mister Jones:

You raise up your head
And you ask, "Is this where it is?"
And somebody points to you and says

"It's his"
And you say, "What's mine?"
And somebody else says, "Where what is?"
And you say, "Oh my God
Am I here all alone?"

Because something is happening here
But you don't know what it is
Do you, Mister Jones?[228]

Meanwhile, far beyond the end of the highway, travelling on way down to the south-west and crossing the border from El Paso in Texas into Mexico, escapism fails to deliver its elusive alternative promise in "Just Like Tom Thumb's Blues":

When you're lost in the rain in Juarez
And it's Eastertime too
And your gravity fails
And negativity don't pull you through
Don't put on any airs
When you're down on Rue Morgue Avenue
They got some hungry women there
And they really make a mess outa you.[229]

With appetites sated then jaded, the exotic suddenly transformed into the sordid, sooner or later home must somehow exert its overriding influence:

I started out on burgundy
But soon hit the harder stuff
Everybody said they'd stand behind me
When the game got rough
But the joke was on me
There was nobody even there to call my bluff
I'm going back to New York City
I do believe I've had enough.[230]

Released in the USA on 30th August and the UK in September, *Highway 61 Revisited* went to Nos.3 and 4 respectively in the album charts of both countries.

From these self-same sessions also emerged his next two singles; the first of which, "Positively 4th Street", is a song so driven by unbridled scorn that listening to it is like eavesdropping half in embarrassment and half in incredulity on the most fractious shouting-match in the world. As the opening verse makes abundantly clear, in Dylan's head it's pay-back time:

You got a lotta nerve
To say you are my friend

When I was down
You just stood there grinning.[231]

And if you can't believe your ears at this put-down, hang on for the rough ride to the closing verses and be left in no doubt of it at all:

I wish that for just one time
You could stand inside my shoes
And just for that one moment
I could be you

Yes, I wish that for just one time
You could stand inside my shoes
You'd know what a drag it is
To see you.[232]

Uncharacteristically, this song has little time for symbolism: it is a viciously direct counter-blast against the paradoxical conservatism of the folk community in general and more specifically that of New York's Greenwich Village, where once upon a long time ago an unknown Bob Dylan had celebrated his signing to CBS Records by renting a sparsely furnished top-floor apartment at 161 West 4th Street and living in sin with his new girlfriend Suze Rotolo.

The hypocrisy that Dylan had come to regard as manifest in the culture of 4th Street rankled with him to the extent that he was unable to resist another sideswipe at it in his stream-of-consciousness sleevenotes to *Highway 61 Revisited*: "… & when Paul Sargent, a plainclothes man from 4th street, comes in at three in the morning & busts everybody for being incredible, nobody really gets angry – just a little illiterate most people get …"[233] Despite inevitably being blind to such nuances of interpretation on first acquaintance, British record-buyers still found "Positively 4th Street" sufficiently enlivening to afford it a nine-week stint in the Top 30, from the end of October to Christmas, giving Dylan his fifth UK hit of the year with a chart high of No.12. (The follow-up single, cut at the same time but re-recorded in October, was "Can You Please Crawl Out Your Window?" – judgement on which, with its UK chart debut in January 1966, is reserved for the next chapter).

It was this accumulation of new material, added to the already impressive legacy of *Bringing It All Back Home*, that was now to become the bedrock of Dylan's set list for his next ambitious project, an extended series of concerts that graduated in the coming months to the status of a 'world tour'. In agreement with Albert Grossman, however, each concert was to be staged in two halves – acoustic, followed by electric – and it was the latter that would continue to engender hostile audience reaction, not only immediately in America but also continuing well into 1966 when he ventured further afield.

Looking for musicians robust enough to work with him, for his initial line-up Dylan recruited two members of five-piece Canadian/American group the Hawks, guitarist Robbie Robertson and drummer Levon Helm; to whom, on the back of their prior participation in that summer's recording sessions, he added the known and trusted Al Kooper on organ and Harvey Brooks on bass guitar. Their first outing together was on 28th August, at Forest Hills in New York, a sell-out concert at which the audience began by being respectful to Dylan as an acoustic soloist but then became increasingly restless and sorely troubled by his electric *alter ego* when he paraded songs such as "Maggie's Farm" or "Ballad Of A Thin Man". As Robert Shelton noted, however, dogged persistence in the face of very vocal opposition eventually paid off: "By the time Dylan did "Rolling Stone", already a hit single, the audience mostly sang along. Critics of Newport '65 and the new music were proved wrong. At Forest Hills, the sound was right, the programming intelligent, the presentation persuasive. The problem lay with the audience."[234]

Even though the same line-up found, encouragingly, that a West Coast audience at the Hollywood Bowl on 3rd September proved to be more open-minded and forgiving, Dylan subsequently decided that for the tour proper, beginning in Austin, Texas on 24th September, he would enlist the support of the Hawks in their entirety. Hence from this point onwards Robertson and Helm were reunited with their three colleagues Rick Danko (bass guitar), Richard Manuel (piano) and Garth Hudson (organ) – to be known in due course simply as The Band – but from the outset, the tour was to be the severest test yet of their resolve:

> Everywhere we went they booed us. It was a very interesting process to pull into a town, set up, play. People come in. They boo you. You pack up. You go on to the next town. You play. The people boo you. And then you just go on. You go all the way around the world with people just booing you every night.[235]

Robertson articulated their rationalisation for carrying on regardless in these straightforward terms: "We would listen to these tapes sometimes after the show, just to see what they were booing at, and … we thought, God, it's not that bad. It's not that terrible. And nobody else sounds this way. It's got something. That was the only thing that enabled us to go on."[236] And Hudson reflected on the fact that they had experienced worse responses in the past: "After the first two or three concerts where they booed, they didn't seem to be throwing anything dangerous and they didn't threaten us out in the hall, or in the alley, so we kept doing it."[237]

But for drummer Helm, seemingly every bit as much a seasoned campaigner on the road as his comrades-at-arms, the constant barracking swiftly became insufferable to him:

> You're used to people going, "Yeah! Bravo!" And instead of that

it's just, Booo! The worst! Get out! Go! Leave! You know. It's a hell
of a sound. At the time it cut me all the way to the bone. I just … I
couldn't take it. I really couldn't. And didn't after a certain time.[238]

Having thus struggled to endure playing for thirty-odd of Dylan's concerts
across the USA and Canada, by the end of November he was so badly affected
that he could take no more and reluctantly bailed out (to be replaced on tour
in the short term by Bobby Gregg, then Sandy Konikoff), thereby turning
his back on performing and not rejoining the Hawks – or the Band, as they
had then become – until early 1968 for the recording of their seminal work
Music From Big Pink.[239] Despite the emotional damage he had sustained in the
course of working with him, Helm still retained huge respect for Dylan's own
studied persistence in the face of such adversity:

> By God, he didn't change his mind or direction one iota … Bob is
> a funny guy like that. He don't care, you know. I like Bob's policy:
> if you bought the ticket, you should be allowed to boo. If you don't
> like it, voice your opinion. But, goddamnit, it's a hard one to take.[240]

If Dylan's shift of musical direction had sharply divided his devotees,
strangely it proved no obstacle to success in parallel for those performers
who sought to emulate his example. One of the most striking No.1s in the
summer of 1965 on both sides of the Atlantic was a deconstruction of "Mr.
Tambourine Man", admittedly reworked in a severely abridged version but
with a bold new electric arrangement by Californian group the Byrds that, to
their great credit, received Dylan's personal seal of approval.

The three founder-members boasted in common earlier apprenticeships within the more accessible popular realms of folk and country music:
Jim McGuinn as accompanist to the Chad Mitchell Trio (before assuming
a similar role in a wholly different genre for Bobby Darin); Gene Clark as
a member of the New Christy Minstrels; and David Crosby as one of Les
Baxter's Balladeers. All having gravitated to Los Angeles, the focal point of
their meeting in the spring of 1964 was Hollywood's Troubadour Club; where
Crosby, in search of fellow musicians with whom he might be able to realise
the tempting promise of a recording career, first encountered McGuinn and
Clark, who had not long come together tentatively as a singing duo, in a
shared appreciation of the Beatles and Peter and Gordon. Crosby in his own
right had already caught the interest of record producer Jim Dickson, who
now took on this trio of guitarists as the Jet Set and set about rehearsing
them regularly during down-time at LA's World Pacific Studios.

Attending that year's Newport Folk Festival, Dickson had seen and
been impressed by Dylan's performance of his new song "Mr. Tambourine
Man"; and, armed with the foresight to see it as a potential hit for one of

his acts, followed this transforming experience up with intermediaries in the music business, thereby managing to obtain an acetate copy of Dylan's earlier recording of it in June.[241] In the months ahead, he persevered with the Jet Set to work over and over again in the studio at coming up with their own marketable version of the song, although initially none of the group found it particularly to their taste.

The trio soon expanded to a quartet through Crosby's recruitment of a drummer – of sorts – Michael Clarke, who, in spite of a childhood passion for drumming, possessed neither any particularly well developed skills in that direction nor, for that matter, an actual drum kit. But, more importantly, it had to be said in his favour that he had the right look:

> He already had the long hair that they were still beginning to
> grow and was everybody's dream to be in one of those groups ...
> Michael didn't have any drums so we set him up with a cardboard
> box which we found in a locker at World-Pacific. They were full of
> empty tape boxes. He put a tambourine on top and made himself a
> couple of tom toms and a snare.[242]

Then, to overcome his dissatisfaction with Crosby's prowess as bass guitarist and boost his role as a harmony singer instead, Dickson added a fifth member to the group, Chris Hillman, whose previous reputation related to his talent as a player of bluegrass music on the mandolin and who therefore now had to learn how to play bass. As producer, Dickson was confident that for his recording purposes both Clarke and Hillman would soon come up to speed. As for Hillman, at Dickson's prompting he summoned up the courage to abandon his hitherto lucrative work as a bluegrass musician and commit himself, with understandable trepidation, to this very different endeavour with the Jet Set:

> I was a mandolin player and didn't know how to play bass, but they
> didn't know how to play their instruments either, so I didn't feel
> too bad about it. None of us were rock'n'rollers; we were all folk
> musicians and, although it was tremendously exciting, it was such an
> alien thing to be getting into ...[243]

The undoubted masterstroke that Dickson pulled off next in the furtherance of his ambitions for the group was to invite Dylan to attend one of their rehearsals of his song in person; and although the date is lost to history, it is most likely to have occurred in late November or early December 1964, at a time when Dylan had several concert engagements in California. Having listened to their still hesitant playing of "Mr. Tambourine Man" and congratulated them effusively ("Wow, man! You can dance to that!"[244]), before departing he amused himself further by jamming on the piano with them, leaving them suitably starstruck. Dickson could not have been more delighted at the outcome: "[Dylan] got them to like him, and once the song came back, it never dropped out of the set again. At the end of the session, I knew I'd won. All the hostility and jealousy over Dylan was gone."[245]

The group's impoverished state in respect of instruments was finally remedied by a speculative investment from a third party, at the suggestion of Dickson's business partner Eddie Tickner; meaning that at long last Clarke could actually have a drum kit and, perhaps more significantly for their future, that McGuinn could buy a 12-string Rickenbacker in deference to the instrument of choice played by his idol George Harrison in *A Hard Day's Night*, the film that the founding trio had found truly inspirational.

The transformation of the Jet Set into the Byrds was completed in November 1964, when Dickson managed to secure a recording contract for them with CBS Records; a contract to which in the first instance only three of them (McGuinn, Crosby and Clark, as vocalists for the group) were parties, in accordance with prevailing company policy at the time, the other two being belatedly incorporated four months later. From the outset CBS sought a name change for the group to avoid conflict with Capitol Records over a UK group also called the Jet Set, whose record release in the USA was imminent, and the Byrds emerged as their new name from protracted discussions between Dickson and McGuinn, importantly capitalised with no less than "the magic 'B' as in Beatles and Beach Boys".[246]

The Byrds' definitive recording of "Mr. Tambourine Man" was made on 20th January, 1965 in the course of their first session at CBS's Hollywood studios, overseen by an up-and-coming young in-house producer, Terry Melcher (only son of actress and singer Doris Day). A combination of their professional inexperience and the continuing non-contractual recognition for now of Clarke and Hillman dictated that Melcher should call upon the services of session players to augment the Byrds' own contributions, including Larry Knechtel on bass and Hal Blaine on drums: as a gruelling day wore on, he was eventually satisfied with Take 22. Also recorded, as the B-side, was one of Gene Clark's own early compositions, "I Knew I'd Want You", a minor-key ballad set in an arrangement that was a conscious American pastiche of the Mersey Sound of the Beatles or the Searchers.

But then, to the Byrds' disappointment, ensued a three-month hiatus while CBS executives prevaricated over the single's release, apparently out of misplaced deference to Dylan (himself, of course, by this time one of CBS's major recording artists and celebrities) and his manager Albert Grossman. Given that Dylan had previously given the Byrds his approval face to face rather than raise any objection, one would have thought further delay at this stage to be unnecessary. Left floundering in the interim to establish themselves as a credible live act, on the back of an increasingly hollow promise of being 'recording artists' as long as no record was forthcoming, the Byrds underwent a turbulent period of self-doubt, to the extent of nearly breaking up. However, once Grossman let it be known that the Dylan camp was content for CBS to proceed, a release date of 12th April was finally scheduled and the pressure on the group eased. On 21st March, they embarked upon the first of a series of residencies at the popular club on Sunset Strip known colloquially as Ciro's (or, to give it its full title from 1964 onwards, Ciro's Le Disc); and whilst there, on the 26th they received yet another personal endorsement from Dylan, who not only came to see them perform that night but also joined in with them on stage for two numbers (as captured in a photograph taken by Jim Dickson that later graced the back cover of their first LP).[247] At a stroke, by this unsolicited gesture of patronage the Byrds' hip credentials with the Hollywood in-crowd were assured.

Three weeks after CBS had released *Bringing It All Back Home*, featuring Dylan's full-length acoustic version of "Mr. Tambourine Man", the Byrds' alternative electric cover of the song came out as a single and shot up the *Billboard* charts to No.1.[248] Issued here a month later, it entered the *NME* Top 30 at No.24, early sales boosted by its pre-release airplay on the pirate station Radio Caroline, and in the week ending 17th July it had become the UK No.1 as well, easily distinguishable by the amplified chiming of McGuinn's 12-string intro: a sound forever frozen in time for me as coming from a fellow Army Cadet's illicit transistor radio while we lolled in the summer sun, flicking the pale yellow broken stems of dead grass off our battledress, idling away a field day at the now long-gone Wedgnock rifle range on the outskirts of Warwick.

Thus catapulted into the limelight, the Byrds were in immediate demand. In addition to further engagements on the Hollywood club circuit, TV appearances, concert dates and even a US tour of their own all soon followed as their new-found fans clamoured to see what many would eventually venerate as the unsurpassed original line-up: Jim McGuinn (lead guitar/vocals), Gene Clark (tambourine/vocals), David Crosby (rhythm guitar/vocals), Chris Hillman (bass guitar), Michael Clarke (drums). For a week in mid-May, they travelled around California as an opening act for the Rolling Stones; and on 3rd July, they were on the same bill as the Beach Boys – and, amongst others, the less than happy Kinks – for the one-night 'summer spectacular' at the Hollywood Bowl. Starting out on 5th July in Denver, Colorado, they toured the Mid-West, ending in Chicago on 31st July but then flying on from there to London the very next day, for a tour of England coinciding with the UK release of their second single and lasting until 20th August.

Their follow-up to "Mr. Tambourine Man" was another Dylan cover, this time of "All I Really Want To Do" from *Another Side Of Bob Dylan*. At home it had failed to impress, only reaching No.40, but in the UK it gave them their second Top Ten hit, reaching No.8 in early September. In both markets, however, it succumbed to unwelcome competition from a rival version by Cher, the female partner of her then husband Sonny Bono in the duo Sonny & Cher who themselves had just scooped US and UK No.1s with "I Got You Babe". Indeed, Jim Dickson would accuse Cher and her management of outright plagiarism, on discovering that she had copied the Byrds' arrangement of the song courtesy of a surreptitious recording made of their performance of it by Bono at Ciro's.

Sadly, the Byrds' English tour was not a success, especially since inept advance publicity had oversold them as America's answer to the Beatles and warned unsuspecting parents of the dangers of rampant 'Byrdmania'. The reality was close to a damp squib and the British music press hammered them for their non-existent stagecraft, inaudible singing and distancing themselves from their audiences. Although they were fêted by members of the Beatles and the Rolling Stones in London's top in-crowd haunts, on the back of their previous month's worth of touring in America they were quickly exhausted by an ill-planned itinerary and often defeated by technical shortcomings. What they thought of as West Coast cool was lost in translation across the pond as aloofness and their appearance on *Top Of The Pops* merely served to emphasise *le difference*:

> McGuinn was positively otherworldly, the consummate method actor, staring deep into the camera lens over those weird rectangular glasses; Crosby smiled seductively, both innocent and mischievous in the same shot; Clark grinned, while slapping the tambourine, occasionally; Hillman barely moved, a statuesque paragon of cool furtiveness, partly hidden beneath his pulled up jacket collar; Clarke, dressed in an English tweed jacket and polo neck, just like McGuinn, affected an abstract disdain, cupping a drumstick in one hand while playing peek-a-boo beneath that long, blond hair. The performance was brilliantly captured by the *Top Of The Pops* crew, who studiously honed in on each individual Byrd as if they were undertaking an ornithological study of a new species.[249]

Thankfully, not everyone was prepared to condemn them out of hand. As the tour drew to its close, they were greeted in Bournemouth by screaming fans, a recording of which by press officer Derek Taylor would later be absorbed into the Byrds' repertoire as an apposite backing track to their 1967 single "So You Want To Be A Rock'n'Roll Star". (In contrast, the planned gig in nearby Portsmouth two days later was cancelled for lack of interest, with only 250 of a possible 4,000 tickets sold.) And when it was all over and they had flown home, there was at least one retrospective attempt made to salvage their good name and shame those who had derided them, in an appreciative piece by Brighton journalist Anne Nightingale:

People who met the Byrds in the flurry of a press conference or the backstage confusion of a one-nighter, put them down as detached and arrogant when spoken to and remote onstage … But in Britain, the Byrds weren't arrogant, just bewildered by the harsh reception from the country they'd set their hearts on visiting.[250]

As it transpired, this was the one and only time the group would be seen in its founding five-man line-up in Britain: when they next visited, in 1967, five had become four.

With impeccably perverse timing, 20th August, the day of the Byrds' departure, saw the UK release by CBS of their first LP, *Mr. Tambourine Man*. Recorded across two sessions in April, it was impressively packaged in a striking sleeve, bearing on its front cover what was, in its day, a novel circular fish-eye lens photograph of the group – complete with optical distortions – in colour by Barry Feinstein, framed within a black border. It seriously looked the business, an object to be coveted for itself irrespective of the music locked within.[251] Out of twelve tracks, four were Dylan songs, "Mr. Tambourine Man" and "All I Really Want To Do" now joined by another two tracks lifted from *Another Side Of Bob Dylan*, "Spanish Harlem Incident" and "Chimes Of Freedom". A further three were by other composers: Pete Seeger's setting of the twentieth-century Welsh ballad "The Bells Of Rhymney", Jackie DeShannon's "Don't Doubt Yourself, Babe" and a tongue-in-cheek reworking of Vera Lynn's wartime classic "We'll Meet Again" (completely alien to English ears but apparently inspired by its recent use in the satiric film *Dr. Strangelove* … and virtually thrown away as the closing track of the album). The remaining five were original compositions, either by Gene Clark alone (the already issued B-sides, "I Knew I'd Want You" and "I'll Feel A Whole Lot Better", plus "Here Without You") or in collaboration with Jim McGuinn ("You Won't Have To Cry" and "It's No Use", the latter a stand-out track for me from the moment I first heard it by virtue of McGuinn's blistering guitar work). Representing a previously unimagined blend of folk and melancholy pop, it sounded that summer as if it had come from another world but it made undeniably compelling listening, for me and all the other fans whose purchases put it in the LP charts for three months, where it peaked at No.7.

Glad to be back in Hollywood, the Byrds were, as noted earlier in this chapter, very swiftly reacquainted with the Beatles at the end of August when the latter took time out from their current US tour to socialise with them. Their time after that was divided between making more records and playing gigs across the States: almost the whole of November, for example, was consumed by a grindingly wearisome tour with "Dick Clark's Caravan of Stars", on which they joined a motley crew including Bo Diddley and CBS rival act Paul Revere & the Raiders. Originally intent on using a Dylan song again for their third single, a brief dalliance with "It's All Over Now,

Baby Blue" gave way to more serious efforts to record "The Times They Are A-Changin'". Their take on the latter was, however, relegated to a track on their second LP, in favour of another Pete Seeger adaptation (this time of verses from the Book of Ecclesiastes), "Turn! Turn! Turn!", drawn from McGuinn's not inconsiderable past folk repertoire. The most majestic yet of all the productions attempted with them by Terry Melcher, it was completed after an unbelievable seventy takes in the course of just one studio session in September; and following its US release on 1st October, it sold a million and gave them their second No.1 hit.

Finding an easy resonance with a young America deeply troubled by the escalation of the Vietnam War and, as a consequence, growing increasingly resistant to being drafted into the armed forces to fight overseas against the Viet Cong, the song had the virtue of being immediately accessible as a peace anthem. Its opening chorus reinforces the long view of God and history:

> To everything (Turn! Turn! Turn!)
> There is a season (Turn! Turn! Turn!)
> And a time for every purpose under heaven.[252]

Each verse then rehearses and invites reflection on a catalogue of man's diverse activities, finally drawing to a heartfelt topical conclusion:

> A time to gain, a time to lose;
> A time to rend, a time to sew;
> A time for love, a time for hate;
> A time for peace, I swear it's not too late.[253]

Released on 29th October in the UK, it floundered, not just because over here it was uprooted from any relevant cultural context but it was also a victim, in a still relatively conservative British market, of its own sophistication (for good measure, the B-side, Gene Clark's "She Don't Care About Time", featured a guitar solo by McGuinn on a theme adapted from Bach's "Jesu Joy Of Man's Desiring"): in the week ending 4th December, it finally achieved a one-week showing at No.28.

Viewed in retrospect, the short-lived popularity of the Byrds in the British charts was attributable to their association with Dylan in the minds of the generality of record-buyers: few had the interest or staying power to follow their progression beyond the point at which they had opted for other sources of material for their singles. In their first flush, they were credited on both sides of the Atlantic as innovators of 'folk-rock', a simplistic label for early attempts to enliven folk music by electric arrangements that, when applied to his own work of the period, Dylan rejected out of hand. Be that as it may, they were certainly the first American group to infuse the UK Top 30 with a new West Coast flavour of pop emanating from the liberal youth cultures of LA and San Francisco. In this regard, they self-evidently set themselves apart from the likes of the Beach Boys, who were solely dependent on Brian Wilson's inner drive; or, for that matter, the Walker Brothers, who, despite having been similarly inspired by the Beatles, opted in February 1965 to leave the Hollywood club scene behind and become Californians-in-exile in London, thereafter shamelessly exploiting the British weakness for lush orchestral arrangements of moody ballads such as "Make It Easy On Yourself" and "My Ship Is Coming In" whilst being photogenic into the bargain.[254]

Where 'folk-rock' tipped over into 'protest', however, controversy was bound to follow; and on the premise that no publicity is bad publicity, "Eve Of Destruction", a record by American singer Barry McGuire (like Gene Clark, another ex-New Christy Minstrel) attracted regular airplay and hostile criticism in equal measure from the moment a pre-release acetate was leaked to an LA radio station. Composed by singer/songwriter P. F. Sloan, it was howled down for its overtly bellicose attitude to world affairs, further heightened by the gravelly quality of McGuire's voice as he rammed the song's unpalatable message home with each thundering chorus:

> And you tell me
> Over and over and over again, my friend,
> Ah, you don't believe
> We're on the eve
> Of destruction. [255]

In his lyrics, Sloan had cast his iconoclastic net wide, with references to "the eastern world ... exploding"; American teenagers being "old enough to kill but not for votin'"; "no one to save, with the world in a grave" after a nuclear apocalypse; even an invitation to "Think of all the hate there is in Red China".[256] While musicians and politicians alike sought to outdo each other in distancing themselves from such redneck sentiments, they nevertheless failed to stop the record being a runaway best-seller. Its rapidly gathering momentum from the onset (even McGuire himself called it "a scary song, because it made it on its own; it had no 'payola', no disc jockey manipulation" [257]) took it all the way to No.1, no less, in America in late summer, then on to No.4 in the UK in October. The notoriety it attracted may have made a name for Sloan but it ended McGuire's career as a solo recording artist before it had hardly begun.

Other folk influences on the UK Top 30 were seen, by and large, as less damaging and controversial. For instance, no outcry attended the temporary accommodation in the lower reaches of the charts for two weeks in May of the archetypal civil rights anthem "We Shall Overcome", as sung by Joan Baez; and at the height of summer, she enjoyed three glorious weeks at No.7 with Phil Ochs's lilting song of protest, "There But For Fortune". (She would briefly revisit the lower 20s in October and December, on safer ground with her respective interpretations of Dylan's "It's All Over Now, Baby Blue" and "Farewell Angelina", the latter the title track of her latest LP from which both singles were taken.)

Meanwhile, her protégé on the rebound, Donovan, needed no support from her on his home ground. Born and brought up originally in Glasgow, from the age of 10 he had resettled with his parents in Hertfordshire, where in his early teens he began to develop his particular interests in jazz, folk and blues. Dropping out of further education in 1962, he took off with best mate Gypsy Dave to Cornwall for the summer, the pair of them cadging casual work and sleeping rough in St. Ives as just two more members of a transient young population then still quaintly termed 'beatniks' but later to be labelled 'hippies'. On his return home, he renewed his efforts to become a competent guitarist, singer and composer and in 1964 was spotted by chance, performing in a club in Southend, by Peter Eden and Geoff Stephens, who offered to manage him professionally. They set up a trial recording session for him and with that successfully under his belt, Stephens first secured him a songwriting and publishing deal then, on the strength of his demo tapes, a slot on television.

For an ambitious young singer/songwriter who had attracted national interest in early 1965 through regular appearances on *Ready Steady Go!* before he even had a record deal, from March onwards he was well served by Pye Records, with the release of three singles, an EP and two LPs all packed in by Christmas. Following his April Top 10 debut with "Catch The Wind", in June he bettered that performance by one place when he took "Colours" to No.5. An appealingly simple folk song to which he provided his own accompaniment on guitar, banjo and harmonica, he set great personal store by it:

> With the release of my second single, 'Colours', I had begun to weave a world of my own into which thousands of fans would enter. I wanted to share a visionary world and found that millions of younger and older fans wanted this too. My music would be more than pop music, more than a dance record, more than a love song.
>
> I thought to myself, it is storytelling, man, and a soundtrack to your changes.[258]

Unfortunately, some fine tuning of his vision of the new minstrelsy was still required, as demonstrated in November when his third single, "Turquoise", a poetic tribute to Baez, had fallen flat and only scraped one week at No.30.

Nevertheless, in the intervening period between "Colours" and "Turquoise" Donovan had made his own foray into that contentious territory between music and political protest with his best-selling EP *Universal Soldier,* entering the charts a fortnight before "Eve Of Destruction" to reach No.12 in September before being finally overtaken by McGuire. (It also spent a total of 30 weeks in the EP charts – then based on a Top 20 – where it reached No.1.) All four tracks had a common anti-war theme, although only one of them, "Ballad Of A Crystal Man", was of Donovan's own composition.

The title song was by Buffy Sainte-Marie, a Canadian/American singer-songwriter, who had been inspired to write it after a stopover in San Francisco where she had witnessed the return of wounded veterans from Vietnam and then brooded on who ultimately bore responsibility for their plight. First and foremost, it conceives of the 'universal soldier' as the hapless functionary of global geo-politics down the ages:

> He's five foot two
> And he's six feet four.
> He fights with missiles and with spears.
> He's all of thirty-one
> And he's only seventeen.
> He's been a soldier for a thousand years.[259]

But after having been delineated as the scapegoat throughout the song, in a final twist the last verse calls the instigator of his actions to account:

> He's the universal soldier
> And he really is to blame.
> His orders come from far away no more.
> They come from here and there,
> And you and me, and brothers,
> Can't you see,
> This is not the way we put the end to war?[260]

The remaining two songs came from the pens of contemporaries of Donovan who, at that time, were less well-known contributors to the burgeoning revival of British folk music: "The War Drags On" by Mick Softley, and "Do You Hear Me Now?" by Bert Jansch. The former, seen as the first British folk song written to challenge the iniquities of the Vietnam War, tells the "story of a soldier named Dan" who "Went out to fight the good fight in South Vietnam" but is finally tormented by an apocalyptic vision of tactical nuclear weapons let loose on the battlefield:

> Last night poor Dan had a nightmare, it seems.
> One kept occurring and recurring in his dreams.
> Cities full of people burning, screaming, shouting loud
> And right there overhead, a great orange mushroom cloud.
> And there's no more war,
> For there's no more world,

And the tears come streaming down.
Yes, I lie crying on the ground.[261]

After such strong meat as this, Jansch's more generalised incitement to
"Freedom fighters" to "speak with your tongues" and "Sing with the might
of the wind in your lungs"[262], though a well-meaning and rousing song in its
own right, seems peculiarly tame by comparison.

As for his two LPs, it was his first, *What's Bin Did And What's Bin Hid*,
released on 21st May, that sold the most copies, spending 16 weeks in the LP
charts and reaching a high spot of No.3. Like so many other debut albums,
it was unashamedly a miscellany thrown together from his still developing
live repertoire, a mix of his own earliest compositions (including an impressively authoritative reprise of "Catch The Wind", minus the backing strings
of the original single that had been used supposedly to broaden its appeal)
and songs gleaned from elsewhere: the homegrown (such as Mick Softley's
critique of the Protestant work ethic, "Goldwatch Blues") as well as the transatlantic ("Remember The Alamo" and Woody Guthrie's "Car Car"). Whilst
it undeniably offered an enjoyable half-hour's listening, in truth its content
lacked focus or bite and attempts at arrangements were minimalist: apart
from Donovan himself, the only musical credits were to ex-Shadow Brian
Locking as bass player, Skip Alan on drums (who incongruously moved on
in November to become the drummer with R&B group the Pretty Things)
and Gypsy Dave (for playing kazoo on "Keep On Truckin'.")

Although the second, *Fairytale*, released five months later, was a much
more assured and mature collection, its sales were inexplicably disappointing:
only two weeks in the LP charts, getting no higher than No.20. Subtitling it
Songs For Sunshine People, Donovan said of it himself that its music "could
be described as coming from the folk-blues tradition, with the exception of
a dimension you might call 'a new way of seeing' that I was developing"[263];
and, furthermore, that it "set the scene for my performance arrival as a 'Bard'
who would present a way of seeing the wonder of the natural world".[264] Rob
Young, author of the monumental history of the British folk revival *Electric
Eden*, less generously sums up his objective thus:

> These benignly stoned odes fondly and naively imagined a long-
> lost, bucolic Avalon where like minds of a forever young Flower
> Generation might sit in peace, singing, dancing, smoking, making
> love and contemplating the universe in a guilt-free environment.[265]

Be that as it may, this time two-thirds of the songs were Donovan's own,
covering a much broader musical spectrum; from the opening track reworking
his hit single "Colours", through the cool jazz of "Sunny Goodge Street"
and the twelve-string embellished delights of "The Summer Day Reflection Song", to the remoter island shores of "Jersey Thursday" and "Belated

Forgiveness Plea", before concluding with the transpositional first-person narrative "The Ballad of Geraldine". I, for one, was greatly taken with its diversity and lyricism, alternating it over and over again on my turntable that Christmas with the Beatles' *Rubber Soul* and Joan Baez's *Farewell Angelina*.

What, however, was not immediately apparent was that the release of *Fairytale* at the end of October had coincided with Donovan seeking to extricate himself from his management deal with Eden and Stephens (who, working in collaboration with Terry Kennedy, had also been responsible for producing his records to date), a move that would pitch him into litigation and blight his recording career for well over a year. Although his autobiography is silent on the split and its attendant machinations, other sources confirm that he opted to sign instead with Ashley Kozak, former jazz musician turned booking agent and manager, who used the voracious Allen Klein as an intermediary to arrive at Donovan's introduction to independent producer Mickie Most. Whilst this relationship with Most and arranger John Cameron would offer him much by way of creative support and inspiration – they started working together at Abbey Road in December – Most was over-zealous in striking a deal with Epic Records for the US distribution of Donovan's new material, since it contravened Pye's existing US licensing arrangement with Warner Brothers. In retaliation, Pye blocked the UK release of his next single and LP for twelve months; meaning that after one frustratingly tantalising performance early in 1966 on BBC TV's new cultural magazine programme *A Whole Scene Going* (presented by Wendy Varnals and Barry Fantoni) of "Sunshine Superman", which I can still recall to this day for its power to make me sit up and take notice of its electrifying originality, in Britain at least he disappeared into a prolonged musical exile.

A far less turbulent dimension of the union of folk influences with pop in 1965 was represented by Australian group the Seekers, in many ways a reincarnation of the long-departed Springfields under the influence and musical direction of Dusty's brother Tom. Founded in Melbourne in December 1962 as a traditional folk group, originally a part-time all-male quartet playing acoustic instruments, by 1964 there had been a change of line-up; three of the founding members (Keith Potger and Bruce Woodley on guitars, and Athol Guy on double bass) now fronted by a female lead singer, Judith Durham (who could also play piano and tambourine). Working their passage from Australia as resident musical entertainers on the *SS Fairsky*, after a long voyage they arrived in England, intending only to take a brief holiday here to see the sights of London before returning home. However, tapes they had sent in advance to agent Eddie Jarrett had enabled him to negotiate slots for them on British television, so that on the very day of their landfall they were whisked off to play on the BBC's popular early evening programme *Tonight* and within a month had made their debut appearance on *Sunday Night At The*

London Palladium; thereafter maintaining a regular television presence from my memory on shows such as *Hoot'nanny* (a pseudo-folk music programme broadcast from Edinburgh that popularised the Corries).

Jarrett formed a production company with Tom Springfield to exploit the Seekers' recording potential and a deal was struck with EMI's Columbia label, resulting in the release of their first UK single in December 1964. The song, "I'll Never Find Another You", was the first of three consecutive hits in the course of 1965 to be composed and produced for them by Springfield. Thus, not unexpectedly, it was traditional in its feel, unashamedly revisiting the themes of earlier hits such as "You'll Never Walk Alone" and "I Remember You" in a renewed endeavour to explore the increasingly unfashionable theme of the constancy of love:

> There is always someone
> For each of us, they say,
> And you'll be my someone
> For ever and a day.
> I could search the whole world over
> Until my life is through
> But I know I'll never find another you.
>
> It's a long, long journey,
> So stay by my side.
> When I walk through that storm,
> You'll be my guide (be my guide) …[266]

Favoured with regular airplay not just on the BBC but also on Radio Caroline (thus demonstrating the breadth of their popular appeal) and entering the Top 30 at No.24 in late January, in the week ending 20th February it displaced the Kinks' "Tired Of Waiting For You" to take the No.1 position, where it stayed for two weeks. Overall, it spent 16 weeks in the charts, up to and including the week ending 8th May, an extraordinary achievement for a hitherto unknown group from overseas. Indeed, for the last four of those weeks it shared chart honours with their follow-up single, "A World Of Our Own", which in its turn rose to No.2 for three out of the four weeks from the week ending 15th May onwards.

After a long hiatus, they struck gold again with their third single, "The Carnival Is Over", majestically slower than their previous two offerings and exhibiting Springfield's long-held passion for music from around the world in his adaptation of a Russian melody. It entered the Top 30 at the end of October and made No.1 in the week ending 4th December, immediately prior to the Beatles' Christmas onslaught with "Day Tripper/We Can Work It Out"; but as with "I'll Never Find Another You", the record had remarkable staying power and altogether lasted 15 weeks in the charts until the beginning of February 1966. The final accolade of the year for the Seekers was to be voted the Best New/Most Promising Group of 1965 in the *NME*'s annual poll, a title they, as the unlikeliest of bedfellows, now held in common with its inaugural winners from the year before, the Rolling Stones.

Just as 1965 witnessed the demise of Mersey Beat as the driving force at the heart of pop, in the wider realms of history it similarly marked the passing of the old guard. January and December respectively saw the deaths of literary greats T. S. Eliot and Somerset Maugham; but way above these in terms of national mourning came the loss, on 24th January, of Winston Churchill, almost ten years on from when, at the age of 80, he had relinquished his second premiership of the twentieth century in 1955. This latter-day Renaissance man – soldier, prize-winning author, statesman and inspirational leader of the country for the duration of World War Two – was duly honoured by a state funeral on 30th January worthy of comparison to those afforded to Nelson and Wellington before him. The sombreness of the occasion was emphasised not only by the black and white pictures tracking the cortege's procession to St. Paul's Cathedral in the course of a live broadcast believed then to have attracted the largest television audience ever to date but also by the unmistakeable hushed tones of the reverential – and revered – long-serving BBC commentator Richard Dimbleby (who himself died in December).

With Harold Wilson in power after Labour's election victory of October 1964, Sir Alec Douglas-Home finally relinquished his role as stopgap leader of the Conservative Party in July, having weathered the aftermath of the Profumo scandal but then being unable to ride out Tory discontent at the loss of a March by-election in a Scottish constituency to Liberal candidate David Steel (who, at 26, became Britain's youngest MP). He was replaced by the almost equally uncharismatic Edward Heath, beating both the favourite for the post, Reginald Maudling, and rank outsider Enoch Powell in the first leadership contest to be determined – under new procedures devised by Douglas-Home – by the votes of fellow MPs. Wilson, however, faced increasing difficulties of his own on the foreign policy front when, on 11th November, Ian Smith, Prime Minister of Rhodesia, the last British colony in Africa, circumvented the Governor-General as the Queen's proxy head of state by announcing UDI (i.e., a unilateral declaration of independence from the Commonwealth) and thereby triggering a constitutional crisis. Unwilling to countenance mounting a military intervention against Smith's illegal white minority regime, Wilson was obliged instead to opt for the imposition of economic sanctions as a punitive measure, the most prominent of these being an embargo on oil exports to Rhodesia, whilst he and his Cabinet reflected further over Christmas on negotiating a face-saving diplomatic outcome.

These, of course, were as nothing compared to the tribulations of US President Lyndon Johnson. Having completed his unelected term of office following the death of President Kennedy, as noted in the last chapter he had submitted himself for election in November 1964 and secured a second term as 36th President with an overwhelming majority over his ultra-right-wing Republican opponent Barry Goldwater. In his campaign, he had "painted Goldwater as a dangerous extremist who might lead the United States into World War III and presented himself as a man of peace", vowing that: "We are not about to send American boys nine or ten thousand miles from home to do what Asian boys should be doing for themselves."[267] Resuming power in January 1965, he was nevertheless already heavily committed to an escalation of American involvement in the Vietnam War, signalled spectacularly on 11th February by the commencement of air raids on targets in North Vietnam, a strategy that achieved euphemistic notoriety as 'Rolling Thunder': "Within weeks, the use of napalm as well as conventional bombs had been approved, and by April 1965 American aircrews, with token participation from the South Vietnamese Air Force, were flying over 3,000 bombing sorties a month against North Vietnam."[268]

This was followed by the landing, on 8th March, of a sizeable force of US Marines to reinforce the garrison at Da Nang airbase, at the southern extremity of the infamous Gulf of Tonkin on the north-western coast of South Vietnam. But on 29th June, a truly historic turning-point was reached when it was reported that US ground troops had been deployed for the first time in direct action against Viet Cong guerrillas:

> In a joint operation with South Vietnamese forces they overran a network of trenches and tunnels in a Viet Cong stronghold 30 miles east of Saigon.
>
> Most of the 173rd Airborne Brigade were flown into the area yesterday by 130 helicopters, but only light contact was made as the guerrillas melted into jungle and deep swamp infested with leeches.
>
> Despite its lack of results the operation was important because it marks the beginning of the regular commitment of American troops in an offensive role.
>
> It follows the announcement three weeks ago that US forces had been authorised to give "combat support" to Vietnamese troops. While this is qualified, in that the Vietnamese must request assistance and the Americans must operate alongside South Vietnamese troops, it is felt in Saigon that the Americans will soon become the major partners.[269]

A month later, Johnson announced that another 50,000 US troops were to be sent to Vietnam, bringing their total to 125,000, an action he justified on the grounds that "we have learned at a terrible and brutal cost that retreat does not bring safety and weakness does not bring peace".[270] However, historian Christian G. Appy reminds us that he had also "privately authorised an additional one hundred thousand by the end of 1965, raising the total to almost two hundred thousand" and "left the door open for further escalations to come".[271]

For all the apparent evidence to the contrary, Johnson was a man deeply troubled by the responsibilities he bore as Commander-in-Chief. In November, at a briefing meeting in the Oval Office of the White House with his Joint Chiefs of Staff, he was incredulous almost to the point of apoplexy at their proposals to heighten the offensive against North Vietnam, his summary of what they had presented to him being dismissively brusque: "So you're going to cut them off, keep them from being reinforced, and then you're going to bomb them into the Stone Age."[272] When they showed no sign of comprehending the depths of the anxieties their plans had raised in him, he uncompromisingly spelt it out for them:

> "I'm going to ask you a question and I want you to give me an
> answer. Imagine that you're me – that you're the President of the
> United States – and five incompetents come into your office and
> try to talk you into starting World War III. Then let's see what kind
> of guts you have with the whole damn world to worry about. What
> would you do?" The silence was overpowering.[273]

After which rebuke, he threw them out, cursing them roundly for having "contaminated my office".[274]

Unfortunately for him, his preferred path at home of legislating to promote greater racial equality and harmony was also strewn with obstacles. As noted by a contemporary report, on 11th August, in a heatwave-stricken Los Angeles:

> … a police patrol arrested a black man for drunken driving. Within
> hours, Watts, an area of the city which is mainly inhabited by
> blacks, was in flames, with roof-top snipers ignoring a curfew and
> shooting at police. Fire and ambulance men were enlisted to contain
> the worst outbreak of racial rioting in the United States since the
> [Second World] War.[275]

It took six days and the deployment of more than 14,000 California National Guardsmen to bring the rioting under control. In that period 3,500 arrests were made, over 1,000 people sustained serious injuries and there were 34 deaths. The estimated cost of the damage to property was in the region of $40 million.

Perversely, if Johnson were to find any comfort, it would be in the undeclared Cold War in the heavens, where America and Russia continued to trade exploratory blows in the ever more rapid acceleration of their respective space programmes. In response to advance notice of American intentions, Russia seized the initiative with the launch on 18th March of the two-man Voskhod 2, crewed by Pavel Belyayev and Alexei Leonov, with the latter becoming the first ever human being to walk in space, for ten minutes "held like a feather in still air, yet travelling at 17,400 mph": "I had never felt anything quite like it before. I was free above the planet Earth and I saw it – saw it was rotating majestically below me. Suddenly in the silence, I heard the words: "Attention, attention! Man has entered open space."[276]

Leonov's triumph, confirmed by live television pictures beamed back to Earth, was perilously shortlived. Firstly, his return to the safety of the space-craft was severely impeded by the unforeseen expansion of his spacesuit, which he had to struggle to depressurise; but once he was finally back inside with Belyayev, the cosmonauts were unable to make the exit hatch completely airtight and in compensation their spacecraft's atmosphere was automatically enriched with a dangerously high level of oxygen. Then they discovered that their automatic guidance and stabilisation system had failed, forcing them to manually control their descent for re-entry, and they landed a thousand miles off track in the Urals, their craft crashing into remote snow-covered forest and jamming between two fir trees off the ground. Soon located by helicopter, they could not, however, be physically extricated by a rescue force on the ground until the following day, narrowly escaping hypothermia after further torment overnight from cabin fans they couldn't switch off constantly circulating cold air from a malfunctioning heating system.

Although the mission's outcome was celebrated as a victory, the prob-lems encountered had been of such magnitude that Russia would not attempt manned spaceflight for another two years. Instead, from May onwards they turned their attention to launching a succession of unmanned probes at and around the Moon (some of which failed on takeoff, others crashed into it and yet another missed it by as much as 100,000 miles), before looking even further afield to Venus. This left the stage clear for NASA to pursue its Gemini programme, which it did both vigorously and audaciously with five manned missions completed by Christmas.

The first of these, Gemini 3, less than a week after the Russian Voskhod flight, ended in farcical recrimination when it was discovered that Gus Grissom had part-eaten a corned beef sandwich smuggled on board by his partner John Young as a jokey 'experiment'. The subsequent outrage expressed at this breach of flight protocol by NASA's medical staff and electrical engi-neers even spread to the US Congress, where several excitable politicians saw an opportunity to grab "newspaper space by shouting that NASA 'had lost all control of its astronauts'".[277] With order reimposed by a strict directive from Co-ordinator of Astronaut Activities Deke Slayton threatening disciplinary action for any such future misdemeanours, the programme proceeded apace. Its highlights included Gemini 4, launched on 3rd June to facilitate the first US spacewalk, by astronaut Ed White (partnered on this flight by James McDivitt); and, on 15th December, the first rendezvous in space, at a final reputed distance of no more than six to eight inches, between Gemini 6A (crewed by Wally Schirra and Tom Stafford) and Gemini 7 (crewed by Frank Borman and Jim Lovell, who themselves spent a record-breaking fourteen days in orbit).

Back in England, however, the common man was less likely to be challenged by the implications of the superpowers' race to master compliant post-war rocket technology than by a more down-to-earth array of ethical and moral considerations. In what many must have seen as a discomforting juxtaposition, reports on 28th October of committal proceedings against Ian Brady and Myra Hindley – on charges relating to the abduction, abuse and murder of a number of children whose bodies they then buried on Saddleworth Moor, to the north-east of Greater Manchester – were swiftly followed on 8th November by the passing into law of the Murder (Abolition of the Death Penalty) Act, thus setting the final seal on Sydney Silverman's Parliamentary initiative of the year before. And lest it be thought that 1965 denoted any specific watershed in the moral laxity of the population as a whole, take heed that on 29th November a middle-aged teacher and housewife from Essex, Mary Whitehouse, announced the foundation of a National Viewers' and Listeners' Association, the latest vehicle in her ongoing campaign as self-appointed public censor to hold the BBC to account for what she saw as the increasingly undesirable content of its programming.

There can be no denying that in 1965 the decade had entered more turbulent times, nor that those growing uncertainties and instabilities were increasingly being reflected in new trends in popular music, especially as the balance of artistic supremacy shifted to and fro across the Atlantic. In particular, despite the seeming disregard for many other dimensions of current affairs that inevitably impinged upon the public consciousness at large, there was no escaping the impact of the growing body of protest against the war in Vietnam on both American and British songwriters and musicians; whilst the ever-expanding influence of the Beatles had cast them as the *de facto* heads of an exclusive, jet-setting transatlantic inner circle. Furthermore, the most successful established acts, together with the sharpest of those newcomers who similarly aspired to greatness, were only too aware that having collectively created a new art form in pop, then their role as mass entertainers could now provide them with a platform, if not to be overtly political, at least to be outspoken, more direct, to shake off what they saw as unnecessary constraints imposed on them by an older order; to which the undisputed key was devoting more time to writing and recording their own compositions.

As this latest realisation, born out of a rising spirit of *laissez faire* amongst the self-made heavyweights of the pop world, slowly came to fruition, at the same time it was, however, all set to bring with it the serious risk of conflict and disaffection in the year to come.

NOTES

1   John Lennon, "The Beatles Anthology" (Cassell, 2000), p.174.

2   Peter Ames Carlin, "Catch A Wave: The Rise, Fall and Redemption of The Beach Boys' Brian Wilson" (Rodale, 2006), pp.61-62.

3   With Paul and Jane Asher then on holiday in Tunisia, the wedding guests on this occasion were John and Cynthia Lennon, George and Pattie Boyd, Ringo's mother and stepfather and Maureen's mother. Afterwards, they all attended a wedding breakfast laid on by Brian Epstein at his house in Belgravia. [See Cynthia Lennon, op. cit., pp.203-204.]

4   John Lennon, "The Beatles Anthology" (Cassell, 2000), p.173.

5   John Lennon, op. cit., p.171.

6   Lennon/McCartney, © 1965 by Northern Songs Ltd.

7   Quoted in Barry Miles, "Paul McCartney: Many Years From Now" (Henry Holt, 1997), p.195.

8   Quoted in Barry Miles, op. cit., p.204.

9   Lennon/McCartney, © 1965 by Northern Songs Ltd.

10   Paul McCartney, "The Beatles Anthology" (Cassell, 2000), p.175. Take 1 from 14th June can be found on *The Beatles Anthology Vol.2* (Apple/EMI, 1996).

11   George Martin, ibid.

12   Ibid.

13   Ian MacDonald, op. cit., p.139.

14   Paul McCartney, "The Beatles Anthology" (Cassell, 2000), p.181.

15   John Lennon, op. cit., p.176.

16   Mark Lewisohn, op. cit., p.199.

17   John Lennon, "The Beatles Anthology" (Cassell, 2000), p.187.

18   Ringo Starr, ibid.

19   From Brian Epstein's manuscript notes reproduced in "The Beatles Anthology" (Cassell, 2000), p.192.

20   John Lennon, ibid.

21   Ringo Starr, ibid.

22 Not that it always followed. Their meeting with the princesses of Motown, the Supremes, at their New York hotel earlier in the tour, although admittedly a promotional set-up on behalf of the girl group, had been a disaster. While "the Beatles … sat around in dirty jeans and T-shirts looking rather out of it", the girls, "decked out in elegant day dresses, hats and jewelry, and each wrapped in fur … couldn't engage them even in small talk." They soon made their excuses and left. [See Mark Ribowsky, "The Supremes: A Saga of Motown Dreams, Success, and Betrayal" (Da Capo, 2009), p.231.]

23 See Joel Whitburn (ed.), "The *Billboard* Book of Top 40 Hits" (Billboard, 9th edition, 2010), pp.866-867.

24 While Richards' principal claim to fame derived from his work with the Hollies, there are other, lost gems to his credit; including a personal favourite of mine, the Quiet Five's exquisite non-hit on Parlophone from April 1965, "When The Morning Sun Dries The Dew".

25 See Ian MacDonald, op. cit., p.146.

26 George Harrison, "The Beatles Anthology" (Cassell, 2000), p.196.

27 Ringo Starr, op. cit., p.197.

28 John Lennon, ibid.

29 Ibid.

30 Lennon/McCartney, © 1965 by Northern Songs Ltd.

31 John Lennon, op. cit., p.193.

32 Paul McCartney, op. cit., p.198.

33 John Lennon, op. cit., p.199.

34 Ringo Starr, ibid.

35 Information collated from: Martin Creasy, "Beatlemania! The Real Story of The Beatles UK Tours 1963-1965" (Omnibus, 2010); and Bill Wyman's personal diaries, as included in Bill Wyman with Richard Havers, "Rolling With The Stones" (Dorling Kindersley, 2002).

36 Reproduced in Bill Wyman with Richard Havers, op. cit., p.165.

37 Keith Richards with James Fox, op. cit., pp.172-173.

38 Jagger/Richards, © 1965 by ABKCO Music Inc. USA/Essex Music International Ltd. London.

39 Keith Richards with James Fox, op. cit., p.174.

40 Andrew Loog Oldham, "2Stoned" (Vintage, 2003), p.183.

41 On which their support acts included Dave Berry and the Cruisers, the Hollies and American girl group Goldie and the Gingerbreads.

42 Keith Richards with James Fox, op. cit., p.176.

43 Jagger/Richards, © 1965 by ABKCO Music Inc. USA/Essex Music International Ltd. London.

44 Jagger/Richards, © 1965 by ABKCO Music Inc. USA/Essex Music International Ltd.

London.

45   Bill Wyman in particular had been caught short on a car journey back from Romford, after they had played the last concert of their UK tour there on the night of 18th March.

46   After the Everlys and Elvis came the Shadows' "Wonderful Land" and Frank Ifield's "I Remember You", both at No.1 for 8 consecutive weeks in 1962. Other than "Tears", the remaining records at No.1 for 6 consecutive weeks were: the Shadows' "Apache" (1960), Cliff's "The Young Ones" (1962) and two from the Beatles, "I Want To Hold Your Hand" (1963-64) and "I Feel Fine" (1964-65). (Although "She Loves You" was also No.1 for 6 weeks, in 1963, this was in two separate stints of 4 and 2 weeks, with a 7-week interval between them.)

47   Jagger/Richards, © 1965 by ABKCO Music Inc. USA/Essex Music International Ltd. London.

48   It was another LP predominantly made up of R&B or soul covers, with only four of the twelve tracks original compositions. Reaching No.2 in the British LP charts, it was the ninth best-selling album of the year.

49   Keith Richards with James Fox, op. cit., p.179.

50   Keith Richards with James Fox, op. cit., p.180.

51   Bill Wyman with Richard Havers, op. cit., p.193.

52   Bill Wyman with Richard Havers, op. cit., p.194.

53   Christopher Sandford, "The Rolling Stones: Fifty Years" (Simon & Schuster, 2012), p.94.

54   Bill Wyman with Richard Havers, op. cit., p.208.

55   Bill Wyman with Richard Havers, op. cit., p.211. Although this episode is recounted in all the standard Stones' biographies, Keith himself obviously attached no significance to it, since he makes no reference to it at all in his 2010 autobiography "Life".

56   Keith Richards with James Fox, op. cit., pp.189-190.

57   Keith Richards with James Fox, op. cit., p.191.

58   Ibid.

59   See Christopher Sandford, op. cit., pp.88 & 95.

60   Eric Clapton with Christopher Simon Sykes, op. cit., p.55.

61   Ibid.

62   Eric Clapton with Christopher Simon Sykes, op. cit., p.59.

63   Ibid.

64   Eric Clapton with Christopher Simon Sykes, op. cit., p.62.

65   Quoted in Christopher Hjort, "Strange Brew: Eric Clapton & The British Blues Boom 1965-1970" (Jawbone, 2007), p.14.

66   Ibid.

67   This is Clapton's own version of the famous urban myth, referenced from his autobiography. It reputedly multiplied from there. Alan Clayson, for example, credits it

with having been written on a toilet wall at the Marquee Club: see his "The Yardbirds" (Backbeat, 2002), p.86.

68   Quoted in Alan Clayson, "The Yardbirds" (Backbeat, 2002), p.77.

69   "Evil Hearted You" was included with the Sun Studios tracks on their US-only LP *Having A Rave Up With The Yardbirds*, released on 20th November 1965.

70   Michael Aldred, LP sleevenotes to *The Kink Kontroversy* (Pye, 1965).

71   Dave Davies, op. cit., pp.78-79.

72   Ray Davies, op. cit., p.224.

73   Dave Davies, op. cit., p.68.

74   Ray Davies, op. cit., p.233.

75   Ibid.

76   Ray Davies, op. cit., pp.233-234.

77   Ray Davies, op. cit., p.204.

78   Dave Davies, op. cit., pp.74-75.

79   Nick Hasted, "The Story of The Kinks: You Really Got Me" (Omnibus, 2011), pp.62-63.

80   At Larry Page's behest, the Kinks had recorded "Ring The Bells" on 30th June at the Gold Star Studios, Hollywood, in the course of their first US tour. Talmy threatened legal action to secure the previously slated release of "See My Friends" and "Ring The Bells" was later re-recorded in London for inclusion on *The Kink Kontroversy* LP.

81   With his wife Rasa at the Imperial Hotel, Torquay in July, following the conclusion of the Kinks' first US tour.

82   Quoted in Nick Hasted, op. cit., pp.65-66.

83   Ray Davies, © 1965 by Edward Kassner Music Co. Ltd.

84   Its companion tracks being Dave's song "Wait Till The Summer Comes Along" and two other songs by Ray, "Such A Shame" and "Don't You Fret". It was, however, released as a single in the USA, where it reached No.13 in the *Billboard* Top 40.

85   Doug Hinman notes a crucial meeting between the three of them on 2nd August: "Simkins advises them that according to his interpretation of their contract Ray is free to sign whatever publishing deal he wishes. Simkins says Ray is not personally bound to Kassner beyond the songs that have been assigned so far, because there was never a signed contract directly between Davies and Kassner." [Op. cit., p.62.]

86   The Kinks, it seemed, were on a downward slide with each successive LP. *Kinks*, with 25 weeks in the LP charts, had reached No.3; as had *Kinda Kinks*, but over a much reduced period of 15 weeks.

87   Dave Davies, op. cit., p.57.

88   Rasa Didzpetris, the German-born daughter of Lithuanian refugees who had settled in Bradford, was married to Ray on 12th December 1964, having first met him earlier that year after a Kinks' gig at the Esquire Club in Sheffield on 19th May.

89   And thus the inspiration for the Kinks' 1969 LP, *Arthur (Or The Decline And Fall Of The*

British Empire).

90   Ray Davies, op. cit., p.255.

91   Nick Hasted, op. cit., p.74.

92   Ray Davies, op. cit., p.266.

93   Dave Davies, op. cit., p.85.

94   Ray Davies, op. cit., p.270.

95   Pete Townshend, "Who I Am" (Harper Collins, 2012), p.298.

96   Pete Townshend, op. cit., p.31.

97   Ibid.

98   Alan Clayson, "Keith Moon – Instant Party: Musings, Memories and Minutiae" (Chrome Dreams, 2005), p.27.

99   Tim Ewbank & Stafford Hildred, "Roger Daltrey: The Biography" (Piatkus, 2012), p.26.

100 Tim Ewbank & Stafford Hildred, op. cit., p.24.

101 Alan Clayson, op. cit., p.29.

102 Pete Townshend, op. cit., p.57.

103 Tim Ewbank & Stafford Hildred, op. cit., p.28.

104 Quoted in Andy Neill & Matt Kent, "Anyway Anyhow Anywhere: The Complete Chronicle of The Who 1958-1978" (Virgin, 2007), p.38.

105 Quoted in Andy Neill & Matt Kent, op. cit., pp.2-3.

106 Arranged, on Kit Lambert's behalf, through the intercession of friend and business associate Russ Conway, who also lent the group his Rolls Royce for the day. [See Tim Ewbank & Stafford Hildred, op. cit., p.50.]

107 Including Clem Cattini, Jimmy Page and vocalists the Ivy League – John Carter, Ken Lewis & Perry Ford.

108 Pete Townshend, op. cit., p.77.

109 Quoted in CD liner notes to *My Generation – The Very Best Of The Who* (Polydor, 1966).

110 Townshend/Daltrey, © 1965 by Fabulous Music Ltd.

111 Andy Neill & Matt Kent, op. cit., p.67.

112 Ibid.

113 Pete Townshend, op. cit., p.83.

114 Pete Townshend, op. cit., pp.83-84.

115 Townshend, © 1965 by Fabulous Music Ltd.

116 There is no unanimity in relevant reference works as to when this incident actually occurred. It is commonly placed later, in October, in closer proximity to the release of "My Generation" as a single. However, in the CD liner notes to the deluxe edition of *My Generation*, Mike Shaw, who worked closely with Kit Lambert and Chris Stamp

as the Who's first production manager, unequivocally dates it to 25th September 1965. This is supported, though not definitively confirmed, by Andy Neill and Matt Kent in their comments on "an ugly backstage incident … resulting in Daltrey being unanimously fired from the group" [op. cit., pp.93-94] while the Who were in Denmark on 25th and 26th September; whereas in October, they record the group as only otherwise having been in Scandinavia (Sweden) for one day, the 10th, without altercation.

117 Tim Ewbank & Stafford Hildred, op. cit., p.80.

118 Tim Ewbank & Stafford Hildred, op. cit., p.81.

119 Tim Ewbank & Stafford Hildred, op. cit., p.69.

120 Which itself had been preceded by the release in October 1964 of another miss, the equally strong "Last Night (I Made A Little Girl Cry)".

121 Under the title "Goodbye My Lover Goodbye" - causing Chris Curtis to claim in later years that it was really about the break-up of a gay relationship.

122 The B-side, "Till I Met You", is, by comparison, stunningly beautiful in its simplicity, with a sparing acoustic accompaniment, composed by John McNally as a love song to his wife Mary though credited by mutual agreement to the whole group.

123 Namely: "Bumble Bee", "Everything You Do", "Magic Potion" and "If I Could Find Someone".

124 Frank Allen, op. cit., p.187.

125 Frank Allen, op. cit., p.188.

126 Quoted by Spencer Leigh in his CD liner notes to *Herman's Hermits & Peter Noone: Into Something Good. The Mickie Most Years 1964-1972* (EMI, 2008).

127 Stefan Granados, CD liner notes to *The Mindbenders: A Groovy Kind Of Love – The Complete LP's & Singles 1966-1968* [RPM, 2010].

128 Founded as an independent label in 1947, Imperial became a subsidiary imprint of Liberty Records from 1963 onwards and was also the US record distributor for the Swinging Blue Jeans and Billy J. Kramer and the Dakotas.

129 Only five of the twelve tracks on *Hollies* were originals, as opposed to the seven included on the preceding *In The Hollies Style*.

130 Quoted in Sean Egan, op. cit., p.80.

131 Eric Burdon, op. cit., p.63.

132 Which can be found on *The Red Bird Story* (Charly, 2011). Mann and Weil had given Allen Klein a copy of Mann's demo, only to find that he had then forwarded it to Mickie Most.

133 Sean Egan, op. cit., p.90.

134 Mann/Weil, © 1965 by Screen Gems/EMI Music Ltd. Its resonance has continued down the years. When I came to leave teaching at Christmas 1982, by which time I had become a sixth-form tutor in a 12-18 comprehensive school in Warwick, it just had to be the piece of music I chose to round off my farewell address to my last-ever sixth-form assembly.

135 Quoted in Sean Egan, op. cit., p.95.

136   The first, self-composed song of that title the group recorded, not to be confused with their later recording in 1967 of an identically titled Les Reed/Barry Mason composition, which reached No.2 that December.

137   And released in the USA as *Having A Wild Weekend*, where it still seems to enjoy something of a cult status.

138   Sister of actress Pam Ferris, Barbara had previously appeared in Michael Winner's *The System*, the 1964 film for which the Searchers had recorded the title song, as mentioned in Chapter 6.

139   Tom McGuinness, CD liner notes to *Manfred Mann: Down The Road Apiece – Their EMI Recordings 1963-1965* (EMI, 2007).

140   Jones, © 1965 by Cooper Music Ltd.

141   Ibid.

142   Quoted in Greg Russo, "Mannerisms: The Five Phases of Manfred Mann" (Crossfire, 1995), p.32.

143   Quoted in Greg Russo, op. cit., p.33.

144   Ibid.

145   Tom McGuinness, CD liner notes to *Manfred Mann: Down The Road Apiece – Their EMI Recordings 1963-1965* (EMI, 2007).

146   Roger Dopson, CD liner notes to *The Rockin' Berries: They're In Town* – The Pye Anthology (Sequel, 1998). Dopson also notes that shortly after the release of "Poor Man's Son", original bass guitarist Roy Austin had left, to be replaced by Liverpudlian Bobby Thomson – who, some years before, had played with Ringo Starr in Rory Storm and the Hurricanes.

147   Ibid.

148   Published by Ovolo, 2008.

149   Also covered by the Searchers at around the same time – to whose harmonies it was possibly better suited – as a track on their fourth LP, *Sounds Like Searchers*.

150   Quoted by John Reed, CD liner notes to *The Spencer Davis Group: Eight Gigs A Week – The Steve Winwood Years* (Chronicles/Island, 1996).

151   Ibid.

152   Born Clive Powell in Lancashire, in the late Fifties Fame had been hired – and renamed – by agent and manager Larry Parnes as a pianist in a band accompanying solo artists on tour such as Marty Wilde, Gene Vincent and Billy Fury, later branching out to play exclusively for Fury with the original Blue Flames before parting company with Parnes in 1962.

153   The original line-up was: Van Morrison (vocals, harmonica & saxophone), Billy Harrison (lead guitar), Alan Henderson (bass guitar), Eric Wrixon (keyboards) and Ronnie Millings (drums). When they decided to further their career in England, Wrixon stayed in Belfast to complete his A Levels and was replaced by Pat McAuley.

154   Morrison, © 1964 by Carlin Music Corp.

155   See Lulu, op. cit., p.76.

156 Jackie McAuley, quoted in Pete Frame, "The Beatles and Some Other Guys: Rock Family Trees of the Early Sixties" (Omnibus, 1997), p.31.

157 Ibid.

158 Morrison, "The Story Of Them", © 1967 by Carlin Music Corp.

159 Paolo Hewitt, "The Small Faces: The Young Mods' Forgotten Story" (Acid Jazz, revised edition, 2010), p.35.

160 Paolo Hewitt, op. cit., p.8.

161 Quoted by Paolo Hewitt, op. cit., p.59.

162 Arden would later admit that he paid substantial backhanders to those in a position to manipulate the weekly chart listings. [See Paolo Hewitt, op. cit., p.62.]

163 *Aka* Boz People or just plain Boz, after group leader Ray 'Boz' Burrell. In a move reminiscent of Tito Burns with Tony Jackson of the Searchers, Arden retained Winston as a solo artist, although he was unrewarded by any chart success in that capacity.

164 Quoted by Paolo Hewitt & John Hellier, "Steve Marriott: All Too Beautiful ..." (Helter Skelter, 2004), pp.105-106.

165 Quoted by Paolo Hewitt, op. cit., p.64.

166 Quoted by Paolo Hewitt, op. cit., p.69.

167 The delay of the film's release until April 1966 rendered any tie-in with the single impossible.

168 This was less than coincidence, the song having been written and recorded by US country singer Buck Owens in direct response to Esso's campaign launched across America in 1964.

169 At the same time, King had also entered the world of pop management and record production with Hedgehoppers Anonymous, who sang his composition "It's Good News Week".

170 Although she featured the song as a support artist on the Beatles' final UK tour in December, her fifteen minutes of chart fame were, sadly, already over.

171 Marianne Faithfull with David Dalton, op. cit., p.46.

172 Marianne Faithfull with David Dalton, op. cit., pp.49-50.

173 Marianne Faithfull with David Dalton, op. cit., p.47.

174 Ibid.

175 Ibid.

176 Marianne Faithfull with David Dalton, op. cit., p.52.

177 In her autobiography, Faithfull states that the year before she became pregnant with her son by Dunbar, she had aborted an unborn child fathered by Gene Pitney; but if one accepts the accuracy of her touring chronology, which offers no evidence of her meeting Pitney until the spring of 1965, then this cannot be so.

178 Marianne Faithfull with David Dalton, op. cit., p.61.

179 Marianne Faithfull with David Dalton, op. cit., p.65.

180   Marianne Faithfull with David Dalton, op. cit., p.80.

181   Quoted in Sharon Davis, op. cit., p.61.

182   Op. cit., p.70.

183   Quoted in Paul Howes, op. cit., p.218.

184   Sandie Shaw, op. cit., p.16.

185   Ibid.

186   Hatch, © 1965 by ATV Music Ltd.

187   Hatch, © 1965 by ATV Music Ltd.

188   Cilla Black, op. cit., p.125.

189   Mark Ribowsky, "The Supremes: A Saga of Motown Dreams, Success and Betrayal"
      (Da Capo, 2009), pp.198-199.

190   The end-result, in fact, of what had originated as a proposed television showcase for
      Dusty, onto which she had planned to invite Martha and the Vandellas as her special
      guests, before events were overtaken by the announcement of the Motown tour.

191   Sharon Davis, op. cit., p.68.

192   Quoted in Keith Badman, op. cit., p.83.

193   Keith Badman, op. cit., p.89.

194   Ibid.

195   Quoted in Keith Badman, op. cit., p.85.

196   Quoted in Keith Badman, op. cit., p.89.

197   In which, of course, "… the Ukraine girls really knock me out/They leave the West
      behind/And Moscow girls make me sing and shout/That Georgia's always on my
      mind." Lennon & McCartney, © 1968 by Northern Songs Ltd.

198   The song is a cover of a 1961 US Top 20 hit by Italian-Americans the Regents.

199   Quoted in Keith Badman, op. cit., p.105.

200   Side 1 of the American version omits "Drive My Car" (opening instead with "I've Just
      Seen A Face") and "Nowhere Man". Side 2 omits "What Goes On" (substituting "It's
      Only Love") and "If I Needed Someone". All four missing tracks were later included
      on the Beatles' next Capitol LP Yesterday … And Today, released on 20th June 1966. [See
      Mark Lewisohn, op. cit., p.351.]

201   Quoted in Keith Badman, op. cit., p.104.

202   Ibid.

203   Robert Shelton, op. cit., p.203.

204   Dylan's own words describing his earlier works, from a TV press conference, San
      Francisco, December 1965, in "Dylan on Dylan: The Essential Interviews", ed. by
      Jonathan Cott (Hodder, 2007), p.78.

205   Robert Shelton, op. cit., p.189.

206   Robert Shelton was moved in admiration to profess: "If given a time limit to illustrate

his gifts, I would play the 23 minutes of side two." See op. cit., p.193.

207 D.A. Pennebaker, transcript of *Dont Look Back* (New Video Group Inc., 2006), p.21.

208 Interview with Nora Ephron & Susan Edmiston, August 1965, in Jonathan Cott, op. cit., p.54.

209 TV press conference, San Francisco, December 1965, in Jonathan Cott, op. cit., p.64.

210 Joan Baez, quoted in Anthony Scaduto, op. cit., pp.196-197.

211 D.A. Pennebaker, op. cit., p.34.

212 TV press conference, San Francisco, December 1965, in Jonathan Cott, op. cit., p.75.

213 Clinton Heylin, "Revolution in the Air {The Songs of Bob Dylan Vol.1: 1957-73}" (Constable, 2009), p.243. The complete line-up responsible was: Mike Bloomfield (guitar), Bob Dylan (rhythm guitar/harmonica), Joe Macho Jr. (bass guitar), Paul Griffin (piano), Al Kooper (organ), Bruce Langhorne (tambourine) and Bobby Gregg (drums).

214 © 1965 by Warner Bros Inc.; renewed 1993 by Special Rider Music.

215 Ibid.

216 Ibid.

217 TV press conference, San Francisco, December 1965, in Jonathan Cott, op. cit., p.64.

218 Quoted in Greil Marcus, "Like A Rolling Stone: Bob Dylan At The Crossroads" (Public Affairs, 2006), p.70.

219 Greil Marcus, for example, is obsessed with the significance of the "drum beat like a pistol shot" that is the first sound you hear on the recording of "Like A Rolling Stone". For him, without it, the rest of the song would be meaningless: "When drummer Bobby Gregg brought his stick down for the opening noise of the six-minute single, the sound – a kind of announcement, then a void of silence, then a rising fanfare, then the song – fixed a moment when all those caught up in modern music found themselves engaged in a running battle for a prize no one bothered to name: the greatest record ever made, perhaps, or the greatest record that ever would be made." [Op. cit., p.3.]

220 Interview with Nora Ephron & Susan Edmiston, August 1965, in Jonathan Cott, op. cit., p.50. Note that this is an interview given no more than two months after Dylan had recorded "Like A Rolling Stone."

221 TV press conference, San Francisco, December 1965, in Jonathan Cott, op. cit., p.73.

222 Three members of the Paul Butterfield Blues Band (Mike Bloomfield on guitar, Jerome Arnold on bass guitar and Sam Lay on drums) were supplemented by Barry Goldberg on piano and Al Kooper on electric organ.

223 Robert Shelton, op. cit., p.210.

224 Murray Lerner, speaking in the course of an interview for BBC TV's *Arena*, added as a bonus feature to the DVD of his documentary *The Other Side Of The Mirror: Bob Dylan Live At The Newport Folk Festival 1963-1965* (Sony/BMG, 2007).

225 TV press conference, San Francisco, December 1965, in Jonathan Cott, op. cit., p.73.

226 © 1965 by Warner Bros Inc.; renewed 1993 by Special Rider Music.

227   © 1965 by Warner Bros Inc.; renewed 1993 by Special Rider Music.

228   © 1965 by Warner Bros Inc.; renewed 1993 by Special Rider Music.

229   © 1965 by Warner Bros Inc.; renewed 1993 by Special Rider Music.

230   Ibid.

231   © 1965 by Warner Bros Inc.; renewed 1993 by Special Rider Music.

232   Ibid.

233   "Notes by Bob Dylan" to *Highway 61 Revisited* (CBS, 1965).

234   Robert Shelton, op. cit., p.215.

235   Robbie Robertson, quoted in Howard Sounes, op. cit., p.231.

236   Ibid.

237   Ibid.

238   Quoted in Howard Sounes, op. cit., pp.231-232.

239   Before he left, however, Helm had contributed with the Hawks to Dylan's re-recording of "Can You Please Crawl Out Your Window?", enabling Clinton Heylin to confirm that this had therefore taken place in early October – prior to his departure. [See Clinton Heylin, op. cit., p.254.]

240   Quoted in Howard Sounes, op. cit., p.232.

241   This was not the version ultimately included on *Bringing It All Back Home* but an earlier out-take from the recording sessions for *Another Side Of Bob Dylan*, on which Ramblin' Jack Elliott joins in with Dylan on the choruses. [See Clinton Heylin, op. cit., p.185.]

242   Jim Dickson, quoted in Johnny Rogan, "Byrds: Requiem For The Timeless Vol.1" (Rogan House, 2012), p.43.

243   Ibid.

244   Quoted in Johnny Rogan, op .cit., p.64.

245   Quoted in Johnny Rogan, op. cit., p.65.

246   Eddie Tickner, quoted in Johnny Rogan, op. cit., p.73.

247   He sang along with them to their cover of his own "All I Really Want To Do" and played harmonica for the Jimmy Reed number "Baby, What You Want Me To Do". [See Johnny Rogan, op. cit., p.101.]

248   Although this was their debut single with CBS as the Byrds, in the summer of 1964 McGuinn, Clark and Crosby had recorded one earlier, unsuccessful single as the Beefeaters for Jac Holzman's Elektra label: "Please Let Me Love You" b/w "Don't Be Long". [See Mick Houghton, "Becoming Elektra: The True Story of Jac Holzman's Visionary Record Label" (Jawbone, 2010), pp.172-173.]

249   Johnny Rogan, op. cit., p.161.

250   Quoted in Johnny Rogan, op. cit., p.173.

251   Johnny Rogan, Byrds' archivist supreme, tortured himself in his teens by buying their first two LPs without having a record player of his own to play them on! Dependent on the occasional generosity or forbearance of older relatives to hear what they had

recorded, he describes how he looked over and over again at the track titles hitherto unknown to him, wondering what they might sound like. [See Johnny Rogan, op. cit., pp.9-10.] However, Greil Marcus documents an earlier and more widespread occurrence of this phenomenon of imbuing silent, unplayed vinyl with mystical properties, in respect of the release in the USA in 1952 of Harry Smith's three-volume *Anthology Of American Folk Music*, as follows: "Many copies of these records were bought by people without phonographs. They bought the discs as talismans of their own existence; they could hold these objects in their hands and feel their own lives dramatised. In such an act, people discovered the modern world: the thrill of mechanical reproduction." [Greil Marcus, "Invisible Republic: Bob Dylan's Basement Tapes" (Picador, 1998), p.121.]

252   Adapted & music by Pete Seeger, © Melody Train Inc. (BMI).

253   Ibid.

254   They were neither brothers nor any of them called Walker, but a trio of talented musicians - Scott Engel, John Maus and Gary Leeds – of whom, when they first met on the emerging Hollywood club circuit in 1962, only Leeds was a native of California, the other two having moved there as children. After he had toured England in 1964 as P.J. Proby's drummer and finding himself totally in awe of the Beatles' success, Leeds instigated a plan with Engel and Maus to relocate from California to London in February 1965 and make their fortune there. Signed to the Philips label, their UK chart debut "Love Her" made No.18 that June, to be followed by the Top 10 smash hit "Make It Easy On Yourself", which reached No.2 in October. At the beginning of December, "My Ship Is Coming In" entered the Top 30 and would peak at No.4 in mid-January 1966.

255   P.F. Sloan & Steve Barri, © 1965 by Universal/MCA Music Publishing.

256   Ibid.

257   Quoted in Matthew Greenwald, "Go Where You Wanna Go: The Oral History of The Mamas & The Papas" (Cooper Square, 2002), p.87.

258   Donovan Leitch, "The Hurdy Gurdy Man" (Century, 2005), p.104. He sang "Colours" as a duet with Joan Baez when he accompanied her to the 1965 Newport Folk Festival and she paid him the further compliment of recording it as a track on her LP *Farewell Angelina*.

259   Sainte-Marie, © 1965 by Peermusic (UK) Ltd.

260   Ibid.

261   Softley, © 1965 by Peermusic (UK) Ltd.

262   Jansch, © 1965 by Heathside Music.

263   Donovan Leitch, op. cit., p.124.

264   Donovan Leitch, op. cit., p.126. He would finally achieve his due recognition in the guise of "Mother Nature's Son" from Paul McCartney and the Beatles on the 1968 'White Album'.

265   Rob Young, "Electric Eden: Unearthing Britain's Visionary Music" (Faber & Faber, 2010), pp.18-19.

266   Springfield, © 1964 Chappell Music Ltd.

267   Christian G. Appy, op. cit., p.113.

268   Richard Burks Verrone & Laura M. Calkins, "Voices from Vietnam" (David & Charles, 2005), p.40.

269   Derrik Mercer (ed.) et al., op. cit., p.932.

270   Quoted in Derrik Mercer (ed.) et al., op. cit., p.934.

271   Christian G. Appy, op. cit., p.113.

272   Quoted in Christian G. Appy, op. cit., p.122.

273   Quoted in Christian G. Appy, op. cit., p.123.

274   Ibid.

275   Derrik Mercer (ed.) et al., op. cit., p.935.

276   Deborah Cadbury, op. cit., pp.286-287.

277   Alan Shepard & Deke Slayton, op. cit., p.180.

Chapter 8

The acrid smoke from bonfires of burning record sleeves and black vinyl was one of the more unmistakable signs of changing fortunes in the world of pop in the summer of '66, as those who had previously carried torches for the Beatles now opted instead to set torches to their previously cherished discs and memorabilia. True, it was an extreme gesture on the part of a strictly limited minority of fans and their elders in the 'Bible Belt' of America's Deep South, but it was indisputably reflective of an international undercurrent of discontent that hastened the Beatles' decision to forsake live performance once and for all for the sanctuary of the recording studio. In its turn, that decision would mark a watershed for the record industry, portending a slow but steady shift of emphasis throughout the remainder of the decade from the singles market to the increasingly esoteric realms of the long-player – or the album, if you will.

The hellfires breaking out in hotspots across Alabama, Texas and elsewhere that August were manifestations of the offence unintentionally given to those with pronounced religious sensibilities by John Lennon, who, at the age of 25, spake thus:

> Christianity will go … It will vanish and shrink. I needn't argue about that; I'm right and I will be proved right. We're more popular than Jesus now; I don't know which will go first, rock'n'roll or Christianity. Jesus was all right but his disciples were thick and ordinary. It's them twisting it that ruins it for me.[1]

Just one of many musings embedded in the course of a lengthy interview with London journalist Maureen Cleave, published by the *Evening Standard* on 4th March as one of the five profile pieces she wrote on the individual members of the group and their manager, Lennon's thoughts provoked relatively little by way of comment at home in England, other than from like-minded crusty reactionaries of the day such as radio and television personality

Gilbert Harding or actor James Robertson Justice. The spark igniting more serious and sustained protest was the re-publication of the article in America on 29th July, in the teen magazine *Datebook*, fuelled in advance by editor Art Unger through his circulation of copies to local radio stations in the southern States. As author Robert Rodriguez explains, Unger had no particular axe to grind on the issue but "recognized media dynamite when he saw it":

> It didn't take long for the most reactionary broadcasters in America to take the bait. Whatever antipathy they had heretofore largely kept in check against the Beatles, their hair and their latent Negro tendencies (evidenced by their fondness for black artists) had at last been unleashed. Not only did a number of stations announce a boycott of Beatles music on the airwaves ("We're not going to forget what they said …"), but plans were soon announced in Birmingham, Alabama, for a public burning of their product. Chapters of the Ku Klux Klan leapt into the fray, undoubtedly pleased at the novelty of having somebody other than blacks and Jews to threaten. All of this might have stayed a local concern, but for the UPI wire service picking up the story and taking it national.[2]

Unger's timing, on the threshold of the Beatles' latest (and last) US tour, could hardly have been worse – or better, depending on your perspective. Helpless and completely wrongfooted far away in London, press and publicity officer for the group, Tony Barrow, describes how it was that with mounting alarm he watched the wildfires spread:

> Presenters and deejays at radio stations in the South … jumped on the bandwagon and urged young fans to rally round and build ceremonial bonfires on which the Beatles' records were burnt. Some of these stations had never played the group's records in the past but were now moved to ban them anyway. In Mississippi an Imperial Wizard of the Ku Klux Klan announced that he believed The Beatles had been "brainwashed by the Communists". Joining in the holy war with enthusiasm, the Grand Dragon of the KKK in South Carolina tied a bundle of the Beatles' albums to a cross, which he then set alight in front of a cheering crowd. To all but the most biased and prejudiced observers, the fires were publicity stunts to raise the profile of the organising broadcasters … Radio station WAQY in Birmingham, Alabama, announced that The Beatles had been banned because "we consider them unacceptable to many lovers of good music". WTUF in Mobile denounced Lennon's statement as "an outright sacrilegious affront to Almighty God". The gospel-orientated Texan station KZEE decided to ban the Beatles "eternally".[3]

But, as Barrow goes on to note with grim fortitude, regrettably the furore could not just be contained within America, for others around the world were soon sounding off: "the South African Broadcasting Corporation banned the playing of Beatles' records, a Spanish station followed suit and there were attempts by sections of the Dutch population to ban the group's records and refuse permission for The Beatles to appear again in Holland".[4]

Cutting short a holiday in North Wales to review the rapidly worsening PR situation, Brian Epstein eventually decided to proceed with the forthcoming US tour 'in spite of all the danger' (as a juvenile McCartney and Harrison once had it). The tour, to which the Beatles flew out on 11th August, was to be prefaced by a press conference in the Astor Towers Hotel, Chicago, for which both Epstein and Barrow solemnly and specifically briefed Lennon beforehand. With all musical considerations suddenly and urgently becoming very much secondary to damage limitation, John in particular endured a seemingly interminable interrogation by a roomful of hostile American reporters, seeking to turn away their wrath and thus save the tour by offering placatory rationalisations that once or twice came close to being an apology:

> If I'd have said, 'Television is more popular than Jesus,' I might
> have got away with it. I am sorry I opened my mouth. I just
> happened to be talking to a friend and I used the word 'Beatles'
> as a remote thing – 'Beatles', like other people see us. I said they
> are having more influence on kids and things than anything else,
> including Jesus. I said it in that way, which was the wrong way. I'm
> not anti-God, anti-Christ, or anti-religion. I was not knocking it. I
> was not saying we are greater or better. I think it's a bit silly. If they
> don't like us, why don't they just not buy the records?[5]

Mercifully, whatever he said in Chicago and even allowing for however ineptly he said it, it suitably served to appease the majority of his critics, much to the relief of his immediate circle. It was just as well, therefore, that the superficiality of John's responses had evaded detection; for after the event, as Tony Barrow observed, "the old Lennonesque resilience replaced the brief show of remorse and he described the bonfire protesters as 'middle-aged deejays burning a pile of LP covers for an audience of 12-year-olds'".[6]

Nonetheless, the principal objective had been achieved and the tour could now proceed as planned, albeit in the face of some residual opposition; to which, by this point in the year, the Beatles were sadly no stranger. For the 'bigger than Jesus' episode was merely the latest in a series of misfortunes to befall them in the course of their ill-fated 1966 touring programme, preceded as it had been by equally impassioned pleas to the Beatles to go home from angry voices raised against them in Japan and the Philippines.

When they left England on 23rd June for what was to be their last 'world' tour, they had already given their last live performance in Britain, although their bill-topping appearance at the *NME* Poll-Winners Concert on 1st May was to be denied to home television audiences by a contractual dispute with independent broadcaster ABC-TV.[7] After opening with three concerts in West Germany (including a return and farewell to Hamburg), they flew on to Tokyo, where they were due to appear for three consecutive nights (30th June – 2nd July) at the Nippon Budokan Hall. Budokan has long since passed into rock history, notably as the 1978 venue for legendary concerts by Bob Dylan, the recordings of which aroused the interest of a whole new generation of his followers, but back in 1966 the Beatles' venture was ground-breaking. Hitherto, the hall had not been put to such mundane use, having been cherished instead as "an almost sacred place, a highly respected shrine dedicated to the presentation of traditional martial arts tournaments including high-level championship sumo wrestling matches".[8] "In the Budokan," as George would later observe, "only violence and spirituality were approved of, not pop music."[9] Incensed at the imminent prospect of its desecration, extreme right-wing Japanese students openly disseminated death threats against the group, although their full import was kept from the Beatles themselves by a fortuitous combination of Tony Barrow's circumspect stewardship and the language barrier.

While the five scheduled concerts subsequently passed off without incident, they were overshadowed by the understandably high level of security imposed by the Japanese authorities on performers and audience members alike, one aspect of which was the creation of a formidable *cordon sanitaire* around the front of the stage; making it difficult for the Beatles to "establish contact with their audience because it meant bridging the vast gap between where they were singing and playing in the empty ground-floor arena and the two layers of seating on the far side of what amounted to a big dry moat".[10] The opening concert was further hampered by recurring difficulties with microphones, resulting in the Beatles delivering one of their poorest ever performances and leading George, in giving voice to their collective disappointment, to express the unthinkable: "Let's face it, this is as good as it gets for us nowadays on tour. We're burning ourselves out on these pointless stage shows when there are better things we could be doing in the recording studios."[11]

Worse was to follow when they left Tokyo on 3rd July for Manila, capital of the Philippines, thanks to the disingenuousness of local concert promoter Ramon Ramos Jr. In drawing up the itinerary for their short visit, planned around the two concerts they set to play on 4th July, Ramos had neglected to consult Brian Epstein on the possibility of the Beatles attending the Presidential Palace to meet the First Lady, Imelda Marcos, and an invited assembly of children. Furthermore, it had been reported in the Filipino press as a firm engagement, in the clear expectation that the Beatles would duly present themselves at the palace on the morning of the 4th. Oblivious to this undertaking made in their name, Epstein was caught off guard that morning when high-ranking military officers arrived at the Beatles' hotel to accompany them to the reception, peremptorily and undiplomatically refusing to co-operate with them. By the time the Beatles were resting in the interval between their afternoon and evening concerts, this unprecedented snub to the First Lady was headline news on Manila TV, prompting public outrage. Tony Barrow was even advised by the British Embassy that death threats had been made against the group. Although he hastily secured a TV slot that same day for Brian Epstein to broadcast a personal apology, it appeared to be deliberately jammed: "almost everything Epstein said was blotted out by unexplained interference so that nobody heard his explanation."[12]

As a consequence, after the conclusion of the second concert the Beatles and their entourage found themselves subject to a variety of intimidations; including the withdrawal of Filipino security arrangements, hostility from hotel staff, impromptu demands for the payment of taxes and a boycott on assisting their departure next day from Manila Airport. Best efforts to board their flight out to Delhi thus rapidly degenerated into an undignified scrimmage. Brian Epstein – whom John held personally responsible for the entire debacle – was "punched in the face and kicked in the groin", while Mal Evans was "kicked in the ribs and tripped up but he staggered on across the tarmac towards the aircraft with blood streaming down one leg".[13] Yet even making the safety of the plane did not bring the longed-for end to the besieged party's problems, as Barrow and Evans were then recalled to the airport terminal to resolve irregularities in official paperwork relating to their arrival in and departure from the Philippines, thus adding still further delay to take-off until late that afternoon. Once safely up and away from the stultifying heat and humidity they had had to endure whilst stuck on the runway, they savoured resentment in equal measure to relief, already seriously persuaded that touring had finally turned sour on them:

> When they got out of the country they said, 'Never again. This is
> it.' They said to Brian then that they would not tour again. Brian
> said, 'Sorry, lads, we have got something fixed up for Shea Stadium.
> If we cancel it you are going to lose a million dollars ...'[14]

Little wonder, then, that George, when asked on his return to London about the group's future plans, should harbour thoughts of self-preservation in replying: "We're going to have a couple of weeks to recuperate before we go and get beaten up by the Americans."[15] Any hopes of recuperation for Epstein himself in taking a holiday in North Wales were, of course, subsequently dashed when he had to be recalled to deal with the 'bigger than Jesus' crisis; and so it was that the Beatles lurched unwillingly into their final US tour.

As it transpired, the Shea Stadium concerts (on 23rd and 24th August) made an overall loss, with thousands of seats remaining unsold. Earlier on, in Cleveland on 14th August, a major failure of crowd control midway through the Beatles' set allowed fans to break through crush barriers and security fences to invade the stage, from which the group had to make a rapid exit to safety until order was restored. (Similar difficulties at the end of their penultimate concert in Los Angeles on 28th August rendered them virtual prisoners in the Dodger Stadium for more than two hours before they could make their getaway in an armoured car.)

On 19th August in Memphis:

> … somebody let off a firecracker while we were on stage. There had been threats to shoot us, the Klan were burning Beatle records outside and a lot of the crew-cut kids were joining in with them. Somebody let off a firecracker and every one of us – I think it's on film – look at each other, because each thought it was the other that had been shot. It was that bad.[16]

Next day in Cincinnati, heavy rain brought with it the fear of electrocution on the inadequate stage, causing the evening concert to be cancelled and a re-run hastily organised for the following morning, before they flew on to St. Louis for that evening's scheduled gig. As anticipated, the tour had all too soon become a desperate, joyless slog but when they reached San Francisco on 29th August, thankfully the end was in sight:

> When we got to Candlestick Park we placed our cameras on the amplifiers and put them on the timer. We stopped between tunes, Ringo got down off the drums, and we stood facing the amplifiers with our back to the audience and took photographs. We knew. 'This is it – we're not going to do this again. This is the last concert.' It was a unanimous decision.[17]

With the assembled 25,000 fans cooled by a strong breeze blowing in from San Francisco Bay, it took the Beatles barely over half an hour to perform their last ever live concert before a paying audience, beginning with "Rock And Roll Music" and ending with "Long Tall Sally" shortly before 10.00 p.m. – both long-standing, classic crowd-pleasers but patently from the pens of others. After the event, on their overnight flight back to Los Angeles, George acknowledged the rite of passage it had represented by famously remarking to Tony Barrow: "That's it then. I'm not a Beatle any more."[18] And John was equally forthright:

> We've had enough of performing forever. I can't imagine any

reason which would make us do any sort of tour again. We're all really tired. It does nothing for us any more – which is really unfair to the fans, we know, but we've got to think of ourselves … The music wasn't being heard. It was just a sort of freak show: the Beatles *were* the show, and the music had nothing to do with it.[19]

As to the music itself, new songs from the Beatles were in short supply in 1966 – a total of just seventeen on the home market, amassed from one single, fourteen original LP tracks and rounded off by the addition to a compilation LP of a cover version only released before in the US. For this was the year in which they broke free of the commercial restraints imposed on them by EMI, as their original contract with the company expired and Brian Epstein prevaricated over its renewal (to the extent that they continued to record for another six months without a valid contract in place, until its re-negotiation was concluded in January 1967). Put at its simplest, they would not be No.1 at Christmas for the first time in four years because they had not opted to record a single for that purpose.

It was also clear from the earliest recording sessions of the year, beginning on 6th April, that precious little of their latest material would be capable of being reproduced live on stage anyway. Of these new songs, "Paperback Writer" (released as a single in the UK on 10th June – and the first since "She Loves You" not to enter the Top 30 straight at No.1) was the only one to be featured in an otherwise heavily retrospective set list that remained more or less unchanged over the course of their final international tours. (As it was, they now had trouble enough out on the road remembering some of their least sophisticated songs from the recent past: Mark Lewisohn notes that during their opening German concert in Munich they had to stop playing "I'm Down" to consult each other on the right words yet still managed to lose their way in it![20]) The B-side, "Rain", was a classic case in point of the Beatles having recorded a song that was incompatible with live performance, given the reliance for striking effect on its incorporation of vocal and instrumental tapes run backwards. And both sides of that single neatly illustrate in their different ways the continuing shift of lyrical emphasis from traditional love songs, albeit set to a rock'n'roll beat, to exploring wholly individualistic preoccupations – Paul creating a fantasy *alter ego*, John matching mood swings to weather pseudo-philosophically through the filter of LSD – in ways that genuinely began to turn pop into a multi-dimensional art form, to be pored over intensively by dedicated listeners in isolation rather than savoured collectively in the raw as one in a seething crowd of thousands.

Other than these two tracks, the sessions produced a body of work encapsulated on their only original LP of 1966, *Revolver*; for which the last track was the first to be recorded and the most revolutionary in concept to date. Inspired by his current reading of *The Tibetan Book of The Dead* as interpreted by the self-proclaimed American prophet of acid, Timothy Leary, John envisaged "Tomorrow Never Knows" as a testimony to the power of LSD to transport him to the realms of higher consciousness. He told George Martin he wanted it "to sound as if I'm singing from the top of a hill; I want to sound like a Buddhist monk, singing from the top of a mountain. Like the Dalai Lama. Distant, but I still want to hear it."[21]

Martin, ably assisted by engineer Geoff Emerick, duly set about the inventive task of harnessing the imperfect technologies of the day in the quest to re-create John's imagined mystical experience, the vocal aspect of which proved the easiest to capture:

> To make him sound like a Buddhist monk, his dearest wish at that moment, we had put his voice through the Leslie loudspeaker of our Hammond organ. A Leslie speaker rotates at different speeds inside the cabinet of a Lowry organ. You can make the speaker rotate faster or slower by depressing a pedal. It gives a kind of doppler, or 'wah-wah' effect. We put his voice into that speaker, 87 seconds into the song, then recorded it through another microphone placed outside the Leslie speaker. It gave this weird impression of a voice that was somehow pulsating, far-off and altogether singular, as he wished.[22]

The accretion of the remaining effects was derived, courtesy of George, from the tamboura, an Indian instrument "like a sitar … which the player strokes continuously to give a never-ending, mesmeric resonation of sounds"[23]; courtesy of Ringo, from "a very heavy off-beat on his bass drum, which had a big woollen jumper stuffed into it by Geoff Emerick to deaden the sound"[24]; and courtesy initially of Paul, from an overlay of random sounds recorded on tape loops, a subsidiary task which all four of them then embraced with enthusiasm:

> They would all bring me in these loops, like cats bringing in sparrows. I would listen to them, play them at different speeds, backwards and forwards, at three-and-three quarters, seven-and-a-half or fifteen feet per second, and select liberally from them. From the thirty or so tapes they brought in, I selected sixteen loops I liked, each about six seconds long …[25]

Realising the alchemy to bring all these disparate elements together involved Martin in commandeering all the massive reel-to-reel tape recorders EMI had *in situ* and remotely conducting their surreal orchestration:

> The tape-recording machines in those days were enormous, big BTR3s. Once one was in place, it could not easily be moved. So we had white-coated operatives standing all over Abbey Road, on every

floor of the building, each in front of a BTR3 with a pencil stuck in a small loop of tape. Each continuous loop was fed through Abbey Road's internal jack plug patching system, down through the intervening walls and floors, out into our studio, and plugged into my mixing console. By raising a fader, I would hear a particular loop going round and round, held in position by a man in a white coat several floors away, playing its cacophony continuously for ever and ever.[26]

Such was the bizarre backdrop to the recording of "Tomorrow Never Knows", redolent as it is with images worthy of plunder by Storm Thorgerson for a latter-day Pink Floyd album cover. There could be no clearer marker than this of the distance the Beatles had travelled in the almost four years since they first set foot over the threshold of Abbey Road, hawking "Love Me Do" as their prime product, for it is, as George Martin reflected, "the one track, of all the songs the Beatles did, that could never be reproduced" since "the 'happening' of the tape loops, inserted as we all swung off the levers on the faders willy-nilly, was a random event".[27] So if you think you hear tormented seagulls punctuating the dirge at intervals, think again, for it is nothing more than a unique electronic trick of the imagination.

Released in the UK on 5th August, *Revolver* marked for me the high point of that summer's LP releases. After the accursed soundtrack to *The Sound Of Music*, it was the best-selling LP of the year and it even broke into the *NME* Top 30 for a month, peaking at No.18 in the week ending 20th August. Like the music within it, the LP sleeve was a clean break with traditional expectations too. Printed only in black and white, the iconic front cover, designed by Klaus Voorman of old Hamburg acquaintance, bears highly stylised pen-and-ink drawings of – in clockwise rotation – John, George, Ringo and Paul, with a manic photo-montage of Beatles' stock shots interwoven in the strands of their hair; while on the back cover, a photograph by Robert Whitaker catches the group relaxing between takes in the studio at their hippest, John sporting the latest retro fashion in 'granny glasses' and the rest wearing shades.

The only disappointment was that two of the tracks from Side 1 were simultaneously released as a spin-off double-A-side single, both of them in their different ways outstanding songs from the full set of fourteen. "Yellow Submarine", coupled with "Eleanor Rigby", failed, like "Paperback Writer" before it, to break into the Top 30 at No.1; but after its entry at No.2, made No.1 in its second week in the charts, staying there for a total of four weeks until mid-September.

"Yellow Submarine" is a jolly song, far and away the jolliest on an LP that has more than its fair share of darker moments, a Goon-Show revival of the by now honoured custom of surrendering one track to Ringo as vocalist and clearly betraying George Martin's previous talents as a producer of comedy records in the nonsensical accumulation of sound effects conjuring up the joys of life "beneath the waves".[28] Dubbed by Ian MacDonald "a sparkling novelty song impossible to dislike"[29], it took twelve hours to record, from 2.30 p.m. onwards on 1st June, and features unattributed contributions from a seeming cast of thousands – including Marianne Faithfull, Brian Jones, and Pattie Boyd (*aka* Mrs. George Harrison, since 21st January), as well as redoubtable Beatle aides Neil Aspinall, Mal Evans and Alf Bicknell.

"Eleanor Rigby", by contrast, is a plaintive story-in-song from Paul, drawing on his family's Catholic heritage and his own subconscious memories of Liverpool (an Eleanor Rigby is buried in the graveyard of St. Peter's Church, Woolton); to which George Martin's arrangement brings an added chill, in the form of what Ian MacDonald perfectly describes as "a wintry string octet".[30] In this melancholy lament for "all the lonely people", the theme of isolation is first illustrated by reference to the title character herself:

Eleanor Rigby picks up the rice in the church where a
wedding has been,
lives in a dream.
Waits at the window, wearing a face that she keeps
In a jar by the door,
Who is it for?[31]

And then extended by the introduction of the necessarily self-sufficient parish priest:

Father Mackenzie, writing the words of a sermon that
no-one will hear,
No-one comes near.
Look at him working, darning his socks in the night
when there's nobody there,
What does he care?[32]

On Eleanor's death, she is "buried along with her name" at a funeral to which "Nobody came", officiated over by Father Mackenzie, "wiping the dirt from his hands as he walks from the grave" after a service that, in the very act of bringing the characters together, has brought neither comfort nor hope: "No-one was saved."[33] Not so much a pop song, then – notwithstanding the votes of *NME* readers acknowledging it as the Best Single of 1966 – as a poem of some consequence set to music – and worthy of study as such.

Paul was also the prime mover in four other songs on the LP. The unashamed celebration of being totally smitten, "Here, There And Everywhere" (sung in "an almost falsetto voice and double-tracked" in earnest imitation of the voice in his head, that of Marianne Faithfull[34]), is later counter-balanced by the depth of sadness in "For No One", the resignation in his voice here further heightened by the sombre French horn accompaniment:

You want her, you need her,
and yet you don't believe her,
when she says her love is dead,
you think she needs you.
And in her eyes you see nothing,
no sign of love behind the tears cried for no one,
a love that should have lasted years.[35]

"Good Day Sunshine", the opener of Side 2, is an unashamedly 'good time' song, one of several that were prevalent that summer, as we shall see as this chapter goes along. Which leaves the rocking "Got To Get You Into My Life", in an arrangement replete with ferocious brass; superficially passing as another love song, yet John thought it was about taking acid and Paul himself said, "It was a song about pot, actually."[36]

In addition to "Tomorrow Never Knows", John was the driving force behind "I'm Only Sleeping", a theme he would later revisit with a vengeance in "I'm So Tired"; "She Said She Said", directly inspired by conversations with the Byrds and Peter Fonda during their 1965 Hollywood chill-out sessions together; "Doctor Robert", a satiric portrait of Dr. Robert Freymann, compliant provider of pills to the idle rich in New York; and finally, "And Your Bird Can Sing", which author Jonathan Gould convincingly maintains was originally conceived as a putdown of Frank Sinatra, who was known to have expressed far from complimentary views on the Beatles and their music.[37]

And then, from George, there were three. Of his two lesser compositions on *Revolver*, he had this to say:

'I Want To Tell You' is about the avalanche of thoughts that are so hard to write down or say or transmit.

I wrote 'Love You To' on the sitar, because the sitar sounded so nice and my interest was getting deeper all the time. I wanted to write a tune that was specifically for the sitar. Also it had a tabla part, and that was the first time we used a tabla player.[38]

Both of these, however, pale into insignificance by comparison with the song that opens Side 1, "Taxman", a rare example for the time of British pop music reflecting contemporary concerns, complete with references to political leaders of the day "Mister Wilson" and "Mr Heath"[39] and written, unusually for George, out of self-righteous indignation:

I had discovered I was paying a huge amount of money to the taxman. You are so happy that you've finally started earning money – and then you find out about tax.

In those days we paid nineteen shillings and sixpence out of every pound … and with supertax and surtax and tax-tax it was ridiculous – a heavy penalty to pay for making money. That was the big turn-off for Britain. Anybody who ever made any money moved to America or somewhere else.[40]

As one of the nation's four most prominent supposed high earners, George was suitably – if somewhat naively – outraged when he realised the vast disparity between his presumed gross and actual net income; although in reality the taxman was well down the chain of predation, after the record companies, music publishers and even that charming Mr. Epstein had all taken their respective cuts of the Beatles' profits. But for George, the taxman obsessively remained the ubiquitous villain of the piece:

> If you drive a car, I'll tax the street.
> If you try to sit, I'll tax your seat.
> If you get too cold, I'll tax the heat.
> If you take a walk, I'll tax your feet.
> Taxman.[41]

To the extent, being equally mindful of the inescapable certainty of death duties, that he could not resist one final flourish:

> Now my advice for those who die,
> Declare the pennies on your eyes.[42]

Alas for George, at the end of the day the taxman still had the last laugh, as John Blaney explains:

> Northern Songs published the song; but unlike Lennon and McCartney the astute guitarist had negotiated a far superior royalty. While Lennon and McCartney were on a 50/50 split, Harrison received 80% of mechanical royalties, 70 from overseas publishing and 66 2/3 from performing and broadcast fees. Ironically, most of the money he made from the song went straight to the Inland Revenue. No wonder he was annoyed.[43]

With their work on *Revolver* completed on 22nd June, the Beatles departed England next day for the start of their summer tours abroad and undertook no further recording at Abbey Road until 24th November. (This meant that over six months would elapse from the joint issue in August of LP and spin-off single until their next new original UK release.) *Revolver* was the last LP to be filleted by Capitol for its release in America (on 8th August), a practice that had increasingly irked the Beatles as being beyond their control: heretofore, they would seek to ensure consistency between the content of British and American record releases as far as possible. Three tracks ("I'm Only Sleeping", "Doctor Robert" and "And Your Bird Can Sing") had already been submitted by George Martin at Capitol's request for inclusion on what ended up, to British eyes, as a wholly random assembly culled from *Help!*, *Rubber Soul* and *Revolver*, plus "Day Tripper" and "We Can Work It Out"; released on 20th June as *"Yesterday"* ... *And Today* and thereby leaving the later US version of *Revolver* with only eleven tracks.

Irrespective of its content, *"Yesterday"* ... *And Today* enjoys greater notoriety in Beatles history for its association with the so-called 'butcher' photo-shoot orchestrated by Robert Whitaker at his Chelsea studio on 25th March. Pictures from this session – showing the Beatles seated in white smocks, festooned with cuts of raw meat and dismembered dolls – were presented, amongst others, to Capitol as potential shots for the LP's front cover and amazingly taken forward as such in an initial print run of perhaps as many as 750,000 copies. (Whitaker sought to justify his approach to his assignment as purely experimental: "People will jump to the wrong conclusions about it being sick, but the whole thing was based on simplicity, linking four very real people with something real."[44] The Beatles themselves were divided: John and Paul for, George and Ringo against.) Nonetheless, widespread shock at the image expressed by distributors and retailers on receipt of advance copies prompted a rapid U-turn on strict orders from the top:

> In accordance with the following statement from Alan W. Livingston, President, Capitol Records Inc., the original album cover is being discarded and a new jacket is being prepared:
>
> "The original cover, created in England, was intended as 'pop art' satire. However, a sampling of public opinion in the United States indicates that the cover design is subject to misinterpretation. For this reason, and to avoid any possible controversy or undeserved harm to the Beatles' image or reputation, Capitol has chosen to withdraw the LP and substitute a more generally acceptable design."[45]

In fact, to minimise production losses, the new cover image (an anodyne shot of the Beatles posed in and around an up-ended cabin trunk) was pasted over the original copies, although a few did slip through the net. The cost to Capitol of recovery from this *faux pas* is believed to have been in the order of $250,000, severely curtailing any profit from sales of what became, despite the uproar, yet another US No.1 album. British fans were treated to a black-and-white version of the 'butcher' shot in a full-page advert for "Paperback Writer" carried by the *NME* on 3rd June.

In the long interim between the end of their US tour and returning to Abbey Road, all four Beatles went their separate ways. John was away filming for two months on location in West Germany and Spain, as Private Gripweed in Richard Lester's adaptation of Patrick Ryan's comic novel *How I Won The War*. George took a six-week vacation in India to extend his personal study of religion, philosophy and music, which included intensive tuition on the sitar from master of the instrument Ravi Shankar. Paul not only composed the score for the Boulting Brothers' film *The Family Way*, in collaboration with George Martin, but also set off on an incognito road trip through France with Mal Evans before flying on with him to Kenya for an African safari. Ringo divided his time between being at home in Weybridge and visiting John out in Spain.

John finally returned to London on 7th November. Invited by John Dunbar, co-owner (with Peter Asher and Barry Miles) of the Indica Gallery, to a new exhibition of conceptual art, he went to view it on the evening of 9th November, where he had his first momentous meeting with the artist concerned, Yoko Ono. Initially bemused by the minimalism of her exhibits, he gradually found himself succumbing to their intriguing qualities: "And that's when we really *met*. That's when we locked eyes and she got it and I got it and that was it … The rest, as they say in all the interviews we do, is history." [46] The repercussions of that meeting were to impact progressively and profoundly on his marriage to Cynthia, his relationships with the other Beatles, his approach to making music; and ultimately would comprehensively reshape his outlook on life, his entire world-view.

For now, when the group reconvened in the recording studio on 24th November, their intention was, in their own time and at their own pace, to work with George Martin on putting a new LP together. First up for their consideration was a song composed by John with time on his hands in Spain, called "Strawberry Fields Forever", an exploration of the inner workings of his mind sparked by those childhood memories of Liverpool he held most dear. The radical approach required to bring it to fruition unquestionably "set the agenda for the whole album"[47], although the final direction they would take to arrive at *Sgt. Pepper's Lonely Hearts Club Band* was as yet unclear. In a series of sessions that then continued intermittently to the end of December, they also worked on two songs from Paul, "When I'm Sixty-Four" (with words now put to a much earlier instrumental composition) and "Penny Lane".

Meanwhile, in the continuing absence of any new product since *Revolver*, EMI had elected to secure their share of the home Christmas market by asking Martin and Emerick to collate a 'greatest hits' LP for Parlophone. The only consolation for otherwise short-changed fans was that it included one track previously unreleased in the UK, a cover of the Larry Williams rocker "Bad Boy", recorded in May 1965 together with "Dizzy Miss Lizzy" and first put out by Capitol on the *Beatles VI* album that June. I cannot have been alone in subsequently picking up on tantalising references to this 'unknown' track from time to time in the small ads section of the *NME*, when offered for sale as a bootleg US import. Released on 9th December as *A Collection*

Of Beatles Oldies (But Goldies), sales inevitably spilled over into 1967, taking it to No.7 in the LP charts over a period of eighteen weeks; but representing, as it did, desperation on the part of the record company, it was also highly symbolic of the distance now perceptibly opening up between the Beatles and their original British fanbase.

As seen in the last chapter, Bob Dylan had already faced down more than his fair share of antagonism from audiences who were, with almost crusading zeal, resistant to his switch from acoustic to electric instrumentation, regarding it somehow as symbolic of his unprincipled abandonment of the protest movement. On 4th February, he returned unabashed with the Hawks to the fray of live performance, resuming his 'world tour' in Louisville, Kentucky and then spending the next two months traversing the United States and Canada. These concert engagements in February and March were, however, also interspersed with recording sessions in, of all the unlikely places, Nashville (at the suggestion of producer Bob Johnston), laying down tracks for the double-LP *Blonde On Blonde*.

Dylan began 1966 hoping that he might sustain a breakthrough as a singles artist, given his successes of the year before, but it wasn't to be. Unfortunately, "Can You Please Crawl Out Your Window?", out in January in both the US and UK, came across as an undistinguished rock'n'roll thrash despite the Hawks' best efforts as backing group, completely lacking the flair or bite of either of its immediate predecessors, and didn't even make it into the *Billboard* Top 40 at home. Relatively speaking, therefore, its impact was greater over here, entering our Top 30 at No.30 in the week ending 29th January but only staying in the charts for three weeks, with a high of No.19. It was followed by the US February release of "One Of Us Must Know (Sooner Or Later)", of interest lyrically for its conciliatory rather than vengeful overtones but another chart failure; leading Dylan not only to conclude that making singles was an unwelcome distraction from the serious business of recording albums but also insisting that the track be included on *Blonde On Blonde* – where it closed Side 1. (Released later in the UK, by the end of April it was briefly threatening to break into the Top 30 but never managed it.)[48]

Dylan brought trusted close associates Al Kooper (on organ) and Robbie Robertson (on guitar) to work with him in Nashville on recording his latest songs over eight days split between mid-February and early March. This core trio was augmented as necessary by an eclectic mix of old-hand session musicians, to whom Dylan was as unknown as they were to him, and who found his largely improvisational approach in the studio completely alien. The most striking example of the way in which, despite their incredulity, they still managed to accommodate him professionally was the first run-through of the marathon "Sad-Eyed Lady Of The Lowlands" (written in florid praise of Sara and finally emerging as a thirteen-minute-long track occupying the whole of Side 4), as described here by drummer Ken Buttrey:

> He ran down a verse and a chorus and he just quit and said, 'We'll do a verse and a chorus then I'll play my harmonica thing. Then we'll do another verse and chorus and I'll play some more harmonica, and we'll see how it goes from there.' That was his explanation of what was getting ready to happen … Not knowing how long this thing was going to be, we were preparing ourselves dynamically for a basic two- to three-minute record. Because records just didn't go over three minutes … After about five, six minutes of this stuff we start looking at the clock, everyone starts looking at each other, we'd built to the peak of our limit and, bang, [there] goes another harmonica solo … After about ten minutes of this thing we're cracking up at each other, at what we were doing. I mean, we peaked five minutes ago. Where do we go from here?[49]

On other occasions, the mood was mercifully not as tense as this, even though unpredictability continued to prevail in the studio. Howard Sounes, for example, offers a possibly apocryphal account of how Dylan plied the ensemble with drink to loosen them up before they set to recording "Rainy Day Women Nos. 12 & 35", indisputably the most uproarious and least disciplined of all fourteen tracks.[50]

The LP as a whole is less infused with anger than you might expect, given Dylan's near-masochistic bloody-mindedness in the face of continuing opposition to his change of style; and as an opening track, "Rainy Day Women Nos. 12 & 35" reveals him having a ball, both literally and figuratively, as he simultaneously laughs in his critics' faces:

> Well, they'll stone you and say that it's the end.
> Then they'll stone you and then they'll come back again.
> They'll stone you when you're riding in your car.
> They'll stone you when you're playing your guitar.
> Yes, but I would not feel so all alone,
> Everybody must get stoned.[51]

While the accompaniment of the drunken marching band surely harks back distantly to the suppressed "Mixed Up Confusion" single, the wordplay on the theme of 'stone/stoned' is set to tease and annoy in equal measure, as the Biblical imagery of stoning as punishment is interwoven with the entreaty to the listener to "get stoned": i.e., drunk, or – in its more modern sense – high on drugs.[52] Seen by the generality of young people as first and foremost a great singalong party record, it gave British broadcasters a headache when it was separated out from the album for release as a single and became a UK No.9 hit in May.

The second track to be issued as a single, "I Want You", takes us back into more familiar Dylan territory in its surreal exploration of a sense of yearning, of love frustrated by a bewilderingly random collection of discordant, interfering misfits:

The guilty undertaker sighs,
The lonesome organ grinder cries,
The silver saxophones say I should refuse you.
The cracked bells and washed-out horns
Blow into my face with scorn,
But it's not that way,
I wasn't born to lose you.
I want you, I want you,
I want you so bad,
Honey, I want you.[53]

Released in the UK in July, in advance of *Blonde On Blonde* complete, it reached No.17 in mid-August; by which time, as we shall see shortly, fate had intervened, making it his last British hit single for another three years.

Of the remaining tracks, five at least stand out, the first of these being "Visions of Johanna". The version to be found here represents the culmination of efforts Dylan had been making since the previous November to complete a satisfactory take of it, thus denoting the particular importance he attached to this song. Once – but no longer – a potent force in his life, the mysterious Johanna continues to exercise an inescapable hold over him, thwarting his every effort at distraction even in the company of others:

Ain't it just like the night to play tricks when you're trying to be so quiet?
We sit here stranded, though we're all doin' our best to deny it
And Louise holds a handful of rain, temptin' you to defy it
Lights flicker from the opposite loft
In this room the heat pipes just cough
The country music station plays soft
But there's nothing, really nothing to turn off
Just Louise and her lover so entwined
And these visions of Johanna that conquer my mind.[54]

Elsewhere, in "Stuck Inside Of Mobile With The Memphis Blues Again", there are distractions a-plenty on offer from that ever-intrusive technicolour cast of sleazy lowlife and whores with hearts of gold, yet all of them, it seems, destined to bring bad luck with no prospect of escape from it:

Now the bricks lay on Grand Street
Where the neon madmen climb.

They all fall there so perfectly,
It all seems so well timed.
An' here I sit so patiently
Waiting to find out what price
You have to pay to get out of
Going through all these things twice.
Oh, Mama, can this really be the end,
To be stuck inside of Mobile
With the Memphis blues again.[55]

The natural end of an affair is played out in "Most Likely You Go Your Way (And I'll Go Mine)", a song that Dylan jokingly said he had "probably written after some disappointing relationship where, you know, I was lucky to have escaped without a broken nose"[56]:

You say you love me
And you're thinkin' of me,
But you know you could be wrong.
You say you told me
That you wanna hold me,
But you know you're not that strong.
I just can't do what I done before,
I just can't beg you anymore.
I'm gonna let you pass
And I'll go last.
Then time will tell who has fell
And who's been left behind,
When you go your way and I go mine.[57]

It is only in the magnificent "Just Like A Woman" that Dylan's thoughts appear to stray perilously close back to the corrosive scenario of "Like A Rolling Stone":

Ev'rybody knows
That Baby's got new clothes
But lately I see her ribbons and her bows
Have fallen from her curls.
She takes just like a woman, yes, she does,
She makes love just like a woman, yes, she does
And she aches just like a woman
But she breaks just like a little girl.[58]

But this time around, fear and loathing are equally distributed between the protagonists, casting a long shadow of uncertainty over their break-up:

When we meet again
Introduced as friends
Please don't let on that you knew me when
I was hungry and it was your world.[59]

Finally, "Leopard-Skin Pill-Box Hat" combines blistering guitar from Robbie Robertson with wit and a whiff of scandal in its salacious commentary on the owner's serial infidelities. For her doctor, for instance, the hat serves to enhance his desire by assuming the status of a fetishistic object:

Well, I asked the doctor if I could see you
It's bad for your health, he said
Yes, I disobeyed his orders
I came to see you
But I found him there instead
You know, I don't mind him cheatin' on me
But I sure wish he'd take that off his head
Your brand new leopard-skin pill-box hat.[60]

Consequently, as she is warned in the last verse, that hat has all too quickly become synonymous with her recklessness in bestowing her favours:

Well, I see you got a new boyfriend
You know, I never seen him before
Well, I saw him
Makin' love to you
You forgot to close the garage door
You might think he loves you for your money
But I know what he really loves you for
It's your brand new leopard-skin pill-box hat.[61]

Blonde On Blonde was warmly received when it was at last released in the UK in August, reaching No.3 in the LP charts and making it the second most popular of his albums in Britain so far, after *Bringing It All Back Home*.

After its completion, Dylan and the Hawks returned to the treadmill of concert dates across America. Although they were able to incorporate some songs from the new album into their repertoire straight away (most commonly "Visions Of Johanna", "Just Like A Woman", "Leopard-Skin Pill-Box Hat" and the lesser "Fourth Time Around" – which, melodically, owed a huge debt to "Norwegian Wood"), they were still constrained by Albert Grossman's stipulation that they must play two sets, one acoustic and one electric, at each concert, thus forcing Dylan to cast his net more widely. Having closed this leg of their tour in Honolulu on 9th April, next stop, from 12th April, was Australia, "even more middlebrow and muddled than Middle America" according to Robert Shelton, where, over the course of the next fifteen days, as he noted pityingly, Dylan "flew from city to city [beginning in Sydney and ending in Perth], meeting reporters who were mostly hostile, inane, callous or uninformed".[62] Others accompanying him or making his passing acquaintance en route were struck by his violent mood swings, how hard he appeared to be driving himself and his reliance on uppers and downers to help him overcome what he later described himself as the "unbelievable" pressures of the tour that "hurt so much".[63] They feared not so much for his health as for his sanity in these circumstances.

After leaving Australia, Dylan made his way to London, via Scandinavia (where he gave concerts in Stockholm and Copenhagen). Arriving on 2nd May, he set up temporary court in the Mayfair Hotel for a brief respite – where amongst those he received as guests were Keith Richards, Brian Jones and Paul McCartney – before flying over to Ireland for gigs in Dublin and Belfast on the 5th and 6th. The tour proper of mainland UK began on 10th May in Bristol and, as it proceeded, the by now familiar resistance to what he and the Hawks had to offer surfaced again. This response, from a Bristol fan, was typical: "They buried Bob Dylan, the folksinger, in a grave of electric guitars, enormous loudspeakers and deafening drums. It was a sad end to one of the most phenomenal influences in music."[64]

Although historically the concert at the Free Trade Hall, Manchester on the 17th (mis-attributed on early bootleg recordings as the "Royal Albert Hall Concert") has ever since been regarded as the most infamous, there is reliable documentary evidence of more widespread disapproval. For instance, on the 14th in Liverpool, a city to which by now the Beatles had long grown strangers, he was barracked by the rebuke that "Woody Guthrie would turn in his grave"[65]; while in Glasgow, where he was taunted by slow handclaps when he played there on the 19th, he narrowly escaped physical assault in his hotel by a waiter whose novel twist on room service was to accuse him to his face of being a "fucking traitor to folk music".[66]

It is Manchester, however, that has gone down to posterity as the zenith of anti-electric sentiment because of the moment, captured on record and film, when Keele University student Keith Butler assured himself of his fifteen minutes of fame by calling Dylan "Judas!" From the start of that night's electric set, something far stronger than unease had been building up amongst the discontented traditionalist segment of the audience, making it, in the words of another, more open-minded sixteen-year-old concertgoer, "quite bewildering and frightening to see them going apeshit".[67] Approaching the conclusion of the set, in the lull immediately following the end of the penultimate number, "Ballad Of A Thin Man", Butler could contain himself no longer and Dylan's response was instantaneous. To his unseen accuser, out in the auditorium, he shouted back, "I don't believe you. You're a liar!" Then to drummer Mickey Jones and the Hawks, now poised for their cue into "Like A Rolling Stone", he spat, "Play fucking loud!" – and, cranking it up, so they did.

The caravan moved on regardless, taking in a diversion to Paris along the way for a concert at the Olympia on the 24th, when it was not so much the music that gave offence as the dressing of the stage for the performers' electric set with a giant Stars and Stripes (pre-dating by several years the iconic opening sequence of *Patton*). Apparently oblivious to the cultural consequences of this patriotic display, Dylan thus found himself denounced by members of the audience protesting against his association – by default – with an imperialist US administration hell-bent on waging war in Vietnam. It might have been as well for him if he had paid more heed to the anxieties he had obviously been harbouring on his outbound flight to France, as evidenced by his asking a French journalist, "Can you tell me what I'm doing in a country where nobody understands a word I say? Do you think they'll boo at the Olympia?"[68]

Two consecutive nights at the genuine Royal Albert Hall in London marked the tour's grand finale on 26th and 27th May, the former attended by the Stones and the latter by the Beatles, with Dylan every bit as combative on stage as he appeared at times to be confused. Leaving England on the 28th with wife Sara for a short restorative break in Spain, on his arrival back in America he retreated to the sanctuary of their family home near Woodstock in New York State and did as little as possible. Obviously exhausted by the ravages of his 'world tour', in large part self-inflicted, he was reluctant to engage in important work-related projects: he was supposed to be making final corrections to the proofs of his prose-poem *Tarantula* prior to its publication, as well as reviewing film footage of the tour (as before, shot by D.A. Pennebaker) in preparation for a proposed TV documentary. Other complications revolved around Albert Grossman's protracted re-negotiation of his recording contract and his plans to send Dylan out imminently on another American tour for the remainder of 1966 into 1967, this time to play more than sixty scheduled concerts.

On 29th July, he suffered an accident on his Triumph motorcycle, the details of which have never clearly emerged although the injuries he sustained were serious enough to put him out of circulation for months, in the process relieving him of all pressures related to business matters or performing. In this regard, it confirms Robert Shelton's contemporary view that although it was "widely reported that Dylan nearly lost his life", it seemed "more likely that his mishap *saved* his life".[69] The accident had occurred as Dylan was riding the bike to a local repair shop:

> It was real early in the morning on top of a hill near Woodstock.
> I can't even remember how it happened. I was blinded by the sun
> … I was drivin' right straight into the sun, and I looked up into it

even though I remember someone telling me a long time ago when I was a kid never to look straight at the sun … I went blind for a second and I kind of panicked or something. I stomped down on the brake and the rear wheel locked up on me and I went flyin' … [Sara] was followin' me in a car. She picked me up. Spent a week in the hospital, then they moved me to this doctor's house in town. In his attic. Had a bed up there in the attic with a window lookin' out. Sara stayed there with me.[70]

The extent and nature of his injuries have never been definitively established. At worst, they may have been as serious as a broken neck: at least, he may have escaped with severe bruising and concussion. Whatever the outcome, his recovery was painfully slow, his withdrawal from the public scene complete; to the extent that, as Anthony Scaduto so succinctly put it, "Dylan remained holed up in his Woodstock home for more than nine months after the accident, refusing to see any but close friends and growing into an American legend at twenty-five."[71] In reality, the wait for his next new release would be much longer, approaching more like eighteen months; by which time he would be a totally changed man in outlook, appearance and even in voice.

If, albeit for different reasons, touring had now become anathema to the Beatles and to Dylan, the same could not be said of the Rolling Stones. For them, superficially 1966 continued in much the same vein as previous years, balancing the requirements of recording with spending a high proportion of their time giving shows around the world. It was, nevertheless, the year when the Jagger/Richards songwriting partnership really came into its own, adding a new LP of totally original tracks to yet another impressive tally of hit singles.

As noted in the previous chapter, work had already commenced at RCA Hollywood in December 1965 on tracks for their forthcoming new album. These included: "Mother's Little Helper", "Doncha Bother Me", "Goin' Home", "Take It Or Leave It" and "Think". However, early in the New Year Decca shelved its planned March release, having taken fright at possible accusations of blasphemy after Andrew Loog Oldham's latest publicity wheeze of announcing its title to the music press as *Could You Walk On The Water?* With the project for the LP's completion now subject to radical change, in the interim another track from the December sessions was released as a single in the UK on 4th February; although the edge was taken off this when on the same day, much to Loog Oldham's discomfort, a less than complimentary profile of Mick Jagger by Maureen Cleave appeared in the *Evening Standard*, beginning as follows:

For some unaccountable reason Mick Jagger is considered the
most fashionable, modish man in London, the voice of today ...
He has said nothing – apart from a few words on the new single
– to suggest he is of today, yesterday or any other day. He remains
uncommunicative, unforthcoming, uncooperative.[72]

"19th Nervous Breakdown" (b/w the Stones' own orchestrated take on
"As Tears Go By") was very much a child of its times, reflecting the shallow
spite of pop's high society in its uncharitable depiction of a neurotic female
hanger-on (whom many believed was based on Jagger's girlfriend at the time,
Chrissie Shrimpton):

> You're the kind of person you meet at certain dismal
> dull affairs,
> Centre of a crowd, talking much too loud, running up
> and down the stairs.
> It seems to me that you have seen too much in too
> few years,
> And though you try, you just can't hide your eyes are
> edged with tears.
> You'd better stop, look around.
> Here it comes, here it comes, here it comes, here
> it comes,
> Here comes your nineteenth nervous breakdown.[73]

Entering the *NME* Top 30 at No.2 in the week ending 12th February, for
the next three weeks it was at No.1, a success the Stones could only savour
at a distance for they had already jetted off for a second Australasian tour,
landing in Sydney on 16th February where they were joined by their principal support act, the Searchers; "a combination", in Frank Allen's opinion,
"almost as bizarre as putting Pearl Carr and Teddy Johnson on the road with
Megadeth ... the good, the bad and the downright unlikely".[74]

Unlike the hapless Bob Dylan, the Stones' popularity in Australia was
well-established, enabling them to take the tour in their stride as was their
wont, whereas the Searchers found themselves driven to distraction by
drummer Chris Curtis, whose behaviour grew ever more erratic and unpredictable as he grappled with his own personal demons. Before reaching
Sydney, they had been playing in the predominantly Catholic Philippines,
narrowly escaping the condemnation of the press in Manila "when Chris
Curtis, on being asked of any unfulfilled ambitions, replied that he wanted to
play Jesus Christ in a movie".[75] He had gone on to create further difficulties
by responding over-attentively to a girl trying to present him with a garland of
flowers at one concert, before recklessly injuring a US serviceman at another
by throwing a malfunctioning microphone in anger off the stage into the

audience. And before the Stones' tour was barely under way, Curtis had made a spectacle of himself twice in one day in Sydney, being temporarily detained by military police for unauthorised entry to a local naval base, as well as passing out – under the influence, unbeknown to the others, of a formidable cocktail of pills – in a TV studio immediately prior to a promotional broadcast (which the other three Searchers then had to complete without him). Barely kept in check for the rest of the tour, lesser mishaps alternating with making pronouncements bordering on the delusional, at its close Curtis quit the group, with the avowed intent of moving full-time into record production. The legacy he left them, courtesy of the time spent with the Stones, was his strong hint that they should record the new Jagger/Richards song "Take It Or Leave It" as their next single; which they did on their return to England, having hesitantly recruited John Blunt as his replacement. Just good enough to give them their last-ever toehold in the Top 30, scraping to No.25 in the week ending 7th May, for the Searchers there was still no escaping the depressing fact that it was a casualty of "the unforgiving bear pit that was the record buying market".[76]

Following the end of the tour in Perth on 2nd March, the Stones flew back to Los Angeles via Fiji, to spend 6th to 9th March recording at RCA Studios. Over the course of these few days, they concentrated on completing another nine tracks towards their new LP, as well as both sides of their next single. Despite the growing rift between him and other group members, Brian Jones set his seal on this intensive burst of activity as a versatile and creative multi-instrumentalist, making a distinctive contribution that even his fiercest critics Loog Oldham and Keith Richards felt bound to acknowledge. A short spell back in England concluded on 26th March with their departure for Amsterdam and a whistlestop European tour (taking in seven venues in five countries) that lasted until 5th April.

Aftermath was released in the UK on 15th April and, after interrupting the supremacy of *The Sound Of Music* as the No.1 album for up to eight weeks, went on to become the fourth best-selling LP of the year. Although to me its overall sound felt downbeat by comparison with the muscularity of the Stones' singles output, its dual appeal lay in combining content full of contrasts with good value for money: in total, its playing time ran to more than fifty minutes. Consider, for instance, the largely improvisational track "Goin' Home", the forerunner, at over eleven minutes long, of what others came to christen the extended jam – which in that guise would habitually become the curse of highbrow pop and an interminable teeth-gritting bore on the excruciating outermost limits of any sober listener's physical endurance. Embellishing Mick's plaintive lament for home comforts with the traditional blues trick of using instruments to mimic the careering motion of a train, it chugged and rolled its way up hill and down dale far beyond the then usual time constraints of the studio, by mutual consent of engineer Dave Hassinger and producer Loog Oldham.

Describing *Aftermath* as "the culmination of the adrenalin rush that had been their first three years as a professional band", Bill Wyman went on to say that it "showed the band's chauvinism in its full flowering"[77]; a trait painfully self-evident in songs like "Stupid Girl", "Under My Thumb" and "Out Of Time". However revisionism may try to dress it up, the astounding arrogance of Jagger's vocals serves only to highlight this common thread of a woman despised. The "stupid girl" of that song's title, for example, has nothing whatsoever to recommend her:

> I'm not talking about the way she digs for gold –
> Look at that stupid girl!
> Well I'm talking about the way she grabs and holds –
> Look at that stupid girl!
> The way she talks about someone else
> That she don't even know herself,
> She's the sickest thing in this world –
> Look at that stupid girl![78]

Forcing a self-willed girl into submission is portrayed as a positive virtue in "Under My Thumb":

> Under my thumb's a squirming dog who's just had her day.
> Under my thumb's a girl who has just changed her ways.
> It's down to me, the way she does just what she's told.
> It's down to me, the change has come, she's under
> my thumb.[79]

And there is no perceptible hint of irony in the last verse, where hypocrisy comes shining through:

> Under my thumb her eyes are just kept to herself.
> Under my thumb, well, I can still look at someone else.
> It's down to me, the way she talks when she's spoken to.
> It's down to me, the change has come, she's under
> my thumb.[80]

As a final threat, the informing premise of "Out Of Time" is that ostracism is the only right and proper punishment for any girl attempting to break free and go it alone:

> You thought you were a clever girl,
> Giving up your social whirl,
> But you can't come back
> And be the first in line.

You're obsolete, my baby,
My poor old-fashioned baby.
I said, baby, baby,
You're out of time.[81]

Nonetheless, the misogyny of such lyrics remained cloaked in invisibility for now – partly, no doubt, because too few people as yet were inclined to listen specifically to the words of pop songs, as opposed to simply appreciating their overall sound – to the extent that Chris Farlowe's hoarse, rasping cover version of "Out Of Time", released courtesy of Loog Oldham's parallel interest in Immediate Records, was happily made a summertime No.1.

Looked at in other ways, "Under My Thumb" and "Out Of Time" bene-fited, as did several other tracks, from the decorous instrumental flourishes added by Brian Jones: to both he contributed the sound of the marimba, an African relative of the xylophone. On "Mother's Little Helper", he played sitar; the dulcimer on "Lady Jane" (to which Jack Nitzsche also added harp-sichord) and "I Am Waiting". This eclecticism on his part does appear, however, to have been more fortuitous than cerebral (as, say, was the case with George Harrison): even the habitually critical Loog Oldham was forced to admit that he "surprised us with his adept picking up of an instrument hitherto unknown to him and coming up with [a] polished gem".[82]

At other times, however, his contribution was positively counter-pro-ductive, as in the March recording session for "What To Do" when he was so wasted that he crashed out for more than two hours, clutching "his guitar like a life preserver" and lying "in a pathetic foetal position on the floor, draining the life out of the room".[83] With the hum from his guitar's amplifier continu-ally playing havoc with the sound levels within the studio, Loog Oldham was finally obliged to make an executive decision:

> I got up off the control room chair, walked into the studio towards Brian and the humming amp. I found the on/off switch, put it in off, yanked the guitar lead out of the amp and walked back into the control room. Nothing needed to be said. It was all part of the gig, the beginning of the last rites, my day would come. We all went back to work, knowing what to do and doing it, even though one of our aircraft was missing in action.[84]

The single they had also recorded in March was released a month after *Aftermath* on 13th May. Within a fortnight, "Paint It, Black", the one track most prominently adorned with Brian's sitar playing, was No.1, as the extraordinary preface for one week only to a resurgence in easy listening that passed the crown on to Frank Sinatra's "Strangers In The Night"! It exudes a sinister mysticism, Mick's half-spoken vocals solemnly exploiting the atten-dant depression of having lost the love of a girl:

I see a red door and I want it painted black.
No colours any more, I want them to turn black.
I see the girls walk by, dressed in their summer clothes.
I have to turn my head until my darkness goes.[85]

And, as this incantation thunders along, Bill augmenting his bass line on guitar with a second bass figure he thumps out on the pedals of a Hammond organ with his fist, the threat of possible retribution is eerily left unresolved by lines like: "I look inside myself and see my heart is black."[86] Is it too fanciful to see concealed here in such imagery the earliest prefiguring of the Midnight Rambler? In retrospect, Bill modestly cites the record as simultaneously marking "the end of the Stones' first phase as a pop band" and representing "a call to arms for every other group that aspired to making it as a rock outfit". [87] Be that as it may, its lasting legacy in pop history is as a quintessential Stones' single of the period, its disturbing blend of excitement and edginess easily setting it apart from the work of any contemporary competitors.

A lengthy hiatus then followed – occasioned principally by yet another major tour of the USA and Canada in June and July – until late September, when on the 23rd the next single, "Have You Seen Your Mother, Baby, Standing In The Shadow?", was released.[88] Its arrival was heralded by what was, in its day, a suitably outrageous publicity shot, taken by US photographer Jerry Schatzberg in downtown New York. The Stones' equivalent of the Beatles' 'butcher' shot and similarly used as a full-page advertisement in the NME, it showed all five group members in drag, with Brian and Bill both in military uniform (the latter seated in a wheelchair with legs contorted) and Charlie carrying it off as Grandma Giles personified. Loog Oldham at his most fanciful suggested to the press that the song was somehow about "the attitude that exists between parents and their children" and that the 'Shadow' of the title represented "the uncertainty of the future [as to] whether we slide into a vast depression or universal war".[89] The accompanying picture, so he went on to claim, was an attempt to convey the "idea of what some of the mothers of today's generation might have looked like in the Shadow of the warring Forties", thereby "parodying the theme".[90] Its propensity to shock and/or amuse appeared, however, to work in inverse proportion to its ability to drum up sales, since with this record the Stones only managed to reach a disappointing No.5 in mid-October.

The August and September sessions from which it emerged had largely been dedicated to recording songs for their next original LP and were the last the Stones would attend at the RCA Studios in Hollywood (from November they reverted to using the Olympic Studios in London). The lyric was impenetrable, the production brash in imitation of Phil Spector's 'wall of sound'. Although it had been worked and re-worked in the studio in increasingly intense efforts to bring it to life, including the addition of trumpets by musical arranger Mike Leander, Keith, as the song's principal composer, still remained dissatisfied with the end result. It was nevertheless considered good enough to be used as the opening track of the compilation LP *Big Hits [High Tide And Green Grass]*, which Decca released in the UK on 4th November in an ultra-sharp gatefold sleeve that also housed ten pages of photographs.[91] Reaching No.4 in its ten weeks in the LP charts in the run-up to Christmas and on into the New Year, sales gratifyingly exceeded those of its prime competitor within that same period, namely *A Collection Of Beatles Oldies (But Goldies)*.

By the beginning of 1966 the Beach Boys, unlike any other top-flight group of the era, had already forced themselves through one year of marked separation between touring and recording and were content for it to continue; the travelling band now casting its net even wider geographically while back home Brian Wilson was lost to the world in his exhaustive preliminaries to the making of their most critically acclaimed LP *Pet Sounds*. From 7th to 23rd January, the performing Beach Boys toured Japan, leaving Brian to work up a varied set of new songs in collaboration with Tony Asher, whom he had engaged as a lyricist. Still perturbed by the profound impact *Rubber Soul* had made upon him, Brian's endeavours were directed towards creating an entirely new genre of pop music. For him this meant setting his face against any further repetition of a formulaic approach to hit-making but it was to provoke confrontation when the rest of the group eventually rejoined him in the studio.

When they all met for their first recording session of the year together on 9th February, Brian already had eight earlier sessions under his belt, in the course of which, from 18th January onwards, he had been engaged with seasoned session musicians in producing a number of instrumental backing tracks. Presented that day with Brian at his most demanding from the outset in attempting to record the intricate vocal harmonies to "Hang On To Your Ego", a song they simply didn't understand, the other group members were confounded. Unsurprisingly, Mike Love (who had, after all, hitherto enjoyed composing credits with Brian for most of their hits) was scornfully disruptive throughout, dismissing the abstraction of the lyric as a joke. A less wounded Al Jardine was at least able to summarise their dilemma more rationally: "We were a surfing group when we left the country at the start of 1966 and we came back to this new music. It took some getting used to."[92]

With everyone's forbearance over time, however, the LP was eventually completed on 16th April, the outcome of an unbelievably long haul of twenty-seven recording sessions in total sprawling over three months and leaving Brian feeling vindicated at last. But to his disappointment Capitol's initial reaction to *Pet Sounds* was lukewarm. Not only did he have to persist in his discussions with the label's senior managers before they agreed to release it but he was also obliged to accede to their request to include a proven hit on it as an extra track. This was the Beach Boys' remake of "Sloop John B", already released by Capitol in America on 21st March in an attempt to recover ground lost by the unsuccessful release on 7th March of one of the new album tracks, "Caroline No", as an advance single.[93] (At home "Sloop John B" quickly climbed to No.3 and sold equally strongly in the UK after its April release here, reaching No.2 in the week ending 21st May. This gave the Beach Boys their second British Top 10 hit of the year so far, having been preceded by the February release of "Barbara Ann", which had made it to No.4 in mid-March.)

Pet Sounds, "not an album constructed for the typical Beach Boys fan of 1966", was released "to a confused public"[94] in the US on 16th May, the main source of that confusion being that its content was seen as *avant garde* in comparison to that of its predecessor, *Recorded 'Live' At A Beach Boys' Party*, which had been much easier on the ear. True, Side 1 did open with a more or less conventional love song, "Wouldn't It Be Nice", looking forward to marriage as the opening of the door onto a life of uninterrupted bliss; but in between that and Track 7, "Sloop John B", what was one to make of the often dissonant intervening songs of introspection or of Track 6, the lounge-music instrumental "Let's Go Away For Awhile"?[95] Side 2 was equally bewildering. After the initial breathtaking revelation of "God Only Knows" (which in America perilously straddled the thin line between acceptability and blasphemy) and the upbeat duo of "I Know There's An Answer" (as "Hang On To Your Ego" had now become) and "Here Today", there came a headlong plunge into Brian's very private world with "I Just Wasn't Made For These Times", its idiosyncrasy enhanced by the futuristic sound of an elec-tro-theremin; followed by another instrumental, this time of a quirkier kind in the form of the proto-ambient music credited as the title track, and finally "Caroline No", with its totally inexplicable fade-out of barking dogs and a passing railroad train.[96] And, for that matter, what, if any, was the hidden significance of the LP's front cover shot, showing the Beach Boys feeding the goats at San Diego Zoo?

Brian's retrospective riposte was to say:

> The music of *Pet Sounds* was created solely for the purpose of making people feel good and making them feel like, 'Hey, that's really cool.' … Good, emotional music is never embarrassing. If you take the *Pet Sounds* album as a collection of art pieces, each designed to stand alone, yet which belong together, you'll see what I was aiming at.[97]

Never destined to be the US No.1 album of Brian's dreams, *Pet Sounds* was unexpectedly far better received in Britain, where a short *extempore* promotional visit to London in May by Bruce Johnston and the group's newly acquired press officer Derek Taylor was crucial to stoking a healthy demand for its release here. (EMI, as Capitol's UK distributor, originally had no plans to issue it until November at the earliest, to coincide with a planned Beach Boys tour. As for Capitol's own interests, the company would soon deem it prudent to hedge its bets against losses on the record by releasing a compilation LP in July, *Best Of The Beach Boys*, much against Brian's wishes.) Basing themselves at the Waldorf Hotel for five days, from 16th to 21st May, Johnston and Taylor ensured that their time was well spent by playing *Pet Sounds* to the highly appreciative aristocracy of the British pop industry (including Mick Jagger, Andrew Loog Oldham, John Lennon and Paul McCartney) as well as to respected music journalists such as Keith Altham and Penny Valentine.

Johnston, furthermore, was also interviewed live by Cathy McGowan when he made an impromptu appearance on *Ready Steady Go!* As word spread from these cleverly cultivated initial endorsements of the record's unique merits, sufficient wider interest was generated to force EMI to reconsider its position and the release of *Pet Sounds* was duly brought forward to 27th June. With a top placing of No.2 in the UK LP charts, it was eventually the fifth best-selling LP of the year; and, as another track stripped out as a single, "God Only Knows" would reach No.2 in the Top 30 for two weeks in late August and early September.

Bruce's timely – and, as it turned out – key intervention to raise the profile of *Pet Sounds* had followed end-on to the conclusion of a Beach Boys' US tour that had begun on 28th April. On 24th June, the group commenced another such tour as the headline act at San Francisco's Cow Palace (where their 'Summer Spectacular' concert line-up included the cream of contemporary West Coast bands – such as the Lovin' Spoonful, Jefferson Airplane and the Byrds – as well as soul singer Percy Sledge and the popular expatriate British duo Chad and Jeremy). For once, a critique of their performance on that occasion struck a curiously jarring note: "The Beach Boys are a very special thing. Their audience response was at least as great as the Spoonful's but they also inspire distaste and many left when they were on-stage. Personally, I can take them on record but in person I find them unbearable."[98] With the closing gig played at Asbury Park in New Jersey on 8th July, they allowed themselves a week's recovery before kicking off a new round of concert dates in Chicago on the 16th that continued through to Atlantic City on the 30th; after which, touring went into abeyance until the end of October, when they would embark on an ambitious trip to northern Europe.

During those periods when the operative unit of the group was away, Brian, as usual by now, was left behind to pursue his own singular preoccupations in the studio. Having completed *Pet Sounds*, his obsessive nature refocused itself for much of the remainder of spring and summer on a song with its origins in the earlier album sessions. (Indeed, his first tentative attempts to record it had consumed an eye-watering twenty-six takes of a potential instrumental backing track on 17th February; which he then scrapped the next day, when he worked on a further twenty-eight takes of a revised version.)

This was "Good Vibrations", originally composed with Tony Asher as one of their intended album tracks but soon set aside by Brian to be addressed at a later date as a project in its own right. In succession to Asher, Brian turned next to Van Dyke Parks as collaborator and lyricist; but while Parks was willing to assist with brand new compositions, he was reluctant to involve himself in rectifying existing work in progress. Thus Mike Love eventually came to Brian's rescue, helping him to revise and refine the lyrics to the point that ultimately it was the two of them who shared the composing credits. The time lavished on this specific enterprise was unprecedented, as neatly documented in summary here by Keith Badman:

> In the early hours of the morning of Thursday September 22nd, after 22 sessions lasting around 94 hours in four different recording studios, Brian's masterpiece is finally completed. His four-year musical apprenticeship has paid off wonderfully. 'Good Vibrations', recorded intermittently since February 18th, is at last finished, complete with that final set of lyrics by Mike Love. Brian has recorded somewhere between 15 and 20 different versions of the song before he is satisfied.[99]

The cost of the endeavour was correspondingly colossal – an estimated $50,000 to arrive at the most expensive single yet made in the short but increasingly colourful history of pop.

In the richness of its instrumental and vocal complexities, "Good Vibrations" far surpasses even the most outlandish arrangements to be found on *Pet Sounds*, with the undulating, throbbing notes of the electro-theremin providing the most distinctive element of all. Its reputation has long since transcended the more mundane facts of its release. Forever frozen in collective consciousness erroneously as the epitome of the so-called 'summer of love', it still comes as something of a shock to remember that, as a much earlier autumn release in both the US and UK, its original achievement had been to metaphorically bring a welcome splash of colour and light to the rapidly darkening days of October and November. A No.1 on both sides of the Atlantic (though not for long: one week in America, two in the UK), its place in modern music history is assured forever by the unique quality of its dazzling, other-worldly take on both the traditional love song and conventional pop record, Brian and Mike having taken their respective leads in weaving a tapestry of sound as the medium through which to distil the elusive essence of a swoon:

> I – I love the colourful
> clothes she wears
> and the way the sunlight
> plays upon her hair.
>
> I hear the sound
> of a gentle word
> on the wind that lifts
> her perfume through the air.
>
> I'm pickin' up good vibrations,
> She's giving me excitations.[100]

But words alone are not enough to sustain this ecstasy:

> I don't know where
> but she sends me there –
> Ah my, my, what a sensation!
> Ah my my, what an elation![101]

Which is where the music has its specific role to play, although its further deconstruction has always proved challenging. There simply is no escaping the fact that in its accretion of multiple layers of sound the resultant opus has to be seen as the pinnacle of Brian's achievements as producer in the primitive tape-splicing era of pre-digital recording.[102] The tragedy of it is, however, that he saw it as a stepping-off point for going yet one better, the threshold of an Icarus-like flight and fall from which, in the long term, he was lucky to recover. As early as 11th May, months before the completion of "Good Vibrations", Brian had temporarily diverted his mini-orchestra of session musicians to run through a preliminary instrumental arrangement of a new song he had composed with Van Dyke Parks, "Heroes And Villains". Work on it was then shelved until the autumn, when it was resurrected in October as one of an extensive folio of songs with which Brian had been preoccupied since August, his main object now being to produce a successor album to *Pet Sounds*. Provisionally entitled *Dumb Angel* in his head, in early September Brian confirmed that the new LP was to be called *Smile*, envisaging it as "a far-out trip through the old west, real Americana, but with lots of interesting humour".[103]

Apparently oblivious to the warning signs implicit in such a glib, if not flaky, overview, Capitol took him at his word and started to plan for its release at Christmas. According to Brian, "Heroes and Villains" would take its rightful place in this ill-assorted American pantheon as both an evocation of the Wild West and a "three minute musical comedy … a record that's better than 'Good Vibrations'".[104] At the same time, however, he was trying to collate other, currently disjointed aspects of his over-arching vision for *Smile*: such as pieces of music symbolising the four natural elements of earth, water, fire and air; or the "Barnyard Suite", "a musical depiction of farm life, replete with animal sounds, hammers and saws, and lyrics about 'eggs and grits'".[105] Sadly, the longer his quest for the unattainable continued, so the weaker became his ability to maintain a grasp on reality, personally and commercially.

Yet there were moments of lucidity amidst the turmoil of his best efforts to impose order on all this creative clutter. On 22nd October, for instance, he made a rare excursion with the rest of the Beach Boys to a two-concert gig at Michigan University, in order to rehearse the group beforehand for their first-ever live performance of "Good Vibrations" – a task on which he spent most of that day with them. The song went down well in front of both houses, Brian himself being persuaded to come out and sing "Johnny B. Goode" as a surprise encore to the second show.[106] But on his homeward flight, he prevailed upon the aircrew to relay a message ahead to his wife Marilyn, to the effect that she should bring some thirty of his closest friends and acquaintances with her to meet him on his arrival back at Los Angeles Airport; where Brian then posed with them all in turn for a sequence of group photographic portraits, his selected favourites from these pictures later adorning the walls at home.

Alas, these tangible outcomes of his carefully orchestrated group encounter proved incapable of warding off his paranoid delusions for long. As his interactions with his immediate social circle grew ever more irrational and eccentric, so it understandably provoked a reaction from those regularly in his company, to "ponder the thin line between divine inspiration and complete lunacy"[107] in the make-up of his personality. Although he remained obsessively dedicated to the completion of *Smile*, at the same time he found this visionary project troubling to the point of over-burdening: even after the conclusion of the forty-third recording session on 28th December, the sad fact was that the end product of all his painstaking micro-assembly – much to Capitol's dismay, no less Brian's – was just as tantalisingly far away as ever.

After Michigan, the performing Beach Boys took their leave of Brian for northern Europe, the opening date of their tour being at the Paris Olympia on 25th October and their set list, as hitherto, inevitably dominated by their back-catalogue of hits, with "God Only Knows" and "Good Vibrations" the only concessions to the group's newer music. Here they played to a disparate audience of "teenage ravers … who started screaming directly the curtain rose … liberally mixed with an incongruous assortment of silent middle-aged devotees" and were seemingly reliant on their compelling harmonic presence to carry them through: "On stage they have no act. Mike Love does a little clowning around when he introduces the numbers, but on the whole it's just a case of standing up and singing – beautifully."[108]

Moving on through West Germany, Denmark and Sweden, they flew into Heathrow on 6th November – the day after "Good Vibrations" had entered the UK Top 30 at No.6 – to scenes redolent of the heights of Beatlemania as they were greeted and then pursued by hordes of screaming fans. That night, they played the first two houses of this, the longest leg of the tour at the Finsbury Park Astoria but again failing to satisfy all of their critics, such as experienced music journalist Ray Coleman: "It just isn't enough for five imageless Americans to stand and sing. They made no attempt to project personality unless it lay in their fresh California sun outfits of blue and white striped shirts and pure white trousers …"[109]

With similar criticisms in England having been directed the year before at the Byrds' lack of stagecraft, and with Dylan almost calculatingly oblivious to what anybody thought of him or his music in live performance, a clearer cultural divide – in terms of audiences' expectations and entertainment value – was thus emerging between already established British acts and the retaliatory new wave of American artists, attended by the faintest whiff of sour grapes. Admittedly, many British groups, from the Beatles onwards, had built up their stage acts from the foundations of passing through the formative mill of Hamburg, where they had been subject to the *mach shau* regime of uncompromising club owners; an experience totally alien to their American counterparts. Yet there is strong evidence to the effect that on their home turf, notably on the West Coast, American performers were equally capable of generating overwhelmingly positive and energetic audience responses: witness, for example, the thriving dance scene in the Hollywood beat clubs of the mid-Sixties. The British concert circuit, predominantly made up of provincial cinemas and theatres, must have seemed quaintly archaic by comparison with the vaster geographical spread in the US of multiple sports arenas, state fairgrounds and university campuses; and it has to be remembered that groups like the Byrds and the Beach Boys or artists of Dylan's stature were well used to playing dedicated concert venues such as the Hollywood Bowl or Carnegie Hall (to which the Royal Albert Hall was the only British equivalent).

Following a circuitous route via Leicester, Leeds, Manchester, Cardiff and Birmingham, accompanied by Lulu as their principal supporting act, the Beach Boys were back in London on 14th November to close the tour at the Hammersmith Odeon. Returning to Los Angeles next day, they were put on notice by Brian that as things currently stood they faced the prospect of much hard work in the studio to finish "Heroes And Villains" and *Smile* by Christmas; pressure intensified by them having to take off again almost immediately for their fourth annual 'Thanksgiving Tour', filling the next eight days with concerts in the north-eastern States and Canada.

With that behind them, they reconvened with Brian at Gold Star Studios on 28th November, when former tensions between him and Mike Love in particular were almost instantly reignited. To Mike, his cousin's whole demeanour and the off-the-wall character of the music with which he was now cajoling the group to engage strongly suggested that in their absence Brian had fallen under the unwelcome influence of others. The ultimate flashpoint was triggered on 6th December at the CBS Studios, at a session in which Mike angrily refused to proceed any further with recording a segment of "Cabin Essence" from *Smile* until he received a satisfactory explanation of the lyric. (He was specifically incensed by the lines "Over and over, the crow cries uncover the cornfield./Over and over, the thresher and hover the wheat field"[110] – perfectly acceptable as possible lost lines from, say, a poem by Dylan Thomas but hardly the stuff of a stand-out track on the Beach Boys' latest LP.) Brian, fearful of direct conflict, called collaborator Van Dyke Parks to come to his rescue; and when he arrived at the studio, he walked head-on into a confrontation with the furious Mike:

"I want you to tell me what it means!" Mike demanded … Van Dyke dodged the issue entirely. "If you're looking for a literal explanation of that line, of any line of verse, I don't have it," he replied simply.

"You don't know what it means?" Mike laughed. "You wrote it and YOU don't know what it means?"

"I have no excuse, sir."[111]

Opting then for discretion as the better part of valour, Parks walked out, and from that moment Brian's beloved *Smile* project began to unravel, although it would take until well into 1967 before it was utterly dead in the water. In the interim, Brian's "appetite for amphetamines and hashish accelerated, and his episodes of paranoia became more profound and frightening".[112] How strange, therefore, that against this undisclosed backdrop of mounting discord in private the Beach Boys should come top of the *NME* poll, by a narrow margin of a hundred votes above the Beatles, as the overall Best Group of 1966.

Pete Townshend, for one, was not immediately enamoured by the Beach Boys' shift away from surf music and provided the British music press with some savage contemporary quotes to make his point. He was initially dismissive of *Pet Sounds* for being reliant on "an audience sympathetic to Brian Wilson's personal problems", going on to suggest that it had been devised "for a feminine audience" by virtue of its content being "too remote and way out".[113] And when presented with "Good Vibrations" in due course, he totally lost his cool:

> Brian Wilson lives in a world of flowers, butterflies and strawberry flavoured chewing gum. His world has nothing to do with pop. Pop is going out on the road, getting drunk and meeting the kids. 'Good Vibrations' was probably a good record but who's to know? You had to play it about 90 bloody times to even hear what they were singing about.[114]

In one sense, of course, these barbs were fuelled by a sense of betrayal, for the Who (especially Keith Moon) were known devotees of surf music, playing it live themselves as well as allowing its style to influence some of their own compositions or their delivery of others' work. But in another, perhaps they reflected an unwilling, subconscious recognition on Townshend's part of the similarities between himself and Wilson. Both were driven by the urge to make grandiose artistic statements through music; both built up their own compositions piecemeal from shimmering fragments of potential tunes that they salted away on demo tapes; both were deeply introspective and self-analytical; both unashamedly sought refuge and escape in recreational drugs. And neither of them envisioned a pop group as constituting a democracy.

After three hit singles to date through producer Shel Talmy's deal with the Brunswick label, in January 1966 the Who's managers Chris Stamp and Kit Lambert went looking for a better deal for the group from parent company Decca. When this was not forthcoming, and with the benefit of legal advice suggesting they could fend off an action for breach of contract, they opted instead to place the Who with promoter Robert Stigwood and his Reaction record label (that he had just set up as a new subsidiary of Polydor). While this paved the way for a succession of exciting new releases, it could not prevent either a long-running dispute with Shel Talmy or extended spoiling action from Decca in the form of seeking to undermine the Who's home market with the reissue of old tracks from *My Generation* as singles.

Reaction opened for business proper on 4th March with the release of "Substitute" (b/w "Circles", *aka* "Instant Party"), the first of several Townshend compositions exploring issues of trust and identity that the Who recorded in the course of this year. It is an intriguing song, replete with images of artifice, in which the protagonist denounces his lover's falsehoods by disclosing that he too has deliberately cultivated a deceptive persona:

> You think we look pretty good together.
> You think my shoes are made of leather.
>
> But I'm a substitute for another guy.
> I look pretty tall but my heels are high.
> The simple things you see are all complicated.

I look pretty young but I'm just back-dated, yeah.

Substitute your lies for facts.
I can see right through your plastic mac.
I look all white but my dad was black.
My brand-new suit is really made out of sack.[115]

The final put-down is that he'd be better off with his mum: "At least I'll get my washing done."[116]

Although advance orders were strong, distribution was suddenly halted by a court injunction, secured by Talmy on the grounds of alleged breach of copyright. (He claimed production rights over both the A and B sides in relation to the Who's last recording session with him at IBC Studios in January; whereas "Substitute" at least had not been recorded until February at Olympic Studios, when Townshend himself had acted as producer.) Thus a re-release was hastily organised for 14th March, this time – with the subtlety of a Loog Oldham at his most contemptuous – with a replacement instrumental B-side by 'The Who Orchestra' entitled "Waltz For A Pig" (actually composed by Ginger Baker during his time with the Graham Bond Organisation). Breaking into the Top 30 at No.19 on 12th March, it eventually made No.7 on 23rd April; a week before the Who played it as one of their two numbers (with "My Generation") in their brief appearance at the *NME* Poll-Winners' Concert.

The spring of 1966 witnessed further turbulence in the group's internal relationships. In March, Pete Townshend had suspected John Entwistle and Keith Moon of seriously considering branching out to form a group of their own; fears that by May were further fuelled by Moon being commissioned in secret to play drums on a solo recording by the Yardbirds' Jeff Beck. At a concert in Newbury on 20th May, Townshend and Roger Daltrey had had to improvise with two subbing musicians from a support act in the absence of Entwistle and Moon. When they finally came on stage, more than two hours late, frayed tempers all too readily snapped: "Keith sustained a black eye and a leg injury requiring three stitches, after being bodily injured by Pete's guitar and Roger's mike stand."[117] Following this clash, Moon declared his intention of leaving with Entwistle, a temporary rift mended after a week of conciliatory efforts behind the scenes by Kit Lambert and Robert Stigwood. As time went on, however, any lingering frustrations more commonly found a safety valve in the premeditated auto-destructive climax to their stage act; as here, for example, at the Windsor Jazz and Blues Festival on 30th July:

> Lambert and Stamp stood in the wings, lighting and throwing smoke bombs onto the stage. A dry-ice machine created artificial mist as Pete smashed his guitar and pushed amplifiers over, Keith scattered his kit and Roger threw microphones and kicked in the

footlights. A section of the crowd broke chairs and damaged canvas screens in response to the group's antics, while others were exuberantly celebrating England's victory in that day's 1966 World Cup Final.[118]

More radical than "Substitute", the next single, "I'm A Boy", examined gender issues through the salutary story of Bill, being brought up as a girl with his three sisters:

Put your frock on, Jean Marie.
Plait your hair, Felicity.
Paint your nails, little Sally Joy.
Put this wig on, little boy.[119]

Bill has learnt the hard way that resistance is futile:

I'm a boy, I'm a boy,
But my ma won't admit it.
I'm a boy, I'm a boy,
But if I say I am, I get it.

So all he can do is dream of the rough-and-tumble boy's life he would lead if only left to his own devices:

I wanna play cricket on the green,
Ride my bike across the stream;
Cut myself and see my blood,
I wanna come home all covered in mud.[120]

One striking feature of this record (marking Kit Lambert's debut as producer) is the rounding-off of the instrumental break after the second chorus by the group vocalising wordless harmonies worthy of the Beach Boys. Townshend later claimed the song originated from a futuristic storyline of his about a society in which parents are able to choose the sex of their children, into which Bill is born by mistake. Nevertheless, at the time of its release, on 26th August, it was issued without the benefit of any such gloss; and when you saw Roger Daltrey sing it straight-faced, you knew you were meant to sit up and take it seriously, as opposed to seeing it in any way as a novelty record. Its release also signalled the Who's ability at last to move on from the lawsuit mounted by Talmy, with whom Stamp and Lambert had finally reached an accommodation: he was to drop his action, in exchange for 5% of the royalties from the group's records for the next five years.

Making its Top 30 entry at No.13 in mid-September, "I'm A Boy" climbed to No.2 for the first two weeks of October, there finding its way to the top of the charts blocked by the posthumous sentimentality of "Distant Drums" by Jim Reeves. It was also one of the numbers the Who chose for their contribution to a special edition of *Ready Steady Go!* that they pre-recorded on 18th October, when theirs was the sole act featured in the programme's second half; although the subsequent 'commemorative' EP of the event, released on 11th November as *Ready Steady Who*, was, in fact, made up of existing recordings of the five tracks concerned to avoid infringing the TV company's rights to the broadcast material.

Side 1 opens with "Disguises", yet another of Townshend's teasing 'puzzle' songs:

> I used to know everything about you
> But today, when I tried to point you
> Out to one of my friends,
> I picked the wrong girl again.
> Don't see you in the crowd any more,
> I think it's you but I can't be sure.
>
> You're wearing disguises.
> Occasionally a girl surprises me
> When she turns out to be you,
> Wearing disguises.[121]

It is followed by a reprise of the contentious B-side "Circles", while on Side 2 there are three cover versions: a parody of the theme to the contemporary *Batman* TV series, plus two West Coast classics – Jan and Dean's hotrod song "Bucket 'T'" and the Beach Boys' "Barbara Ann" – on both of which surf music fanatic Keith Moon sings the lead vocals. At a time when sales of EPs were headed into decline, *Ready Steady Who* still managed a respectable one week at No.30 in the singles chart in the week ending 19th November.

As the end of the year approached, 9th December saw the simultaneous issue by Reaction of a new single, "Happy Jack", and the Who's second LP, *A Quick One*, both firmly rooted in Townshend's not always comfortable childhood memories.

In his autobiography, he describes "Happy Jack" as "a nonsense song I wrote about a village idiot from the Isle of Man ... partly inspired by 'Eleanor Rigby'" and says that his intention in the lyric was to create a "Kafkaesque" atmosphere.[122] It is without question a left-field take on revisiting the long annual holidays he spent on the Isle of Man as a boy, while his father Clifford played saxophone and clarinet through summer seasons there with the Squadronaires dance band. The title character, akin to Keith Waterhouse's Uncle Mad in his first novel *There Is A Happy Land*, attracts the curiosity and taunts of children whilst remaining locked in his own unassailable world:

> Happy Jack wasn't old but he was a man.
> He lived in the sand at the Isle of Man.

The kids all would sing, he would take the wrong key,
So they rode on his head in their furry donkey,
But they never stopped Jack, nor the waters' lapping
And they couldn't distract him from the seagulls' flapping.

The kids couldn't hurt Jack,
They tried and tried and tried.
They dropped things on his back
And lied and lied and lied and lied and lied.

But they never stopped Jack, nor the waters' lapping
And they couldn't prevent Jack from feeling happy.[123]

Advertised in the *NME* by a grotesque Ralph Steadman pen-and-ink caricature of the group, the record made a lowly arrival in the pre-Christmas
charts at No.25, before rising to No.3 a month later. (Unaccountably, given
the obscurity of its content, later still in 1967 it would even go on to give the
Who their first US hit in the *Billboard* Top 40.)

    A Quick One, however, was, in compositional terms, an atypical collab-
orative effort, to which Townshend contributed only four of the ten tracks.
With an advance on the music publishing rights, negotiated by Stamp and
Lambert to cover the recording costs, conditional upon all four group
members writing songs, this brought forth a predictably eclectic mix. From
John Entwistle came "Boris The Spider" and "Whiskey Man" (the two most
atmospheric tracks of the whole set); from Keith Moon, "I Need You" and
the manic instrumental "Cobwebs And Strange"; and from Roger Daltrey,
"See My Way". A surf-inspired cover version of Martha and the Vandellas'
"Heatwave" was thrown in for good measure but it was the concluding,
Townshend-composed suite of tracks that truly marked the LP out for crit-
ical attention.

    In the scope of 9 minutes 10 seconds, the mock operetta "A Quick One,
While He's Away" tells the story of "the unnamed heroine [who] pines for
her absent lover, selects Ivor [The Engine Driver] as a substitute, regrets
her folly when her man returns, confesses her indiscretion and is ultimately
forgiven".[124] Townshend disclosed much later that it was imbued with "dark
reflections of my childhood"[125] with their origins in the deep unhappiness he
had experienced from the age of five, when his mother had been unfaithful
to his absentee father and he had been sent away from home to live temporarily with his maternal grandmother:

    [She] took in men from the bus garage and the railway station
    opposite her flat all the time, and I still have nightmares in which
    my bedroom door opens in the middle of the night and a shadowy

man and woman stand watching me, the perfume of eroticism in the air.[126]

That was why the finale of the piece, "You Are Forgiven", held particular significance for him: "When I sang this part live on stage, I would often become more furious, thrashing at my guitar until I could thrash no more, frantically forgiving my mother, her lover, my grandmother, her lovers, and most of all myself."[127]

To me, the glossy album cover was a beautiful artefact to possess in its own right, the front of the sleeve bearing one of Alan Aldridge's earliest pyschedelic illustrations, depicting each group member in rotation with their instruments and the title of one of the songs they had written streaming away from them to the four corners, its vivid airbrushed colours shining out against a black ground. With the innovative structure of its title track as its unique selling point, *A Quick One* proved more popular in sales terms than *My Generation*, enjoying a longer run in the LP charts than its predecessor to eventually reach No.4.

Having rampaged through Scandinavia, France and West Germany on a tour from late October into November, the Who rounded off their year in typically robust style on 20th December by joining a host of stars bidding farewell to the last-ever edition of *Ready Steady Go!*, the programme to which they more than most had good cause to be grateful for its patronage; before taking to the stage at the Roundhouse on New Year's Eve at an event billed as "Psychedelicamania", where reportedly:

> The strobe lights in use interfered with Pete's playing, and three
> power cuts and several lighting failures didn't improve his mood.
> This resulted in a particularly savage guitar and amp smashing
> display, with shards flying into the audience, prompting a flurry of
> aggrieved letters to *Melody Maker*.[128]

Every bit as unpredictable as the Who, the Kinks would find 1966 equally tempestuous. A year in their history forever distinguished by the release of an impressive trilogy of ground-breaking hit singles, it was also a year in which Ray Davies was, as he had feared, driven to near-breakdown by mounting personal and commercial pressures before he was able to seize greater control of the group's output and artistic direction.

With "Till The End Of The Day" on the slide down the charts from January into February, the Kinks returned to the studio, working over several days on a potential new single of a wholly different character yet struggling to complete a final take with which they all felt content. This was the social satire aimed at the gadflies of Swinging London, "Dedicated Follower Of Fashion", that in the end Pye rush-released on 25th February and made it to No.4 in April. Reputedly written by Ray to vent his spleen at being insulted about his dress sense by a party guest, it shifted the group's focus back from hard rock to the barbed observational humour that with seeming effortlessness had earlier informed "A Well Respected Man". While the lyric predominantly highlights one individual, who "flits from shop to shop just like a butterfly", at its heart the song is scornful of all those seduced by the contemporary hype conferring exclusivity upon the garish boutiques of Carnaby Street:

> They seek him here, they seek him there,
> In Regent Street and Leicester Square.
> Everywhere the Carnabetian army marches on,
> Each one a dedicated follower of fashion.[129]

Soon after its release, however, immediately following the Kinks' return from a brief tour of Switzerland and Austria at the beginning of March, Ray was overcome by nervous exhaustion and forced to recuperate for several weeks at home. The depression with which he was now afflicted robbed him at a stroke of the ability to share others' delight in the song's music-hall jollity:

> With 'A Dedicated Follower Of Fashion' such a hit, people started
> coming up to me in the street and singing the chorus in my face:
> 'Oh yes he is, he is, oh yes he is,' as if to say that I knew who I was.
> Unfortunately, my inner and somewhat distorted sense of reality
> told me that this was not who I wanted to be: I didn't know who I
> was. I didn't care that everybody loved the song or that it was being
> quoted on television and in the tabloids as a comment on the times.
> I saw myself on Top Of The Pops and tried to throw the television
> out of the kitchen window. In the end, I compromised with my
> concerned relatives and put the television in the gas oven. The cord
> was still attached to the wall and through the glass in the oven I was
> still performing. 'Oh yes he is, oh yes he is.' After that I declared I
> was going to bed and woke up a week later with a moustache and a
> beard.[130]

To fulfil the group's next touring commitments later in the month in Belgium, Dave Davies was obliged to assume the role of leader and Mick Grace was temporarily taken on as stand-in for Ray; but on their return, in Ray's continuing absence a string of UK concerts had to be cancelled.

This was just as well, for in the depths of his despair Ray's frustrations had erupted into violence towards others, as evidenced by the following notes from his diary, maintained during his illness by his wife Rasa:

> Tuesday, 15 March. Ray very ill. Doctor came to see him. Said
> needed extreme rest and quiet. Ray very depressed and very ill.

Many pills – sedatives and sleeping pills. Psychiatrist came (Rasa black eye). Ray nearly had nervous breakdown. Family interfering very much. Fight with Rasa. Fight with Gwen [the youngest of Ray's sisters]. Gwen hit Ray while he was helpless in bed. Ray nose-bleed, extremely upset. Ray's mother came over and caused a terrible scene. He had terrible argument with them.

Thursday, 17 March. Ray went to Robert [Wace]'s office, punched Brian Somerville in face. Doctor came.[131]

Unsurprisingly, the assault on Somerville (who had shown little sympathy for Ray's predicament) prompted his resignation as the Kinks' publicist but the period of enforced rest that then ensued was ultimately to Ray's benefit: "In the music press they were saying that I had become a recluse and there were even rumours that I had left the group. But the break allowed me time to stay at home and write songs, some of which were therapeutic, others for the next Kinks album."[132]

Later claiming in an interview to have written as many as forty new songs during this period of gradual recovery from his mental turmoil, Ray's welcome revival in creativity would now aptly encompass the composition of "Sunny Afternoon" as well as a slew of tracks for the LP *Face To Face*. "Sunny Afternoon" – emanating from the same sense of grievance informing George Harrison's "Taxman" – was intended to be "a topical song about the new taxes the Labour Government was bringing in to relieve the wealthy of all their hard-earned cash", that Ray enlivened by turning "the narrator into a scoundrel who fought with his girlfriend after a night of drunkenness and cruelty".[133] When he first played the tune through for Dave, his brother was instantly taken with it:

Ray insisted I get my guitar and listen to an idea he had. A noticeably forlorn-looking Rasa stood by his side as he sat by the piano and started to play in octaves the descending line of what was soon to become the main riff … He played the riff again, I doubled the line with my guitar, and he sang the rough first verse of it.

I got that now familiar chill up my spine and knew that this was something special. It was the same way I felt when I first heard 'You Really Got Me'. A mysterious magic had visited the three of us in that little house in Fortis Green.[134]

By early April, Ray was well enough to rejoin the rest of the group for the resumption of recording sessions with Shel Talmy at Pye's Marble Arch Studios, shortly afterwards taking to the stage again for live performances (including trips to France and the Netherlands). "Sunny Afternoon" was recorded on 13th May, the good-time feel of the arrangement enhanced by contributions from respected session man Nicky Hopkins on piano and melodica. Deliberately released by Pye on 3rd June to coincide with the onset of summer, it displaced the Beatles' "Paperback Writer" when it reached No.1 in mid-July, before itself being dislodged after two weeks by Chris Farlowe's cover of "Out Of Time". It was, as both Ray and the record company had suspected, the perfect catchy, seasonal hit:

> The taxman's taken all my dough
> And left me in my stately home,
> Lazing on a sunny afternoon.
> And I can't sail my yacht,
> He's taken everything I've got.
> All I've got's this sunny afternoon.
>
> Save me, save me, save me from this squeeze.
> I got a big fat momma trying to break me.
> And I love to live so pleasantly,
> Live this life of luxury,
> Lazing on a sunny afternoon
> In the summertime,
> In the summertime,
> In the summertime.[135]

For those of us who were all too willing purchasers, however, the single did offer a startling bonus in the radically different B-side, the proto-punk "I'm Not Like Everybody Else", seen by some as "a manifesto for the band".[136] With its clanging, snarling guitars, plus the hypnotic swirl of an electric organ intermittently discernible in the middle distance of the mix, the arrangement is every bit as challenging as Dave's aggressive lead vocals and the uncompromising chant of the chorus:

> I'm not like everybody else,
> I'm not like everybody else,
> And I don't want to ball about like everybody else,
> And I don't want to live my life like everybody else,
> And I won't say that I feel fine like everybody else
> 'Cause I'm not like everybody else,
> I'm not like everybody else.[137]

Happening to coincide with the release of "Sunny Afternoon", the Kinks were booked for a gig in Morecambe on 3rd June. Afterwards, travelling separately from others with the group's kit to their overnight stop at a B-and-B in Manchester, Pete Quaife and road manager Jonah Jones were both injured in a collision with a lorry on the M6 and admitted to hospital in Warrington. At short notice, therefore, bass player John Dalton was recruited as Pete's temporary replacement, although in the event he actually retained that stand-in role for five months, thereby touring extensively with the Kinks in the UK as well as around Europe. He was even briefly taken on permanently, after Pete ended a prolonged convalescence by announcing his intention to marry and settle in Denmark, and his formal resignation with effect from the end of September; but his services were dispensed with (at least for the foreseeable future) in November, after Dave managed to persuade Pete to rejoin them.

With unresolved contractual difficulties from Ray's precipitate actions of the year before still bedevilling the Kinks' relationship with Pye, once the recording of *Face To Face* had been all but completed by the end of June, the record company postponed its release for the time being; opting in the interim to issue a compilation LP of past singles and EP tracks, *Well Respected Kinks*, on its Marble Arch budget label on 2nd September. For fans like me, who had missed out on collecting some of their earlier work, it was well worth the duplication of one or two tracks to buy their greatest hits at cut-price; and, as the only Kinks LP of the year so far, it proved immensely popular, peaking at No.5 in the course of an unbroken thirty-one weeks in the LP charts – paradoxically, by far the longest chart-run achieved by any of their albums.

Through transatlantic shuttle diplomacy from July onwards, Allen Klein was engaged by Robert Wace and Grenville Collins, with Ray's approval, to renegotiate the Kinks' recording contracts in both the US and UK, as well as to seek a settlement of Ray's ongoing dispute with Kassner over his composer's royalties. By October Klein had at least got as far as agreeing new five-year contracts for the group with Reprise in America and Pye in Britain, thus finally clearing the way for Pye to sanction the UK release of *Face To Face* on the 28th of that month. Of all their LPs to date, it offered the most coherent set of songs yet, unified, of course, to a great extent by the fact that the majority had been composed during Ray's enforced sabbatical. "Sunny Afternoon" was included, complemented by two near-companion pieces, "A House In The Country" and "Most Exclusive Residence For Sale"; while "Too Much On My Mind" and "Rainy Day In June" clearly reflected different facets of the depths to which he had sunk in his illness, and "Rosy Won't You Please Come Home" betrayed a yearning to be reunited with his sister in Australia. In contrast, on the lighter side were songs such as "Holiday In Waikiki", revisiting the closing moments of last year's US tour; and "Dandy", a suitably up-tempo, rumbustious portrayal of a perpetual womaniser: "It was about someone, probably me, needing to make his mind up about relationships. Also about my brother who was flitting from one girl to another. It's a more serious song than it seems. It's about a man trapped by his own indecisions and lack of commitment."[138]

Tired of the unimaginative staged photographs Pye had used on the sleeves of their earlier albums, Ray had even had a hand in designing the LP cover this time, depicting "this kind of theatrical mask with the head lifted up and butterflies fluttering out from the inside. Huge butterflies all over the cover and just the word 'Kinks' on the front".[139] In its final realisation, the non-photographic cover, true to Ray's wishes, is awash with bright primary colours, revolutionary in its day but now instantly recognisable as classic mid-Sixties' graphic art. Heavily outsold anyway by *Well Respected Kinks*, *Face To Face* turned out to be the least successful of their original LPs so far but nevertheless deserved to do much better than its short chart run of 11 weeks and highest placing of No.12 might suggest.

Next to be released, on 18th November, was their last single of the year, "Dead End Street", unusually for pop of the period a song belying a strong sense of social conscience. Dave generously described it as:

> … the epitome, to me, of what the Kinks were all about. A song full of character, pathos, yet containing an underlying sense of hope. Reflecting a fondness for the past but at the same time expressing a determination and yearning for change. Anguished voices calling to a heartless world. A world where the plight of the ordinary person mattered little.[140]

Ray was even more forthright in attributing its origins to finding that delicate balance between expiating his own sense of guilt and humbly setting his art to work in the service of protest:

> … I think the sixties were a con: the establishment still ruled the country … The sixties were like a carrot held up to youth to distract us so that we would not rebel against the ruling classes and all the backhanders and corruption that were actually present in politics. The countryside was being eroded and trees pulled up in order to build motorways, factories were being closed, coal mines were being ear-marked for the chop … I was becoming aware of the thousands of people who were being given the shit end of the stick in the sixties. They were the people who would be left behind without work when the party was over, without a place in society. My job lasted from record to record. The sick thing was, that I was heralded as a standard-bearer for that deceitful time. I was writing songs and the country was gradually being sold out. Cheated.[141]

He succeeded, as it has turned out, in writing a song of timeless quality, remaining as sadly relevant today as it ever was. Thirty years earlier, George Orwell had famously encapsulated the degrading essence of inter-war poverty in the image of a young woman he had spied momentarily from a train:

She looked up as the train passed, and I was almost near enough to catch her eye. She had a round pale face, the usual exhausted face of the slum girl who is twenty-five and looks forty, thanks to miscarriages and drudgery; and it wore, for the second in which I saw it, the most desolate, hopeless expression I have ever seen. It struck me then that we are mistaken when we say that 'It isn't the same for them as it would be for us', and that people bred in the slums can imagine nothing but the slums. For what I saw in her face was not the ignorant suffering of an animal. She knew well enough what was happening to her – understood as well as I did how dreadful a destiny it was to be kneeling there in the bitter cold, on the slimy stones of a slum backyard, poking a stick up a foul drain-pipe.[142]

Now Ray and the Kinks served up "Dead End Street" as a reminder that, for all the Sixties' self-congratulation, post-war decadence had neither vanquished that grinding poverty nor yet brought real hope to those on the breadline:

There's a crack up in the ceiling,
And the kitchen sink is leaking.

Out of work and got no money,
A Sunday joint of bread and honey.

What are we living for?
Two-roomed apartment on the second floor.
No money coming in.
The rent collector's knocking, trying to get in.

We are strictly second class,
We don't understand
(Dead end!)
Why we should be on Dead End Street.
(Dead end!)
People are living on Dead End Street,
(Dead end!)
Gonna die on Dead End Street.[143]

Almost in the spirit of a New Orleans funeral march, the arrangement incorporated a sleazy trombone in the extended fade-out; and a Pythoneseque promotional film (that the BBC refused to show on *Top Of The Pops*) cast the Kinks as undertakers, bearing a coffin into a terraced house where Dave doubled as a grieving widow.

The B-side, "Big Black Smoke", was, according to Dave, the perfect match in "atmosphere, sound and feeling", telling the modern story of "a young girl who leaves her country home in search of something more exciting in the city".[144] Positively Dickensian in its feel, the heroine of the song is the:

Frailest, purest girl the world has seen,
According to her Ma, according to her Pa,
And everybody said
That she knew no sin and did no wrong
Till she walked the streets of the Big Black Smoke,
Of the Big Black Smoke.[145]

She does, however, end up spending her money on "purple hearts and cigarettes" before falling into the clutches of no-good Joe who "took her money for the rent/And tried to drag her down".[146] Beginning with a fade-in of church bells symbolic of the wicked capital city, the track concludes, like the A-side, with an extended fade-out, this time reprising the bells but building up an atmospheric cacophony by adding in the repeated 'Oyez!' of a town crier. The most thought-provoking and imaginative single of the year from the Kinks, it clambered its way up to and hung onto the No.8 position for three weeks over Christmas and the New Year despite finding itself in decidedly mixed chart company.

Between them, headlining acts of the calibre of the Rolling Stones, the Who and the Kinks confirmed that by 1966 the epicentre of British pop had irretrievably shifted well south of Watford. As if to underline the demise of Merseybeat, the Cavern itself was forced to close on 28th February and seized by bailiffs, after Ray McFall was driven into bankruptcy by his inability to meet the costs of complying with an order from Liverpool City Council to rectify the club's inadequate sanitation. When local MP Bessie Braddock failed to get a rescue bid off the ground, the Official Receiver put the club up for sale; and on 18th April it was bought by café-owner Joe Davey, who revamped it in partnership with butcher Alf Geoghegan. It was officially reopened on 23rd July by another Liverpool MP, Prime Minister Harold Wilson, who, as the country's then best-known pipe-smoker, received a commemorative gift of "a pipe made out of wood from the Cavern's original stage".[147] And just as the Cavern's glory days were behind it, so the charts now said farewell to the last of the Mersey performers who had benefited from the halo effect of being members of the Beatles' extended musical family.

Stalwarts of the Cavern from the outset, the Swinging Blue Jeans scraped into the charts for one last time after a string of misses. Their cover of Dionne Warwick's "Don't Make Me Over" (composed, inevitably, by Bacharach and David) gave them a final, fleeting entry at No.30 for the week ending 19th February. The Merseybeats had split up in 1965, despite the best efforts of the group's new managers Chris Stamp and Kit Lambert to revive their fortunes, thus leaving Billy Kinsley and Tony Crane to carry on in their stead as the Merseys. Their one and only hit came with the release of their debut single as a duo in April, "Sorrow", an American composition originally recorded as a B-side by the McCoys. It spent a total of ten weeks in the Top 30, three of those in June at its peak position of No.5, but its success was not destined to be repeated, even with a follow-up song by Pete Townshend, "So Sad About Us" (which the Who, of course, later recorded themselves as a track on *A Quick One*). And, as we saw earlier in this chapter, the Searchers had bowed out of the charts in May.

Nonetheless, there were other mid- to long-term survivors who fared better, even in the face of changing musical tastes, including some who had already been through break-ups and re-formations. The Mindbenders, for example, overcame their rift with former frontman Wayne Fontana in spectacular style in late January with their first single in their own right, "A Groovy Kind Of Love", which eventually occupied the No.3 slot for three weeks from the end of February and went on to be a No.2 hit in the US. Subsequent releases were never going to be so popular; but they did have two lesser hits, "Can't Live With You, Can't Live Without You" (reaching No.22 for two weeks at the end of May/beginning of June) and "Ashes To Ashes"[148] (No.16 in September). As for Fontana himself, he returned to the charts in May with "Come On Home", which took him to a respectable No.14 in June; and "Goodbye Bluebird", which less encouragingly only managed a week at No.30 in September.

For their first Decca single after jumping ship from Columbia, the Animals chanced their arm with "Inside Looking Out", an Eric Burdon/Chas Chandler adaptation of a traditional American prison song. Tom Wilson, highly respected for his work in the past with Bob Dylan, was assigned to them as their new producer and, compared to the run of hits they had experienced with Mickie Most, this was a much darker and heavily blues-oriented number; with, in Sean Egan's words, "instrumentation … as brutal as the prison regime the song describes".[149] In the week ending 19th February, with the Stones' "19th Nervous Breakdown" newly at No.1, it jumped straight into the Top 30 at No.11 but could not sustain that early promise and a week later it had already peaked, at No.6. That same month, an utterly disenchanted John Steel gave his notice to quit, fearing that a break-up of the group was imminent and feeling, as a married man and father, inadequately rewarded for the long hours he had put in on the road away from home: "We just worked continually and we were still getting the same basic retainer as we were a couple of years before. Where was the money? All this bloody work and all the records sold. I never saw a big cheque yet. I was just fed up."[150]

Burdon dispensed with the formalities of audition for Steel's replacement by making a direct approach to Barry Jenkins of the Nashville Teens, and Jenkins duly made his first appearance as the Animals' new drummer on 15th March. Chas Chandler, however, who had taken Steel's loss hard, resented the change: "If anything, the real sound of the Animals was the swing of John's drumming. I think that's what distinguished us from other bands at the time. And when Barry Jenkins came in, we were just another rock band and I literally lost interest overnight."[151] And, as if to prove Steel prescient, the new line-up was not destined to last the year, even though the Animals' next single, the Goffin & King song "Don't Bring Me Down", was probably the best record they had made since "House Of The Rising Sun".

Recorded on portable equipment shipped out to the Bahamas where the group were taking time out from touring, it not only features a distinctive riff by Hilton Valentine on lead guitar, much enhanced by fuzz-box and reverb, but also gives particular prominence to Dave Rowberry's playing on piano and organ (despite the latter being recorded through a radiogram speaker in the absence of an amplifier). Going straight into the Top 20 at No.17 on its release in June, two weeks later it had matched "Inside Looking Out" by peaking at No.6 – one place below the Merseys' "Sorrow", two below the Stones' "Paint It, Black". But by the time another chart entry was credited to 'Eric Burdon & The Animals' in October (their last Decca single, "Help Me Girl", which got to No.19 in mid-November), the group existed in name only: Burdon had broken it up, claiming not to have the support of the others to "help me realise further new concepts and new materials"[152], and – temporarily – gone solo, filling the void with session musicians as a stop-gap.

Increasingly seduced by the burgeoning association between drugs and rock music on the West Coast of America, with which he had grown familiar through frequent tours of the US, in the autumn Burdon set about recruiting members of a band that would become known as the New Animals; turning his back in the process on any last vestige of his historic musical connections to Tyneside. Keeping Barry Jenkins on drums, the others he signed up were: John Weider (guitar & violin), Danny McCulloch (bass guitar), Vic Briggs (guitar) and Tom Parker (keyboards). While Parker was retained for only a few weeks (after which Weider also picked up keyboard parts as necessary), the remainder worked up an act in rehearsals with Burdon before playing their first concert together at Birmingham University on 25th November. In December, Tom Wilson joined them at Olympic Studios in London to produce their first single, one of Burdon's own compositions that he hoped would usher in an entirely different sound in 1967; that of "*the* English West Coast psychedelic band".[153] Looking back, it was no surprise to John Steel:

> Knowing Eric, he was probably trying to get away from his Geordie-ness. He always fantasised about being a black American, so it's quite within his psychological make-up to completely put his Geordie-ness in a hole somewhere and forget it and be at least a

Londoner rather than a North-Easterner. As soon as he was able to, he achieved his teenage dream of living in America. Now he considers himself almost to be American, I think. He just did it in stages.[154]

Of all the original Animals, the only one to profit from their demise was the first one out of the door, Alan Price. Cushioned by his royalties from "House Of The Rising Sun", he was able to persevere gamely with his Set in parallel to the declining fortunes of his former bandmates, intermittently turning out popular recycled versions of old blues and light jazz standards: "I Put A Spell On You" (No.12 in April) and "Hi-Lili, Hi-Lo" (No.10 in August). Although the others were supposed to receive a final pay-off in return for formally agreeing to disband in September, it was never forthcoming. When it came to the crunch, Chas Chandler discovered that the money to fund it, supposedly salted away by manager Mike Jeffrey for safe keeping in a Bahamian tax haven, had mysteriously disappeared. Yet strangely this did not deter Chandler from maintaining a business relationship with Jeffrey as he made the move from performing into management and the two of them set about the task of launching an extraordinary new talent onto the British pop scene.

Chandler had fallen on his feet through a chance encounter in July at New York's Café Wha? in Greenwich Village with a young black guitarist, there going under the name of Jimmy James as leader of a band called the Blue Flames and tearing the house down with his unorthodox, showy style of playing:

> That afternoon at the Café Wha? [Jimmy] was just an explosive kid whose potential struck me. As much as his version of 'Hey Joe' impressed me, what convinced me of his talent was another song that he did that first day, 'Like A Rolling Stone'. I knew Dylan well and loved his material, but 'Like A Rolling Stone' was the first of his songs that I didn't quite get. It was something about the way Dylan had sung the song. I never felt he expressed it properly. When [Jimmy] sang the song, he did it with tremendous conviction and the lyrics came right through to me. My initial impression, having heard him play 'Hey Joe' and 'Like A Rolling Stone', was that I couldn't see his career going in any other way but the place between those two songs. That was where it had to go.[155]

In reality, 'Jimmy James' hailed from Seattle, in the far north-west of Washington State (where he had been born Johnny Allen Hendrix, later to be renamed James Marshall Hendrix when his father Al returned from military service overseas and assumed parental responsibility for him). Although at

this juncture still only twenty-three, he was already a seasoned semi-professional musician who had toured the States extensively in bands backing the
like of the Isley Brothers, B.B. King, Sam Cooke, Solomon Burke and Little
Richard before playing in New York clubs with groups such as Curtis Knight
and the Squires or Joey Dee and the Starlighters. Branching out on his own
with the Blue Flames had not, however, proved lucrative: in his own words,
he was "living off sympathy"[156] until Chandler happened upon his act and
subsequently proposed becoming his manager. Once free of his own role as
an Animal, Chandler returned to New York in September and on the 23rd
boarded a flight back to London with his protege in tow, henceforth to be
known as Jimi Hendrix.

For all his good intentions, Chandler took his project forward on a
shoestring and was reliant on subterfuge to obtain both a new passport for
Hendrix (who had been rootless for years) and a temporary visa for him
to enter England as a visitor. Once Jimi was in this country, Chandler then
had to prevail upon Mike Jeffrey to secure the necessary work permit for
him, without which he was unable to perform in public – which Jeffrey duly
conjured up with no questions asked. Through overlapping auditions with
those Eric Burdon was holding to find his New Animals, Chandler recruited
a backing band of Noel Redding (bass guitar) and Mitch Mitchell (drums);
and thus the Jimi Hendrix Experience was born.

As Hendrix made a number of cameo appearances at the 'in' clubs of
London, his instantly perceived skill as a virtuoso guitarist rapidly spread
praise and unease in equal measure through the higher ranks of British pop
nobility but the Experience's first public concerts in October were actually
in France, playing in support of Johnny Hallyday on a short four-venue tour
that ended at the Paris Olympia. A few days later, on 23rd October, they went
to De Lane Lea Studios to record their first A-side, "Hey Joe"; although on
this occasion Chandler, now acting as producer, was so strapped for cash
that he could barely afford the studio time to lay down just this one track.
(Because Redding had previously been a guitarist rather than a bass player,
he was still struggling to make the transition, so unbeknown to him Chandler later overdubbed the bass part himself. Chandler did nevertheless offer
Redding further advice on his technique as a matter of course as he went
along, for which he was genuinely grateful.) They then had to wait another
ten days before going back into the studio to record the B-side, "Stone Free",
composed by Hendrix (at Chandler's suggestion) to maximise his earning
potential through additional publishing royalties.

After Kit Lambert had seen Hendrix playing at the Scotch of St. James,
he was only too eager to offer Chandler a recording contract for him. Having
earlier moved the Who to the Reaction label, Lambert and Stamp were now
in the final throes of setting up their own independent company, Track

Records, and agreeing a distribution deal through Polydor. Track would not, however, be fully operational until the New Year, meaning that the release of "Hey Joe" on 16th December went out on the Polydor label. Bolstered by promotional television appearances either side of Christmas on *Ready Steady Go!* and *Top Of The Pops*, all that remained was the anxious wait to see what impact, if any, it might have on the charts. The fate of Chandler's inspired gamble now lay in the unpredictable hands of the record-buying public.

While the Animals had gone under, Manfred Mann continued to demonstrate a chameleon-like capacity to adapt and survive. The year began badly when the group's transport, with Jack Bruce at the wheel, was involved in a road accident on 13th January on the return journey from a gig at Hull University. The chief casualties were Mann, who sustained bruised ribs from which he soon recovered, and Paul Jones, for whom a broken collarbone meant a longer period of convalescence. Pending the return of their vocalist (who, as we saw in the last chapter, was waiting to leave the group anyway), Mann and Hugg capitalised on the strengths of the Manfreds' augmented line-up by pressing on with a project first mooted before Christmas; namely, to record jazzy instrumental covers of recent hits.

Two studio sessions later, they had come up with four tracks that were released in June as an EP, *Instrumental Asylum*, with credits for the arrangements split between Hugg and Bruce. My personal favourite always was – and still remains – their athletic take on "I Got You Babe"[157], driven along at a cracking pace by the sax and trumpet of Lyn Dobson and Henry Lowther respectively, underpinned by a sophisticated bass line from Jack Bruce (who was also responsible for arranging this track). Embedded within the sleeve notes by Tom McGuinness were to be found the strongest indications yet of their collective frustrations:

> … MANFRED WANTS NEW *MENN* – a group is a growing, changing thing – members come and go – it's got to be that way – *develop or stagnate* … *Jacklynandhenry* have helped to pinpoint our limitations. We were coasting, taking it easy, bored and boring. Now, at least, *againalready*, we're trying to extend ourselves. If it succeeds, we'll be lucky and happy. If not, well we will have tried.[158]

The irony of his commentary was that by the summer, when it finally emerged into the public arena, Manfred Mann's time with the HMV label and John Burgess was already up. The intervening period had been beset with concerns mutually shared by Burgess and the group as to the long-overdue follow-up to "If You Gotta Go, Go Now". Although still several weeks off being fit enough to sing on stage, Jones had returned to the fold and the studio on 24th January, but only six more recording sessions were to follow, during which agreement on that next single remained as elusive as ever. It was not until the last session of all, on 18th March, that they at last recorded their penultimate HMV single and valedictory No.1 hit, "Pretty Flamingo". This came out on 15th April (a week after the release of the slightly quirky and musically unbalanced EP *Machines*[159]) and held the No.1 slot for three weeks in May before being deposed by "Paint It, Black".

There now followed a messy and protracted period of disengagement and recovery, made more complicated by simultaneously having to honour a heavy schedule of concert dates up and down the country. As the midsummer deadline for the renewal of Manfred Mann's contract with HMV drew closer, the company confirmed that it only wanted to retain Jones, as a solo artist, adding new urgency to the group's search for a replacement vocalist and another record deal. To add to the confusion, it further transpired that Jack Bruce had secretly been engaged in discussions with Ginger Baker and Eric Clapton about forming a new group with them and he too would be leaving.

To hold things together in the face of this disruption, the triumvirate of Mann, Hugg and McGuinness had a mountain to climb, especially since they now also decided to dispense with Lowther and Dobson. Whilst denying growing rumours of Jones's departure, and keeping the singer himself out of the loop, they opted to replace him with Mike D'Abo, whom they had seen on television and in live concert with A Band Of Angels, a lesser-known group he had founded at Harrow School. On the same day, 8th June, that they undertook a trial recording session with D'Abo (the last in which Bruce would take part), the group convened a press conference (attended by Jones) to announce the signing of a new record contract with Fontana. Three days later, *Melody Maker* went public with details of the new Bruce/Baker/Clapton line-up. Bruce played his last gig with Manfred Mann on 27th June and was replaced by Klaus Voorman, erstwhile bass player with the short-lived Paddy, Klaus & Gibson and designer of the *Revolver* sleeve for the Beatles. By the beginning of July, Voorman had first participated in recording sessions with the 'new' Manfreds (i.e., Mann, Hugg, McGuinness and D'Abo), then played live with the 'old' Manfreds (i.e., Mann, Hugg, McGuinness and Jones).

As Jones saw out his time with Manfred Mann in July fulfilling concert engagements, the release of the group's debut single for Fontana, recorded without him on 30th June, drew ever closer. In a pre-emptive strike on 1st July, HMV released the last Manfred Mann single on that label. "You Gave Me Somebody To Love", credited to the group but in effect a glorified solo by Jones, had originally been recorded more than a year ago and failed to reach the Top 30. On 29th July, however, Fontana released "Just Like A Woman", their cover version of the Dylan track from *Blonde On Blonde* as produced by Shel Talmy and sung by Mike D'Abo, immediately causing Manfred himself some temporary embarrassment:

I actually remember driving to our last gig with Paul when 'Just

Like A Woman' was played on the radio – it was really awkward. We actually had our first single with D'Abo being played before the last gig with Paul was finished. No one said a word. At that time there was a really bad vibe in the group. We felt our whole career was over because of Paul's decision to leave. As it turned out, we were completely wrong about this.[160]

Whilst its climb up the charts was relatively slow, it did eventually reach No.13 in mid-September; but its successor, "Semi-Detached Suburban Mr. James", fared much better. Now distinctively featuring Mann on the mellotron, it rose to No.3 in November, overtaking on the way the first official solo single from Paul Jones, "High Time", which peaked at No.6. A reversion in December to jazz-pop with the *Instrumental Assassination* EP was, however, poorly received, a singular failure to recapture the warmth, colour and verve of the earlier *Instrumental Asylum*.[161]

Meanwhile, in parallel to these new developments, HMV persisted in its efforts to secure some final returns from their back catalogue by putting out a compilation LP, *Mann Made Hits*, in September; and next month followed it with the *Aswas* EP, pointedly billed on its front cover as being by 'Manfred Mann with Paul Jones', the sleevenotes to which (jointly written by Tom McGuinness and John Burgess as a mock history of the original group) attempted something vaguely resembling, yet not quite achieving, closure:

For three long years they grew and prospered under the guidance of John the Burgess until the black day when the cult of Elessdee grew stronger than soft words and became master. Angry words and lost souls, Michael from the house of Vickers, Paul of Jones went their own ways and sadly the five became three.

These three wandered into the wilderness to seek other companions. Leaving behind them on this appropriately black image the last hitherto unheard sounds of the original five "ASWAS", who once dwelt together in the light of Mingus and Aranbee.[162]

When he left Manfred Mann, Jack Bruce had been with them for only seven months. Soon after *Melody Maker* had broken the news of Bruce's collaboration with Ginger Baker and Eric Clapton, Robert Stigwood formally announced that: a) he would be managing the trio, to be known as 'The Cream', b) they would be recording on his Reaction label, and c) they would make their performing debut at the Windsor Jazz and Blues Festival on 31st July. Beginning in May by sounding out Clapton, Baker had been the *de facto* architect of the new group. Although they were then both agreed on bringing Bruce on board, a pre-requisite to this involved an act of magnanimity on

Baker's part, since repeated arguments between them the previous September as members of the Graham Bond Organisation had led to Bruce leaving. With apologies given and accepted on both sides, preparations could be taken forward and clandestine rehearsals got under way; but *Melody Maker's* June scoop, instigated by an over-eager Baker, not only blew Bruce's cover but also Clapton's. Less forgiving and amenable than Manfred Mann, John Mayall sacked Clapton from the Bluesbreakers there and then, although the reality was that he was obliged to work out a month's notice in concert engagements.

It was desperately unfortunate that Mayall had been forced into his decision barely a month after the recording of the seminal LP *Blues Breakers – John Mayall with Eric Clapton* (better known as *The 'Beano' Album* for its cover shot of the group in which Clapton is seen studiedly reading the comic). By its release date of 22nd July Clapton was no longer a member of the group, yet it was the power of his "ferocious but inspired guitar work"[163] in particular that attracted favourable reviews of the album across a wide spectrum of the music press. Little did the journalists know that in the studio he had insisted throughout on playing at "club volume-levels"[164], to capture the sound he wanted, much to the consternation of producer Mike Vernon and engineer Gus Dudgeon. Long since regarded as a classic of its genre, it was the first blues album of the Sixties to cross over into the pop music market when it rose to No.6 in the LP charts; but it would later be succeeded by an equally stunning LP of a different complexity, following Mayall's inspired choice of Peter Green as Eric Clapton's replacement.

Irrespective of Stigwood's advance publicity, Clapton confirms in his autobiography that it was Manchester's Twisted Wheel Club that hosted Cream's first live performance, on 29th July, as a trial run on a quiet night for the more auspicious Windsor Festival slot two days later, where they played to an enthusiastic estimated crowd of 20,000 seemingly undaunted by torrential rain. From then until Christmas, a long and at times awkward shakedown period given that they saw themselves as a musical co-operative with no one person designated as their leader, the hard graft of establishing a repertoire in their own right on the club circuit alternated with tentative recording sessions. In their first interview with Chris Welch of *Melody Maker*, Clapton suggested they would be playing "blues ancient and modern", whereas Bruce plumped instead for what he termed "sweet and sour rock and roll"[165]; but much later Clapton would admit in retrospect that:

> Musically, we didn't really have a plan. In my mind, when I had fantasised about it, I had seen myself as Buddy Guy, heading a blues trio with a very good rhythm section. I didn't know how Ginger and Jack saw it in their heads except I'm sure it would have been more jazz-orientated. Since Stigwood probably had no idea

what we were doing either, it is clear that the whole project was a colossal gamble. The very idea that a guitar, bass and drum trio could make any headway in the era of the pop group was pretty outrageous.[166]

That he was uncertain as to Cream's prospects as a trio from the very beginning of the venture was understandable and, if he had looked hard enough, he would, of course, have found at least one discouraging lesson from recent history in the fate of the Big Three (see Ch.5). Clapton's confidence would be shaken further at a gig at London Polytechnic on 1st October, where his decision to allow the newly arrived and as yet unknown Jimi Hendrix to sit in with them had a totally unexpected outcome. Chas Chandler, who had gone backstage to introduce Hendrix to the group, asked Clapton as a favour if he could join them in a number. It is worth bearing in mind, in reading Clapton's recollection of what happened next on first acquaintance, that he was Hendrix's junior by well over two years:

> The song Jimi wanted to play was a Howlin' Wolf song called
> 'Killing Floor'. I thought it was incredible that he would know how
> to play this, as it was a tough one to get right. Of course Jimi played
> it exactly like it ought to be played, and he totally blew me away.
> I mean if you're jamming with someone for the first time, most
> musicians will try to hold back, but Jimi just went for it. He played
> the guitar with his teeth, behind his head, lying on the floor, doing
> the splits, the whole business. It was amazing, and it was musically
> great too, not just pyrotechnics … The audience were completely
> gobsmacked by what they saw and heard too. They loved it, and I
> loved it too, but I remember thinking that here was a force to be
> reckoned with. It scared me, because he was clearly going to be a
> huge star, and just as we were finding our own speed, here was the
> real thing.[167]

Future competition notwithstanding, Cream persevered and played their way through what simply became "a blur of seemingly endless club dates".[168] They had started recording together in August, although their management deal with Robert Stigwood, as yet inexperienced as a producer, failed to give them instant access to top-flight facilities, limiting them at first to Rayrik then to Ryemuse, two lesser-known studios in the Chalk Farm and Mayfair districts of London respectively. Baker and Bruce were particularly keen to record material of their own alongside classic blues numbers like Willie Dixon's "Spoonful" or Muddy Waters' "Rollin' And Tumblin'" but were quick to acknowledge that neither of them were competent lyricists. At Baker's request, therefore, they were assisted by jazz-and-poetry performance artist Pete Brown, whose earliest input was to work with Bruce on a song that was to become Cream's first single.

Stylistically, "Wrapping Paper" is, however, probably the least typical of any Cream track. Brown, in fitting words to a tune that Bruce claimed to have composed at least two years earlier, came up with the obscurest of concepts:

> It's about two people who can only meet in a picture on the wall
> in an old house by the sea. There was also the image of wrapping
> paper in the gutter in some sort of out-of-season holiday town.
> For some reason, I was spending a lot of time in deserted
> seaside resorts. I also crammed into the song just about every
> cinema image I had ever thought of, with the result that it's fairly
> incomprehensible.[169]

As recorded, it comes across as a low-key, breathy set of vocals, with little or nothing of instrumental flair to lift it, yet it was deemed to be sufficiently out of the ordinary to be worth a shot at the charts. Released on 7th October, its saving grace was that it did at least allow Cream to break into the Top 30, entering the charts in the week ending 29th October (at the same time as Manfred Mann's "Semi-Detached Suburban Mr. James" and Eric Burdon's "Help Me Girl") but only keeping them there for two weeks all told, with No.25 the highest position it could manage.

With that behind them, they pressed on with putting together their first LP, which, in Baker's words, "wasn't exactly a big budget album"[170]; although amazingly, considering the potentially incendiary egos involved, they lacked between them the fundamental drive and inspiration to make it something of quality – as Clapton explained:

> Stigwood was the producer, and neither he nor any of us had
> any idea how to make a record. We'd run down a tune and play it
> through a couple of times and say, 'Did you get that?' There was
> no polish to it, although we may have done a bit of overdubbing.
> Mayfair [Studio] was only about sixteen foot square, with a control
> room next door, and no glass to look through. Really though, we
> were just having fun and weren't taking it seriously at all. And it's
> unusual for me to admit that, because up till then I'd been extremely
> serious about the way the music should be. We weren't concerned
> with making a record, listening to mixes, or anything like that.[171]

The result was *Fresh Cream*, not merely their first LP but the first of only three in total to be credited to Reaction's catalogue in its brief life; sharing 9th December as a release date with their second single, "I Feel Free" (a qualitatively different Bruce/Brown collaboration), as well as with the Who's "Happy Jack" and *A Quick One*. The album attracted a muted welcome from the critics, suffering in the eyes of some by comparison with *Blues Breakers*, but nevertheless made a worthy debut in the LP charts by Christmas, eventually reaching No.6; whereas judgement on the success or otherwise of "I Feel Free" would have to be suspended until the New Year.

Putting the advent of Jimi Hendrix and Cream to one side, other significant blues-based acts – principally the Spencer Davis Group and the Yardbirds – had also taken their music in new directions in 1966. After following the Beatles' "Day Tripper/We Can Work It Out" into the No.1 slot for three weeks in January with "Keep On Running", the Spencer Davis Group retained their faith in songs composed by Jackie Edwards for their next two hits: "Somebody Help Me" (delivering their second No.1 in the week ending 16th April), and "When I Come Home" (reaching No.14 at the end of September).

But by the autumn playing to a tried and trusted formula had lost any of its residual appeal, and instrumental B-sides like "Stevie's Blues" and "Trampoline" that prominently featured 18-year-old Steve Winwood's prowess on Hammond organ simply served to demonstrate that he was growing increasingly restless. (Indeed, he had already been paid the compliment in March of being invited, along with prominent others equally feeling the wanderlust, to contribute to a strictly one-off recording session organised by Paul Jones and Eric Clapton, in which he had participated – under the pseudonym of 'Steve Anglo' – together with fellow band member Pete York, Jack Bruce and pianist Ben Palmer. The pick of the results, credited to 'Eric Clapton and the Powerhouse', were included on a blues and rock compilation LP, *What's Shakin'*, released on the US Elektra label in August.) Older brother Muff was only too well aware of how fragile relationships within the group were becoming:

> Steve was losing interest. Because he was young and had never had
> a real growing up life, he was fed up. Suddenly, he didn't want to get
> up in the morning and play a gig. He wanted to break out. It was
> getting dicey and I guessed it wouldn't be long before we'd split up.
> Although we didn't for a while, it was on the cards, because there
> was such a disparity of ages – Spencer was ten years older than
> Steve and five years older than me and Pete. For a group, it's rare
> to have such a wide gap. Also brothers aren't the best people to
> mould a group together … We decided amongst ourselves to give it
> another so many months.[172]

After a temporary diversion to play themselves in the comedy musical film *The Ghost Goes Gear*, with Nicholas Parsons as the lead professional actor, the group were finally forced to consider their follow-up to "When I Come Home". Telling Chris Blackwell that they were weary of Jackie Edwards numbers, his response was to challenge them to write a song of their own.

When they prevaricated, Blackwell, with two days left before a scheduled studio session, confined them to a rehearsal room at the Marquee Club under strict orders to come up with the goods. Muff Winwood again:

> We started to mess about with riffs and it must have been eleven
> o'clock in the morning. We hadn't been there for half an hour,
> and this idea just came. We thought, bloody hell, this sounds really
> good. We fitted it all together and by about twelve o'clock, we had
> this whole song. Steve had been singing, 'gimme some loving' – you
> know, just yelling anything, so we decided to call it that. We worked
> out the middle eight and then went to a café, that's still on the
> corner down the road.[173]

Recorded the next day, and instantly recognisable by its opening trading of throbbing bass riff for shattering organ chords between the brothers Winwood, "Gimme Some Loving" entered the charts in early November at No.14 and two weeks later had risen to No.2, denied the top spot by the Beach Boys' "Good Vibrations". Coupled with yet another instrumental B-side, "Blues In F", this fourth hit single in twelve months was strong enough to set the seal decisively on their popularity with *NME* readers, who in the annual poll voted both the Spencer Davis Group the Best New Group of 1966 and Steve Winwood the Best New Singer, their ardent fans little realising then that the existing line-up had only one more hit left in the bag.

In contrast, the Yardbirds, on record at any rate, were moving further into the realms of the psychedelic, courtesy of lead guitarist Jeff Beck. Their first new release of the year, on 25th February, was a coupling of recordings they had made several months earlier in America: the A-side, "Shapes Of Things", being a group composition (flung together by – and credited to – Paul Samwell-Smith, Keith Relf and Jim McCarty, before being refined instrumentally by Beck), and the B-side, "You're A Better Man Than I", written by Manfred Mann's Mike Hugg. Both tracks feature stand-out guitar breaks by Beck. The former, as well as including feedback, clearly displays the topical Indian influence of the times: "I was happy making silly noises. I'd get carried away. I'd slacken off the bottom two guitar strings and press them against the pickup and play a kind of sitar thing, with wobbles."[174] But the latter is a *tour de force* to raise the hairs on the back of your neck, as it swoops, glides and reverberates between the bass and treble registers, and at its most powerful, in my submission, if listened to in a darkened room, as I habitually savoured it from first purchase in my late teens.

In the same week (beginning 26th March) as the Spencer Davis Group's "Somebody Help Me" entered the charts, "Shapes Of Things" reached its highest position of No.4; to be followed in May by "Over Under Sideways Down". Whereas "Shapes Of Things" had bemoaned the loss of habitable land through endless wars to a militaristic beat, this was altogether a more frivolous composition (credited to all five group members) that was one of the first songs of the era to openly celebrate the rock'n'roll lifestyle:

> Cars and girls are easy come by
> In this day and age.
> Laughing, joking, drinking, smoking,
> Till I've spent my wage.
> When I was young, people spoke of immorality.
> All the things they said were wrong
> Are what I want to be.[175]

Although it seemed to chime perfectly with the mood of the times, it was the least successful of their hit singles to date and surprisingly failed to reach the Top Ten when it stalled at No.13 at the end of June; by which time Paul Samwell-Smith had left the group.

He had been driven to despair by the crushing weight of a combination of unfortunate circumstances. These included the frustration he had experienced from April to the beginning of June in trying to co-produce and record their new LP (to be released on 15th July as *Yardbirds*, but commonly known as *Roger The Engineer* after the caricature on the front cover by Chris Dreja), a shambolic, under-rehearsed undertaking for which the group had composed the songs on the hoof as they went along; as well as the all-too familiar sense of having been on the road endlessly for little or no financial reward. The final straw for him, however, came at a concert at Queen's College, Oxford on 18th June, when he and Jeff Beck had had to take over the vocals from an almost totally incapable Keith Relf, who, "muzzy with liquor", confronted the audience with "belching, swearing, and stumbling about aimlessly before sinking to the floor".[176] After this debacle, he told the others he was off: "I knew there must be something better in life – and there was."[177] He opted instead to pursue composing and producing.

Samwell-Smith was almost immediately replaced by ubiquitous session musician Jimmy Page, who made his first appearance with the Yardbirds at their very next gig, at the Marquee Club on 21st June. There then followed a brief, legendary period when the group effectively had two equally outstanding lead guitarists in Page and Beck. However, by the end of November, as they approached the end of a second punishing tour of the US within the space of four months, with quarrels abounding, the others had come to realise that "having two [lead] guitarists was no longer a great idea"[178] and Beck, on the pretext of tonsillitis, pulled out *pro tem*; to be fired in his absence when it subsequently emerged that instead of recuperating he had been whooping it up in Los Angeles. There is precious little recorded output to show for what soon became an uneasy, then toxic, partnership, other than the extraordinarily dynamic but failed single, "Happenings Ten Years Time Ago", that was released on 21st October yet inexplicably never made it into the Top 30. With its lack of success, and the group now reduced to a quartet, UK hits irrevocably became a thing of the past for the Yardbirds.[179]

At the lighter end of the pop spectrum, however, Manchester exiles Herman's Hermits showed no signs of ceasing to rack up the hits, even if their chart placings at home from one record to the next proved to be inconsistent. After the Top 10 success of "A Must To Avoid" in January, their fortunes dipped with their next two singles. "You Won't Be Leaving" only stayed in the Top 30 for four weeks in April, peaking at No.20; to be followed by "This Door Swings Both Ways", which entered the charts in July to achieve a highest placing of No.21 over five weeks. Then, in a bid to round the year off in style, in November they were back in the Top 10 again, this time at No.9 with the catchy Graham Gouldman song "No Milk Today"; but miscalculated by chasing it up with another title from the same pen, "East West", that scraped a solitary week at No.30 in December. Their US catalogue nevertheless remained their strength throughout 1966. All six singles released in America made the *Billboard* Top 30 and of the four that reached the Top 10, they included a No.3 hit with "Listen People" and a No.5 with their cover of Ray Davies's "Dandy" from *Face To Face*.

For their fellow Mancunians the Hollies, meanwhile, the opposite situation, of retaining a strong fanbase in the UK while struggling to break into the American market, still applied. Badly needing to recover from the stunning indifference shown towards "If I Needed Someone" before Christmas, they recorded their next single in January at the suggestion of Tony Hicks, who had come across a new song co-written by US composer 'Chip' Taylor. "I Can't Let Go", released in mid-February, came up trumps when it took them all the way to No.1 within a month but it gained additional significance in the group's history as the last single to feature bass player Eric Haydock, who was fired in March after several months of ill-concealed disenchantment and unco-operativeness on his part. While Haydock slunk away to form an unsuccessful six-piece band of his own, Haydock's Rockhouse, in the short term the Hollies were obliged to engage temporary stand-ins, amongst them Jack Bruce (who, on 10th May, sat in on their recording with Peter Sellers of the title song for his forthcoming film *After The Fox*) and Klaus Voorman. When it was formally announced on 18th May that his permanent replacement was to be Bernie Calvert from the Dolphins (thereby rejoining former bandmates Tony Hicks and Bobby Elliott), this just happened to coincide with the recording of their next single, "Bus Stop".

A more assured composition by Graham Gouldman than "Look Through Any Window", his previous offering for the Hollies, in its homely yet effective narrative of modest courtship "Bus Stop" had all the key ingredients of a picture romance story from any teen magazine of the day to readily capture the mass record-buying market:

> Bus stop, wet day, she's there, I say,
> "Please share my umbrella."
> Bus stop, bus goes, she stays, love grows
> Under my umbrella.
>
> All that summer we enjoyed it,
> Wind and rain and shine.
> That umbrella, we employed it.
> By August she was mine.[180]

In the week beginning 25th June, it broke into the charts at No.19, its closest competitor amongst the other new entries being (at one place higher) "Get Away" by Georgie Fame and the Blue Flames, with which it then engaged in a joint race for the Top 10. Two weeks later, the Hollies appeared to have beaten Fame by reaching No.3, but they had peaked and the following week had to surrender the slot to him. Yet there was further good news to come later in the summer, when "Bus Stop" finally gave them their long-awaited breakthrough in America by reaching No.5.

June also saw the release of their fourth LP, *Would You Believe*, the last album on which the Hollies would still be reliant on crowd-pleasing rock'n'roll standards, such as "Sweet Little Sixteen" or "I Take What I Want", as fillers. In August, they moved on significantly by embarking on recording a string of their own songs, sessions that were eventually completed in October and indicative of a new level of trust in their abilities from producer Ron Richards. From this material came *For Certain Because*, the first of a trilogy of LPs to be made up entirely of original compositions, two of these tracks being extracted in advance for the next single. "Stop! Stop! Stop!" (b/w "It's You") is instantly recognisable as a rare showcase for the amplified banjo-picking of Tony Hicks. Based on an imaginative reconstruction of the entertainment they had witnessed in a New York nightclub, its tale of a besotted customer losing his self-control at the sight of a belly-dancer introduced a rare exotic note to the charts at the onset of a typically dreary British autumn:

> See the girl with cymbals on her fingers
> Entering through the door,
> Ruby glistening from her navel
> Shimmering around the floor.[181]

In the Top 30 chart for 15th October, it was the highest British new entry of the week at No.16 – above "No Milk Today" from Herman's Hermits (No.21), "High Time" by Paul Jones (No.22) and Cliff Richard with "Time Drags By" from his latest film *Finders Keepers* (No.24) – and out-performed them all by going on to reach No.2 at the beginning of November.[181]

Released in December, for me *For Certain Because* made a very welcome alternative Christmas present in the absence of anything new from the Beatles. Stylistically and lyrically, it showed the Hollies off at their most diverse yet, including three tracks sung by Allan Clarke on Side 2 with strikingly different arrangements by ex-Manfred Mike Vickers. "High Classed", a tale of love beset by social inequalities, was treated to a syncopated makeover, looking back to the jazz age with muted trumpets, slide trombones and Chinese skulls; "What Went Wrong" was fleshed out with a full orchestra, topped and tailed by timpani; while to the accompaniment of twelve-string acoustic guitar and the tramp of marching feet, "Crusader" re-created the mediaeval atmosphere of a weary knight returning home from the wars. Elsewhere, on Side 1 Graham Nash excelled with the Latin-tinged "Tell Me To My Face" before baring his soul with "Clown", updating in miniature the classic paradox of "On With The Motley" and concluding with the sound of an out-of-tune jack-in-the-box winding down before snapping shut. All told, it was an unashamedly well-crafted set, deserving of far higher sales than its lowly No.23 in the LP charts suggested, and demonstrated a willingness to explore the realms of commercialism without necessarily selling out.

For the Small Faces, however, resisting the pressure to make records that would sell well irrespective of content was beginning to be a matter of principle. Looking ahead to their first release of the New Year, manager Don Arden had handed them an almost surefire No.1 on a plate, in the form of an infectiously catchy song co-written to order by Kenny Lynch and Mort Shuman, "Sha-La-La-La-Lee", but it grated on them for running counter to their personal preferences for soul and rhythm and blues. Steve Marriott especially resented the fact that, in the making of the record, Kenny Lynch was so intrusive: "He wrote it and produced it and ended up bleedin' singing on it, doing backing vocals."[182] Kenney Jones thought it was "a bit of an iffy number", while Ronnie Lane summed it up as "a good Saturday night dance record but [not] what we were really good at", seeing their enforced acceptance of it by Arden as marking "when the rot began to set in".[183] Yet nonetheless, from its release on 29th January it sold well, making No.2 in the week beginning 12th March beneath the Hollies' "I Can't Let Go". The unwelcome knock-on effect for the group was that its very popularity led to them being stereotyped as "a teenybopper band": "It explains why their talent was never fully recognised at the time. The press simply couldn't see the band for the screams."[184]

Ironically, there was a pay-off, in that Arden, now surer of his money, was more receptive again to them recording an original Marriott/Lane composition as a follow-up A-side, provided that it was still broadly in the same groove. They duly delivered "Hey Girl", which was at least a Top 20 hit through May and June, peaking at No.12. In the space of no more than five days at the IBC Studios in mid-February, with Glyn Johns as engineer, the Small Faces had also put together their eponymous first album, which Decca released in May the week after "Hey Girl" and which gratifyingly took them to No.3 in the LP charts.

The pressure of constant touring at home and abroad, a demanding schedule enough without also having to shoehorn in promotional TV appearances and recording, eventually forced both Marriott and Lane to seek several days' respite in June due to sheer physical exhaustion; as dramatically evidenced by Marriott passing out on 10th June during the group's slot on *Ready Steady Go!* But on their return, it was straight back onto the treadmill, typically as follows:

> There was Burnley, Sheffield, London, Purley, then onto Reykjavik in Iceland, back after two days, a quick BBC interview Saturday, off to Germany on Sunday, a week of gigs there and then back to England and up to Hull, back to London, onto the Isle of Man, then Maryport, Luton, Nottingham, Blackburn, London, Coventry, Plymouth and at the end of July, the Sixth National Jazz and Blues Festival held at Windsor racecourse.[185]

Somewhere in amongst that blur of commitments, they fitted in the recording of their next single, this time, almost by accident, miraculously managing to contrive an outcome of which they were all genuinely proud. For once, as Marriott explained in an interview for *Record Mirror*, Arden served both as critic and muse:

> When we were doing a session, Don [Arden] came in to watch us. Don gets the hump if he doesn't hear a hit. You can play him the melody but he can't hear the end product right away. We could see he was fed up.

> So I just played him an idea I had. The organ hadn't played it, the drum hadn't played it, the bass hadn't played it, but I'd thought about it so I let him hear it. He liked it so we re-wrote it on the spot and it turned out to be 'All Or Nothing'.[186]

Arden had every right to be pleased, for "All Or Nothing" provided the Small Faces with a potentially lucrative No.1 hit in mid-September, when it brought the Beatles' four-week run at the top with "Yellow Submarine/ Eleanor Rigby" to an end (but after only one week it fell victim in its turn to the middle-aged, posthumous mellowness of "Distant Drums" by Jim Reeves.) It should have proved to be the means of opening the door to America but the US tour Arden promised them never happened. It was not long, therefore, before the group's relationship with their maverick manager started to turn sour. For one thing, they began to question why they were seeing so little of the money they were earning, which Arden neatly side-stepped on the pretext of opening a bank account on which they exclusively could draw – whilst leaving himself as the sole signatory. Furthermore, when they put out feelers to Robert Stigwood as a possible replacement, Arden and his heavies paid him a visit, firmly intending to "nail this impresario to his chair with fright".[187] It was by no means a courtesy call, culminating as it did in Arden threatening to throw Stigwood off the fourth-floor balcony of his office for presuming to meddle in his business affairs.

As matters thus went from bad to worse, the last straw was Decca's release of the Small Faces' next single without their knowledge. Since the beginning of October, the group had completed a nine-day tour of Sweden, followed by another marathon tour of UK concerts (with, amongst others, the Hollies and Paul Jones), and in early November were grateful to be travelling home at last from Newcastle to London down the A1. Paolo Hewitt and John Hellier take up the story:

> Steve Marriott asks that the car radio is switched on. His former girlfriend Adrienne Posta is being interviewed on the BBC and he wants to hear what she has got to say for herself.
>
> Towards the end of the interview, the interviewer, Barry Aldis, unexpectedly mentions Marriott. Steve shuts up everyone in the car, leans forward to catch what is being said. Countryside speeds past his window.
>
> 'By the way Adrienne,' Aldis announces in his best BBC voice, 'the Small Faces have a new single out this Friday, entitled 'My Mind's Eye'.'
>
> Aldis then plays the song from [a] demo tape Marriott left at Arden's office prior to the tour's commencement. Neither manager [nor] record company had told the band about the record's release.[188]

When they reached London, the group went straight to Arden's Carnaby Street office to have it out with him; and a month later, on 8th December Marriott announced – notwithstanding that in that self-same week "My Mind's Eye" had climbed to a more than respectable No.4 – that they had a new manager in Harold Davison, an arrangement that turned out to be good in name only since it failed to stick much beyond Christmas: "We didn't get out of the contract with Don Arden, it was sold to Harold Davison who then sold it in turn to Andrew Oldham … We were sold – that's what we felt like, pounds of flesh. Like a cattle market."[189]

Of the various other British groups breaking into the 1966 charts, there was a cluster on the Fontana label that attracted particular attention, in spite of the generally derivative and lightweight nature of their offerings. For sheer durability, first mention should rightly go to Dave Dee, Dozy, Beaky, Mick and Tich, who consistently kept clocking up hits from their first Top 30 entry in December 1965 all the way through to the summer of 1969 and Dee's separation from the rest of the group. Formed in Salisbury as Dave Dee and the Bostons in 1961, when Dee's full-time occupation (as Dave Harman) was that of policeman[190], they braved a 1962 season at the Top Ten Club in Hamburg before returning to England, to resume the more mundane round of playing at local concerts and in holiday camps. Signed up by Ken Howard and Alan Blaikley in 1964 after sharing a bill with the Honeycombs in Swindon, they were rebranded as performers according to their individual nicknames by their new songwriters/managers and eventually had a hit, at the third time of trying, with "You Make It Move", which ended up at No.19 in the first Top 30 of 1966. There then followed four Top 10 hits in a row, all of them serviceably formulaic confections with irritatingly catchy hooks: "Hold Tight" (No.3 in April), "Hideaway" (No.8 in July), "Bend It" (No.2 in October – the innuendo played upon for all it was worth, but nevertheless a casualty, like the Small Faces' "All Or Nothing", of Jim Reeves stuck forever at No.1 that autumn) and "Save Me" (No.3 by January 1967).

To their credit, Dave Dee, Dozy, Beaky, Mick and Tich made little pretence of being anything other than good fun and were rewarded handsomely for it. The same might also be said of the New Vaudeville Band, an *ersatz* group assembled as a front for the songs of composer Geoff Stephens who, five years on from the heyday of the Temperance Seven, revived Twenties' kitsch most successfully with "Winchester Cathedral"; which, at its peak at No.4 in October, made strange meat indeed in a sandwich between the Who's "I'm A Boy" at No.3 and the Stones' "Have You Seen Your Mother, Baby, Standing In The Shadow?" at No.5.

And then there were the Troggs, a jobbing four-piece group from Andover who, on the back of a record deal secured for them by Larry Page, left an indelible mark on the music of the decade with their chart debut "Wild Thing", No.2 at the end of May to the Stones' No.1 with "Paint It, Black". Based on a demo by American composer 'Chip' Taylor, with an ocarina solo in place of his original whistling, and recorded at Olympic Studios end-on to one of Page's own self-indulgent orchestral sessions, it was the unexpected success of this simplistic rock number that led the group to turn professional; and when it went on to become the US No.1 for two weeks, their new-found status as rough-and-ready pop celebrities was confirmed.

Ex-bricklayer Reg Presley (born Reg Ball) was a great admirer of the Kinks and his vocal style could often be as mannered as that of his hero Ray

Davies, inclining to recitation as much as singing: his backing was provided by Chris Britton on lead guitar, Pete Staples on bass guitar and Ronnie Bond (born Ronnie Bullis) on drums. Between them, they had cautiously developed a capacity to turn out songs of their own but it was Presley's compositions that were most readily taken up as A-sides and their next two singles, "With A Girl Like You" and "I Can't Control Myself", were both from his pen.[191] The former gave them a UK No.1 in August, while the latter – the first of their releases to be moved across from Fontana onto Page's own new Page One label – went to No.3 for three weeks from October into November, causing consternation to some for the raciness of its lyric ("I can't stand still 'cause you've got me going./Your slacks are low and your hips are showing.").[192] For their last single of the year, however, "Any Way That You Want Me", they demurely rang the changes with a ballad from 'Chip' Taylor that incorporated cellos in its arrangement. Released in December and having entered the charts by Christmas, it would reach No.6 the following January.

Despite the apparent healthiness of all this home-grown activity, there was no escaping the fact that in 1966 the tide had turned again in renewed favour of bringing diverse American influences to bear on the British music scene and the pockets of record-buyers. Some, as already noted in passing, were just inexplicably retro and only of appeal to a much older demographic, such as Frank Sinatra and Jim Reeves. Others were straight imports of one-hit wonders, like "Ballad Of The Green Berets" by S/Sgt. Barry Sadler (a patriotic counterblast from a veteran of Vietnam to Barry McGuire's "Eve Of Destruction" and all other anti-war songs, as well as a US No.1 for five weeks, that over here, completely out of context, made No.24 in April) or Napoleon XIV's tastelessly demonic novelty song "They're Coming To Take Me Away, Ha-Haaa!" (which, at the end of August, at No.4, was the highest American placing in the UK Top 30 after the Beach Boys' "God Only Knows" at No.2). There was further consolidation of the popularity of Tamla-Motown groups like the Supremes, with two Top 10 hits in the course of the year ("You Can't Hurry Love", a No.3 in October; followed by "You Keep Me Hangin' On", No.5 in December), and the Four Tops, whose "Reach Out I'll Be There" finally wrested the No.1 spot away from Jim Reeves at the end of October. And there was grand theatre, not just from the expatriate Walker Brothers (with their spring No.1, "The Sun Ain't Gonna Shine Any More"), but also from Ike and Tina Turner (with the Phil Spector production of all time, "River Deep – Mountain High", a No.4 hit in July).

In addition, in the wake of the Byrds came a mixed bag of other groups who shared their aspiration to elevate the status of US rock music; notably the Lovin' Spoonful and The Mamas & The Papas. Before examining these very different contributions, however, it is worth reflecting on the increasingly oblique influence of the Byrds themselves, a group I much admired in their earliest incarnations but who were by this time destined to have only one more fleeting glimpse of a UK hit, in the form of the unparalleled magnificence of "Eight Miles High". Attracting little airplay over here as chart absentees, they had suddenly become a group whose progress I was now reduced to following solely through the advertisements and occasional sniping reviews appearing in the *NME*. In these circumstances, it speaks volumes for the power of CBS Records' publicity department that even the small local retailers where I lived continued to buy in each new release of theirs as it came along, although there can have been no profit for them in the penny-number sales they accrued.[193]

Pending the UK release of their second LP, *Turn! Turn! Turn!*, CBS stripped out the tracks "Set You Free This Time" and "It Won't Be Wrong" for release on a single in February; the former, as the original A-side, being a highly unorthodox love song written by Gene Clark late one night in London during the Byrds' 1965 tour, its essence perfectly captured by Johnny Rogan as follows: "The vocal is tender and humble, yet the subtext is quiet vengeance. Even the song's title presents rejection as if it were an act of kindness."[194] Unfortunately, as "a love song whose opening sentence was 24 words long and full of complex recriminations and romantic neuroses"[195], it soon became clear to CBS that it was going nowhere and was flipped to the B-side.

The LP followed at the end of March, displaying more of a blend of folk and country influences than had previously been evident on *Mr. Tambourine Man*. Jim McGuinn had included his reworking of "He Was A Friend Of Mine" (turning it into a personal tribute to President Kennedy) and there was a cover of "Satisfied Mind" that came across a little awkwardly if you already knew its purer rendition by Joan Baez on *Farewell Angelina*. The reliance on Dylan as their bedrock was sustained by alternative versions of "Lay Down Your Weary Tune" (an unreleased composition of his from 1963) and "The Times They Are A-Changin'". Side 2 opened brilliantly with another Gene Clark gem in "The Whole World Turns Around Her" but fell flat with the final track, a supposedly 'humorous' electric arrangement of Stephen Foster's "Oh! Susannah" (added in on the back of a private joke between McGuinn and Dylan). All in all, it was far more introspectively American in its slant than *Mr. Tambourine Man*, which in places had truly rocked, and as such an acquired taste even for a dedicated British fan like me.

After they had completed *Turn! Turn! Turn!* in the autumn of 1965, there followed a period of instability for the Byrds, coloured by internal political intrigue and starting with a request to CBS from manager Jim Dickson to remove their record producer Terry Melcher. Pending his replacement, Dickson once again assumed the mantle of production and on 22nd December oversaw a session at RCA's Hollywood studio when they recorded two stunning tracks in psychedelic mode and therefore of an altogether different genre from any they had ever attempted before: "Eight Miles High" and "Why". In facilitating this, however, Dickson had been precipitate and the songs had to be re-recorded for CBS anyway in January for the sake of contractual propriety, this time with company man Allen Stanton in the control booth.

Credited collaboratively to Clark, McGuinn and Crosby, "Eight Miles High" was both of its times and way ahead of them, with a lyric ostensibly about the group's flight to and impressions of London weaving its way in and out of fearsome improvisational guitar-playing inspired by jazz saxophonist John Coltrane. "Why", credited to McGuinn and Crosby alone, went to another extreme entirely by emulating the sound of the sitar in soaring guitar solos born out of electronic trickery; McGuinn's 12-string Rickenbacker being fed through a gizmo he had cobbled together, combining "an amplifier from a Philips portable record player and a two-and-a-half inch loudspeaker from a walkie-talkie placed in a wooden cigar box which ran on batteries".[196]

Released in March in America and May in the UK, "Eight Miles High" (b/w "Why") marked then and still remains to me today one of the most evocative and powerful couplings of any Sixties' single.[197] Its progress up the US charts was, however, brought abruptly to a halt by a damning entry in a weekly trade paper, Bill Gavin's Record Report. Circulated widely across America to a multitude of radio stations, it recommended the withdrawal from playlists of both "Eight Miles High" and Dylan's "Rainy Day Women Nos. 12 & 35" for their implicit "encouragement and/or approval of the use of marijuana or LSD".[198] The group fought valiantly, if in vain, against the condemnation, a despairing McGuinn at one point driven to comment caustically: "We could have called the song 'Forty-Two Thousand Two Hundred and Forty Feet', but somehow this didn't seem to be a very commercial song title and it certainly wouldn't have scanned."[199] In Britain, on the other hand, the drug connotations of the word 'high' proved to be rather less troublesome than indifferent and/or uncomprehending reviews of the record in our music press. With little active encouragement, then, from the four main music papers of the day and a corresponding lack of exposure on the BBC, the best chart position it could hope for was a lowly No.28, for one week only, in June – after which the Byrds never appeared in the UK Top 30 again for the remainder of the decade.

Equally significantly, the record marked the last contribution to the Byrds by Gene Clark, who had officially left the group in March. For general consumption, it was ironically his fear of flying that was cited as the main reason for his departure; and it was certainly true that on 22nd February he had disembarked before take-off from a flight the group were due to make from Los Angeles to New York, after suffering a catastrophic panic attack.

But there were other undercurrents contributing to his anxiety. For one, his position as the principal earner of royalties for his composing talents was increasingly resented by the other group members, immediately precluding any possibility of an accommodation akin to that reached by Brian Wilson with the rest of the Beach Boys, for example. For another, the insecurity of his personality led him all too easily to be the target of bullying behaviour by David Crosby. When CBS closed ranks after the event, issuing a directive to the effect that all extant publicity shots should be doctored forthwith to show the group as a quartet, publicity officer Derek Taylor at least showed greater compassion towards Clark by issuing a statement in which he said:

> He left not because of a row, and not because he was fired. He left because he was tired of the multitude of obligations facing successful rock'n'roll groups. Tired of the travel, the hotels and the food. Tired of the pursuit of the most relentless autograph hunters, weary of the constant screaming. Bothered by the photographs and interviews, and exhausted by the whole punishing scene. [200]

And he generously concluded thus:

> Gene will always be a Byrd. For he wrote Byrd songs and, indeed, 'Eight Miles High' was his hymn to London – to the very strange and mystical impact the city had on the Byrds when they arrived last year to justify the intriguing reputation they had earned so swiftly with 'Mr Tambourine Man'.[201]

Hence only four Byrds rode the magic carpet on the striking cover photo of their next LP, *Fifth Dimension*, a September release in the UK. The preceding single from which the album took its title, "5D (Fifth Dimension)", marked McGuinn's first serious attempt to step up to the plate as a composer now that Clark was gone, but his earnest explanations of the song's ambitious scope confused as much as they clarified: "It's sort of weird but … what I'm talking about is the whole universe, the Fifth Dimension which is height, width, depth, time and something else. But there are definitely more dimensions than five. It's infinite. The Fifth Dimension is the threshold of scientific knowledge."[202]

Conceptually, therefore, rather than either musically or lyrically, he had stumbled into the same mystical territory that John Lennon sought to delineate in "Tomorrow Never Knows", and so "5D (Fifth Dimension)" is best understood as McGuinn's own personal account of how he too had surrendered to the void:

> Oh, how is it that I could come out to here and be still floating?
> And never hit bottom and keep falling through,
> Just relaxed and paying attention?

All my two-dimensional boundaries were gone,
I had lost to them badly.
I saw the world crumble and thought I was dead,
But I found my senses still working.[203]

The B-side, "Captain Soul", was a rarity as a Byrds' instrumental – the first, in fact, they had recorded, with its origins in their improvisation on the riff of Lee Dorsey's contemporary hit "Get Out Of My Life Woman", and McGuinn later credited drummer Michael Clarke in particular as championing the cause of this track. Chris Hillman thought of the title and Clarke himself made the additional contribution of a mightily atmospheric piece of harmonica-playing. Always one of my personal favourites from the moment of its release, I plainly remember my anger when Derek Johnson, record reviewer for the *NME*, who probably barely listened to most of the records he wrote about every week, made a carping remark about its poor quality. I was so incensed that I wrote a letter of complaint to the paper, pointing out what I saw as its strengths and that, by the way, he hadn't previously seen fit to denigrate the far less than impressive instrumental on the B-side of the Yardbirds' "Over Under Sideways Down", "Jeff's Boogie"! My protests fell, of course, on deaf ears.

Both these tracks and "Eight Miles High" (though not "Why") were included on the LP, which offered, in the words of one American reviewer, "songs ranging from the weirdly experimental to the beautiful":

> Often sounding like a hive of super-amplified bees, The Byrds have strongly influenced the rock'n'roll trend toward massively overlaid agglomerations of electronic noisemakers. Incoherence occasionally riles this type of sound, but The Byrds generally seem to control it better than their pale followers.[204]

Moving out towards the experimental end of the continuum were two more tracks in the freer musical spirit of "Eight Miles High" – "I See You" and "What's Happening?!?!" – but even further out beyond them lay "2-4-2 Fox Trot (The Lear Jet Song)"[205], a simple chant in praise of, literally, belonging to the jetset with your own private aeroplane, to which McGuinn and Crosby eagerly applied the overlay of a multiplicity of effects:

> It's another expansion for us. It's another direction that we've gone into. We've mixed the sound of the jet and the sound of the people talking on the radio and the sound of the instruments, and the entire sounds – all the sounds that you would go through if you were taking off in a Learjet. We mixed them with music, with songs, with words, and everything.[206]

Despite their naïve enthusiasm for their experiment, they were nevertheless forced to admit that, given the inadequate state of recording technology at the time, poor quality of reproduction (especially in the almost universal mono format of the day) rendered the sound of the jet engine down to the level of something far humbler. McGuinn was definitely not amused:

> It was not a vacuum cleaner, it was a Learjet. We went out to the airport with an Ampex tape recorder and recorded the jet starting up. I really resent the fact that some people think it's a vacuum cleaner. But, then again, I guess they sound pretty much the same on record.[207]

Heading in the opposite direction, both modern and traditional folk idioms were brought into play: the former represented by the doleful "I Come And Stand At Every Door" (translated by Pete Seeger from a poem by Nazim Hikmet Ran about the spirit of a child killed at Hiroshima), the latter by adaptations of "Wild Mountain Thyme" and "John Riley" (as previously popularised by Joan Baez), to which they added strings. More or less equidistant between these extremes were McGuinn's playful "Mr. Spaceman" [208] (he was as obsessed with space travel as he was with flight) and Crosby's galloping take on "Hey Joe", which, although popular with other West Coast groups, at the time of release was still an obscure song over here in advance of Jimi Hendrix's arrival in England and did not find favour with manager Jim Dickson: "A song about a guy who murders his girlfriend in a jealous rage and is on the way to Mexico with a gun in his hand. It is not what I saw as a Byrds' song."[209]

Compared to the safe and staid *Turn! Turn! Turn!*, taken as a whole – and making due allowances for its sometimes misplaced eccentricities – *Fifth Dimension* was a box of delights, although sadly its strengths were not apparent to the generality of potential UK purchasers. Its sales over here warranted no more than two weeks in the LP charts and a correspondingly dismal highest placing of No.27 (whereas its duller predecessor had reached No.11 over five weeks). Nevertheless, the very existence and availability in Britain of such a contemporary body of work from the Byrds, although it largely went unrecognised, was one positive indicator of how, if you chose, you could now expand your musical tastes way beyond the original confines of the 'hit parade'. It was irrelevant – as, indeed, it always had been – that the Byrds were not the new Beatles. What mattered far more was that record companies and retailers should acknowledge at last that even releases with poor sales prospects had their place in the grander scheme of things; and by so doing, they initiated a major shift in the marketing of pop music that could only be of benefit to the customer.

The Lovin' Spoonful's breakthrough in Britain came in the late spring of

1966 with "Daydream", a No.2 hit record in May vying with the Beach Boys' "Sloop John B" for the top of the charts but both groups in the end forced to concede that victory to Manfred Mann's "Pretty Flamingo". Formed in 1965 in Greenwich Village, its laid-back members were: John Sebastian (lead vocals, guitar, autoharp & harmonica), Zal Yanovsky (guitar), Steve Boone (bass guitar & piano) and Joe Butler (drums), who, according to the sleevenotes of their first LP, were wont to "dress like comic book characters" and "move like a carton of ping pong balls on their way to some great party somewhere".[210] Sebastian, as a talented multi-instrumentalist, composer and arranger, was the driving force behind the group, whose early reputation as impoverished musicians' musicians was built upon their residency at the Village's Night Owl Café.[211] Their speciality lay in being able to create a distinctive amalgam of rock, folk, blues, jug band and country influences, branded 'good time music' by the record company that finally took them on, Kama Sutra.

An initial distribution deal with Pye brought them belatedly to the UK, for "Daydream" was their third US Top 40 hit (after "Do You Believe In Magic" and "You Didn't Have To Be So Nice"). Although it sounds like the archetype of recording at its most casual, complete with indolent whistling towards the end, the apparently simplistic structure of "Daydream" was a contrivance. Whilst they were on tour in 1965 with the Supremes, Sebastian had originally attempted to write a song of his own to the beat of their early hits, like "Where Did Our Love Go" or "Baby Love", but in the studio somehow it proved frustratingly difficult for him and Yanovsky to record their guitar parts. After more than twenty takes, producer Eric Jacobsen came to the rescue:

> … to play them a perfectly solid performance assembled with
> scissors and splicing tape from the best parts of the various takes!
> Joe Butler added spoons and an orchestral "slapstick" whip. Steve
> tickled the ivories in his first featured piano part on an album. Zal
> overdubbed his Thunderbird electric guitar. John sang lead and
> whistled. Like a charm, it worked. As Sebastian put it, "'Daydream'
> is, in fact, a splicing wonder."[212]

Kama Sutra then issued their US No.1 hit, "Summer In The City", as their follow-up in Britain. The song owed its existence to John Sebastian's younger brother Mark, whose original couplet "But at night it's a different world/Go out and find a girl"[213] had sparked his sibling's interest in writing a contextual back-story. Reaching No.7 in August, it too had benefited from studio magic in its re-creation of the heat-baked, traffic-choked heart of New York, courtesy this time of CBS recording engineer Roy Halee, who:

> … selectively splashed the track with reverb from the eighth floor

stairwell, Zally contributed "some of my best chakka chakkas" on guitar, veteran arranger/composer/session man Artie Schroeck was on hand to play the electric piano riff that John wrote, and a sound effects man added the city noises. Boone recalls him "sitting crossed leg on the floor with his little portable reel to reel and boxes of tapes of car horns and pneumatic drills. It was pretty primitive but it was just magical watching this guy work."[214]

The scene thus evoked was not dissimilar to the organised chaos visited upon Abbey Road by the Beatles during their recording of "Yellow Submarine", that now just happened to be perched six places above "Summer In The City" at No.1.

A month after "Daydream" had entered the Top 30, another American group, The Mamas & The Papas, made their British chart debut on the RCA Victor label in an altogether different style with "California Dreamin'". Itinerant musicians John Phillips and his wife Michelle had been performing together with Denny Doherty as the New Journeymen and had gravitated to the Virgin Islands in the summer of 1965, eking out a meagre existence on credit in the Caribbean sun. They were joined there by Cass Elliot, who was seeking a reunion with Doherty after the two of them had previously sung together in the early Sixties (with John Sebastian and Zal Yanovsky) as the Mugwumps. Having now come together informally as a four-part harmony group, in which Cass's membership was as yet barely tolerated, they were then unexpectedly forced to flee St. Thomas Island, to avoid the Governor's wrath after he had discovered they had turned his son onto LSD. After flying back to New York, with tickets fortuitously paid for from the proceeds of a one-off gambling win by Michelle at the card tables of the Carib Hilton Casino, they relocated to Los Angeles but here again they were penniless and forced to live a hand-to-mouth existence, taken in by friends and crashing out on the floor of their apartment:

> While John and Denny took to stealing cuts of meat from supermarkets during the day so there'd be something to eat for dinner, there was nothing to do in the evenings as they had no money with which to go anywhere or do anything. All that was left was to sit around the flat by candlelight and sing.[215]

However, the prospect of an end to their poverty finally presented itself when they were signed up later that year to a recording contract in their own right with producer Lou Adler, having originally auditioned for him as backing singers for Barry McGuire (an old acquaintance of Cass). As part of the deal, John extracted from Adler not only the promise of the purchase of a car for the group's use but also an advance payment of $5000, with which they were at last able to rent a place of their own.

It was at this point, then, on the threshold of their recording career, that they decided to call themselves The Mamas & The Papas, from the slang terms for women and men used by Hell's Angels, but Cass explained that their group name had other resonances too: "We wanted a name that would indicate that there were both men and women in the group, because it was the first group that actually was sexually integrated – so you might speak."[216] Nevertheless, their bohemian lifestyle brought with it a legacy of interpersonal tensions that constantly threatened to destabilise their working relationship. Although John and Michelle were married, Michelle and Denny also lusted after each other, a situation further complicated by Cass having a long-standing crush on Denny. Add to this the fact that, musically speaking, John was an obsessive perfectionist, using his roles as principal songwriter and arranger to dominate the other three, and you rapidly arrive at an inherently unstable situation.

Even the story of the genesis of "California Dreamin'", arguably their best-known and most iconic song, was tainted by disagreement between John and Michelle as time passed. It has its origins in the winter of 1963 when they were together in New York and is credited for publishing purposes to both of them, but whereas John subsequently claimed to have written the majority of it without Michelle's assistance, she has always remained clear that she made a very specific contribution by writing the second verse herself:

> Stopped into a church
> I passed along the way.
> Well, I got down on my knees
> And I pretend to pray.
> You know the preacher liked the cold,
> He knows I'm gonna stay
> California dreamin'
> On such a winter's day.[217]

A No.4 hit in America, it was only in the British charts for four weeks from mid-May and in that time climbed no higher than No.24. This is largely because the week after its entry to the Top 30 it was spectacularly overtaken by a second release, "Monday Monday". Already a US No.1, it went straight in at No.12 and quickly shot up to No.3, where it stayed for three weeks in June.

In August came their third UK hit in a row, "I Saw Her Again", which made No.14, but embedded in the lyric were clues as to the recent worsening state of personal affairs within the group. The 'her' of the title was Michelle and the song was John's indirect means of challenging Denny to a vocal duel, by forcing him to confront his guilt:

> I saw her again last night

And you know that I shouldn't
Just string her along, it's just not right.
If I couldn't, I wouldn't.

But what can I do? I'm lonely too
And it makes me feel so good to know
She'll never leave me.[218]

Michelle's infidelity with Denny had, however, been the least of her problems, for she had latterly begun an affair with ex-Byrd Gene Clark. When he conspicuously attended a Mamas & Papas concert, taking a seat on the front row, it was the last straw for John Phillips. He ordered Cass and Michelle to move out of Clark's eye-line and join him and Denny on the other side of the stage, where, in Michelle's words:

> … we continued singing and we continued the concert, but in the pit of my stomach I was terrified. Even though John had not caught us, he 'caught' us in the same way he had caught me with Denny. He didn't catch me in any kind of compromising situation. It was *thick* with guilt. He chased me right out into the parking lot. I was headed for my car. It was my birthday, June 4th, 1966. He came running out as I was getting into my car, and he said, "You're *fired!*" I said, "I really don't think that you have the authority to do that, John." He said, "Oh, really? Happy Birthday. Good-bye."[219]

As good as his word, John then prevailed upon Denny and Cass to choose between him and Michelle to sustain the group's future. They sided with him and on 28th June Michelle was sent a formal letter of dismissal, signed by all three of them:

Dear Michelle,
   This letter is to advise you that the undersigned no longer desire to record or perform with you in the future. Moreover, the undersigned desire to terminate any business relationship with you that may have heretofore existed.[220]

In order to fulfil recording and touring commitments, that included a short visit to London, she was replaced, at Lou Adler's suggestion and supposedly on a permanent basis, by Jill Gibson; whom John expected to be equally submissive to his will and who "would have been more comfortable on stage if John hadn't pushed me to get stoned before going on".[221] After a couple of months, however, he relented and Michelle was reinstated, on the understanding that, as she said: "Everything had to be forgotten, and all of the bad stuff had to be swept under the rug and never spoken about again, which is how we dealt with it."[222]

Paradoxically, one of the other most popular American songs to enjoy repeated airplay on the radio in Britain in 1966 was not a hit single here for its original recording artists, despite having been a million-selling No.1 for them the year before in the US. By the time the Bachelors' cover version of Paul Simon's song "The Sound Of Silence" reached No.4 in the *NME* chart for the week ending 23rd April, Simon & Garfunkel had, however, made their own Top 30 debut with "Homeward Bound", destined to rise to No.11 in early May, and were beginning to exert an intense influence as polished performers in a modern folk idiom.

Paul Simon and Art Garfunkel both hailed from New York, where they had been close neighbours in the outer-city district of Queens and first thrown together at school as the White Rabbit and Cheshire Cat respectively in a musical production of *Alice in Wonderland*. In 1957, as teenagers in high school, calling themselves Tom & Jerry, they had cut a record of Simon's own early composition "Hey Schoolgirl" in imitation of the Everly Brothers. As a one-hit wonder, it made No.49 in the *Billboard* Hot 100, gave them a TV appearance on Dick Clark's *American Bandstand* and earned them a net profit of $1000 each; after which Art settled back down to his pre-university studies, while Paul still dreamt of making it big in music and went on to working part-time at the Brill Building, recording demos of new songs by its in-house composing teams.

Reunited in the early Sixties, the duo were ready to try their luck again, this time on the coat-tails of the folk movement re-energised in Greenwich Village by Bob Dylan's emergence. In late 1963, they performed – as Kane & Garr – at Gerde's Folk City, singing three of Simon's most recent compositions, including "The Sound Of Silence". As luck would have it, in the audience that night was CBS producer Tom Wilson, out talent-spotting, and his interest was initially aroused by one of Simon's other songs, "He Was My Brother", that he thought might be suitable for a new group he was working with at the time. But Simon was unwilling to sell Wilson the rights to that song, pressing instead for the pair to be given an opportunity to audition for him. When Wilson agreed and arranged a test session in the studio for them, they reprised "The Sound Of Silence" and thereby secured the offer of a recording contract.

Under Wilson's supervision, in March 1964 they recorded an LP, *Wednesday Morning, 3 A.M.*, on which traditional ballads were in the majority, together with the almost obligatory cover of Dylan's "The Times They Are A-Changin'" and five of Simon's own songs, "The Sound Of Silence" being one. They were adamant that they should henceforth be known as Simon & Garfunkel but when they reappeared at Folk City at the end of the month to promote themselves as CBS's latest signings, their reception was less than friendly. Robert Shelton and Bob Dylan, by now more than influential figures in the Village and beyond, were openly unimpressed:

> Dylan and I were at Folk City as Simon & Garfunkel came on. Simon cast a hostile look Dylan's way. Onstage, Simon & Garfunkel began to sing ethereal choirboy harmonies that sounded seriously out of place at Gerde's home of weatherbeaten ethnic songs. At the bar, Bob and I, who had been doing quite a bit of drinking, had an advanced case of giggles over nothing. We weren't laughing at the performance, but Simon was furious. Afterward, Simon acted as though there were a Dylan cabal against him, while Dylan tended to ignore Simon.[223]

And they met similar indifference or hostility elsewhere from dyed-in-the-wool folk reactionaries, as recalled by Village veteran Dave Van Ronk:

> … they were in a pretty tough situation, because they had already had a Top 40 hit as teenagers, and as far as the music was concerned, they were over the hill, but the mouldy fig wing of the folk world despised them as pop singers. I remember hearing them down at the Gaslight, and nobody would listen. I thought they were damn good, but the people who wanted to hear Mississippi John Hurt and Dock Boggs wanted no part of Simon & Garfunkel.[224]

To avoid the further embarrassment of their album's probable failure on issue, they decided to split once more; Garfunkel returning to university, Simon making a clean break and taking off for Paris where, through a chance encounter while busking, he was invited to visit England and try his hand on the folk circuit there. So from April to September 1964, he worked his way outwards from clubs in Essex and London to travel around the country, writing songs as he went, such as "Kathy's Song" (dedicated to his new English girlfriend and muse, Kathy Chitty) and "Homeward Bound" (reputedly written whilst waiting for a train on Widnes Station). Then, ahead of CBS's much-delayed release of *Wednesday Morning, 3 A.M.* that October, he was summoned back to New York by Tom Wilson. Accompanied by Kathy, he made her his first priority, taking her on a trip across the States (immortalised in his song "America"), before seeing her off on her flight back home and finally rejoining Wilson (and Garfunkel) on standby for official promotional duties as requested. But as Simon had previously feared, the album was a flop, selling only 3,000 copies, and by the end of the year he decided to return again to England.

Second time around, he tried his hardest to use his time here in 1965 to his best advantage, broadening his repertoire by fraternising with some of the leading lights of the British folk scene, such as Bert Jansch and Martin Carthy (both of whom tolerated him but found him precocious, if not arrogant), and setting up a music publishing deal for his own songs. After a friend of his in London, Judith Piepe, had, unbeknown to him, sent a tape she had compiled from his demos to the BBC and some of this material was broadcast, under his latest pseudonym of Jerry Landis, it created a new groundswell of interest in his work. To capitalise on this, CBS determined that Simon should record a new solo album and in June Tom Wilson was despatched to London to oversee the project, which entailed the use of a studio in Bond Street for a single one-hour session at minimal cost. For all this flurry of activity, the outcome was disappointing yet again, as *The Paul Simon Songbook*, whilst artistically gratifying to Simon himself, failed to break into the LP charts following its August release.

Meanwhile, back in America, the virtually forgotten *Wednesday Morning, 3 A.M.* had been lighted upon by a Boston radio station and the original version of "The Sound Of Silence" given a late-night airing to a receptive student audience. When other stations along the eastern seaboard followed suit and CBS promotions staff were suddenly alerted to a growing demand for a single of that track, Tom Wilson responded by unilaterally producing an updated version, employing session men to overdub the simple acoustic arrangement with electric guitars and drums in a mix overseen by engineer Roy Halee. Now, at long last, without either their prior knowledge or physical participation, Simon & Garfunkel had been handed a hit on a plate.

As it made its way up the US charts in the autumn of 1965 to No.1, the new single's success first came to Simon's attention when he chanced upon export copies of the two most popular American music papers, *Billboard* and *Cashbox*, and saw it mentioned in their respective listings. Then Garfunkel was in touch with him to share the news, swiftly followed by a complimentary copy of the record sent to him by Wilson – which he detested at first hearing. Yet he couldn't bear to forego the longed-for prospect of a worthwhile career in music that was now beckoning him back to New York, to pick up with Garfunkel where they had left off. So it was that in January 1966 he said his farewells to England and flew home, to "a partnership he hadn't wanted rekindled as a result of a remix he had not made whose enhanced performance he did not like".[225]

On his return, the pressure from CBS to maintain sales on the back of "The Sound Of Silence" was so great that he and Garfunkel were almost immediately required to join Wilson and Halee in the studio to record a full album; although in the circumstances, their starting-point was a reworking, with new electric arrangements, of material culled from *The Paul Simon Songbook*, and Wilson would subsequently hand over production to his colleague Bob Johnston. The resultant *Sounds Of Silence*, released in February in the US and March in the UK, sold strongly in both countries and it was this LP rather than their early singles that was chiefly responsible for breaking Simon & Garfunkel as an act in Britain in the vanguard of a modern folk revival but was to be followed by some faltering steps. The album's concluding track, "I Am A Rock", struggled to make headway as their next UK single, unsurprisingly only reaching No.24 by late July given that it was heavy on intellectual angst:

> I've built walls
> A fortress, steep and mighty
> That none may penetrate
> I have no need of friendship
> Friendship causes pain
> It's laughter and it's loving I disdain
> I am a rock
> I am an island.[226]

And after that in September came "The Dangling Conversation", another undeniably clever and cerebral song about the end of a relationship:

> And you read your Emily Dickinson
> And I my Robert Frost
> And we note our place with bookmarkers
> That measure what we've lost
> Like a poem poorly written
> We are verses out of rhythm
> Couplets out of rhyme
> In syncopated time
> And the dangling conversation
> And the superficial sighs
> Are the borders of our lives.[227]

An obvious miss from the outset for all that it was beautifully sung, it always deserved to be savoured in solitude as an LP track rather than to be completely abandoned as a more than fragile single in a chart free-for-all then favouring the robustness of the Small Faces, the Troggs, the Who and the Spencer Davis Group or even the very different American genres represented by the Supremes, the Lovin' Spoonful and The Mamas & The Papas. It was far more appropriately housed in October within the covers of *Parsley, Sage, Rosemary And Thyme*, the title of their next LP echoing the chorus of the first track, "Scarborough Fair/Canticle" (which, though credited to P.Simon/A. Garfunkel on the record label, was, of course, strictly speaking no more than an arrangement of a traditional English folk song Simon had gleaned from Martin Carthy).

While this album is the source of lighter ephemera like "The 59th Bridge Street Song (Feelin' Groovy)", it also contains three much heavier tracks reflecting deeper and darker aspects of Simon's persona. "The Big Bright Green Pleasure Machine" is a quick-tempo send-up of the consumer society in the form of an aggressive advertising jingle for the latest must-have accessory. "A Simple Desultory Philippic (Or How I Was Robert McNamara'd Into Submission)" is Simon's alternative take on "Subterranean Homesick Blues", name-checking the controversial US Secretary of State for Defence in the course of a splenetic catalogue of contemporary influential figures that includes openly mimicking Dylan's habitual mode of delivery at one point as well as his thought-processes:

> I knew a man, his brain so small
> He couldn't think of nothing at all
> He's not the same as you and me
> He doesn't dig poetry
> He's so unhip
> When you say Dylan, he thinks you're talking about Dylan Thomas
> Whoever he was
> The man ain't got no culture
> But it's alright, ma
> Everybody must get stoned.[228]

But it is in the concluding track, "7 O'Clock News/Silent Night", that he seeks to make an overtly political statement. In what Robert Shelton called one of Simon's "most doubting songs", the traditional Christmas carol is "drowned out by the voice of a radio announcer reading the day's news about war and discrimination"[229], this sound collage steadily building to a crescendo of disaffection:

> In Washington the atmosphere was tense today as a special
> Subcommittee of the House Committee on Un-American
> Activities continued its probe into anti-Vietnam War protest.
> Demonstrators were forcibly evicted from the hearings when they
> began chanting anti-war slogans.
> Former vice president Richard Nixon says that unless there is a
> substantial increase in the present war effort in Vietnam, the US
> should look forward to five more years of war.
> In a speech before the Convention of the Veterans of Foreign Wars in
> New York, Nixon also said opposition to the war in this country is
> the greatest single weapon working against the US.
> That's the 7 o'clock edition of the news. Good-night.[230]

Although the LP, in many ways a bewildering successor to the more evenly melodic *Sounds Of Silence*, failed to find favour with British record-buyers first time around, it did achieve greater recognition on its reissue in 1968, by which time Simon & Garfunkel's fortunes here had significantly revived.

Some of Simon's lighter compositions were given an airing by the Seekers, beginning with their single "Someday, One Day", the follow-up to

"The Carnival Is Over" that brought them back into the charts in April and climbed to No.14 by early May. For their second LP, *Come The Day*, released in November, they also recorded "I Wish You Could Be Here" and "Red Rubber Ball" (the latter a joint composition with group member Bruce Woodley dating from Simon's earlier days in London, and clearly the only one of these three in which he took sufficient pride to include it in the 2008 published collection of his lyrics). But it was Tom Springfield's song "Walk With Me" that gave the Seekers another No.14 hit in October, before they turned to Malvina Reynolds for the pre-Christmas kitsch of "Morningtown Ride", a sentimental blockbuster of a lullaby clocking up twelve weeks in the Top 30 that included three at No.2, blocked at No.1 by Tom Jones and his equally discomforting "Green Green Grass Of Home".

Following the thread of successful electrified folk on the CBS label back from Simon & Garfunkel – always allowing, of course, for the fact that strictly speaking they were unwilling accomplices, with such arrangements imposed on them for commercial considerations – took you in pretty short order to the Byrds and Bob Dylan. The genre was, however, set to receive fresh impetus from another direction entirely by the end of 1966 when Pye's contractual wrangles with Donovan in the UK were resolved to finally allow the release in December, all but a year on from when it was recorded, of "Sunshine Superman". By that time, the US deal Mickie Most had negotiated for him with Epic Records meant that it had already enjoyed runaway success in America, a July release over there leading to sales of 800,000 within six weeks and a No.1 hit in September, and had been followed by an LP of the same title (that Donovan would later modestly refer to as "the first record of the New Age"[231]), as well as a No.2 million-selling single in the form of "Mellow Yellow". Yet Donovan's love affair with the States, which he had pursued with vigour in the first half of the year, was abruptly curtailed by a police raid on his flat in London; leading to his conviction in July, together with Gypsy Dave, for the possession of cannabis and thus denying him the requisite US entry visa.

All too conscious of the very real danger that "the 'Now Music' of Donovan would soon become the 'Then Music'"[232], he would be relieved and gratified to find that he had not been abandoned by his British fans when, in the week beginning 10th December, "Sunshine Superman" entered the Top 30 and went on to spend a solid month at No.4. Indeed, in the chart for Christmas Eve, it was the highest placed genuine rock record of the season, positioned as it was immediately below a festive triumvirate of Val Doonican, the Seekers and Tom Jones. Donovan's own economical description of it is as follows:

... a three-chord Latin rocker, scored for two basses, one

acoustic and one electric. The drummer was Bobby Orr and the percussionist Tony 'The Maltese Falcon' Carr. The electric guitars were Jimmy [Page] and Eric [Ford] ... The new sound of rock harpsichord was played by John Cameron. I ... played the acoustic Gibson J-45 ...[233]

The richness and varied textures of Cameron's arrangement meant that with this record alone Donovan had moved light years away from the early naivety of "Catch The Wind" to the fringes of psychedelia. In his imagination he was reborn as a super-hero, using the song as a vehicle to express the depth of his love for Linda Lawrence, with whom he had embarked upon a relationship after she had split up with Brian Jones but from whom he was now separated by thousands of miles: unable to commit to him, she had gone to live in Los Angeles. Hence the superhuman effort required to bring her back to his side:

Sunshine came softly through my window today,
Could've tripped out easy but I've changed my way.
It'll take time, I know it, but in a while
You're gonna be mine, I know it,
We'll do it in style
'Cause I've made my mind up you're going to be mine,
Any trick in the book now, baby, that I can find.[234]

The B-side, "The Trip", was, aptly enough, one outcome of recording sessions in Hollywood during April and May, before Donovan was declared *persona non grata*, an hallucinatory account of a drive down Sunset Boulevard under the influence of mescaline – on a trip, therefore, passing the flashing neon lights of The Trip, the legendary beat club where he had been booked to play for ten nights:

We was a-d-d-drivin' a-downtown LA
About the midnight hour.
An' it almost a-b-b-blew my mind,
I got caught in a coloured shower.
The lights they were a-twinklin' on Sunset,
I saw a sign in the sky.
It said t-t-t-trip, a-trip, a-trip,
I couldn't keep up if I tried.
We stopped at a reality company,
To get some instant sleep,
And the driver turned, he said a-welcome back,
He smiled and he said, 'Beep-beep'.
What goes on, chick, chick?
What goes on, I really wanna know?[235]

Coming in at a combined playing length just short of eight minutes, the pairing of these two tracks on one single was, to me, every bit as inspired as that of the Byrds' "Eight Miles High"/ "Why". Not merely proving that Donovan was capable of both reinvention and dazzling originality, it went even further by arousing great expectations of the LP that was as yet still unavailable here and for which British fans would have a further agonised wait until the summer of 1967.

In stark contrast to this trans-continental nurturing of progressivism amongst male musicians, the most significant British female artists remained subject to more conservative influences and firmly steered in the safer direction of mass light entertainment. By 1966, however, the competition for those still standing had been even further reduced. Firstly, Decca's loss of Lulu to Columbia was not to result in any immediate new challenge from her: she was temporarily lured away from recording by an acting role as schoolgirl Barbara 'Babs' Pegg in James Clavell's film adaptation of E.R. Braithwaite's *To Sir, With Love*, starring Sidney Poitier. Marianne Faithfull, too, was out of contention as she struggled, with varying degrees of success, to adjust to motherhood and a marriage slowly being destabilised by husband John Dunbar's growing preoccupation with the counter-culture of drug-taking. This left, in ascending order of popularity as measured by new chart-placings, Sandie Shaw, Petula Clark, Cilla Black and Dusty Springfield; plus a short-lived interloper from the States in the form of Frank Sinatra's daughter Nancy.

Sandie Shaw's continuing partnership with Chris Andrews delivered three more Top 30 hits for her; of which the first, "Tomorrow", was far and away the most successful, as the only one to reach the Top 10 (at No.10) in February. It was followed by "Nothing Comes Easy", a No.15 in June, and a disappointing No.25 in December with "Think Sometimes About Me", which represented a change in style towards the ballads more readily associated with Dusty Springfield. Her running mate on the Pye label, Petula Clark, similarly maintained her productive relationship with Tony Hatch, although she disapproved strongly of his actions in leaving his wife for Jackie Trent and now working with her as his songwriting collaborator. It was, therefore, heavily ironic that both her Top 10 hits of the year should be beholden, in their lyrical content, to her composers' expressions of love for one another: "My Love" (No.4 in February, but also her second US No.1) and "I Couldn't Live Without Your Love" (No.7 in July, which she promoted in the course of a series of BBC TV spectaculars, *This Is Petula Clark*).

In retrospect, Cilla Black's crowning achievement of 1966 would easily be seen as her recording of the Bacharach & David title song for the film *Alfie* (starring Michael Caine, with Julia Foster and Jane Asher), yet in chart terms it was only the third most popular of her four hits that year. Preceded by "Love's Just A Broken Heart" reaching No.3 in February, "Alfie" was sprung on her when she was expecting to record a new Italian ballad as the follow-up, but, with no prior knowledge of the planned film to which it related, it was not a song to which she took on first hearing:

> Because I really didn't want to record the song, but didn't want to say an outright 'no', I thought I'd be really difficult for a change and start putting up barriers. So first of all I said I'd only do it if Burt Bacharach himself did the arrangement, never thinking for one moment that he would. Unfortunately the reply came back from America that he'd be happy to. So then I said I would only do it if Burt came over to London for the recording sessions. 'Yes' came the reply. Next I said that as well as the arrangement and coming over, he had to play on the session. To my astonishment it was agreed that Burt would do all three – do the arrangement, fly in and play! So, by this time, coward that I was, I really couldn't back out.[236]

Unbeknown to her, the composers themselves had originally been resistant to accepting the commission from the film-makers for the song, turning it down twice before Hal David finally read the script and lighted on the phrase 'What's it all about?' as his way into it.[237] Director Lewis Gilbert had then identified Cilla as his preferred singer, to complement a British production aimed at British filmgoers.

The session at Abbey Road, with Bacharach conducting a full orchestra and George Martin producing, was long and arduous. By Cilla's recollection, she was required to attempt at least eighteen takes: by Bacharach's there were even more, possibly as many as twenty-eight or twenty-nine, and Martin eventually rescued her by calling a halt on her behalf, impressing on Bacharach that in his opinion the best take had already been laid down much earlier in the proceedings. Martin would later rank "Alfie" as the recording with Cilla of which he was proudest, while Bacharach would magnanimously concede that he had been pushing for perfection and found it:

> I don't know what Cilla was used to in the studio but I know what I was used to. I just went and I guess I kind of challenged her and beat her up a lot and kept making her do one take after another. My feeling always has been that you just keep going if you're at 9½ and you want to try to get 10. It was great with Sir George sitting in the booth and he couldn't have been nicer letting me just do my maniacal behaviour and my work. Cilla was great and wound up delivering a killer vocal as she did on many of my songs.[238]

For all the time and money spent on it, and for all the undoubted subtlety and quality of Cilla's performance, "Alfie" still lost out to some of her less prestigious recordings by climbing no higher than No.7 in April; four places lower than its predecessor and two places lower than its successor, the post-poned Italian ballad "Don't Answer Me", that took her to No.5 in June. A second Italian composition, "A Fool Am I", would follow in the autumn, peaking at No.11 in November. She had ended 1965 by going into panto-mime: she would round off this year by co-starring with Frankie Howerd in a revue scripted by Ray Galton, Alan Simpson and Eric Sykes, *Way Out In Piccadilly*.

1966 was the third year in a row in which readers of the *NME* voted Dusty Springfield Best UK Female Singer and the second in which they had also declared her Best International Female Singer. But unlike 1965, when those votes had been cast against the odds, this time round they reflected an altogether more positive chart history of four hit singles, including a truly memorable No.1. And in this regard fortune favoured Dusty again over Cilla, even though, in terms of the total number of weeks their respective records spent in the Top 30 throughout the year, the two of them were level, at thir-ty-two weeks each.

She opened the year with what she regarded as "a sustainer, a pot-boiler"[239] to hold her place in her public's consciousness, the upbeat "Little By Little" (from the composers of "In The Middle Of Nowhere") that gave her a No.16 hit in February. Then came the extraordinary triumph in April of being at No.1 for two weeks, with the high orchestral drama of "You Don't Have To Say You Love Me"; a ballad that had first taken her fancy at the 1965 San Remo Song Contest, when she had seen it performed in its original Italian by its composer, Pino Donaggio. She was determined to record it herself and had hoped to be able to write an English lyric of her own, but the responsibility for this passed eventually to Vicki Wickham, assisted by Yardbirds' producer Simon Napier-Bell, who wrote new words to fit the mood of the music rather than attempt something approaching a literal translation from the Italian. In the end, they found themselves working to a tight deadline before Dusty was due to go into the Philips Studios in early March and no-one, as Napier-Bell explains, was confident of the outcome:

> Dusty said that she wasn't certain that she liked the new lyrics [Wickham and Napier-Bell had thought them corny] and was quite half-hearted about doing a ballad and had to be pushed by everybody. She really wanted to sing soul but they wouldn't let her and eventually she was persuaded. I'm not talking about me and Vicki but about Johnny Franz, her producer at Philips, who suggested she sang it and then they would decide. She sang it – they decided! Great singers can take mundane lyrics and fill them with their own meaning. Vicki and I had thought that our lyric was about avoiding emotional commitment but Dusty stood it on its head and

made it a passionate lament of loneliness and love.[240]

He also discloses that in the process of recording an overdub onto the backing track Dusty, highly self-critical as ever, "complained about the echo on her voice":

> … and when the engineer went to the basement to adjust it, he noticed how good the natural echo sounded in the stairwell of the building. Five minutes later, Dusty was half way up it, leaning out from the stairs, singing into a mic, hanging in space in front of her. There, standing on the staircase at Philips studio near Marble Arch, singing into a stairwell, Dusty gave her greatest performance, perfection from first breath to last, as great as anything by Aretha Franklin or Sinatra or Pavarotti.[241]

In a very real sense, this supercharged act was impossible to follow; and for the future, Dusty would reserve it to the finale of her live appearances because she found it "such a killer vocally".[242] Nevertheless, in the summer Dusty did release a worthy successor in Goffin & King's "Goin' Back", the tenderness of her interpretation drawing praise from Carole King herself as the only truly worthwhile performance of the song. At the end of July it peaked at No.11; after which she reverted that autumn to another bold ballad, this time by Clive Westlake, "All I See Is You", closing her year's run of hits in October at No.8.

Dusty had seen out the previous winter in the relative obscurity of the Northern club circuit but in the course of 1966 her profile as an entertainer was to be greatly enhanced by hosting her own TV show, *Dusty*, a series of six programmes broadcast by the BBC through August and September. In November, however, she faced one of her biggest challenges when she had to confront and overcome the unreconstructed chauvinism and bullying attitude of American jazz bandleader and drummer Buddy Rich, with whom she had to share a fortnight's billing at Basin Street East in New York. Arguments broke out between them on her arrival two weeks before the engagement, over his refusal to allow her rehearsal time with his musicians, and continued from night to night through the run over which one of them should be top of the bill, with Rich hogging the stage and making defamatory remarks about her before her entrances. Her perseverance and fortitude in withstanding this offensive onslaught were at least recognised by Rich's bandsmen, who presented her with a farewell gift of a pair of boxing gloves inscribed to 'Slugger Springfield'. Bloodied but unbowed, on her return to England she understandably sought light relief by spending nine weeks at the Liverpool Empire from 23rd December, in a cameo role in the pantomime *Merry King Cole*.

Dusty was only one of two female singers – and the only British female artist – to reach No.1 in 1966, her achievement in April with "You Don't Have To Say You Love Me" being predated in February by that of Nancy Sinatra, with a song of an entirely different complexion, "These Boots Are Made For Walkin'". A US No.1 and an international million-seller into the bargain, this catchy, semi-comic pseudo-feminist rant against men's infidelity, composed and produced for her by Lee Hazelwood, was instantly distinguishable by its repetitive descending bass line and stinging brass accompaniment, and a fast mover for an artist with no previous track record in the UK: it went from a chart entry at No.16 to No.1 in just three weeks. A good record to dance to, it also had staying power, holding on to the No.2 slot for three consecutive weeks after being displaced at the top by the Rolling Stones with "19th Nervous Breakdown" and completing a chart run of twelve weeks overall. It was not so popular here, however, that the UK market would any longer readily support a formulaic follow-up and its pale imitation (this time minus the dominant bass), "How Does That Grab You, Darlin'?", could only manage five weeks in the Top 30 from late April into May and do no better than No.20. Thus her challenge to home-grown talent evaporated almost as soon as it had arisen and she now faced several months' wait before being restored to UK chart favour.

Aside from England's sporting triumph in the 1966 World Cup, the focus of international interest in current affairs lay elsewhere; in America, in the ongoing prosecution of the Vietnam War and, from the late summer onwards, in China, where Chairman Mao Tse-tung had decreed that political and social reforms would henceforth be led by a Cultural Revolution. By ushering in the oppressively radical era of the Red Guards, whilst simultaneously skilfully deploying soundbite propaganda through the worldwide dissemination of his personal doctrine (his 'thoughts') in his Little Red Book, Mao was determined to impress and intimidate the West with his re-assertion of hard-line Communist orthodoxy:

> The chief targets of the campaign are Communist party officials,
> and workers in artistic and educational institutions guilty of
> "revisionist" attitudes and "bourgeois reactionary thinking".
> Schools are being shut and hundreds of teachers and other
> intellectuals are being paraded by Red Guards through the streets
> wearing dunces' caps.[243]

Although apparently hell-bent on tidying up his own backyard, neither did Mao miss any opportunity to promote his own place in the world order by rallying his true followers to denounce the 'paper tigers' of Western imperialism, whom he accused of threatening China with nuclear annihilation.

In the race to the moon between the USA and USSR, any advantages gained by one or other of the participants continued to be offset by setbacks encountered. On 14th January, as the Russians contemplated how to regain the initiative following the Americans' successful rendezvous between two Gemini spacecraft a month earlier, the future direction of their space programme was temporarily threatened by the unexpected death of Sergei Korolev, who failed to survive a major operation for the removal of an abdominal tumour. In life his identity and role had been kept secret but President Brezhnev decreed that in death his achievements should finally be publicly celebrated as befitted a hero of the Soviet Union and he should be given a lavish state funeral in Moscow.

Korolev was succeeded by his deputy, Vasily Mishin, now charged with overseeing the development of the N-1 rocket as the launch vehicle for the Soyuz spacecraft as well as pressing on with the Voskhod programme, both endeavours fraught with difficulties. However, it would very soon fall to the unmanned Luna programme, running in parallel with the projects Mishin had inherited, under the control of Georgi Babakin, to deliver the next great leap forward. Launched on 31st January, Luna 9 made a successful moon landing on 3rd February "and within fifteen minutes it took its first picture of the lunar surface: a panorama of the surrounding landscape":

> The pictures were of poor quality but clearly showed rocks and
> craters. The fact that the [probe] was successfully placed on the
> surface ended the speculation that any landing object would sink
> into the regolith (the layer of fine dust that covers almost the entire
> surface). The pictures were intercepted by the radio observatory
> at Jodrell Bank and with the help of equipment borrowed from
> the *Daily Express* were transmitted to the world, stealing the Soviet
> thunder.[244]

From March to December, with due adjustment to transmission frequencies to keep the Russian data for their eyes only in future, a further four Luna probes were launched, the last of which, Luna 13, repeated Luna 9's success and made a soft landing on Christmas Eve, sending back new panoramic photographs of its surroundings and findings as to the composition of the moon's surface.

After the launch of Luna 9, in February Mishin sent up two dogs in a Voskhod spacecraft into orbit for a test flight lasting twenty-two days, but on their return to earth, the animals were found to have suffered severely from the effects of prolonged weightlessness – "wasting muscles, dehydration, calcium loss and problems in walking"[245] – from which it took them over a week to recover. As a consequence, Mishin was forced to cancel a manned spaceflight scheduled for March that had been intended to coincide, for propaganda purposes, with the Communist Party Congress; and after intensive ground-testing of Soyuz revealed an alarming number of systems defects to be remedied, running into four figures, the year was to see no more manned Russian missions.

The Americans, by contrast, forged ahead relentlessly, completing the Gemini phase of their manned space programme with five missions between March and November, extending the testing of rendezvous and docking procedures between spacecraft and refining the capabilities of astronauts to move and work in space (termed, in NASA's deathless prose, as EVA, or extra-vehicular activity). This is not to deny, however, that between them the missions threw up unexpected problems, beginning with the flight of Gemini 8 on 16th March, when a planned fifty-three orbits had to be curtailed after only seven, ten hours after lift-off, to save the lives of the crew, the commander Neil Armstrong and his co-pilot Dave Scott. The euphoria of achieving an historic first hard dock with the unmanned Gemini Agena Target Vehicle dissipated with alarming rapidity when they realised that the joined spacecraft were unstable and starting to spin out of control. When undocking failed to stop the manned Gemini capsule from spinning, Armstrong then deduced that it was being caused by the continuous firing of an auxiliary jet thruster, which had jammed open during earlier alignment manouevres, and called for urgent action if the astronauts were not to black out. As their spacecraft "turned into a tumbling gyro"[246], the only option open to them, in Armstrong's judgement, was to fire up the re-entry control system, thus aborting the mission and taking them back to earth; where they eventually splashed down safely in the Pacific Ocean, some 500 miles east of Okinawa.

On the next three flights, the principal issues of concern arose from difficulties encountered by astronauts in controlling their own movements once out of their spacecraft and committed to EVA. On the Gemini 9 mission in June, a year after Ed White had carried out the first US spacewalk during the flight of Gemini 4, Gene Cernan was due to replicate his achievement but for a much longer period of over two hours, during which time he was also supposed to be testing a jet pack designed by the Air Force known as an AMU (Astronaut Manouevring Unit). This was stowed in an external equipment storage bay to the spacecraft's rear. To reach it, Cernan, tethered only by a twenty-five-foot lifeline, had to make an unaided traverse of some fifteen feet along Gemini's hull: the slipperiness of the metal surface and the absence of any guiderails or handholds meant that it took him all his strength and virtually an hour to complete what had superficially appeared to be a straightforward move from A to B.

After conferring with command pilot Tom Stafford, Cernan rested awhile before attempting to don the AMU, but soon discovered that:

> The job demanded more than just slipping into simple straps. He
> needed to make electrical connections, and he found that every

move was more time-consuming than he had counted on ... Soon
he was severely overworking his own chest pack, which circulated
oxygen through his suit and also removed excessive moisture from
his body. He perspired. Fog collected inside his helmet visor and
froze, and he endured excessive heat, perspiration, and ice all at the
same time. He was barely able to see through the visor, a potentially
lethal situation for a man turning like a bloated rag doll in vacuum
several feet from the security of his spaceship cabin.[247]

Reporting Cernan's plight to Mission Control in Houston, Stafford confirmed
"It's no go on the AMU!" and waited in trepidation for his companion to
return safely to him inside the craft; which, against all the odds, with his heart
monitored as racing at times as high as 180 beats per minute, he managed
after an agonising, record-breaking spacewalk over two hours long. Once he
was back in and Stafford had slammed the exit hatch shut, Cernan thankfully
"got back in his seat, raised his visor, and his face was pink, like he'd been in
a sauna ... Turns out he lost about ten and a half pounds in two hours and
ten minutes outside." [248]

Although proving the worth of the AMU was abandoned for the time
being, similar difficulties of manouevrability and a build-up of condensation
inside their space suits beset both Mike Collins (on Gemini 10) and Dick
Gordon (on Gemini 11) during their EVAs in July and September respectively. It was not until the final mission, Gemini 12, in November that Buzz
Aldrin was able to demonstrate that, with the application of careful fore-
thought and the right tools, it was possible to carry out an efficient and effective spacewalk:

He took along with him ... special devices like a wrist tether and a
tether constructed in the same fashion as one that window washers
use to keep from falling off ledges ... One of his neatest tricks was
to bring along portable handholds he could slap onto either the
Gemini or the Agena to keep his body under control. A variety of
space tools went into his pressure suit to go along with him once he
exited the cabin.[249]

Consequently, he exhibited no signs of over-exertion as he carried out an
impressively varied range of EVA tasks. By his analytical approach to overcoming what had gone so badly wrong for his colleagues and by consciously
conserving energy as he worked his way through his schedule of physical operations, Aldrin had single-handedly helped to bring the Gemini programme
to a triumphant conclusion and thus went on to eagerly anticipate the part
he might play in the next phase of the race to the moon, codenamed Apollo.

Regular coverage of the astronauts' increasingly spectacular achievements afforded President Johnson at least a temporary measure of distraction

from his preoccupation with weightier affairs of state at home and abroad. With the promotion of racial equality remaining highly contentious, riots broke out again in July, this time affecting communities in Chicago, New York and Cleveland. Generational issues too came to the fore in Los Angeles in November, when long-running clashes between, on the one hand, the teenagers who frequented the Hollywood beat clubs and, on the other, the alliance of the civic authorities and business interests seeking to redevelop the area for other purposes culminated in the so-called 'Riot on Sunset Strip', as immortalised in Buffalo Springfield's "For What It's Worth" (a song composed *in situ* by eye-witness Stephen Stills). Even so, such disturbances paled into insignificance by comparison with the sustained and damaging impact of the Vietnam War.

US troop numbers in Vietnam increased sharply from the end of 1965, when they stood at 184,000, to a total of 385,000 by the end of 1966, while the full-year budget to fund the war rose accordingly to an estimated $12.7 billion. Beyond pressing considerations of achieving strategic military objectives, however, South Vietnam's Premier Ky also held the US President accountable for the economic decline of his country as it was overwhelmed by a combination of the importation of western goods and services in support of the military and the creation of a lost generation of dispossessed refugees and war orphans:

> President Johnson had promised to extend his 'Great Society' to Vietnam, to provide 'food', 'shelter' and 'job opportunities'. Premier Ky now pressed for massive economic aid, and on 8 February 1966 the two allies met halfway in Honolulu to plan victory in 'the other war'. Johnson agreed to commit immediately 750 million dollars (one fifteenth of the military bill) to start building an industrial base in the South. Johnson told Ky, 'We are determined to win not only military victory but victory over hunger, disease and despair.' Ky promised to bring about a social revolution.[250]

Once it became clear that the additional promised money and materials were being diverted wholesale from their intended targets by high-ranking South Vietnamese army officers cutting corrupt deals on a scale worthy of Joseph Heller's Milo Minderbinder, it prompted a Buddhist-led campaign of anti-American protest in northern provinces of the country that had to be suppressed by Ky himself, in command of a force of South Vietnamese Marines. It served as an ill omen of the inherent distrust of US imperialism in all its manifestations by the indigenous population, undermining in the process the willingness of South Vietnamese foot-soldiers to fight for their country alongside their American 'allies'. As one contemporary observer expressed it:

From the point of view of the peasants, why should they die to preserve the comfort and property of the urban ruling elite, whose representatives are their commanders, rarely seen at the heads of the columns or among them in dangerous and critical situations?[251]

Yet the overall theatre commander, General Westmoreland, still viewed the war as winnable, given the enormous wealth of firepower and technology at his disposal not just to slaughter the enemy but to reshape the very landscape to his seeming advantage, a fearsome armoury that soon spawned its own distinctive linguistic sub-culture, resplendent in the camouflage of euphemism:

> The 'Daisy-Cutter' – a 15,000 lb monster bomb – would blow a
> hole on a hilltop 300 feet in diameter or 'the size of the Rosebowl'
> to create an instant firebase. 'Jolly Green Giants' – Sikorsky
> helicopters – would ferry in huge 105mm howitzers and this
> artillery would glint in star formation from the heart of the jungle,
> thundering in every direction … squadrons of giant 'Rome' plows,
> looking like a centurion's prong, were trying piecemeal to bulldoze
> the jungle; 'Agent Orange' defoliants were burning off the foliage;
> 'People Sniffers' or electronic sensors shaped like small trees were
> strewn over the forests to transmit sounds of men or vehicles, while
> 'Huey' platoons vaulted from sighting to sighting supported by the
> new 'Cobras' of the jungle – helicopter gunships with nose-painted
> fangs. At night there was 'Spooky', a prop-plane carrying enough
> flares to floodlight a mile radius while firing 6,000 rounds a minute
> and also known as 'Puff, the Magic Dragon'.[252]

Such expansions of the American arsenal came about in addition, of course, to the continuation of the 'Rolling Thunder' bombing campaign against key targets in North Vietnam, now coupled with the deployment of B-52 bombers to halt incursions by the Viet Cong down its arterial supply route, the Ho Chi Minh Trail, a response that could by no stretch of the imagination be considered either militarily or cost-effective:

> Bombing by co-ordinates, a B-52 could unleash more than a
> hundred 750-pound bombs within thirty seconds, cutting a scythe
> through the forest a mile long and a quarter-mile wide. But the
> estimated kill ratio was one infiltrator for every 300 bombs – or
> 100 tons – at a cost of $140,000. US military records show that in
> the peak year when an estimated 150,000 North Vietnamese were
> sent South, 171,000 tons of bombs were dropped over the Trail, or
> about one ton for every suspected infiltrator. If the kill ratio was
> correct, then the B-52s were accounting for fewer than one in every
> hundred infiltrators – perhaps 1,500 men that year at a cost of

more than two billion dollars.[253]

And none of this prevented the full-year US death toll in 1966 from rising to a new high of 6,350. As media involvement had grown in proportion to the escalation of the conflict, encompassing regular television as well as radio reporting of combat in the field, questioning of the efficacy of conducting a conventional war on such a vast scale against an elusive army of ideologically driven peasant guerrillas had inevitably became more open and vocal (Simon & Garfunkel's "7 O'Clock News/Silent Night" being one of its more considered manifestations). John Laurence, who spent five years in Vietnam as a war correspondent for CBS-TV, took the pragmatic view that reporting the news had to take precedence over attempting any interpretation of events:

> In Saigon, most reporters tried to cover the war honestly. They did not usually worry about the effect their reporting might have on public opinion in the United States. Trying to figure out what the public needed to be told or not told for morale reasons was outside the responsibility of a daily news reporter's job. It made everything too complicated ... As most journalists saw it, Americans were better able to form opinions based on accurate information reported by a fair but critical press in Vietnam. Anything else was misleading, dishonest, and, in wartime, dangerous.[254]

Yet he was forced to concede that its cumulative effect was to be profoundly disturbing:

> The war was undermining the nation's propriety, the integrity of its culture, its political cohesion. The war corrupted everything it touched. Television images of the slaughter touched the eyes of millions of viewers, bringing the horror home. The effect of that transference, night after night ... was more apocalyptic than anyone knew.[255]

There were mass anti-war demonstrations in major cities across the United States on 26th March and again in Washington on 15th May. While Joan Baez actively promulgated witholding tax payments in protest against expenditure on the war, heavyweight champion boxer Cassius Clay (*aka* Muhammad Ali) proclaimed himself a conscientious objector and faced trial for draft evasion. The power of celebrity to challenge Johnson's administration was beginning to make itself felt.

In the shrinking global village, it was only to be expected that disquiet in America should readily be communicated to Britain, where Michael Foot, writing in the left-wing journal *Tribune* in June, stated baldly: "We and our Labour government share the guilt for the continuance of the infamy [of

Vietnam]."[256] His sense of outrage was similarly shared by Harold Wilson's deputy, George Brown, who constantly subjected the Prime Minister to criticism on the point, even to the extent of (albeit hollowly) threatening resignation over it; and in July, some 4,000 demonstrators gathered outside the American Embassy in London to voice their protests. Yet Wilson remained unruffled, more secure than ever in his position following a landslide victory for Labour in the general election of 19th March (that now, incidentally, confirmed him in office for the remainder of the decade). Embattled thereafter by a national seamen's strike, the struggle to impose wage restraint through an unwieldy prices and incomes policy and, to cap it all, a threat to the stability of sterling, he still happily seized upon his invitation to re-open the Cavern as a sign of public confidence in him, even though he was known not to have played any part in its rescue:

> You don't realise that I am not so unpopular as everybody thinks
> ... I was in Liverpool last weekend and I went to the Cavern, where
> the Beatles first played, to be present at its reopening and the whole
> place stood and cheered me.[257]

Compared to the complexities of world foreign policy with which President Johnson was grappling, those faced by Wilson were small beer indeed. By means of a resolution passed by the UN General Assembly in December 1965, Argentina had forced Britain to entertain negotiations over the future sovereignty of the Falkland Islands, in colonial terms hitherto "the most somnolent of sleeping dogs".[258] Talks were proceeding at a snail's pace, conducted largely in secret by senior diplomats, but the merest hint of trouble in store for the future came at the end of September. The residence of the British Ambassador in Buenos Aires, then host to a royal visit from Prince Phillip, came under fire from gunmen in a drive-by shooting. Further afield, a group of twenty armed nationalists, grandly proclaiming themselves the New Argentina Movement, hijacked a plane and landed it on the racecourse at Port Stanley. Claiming to have arrested the British officials who first attended the scene, these activists were swiftly overcome by the Royal Marine detachment based on East Falkland and sent back to Argentina, where unsurprisingly they were regarded in some quarters as national heroes.[259]

Elsewhere, the continuing dilemma over how to end the unconstitutional regime in Rhodesia was proving highly resistant to resolution, as the rebel government circumvented British sanctions on the importation of oil and other essential supplies with the connivance of Mozambique and South Africa. In a gesture reminiscent of the Victorian heyday of gunboat diplomacy, at the beginning of December Wilson invited Ian Smith to talks on board HMS *Tiger*, stationed off Gibraltar; apparently extracting concessions from him, only to find that Smith and his cabinet rejected them out of hand immediately afterwards, thus heralding an ignominious extension of the stalemate.

It was little wonder, therefore, that at home in Britain Wilson should prefer the alternative populist image he had created for himself, now coinciding happily as it did with a rising groundswell of American plaudits for 'London: The Swinging City', the proclamation used as a banner headline on the cover of *Time* magazine for its issue of 15th April. He even received a laudatory namecheck in Piri Halasz's full-length feature generating the cover story:

> In Harold Wilson, Downing Street sports a Yorkshire accent, a
> working-class attitude and tolerance towards the young that includes
> Pop Singer Screaming Lord Sutch, who ran against him on the
> Teen-Age Party ticket in the last election … [260]

The prime focus of the article was, however, what Halasz perceived as the coming together in London of egalitarianism and style, as symbolised by the capital's "new and surprising leadership community: economists, professors, actors, photographers, singers, admen, TV executives and writers – a swinging meritocracy".[261] Unlike Ray Davies, here was no hint of ridicule in her depiction of the "Carnabetian army", just open-mouthed, unqualified admiration:

> In this century, every decade has had its city. Today, it is London,
> a city steeped in tradition, seized by change, liberated by affluence,
> graced by daffodils and anemones, so green with parks and squares
> that, as the saying goes, you can walk across it on the grass. In
> a decade dominated by youth, London has burst into bloom. It
> swings; it is the scene.[262]

The 'look' conceived in London for young women to grace 'the scene' had its origins in the King's Road fashions of Mary Quant, the designer credited, amongst other things, with the creation of the mini-skirt and waterproof mascara (and awarded an OBE in the 1966 Birthday Honours List – Harold Wilson again showing he was never one to miss a trick); complemented by the 'shape', the innovative bob hairstyle dreamed up for Quant personally by stylist Vidal Sassoon, and now embodied in the fashion shoots of the latest model, Lesley Hornby from Neasden, named as "THE FACE OF '66" by the *Daily Express*[263] and dubbed 'Twiggy' for the almost skeletal slightness of her figure.

In the arts, April marked the passing of two distinguished British authors, C.S. Forester and Evelyn Waugh. In the theatre, the London *Evening Standard* conferred its annual Drama Award for best play upon *Loot*, an irreverent black comedy by maverick playwright Joe Orton first performed in September, in which Michael Bates, as the totally unscrupulous Inspector Truscott of the Yard, looked for the hidden proceeds of a bank robbery as well as trying to entrap a serial killer in the context of the death and funeral of a Mrs. McLeavy; and, of course, as befitted his office as censor, the Lord Chamberlain had taken the necessary steps to ensure that public decency should not be offended:

> The Lord Chamberlain grants a licence to the play subject to the following conditions:
>
> (i) The corpse is inanimate and not played by an actress.
>
> (ii) On page 79 the [funerary] casket is wiped with a handkerchief. The Lord Chamberlain is particularly anxious that no stain shall appear on the handkerchief.[264]

Amongst the most notable of the year's films were, as noted earlier, *Alfie*, a modern tale of sexual dalliance and consequences (on general release from March), followed, in April and December respectively, by two historical blockbusters: David Lean's epic adaptation of Boris Pasternak's *Dr. Zhivago* (starring Omar Sharif and Julie Christie) and Fred Zinnemann's rendition of Robert Bolt's play *A Man For All Seasons* (starring Paul Scofield as Sir Thomas More, for which he received the Oscar for Best Actor). More controversially, a drama-documentary for television directed by Peter Watkins and graphically portraying the aftermath of a nuclear attack on Britain, *The War Game*, was given its first screening at the National Film Theatre in February (having previously been denied a showing by the BBC on the grounds of its potential to shock and distress) and subsequently won an Oscar for Best Documentary Feature of 1966.

Yet for hard evidence of man's inhumanity to man, there was truly nothing to compare with the catalogue of base amorality revealed in the reporting of the trial of the unrepentant Ian Brady and Myra Hindley at the Old Bailey, that began on 19th April and ended on 6th May, with Brady sentenced to three concurrent life sentences for murder and Hindley to two. April had also seen the eventual arrest in Kent of Jimmy White, one of the Great Train Robbers who had been on the run from the outset and had lived incognito for a majority of the past two-and-a-half years as a hill farmer in Derbyshire. At his trial in Leicester in June, after pleading guilty to robbery, he was sentenced to eighteen years' imprisonment. For others, however, there were no prisons big enough: on 22nd October, George Blake, convicted in 1961 of espionage, scaled the walls of Wormwood Scrubs (using a home-made ladder reinforced with knitting needles) and was spirited out of the country, later arriving in Moscow via East Berlin with his escape purportedly having been financed by film director Tony Richardson (the then husband of Vanessa Redgrave). It seemed hardly deserving of a headline, coming as it did the day after the shock at the loss of 144 people, 116 of them young children, in the South Wales village of Aberfan, when Pantglas Junior School and neighbouring houses were buried beneath a vast landslide of unstable mining waste.

1966 was a topsy-turvy year, characterised by the pronounced resurgence in Britain of American culture and attitudes whilst at the same time owing the uplift in national pride implicit in the celebration of 'Swinging London' to hyperbolic American deference. Our world view was being as radically reshaped by our growing exposure to newscasts of the Vietnam War as it was in another dimension by the exploits of the Gemini astronauts, already beginning to transmute before our eyes into the archetypes of Bowie's Major Tom. With the Beatles' decision to call time on live performances and Brian Wilson's idiosyncratic pursuit of the virtually inexpressible, at one level pop music as pure entertainment had veered off sharply at a tangent from whatever passed for the mainstream of the day, to be guided in future by the extent to which imaginative genius could either work within or overcome the constraints of increasingly inadequate technology: for them, the studio must now also double as their concert hall. For others, hard-grafting bands like the Rolling Stones, the Kinks or the Who, a combination of performance and recording was to be maintained almost at any price, as much out of economic necessity as to sustain and invigorate creativity. Although the single might still be the quick-fix ticket to success, it offered so many fewer opportunities than the album to raise the overall standard and comparative value of pop music, as evidenced by the steady accretion of dross throughout the year in the Top 30. Psychedelia and the counter-culture were already beckoning both the initiated and the unwary down new, as yet largely unexplored avenues, tempting virtuosi to dream of turning guitar bands into weapons of mass distraction. If there was a revolution in the offing, there was to be no place in it for girls, barring enraptured bedfellows and honorary muses; and as for girl acts – well, they were pretty much irrelevant, even if they showed some talent, and best kept within recognised bounds as decorative appendages to the lucrative easy listening market. So who would be the next casualties and who would reign triumphant? Where would it all end?

NOTES

1   Quoted in Maureen Cleave, "How Does A Beatle Live? John Lennon Lives Like This", Evening Standard, 4th March 1966; reprinted in Sean Egan (ed.), "The Mammoth Book Of The Beatles" (Robinson, 2009), p.104.

2   Robert Rodriguez, "Revolver: How The Beatles Reimagined Rock'n'Roll" (Backbeat, 2012), pp.169-170.

3   Tony Barrow, "John, Paul, George, Ringo & Me" (Andre Deutsch, 2nd edition, 2011), pp.211-212.

4   Ibid.

5   John Lennon, quoted in "The Beatles Anthology" (Cassell, 2000), p.226.

6   Tony Barrow, op. cit., p.216.

7   The appearance of the Rolling Stones immediately before the awards ceremony was withdrawn from the broadcast of the concert on the same grounds.

8   Tony Barrow, op. cit., p.189.

9   Ibid.

10   Tony Barrow, op. cit., p.193.

11   Quoted in Tony Barrow, op. cit., p.194.

12   Op. cit., pp. 206-207.

13   Tony Barrow, op. cit., p.208.

14   George Martin, quoted in "The Beatles Anthology" (Cassell, 2000), p.221.

15   Quoted in Tony Barrow, op. cit., p.210.

16   John Lennon, "The Beatles Anthology" (Cassell, 2000), p.227.

17   George Harrison, "The Beatles Anthology" (Cassell, 2000), p.229.

18   Quoted in Tony Barrow, op. cit., p.220.

19   John Lennon, "The Beatles Anthology" (Cassell, 2000), p.229.

20   See Mark Lewisohn, op. cit., pp.226-227.

21   Quoted in George Martin with William Pearson, "Summer of Love: The Making of Sgt. Pepper" (Macmillan, 1994), p.79.

22   George Martin with William Pearson, op. cit., p.81.

23   George Martin with William Pearson, op. cit., p.79.

24   Ibid.

25   George Martin with William Pearson, op. cit., p.80.

26   George Martin with William Pearson, op. cit., pp.80-81.

27   George Martin with William Pearson, op. cit., p.82.

28   Lennon/McCartney, © 1966 by Northern Songs Ltd.

29   Ian MacDonald, op. cit., p.183.

30   Ian MacDonald, op. cit., p.180.

31   Lennon/McCartney, © 1966 by Northern Songs Ltd.

32   Ibid.

33   Ibid.

34   See Barry Miles, "Paul McCartney: Many Years From Now" (Henry Holt, 1997), p.286.

35   Lennon/McCartney, © 1966 by Northern Songs Ltd.

36   Paul McCartney, "The Beatles Anthology" (Cassell, 2000), p.209.

37   See Jonathan Gould, "Can't Buy Me Love: The Beatles, Britain and America" (Piatkus, 2008), pp.359-360.

38   George Harrison, "The Beatles Anthology" (Cassell, 2000), p.209.

39   Harrison, © 1966 by Northern Songs Ltd.

40   George Harrison, "The Beatles Anthology" (Cassell, 2000), p. 206.

41   Harrison, © 1966 by Northern Songs Ltd.

42   Ibid.

43   John Blaney, "Beatles For Sale: How Everything They Touched Turned To Gold" (Jawbone, 2008), pp.115-116.

44   Quoted in David Pritchard & Alan Lysaght, op. cit., p.205.

45   Letter of 14th June 1966 from Capitol's Press & Information Services Manager, reproduced in "The Beatles Anthology" (Cassell, 2000), p.205.

46   John Lennon, "The Beatles Anthology" (Cassell, 2000), p.235.

47   George Martin with William Pearson, op. cit., p.13.

48   It was credited with reaching No.33 in the *Record Retailer* composite Top 40 in the week ending 5th May.

49   Quoted in Clinton Heylin, "Bob Dylan: Behind The Shades" (Faber, 3rd edition, 2011), p.241.

50   See Howard Sounes, op. cit., pp.244-245.

51   Bob Dylan, © 1966 by Dwarf Music; renewed 1994 by Dwarf Music.

52   There is a reputed Biblical – if tenuous – source of the song's title, in Proverbs Ch.27, V.15: "A continual dropping in a very rainy day and a contentious woman are alike." However, in contradiction of some critics who have picked up on this, I can see no relation in the immediate surrounding text to the issue of edicts on stoning as a punishment.

53   Bob Dylan, © 1966 by Dwarf Music; renewed 1994 by Dwarf Music.

54   Bob Dylan, © 1966 by Dwarf Music; renewed 1994 by Dwarf Music.

55   Bob Dylan, © 1966 by Dwarf Music; renewed 1994 by Dwarf Music.

56   From Bob Dylan's own CD liner notes to *Biograph* (Columbia Legacy, 1985: remastered 2011).

57   Bob Dylan, © 1966 by Dwarf Music; renewed 1994 by Dwarf Music.

58   Bob Dylan, © 1966 by Dwarf Music; renewed 1994 by Dwarf Music.

59   Ibid.

60   Bob Dylan, © 1966 by Dwarf Music; renewed 1994 by Dwarf Music.

61   Ibid.

62   Robert Shelton, op. cit., p.251.

63   Quoted in Clinton Heylin, "Bob Dylan: Behind The Shades" (Faber, 3rd edition, 2011), p.251.

64   Quoted in Johnny Black, "Dylan in 1966", first published in *Mojo*, October 1998; reprinted in Sean Egan (ed.), "The Mammoth Book Of Bob Dylan" (Robinson, 2011), p.111.

65   Quoted in Clinton Heylin, op. cit., p.254.

66   Quoted in Clinton Heylin, op. cit., p.253.

67   Quoted in Johnny Black/Sean Egan (ed.), op. cit., p.117.

68   Quoted in Clinton Heylin, op. cit., p.257.

69   Robert Shelton, op. cit., p.259.

70   Quoted in Clinton Heylin, op. cit., p.267.

71   Anthony Scaduto, op. cit., p.247.

72   Quoted in Andrew Loog Oldham, "2Stoned" (Vintage, 2003), p.258.

73   Jagger/Richards, © 1966 by ABKCO Music Inc.

74   Frank Allen, op. cit., p.200.

75   Frank Allen, op. cit., p.198.

76   Frank Allen, op. cit., p.211.

77   Bill Wyman with Richard Havers, op. cit., p.232.

78   Jagger/Richards, © 1966 by ABKCO Music Inc.

79   Jagger/Richards, © 1966 by ABKCO Music Inc.

80   Ibid.

81   Jagger/Richards, © 1966 by ABKCO Music Inc.

82   Andrew Loog Oldham, op. cit., p.89.

83   Ibid.

84   Andrew Loog Oldham, op. cit., p.90.

85   Jagger/Richards, © 1966 by ABKCO Music Inc.

86   Ibid.

87   Bill Wyman with Richard Havers, op. cit., p.234.

88   This also happened to be the first day of a UK tour, on which Ike and Tina Turner were booked as the main support act, with an opening concert at the Royal Albert Hall.

89   Quoted by Patrick Doncaster in *Daily Mirror*, 15th September 1966, and reproduced in Bill Wyman with Richard Havers, op. cit., p.242.

90   Ibid.

91   This LP had originally been released in the US by London as long ago as 2nd April, so different content for the UK version (including "Have You Seen …?" and "Paint It,

Black") was in part simply a reflection of that passage of time.

92   Quoted in Keith Badman, op. cit., p.115.

93   The performing credit on this was to Brian Wilson alone, not to the Beach Boys.

94   David Leaf, CD liner notes to *Pet Sounds* (Capitol, remastered 1990), p.20.

95   Described by Brian as "the most satisfying piece of music I've ever made" and possibly to be seen as his own personal homage to Burt Bacharach, Keith Badman notes that for the session on 19th January it was all too evident that he had "consigned straightforward, regimented recordings to the past: today he employs 12 violins, four saxophones, piano, oboe, flute, cello, viola, vibes – and a guitar with a Coca-Cola bottle sliding across the strings." [Op. cit., p.111.]

96   A touch surely complimentarily referenced by the Beatles in the lead-in to and fade-out from "Good Morning, Good Morning" on *Sgt. Pepper's Lonely Hearts Club Band*.

97   Quoted in Keith Badman, op. cit., p.134.

98   Ralph J. Gleason, writing in the *San Francisco Chronicle*; quoted in Keith Badman, op. cit., p.139.

99   Op. cit., p.147.

100 Wilson/Love, © 1966 by Irving Music Inc./BMI.

101 Ibid.

102 See, for example, Keith Badman, op. cit., pp.147-148, for a detailed analysis of just how Brian constructed the complex master track.

103 Quoted in Keith Badman, op. cit., p.147.

104 Quoted in Keith Badman, op. cit., p.153.

105 Ibid.

106 Peter Ames Carlin, writing some time after Keith Badman, suggests instead that Brian contributed to an encore of "Barbara Ann". [See Peter Ames Carlin, op. cit., pp.107-108.]

107 Peter Ames Carlin, op. cit., p.110.

108 Wendy Varnals, quoted in Keith Badman, op. cit., p.155.

109 Quoted in Keith Badman, op. cit., pp.159-160.

110 Wilson/Parks, © 2011 by Capitol Records, LLC.

111 Peter Ames Carlin, op. cit., p.117.

112 Ibid.

113 Quoted in Keith Badman, op. cit., p.139.

114 Quoted in Keith Badman, op. cit., p.156.

115 Townshend, © 1966 by Fabulous Music Ltd.

116 Ibid.

117 Andy Neill & Matt Kent, op. cit., p.124.

118   Andy Neill & Matt Kent, op. cit., p.131.

119   Townshend, © 1966 by Fabulous Music Ltd.

120   Ibid.

121   Townshend, © 1966 by Fabulous Music Ltd.

122   Pete Townshend, op. cit., pp.99-100.

123   Townshend, © 1966 by Fabulous Music Ltd. A previously unreleased acoustic version, with Townshend on cello, was issued as a bonus track on the 1995 remastered edition of *A Quick One*.

124   Chris Stamp, CD liner notes to *A Quick One* (Polydor, remastered edition 1995).

125   Pete Townshend, op. cit., p.101.

126   Pete Townshend, op .cit., p.102.

127   Pete Townshend, op. cit., p.103.

128   Andy Neill & Matt Kent, op. cit., p.143.

129   Ray Davies, © 1966 by Carlin Music Corp.

130   Ray Davies, op. cit., p.279.

131   Ray Davies, op. cit., p.274.

132   Ray Davies, op. cit., p.283.

133   Ray Davies, op. cit., p.285.

134   Dave Davies, op. cit., p.93.

135   Ray Davies, © 1966 by Carlin Music Corp.

136   Daniel Rachel, CD liner notes to *Face To Face* (Sanctuary, remastered deluxe edition, 2011), p.13.

137   Ray Davies, © 1966 by Carlin Music Corp.

138   Ray Davies, quoted by Daniel Rachel, CD liner notes to *Face To Face* (Sanctuary, remastered deluxe edition, 2011), p.14.

139   Quoted by Keith Altham in his interview with Ray for *NME*, 8th July 1966, and reproduced in "The Ultimate Music Guide: The Kinks" (*Uncut*, Winter 2012), p.29.

140   Dave Davies, op. cit., p.100.

141   Ray Davies, op. cit., pp.311-312.

142   George Orwell, "The Road to Wigan Pier" (Penguin, 1963 reprint), pp.16-17.

143   Ray Davies, © 1966 by Carlin Music Corp.

144   Dave Davies, op. cit., p.100.

145   Ray Davies, © 1966 by Carlin Music Corp.

146   Ibid.

147   The other guests of honour on this occasion being: "his wife Mary, his son Giles, Bessie Braddock, Ken Dodd and the Lord Mayor of Liverpool." Spencer Leigh, "The

Cavern: The Most Famous Club in the World" (SAF, 2008), p.158.

148   Composed by Toni Wine & Carol Bayer Sager, not to be confused with David Bowie's No.1 hit of 1980.

149   Sean Egan, "Animal Tracks – The Story of the Animals: Newcastle's Rising Sons" (Askill Publishing, revised edition, 2012), p.100.

150   Quoted in Sean Egan, op. cit., p.102.

151   Quoted in Sean Egan, op. cit., p.108.

152   Quoted in Sean Egan, op. cit., p.119.

153   Eric Burdon, quoted in Sean Egan, op. cit., p.140.

154   Quoted in Sean Egan, op. cit., p.139.

155   Chas Chandler, quoted in John McDermott with Eddie Kramer & Billy Cox, "Ultimate Hendrix" (Backbeat, 2009), p.20.

156   Quoted in interview with Keith Altham for *NME*, 14th January 1967.

157   The other three tracks being: "Still I'm Sad", "My Generation" (arranged by Mike Hugg) and "(I Can't Get No) Satisfaction" (arranged by Jack Bruce).

158   Sleevenotes to *Instrumental Asylum* EP (HMV, 1966).

159   The title track, composed by Mort Shuman, satirises a future dominated by automation and computers. The only original composition included on *Machines* was "She Needs Company", written by Paul Jones, which had previously – albeit briefly – been considered as the next single. I have taken the EP's release date of 7th April from what I regard as the definitive EMI discography included in the liner notes to the CD compilation *Manfred Mann: Down The Road Apiece – Their EMI Recordings 1963-1966* [EMI, 2007], although other listings published elsewhere differ.

160   Quoted in Greg Russo, op. cit., p.37.

161   The four contemporary hits reworked on this very cold offering indeed were: "Sunny", "Wild Thing", "Get Away" and "With A Girl Like You".

162   Sleevenotes to *Aswas* EP (HMV, 1966). As with *Machines* before it, the only original group composition in this set, "It's Getting Late", had also been considered then rejected as a possible single earlier in the year.

163   Review from *Disc* magazine, quoted in Christopher Hjort, "Strange Brew: Eric Clapton and the British Blues Boom 1965-1970" (Jawbone, 2007), p.58.

164   Quoted in Christopher Hjort, op. cit., p.48.

165   Quoted in Christopher Hjort, op .cit., p.57.

166   Eric Clapton with Christopher Simon Sykes, op. cit., p.80.

167   Eric Clapton with Christopher Simon Sykes, op. cit., p.84.

168   John Platt, "*Disraeli Gears: Cream*" (Schirmer, 1998), p.26.

169   Quoted in John Platt, op. cit., p.30.

170   Quoted in John Platt, op. cit., p.36.

171   Ibid.

172 Quoted by John Reed, CD liner notes to *The Spencer Davis Group: Eight Gigs A Week – The Steve Winwood Years* (Chronicles/Island, 1996).

173 Ibid.

174 Jeff Beck, quoted in Alan Clayson, "The Yardbirds" (Backbeat, 2002), p.92.

175 Dreja/McCarty/Beck/Relf/Samwell-Smith, © 1966 by Yardbirds Music Ltd.

176 Alan Clayson, op. cit., p.99.

177 Ibid.

178 Chris Dreja, quoted in Alan Clayson, op. cit., p.108.

179 Keith Relf also released two unsuccessful solo singles in 1966: "Mr. Zero" in May and "Shapes In My Mind" in November.

180 Graham Gouldman, © 1966 by Hournew Music Ltd.

181 Clarke/Hicks/Nash, © 1966 by Gralto Music Ltd.

182 Quoted in Paolo Hewitt, "The Small Faces: The Young Mods' Forgotten Story" (Acid Jazz, revised edition, 2010), p.70.

183 Quoted in Paolo Hewitt, op. cit., p.74.

184 Paolo Hewitt & John Hellier, "Steve Marriott: All Too Beautiful …" (Helter Skelter, 2004), p.110.

185 Paolo Hewitt & John Hellier, op. cit., p.116.

186 Quoted in Paolo Hewitt & John Hellier, op. cit., p.120.

187 Quoted in Paolo Hewitt, "The Small Faces: The Young Mods' Forgotten Story" (Acid Jazz, revised edition, 2010), p.93.

188 Paolo Hewitt & John Hellier, "Steve Marriott: All Too Beautiful …" (Helter Skelter, 2004), pp.130-131.

189 Steve Marriott, quoted in Paolo Hewitt & John Hellier, op. cit., p.133.

190 Alan Clayson notes that as a police cadet Harman was charged with the safe keeping of Eddie Cochran's personal effects after his fatal West Country car crash in 1960. [See Alan Clayson, "Call Up The Groups!" (Blandford Press, 1985), p.100.]

191 As were five tracks on their first LP *From Nowhere The Troggs*, released on Fontana in July, which also contained their takes on reliable US standards like "Ride Your Pony", "Louie Louie" and "Jaguar And Thunderbird".

192 R. Presley, © 1966 by Dick James Music Ltd.

193 Christopher Hjort cites a useful summary of CBS's UK marketing strategy of the period from the company's PR officer Sue Horwood, in an interview given to *Record Mirror*: "We release 200 [singles] a year, about four a week. They all get equal promotion. We spend as much as we can afford. On every single we do a press release, and 250 have to be sent out every week. Fifty review copies are sent to national newspapers, trades and provincials. We send about 250 pictures as well." [See Christopher Hjort, "So You Want To Be A Rock'N'Roll Star: The Byrds Day-By-Day 1965-1973" (Jawbone, 2008), p.103.]

194 Johnny Rogan, "Byrds: Requiem For The Timeless Vol.1" (Rogan House, 2012), p.226.

195 Johnny Rogan, op. cit., p.248.

196 Quoted in Johnny Rogan, op. cit., pp.244-245.

197 The original mono mixes, as on the single, are the superior versions; especially of "Eight Miles High", which in the stereo version loses Michael Clarke's faint concluding drum roll.

198 Quoted in Johnny Rogan, op. cit., p.254.

199 Ibid.

200 Quoted in Johnny Rogan, op. cit., pp.279-280.

201 Ibid.

202 Quoted in Johnny Rogan, op. cit., p.288.

203 McGuinn, © 1966 by Essex Music Ltd.

204 Quoted in Christopher Hjort, op. cit., p.102.

205 The title refers to the registration number of the personal aircraft of company chief John Lear, a friend of McGuinn and Crosby. [See Johnny Rogan, op. cit., p.298.]

206 David Crosby, quoted in Johnny Rogan, op. cit., p.298.

207 Ibid.

208 As well as "5D (Fifth Dimension)" and "Captain Soul", CBS also issued "Mr. Spaceman" (b/w "What's Happening?!?!") as a taster single from the LP. Released here a fortnight before *Fifth Dimension* came out, it made no impression on the charts, although in America it did scrape into the Top 40.

209 Quoted in Johnny Rogan, op. cit., p.296.

210 Peter Stampfel & Antonia John, reproduced in CD liner notes to *The Lovin' Spoonful: Do You Believe In Magic* (Buddha/BMG Heritage, 2002).

211 Hence the origin of their outstanding instrumental, "Night Owl Blues", a bewitching delight in its full-length version as a bonus track on the CD reissue of *The Lovin' Spoonful: Daydream* (Buddha/BMG Heritage, 2002).

212 Dennis Diken, CD liner notes to *The Lovin' Spoonful: Do You Believe In Magic* (Buddha/BMG Heritage, 2002).

213 J. Sebastian/M. Sebastian/S. Boone, © 1966 by Faithful Virtue Music (renewed 2003 by BMG Music).

214 Dennis Diken, CD liner notes to *The Lovin' Spoonful: Hums Of The Lovin' Spoonful* (Buddha/BMG Heritage, 2003).

215 Eddi Fiegel, "Dream a Little Dream of Me: The Life of 'Mama' Cass Elliot" (Pan, 2006), p.163.

216 Quoted in Eddi Fiegel, op. cit., p.169.

217 J. Phillips/M. Phillips, © 1966 by MCA Music Ltd.

218 J. Phillips/D. Doherty, © 1966 by MCA Music Ltd.

219 Quoted in Matthew Greenwald, op. cit., p.133.

220   Reproduced in Matthew Greenwald, op. cit., p.135.

221   Quoted in Matthew Greenwald, op. cit., p.141.

222   Quoted in Matthew Greenwald, op. cit., p.175.

223   Robert Shelton, quoted in Marc Eliot, "Paul Simon: A Life" (John Wiley, 2010), pp.46-47.

224   Quoted in Marc Eliot, op. cit., pp.47-48.

225   Marc Eliot, op. cit., p.66.

226   Simon, © 1965, 1993 by Paul Simon Music.

227   Simon, © 1966, 1994 by Paul Simon Music.

228   Simon, © 1965, 1993 by Paul Simon Music.

229   Robert Shelton, article for *New York Times* of 28th August 1966, reproduced as LP sleevenotes to *Parsley, Sage, Rosemary And Thyme* (CBS, 1966).

230   Simon, © 1966 by Paul Simon Music.

231   Donovan Leitch, op. cit., p.188.

232   Donovan Leitch, op. cit. p.180.

233   Donovan Leitch, op. cit., p.139.

234   Donovan Leitch, © 1966 by Southern Music.

235   Donovan Leitch, © 1966 by Southern Music.

236   Cilla Black, op. cit., p.138.

237   The phrase also stuck with Michael Caine and Cilla Black, who both used it as the title of their respective autobiographies.

238   Quoted in CD liner notes to *Cilla Black – Completely Cilla: 1963-1973* [EMI, 2012].

239   Quoted in Lucy O'Brien, op. cit., p.96.

240   Quoted in Paul Howes, op. cit., pp.276-277.

241   Quoted in Paul Howes, op. cit., p.277.

242   Quoted in Sharon Davis, op. cit., p.86.

243   Derrik Mercer (ed.). op. cit., p.951.

244   Rick Stroud, "The Book of The Moon" (Doubleday, 2009), pp.194-195.

245   David Whitehouse, "One Small Step: The Inside Story of Space Exploration" (Quercus, 2009), p.77.

246   Neil Armstrong, quoted in James R. Hansen, "First Man: The Life of Neil Armstrong" (Simon & Schuster, 2005), p. 260.

247   Alan Shepard & Deke Slayton, op. cit., pp.187-188.

248   Tom Stafford, quoted in David Whitehouse, op. cit., pp.79-80.

249   Alan Shepard & Deke Slayton, op. cit., p.189.

250 Michael Maclear, op. cit., p.196.

251 South Vietnamese journalist Ton That Thien, quoted in Michael Maclear, op. cit., p.200.

252 Michael Maclear, op. cit., pp.212-213.

253 Michael Maclear, op. cit., p.247.

254 John Laurence, "The Cat From Hue" (Publicaffairs, 2002), pp.336-337.

255 John Laurence, op. cit., p.395.

256 Quoted in Dominic Sandbrook, "White Heat: A History of Britain in the Swinging Sixties" (Abacus, 2007), p.282.

257 Quoted in Dominic Sandbrook, op. cit., p.297.

258 Max Hastings & Simon Jenkins, "The Battle for The Falklands", (Michael Joseph, 1983), p.15.

259 Contemporary press reports suggested that, less heroically, they had in fact surrendered after twenty-four hours to a Catholic priest in Port Stanley.

260 Quoted in Dominic Sandbrook, op. cit., p.259.

261 Quoted in Dominic Sandbrook, op. cit., p.258.

262 Quoted in Dominic Sandbrook, op. cit., p.259.

263 See Shawn Levy, "*Ready Steady Go!* Swinging London and the Invention of Cool" (Fourth Estate, 2002), p.240.

264 Joe Orton's note to first edition of *Loot* (Methuen, 1967).

Chapter 9

1967

If you've managed to keep up with me thus far on the journey, then it should not have escaped your attention that even up to this point a hell of a lot had already happened in the Sixties. I say this quite deliberately here and now, because the revisionist pop documentary-makers and cultural historians habitually represent 1967 as the *sine qua non*, the epicentre of the decade, blinded to a wider view of time passing by the year's encapsulation of 'The Summer of Love'. 1967 may be many things but it was categorically not the musical zenith of the decade, against which everything else paled into insignificance: nevertheless, it was, I grant you, a year in which serious pop music unquestionably and irrevocably entered a new phase, as the emergence of the concept album now threatened to fatally erode the previous supremacy of the hit single.

Before I move on, however, let me suggest that the critical years of change were already in the past and that the fulcrum of the Sixties probably lies somewhere along the continuum between 1964 and 1965, at a delicate point of balance between 1963, the golden year of Merseybeat, and 1966, the year America bit back – by when it was a shock to the system to discover that when the Byrds sang about a "Rain-grey town/Known for its sound" in "Eight Miles High"[1], they were referring not to Liverpool but to London instead.

On closer examination, 'The Summer of Love' proves to be something of a misnomer – in Britain, at any rate, where it was loosely applied to a conceptual approach characterising the mid-summer output at the higher end of pop music that reached its high-water mark in August when Scott McKenzie made it to No.1. In America, on the other hand, the phrase was more particularly associated with the growth of counter-cultural unrest on the West Coast and thus covered both a new alignment of unapologetically overt recreational drug use with non-violent protest as well as a series of specific events – or 'happenings' – culminating in the Monterey Pop Festival that June.[2] And, as I pointed out in the last chapter, not all the music retrospectively lumped into the period (mostly through latter-day repackaging of mid-Sixties' songs in CD compilations) had its origins in 1967 anyway, "Good Vibrations" being a classic case in point. Suffice it to say that for those in the industry most uncritically engaged by it, like publicist Derek Taylor, 1967 would hold fond memories years later for having been "simply fabulous, bathed in ever-loving sunshine, cooled by light breezes, full of colour and delight ... a year to treasure beyond measure".[3]

But musically speaking, 1967 was just as much a year of fragmentation as it may superficially have appeared to be one of unity of purpose. The clearest illustration of this from my own memory comes from that autumn, when I was in my first term of teacher-training in Birmingham and the two records most often played in the students' common room every lunchtime were LPs: at one extreme, the Beatles' *Sgt. Pepper's Lonely Hearts Club Band* and, at the other, *The 5000 Spirits Or The Layers Of The Onion* by the Incredible String Band (cited by Paul McCartney as his "most treasured album" of the year[4] and viewed by those who brought it to market as "the *Sgt. Pepper* of the folk world"[5]). Both had – and still have – prized places in my record collection and others, such as folk musicologist Rob Young, were equally struck by the contrast in their styles and presentation:

> In the summer of 1967 millions may have been halted in their
> tracks by the sonic fictions of *Sgt. Pepper's Lonely Hearts Club Band*,
> but the Incredible String Band's *5000 Spirits Or The Layers Of
> The Onion* ... was an infinitely more intimate and disorienting
> happening, a perky potlatch of ideas and space shanties that
> teased and eluded interpretation as deftly as the White Rabbit of
> Wonderland.[6]

Of course, for those of us already loyally fixated on the Beatles come what may, the road to *Sgt. Pepper* was infinitely easier and more straightforward to follow than the crooked byways that ultimately led to *The 5000 Spirits*. After what seemed like an interminable interval of more than six months following the release of "Yellow Submarine"/"Eleanor Rigby" the preceding August, by 17th February it was long overdue for a new Beatles' single to come out – the double-A-sided "Strawberry Fields Forever"/"Penny Lane". (These two songs had been hived off by George Martin from the group's ongoing recording sessions, in order to maintain, at Brian Epstein's insistence, some temporary form of commercial presence during the long wait for the next album.) Aside from its musical content, it broke new ground for a UK single by being issued in a picture sleeve, a marketing ploy for 7-inch records hitherto exclusively reserved for EPs: on the front, a still from the promotional film shot at the end of January in the grounds of Knole Park, near Sevenoaks in Kent, a portrait in muted colours of the now hirsute quartet mounted within a classical gilded picture frame, and on the back a mocked-up page from a family photograph album, linking pictures of each group member from their childhood to the two nostalgic song titles.

Given the Beatles' extraordinary legacy even to this point in their musical development, "Strawberry Fields Forever" was neither immediately accessible nor conventionally melodic, its stream-of-consciousness lyric and other-worldly production perhaps most closely related to "Tomorrow Never Knows" (although Ian MacDonald saw it rather as a sibling of "She Said She Said"[7]). Just what was John on about?

> Always, no sometimes, think it's me,
> But you know I know when it's a dream.
> I think I know I mean a 'Yes'.
> But it's all wrong.
> That is I think I disagree.
> Let me take you down,
> 'Cos I'm going to Strawberry Fields.
> Nothing is real
> And nothing to get hung about.[8]

In reality, the extensive grounds of Strawberry Field (singular), an orphanage run by the Salvation Army, were to the rear of 251, Menlove Avenue, Liverpool 25, where John had lived with and been brought up by his Aunt Mimi, offering the imaginative boy Lennon an additional, secret space to play in and explore. The lyric was, therefore, informed in part by John's nostalgic reiteration of simpler, carefree days, pulled together in solitary moments while he was on location out in Spain, and its personal significance to him is more than amply demonstrated by the demands he heaped upon George Martin's shoulders as producer to deliver what he was prepared to accept as a final take. Instrumentally, it became more and more complex, with the accretion of mellotron, cellos and the exotic harp-like sound of an Indian swordmandel; but even after having devoted an exorbitant fifty-five hours of studio time to completing the track, John still remained dissatisfied with the outcome.

"Penny Lane" was a similarly backward-looking reconstruction by Paul of the townscape in and around Liverpool 15 where he had grown up and hung out with John in his youth:

> When I came to write it, John came over and helped me with
> the third verse, as was often the case. We were writing childhood
> memories: recently faded memories from eight or ten years before,
> so it was a recent nostalgia, pleasant memories for both of us. All
> the places were still there, and because we remembered it so clearly
> we could have gone on.[9]

Gentler on the ear, as the majority of Paul's compositions tended to be, he lent a distinctive orchestral grandeur to the piece with the addition of woodwind and brass instruments, the most striking being the piccolo trumpet played by classical musician David Mason. "Observed with the slyness of a gang of kids straggling home from school"[10], the barber, the banker, the fireman and the pretty nurse are magically restored to life complete with all their random, adult preoccupations ("very strange") and, lo and behold:

> Penny Lane is in my ears and in my eyes,
> There beneath the blue suburban skies …[11]

For all the effort that went into creating both sides, the record – for a Beatles' record, anyway – was no more than a qualified success, in the eyes of the soothsayers and prophets of doom of music journalism. The first of their singles on Parlophone since "Love Me Do" not to make No.1, it entered the charts in the week ending 25th February at No.3, took two weeks to get up to No.2 but in another two weeks was on the slide, down to No.5.[12] (In total, it enjoyed a chart run of nine weeks.) Much was made at the time of the fact that their route to No.1 had been blocked by new balladeer Engelbert Humperdinck's "Release Me"; the longer, more sympathetic view being that it was no more than further proof, if proof be needed, of the retrograde trends now being exhibited by the Top 30 as a whole, following in the wake of Tom Jones's No.1 of Christmas and the New Year with "Green Green Grass Of Home".

While their latest single made its imperfect way up and down the charts, the Beatles continued with the serious business of recording their new album, sticking loosely to Paul's original concept of the group adopting alternative identities, an idea that had come to him on the return flight from Kenya with Mal Evans the previous November: "I thought we can run this philosophy through the whole album: with this alter-ego band, it won't be us making all that sound, it won't be the Beatles, it'll be this other band, so we'll be able to lose our identities in this."[13] The lukewarm reactions of the other three during and after the marathon recording process involved in bringing it to fruition suggest, in their various ways, that they struggled to share Paul's enthusiasm for his vision (especially ironic in George's case, since he so clearly revisited it for his own purposes in the late Eighties when he prevailed upon Bob Dylan, Jeff Lynne, Roy Orbison and Tom Petty to record with him as the Traveling Wilburys). Furthermore, only three out of the album's thirteen songs explicitly relate to it: namely, the title track, Ringo performing "With A Little Help From My Friends" in character as the "one and only Billy Shears"[14], and the reprise of the title track towards the end of Side 2. As Ringo himself bluntly put it:

> It had started out with a feeling that it was going to be something

totally different, but we only got as far as Sgt. Pepper and Billy
Shears ... and then we thought: 'Sod it! It's just two tracks.' It still
kept the title and the feel that it's all connected, although in the end
we didn't actually connect all the songs up.[15]

The amalgamation of the disparate elements that went to make up *Sgt.
Pepper's Lonely Hearts Club Band* into a more or less cogent fiction was ultimately down to George Martin, who as producer determined the tracks'
final running order, "just about [managing] to convince us that we have
been listening to a rounded and coherent performance, when we have in
fact been listening to a series of little side-shows, each with its own distinct
personality".[16] Even so, this degree of assuredness is itself undermined by
the pictorial inconsistency of the LP sleeve, on which the only Beatle 'character' shown wearing sergeant's stripes is Ringo – posing not, of course, as
bandleader Sgt. Pepper but Billy Shears.

Beginning in late November 1966 and ending in early April 1967, the
making of *Sgt. Pepper* devoured the longest sequence of recording sessions yet
that the Beatles had ever attempted. According to engineer Geoff Emerick,
it took 700 hours, or the equivalent of twenty-nine full days, to complete –
compared to the now seemingly paltry 9 hours 45 minutes taken to record
their first LP, *Please Please Me* – at a massive estimated cost, for its day, of
£25,000. Just the costs incurred in creating the gatefold sleeve in which to
house it, over which the Beatles (largely through Paul) had decided to exercise total editorial control, were in the order of £3,000. Harking back to his
own early record-buying days in Liverpool, Paul was insistent that would-be
purchasers should get value for money, which for him extended even to stip-
ulating the quality of cardboard to be used in the sleeve's manufacture; and
inevitably faced in response with constant quibbles from EMI's administra-
tors and accountants about these subsidiary production costs, he stood his
ground. Although it is debatable how far the sleeve alone actually worked as
a marketing tool to boost sales, there was no denying its originality and the
design of the front cover has long been celebrated as a work of art in its own
right; commissioned from notable pop artist Peter Blake, assembled with
the assistance of his then wife Jann Haworth and photographed by Michael
Cooper in his Chelsea studio.[17]

The Beatles solemnly pose as Lonely Hearts Club bandsmen in their
garish pseudo-military uniforms (Paul and George frivolously flaunting their
MBEs), behind a bass drum bearing the LP's title in antiquated showman's
lettering.[18] They look straight ahead, an ornamental border beneath the level
of their gaze planted with crimson flowers spelling out 'Beatles' and cream
hyacinths in the crude shape of a guitar. Ranged around and behind them
are waxworks of themselves (suited and booted as they once were, on loan
from Madame Tussaud's) and a whole host of talismanic images and objects.

They include in-jokes, such as the portable television, then deemed by John to be most precious to him, or the doll whose home-knitted jumper bears the legend "Welcome The Rolling Stones" across the chest and "Good Guys" down the left sleeve. Aesthete and playwright Oscar Wilde peers over John's right shoulder, while Johnny Weissmuller (cinema's earliest Tarzan) looms up behind Ringo and Paul, and to George's left stand Marlene Dietrich and Diana Dors. Saddest of all, towards the top left-hand corner of this illustrious gathering of idols and heroes, an uncomprehending Stuart Sutcliffe looks on.

Open out the gatefold and you are greeted by the warm colours of a head-and-shoulders photographic study of the Beatles, still in costume but this time looking a little more relaxed, against a sunshine yellow background. Inside one half of the gatefold, a cardboard sheet of Blake/Haworth-designed Sgt. Pepper cut-outs, all printed on a vivid green ground (one compromise Paul was forced to accept on the grounds of cost, instead of his original idea of a packet of badges and stickers). Inside the other, the record itself, housed in a paper liner designed by Dutch psychedelic artists Simon & Marijke (*aka* The Fool) bearing a succession of stylised overlapping wave-like shapes in diminishing shades of maroon.[19] On the back cover, bright vermilion save for yet another, smaller costume portrait of the group rising from the centre of the bottom edge, another innovation: instead of just a plain track listing (that, shorn of sleevenotes, had been in place from *Help!* onwards), the complete lyrics of all the songs – and, in the bottom right-hand corner, the finishing touch of quality assurance with an apposite quotation of "A splendid time is guaranteed for all" from "Being For The Benefit Of Mr. Kite!".[20] Taken altogether, truly no product packaging like it had ever been seen before in the modern history of popular music.

Sgt. Pepper was officially released on Thursday, 1st June, but by pure chance I found myself one of the first people in the country to buy a copy, two days earlier on 30th May. I had spent the preceding extended weekend (then known as the Whitsun Bank Holiday) camping in the Lake District on an annual school mountain-walking trip but travelling for this last time in the company of a fellow sixth-former who had his own car, an Austin A40 Farina. When he chose to divert on the way home to visit relatives on the Lancashire coast at Thornton Cleveleys, he left me to my own devices for an hour or so in Blackpool; and hence I could not believe my luck when, with time on my hands, I happened upon the brand-new LP already on display in the window of a small independent electrical and record shop in a side street and unhesitatingly went straight in and bought it. After which:

> *Pepper* sold 250,000 copies in the first week of going on sale in the UK. Within one month, it had sold more than 500,000 copies. By the end of August it had sold over two-and-a-half million copies in

the United States. In Britain, it stayed at number one in the album charts for twenty-seven weeks, in the US for nineteen weeks ... It just kept on selling and selling.[21]

Considered a *tour de force* from the outset both within the music profession and by Beatles fans, it ultimately became the UK's best-selling LP of the decade, its sheer complexity and ingenuity attracting widespread admiration but precious little imitation. When Jimi Hendrix famously opened his show at the Saville Theatre on 4th June with his own interpretation of the title track, the gesture could not fail to be received by one audience member in particular, Paul McCartney, as anything but "the ultimate compliment".[22] There were rapid releases of covers of "With A Little Help From My Friends" by London duo the Young Idea, the briefest of one-hit wonders in late July with a week at No.29, and less successfully by Joe Brown[23], but nothing else until its revival the following year in the guise of a throat-tearing blues number by Joe Cocker, inspiring love and hate in equal measure, that made it all the way to No.1 that November, months before its reprise in his set at the Woodstock Festival of 1969.

As George Martin had observed, each song was best regarded as a sideshow, a separate entity, and there was nothing conventional about any of them. If you looked for a love song, you looked in vain. The lyrical content had broadened out beyond even that of *Revolver* to explore the human condition from a variety of oblique angles, many of the compositions randomly owing their origins to chance. The source of "Lucy In The Sky With Diamonds" was Julian Lennon's drawing of his best friend, that he brought home from school to show John and Cynthia. "Being For The Benefit Of Mr. Kite!" is what today we would call 'found art', the song adapting the text of a nineteenth-century poster in John's possession for a show in Rochdale by Pablo Fanque's Circus Royal. Newspaper reports not only inspired "She's Leaving Home" but also much of "A Day In The Life". "Good Morning, Good Morning" was John's deeper reflection on a contemporary TV advertisement for Kellogg's Corn Flakes.

If not love, then flirtation was certainly evident in both "Lovely Rita" (looking to make a traffic warden, in Paul's words, "a figure of fun instead of a figure of terror"[24]) and "When I'm Sixty-Four" (projecting a congenial relationship far into the future). "Getting Better" skirts less comfortable territory, acknowledging the slow recovery from past shameful behaviour:

I used to be cruel to my woman,
I beat her and kept her apart from the things that she loved.
Man I was mean but I'm changing my scene
And I'm doing the best that I can.[25]

Conversely, "Fixing A Hole" (attributed by Paul to the beneficial influence of marijuana) is about preserving your well-being by maintaining an independent frame of mind. This leaves George's intense philosophical entreaty "Within You Without You" (described by Ian MacDonald as "the conscience of *Sgt. Pepper's Lonely Hearts Club Band*: the necessary sermon that comes with the community singing"[26]), combining classical Indian and Western instrumentation, that even its composer and performer recognised would need some sort of lift at its conclusion:

> George wanted to dub some laughter on to the end of the song. He didn't want people to feel he was being over-earnest, boring for Britain about the meaning of life, and we found a bit of tape that had the four Beatles cracking up with laughter at the end of some take or other. This spontaneous hilarity was dropped in at the end of the song, and George was happy.[27]

It was all the more extraordinary for being the substitute for George's original satiric contribution to the album, "Only A Northern Song", rejected by George Martin as inferior and imbued with the bitterness of the Beatles' 'invisible man':

> It doesn't really matter what chords I play
> What words I say or what time of day it is
> As it's only a Northern song.
> It doesn't really matter what clothes I wear
> Or how I fare or if my hair is brown
> When it's only a Northern song.[28]

On its completion, *Sgt. Pepper* incorporated two other novelties. With the blending on each side of one track into the next without interruption, it heralded the introduction of the segue into the lexicon of pop. And at the end of Side 2, after the last lingering echoes of the climactic piano crescendo at the finale of "A Day In The Life" had subsided, there was a tantalising snatch of a message in the run-out track before the playing arm on the turntable lifted the stylus off the record – if, that is, you were blessed with a record-player that efficient. (Paul later recalled that after some five hours of random recording, what they finally chose was a repetition of the phrase "Couldn't really be any other".[29] Whatever it was, in truth the majority of people buying and playing the album couldn't hear it, either clearly or in its entirety, thus giving rise to endless, mindless speculation about its content and 'meaning' ever since.)

Interpretation of their intentions was also critical to a decision made at the highest levels of the BBC in advance of the album's release that under no circumstances would it be broadcasting "A Day In The Life", occasioning an apologetic letter of explanation from Frank Gillard, Director of Sound Broadcasting, to EMI's Chairman, Sir Joseph Lockwood:

I never thought the day would come when we would have to put a ban on an EMI record, but sadly, that is what has happened over this track. We have listened to it over and over again with great care, and we cannot avoid coming to the conclusion that the words "I'd love to turn you on", followed by that mounting montage of sound, could have a rather sinister meaning.

The recording may have been made in innocence and good faith, but we must take account of the interpretation that many young people would inevitably put upon it. "Turned on" is a phrase which can be used in many different circumstances, but it is currently much in vogue in the jargon of the drug-addicts. We do not feel that we can take the responsibility of appearing to favour or encourage those unfortunate habits, and that is why we shall not be playing the recording in any of our programmes, Radio or Television.[30]

Having taken a short break in America at the beginning of April to celebrate Jane Asher's twenty-first birthday with her (while she was touring in a Bristol Old Vic production of *Romeo And Juliet*), Paul had returned to England with an outline proposal for the next Beatles' project, a musical film for television based on "a very simple idea ... to get on a bus with a few friends, drive around, improvise a few scenes and film everything that happened ... it would bring the Beatles before their hungry public again and it would also provide the vehicle for some new songs".[31]

These were the barest of bones for the storyboard of *Magical Mystery Tour*, for which, by 25th April, Paul had secured Brian Epstein's support, already composed the title song and prevailed upon the other three Beatles to embark upon a new round of recording. Work continued fitfully on this (and, as it happened, with a variety of other songs unconnected with the project) until 14th June, when attention turned perforce to urgent preparations for a prestigious television broadcast in nine days' time. Despite its present misgivings about the final track of *Sgt. Pepper*, the BBC had, several months earlier, commissioned the Beatles to contribute and perform a unifying theme song for a landmark programme, *Our World*. Using live satellite links, it was conceived as:

> ... the first ever world television programme in which twenty or more countries will join together to create and present a single programme to a potential audience of 500,000,000 viewers. It will be a two hour programme on the theme of man and his world; and one section will show mans' [*sic*] greatest current achievements in the field of art and entertainment ... Within this section we would like to offer from Britain the subject of the Beatles at work. Ideally,

we would like, since the occasion seems big enough to warrant this, to hear them in a recording studio actually making a disc. This would be live Outside Broadcast coverage, and would, I hope, give us the first ever public airing of their next single.[32]

The song written for the occasion was a new composition by John, "All You Need Is Love". Those closest to the Beatles, like Brian Epstein or George Martin, appeared to be totally smitten with it. At the time, Epstein described it as "an inspired song, because they wrote it for a worldwide programme and they really wanted to give the world a message. It could hardly have been a better message. It is a wonderful, beautiful, spine-chilling record".[33] While Martin was to write of it, even years later:

> If *Sgt. Pepper* was the definitive hippy symphony, 'All You Need Is Love' was the hippy anthem par excellence; its message is positive; in fact it is viciously idealistic. It is John Lennon, in full awareness of the power of television and popular music as the means of mass communication, putting over his vision of a universe free of war, hatred, poverty and problems. The song presents the possibility of a perfect world, and insists on the ripeness for change of the very imperfect world he saw around him, on its willingness to change.[34]

In the cold light of history, however, not everyone has been so kind about it. Ian MacDonald, having called it up front "One of the Beatles' less deserving hits", went on to castigate them for performing the song on television "knee-deep in garlanded hangers-on", before delivering his final damning judgement as follows: "Lennon's lyric for ALL YOU NEED IS LOVE shows the rot setting in: a shadow of sense discernible behind a cloud of casual incoherence through which the author's train of thought glides sleepily backwards."[35]

As a viewer on the day (Sunday, 25th June), for my money it temporarily brought life and a sense of frivolity to a programme that, whilst admittedly technically innovative, was otherwise inclined to be self-congratulatory and culturally overbearing. It was a simple song of necessity, in a valiant attempt to overcome international language barriers (as reinforced by the multi-lingual placards the Beatles displayed to camera), and as such it was bound to have a naive singalong quality. The party atmosphere prevailing on the day in Abbey Road's Studio One amongst the pop celebrities and friends who joined in the choruses simply added to the fun and made the occasion more memorable (as indeed it became, by virtue of being the Beatles' last live television performance.) There surely never was such a grandstand for a preview of a new single and all the doubts previously entertained about the highly experimental approach of "Strawberry Fields Forever" were cast aside when, a week after its release, "All You Need Is Love" (b/w "Baby You're A Rich Man") was swept on a summertime wave of euphoria straight into the charts for 15th July at No.1, where it held fast for a month. As far as their all-for-giving fans were concerned, at least, the Beatles were back on top form.

They spent much of July and August dabbling in non-musical diversions, individually and collectively. For a while John lured them into toying with the idea of buying a Greek island as a communal hideaway (at the suggestion of his new acquaintance Alexis Mardas – *aka* 'Magic Alex' – a supposed electronics expert) but the plan faltered once it emerged that the ruling Greek military junta intended to make political capital out of their investment. Then George and Pattie took off for a short holiday in California, renting a house located on Hollywood's Blue Jay Way. When they travelled, on 8th August, over to the Haight-Ashbury district of San Francisco, to see for themselves the supposed heartland of American counter-culture, it proved to be an epiphany for George:

> I went there expecting it to be a brilliant place, with groovy gypsy
> people making works of art and paintings and carvings in little
> workshops. But it was full of horrible spotty drop-out kids on
> drugs, and it turned me right off the whole scene. I could only
> describe it as being like the Bowery, a lot of bums and drop-outs,
> many of them very young kids who'd dropped acid and come from
> all over America to this mecca of LSD.[36]

Startled into the realisation that all was not the romanticised harmony and light, he resolved there and then to turn his back on drug-taking and seek out another road to self-enlightenment:

> That was the turning-point for me – that's when I went right off
> the whole drug cult and stopped taking the dreaded lysergic acid …
> It made me realise: 'This is not it.' And that's when I really went for
> the meditation.[37]

After their return to England, on 24th August they attended a lecture at the London Hilton Hotel by Maharishi Mahesh Yogi, a high-profile, self-publicising proponent of transcendental meditation, to which they were accompanied by John, Paul and Jane Asher. Only too well aware of the drawing power celebrities of this magnitude could lend to his cause, the Maharishi immediately afterwards invited the Beatles and their significant others to join him and his disciples over the imminent Bank Holiday weekend at the University College in Bangor, North Wales, where he was launching a ten-day course of lectures and workshops. If, however, they went there in the hope of seeking respite from the peculiar pressures of their hothouse world, it was to be short-lived.

Travelling to Bangor on Friday the 25th, accompanied by Mick Jagger and Marianne Faithfull, their seclusion was catastrophically disrupted on Sunday the 27th by the breaking news that Brian Epstein had been found dead at his house in Belgravia, obliging them all to decamp and return to London. The shock of the event betrayed itself in the numbed, banal first responses that they unguardedly gave to news-hungry reporters, as Ringo intuitively understood: "Your belief system gets suspended because you so badly don't want to hear it. You don't know what to do with it." [38] Part of the Beatles' acute discomfort lay, of course, in having to confront the fact that Epstein's role as their manager had effectively been marginalised since their decision to abandon touring and live performance; and, as Tony Barrow remarks, at the end of May they had further distanced themselves from him when they had "quietly and without publicity registered a new company called Apple Music Limited … Knowing about this can only have deepened Epstein's despondency, despite the fact that they made the token gesture of naming him as a director."[39]

Compared to the present day, his funeral took place in indecent haste: he was buried on 29th August in Liverpool, after a private family service attended by none of the artists he had represented. At the subsequent inquest, the Westminster Coroner pronounced a verdict of accidental death. Although speculation was rife that Epstein may have committed suicide, those closest to him all held to the view that he had, in a befuddled state late at night, inadvertently overdosed himself with sleeping pills "on top of his customary tumbler of vodka and other assorted shots of booze".[40]

In business terms, it left a managerial vacuum at NEMS Enterprises that, for the time being, the Beatles were unwilling to see filled by anyone else: "there were all sorts of vultures flapping their wings over the body, but nothing really materialised."[41] Robert Stigwood, who had merged his own company with NEMS earlier that year, promptly made a play for the position but was turned down flat. Irrespective of Epstein's untimely death, the current contract with NEMS to manage the group's affairs came to an end in September and was not renewed. Instead, the Beatles decided to look after their own business interests under their newly-created Apple umbrella, relying initially on advice from Neil Aspinall, who had rashly offered on their behalf to explore and determine the present state of their finances. Aspinall's task, however, would prove to be complex, time-consuming and thankless from the very outset:

> We didn't have a single piece of paper. No contracts. The lawyer, the accountants and Brian, whoever, had that. Maybe the Beatles had been given copies of various contracts, I don't know. I know that when Apple started I didn't have a single piece of paper. I didn't know what the contract was with EMI or with the film people or the publishers or anything at all. So it was a case of building up the filing system, finding out what was going on.[42]

That aside, Paul appeared to be the most confident of the four that they were capable of taking charge of their own destiny, on the strength alone of their growing autonomy in the recording studio. At the beginning of September, therefore, he had proposed they should press on with putting *Magical Mystery Tour* together (the plan immediately before Epstein's death having been that they should travel back with the Maharishi to India, a trip they all now felt obliged to postpone). So recording of the songs resumed on 5th September; and location filming commenced on the 11th, when the Beatles' entourage descended on the West Country, to be concluded at last, after a protracted period of mostly jovial chaos, on 3rd November.

To say the project was poorly planned from the outset would be a generous understatement. Although Paul assumed the *de facto* role of director, this did not denote that he had any greater qualifications to do so than anyone else but was more a reflection of his penchant for the *avant garde*, as well as of his unquenchable optimism and enthusiasm; whereas George in particular admitted he was ambivalent towards the whole enterprise: "It was very flimsy, and we had no idea what we were doing. At least, I didn't. I had no idea what was happening, and maybe I didn't pay enough attention because my problem, basically, was that I was in another world."[43]

There was no shooting script as such: the approach taken was to be entirely improvisational, in the supposed interests of spontaneity. ("There wasn't a script for *Magical Mystery Tour*," said Paul, "you don't need scripts for that kind of film. It was just a mad idea."[44]) This was all very well but left some critical gaps that had to be filled retrospectively. For example, after a fortnight out on the road, it was blithely assumed that editing could begin on 25th September and would probably take no more than a week: it would eventually take eleven. Neil Aspinall gives an indication of the problems that were soon exposed and their solutions:

> When John and Paul were editing the damned thing, they found out that nobody had filmed any linking shots. There wasn't one shot of the bus from the outside. So I said that I'd do it. I got Nick Knowland as cameraman, and Mal [Evans] and I got the bus out again, put all the posters on the side, and drove off into the sunset.
>
> We stopped by a little gypsy camp. I got a couple of children to wave at the bus going past, and because there was nobody on board, I told the bus driver to drive fast. We did those shots with the bus driving up and over the camera, then of it going away. So, now we had a few links. That sort of thing was going on all the time, and I keep thinking, 'When did they do the music?'[45]

Fitting all the music in was, as Neil suspected, another omission that had to be rectified; occasioning Paul to fly off to Nice in France for the 30th and

31st of October, to shoot a film insert for his song "The Fool On The Hill"[46], and the commandeering of Ringo's house and gardens in Weybridge on 3rd November to complete the filming of George's song "Blue Jay Way".

Boiled down finally to a film lasting 53 minutes, Paul then faced the task of negotiating a deal for it to be televised, but with a clear preference for it to be shown by the BBC, so as to gain the widest possible networked audience, he was already at a disadvantage in meeting with Paul Fox, Controller of BBC1, to discuss terms. Fox, whilst accepting of the Beatles' popularity, thought it a "pretty strange film"[47] and beat Paul down to a relatively low offer of £9,000; which he further qualified by insisting on the removal of the love scene on a Cornish beach between two of the older actors, Ivor Cutler ("Buster Bloodvessel") and Jessie Robbins ("Auntie Jessie").[48] Desperate to secure a prime-time viewing slot with the BBC on Boxing Day evening, Paul conceded.

It was duly shown on 26th December from 8.35 to 9.25 p.m., in what Paul had christened "the Bruce Forsyth slot"[49], but bucking this trend was in large part its undoing, as Kevin Howlett explains: "Light entertainment had been expected – not an experimental fantasy. After all, it was preceded by a variety show hosted by Petula Clark and normal service was resumed after *Magical Mystery Tour* with a film called *The Square Peg* starring comedian Norman Wisdom."[50] Apart from the fact that even to Beatles fans there was no discernible storyline, the film also suffered from having been made in colour but being transmitted in black and white, which considerably reduced its visual impact.

Next morning, the majority of television critics of the national newspapers panned it, and for a while it was open season for debunking the Beatles as a formerly respected national institution now badly fallen from grace. The BBC's own audience research report was equally disheartening, stating baldly that "three quarters of the sample could hardly find a good word to say for the programme"[51] and noting that even its musical content had not generally been well received: "altogether, the programme would seem to have been a monumental 'flop', viewers apparently finding it hard to decide who was most to blame – the Beatles for producing such stuff or the BBC for showing it."[52]

The Beatles had also come unstuck with their plans to promote their Christmas single by way of a short film clip shot for the purpose on 10th November at the Saville Theatre. "Hello, Goodbye" had already taken a month to record and mix; and now, under Paul's direction, three different versions of their stage performance of the song were filmed, in colour. Unfortunately, neither Paul nor anyone else had appreciated that by miming to the record they would place themselves in contravention of the ban then imposed by the Musicians' Union on the televising of non-live music.

Consequently, none of the British television companies could show such a film – forcing Johnnie Stewart, producer of the BBC's *Top Of The Pops*, for example, to improvise supporting clips from still photographs and older stock footage.

"Hello, Goodbye" was released on 24th November, entering the charts the following week at No.3 before jumping up to No.1 for the duration of six weeks over Christmas and the New Year. Bizarrely, it was coupled with "I Am The Walrus", which defied interpretation in advance of the release of either the soundtrack or the film of *Magical Mystery Tour* (from which, of course, it had been taken) and was covertly banned from BBC airplay. A BBC internal memo of 27th November distributed over Paul Fox's signature stated:

> The lyrics contain a very offensive passage and … [it has been] agreed not to play it on radio or television.
>
> Although not officially banned, it will not be heard on "Top of the Pops" or "Juke Box Jury".
>
> I should be grateful if you would ensure that any other possible outlets are similarly blocked off.[53]

The "very offensive passage" that had been detected amidst the jumbled surrealism of "I Am The Walrus" were the lines:

> Crabalocker fishwife pornographic
> priestess boy you been a naughty girl,
> you let your knickers down.[54]

In a song packed full of ridicule and loathing by John, at worst it could, even in those more prudish times, be regarded as no more than an immature outburst of rude words and certainly not intended to be thought of as either depraved or corrupting. That said, you still have to bear in mind that in the context of 1967 another phrase from the song – "stupid bloody/ Tuesday man" – would have been considered equally unacceptable then by many adults for its use of the 'b' word, irrespective of the greater exposure to swearing brought latterly to the television screen by Johnny Speight's patriarchal bigot Alf Garnett in *Till Death Us Do Part*.[55]

Precious little more light was shed on the subject by the release of the *Magical Mystery Tour* soundtrack on 8th December. Issued as a double EP in a revolutionary format that housed the two discs in a lavish, fold-out storybook sleeve in full colour (containing cartoon strips, stills from the film and the lyrics of all the songs), by the end of the month it was sitting at No.2, where it underpinned "Hello, Goodbye" at No.1 for two weeks. That the content of the film was essentially impulsive window-dressing for a new set of Beatles' tunes makes it even more inexplicable, therefore, that there should have been an almost total mismatch between the order in which the songs appeared on film and on record. At the heart of both, however, sits the inescapable presence of "I Am The Walrus", its filming on location (against the back-drop of the huge concrete bomb-blast walls at West Malling airfield in Kent) serving to heighten its surreal impact as the Beatles don animal masks for part of their performance and the play-out is graced with images of both eggmen and policemen parading in a row. Credited by Ian MacDonald as being "the most idiosyncratic protest-song ever written"[56], he characterises it as John Lennon's "ultimate anti-institutional rant – a damn-you-England tirade that blasts education, art, culture, law, order, class, religion, and even sense itself".[57] With its sonorous orchestration, aggressive chanting ("GOO GOO GOO JOOB") and fade-out to a sample of off-station radio broadcasts ending with an extract from *King Lear*, it was as far removed as imaginable from the Beatles' dual heritage of rock'n'roll and Merseybeat; as too were George's doleful contribution, "Blue Jay Way" (locked in a miasma of minor keys and shivering cold blue notes), and the mellotron-dominated instrumental "Flying".[58]

Thank goodness, then, that Paul could always be relied upon to deliver songs of greater mass appeal, as he did here firstly with "The Fool On The Hill", and then with the film's grand finale, "Your Mother Should Know". On screen, the latter brings the Magical Mystery Tour to a worthy end with a pseudo-Busby-Berkeley confection of glamorous ballroom dancers, marching Air Cadets and the Beatles themselves descending a glittering staircase, resplendent in white tuxedos before their final transformation, over the closing credits, into the omniscient magicians.[59] In his commentary on the restored print of the film released in 2012, Paul has generously acknowledged his indebtedness to the cinematic techniques of Richard Lester (their director for *A Hard Day's Night* and *Help!*); but with hindsight, *Magical Mystery Tour* failed originally because it predated the kaleidoscopic discontinuity of *Monty Python's Flying Circus* by almost two years. Had it succeeded the first series of *Python*, it may still not have been comprehensible but at least it would have been better received by an audience already primed for non-sequiturs and madly grinning waiters piling spaghetti onto diners' plates with a garden spade. Out of any such context, the conflict it posed for viewers that late December evening is unwittingly summarised in the film itself by the paradox voiced by Ivor Cutler, who, in character as Buster Bloodvessel posing as the Courier seconds before the introduction to "I Am The Walrus", solemnly urges the coach party "to enjoy yourselves, within the limits of British decency".[60] Yet by the tenets of 1967, adhering to the latter actually meant, for the majority, sacrificing the former.

The Beatles' newest struggles to align their artistic pretensions with "the limits of British decency" were, however, as nothing compared to the mire into which the Rolling Stones were dragged for much of the year, courtesy of their tangled personal relationships and incautious fantasy lifestyle, to the extent that making music rapidly became a secondary consideration for them. Like the Beatles, they also suffered the loss of their manager, although in far less distressing circumstances, and were temporarily rudderless as they attempted to bring new order to their muddled business affairs – of which they had hitherto remained largely ignorant.

Musically, the year started ordinarily enough: a new single, a new LP. The A-side of the single, "Let's Spend The Night Together", was not, however, to have an easy ride in view of the suggestiveness of its title; and was subjected to censorious comment from the moment of its UK release on Friday, 13th January. When they flew to New York that weekend to promote it on US television, Ed Sullivan refused to allow them to perform it on his show as recorded, forcing them into the compromise of changing the lyric to "Let's Spend Some Time Together"; and over there it was only the B-side, "Ruby Tuesday", that made it into the *Billboard* Top 40, eventually snatching a week at No.1.

The following Friday saw the UK release of *Between The Buttons*, their latest LP of original material yet disappointingly lacking the drive and imagi-nation of its acclaimed predecessor *Aftermath*. Part of its problem was that its recording had been disjointed, with tracks initially laid down at RCA Holly-wood in August 1966 and then completed at Olympic Studios in London in November and December. Its major failing, however, was the fact that taken as a whole its collection of twelve songs came across as a derivative ragbag, in which the Stones themselves seemed largely to be going through the motions of making an album and taking no particular pride in it. Only the opening track, "Yesterday's Papers", was remotely in the same vein or even near the same quality as the songs on *Aftermath*, and there was admittedly a sinister spark of originality in the continental arrangement of "Back Street Girl", a song dedicated to a married man's guilty pleasure. Otherwise, overtones of other contemporary acts were liberally distributed across both sides (the Who, the Kinks, the Small Faces, Dylan, Bo Diddley) and the final track on Side 2, "Something Happened To Me Yesterday", was packed full of self-in-dulgent in-jokes: it was all too obvious they were having a laugh. Archivist of their recording sessions Martin Elliott got it exactly right when he said that on *Between The Buttons* the Stones "were recording products that they thought the 'Carnaby Street' public would like and not concentrating on extending their artistic repertoire and swaggering performances".[61]

To combine promotion of both single and album, the Stones were booked to appear on *Sunday Night At The London Palladium* on 22nd January[62] but courted further controversy by refusing to take part in the programme's traditional finale, when all the show's performers took to a revolving stage and waved goodbye to the audience as the closing credits rolled. In its trivial way, this incident proved to be the beginning of the end of Andrew Loog Oldham's influence over his protégés, as Mick and Keith held out against even his efforts at diplomacy:

> The show's producer, Albert Locke, told the band they were insulting everything the Palladium and 'centuries of show-business' stood for. Mick told Locke to fuck off. Keith, also blunt, added that it was 'just this sort of shit' they'd been fighting for five years. Andrew Oldham, whose own showbiz blood perhaps ran deeper than anyone supposed, sided with the producer and called the Stones' behaviour 'atrocious'. Jagger and Richards in turn yelled at Oldham, who walked out.[63]

Inevitably the popular press construed it as another outrageous example of the Stones' contempt for the Establishment and grew emboldened to make further mischief for the group at the earliest opportunity. In this hostile atmosphere, it was all too easy to lose sight of the music. Sales of the single were split between both sides: "Ruby Tuesday" peaked at No.20 at the end of January, while "Let's Spend The Night Together" went on up to No.2 in the week ending 11th February. Despite its inherent weaknesses, *Between The Buttons* (the sales of which overlapped with continuing strong sales of the previous November's *Big Hits* compilation) would ultimately reach No.3 in the LP charts. From Sunday, 12th February onwards, however, such mercenary considerations were rendered strictly irrelevant, when the police raided Redlands, Keith's country home near West Wittering in Sussex, armed with a warrant to search the property for drugs.

It was the unwelcome culmination of a weekend party thrown by Keith, whose house guests included Mick and Marianne Faithfull (now a couple since Mick had broken up with Chrissie Shrimpton in December), together with: "art dealer Robert Fraser, Fraser's Moroccan servant Ali [*aka* Mohammed Jajaj], photographer Michael Cooper, antique dealer Christopher Gibbs, David Schneiderman (a Canadian also known as Acid King David) and Nicky Cramer, a hippy from Chelsea".[64] George and Pattie Harrison were also brief visitors early that Sunday evening, leaving just before 8.00 p.m. to return to their own home in Esher. Their departure was timely, for by 8.10 p.m. the police had arrived in strength and, led by a Chief Inspector Dineley, demanded entry. As Christopher Gibbs, one of those now under intense scrutiny, succinctly expressed the total shock of it: "No one was expected that night. Then all of a sudden these people in blue came flooding in. It was a rather dream-like experience."[65]

In the course of the next hour, the police conducted a thorough search, paying as much attention to the demeanour of their suspects as they did to the possible presence and/or concealment of narcotics on the premises. The one partygoer whose reputation would suffer most from this was Marianne Faithfull, who at the time of the police's arrival happened to be naked, save for a large fur rug she had wrapped around herself after taking a bath[66]:

> And then came the farcical scene on the stairs when the lady constable wanted to search me. I dropped the fur rug just for a second. It wasn't one bit lascivious, just a quick flounce done very gracefully, almost like a curtsey, so they could see I had no clothes on and that's all. I thought it was so hysterically funny. This woman wanted to take me upstairs to search me when I had nothing on but the fur rug. It was a great moment. I was on the stairs, surrounded by all my best friends, Christopher, Robert, Mick, Keith, all these people I adored, and twelve cops and a policewoman. I must have thought I'd make a dramatic moment of it. I couldn't help myself. I always have been an incorrigible exhibitionist. Subsequently I learned how to channel my exhibitionist fix by getting up on stage, but in those days I hadn't sort of worked that all out yet. It was the gulf between us on acid and them with their notepads that made it seem so hilarious at the time. It didn't seem quite so funny later. I certainly got paid back in spades.[67]

The police found and removed for forensic analysis a variety of substances (including amphetamines, heroin and cannabis retrieved from searches of Mick, Robert Fraser and David Schneiderman respectively) and on their departure, Keith was formally advised that even if the drugs could not be identified as belonging to specific individuals, he would still be considered responsible for allowing their consumption under his roof. A clear indication of the paucity of journalistic media at the time can be gained from the fact that it was not until the publication of the Sunday papers the following weekend (i.e., 19th February) that the story broke, principally – though not exclusively – in the *News Of The World*.

There then followed an anxious period of waiting, in anticipation of what charges the police might bring and against whom, during which, in Loog Oldham's notable absence, Allen Klein stepped in and took responsibility for organising preliminary legal advice for Mick and Keith. Loog Oldham himself later admitted to having gone "missing in California as soon as I heard the news"[68] and thereafter discovered a previously well-hidden streak of pragmatism: "After a while I returned to England quietly and remained silent over the bust. On the one hand I was terrified I would be busted myself, and on the other I felt that the Stones had asked for it by their behaviour both on and off stage in the past few months."[69]

To avoid the rising clamour, for their part the Stones opted to leave England for a while, embarking with their entourage from 25th February onwards on a chaotic continental excursion ending up in Tangier and, finally,

Marrakech. Its particular significance for the future of the group would lie in the ever-deeper rift it created between Brian and Keith, Keith having seized the opportunity en route to make his move on Brian's girlfriend Anita Pallenberg and destroy their relationship.

Once back home, on 17th March the solicitors acting for Mick and Keith, and separately for Fraser, were notified by the police that formal summonses were to be served on their clients to appear at Chichester Magistrates' Court in May. (Schneiderman had fled the country immediately after the raid on Redlands, apparently going to ground in Spain.) These were highly inauspicious circumstances in which to contemplate resuming concerts but nonetheless the Stones were committed to an imminent European tour, opening in Sweden on 25th March, and the show must go on. Needless to say, the adverse publicity that preceded them meant they were subjected to intense scrutiny by customs officials (action that, strangely, they found unduly oppressive) as they travelled from venue to venue; their complex itinerary taking them from Sweden to West Germany, then on to Austria, Italy, France, Poland, Switzerland and Holland, before concluding in Greece on 17th April.

On this occasion, many of the concerts prompted serious disturbances, inside and outside the auditoria, so that press reports of their performances incorporated an unseemly catalogue of carnage. In Orebro, Sweden, for example, Reuters reported that some 2,000 fans had thrown "bottles, stones, chairs and fireworks at the stage".[70] In Vienna's Stadthalle, smoke bombs were added to the list of projectiles; in Warsaw, outside the Palace of Culture a rioting crowd of thousands of fans denied tickets had to be dispersed with tear gas; while in Zurich, the correspondent for the *Daily Mirror* witnessed "screaming teenagers [ripping] up chairs and iron railings, which they hurled at the baton-waving police".[71] At the end, the majority of the Stones were lucky to leave Athens for home just before the onset of the Greek military coup that dethroned King Constantine and drove him into exile. Bill Wyman, however, having decided to stay on for a private holiday near Athens with his new girlfriend Astrid Lundstrom[72], found himself temporarily stranded by this turn of events and had to wait another week before being able to fly back to London.

On 10th May, Mick, Keith and Fraser appeared before Chichester magistrates at a preliminary hearing to answer the charges levelled against them. Mick was charged with possession of amphetamines, Keith for allowing Redlands to be used for the smoking of cannabis and Fraser for possession of both heroin and amphetamines. (A further charge against Schneiderman, of possessing cannabis, was read out *in absentia*.) All three defendants present pleaded 'not guilty' and were remanded on bail to appear at the West Sussex Quarter Sessions in June (the date for their trial subsequently being set as the 27th).

Extraordinarily, though quite possibly not by coincidence, that same afternoon police, this time led by Detective Sergeant Norman Pilcher[73], raided Brian's London flat in search of drugs, finding him at home with his friend 'Stash' (*aka* Prince Stanislaus Klossowski de Rola). A steady stream of telephone calls both occupants had fielded throughout the day from journalists strongly suggested that the press had been forewarned of what was to come, much to Keith's later disgust:

> The stitch-up was orchestrated and synchronised with rare
> precision. But due to some small glitch of stage management, the
> press actually arrived, television crews included, a few minutes *before*
> the police knocked on Brian's door with their warrant. The police
> had to push through the army of hacks that they had summoned to
> get to the door. But this collusion was barely noticeable in the farce
> that unfolded.[74]

A large number of potentially incriminating exhibits were duly garnered and removed. For now, both Jones and de Rola were charged that evening with possession of cannabis and bailed to appear next morning at West London Magistrates' Court, when they were again remanded on bail to a further hearing on 2nd June and then elected for trial by jury – which was not to be listed until 30th October.

Any incentive for the group to work on new recordings was effectively negated in the first instance by the looming threat of the pending Redlands trial, although some perfunctory efforts towards a possible new album were made from time to time at Olympic Studios in the intervening period. Everything governing the Stones' future viability as a headline act therefore now hung on the unknown outcome of 27th June. Two days before their fate was due to be determined, Mick and Keith, together with Marianne, sought diversion and temporary solidarity in the company of the Beatles and a host of other friends, all joining in the chorus of "All You Need Is Love" as the song was beamed live around the world.

The trial process in its entirety, exhaustively documented in Simon Wells's 2011 book on the subject, consumed three days: the cases against Mick and Robert Fraser being disposed of on the first day, the case against Keith then occupying the next two days, all being heard at the Quarter Sessions by a bench of three Justices of the Peace and a presiding Judge, one Leslie Block. Mick and Keith's defence counsel was the distinguished barrister Michael Havers QC, while Fraser was represented by William Denny QC.

Mick's trial was over in indecent haste by mid-afternoon, without the singer himself giving evidence. The amphetamines the police had found in a pocket of his jacket at Redlands had not actually been procured in connection with Keith's house party but had, through an oversight on Marianne

Faithfull's part, been obtained by her in Italy, where Mick had joined her in January at the San Remo Song Festival, and secreted in his coat for safe keeping on their return journey together to England. In Italy they were not illegal but in England they were, unless prescribed by a doctor. Thus Havers, perhaps over-optimistically, attempted to mount a defence on the premise that Mick's doctor, Raymond Dixon-Firth, would, if asked, have willingly prescribed them; in view, for instance, of their anti-travel sickness properties. Despite Dixon-Firth's testimony to the fact that he had previously been consulted by Mick as to the dosage and safety of such pills, Judge Block was having none of it and in his summing-up directed the jury in accordance with his own view that the doctor's evidence was not worthy of their consideration as a valid defence. The jury retired – for barely five minutes – and on their return delivered a 'guilty' verdict. The judge then directed that sentencing be deferred until after the two cases still outstanding had been heard, during which period Mick should remain in custody.

With Mick's case concluded, next it was Robert Fraser's turn to come before the court. Fraser had latterly decided to plead guilty to the charges against him, so his defence counsel was solely occupied with submitting a plea in mitigation on his behalf, couched in terms of expressing Fraser's shame at his addiction and his sincere intent to seek professional help to overcome it. As with Mick, Judge Block deferred passing sentence, meanwhile also placing Fraser in custody. That left only sufficient time for Keith to enter his 'not guilty' plea and to be bailed before the court adjourned for the day.

On 28th June, the morning papers had already taken delight in publishing photographs of Mick being driven away from the court in handcuffs to be remanded overnight at Lewes Prison. When Keith's trial opened, the prosecution case against him made great play of the state in which the police had found Marianne Faithfull (anonymised as 'Miss X') when they had entered Redlands, attributing her disinhibited behaviour that night to the all-pervading influence of cannabis within the house. In his opening address in Keith's defence, Havers first made so bold as to assert that the raid was nothing more than the result of collusion between the police and the *News Of The World*[5], and that Schneiderman ("a stranger at the party, a stranger conveniently from across the sea, and loaded to the gunwales with cannabis"[76]) had been employed by the paper purely as an *agent provocateur*. He then went on to challenge the circumstantial nature of the evidence regarding 'Miss X' head-on: "She was a girl who remained technically anonymous, but the consequence of this was that she is described as a drug taking nymphomaniac, with no chance of saying a word in her defence or cross-examining anybody … I am not going to allow this girl into the witness box. I am not going to tear that blanket of anonymity aside and let the world laugh or scorn as they will."[77]

At this point the day's proceedings were adjourned, letting the press-hounds well and truly off the leash that evening and next morning with a rash of front-page stories juxtaposing pictures of Marianne with headlines such as "Naked Girl At Stones Party" or "Nude Girl At Party".[78] Her reaction was predictable: "My life had been stolen from me and sold to the gutter press. I became very detached, I was in shock. I can see that in photographs taken of me at the time. I have a perpetually stunned look on my face, as if to say: I can't believe this is happening!"[79]

However, when Keith took the witness stand himself on 29th June to give evidence, he behaved honourably by making what effort he could to portray Marianne in a less sensational light. Under cross-examination, he rebuked prosecuting counsel Malcolm Morris QC for ascribing "petty morals" to him in respect of her behaviour, going on to say of the infamous rug: "I thought the rug was big enough to cover three women. There was nothing improper in the way she was wearing it."[80] Furthermore, he robustly reiterated his belief in the raid on his home being the product of a conspiracy between the *News Of The World* and the police. It was all to be in vain: the jury took just over an hour to find him guilty as charged.

As the end of the afternoon approached, all three accused were brought back into court for sentencing. For allowing cannabis to be smoked in his house, Judge Block first reminded Keith that the current maximum penalty was up to ten years in jail, before sentencing him to twelve months' imprisonment and ordering him to pay £500 towards the prosecution's costs. He then sentenced Robert Fraser to six months' imprisonment for possessing heroin, with an order to pay £200 in costs. Finally, he came to Mick, for whose possession of amphetamine ("a potentially dangerous and harmful drug"[81]) he handed down a three-month sentence of imprisonment and, like Fraser, an order to pay £200 in costs. While Keith and Fraser were taken from the court to Wormwood Scrubs, Mick was transported separately to Brixton Prison.

For Mick and Keith, Havers made swift work the following day on their behalf at the High Court of seeking leave to appeal against their sentences, which, after a hearing lasting less than half an hour, was granted forthwith; each being freed subject to bail of £5000, additional sureties of £1000 and the surrender of their passports. (While Denny similarly secured a right of appeal for Fraser, the court was not minded to agree to his release on bail and he was therefore obliged to remain in prison.)

Keith devotes precious little space in his autobiography to the whole episode but had this to say in retrospect about Judge Block's harshness towards him in particular:

> What a ludicrous sentence. How much do they hate you? I wonder who was whispering in the judge's ear. If he had listened to wise

information, he would have said, I'll just treat this as twenty-five quid and out of here; this case is nothing. In retrospect, the judge actually played into our hands. He managed to turn it into a great PR coup for us, even though I must say I didn't enjoy Wormwood Scrubs, even for twenty-four hours. The judge managed to turn me into some folk hero overnight. I've been playing up to it ever since.[82]

Acknowledging the uncomfortable truth that the Stones had, in Keith's words, become "the focal point of a nervous establishment"[83], reactions to the sentences from their more vocal supporters combined outrage with bravado; for, after all, who knew tomorrow whose name might next be in the frame? Amongst the pop fraternity, the Who, with the full backing of Kit Lambert and Chris Stamp, made a high-profile attempt to channel public sympathy by hurriedly recording covers of "The Last Time" and "Under My Thumb" (on the evening of 28th June, pre-sentencing), which Track Records then rush-released with a provocative advertisement that appeared in the *Evening Standard* on 30th June:

> The Who consider Mick Jagger and Keith Richards have been treated as scapegoats for the drug problem and as a protest against the savage sentences imposed on them at Chichester yesterday, the Who are issuing today the first of a series of Jagger/Richards songs to keep their work before the public until they are again free to record themselves.[84]

The impact of the gesture was, however, diminished virtually instantaneously by their release on bail pending appeal and, perhaps tellingly, the single never sold in sufficient numbers to reach the Top 30.

The trials and their outcomes had also alarmed the liberal intelligentsia and possibly the most gratifying public response of all came in the form of an impassioned libertarian editorial in *The Times*, written by William Rees-Mogg under the title "Who Breaks A Butterfly On A Wheel?" and published on 1st July.[85] Although referring solely to the plight of Mick Jagger, he concentrated his fire on what he saw as a wholly disproportionate miscarriage of justice enacted in Chichester, observing that "Mr. Jagger's is as about as mild a drug case as can ever have been brought before the courts".[86] And he concluded that Mick had suffered unduly as a consequence of his status as a pop star provoking a backlash: "There must remain a suspicion in this case that Mr. Jagger received a more severe sentence than would have been thought proper for any purely anonymous young man."[87]

On 31st July, matters were finally resolved for Mick and Keith at the Court of Appeal, where Lord Chief Justice Parker presided over their hearings.[88] Having recently contracted chickenpox, Keith was deemed to be infectious and hence was not physically present in court: he had to wait in isolation elsewhere in the building while his hearing proceeded in his absence. The appeal was granted in his favour, the judges being concerned that the police had not furnished substantive proof of the smoking of cannabis *per se* at Redlands and that Judge Block had not directed the jury appropriately on the relevance of the evidence of Marianne's reported state of undress to the charge against Keith. Thus regarding his conviction as unsafe, it was quashed.

As for Mick, it appeared initially that he would fare less well. Upholding the point in law that amphetamines were only legal in England if prescribed and confirming Judge Block's view that Dr. Dixon-Firth's conversations with Mick alone could not be deemed to be a prescription, the judges dismissed his appeal. Examining the latter point further, however, in terms of the evidence of consultation between doctor and patient as powerful mitigation, they concurred in determining that his sentence be reduced, to a conditional discharge; but lest he thought he was now being treated more leniently, there was a salutary sting in the tail of Lord Parker's judgement:

> … because you are, whether you like it or not, an idol of a large
> number of the young in this country. Being in that position you
> have very grave responsibilities, and if you do come to be punished
> it is only natural that those responsibilities should carry a high
> penalty.[89]

And in this regard, by warning him not to transgress again, he did appear to be reflecting the mood of the country at large; for when Mick was interviewed that evening on ITV's *World In Action*, as Dominic Sandbrook reminds us, "the programme began with the stunning statistic that in [a] survey more than eight out of ten young people thought that he deserved his prison sentence".[90]

Seven months on from "Let's Spend The Night Together", Decca released the next Stones' single, "We Love You" (b/w "Dandelion") on 18th August, a musical piece of irony intended to draw a line under Mick and Keith's harrowing experiences at the mercy of the law:

> We don't care if you hound we
> And lock the doors around we
> We've locked it in our minds
> 'Cos we love you
> We love you.[91]

Recorded in June (pre-trial) and July (pre-appeal), serious efforts were made in its arrangement to conjure up Wordsworth's "shades of the prison-house" [92], with Bill Wyman enthusiastically sourcing from a sound effects library those all-important extra touches of authenticity: a warder's footsteps along stone corridors and cell doors being slammed shut. Notwithstanding his own very real preoccupations as distinct from those of his colleagues, Brian also came good, with a virtuoso performance on the mellotron. The recording was rounded off by Nicky Hopkins on piano and backing vocals from John Lennon and Paul McCartney (repaying Mick and Keith for their contribution to "All You Need Is Love"). Peter Whitehead was drafted in to direct a complementary promotional film, featuring Mick, Marianne and Keith in a courtroom setting, mockingly re-enacting the trials of Oscar Wilde; a film that, sure enough, the BBC declined to show. Entering the Top 30 at No.13, "We Love You" peaked at No.4 soon thereafter, in early September, and was to go down in history as the last Stones' single officially credited to Andrew Loog Oldham as producer.

The break-up between the Stones and Loog Oldham was soon to follow. Pressing on with his ambition to establish Immediate Records as a forward-thinking independent label, he had steadily relinquished his former hands-on control of the group he had thrust from nowhere into the spotlight of pop notoriety. Events of recent months had further served to highlight the personal differences of outlook widening the gulf between them; and where Loog Oldham now feared to tread, for self-preservation as much as anything, the Stones had found in his stead a ready and willing ally in Allen Klein. In the end, the foundering of their relationship was symbolically demonstrated by the way the Stones threw caution to the wind in their troubled summer of '67 and returned to Olympic Studios hellbent on pursuing their own musical direction. The early sessions, intended to lay down the foundations of their next LP, *Their Satanic Majesties Request*, were deliberately contrived to irk Loog Oldham and drive him away, as witnessed by recording engineer George Chiantz:

> ... the Stones had come to the conclusion that they'd probably
> got most of the ideas they were going to get out of Andrew and
> wanted to go a different way ... The Stones hadn't even begun to
> finish the songs. The vocals hadn't been written; the tracks were
> being done with no idea of what the vocals were even likely to
> be. The tracks were largely composed in the studio and there was
> an enormous amount of time-wasting. The studio staff thought
> Andrew was being pushed out by the Stones who saw Andrew's
> world as something they really didn't want to relate to – too
> cramped for them to expand into ... Andrew was out of the club
> suddenly and they didn't want to work with him.[93]

It was a perception that Mick was to confirm later in an interview for the American music journal *Rolling Stone*, in which he also admitted that drugs too had their part to play:

> The whole thing, we were on acid ... It was really silly but we

enjoyed doing it. Also we did it to piss Andrew off, because he was such a pain in the neck. Because he didn't understand it. We wanted to unload him, we decided to go on this path to alienate him. Without actually doing it legally, we forced him out. I mean, he wanted out anyway. We were so out of our minds.[94]

The strategy worked. After yet "another night of nothing recorded, just a lot of drugfoolery and clever asides", Loog Oldham walked out of Olympic Studios and never went back: "Nobody noticed, nobody said goodbye."[95] A terse statement issued by the Stones' publicist Les Perrin on 27th September formally signalled the end of their four-year-long partnership:

> The Stones have parted from their recording manager because the band have taken over more and more of the production of their own music. Andrew Oldham no longer has any connection whatsoever with the Rolling Stones.[96]

With the Stones now wholly reliant on Allen Klein as their business manager, they turned to Olympic's Glyn Johns to support them as they saw fit through the tortuous process of completing and producing their psychedelic album, proceedings that were inevitably interrupted by Brian's trial.

This was held on 30th October at the Inner London Court of Sessions, where Brian and 'Stash' de Rola were brought before a bench of four magistrates, chaired by one Reginald Seaton. Brian having pleaded 'not guilty' to charges of possessing cocaine and methedrine, these were, perhaps somewhat surprisingly, dropped by the prosecution. He had, however, been advised by his defence counsel, James Comyn QC, to plead 'guilty' to the two remaining charges of possessing cannabis and allowing cannabis to be smoked at his flat; and in these circumstances, the prosecution dropped the related charges against de Rola.

Comyn thus endeavoured to make as effective a plea in mitigation prior to sentencing as possible, citing both Brian's musical talents and his sensitive disposition. He called an expert witness, psychotherapist Dr. Leonard Henry, to testify to the fragile state of Brian's mental health (which, in his professional opinion, should have precluded him from being sent to prison), before calling Brian himself to express remorse and affirm his intention to renounce drugs. All his efforts appeared, however, to fall on deaf ears. After withdrawing to deliberate for an hour and a half, the bench had reached its decision, which was then delivered by Seaton in unequivocal tones:

> I would be failing in my duty if I failed to pass a sentence of imprisonment. These offences to which you have pleaded guilty are very serious … You occupy a position by which you have a large following of youth and therefore it behoves you to set an example. You have broken down on that. I take into account the

fact that you are a person of good character and have admitted your responsibility for these offences.[97]

He sentenced Brian concurrently to nine months' imprisonment for allowing his flat to be used for the smoking of cannabis and three months for possession, and made an order of costs against him of 250 guineas. After Comyn had made an unsuccessful application for bail, he pressed for and was granted the right of leave to appeal, but none of this was of immediate assistance to Brian, who was then removed to Wormwood Scrubs, following in the footsteps of Keith and Robert Fraser. To his great relief, he was released the following day, after a High Court hearing ruled that he could proceed to appeal against his sentence, subject to bail of £250 and two additional sureties in the same amount and, most significantly, subject to the condition that he should submit himself to independent psychiatric examination.

At the subsequent appeal hearing on 12th December – presided over, as for Mick and Keith, by Lord Chief Justice Parker – the court received no less than four different psychiatric reports on the state of Brian's mental health, chief amongst which was that of Dr. Walter Neustatter, who concluded that:

> Mr. Jones is, at present, in an extremely precarious state of emotional adjustment as a result of his unresolved problems with aggressive impulses and sexual identification … He thus urgently needs psychotherapy to assist in mustering his considerable personality resources and capacity for insight to contain his anxiety. Otherwise, his prognosis is very poor. Indeed, it is very likely that his imprisonment could precipitate a complete break with reality, a psychotic breakdown and significantly increase the suicidal risk for this man.[98]

The Appeal Court's decision was that the concurrent sentences of imprisonment should be overturned, to be replaced by a £1,000 fine, a three-year probation order and the further condition that Brian should continue to consult his personal therapist, Dr. Anthony Flood (one of the other psychiatrists giving evidence as an expert witness). For the avoidance of any doubt on Brian's part, Lord Parker concluded his pronouncement of the appeal judges' ruling by roundly admonishing him:

> Remember this is a degree of mercy which the court has shown. It is not a let off. You cannot go boasting about saying you have been let off. You are still under the control of the court. If you fail to cooperate with the probation officer or Dr. Flood, or if you commit another offence of any sort, you will be brought back and punished afresh for this offence. You know the sort of punishment you will get.[99]

Brian's freedom was granted four days after the release of *Their Satanic Majesties Request*, the Stones' controversially shapeless, aimless album that immediately attracted invidious comparisons with *Sgt. Pepper's Lonely Hearts Club Band*. Even its extravagant front cover, bearing a 3-D holographic image of the Stones in outlandish costumes, seated in the midst of a fantasy landscape, was construed as a parody of the Beatles' cover for *Sgt. Pepper*, having as it did Michael Cooper as photographer in common.[100]

On completion, it was, as Andrew Loog Oldham must have spotted in horror a mile off, the very antithesis of commercialism. To say that it had any particular merit as a whole would be tantamount to congratulating the Emperor on the cut of his new clothes. It only served to confirm that artistically the Stones were bankrupt, taking them nowhere except into an hallucinatory cul-de-sac of their own self-conceit. (The LP's very title constituted a two-fingered salute to the Establishment that had so narrowly failed to crush them, a satiric corruption of the wording to be found inside the front cover of every British passport.[101]) Keith was to be brutally honest about it, dismissing it years later as "a bit of flimflam".[102] Ian Stewart, whose services on keyboard were mostly usurped on this occasion by Nicky Hopkins, viewed it charitably as Brian's swansong:

> The only time Brian looked like coming into his own, was when they did that awful *Satanic Majesties*, where he got the chance to dabble with the mellotron. It was a terrible shame. He'd do anything. He would turn up at the studio with saxophones and he even played harp on a number. There was one in the back of the studio for an orchestral session. He sat down and fiddled with it, and got something out of it fairly easily. The talent and ability were there, but he just screwed himself up.[103]

As with *Between The Buttons*, no tracks were reissued in the UK as singles (although the two arguably most melodic songs of the entire set, "In Another Land" – credited only to Bill Wyman, its composer – and "She's A Rainbow"[104], were both released as singles in the US in the course of December); and similarly, it was to reach No.3 in the UK LP charts. Hidden somewhere deep within the chaos was a futuristic theme struggling to get out, signalled by the inclusion of "2000 Man" and "2000 Light Years From Home" (the latter drafted initially by Mick during his spell in Brixton); but these songs bear no relation at all to the spaced-out opening track "Sing This All Together" or its interminable companion piece of incoherent jamming, "Sing This All Together (See What Happens)", that closes Side 1. And at the end of Side 2, there could not be a more complete disjunction, as the far-flung galaxies of "2000 Light Years From Home" are abruptly abandoned in favour of a Soho clip-joint, into which Mick endeavours to entice us with the leering, nod-and-a-wink "On With The Show".

The best that can perhaps be said about the album now is that it brought the most turbulent and potentially catastrophic year in the Stones' career to date to an unremarkable end. If, however, any of the group troubled themselves to take stock of what and how they had survived in the past twelve months, it was virtually impossible to avoid drawing what Keith identified as the "alarming and evident" lesson to emerge from it all; namely, that "the Rolling Stones had run out of gas".[105]

The Stones were not, of course, alone in having lost their way in 1967. Others, for different though sometimes no less spectacular reasons, were slipping, or had slipped from view. Bob Dylan was without a doubt the most prominent absentee of the year, spending his time at home in Woodstock in enforced recuperation from the combined effects of exhaustion and his motorcycle accident to which he had succumbed in 1966. Fading memories of what had been up to that point a startling career were briefly evoked by the premiere in San Francisco on 17th May of D.A. Pennebaker's film *Dont Look Back*, a contradictory title if ever there was one, since self-evidently it could do no more than offer a backward glance to Dylan's world as it had been two years ago to the day, one now so far distant from the life that its central figure was currently in the painstaking process of rebuilding to start afresh. With contract renewal negotiations still to be concluded and no new recordings available, CBS played for time by issuing a compilation album, *Bob Dylan's Greatest Hits* (or, more accurately, a sampler of twelve best-known tracks from his back catalogue, of which two-thirds were taken from *Bringing It All Back Home* and *Blonde On Blonde*); which broke into the UK LP charts in January, proving from then onwards to be a steady seller and an immensely popular entry route into his music for many. When I enthusiastically bought it with a record token my father had passed on to me as surplus to his requirements, he was less than impressed. "If I'd have known you were going to buy that with it," he said to me, long-sufferingly, "I'd have kept it myself."

What was being perpetuated through 1967, therefore, was the image of the old, tempestuous Dylan; whereas what lay in store – but as yet publicly unrevealed – was his reincarnation as a more mellow, contemplative artist, now minus the choking anger of a singing voice that Jimi Hendrix jokingly claimed his worst critics had likened in the past to that of "a broken-leg dog".[106] During the spring and summer, possibly beginning as early as February, Dylan stepped out on the road to recovery by immersing himself in domestic music-making with the Band, either in his own home or in the basement of the house the Band had rented nearby, the house known locally as 'Big Pink'. What started as sessions in which they collectively explored and enjoyed playing together a wide range of traditional American folk music gradually expanded to encompass a dazzling variety of new compositions:

some little more than humorous jottings, others showing far greater depth and potential. (A much-edited and historically suspect cross-section of these works would not officially be made available to curious fans until the anachronistic release in 1975 of the double album *The Basement Tapes*.) Most, though by no means all, were privately recorded as they went along and a demo tape of ten of the strongest ones was eventually submitted to Dwarf Music (the publishing company Dylan had set up jointly with Albert Grossman), for the interest and consideration of other recording artists. As Dylan himself recalled, they were noteworthy for running entirely counter to the prevalent trends of the day:

> They were written vaguely for other people … I don't remember anybody specifically those songs were ever written for. They must have been written at that time for the publishing company … We must have recorded fifty songs at that place. At that time psychedelic rock was overtaking the universe and we were singing these homespun ballads.[107]

Yet several were seized upon eagerly and brought to a wider public in a variety of styles. In America, four years after they had been in the vanguard of popularising some of his earliest songs, Peter, Paul and Mary now recorded "Too Much Of Nothing" and made it into the *Billboard* Top 40 by Christmas (where it peaked at No.35). Moving on into 1968, as we shall see in the next chapter, the Byrds would gladly embrace "You Ain't Going Nowhere" and "Nothing Was Delivered" as new album tracks[108]; while in Britain, Manfred Mann would opt for "The Mighty Quinn" and Julie Driscoll with the Brian Auger Trinity would produce an extraordinarily cool, definitive interpretation of "This Wheel's On Fire". Much later still, Dylan's own versions of "The Mighty Quinn", "I Shall Be Released", "You Ain't Going Nowhere" and "Down In The Flood" (the latter three ostensibly re-recorded) would be included amongst the 'new' tracks on the 1971 compilation double-album *More Bob Dylan Greatest Hits*.

Whilst the *Basement Tapes* sessions with the Band had served their therapeutic purpose of easing Dylan back into composing and recording in a suitably relaxed, unstructured way, they proved to be largely unrelated to the project he undertook next. The renewal of his contract with CBS having finally been agreed with effect from 1st July, come the autumn Dylan was reunited with producer Bob Johnston in Nashville, to spend six weeks through October and November writing and recording a set of songs entirely different in their feel and scope for a new album, *John Wesley Harding*. Putting the splenitive urban passion of *Blonde On Blonde* far behind him, Dylan would now take on the persona of "a man who has arisen from Armageddon unscathed but sobered, to walk across an allegorical American landscape of small, poor communities working a dusty, fierce terrain".[109] Instead of the Band, here he opted to strip his supporting musicians down to a bare minimum – Charles McCoy (on bass) and Kenny Buttrey (on drums), plus Pete Drake on steel guitar for just two of the twelve tracks – with Dylan making his own contributions on guitar, harmonica and piano; abandoning his "floundering search for some intangible juiced-up mystic rock'n'roll moment" in favour of a "taut asceticism".[110] As an LP released in 1968, however, further evaluation of its contents and their impact is properly reserved to Ch.10.

If, in the making of *John Wesley Harding*, Dylan was indicating as clearly as he could that he would soon be capable of re-entering the public arena as a changed man, events of 1967 conspired to push Brian Wilson totally in the opposite direction. Intent on piling artifice upon artifice to perfect *Smile* and "Heroes And Villains" to his unattainably high standards, Brian only succeeded in driving a deeper wedge between himself on the one hand and, on the other, not just the rest of the Beach Boys but his composing collaborator Van Dyke Parks too. It was a fatal error on his part to assume that the wider world appreciated his musical genius and thus would wait patiently for its next manifestation. In March, Derek Taylor, in his guise as a regular columnist from America for the British music press, tried his best to mount a desperate rearguard action in defence of the still conspicuously absent "Heroes And Villains":

> Brian Wilson does not believe there is a delay. And, in fact, there isn't. The Beach Boys were set no deadline, delivered no ultimatum nor offered any threats. The group's power is such that they make their records in their own good time and release them when they're good and ready. Wilson's only concern is that when the music is ready, it is also good. And the very power which enables them to take time is based on a greatness of their past product.[111]

Whereas there was nothing fundamentally wrong with this rationalisation of events – the same argument might, after all, have equally been employed in defence of the Beatles or the Rolling Stones – it seemed that the Beach Boys as a brand no longer commanded sufficient credibility to warrant Taylor's apologia for them resting on their laurels.

Troubles in the studio came to a head on 14th April, when Van Dyke Parks walked out for good, still smarting from Mike Love's scathing criticism of his obscure contributions to *Smile* and no longer willing to be subordinate to Brian, but this was only one of the mounting difficulties threatening to overwhelm the group. At the end of February, they had instigated legal action against Capitol Records, with a view to ending their contract with the company and claiming an estimated $225,000 worth of unpaid royalties on past record sales. And on 26th April, before the live band was due to play a concert on Long Island, Carl Wilson, now aged 20, was arrested for draft-dodging and ordered to appear in court in Los Angeles on 1st May, the day on which he should have been flying to Ireland with the rest of the Beach Boys in readiness for a European tour.

To add insult to injury, on 28th April, in the continuing absence of "Heroes And Villains", Capitol unilaterally decided to release a two-year old track, "Then I Kissed Her" (a revamp of the Crystals' US hit from 1963 that the Beach Boys had recorded for their *Summer Days (And Summer Nights!!)* LP) as their new single in the UK. Although Brian and the group may have been fuming, sales were seemingly unaffected by the jarring discrepancy between this record (historically a companion piece to "California Girls" and "Help Me Rhonda") and its immediate predecessor "Good Vibrations", to the extent that by 3rd June it had climbed to No.5.

Carl belatedly rejoined his colleagues in Dublin on the night of 2nd May, in time to play a much-delayed second house with them at the Adelphi Theatre. (The previous day he had submitted a 'not guilty' plea to the Los Angeles Federal Court and been released on bail of $40,000, pending his trial proceeding on 20th June.) He had possibly arrived not a moment too soon. A review of the first house in *Melody Maker* exposed serious shortcomings as follows:

> … the absence of brother Carl brought chaos and uncertainty for The Beach Boys and certain disappointment for the first-house audience. As Carl was jetting across the Atlantic, Al, Mike, Bruce and Dennis took the stage. It was, to be as polite and charitable as possible, a disaster. The audience wanted Carl, but not as much as the four men who were struggling to make do without him. They seemed at a complete loss, like some amateur group struck with stagefright at the local talent contest.[112]

When Carl at last "puffed on stage" partway through the second house, the same review grudgingly conceded that "From then on it was the same act, if rougher, that audiences heard on the last tour".[113] As the tour rolled on, there were further brickbats to come. Nick Jones, writing for *Melody Maker*, tellingly had this to say of their concert at the Hammersmith Odeon on 4th May:

> Maybe it is the polished perfection and the wealth of sound and orchestration that one is used to on their records that makes the live Beach Boys' group sound so comparably amateurish, floundering weakly as though their umbilical cord to Brian Wilson had been severed. One expects a group as experienced as The Beach Boys (and years of touring the States would be a good training ground) to have far more presence on stage. As the curtain slides up, the

impact should strike you dumb. But one just hears the disjointed, empty, nervous instrumental sound.[114]

He concluded his piece by throwing them an ominous lifeline:

> The time has come to get The Beach Boys in perspective. Their live performances aren't as outstanding as I, for one, was led to believe … They are good but not great and it's time they devoted their lives to recording studios and not live performances.[115]

Two days later, however, Derek Taylor would be reported as saying that *Smile* had run its course:

> In truth, every beautifully designed, finely wrought inspirationally-welded piece of music, made these last months by Brian and his Beach Boy craftsmen, has been SCRAPPED. Not destroyed, but scrapped. For what Wilson seals in a can and destroys is scrapped. As an average fan of The Beach Boys, I think it is utterly disappointing.[116]

Paradoxically, the next day the Beach Boys would be playing the *NME* Poll Winners' Concert to possibly the greatest acclaim of the tour and receiving their award as the World's Best Vocal Group of 1966.

If, strictly speaking, Taylor's announcement had been premature, it was only another two weeks until Brian – with the live group still away on tour until the end of the month – personally admitted defeat by not showing up to a recording session scheduled for 19th May and consequently Capitol refused to underwrite any more studio time towards the album's completion. *Smile* was officially dead in the water (although the group soon rallied round to salvage something from the wreckage by embarking on an alternative, less ambitious album entitled *Smiley Smile*.) For Brian, it marked the prelude to a long descent through the coming months into ever-deeper withdrawal from the world and a nervous breakdown. For now, he still had to endure a buffeting from his ever more vocal critics, riding out the storm until his astrologer identified Tuesday, 11th July as the most propitious day on which to unveil "Heroes And Villains", a final take of which he had at long last sanctioned on 14th June. Late that night, impulsively and unannounced, accompanied by the rest of the group and loyal close acquaintances such as Terry Melcher, he took an acetate copy of the record to a local radio station in Los Angeles and offered them an exclusive first play on air. To his horror, the duty DJ baulked at it and had to be pressed to seek approval from higher management before he would circumvent his given playlist, a rejection that Melcher saw all too clearly came as a debilitating shock to Brian.

Subsequently released on the Beach Boys' own new Brother label (a subsidiary of Capitol) in America on 31st July (where it reached No.12) and in the UK by Capitol on 18th August (where it would reach No.10), in the end "Heroes And Villains" was attended by a tremendous sense of anti-climax that, over here, not even another promotional visit by Bruce Johnston had the power to forestall. Taking so long to see the light of day after "Good Vibrations", its unfathomable lyric (conceived in large part as Brian's homage to the golden age of the Wild West), combined with its undeniably sublime harmonies and striking changes of tempo, rendered it, somewhat bemusingly, just too clever for its own good. The decline of UK interest in the Beach Boys' records was, however, further underlined by the far from successful November release of "Wild Honey" as their next single, which entered the Top 30 for one week only at No.30, then dropped out of the charts and came back after a fortnight for one more week at its peak of No.29.

Back in the USA, it might have been safe to assume that live performances there still had the potential to generate support for the group; especially with Carl restored to full, unfettered participation after his court appearance in June, when his claim to be a conscientious objector had been accepted and he was cleared of failing to present himself for military service.[117] Yet Carl's anxieties beforehand about the outcome had been used as one of the reasons why the Beach Boys withdrew at the last minute from the Monterey Pop Festival, strategically an ill-considered decision that lost them a massive amount of goodwill. Trying to bounce back, at the end of August the live band staged a two-day Summer Spectacular concert in Honolulu (for which Bruce temporarily stood down, to allow Brian to join the line-up) and the annual Thanksgiving Tour followed in November. But they were far from out of the woods yet. Writing in *Rolling Stone* in December, Jann Wenner, having labelled them "a totally disappointing group" for passing on Monterey, then twisted the knife:

> … in person they are nowhere near their records, especially with their surfing material. To please their fans, they do their old material but they make fun of it. Their old material is fine and they should do it with pride that they have every reason to take. But instead they make fun of it on stage. The Beach Boys are just one prominent example of a group that has gotten hung up on trying to catch The Beatles. It's a pointless pursuit.[118]

It was, of course, a gross simplification for effect to suggest that the Beach Boys had only lost ground to the Beatles. In truth, they were also fighting increasingly desperate rearguard actions against rising new trends in American pop and rock. On their own doorstep of the West Coast, for example, the burgeoning counter-culture of Los Angeles and San Francisco favoured the broad church of psychedelia in preference to earlier, naïve preoccupations with songs of surf or drag-racing. The first two singles from the Electric Prunes, "I Had Too Much To Dream Last Night"[119] and "Get Me To The World On Time", had been Top 40 hits in January and February respectively. The Doors had not only had a debut, million-selling No.1 hit for the first three weeks of July with "Light My Fire" but had also delivered two best-selling albums: *The Doors* (released in January) and *Strange Days* (in September). Jefferson Airplane, who had played Monterey, had Top 10 singles hits that summer with two tracks from their best-selling album *Surrealistic Pillow*: "Somebody To Love" and "White Rabbit", the latter a menacing blend of *Alice in Wonderland* and a trip on LSD. CBS launched Moby Grape with a mad experimental flurry of five simultaneous singles, including the frenetic "Omaha" (b/w "Hey Grandma"). Stablemates of the Doors on the Elektra label, Love built on the early promise of their eponymous first album by recording *Da Capo*, notable both for "The Castle" on Side 1 and the complete devotion of Side 2 to the improvisational "Revelation" (which, to the band's disgust, was completely mangled in the editing of the final mix). All of the above caught my attention eventually, no thanks to long lead-in times and widely differing degrees of promotion in the UK, where their sales were generally poor (the only one to make a Top 30 showing here being the Electric Prunes' "Get Me To The World On Time", No.28 for one week in May).

Then there was the complete polar opposite to the heaviness of this contingent, in the form of the Monkees, a phenomenon of commercial enterprise capitalising on the power of a made-for-purpose television series to sell millions of records in both America and Britain. Much derided as an *ersatz*, as opposed to professional, group, nevertheless the Monkees, initially with the help of their backers, did carve out for themselves an unprecedented niche in pop history. Micky Dolenz firmly makes the point in his autobiography that all four members of the group were auditioned first and foremost as potential television actors, not musicians:

> In retrospect, it's apparent that Bob [Rafelson] and Bert [Schneider] weren't trying to "cast" the show in the traditional sense, i.e., attempting to find actors to fit already established roles, but were looking for unique multitalented personalities who would be distinct, dynamic, yet be able to work together without stepping on each other's toes and, hopefully, develop a rapport that would translate onto the screen.[120]

As luck would have it, between them the four had a breadth of both acting and musical talent to offer; but until they rebelled and bit the hand that had fed them, those producing the television show – and those producing the music for the television show – primarily saw that as irrelevant. Rafelson and Schneider, working with music publisher and promoter Don Kirshner, had their own grandiose plans for weekly episodes of non-sequential comic misadventures targeted on a pre- or early-teen audience, that would also create, through incidental music professionally written to order, a ready-made hit factory; and Dolenz remains insistent that in the beginning there was a mis-reading by the programme's critics of who and what the Monkees were supposed to be:

> It's often been said that the Monkees were America's answer to the Beatles. Nothing could be further from the truth. That would be like saying *Star Trek* was Hollywood's answer to NASA's space program. No matter what's been said or contended, *The Monkees* was a TV show *about* a group; about *all* the thousands of groups that were budding up around the States at the time …[121]

At the outset, Kirshner employed composing duo Tommy Boyce and Bob Hart to write the potential hits: they in turn assembled a group of session musicians they nicknamed the Candy Store Prophets to record them, to which the newly recruited actors would lend their voices on cue. The first Monkees' A-side, "Last Train To Clarksville" (b/w "Take A Giant Step", by Gerry Goffin and Carole King), at least boasted a vocal by Dolenz, had the youth appeal of a mildly anti-war lyric and was released in America on 16th August 1966, in advance of the launch of the TV series on 12th September. Roll forward a mere three weeks on into the series and Kirshner was rushing their eponymous debut album (a sampler of just about every current style in US pop) into the record stores. On the TV screen, at any rate, the Monkees' line-up was: Davy Jones (vocals & tambourine), Mike Nesmith (guitar), Peter Tork (bass guitar) and Micky Dolenz (vocals & drums). On vinyl, their contributions were reduced to the bare minimum. And yet by early November, "Last Train To Clarksville" was the US No.1 and *The Monkees* had topped the US album charts.

With the TV show coming to British screens later (from January 1967 onwards), it was on the strength of their music alone that the Monkees were first promoted in the UK and made their breakthrough with their second single, "I'm A Believer". Although "Last Train To Clarksville" had been released here earlier and rightly attracted some airplay – it was, after all, a good pop record with a distinctive, clanging guitar riff – it only charted after its successor had broken into the Top 30. "I'm A Believer", composed by the as yet unknown Neil Diamond, had swiftly become the Monkees' second No.1 in America (for seven weeks in a row), on the back of well over a million advance orders; and was soon set to repeat high-volume sales in Britain. Trying to buy it myself from no end of shops in and around Birmingham as a must-have single to play at a party I was planning for friends, it was one of the very few singles that took me ages to get my hands on:

almost everywhere I tried, either in big store chains or independent retailers, it was consistently sold out. It entered the UK Top 30 in the week ending 7th January at No.29; next week, was No.2; and the week after that, it was No.1, a position it held for a month. Having displaced Tom Jones, it then further achieved the distinction of being the only No.1 single by a group – as opposed to solo artists – in 1967 until the week ending 20th May, when the Tremeloes' "Silence Is Golden" became the second. It also sported a gritty composition from Boyce and Hart as the B-side, "(I'm Not Your) Stepping Stone", making it even better value. (On the coat-tails of this success, "Last Train To Clarksville", almost apologetically, finally made it into the lower reaches of the charts for two weeks at the beginning of February, peaking at a disappointing No.26.) In parallel, *The Monkees* entered the LP charts on 28th January, the same week as the Rolling Stones' *Between The Buttons*, but significantly outselling and outpacing its competitor: out of a total of thirty-six weeks in the charts, it was No.1 for seven.

Not discernible to their record-buying or viewing fans, for all their instant popularity, the Monkees nevertheless grew rapidly disenchanted with the commercial manipulation to which they were unavoidably subjected. They had been hired only as actors, their interests were not protected by any agent or manager, yet they were now determined to prove their worth as a pop group *per se* and so, starting in Honolulu in December 1966, they pushed themselves into playing concerts as a live band. Matters came to a head while they were on tour early in 1967 when Don Kirshner authorised the release of a second LP, *More Of The Monkees*, which, just like the first album, was a massive best-seller but again only utilised their vocals. Of the four, Mike Nesmith and Peter Tork had felt most keenly that their respective musical talents had hitherto been suppressed and had begun to agitate for more input into future recording sessions. Underwhelmed by what they felt was the indifferent quality of the new album put out in their names, they returned from a concert in Cleveland, Ohio to the RCA Studios in Hollywood and, taking their lead from Nesmith, convened a session of their own. One of the tracks they recorded then was "The Girl I Knew Somewhere" (a Nesmith composition); and in late February, in a move designed to placate the more dissident elements within the group, TV producers Rafelson and Schneider invited the Monkees to re-record it as the possible B-side of their next single.

Don Kirshner, however, wilfully ignored this conciliatory gesture by simultaneously putting out a third single on his own authority, "A Little Bit Me, A Little Bit You", another song commissioned from Neil Diamond, on which the only direct contribution from any of the Monkees was the vocal by Davy Jones, b/w "She Hangs Out": it was a step too far. Siding with the Monkees, Rafelson and Schneider immediately dispensed with Kirshner's services, recalling the single and re-releasing it coupled with "The Girl

I Knew Somewhere" as promised; and from this point on, for good or ill, the Monkees shouldered responsibility for their own musical output. When released in the UK, the reissued single gave them their third hit in a row, entering the Top 30 at No.8 in April and climbing to No.3 by the end of the month, with three more to follow by the end of the year.

Of those remaining three, the first had an unintentionally colourful history. Released here in the summer as "Alternate Title", its original given title as a composition by Dolenz (for their first 'original' album *Headquarters*) had been "Randy Scouse Git". Commemorating his experiences on a promotional trip to England in February, it included an amicable reference to hanging out with the Beatles ("The four kings of EMI/Are sitting stately on the floor"[122]) and took its title from Alf Garnett's slighting description of his good-for-nothing son-in-law in *Till Death Us Do Part* – which RCA Victor, as their British record label, ruled out as unacceptable. As it shot up the charts to No.2 in July, it was denied the No.1 slot by the Beatles' release of "All You Need Is Love". It was at its last gasp in the Top 30 in August when it was succeeded by "Pleasant Valley Sunday", a No.10 hit at the start of September which was then overtaken by the Beach Boys' "Heroes And Villains". Finally in November came "Daydream Believer" and a return to earlier form, as it sold strongly in the run-up to Christmas and on into the New Year, clawing its way up to No.2 in January 1968 beneath the Beatles' "Hello, Goodbye".

It could so easily just have been an urban myth but musicologist Johnny Rogan credits Jim McGuinn and Chris Hillman with having the Monkees' bandwagon at least partly in mind when they wrote the song "So You Want To Be A Rock'n'Roll Star" for the Byrds, quoting McGuinn as follows:

> Some people have accused us of being bitter for writing that song, but it's no more bitter than 'Positively 4th Street'. In fact, it isn't as bitter as that. We were thumbing through a teen magazine and looking at all the unfamiliar faces and we couldn't help thinking: 'Wow, what's happening ... all of a sudden here is everyone and his brother and his sister-in-law and his mother and even his pet bullfrog singing rock'n'roll.' So we wrote 'So You Want To Be A Rock'n'Roll Star' to the audience of potential rock stars, those who were going to be, or who wanted to be, and those who actually did go on and realise their goals.[123]

As we saw in the last chapter, the Byrds' glory days in the UK charts had already passed, so as a single the song made no impact, despite an innovative arrangement incorporating jazz trumpeter Hugh Masekela into the mix. (It was released in Britain on 17th February, the same day as the Beatles' "Strawberry Fields Forever/Penny Lane": I bought both records together and was hard-pressed to decide which of them I enjoyed the most.) It did, however, live again as a strong opening track for their highly regarded but commercially unsuccessful fourth LP *Younger Than Yesterday*, released here on 7th April with its title an allusion to their cover of Dylan's song "My Back Pages" also included on the album.

"So You Want To Be A Rock'n'Roll Star" embodies both a cautionary tale and a critique. At first sight, it looks too easy:

> So you want to be a rock'n'roll star?
> Then listen now to what I say.
> Just get an electric guitar
> Then take some time
> And learn how to play.[124]

But to secure a recording contract, understand that there is a Faustian deal to be done:

> Sell your soul to the company
> Who are waiting there to sell plastic ware
> And in a week or two,
> If you make the chart,
> The girls'll tear you apart.[125]

After which any time left to yourself, to reflect on the consequences of your action, will be at a premium:

> The price you paid for your riches and fame:
> Was it all a strange game?
> You're a little insane.
> The money, the fame and the public acclaim –
> Don't forget who you are,
> You're a rock'n'roll star.[126]

The song was way ahead of its time, pre-dating other sideswipes at the industry that spawned it – like David Essex's "Gonna Make You A Star", Pink Floyd's "Have A Cigar" or Dire Straits' "Money For Nothing" – by years; and, as Rogan observes, it captured "with chilling precision" the dilemma now confronting the Byrds themselves, "caught somewhere between a new age spirit of rebellious disenchantment and an old-world view that demanded they fulfil their appointed role in the pop circus".[127]

In fact, the making of *Younger Than Yesterday* reflected the rapidly changing dynamics within the group, as McGuinn and Hillman assumed a more prominent role in the face of David Crosby's growing unrest and discontent. This time round, Crosby's own direct contributions as a composer were much reduced. The achingly beautiful "Everybody's Been Burned" was a reworking of a song he had written before the Byrds had even formed and "Mind

Gardens" was an engagingly bleak, if stoned, prose poem he embellished experimentally with a tape of a 12-string guitar played back in reverse. Two other tracks were jointly credited to him and McGuinn: "Renaissance Fair", an all-too short impressionistic gem recalling a mock mediaeval event staged near Los Angeles in the spring of 1966, and – at his insistence – a remake of "Why", that turned out to be far less powerful than the original. While McGuinn indulged himself with another novelty song about space, "CTA-102", complete with interstellar sound effects and mock alien conversation, Hillman went into overdrive with four songs of his own ("Have You Seen Her Face", "Time Between", "Thoughts And Words" and "The Girl With No Name") that in their arrangements traded country influences with psychedelia. Crosby had not personally been in favour of recording "My Back Pages", seeing it as retrograde to fall back on Dylan, but was overruled by the other two.

That they had reached some sort of crossroads in their career was evidenced by a contemporary American reviewer of the album, Sandy Pearlman, who ventured this opinion of them:

> Everybody knows that the Byrds are an odd case. After all, only the Byrds, amongst modern rock stars, have managed to change their status from stardom to cultural heroism – that is, as one 45 after another didn't make it, their quality still kept up. And this maintained the fierce loyalty of the small hard-core of several hundred thousand knowing fans. Not enough to make them traditional rock stars – a category wherein the charisma depends upon the quantity – but enough to keep their name in circulation.[128]

It was a perceptive summation of their current standing in relation to their more successful contemporaries; and the uncomfortable truth they now had to deal with was that Crosby wanted out. Having by this stage become a regular partaker of acid, Crosby had eagerly embraced the fuzzy anarchy of hippiedom, apparently untroubled by all its attendant contradictions and inconsistencies; as conveyed by the sentiments of two of his last compositions in his time with the Byrds, "Lady Friend" (in which the supposed free-thinker bemoans the inconstancy of women) and "Triad" (in which he advocates sustaining a *ménage a trois*). His rapidly declining sense of loyalty to the Byrds showed itself more and more frequently on stage through his domineering behaviour towards the rest of the group and his poor playing as a live performer, as it pained Jim Dickson to witness at first hand:

> When the Byrds first broke on to the scene in Hollywood, just about everybody was on their side. They were the only game in town. By 1967 they couldn't draw flies. A lot of that had to do with the bad performances that disappointed people and a lot had to

do with who they turned out to be. Loads of people in Hollywood have egos that they mostly try to control and be civilised about. There's a guy in the Byrds who's got a bigger ego than any movie star, than any musician, than *anybody*. People got soured. It's not important enough for them to put up with. I put up with a lot from David Crosby, the group put up with a lot from David Crosby, but people outside got tired of putting up with David Crosby.[129]

Matters came to a head at the Monterey Pop Festival. When the Byrds played their set on the evening of Saturday, 17th June, Crosby was deemed to have seriously crossed a line by adding a political dimension to some of his on-stage announcements, linking the taking of LSD to the achievement of world peace and, looking in another direction altogether, urging the wider investigation of the conspiracy theory to explain President Kennedy's assassination. Next day, he stepped even further over that line by joining in as an additional member of Buffalo Springfield for the whole of their set. For McGuinn and Hillman, it was the ultimate snub, as Hillman explained:

He wasn't happy in the Byrds, and at the time we were working in the studio, he'd take our tapes and run off and play them for the Springfield. So he took the opportunity to jump on stage with them. McGuinn and I were ready to strangle him at that point after he made some stupid comment about Kennedy and the Warren Commission that was totally inappropriate. I don't think we were officially notified that he was going to join them onstage but we heard rumours.[130]

From here onwards, relationships within the group rapidly deteriorated and arguments abounded, particularly in the course of preparing material for and recording their fifth album, *The Notorious Byrd Brothers*. On 14th August, for example, during a session at the CBS Studios to record one of Crosby's latest songs, "Dolphin's Smile", Crosby launched into a tirade against Michael Clarke, tongue-lashing him for his under-rehearsed drumming and general lack of musicianship. But the final straw came in early September, when McGuinn (by now calling himself Roger, not Jim any more[131]) threw Crosby out of the studio for refusing to participate in the recording of Goffin & King's "Goin' Back", a song chosen for inclusion on the album in preference to "Triad". Producer Gary Usher was unavoidably present:

I just think this had been coming for a long time and McGuinn got to the point where he couldn't take any more, so finally he said, 'Crosby, I've had enough of your bullshit, if you don't want to be part of this song and the group just get your ass out of here. We don't want you, or even need you.' Well, that did it. Crosby turned red and you could sense him burning. He just picked up his guitar and walked out of the studio.[132]

Crosby's last public appearance as a Byrd was at the Fillmore Auditorium in San Francisco on 9th September, the end of a three-day billing marred the previous night by Crosby, enraged by having to play a longer-than-usual set, assaulting road manager Jim Seiter upon leaving the stage; and in the course of the following week, McGuinn and Hillman drove over to his house and sacked him from the group. This effectively meant that the UK release of "Lady Friend" as a single on 1st September (sadly only compounding its original failure to chart in the US) would have to serve for British fans as the epitaph to Crosby's membership of the Byrds. The gap he left was filled temporarily when the surviving trio invited Gene Clark back into the fold, but it quickly proved to be an unsatisfactory arrangement. Stricken again by his old extreme anxieties about performing with the group (the quality of his playing second time around fell far short of their expectations) and flying with them to long-distance engagements, his return was short-lived.

Thus reduced to a trio again in a matter of weeks, they pressed on with completing the recording of *The Notorious Byrd Brothers*, a task now made more complex by their earnest desire to airbrush out most, if not all, of Crosby's earlier contributions to it. By the time it came to be released in the New Year, it would, however, turn out to be testimony to yet another casualty – drummer Michael Clarke, who was dropped by McGuinn and Hillman in December. To all intents and purposes, he had made himself redundant. Not having presented himself for the making of all the album tracks, he had perforce been replaced on several of them by session musician Jim Gordon, added to which his recent obvious all-round loss of interest in the Byrds' future had made him a passenger. Unlike Crosby, he left his former colleagues with no show of ill-will towards them; "a victim," according to Johnny Rogan, "of his own carefree approach, both to the music and the business side of the Byrds … remarkably blasé about his departure [and] fully cognisant that it had largely been self-inflicted".[133]

Further study of American fortunes in the British charts throughout 1967 reveals continuing support for Motown acts such as the Four Tops, the Supremes, Martha & the Vandellas and Gladys Knight & the Pips, balanced by a pronounced selectivity of interest in other acts that not so long ago had been headline-grabbers. The Lovin' Spoonful, for instance, proved unequal to the task of repeating their past successes with "Daydream" and "Summer In The City", making only one disappointing showing in the Top 30 with "Nashville Cats", an amusing but highly context-specific take on the US country music industry scraping to No.26 in January; and the original line-up passed into oblivion over here with the failure of its follow-up, "Darlin' Be Home Soon", a song written by John Sebastian for the Francis Ford Coppola film *You're A Big Boy Now*.

The Mamas & The Papas were also fast approaching the end of what publicist Derek Taylor was to dub in the autumn their "First Golden Era", by which time they had "found that they can no longer carry on without the search for peace and new artistic expression as a group".[134] After a long interval, they returned to the Top 30 in April with "Dedicated To The One I Love", a song they made quintessentially theirs (despite it being a cover of a song previously recorded in America by the Royales and the Shirelles) by gracing it with a delicate lead vocal from Michelle Phillips, and it would reach No.2 in May. Then in August came the valedictory "Creeque Alley", destined only to peak at No.12, offering a tongue-in-cheek retrospective of their formative years, complete with gratuitous name-checks for "McGuinn and McGuire just a-catchin' fire/In LA, you know where that's at".[135]

To that point alone, the year had thrown up many distractions along the way: Cass Elliot unexpectedly disclosing her pregnancy and giving birth to a daughter in April; John and Michelle diverting much of their energy for months with producer Lou Adler into mounting and co-ordinating the Monterey Pop Festival in June; and the re-emergence of interpersonal disputes seriously threatening their fulfilment of a contractual liability to record a new album (which they were ill-advisedly attempting to do in a bespoke studio newly installed in John and Michelle's house in Bel Air, where drug-fuelled chaos was the order of the day). After giving acclaimed performances at New York's Carnegie Hall in July and the Hollywood Bowl in August, but thereafter making minimal progress with their recording, on a whim they decided to take a break and sail from New York to Europe on the cruise liner SS *France*.

On docking in Southampton on 5th October, Cass was arrested before she could even disembark, charged with theft and non-payment of her bill in respect of a previous stay in a London hotel suite. Although the charges were dropped the next day on her appearance before magistrates (the misdemeanours more likely attributable to a former boyfriend who had been accompanying her on that occasion), the episode cast an ominous shadow over the trip, leading them to cancel a proposed concert at the Royal Albert Hall. In the end, further arguments between herself and the impossible John (yet again at odds with Michelle over her fidelity) drove an exasperated Cass, two weeks later, to inform a reporter from *Melody Maker* that the group was breaking up: "'We thought that this trip would give the group some stimulation,' she said, 'but this has not been so.' She then added that the group felt they were just repeating themselves and had done all they could." [136] With their record company still insisting on delivery of the next album, thus forcing the group to reunite on their return home, Cass's announcement may have been inadvertently presumptuous but it was nevertheless a serious statement of intent on her part, giving firm notice of her imminent departure.

It was just as necessary, as ever, for homegrown acts to demonstrate their staying power or go under. Firstly, spare a thought in passing for the Shadows, long going out of style as interest in pure instrumentals had dwindled, who reached an unwelcome milestone on 22nd April with their last entry of the decade in the Top 30. Just short of seven years on from their chart debut with "Apache", their version of the theme from the film *Maroc 7* came in at No.30 and within five weeks had dropped out again, after peaking at No.25. The follow-up in September, the jazzier "Tomorrow's Cancelled", was a miss; and so things seemed set to continue for them for the foreseeable future.

Meanwhile, other well-established groups retaining a stronger grip on occupying the middle ground of popularity vied with each other for sales and attention in the interests of staying alive, even though their sources of inspiration might be wildly divergent. Take, for example, the Kinks and the Who, whose first two new singles of the year stayed in close contention as spring turned to summer. First up were the Who (now recording on Lambert and Stamp's new Track Records label) with the release on 21st April of their follow-up to "Happy Jack", "Pictures Of Lily". How for one minute it ever evaded the overactive imagination of the BBC censors is anybody's guess, for, as Pete Townshend explains, he imbued it with far deeper meaning than just a song about a set of historic postcards that he happened upon in the flat of his girlfriend Karen Astley:

> On Karen's bedroom wall were three Victorian black-and-white postcard photographs of scantily dressed actresses. One was the infamous Lily Langtry, mistress of Prince Edward, later King Edward VII, and one sunny afternoon while Karen was at work I scribbled out a lyric inspired by the images and made a demo of 'Pictures Of Lily'. My song was intended to be an ironic comment on the sexual shallows of show business, especially pop, a world of postcard images for boys and girls to fantasise over. 'Pictures Of Lily' ended up, famously, being about a boy saved from burgeoning adolescent sexual frustration when his father presented him with dirty postcards over which he could masturbate.[137]

It was already climbing the charts by 5th May (then at No.12) when the Kinks' latest offering, "Waterloo Sunset", was released. This offered the more superficially benign fantasy of the weekly tryst between Terry and Julie, as observed every Friday night by the song's lonely narrator scanning the river and rooftops of central London. Ray Davies was later to say of it: "It is a voyeuristic lyric. But it's not about a seedy voyeur looking out of his window.

He just knows that what he's looking at is an idyllic situation, and he won't be able to fit into it. So he's staying away."[138]

Striving to convey his gathering realisation of impending societal change in the air, Ray had originally planned to write "a song about Liverpool that implied that the era of Merseybeat was coming to an end" but then came up with an alternative idea, "not only because that gave me a bigger canvas to work on but because it was about London, the place where I had actually grown up".[139] Its content remained his preciously-guarded secret right up till the day of recording:

> On 13 April I took Rasa, Pete and Dave into number 2 Studio at Pye and we stood round the microphone and put on our backing vocals. I still didn't tell them what the lyrics would be about. Simply because I was embarrassed by how personal they were and I thought that the others would burst out laughing when they heard me sing. It was like an extract from a diary nobody was allowed to read. But when I finally put the vocal on later that evening everything seemed to fit and nobody laughed … Terry meets my imaginary Julie on Waterloo Bridge, and as they walk across the river darkness falls and an innocent world disappears.[140]

In the week ending 27th May, "Waterloo Sunset" reached No.2, trouncing "Pictures of Lily" by two chart places but fended off from the No.1 slot by the Tremeloes, just as The Mamas & The Papas had been the week before. For Ray, then embroiled in a High Court hearing to disentangle the myriad complications of contractual issues and his music publishing rights, in his own mind it immediately assumed the symbolic status of "something that [his lawyers] would never understand because they had forgotten their own innocence".[141] Commended at the time by music journalist Penny Valentine to managers Robert Wace and Grenville Collins as "the best record [Ray] would ever make"[142], it remains to this day one of the most affectionately remembered Kinks songs, instantly recognisable by its tumbling opening chords. Although Ray likened the meeting of Terry and Julie to Henri Cartier-Bresson's famous photograph of the Parisian couple kissing in the street, "Waterloo Sunset" is predominantly cinematic in its conception, its focus constantly shifting back and forth between close-ups of its three protagonists (the narrator, Terry and Julie) and wide-screen shots (of the Thames, of "Millions of people swarming like flies round Waterloo Underground"[143]) before dissolving into that final sublime sunset.

It was to be rapidly followed not by another Kinks single but the first solo outing by Ray's brother Dave, "Death Of A Clown". According to Dave: "The song was a metaphor for my real feelings. The pretence and illusion that surrounded me at the time. Finding myself squashed in between the unreal world of show-business and its parasites; its unquenchable demands on me, both socially and creatively, and of my inner shyness and personal insecurities."[144] Assisted in its recording by Ray and Rasa, as well as the other Kinks and Nicky Hopkins, Dave was suitably gratified in August when it reached No.4 (although his second single, released on 24th November, "Susannah's Still Alive", did not fare as well, peaking at No.20 in the first chart of the New Year).

Later, however, the paths of the Kinks and the Who were set to converge once more, with the simultaneous release on 13th October of "Autumn Almanac" and "I Can See For Miles", the two records poles apart in virtually every way imaginable. Ray Davies's main source for the composition of "Autumn Almanac" had been his reflections on the dedication of his gardener Charlie:

> During the summer a little hunchbacked man came to the house
> twice a week to do my back garden. He was the same hunchback
> I had seen walking the streets when I was a child … He tended
> the garden with loving care, and as the seasons changed he swept
> up the dead leaves and prepared the garden for the next life cycle.
> Watching him always made me feel optimistic about the future; that
> there was always a better day coming.[145]

In a contemporary interview with the *NME*'s Keith Altham, Ray described "Autumn Almanac" as a love song of sorts, one that celebrated the purely selfish intensity of possessiveness (in this case, of the knowledge of the seasons). In stark contrast to its reassuringly sentimental touches, through its very English references to "Tea and toasted, buttered currant buns" and "Roast beef on Sundays, all right"[146], Pete Townshend had mined the savage seams of jealousy to write "I Can See For Miles":

> On one of the Who's many trips away I began imagining that my
> fabulous new girlfriend Karen was deceiving me … It was this kind
> of paranoid, unhinged thinking that spurred me to write 'I Can See
> For Miles', one of my best songs from this period. The first lyric
> was scribbled on the back of my affidavit in the case between [Shel]
> Talmy and Polydor. Perhaps that's why the song, about the viciously
> jealous intuitions of a cuckolded partner, adopts the tone of a legal
> inquisition.[147]

He looked upon the song "as a secret weapon", believing that "when it was properly recorded and released as a Who single" it would simply "flatten all opposition".[148] Both lyrically and instrumentally, it is possibly the most arrestingly sinister of all their Sixties' singles, Townshend's smouldering guitar work the perfect menacing complement to Daltrey's relentless delivery of his words of warning:

I know you've deceived me, now here's a surprise.
I know that you have 'cos there's magic in my eyes.[149]

A magic so strong, in fact, that leaves the hapless unfaithful partner literally nowhere in the world to hide:

The Eiffel Tower and the Taj Mahal are mine to see on clear days.
You thought that I would need a crystal ball to see right through the haze.
Well, here's a poke at you,
You're gonna choke on it too.
You're gonna lose that smile
Because all the while
I can see for miles and miles …[150]

Still convinced that his self-styled "masterwork" would "sweep [the Who] to eternal glory"[151], Townshend was to be more than bitterly disappointed to find that in its eight-week chart run it failed to reach the Top 10, stalling at No.13 on 11th November (after recovering from a three-place backward slide in sales from No.16 to No.19 the week before). "The day I saw it was about to go down without reaching any higher," he said, with feeling, "I spat on the British record-buyer. To me, this was the ultimate Who record, and yet it didn't sell." [152] From the moment of chart entry for both records on 21st October, however, "Autumn Almanac" was consistently ahead of it all the way, sharing 11th November as the date on which it too reached its high point (of No.5) and securing nine weeks overall in the Top 30 (as opposed to the Who's eight).

The tables were only turned in the LP charts, where outcomes were strikingly different. *Something Else By The Kinks*, released on 15th September, was the first album produced by the Kinks themselves after severing their links with Shel Talmy; and apart from including the hit singles "Waterloo Sunset" and "Death Of A Clown", is most notable for the songs "David Watts" and "Two Sisters" (the latter a thinly-disguised exploration of the relationship between the two Davies brothers). The original sleevenotes are of particular interest for their comic take on what by now were becoming the increasingly familiar characteristics of the Kinks' music-making:

Welcome to Daviesland, where all the little kinklings in the magic Kinkdom wear tiny black bowlers, rugby boots, soldier suits, drink half pints of bitter, carry cricket bats and ride in little Tube trains. Here all the little lady kinklings wear curlers in their hair, own fridges and washing machines, fry bacon and eggs, and take afternoon tea.
Gulliver-like Ray Davies stoops to pluck a small mortal from his musical World – turns him upside down to see where he was made – and replaces him firmly but gently in that great class society

where all men are equal but some are more equal than others.[153]

Lacking, much to Ray's regret, comparable promotion from Pye to that afforded their singles, *Something Else* barely registered its presence, with only two weeks in the charts and a highest placing of No.35. Just as in 1966 *Face To Face* had been outsold by the cut-price compilation *Well Respected Kinks*, so history would repeat itself when Pye issued a second compilation LP, *Sunny Afternoon*, on its Marble Arch label on 17th November, that would in due course reach No.9.

The Who's LP of the year, released on 15th December, was *The Who Sell Out*, fancifully constructed around the concept of a continuous radio broadcast, the songs (including "I Can See For Miles") interspersed with both genuine and mock advertising jingles. Its sleeve even boasted panels featuring each of the four group members as models in advertisements for contemporary products, namely: Odorono underarm deodorant (Townshend), Heinz baked beans (Daltrey), Medac anti-acne cream (Moon) and the Charles Atlas body-building course (Entwistle).

It stood or fell as a timely and affectionate tribute to the passing of the pirate radio stations – Radio London in particular – following their outlawing by the implementation of the Marine Broadcasting Act with effect from 15th August. (The station's title was a misnomer: although it beamed its broadcasts to the London area, it was actually based off-shore in the North Sea, on a converted US minesweeper, the MV *Galaxy*.) For Tony Blackburn, one of its leading DJs until its closedown, "Radio London was a model business venture that enabled me to have the time of my life"[154]; and the contents of the album mirrored the station's winning format of alternating commercials with records from its *Fab 40* playlist, as described here by Blackburn:

> Essentially, the American-style formula went like this. Seven records would be played every half an hour – two from an A-list selected from the Top 10, two from a B-list consisting of records from Number 11-40, plus a climber, an American hit and an oldie, what we called a 'revive 45'. Each disc would be plucked from a box, spun, then placed at the back of the box so it didn't come round again for another three hours. Rotating that simple formula throughout the day lent a remarkable consistency to the station. My only reservation was that the *Big L* sales team was so successful in pulling in advertising that sometimes we only had time to play three records in one half-hour slot.[155]

Blackburn and Townshend alike specifically nurtured respect for and were inspired by the station's jingles:

> Jingles had been a distinctive feature of American radio since the '50s, and the essential idea was that they utilised a musical style

entirely different to the music played on the station so they'd stand out. The PAMS jingles [favoured by the pirates but produced to order by a company based in Dallas] had their own particular style; essentially brassy and jazz-tinged, overlaid with fast, Easy Listening vocal harmonies.[156]

Despite Townshend subsequently bemoaning *The Who Sell Out* as a "half-cooked package"[157], once copyright issues with manufacturers and PAMS had been settled (a process that had delayed its release by a month), it sold slowly but steadily, eventually making No.11. (Although Townshend had banked on its greater appeal to US radio stations as "a tribute to their power and influence", on its January release in America, "Joe Bogart, director of WMCA, New York's biggest radio station, called [it] 'disgusting' and said he had 'grave doubts anyone would play it'".[158] Its highest position thereafter in the *Billboard* album charts would be No.48.)

Like the Who, the Small Faces too had changed record labels, although in their case it was also linked to a change of management. Despite their initial discontent at having been 'sold on' to Andrew Loog Oldham by Don Arden via Harold Davison, they were soon openly expressing an unexpected gratitude for the radically different working atmosphere they encountered at Immediate Records from 1967 onwards. Most significantly, after their bruising experiences in the recent past with the domineering Arden, Loog Oldham's approach towards them was refreshingly 'hands off'. Not only was he happy to leave the future production of their own records to them but he was also openly encouraging of Steve Marriott and Ronnie Lane's potential value as in-house songwriters to other artists on the company's books, prompting this warm recollection from Marriott in a later interview for the *NME*:

> We wanted to go to Immediate because Oldham offered us every freedom besides being a management company. Their interests were selling records and nothing more than being a record label. They knew that if they let us loose and gave us the reins then we could write better material and last longer. Oldham knew we could and would write stuff that lasted forever which, quite frankly, a lot of it has and still will. They were very shrewd people in that sense. It was a good move.[159]

Those few artists for whom Marriott and Lane did write initially included Chris Farlowe, the Apostolic Intervention (backing group to female soloist P.P. Arnold but subsequently renamed the Nice by Loog Oldham[160]) and Billy Nicholls. As for work on their own behalf, a formal period of transition remained to be observed before any new record could be released directly

on the Immediate label; which is why in March the Small Faces' first single
of the year, "I Can't Make It", was issued under licence by their old label,
although Decca understandably displayed little or no interest in promoting it
and, into the bargain, the BBC took against it for supposedly being suggestive. As a result, its yo-yo-like progress over four weeks in the Top 30 from
11th March onwards was decidedly uninspiring: in at No.21, then down to
No.29, back up to No.21 and finally down and out at No.30. Then, in a bid
to recoup their losses, in May Decca unilaterally put out an earlier number,
"Patterns", as a second single, which failed to chart at all; quickly following
this up in June with a compilation album culled from their back catalogue,
From The Beginning, which did make No.17 in the LP charts.

Come the day, on 2nd June, when the latest number from the Small Faces
was at last to be released directly on the Immediate label (making it the fiftieth
single to be issued by the company), it turned out to be a jaunty, self-indulgent joke at the expense of the broadcasting establishment. To those in the
know, "Here Comes The Nice" was the open flaunting in song of a habit, the
'nice' of the title being contemporary slang for both the best-quality drugs
and an up-market drug dealer:

> Here comes the nice, looking so good.
> He makes me feel like no-one else could.
> He knows what I want, he's got what I need.
> He's always there if I need some speed.[161]

Far worthier of a ban in relative terms than "I Can't Make It", amazingly
its explicit references to drugs somehow escaped censure and it sold well
enough to reach No.10 for two weeks at the beginning of July.

With a debut *Small Faces* album on Immediate also released by the end
of June (in retaliation for Decca's *From The Beginning*, that nevertheless still
outsold it), attention then quickly turned in August to the incomparable "Itchycoo Park", undoubtedly one of the outstanding singles of the psychedelic
era if not of the whole decade. It displayed its hallucinatory colours sufficiently vividly on its sleeve, with mentions of getting high and being hung
up, to attract an instant ban on release from the BBC, which was rescinded
in the face of a clever counter-claim concocted by Steve Marriott and Tony
Calder: "We told the BBC that 'Itchycoo Park' was a piece of waste ground in
the East End that the band had played on as kids. We put the story out at ten
and by lunchtime we were told the ban was off."[162] Kenney Jones would lend
greater credibility to this supposed fiction by narrowing its location down
to "an area in Ilford which was a bombsite, an area of wasteland all wild
and overgrown that ran down to the railway lines, which are full of stinging
nettles (hence the title the locals bestowed on the area)".[163]

In the song, however, Itchycoo Park is portrayed as an idyllic refuge from the cares of the world – as emphasised by its ringing chorus line, "It's all too beautiful" – and a bolthole for disenchanted youth:

I'll tell you what I'll do
(What will you do?)
I'd like to go there now with you.
You can miss out school.
(Won't that be cool?)
Why go to learn the words of fools?[164]

In addition to the self-assuredness of its lyric, the record was also ground-breaking technically, thanks to the input of recording engineer George Chiantz at Olympic Studios, who had been experimenting with and perfected the creation of an effect known as phasing ("the technique of distorting a certain instrument by means of echoing and lengthening its recorded sound"[165], achieved by mixing the input from more than one tape machine run simultaneously but at differing speeds). The resultant washes of sound serve to add a totally new dimension to the song's surrealism.

By 23rd September, "Itchycoo Park" had climbed to No.3, just one of a host of psychedelic singles clustered in and around a Top 10 otherwise incongruously topped for weeks by Engelbert Humperdinck's "The Last Waltz", and it spent twelve weeks overall in the Top 30. It was succeeded in December by "Tin Soldier", originally written for P.P. Arnold and thus a more typical example of Marriott's preferred soul style of singing, building up to a crescendo from a subdued start. Already in the charts for four weeks by New Year's Eve, it would carry over well into 1968, ultimately peaking at No.10 at the end of January.

Acts like the Who and the Small Faces lent an intimidating edge to the popular music of 1967 that put clear blue water between them and other, by now veteran artists, who were now corralled within the middle ground of anodyne, if not formulaic, pop. While many of the latter habitually turned out good, listenable and/or danceable records, to which no-one could raise any particular objection, it established almost an underclass of chart fodder. Manfred Mann was one group that all but came to grief in this fallow period, as the hits temporarily dried up. Their sole Top 30 entry of the year (on which Manfred had rung the changes by prominently featuring a mellotron in the arrangement) was "Ha! Ha! Said The Clown", climbing to No.4 in April. Thereafter they were ill-advised in their choice of material. Neither of their two subsequent singles – the instrumental "Sweet Pea" (released in May) nor "So Long Dad" (released in August) – charted, seemingly casting them adrift.

The Hollies too seemed to have become locked into satisfying the singles market with more predictable songs, tending to save their more adventurous excursions for LPs that inexplicably failed to attract much attention. "On A Carousel", released in February, and "Carrie Anne", released in May, well-crafted as only to be expected by now but neither of them lyrically demanding, were both Top 10 hits (Nos. 5 and 3 respectively). When persuaded, however, by an increasingly frustrated Graham Nash to attempt something more challenging, in the form of "King Midas In Reverse" (gloriously over-produced by Ron Richards with added orchestration in their absence on tour and released in September), the exercise came to grief, resulting in a highest placing of only No.18:

> The worst backlash from the record was what it did to my relationship with the Hollies. Afterward, they no longer trusted my judgment. I suggested any number of songs to pursue as a follow-up, but they backed away from all of them. It was as if my miscalculation with "Midas" had cursed our hit-making prowess. Rationally, they knew that it wasn't my fault, but their minds were made up. And I literally gave up trying. Who wants to fight?[166]

As a direct consequence, Nash's seduction by the freer spirits of the West Coast, such as David Crosby and 'Mama' Cass Elliot, was all but complete. Yet his influence had strongly pervaded the Hollies' two LPs released that year which, added to the preceding *For Certain Because*, constitute a rarely-celebrated trilogy of excellence. *Evolution*, which came out in June, admittedly did achieve a measure of recognition by reaching No.13 in the LP charts; with a rash of forceful songs like "Have You Ever Loved Somebody", "Then The Heartaches Begin" and "Leave Me" all equally displaying the potential to be strong singles, and with Mike Vickers once again acting as orchestral arranger. *Butterfly*, on the other hand, unplaced in the charts on its release in November, remains a largely unrecognised masterpiece to all but the discerning few and is awash with beautiful songs beautifully arranged: "Dear Eloise", for example, or "Postcard", "Maker" and "Butterfly" itself (the title track which actually closes the album) – the latter two resplendent in all their psychedelic finery. It marked both a high point and a watershed in the Hollies' fortunes to date.

If you were looking for more excitement than the generality of old reliables could muster, then it was unquestionably to be found in the new music and wild stageshows of Birmingham group the Move. Formed in February 1966 from an *ad hoc* amalgamation of members from three different Birmingham bands (Mike Sheridan and the Nightriders; Carl Wayne and the Vikings; and Danny King and the Mayfair Set), the Move's original line-up was: Carl Wayne (vocals), Roy Wood (guitar & vocals), Trevor Burton (guitar & vocals), Chris 'Ace' Kefford (bass guitar & vocals) and Bev Bevan (drums). Signed up by Moody Blues' manager Tony Secunda, they quickly made a name for themselves as a live act that simply refused to be ignored:

> With a floor-shaking energy, inspired both by The Who and the
> emerging Tamla sound, overlaid with brilliantly effective four-
> and five-part harmonies, the band's musical skills were awesome
> enough. Add into the mix one of the first, pre-psychedelic light
> shows, stagecraft that involved exploding televisions, effigies of
> Adolf Hitler and a wildly swinging axe and it's not difficult to
> imagine why The Move's reputation spread so rapidly through
> clubland.[167]

After Secunda had brought them to London, to play a residency at the Marquee Club, and refashioned their image as mobsters in sharp suits, he negotiated a recording contract for them with producer Denny Cordell on the Deram label (a new subsidiary Decca had established in September 1966). The search for a commercial alternative to their stage set of soul and R&B covers provided Roy Wood with an opportunity at last to attempt writing hit songs for the group. Their debut chart single in January 1967, "Night Of Fear", was a heavy rock adaptation by Wood, combining his over-active imagination after a sleepless night with a theme from Tchaikovsky's *1812 Overture*, that had shot up to No.3 by 4th February. This was followed in April by "I Can Hear The Grass Grow", built, according to the Move's photographer Robert Davidson, on the unlikeliest foundations of a reader's letter to what passed in those days as a risqué magazine:

> Above my studio were the offices of the naturist magazine *Health
> & Efficiency*, and somebody had sent in a letter that said, "I listen
> to pop music on the radio because where I live it's so bloody quiet
> that I can hear the grass grow." I said to Roy, 'Wouldn't that make a
> great song title?', and he went off and wrote the song.[168]

In Wood's hands, however, the lyric took on distinctly hallucinatory qualities:

> My head's attracted to
> A magnetic wave of sound
> With the streams of coloured circles
> Making their way around.
> I can hear the grass grow,
> I can hear the grass grow,
> I see rainbows in the evening.[169]

Appealing to a wide enough audience to reach No.7 in May, it marked the end of the Move's brief encounter with Deram, as Secunda and Cordell transferred their allegiances to another label that summer, the grandly-named EMI subsidiary Regal Zonophone. (Acquired by EMI in the inter-war years, it had been defunct since the late Forties, until its premature revival in 1964 with just one hit to its name then, "It's An Open Secret" by the Salvationist group the Joy Strings.)

The Move's first single on Regal Zonophone, recorded in July, was another highly fanciful composition by Roy Wood, "Flowers In The Rain". It enjoys a place in pop history for three very different reasons. Firstly, in its own right, it was a No.3 hit in September. Secondly, it had the distinction of being the first record to be played on air when the BBC launched Radio 1 at 7.00 a.m. on Saturday, 30th September.[170] Selecting it to open his brand-new breakfast show, Tony Blackburn would later describe it as:

> … a bright cheery record that certainly fitted the bill that first Saturday morning. I particularly liked the fact that it began with that crashing rainstorm effect, and its opening phrase, "Woke up one morning half-asleep", was just the job for a 7am start! It was important, too, that we launched Radio One with a British record. Yes, for the first time in my life, I think I actually put a bit of thought into something.[171]

So far, so good. But, thirdly, it achieved notoriety, with unforeseen financial consequences, when Secunda devised and circulated a promotional flyer in the form of a postcard with a cartoon "depicting then Prime Minister Harold Wilson in a supposedly compromising situation with his secretary".[172] Wilson successfully sued for libel and extracted a salutary settlement, requiring both the royalties from the record and those due to Wood as composer to be paid in perpetuity to charity. Smarting from this significant loss of income as a result of Secunda having pulled this stroke unbeknown to them, the group parted company with him soon afterwards. (Common sense would also prevail when "Cherry Blossom Clinic", Wood's over-the-top depiction of the treatment of psychiatric illness, was pulled as a possible follow-up.)

If, as an alternative, you wanted seriously powerful music to stretch you intellectually but without the accompanying aggro, then Cream were likely to fit your bill. Where "Wrapping Paper" had been far too esoteric as a debut single, "I Feel Free" was an absolute triumph by contrast, an arresting song about the liberating effects of music and dancing:

> Dance floor is like the sea,
> Ceiling is the sky.
> You're the sun and, as you shine on me,
> I feel free, I feel free, I feel free.[173]

Entering the Top 30 in the first chart of the New Year at No.24 (three places above "Night Of Fear"), by the end of January it was at its high point of No.11. By the time their next single, "Strange Brew", was released, on 26th May, however, the group's attitude had undergone a marked transformation, mainly – though not exclusively – as a result of their exposure to American influences.

In advance of playing a series of concerts in New York at the end of March (a joint booking negotiated for them and the Who by Robert Stigwood), earlier that month they had commissioned Simon & Marijke to totally restyle them in a psychedelic image, from their clothes down to the decoration of their instruments and amplifiers; the previously conservative Eric Clapton even going so far as to adopt a frizzy Afro hairdo. When they arrived in New York, on the first-ever American visit any of them had made, they were pitched into a gruelling eight days (five shows per day, running from 10.15 in the morning to 11.30 at night) as an unknown support act on the bill of Murray the K's "Music in the Fifth Dimension" extravaganza; but before returning to England after this week of madness, Stigwood had secured two days' session time for them at the Atlantic Studios in Manhattan.

Here, on 3rd and 4th April, they worked under the direct supervision of Ahmet Ertegun, the legendary head of Atlantic Records – who, by all accounts, showed little initial enthusiasm for their brand of music – together with producer Felix Pappalardi and engineer Tom Dowd. Overnight between the two sessions, Pappalardi, aided by his wife Gail Collins[174], came up with the melody and lyric of a new song for the group, no mean feat as Clapton acknowledged when it was presented to them next morning:

> … he took home with him the tape we had previously recorded
> of 'Lawdy Mama', which was a standard twelve-bar blues, and
> came back the next day having transformed it into a kind of
> McCartneyesque pop song, complete with new lyrics and the title
> 'Strange Brew'. I didn't particularly like the song, but I respected the
> fact that he had created a pop song without completely destroying
> the original groove. In the end he won my approval, by cleverly
> allowing me to include in it an Albert King-style guitar solo.[175]

Recording of what was to become the B-side of the new single, "Tales Of Brave Ulysses" (a striking composition co-written by Clapton and a new London acquaintance of his, Martin Sharp), together with a host of other tracks that would make up their next LP, would be deferred until Cream made a return visit to Atlantic from 12th to 15th May.

Sharing its chart entry date of 17th June with "Here Comes The Nice" – but ten places below the Small Faces, at No.29 – "Strange Brew" rose to No.12 at the beginning of July. Its subject matter (similar to the Rolling Stones' "Stupid Girl" or "19th Nervous Breakdown" before it) is the threat posed by a seriously dangerous woman spiralling out of control:

> She's a witch of trouble in electric blue.
> In her own mad mind she's in love with you (with you).

Now what you gonna do?
Strange brew, killin' what's inside of you.[176]

At the time, Clapton was non-committal about it, even going so far as to suggest that he would have preferred to see the A- and B-sides of the record reversed but had bowed to others' assessments of the tracks' relative commercial merits. Yet the truth was that Cream's heart was not – nor ever really had been – in making singles and eventually they determined not to record any more, as all three group members confirmed in a November radio interview. It was a position Clapton would only marginally qualify a fortnight later when interviewed for *Melody Maker*: "It's not definite that we won't ever release a single again. The main reason for not wanting to do them is that we are very anti the whole commercial market."[177] Even more irritatingly, having thus indicated a strong preference for investing time in recording complete albums, Clapton went on to effectively disown *Disraeli Gears*, which had just been released (on 10th November):

> It's a good record, a great LP, but it was recorded last May and it's not really indicative of what we are doing now … It's an LP of songs and there is no extended improvisation anywhere. That's why we are rushing to do our new album, which we will record in America, and hope to have out at Christmas.[178]

Both "Strange Brew" and "Tales Of Brave Ulysses" are included on the album, together with one of Cream's most evocative and potent of all their tracks, "Sunshine Of Your Love", haphazardly composed in early 1967 by Jack Bruce and Pete Brown:

> Jack and I had been working all night, if not longer. Probably the second or third night in succession. We'd already done one good thing, but nothing was happening and I think we'd maybe had some sort of disagreement, which has been known to happen. Anyway, Jack suddenly grabbed his upright bass and said, 'What about this?' and he just played the riff of 'Sunshine'. And at that moment I looked out of the window, and it was getting light, and I sat down and started writing, 'It's getting near dawn, when lights close their tired eyes,' and all that stuff. And there it was. I wasn't there when the actual 'Sunshine of Your Love' hook was added, which I never actually liked.[179]

Elsewhere, there are other touches belying a stronger transatlantic influence. "Dance The Night Away" is openly a tribute to the Byrds, with Clapton on 12-string guitar (but, more surprisingly, according to Bruce, the sound of the Monkees is one dimension of the arrangement of "SWLABR (She Was Like A Bearded Rainbow)", one of Pete Brown's obscurer compositions).

"Take It Back", for all its party atmosphere, reflects the contemporary preoccupation of the young US male with evading the draft, Bruce confirming that "it was about burning a draft card, and I had the line, 'Take it back, get that thing right out of here,' about receiving a draft card."[180] And the final track, "Mother's Lament", was added on for good measure as a Cockney party-piece with which Clapton and Baker had entertained captive audiences in American bars (in the same misguided spirit as the Byrds thinking that a send-up of "We'll Meet Again" would be a fittingly witty conclusion to *Mr. Tambourine Man*).

Nick Jones, writing in *Melody Maker* on 30th December, suggested that *Disraeli Gears* fell between two stools, pleasing neither "the blues fans who were dissatisfied with the lack of obvious blues numbers" nor "some of the highly imaginative hippies – whose insatiable appetites demanded 'further out' material".[181] Nonetheless, on the record racks it was easily distinguishable by virtue of the fluorescent psychedelic collages adorning its sleeve (designed by Martin Sharp) and it sold far better than *Fresh Cream* by reaching No.5 in the course of its 42-week-long run in the LP charts.

But the real issues for Cream – more specifically, Clapton – lay elsewhere. His discomfiture with singles in particular and his desire to play longer improvisations than the discipline of session time in the studio would habitually allow had their origins in his displacement by Jimi Hendrix as the top-ranking rock and blues guitarist. With the music press and radio presenters understandably and repeatedly drawing comparisons between the two acts, the two supposed power-trios, Clapton was wrongfooted time and again by being obliged to comment on Hendrix's records and he could not escape the fact that the Jimi Hendrix Experience *was* more popular in Britain than Cream. When that summer Hendrix went on to cause a sensation with his stage act at the Monterey Pop Festival (an event from which Stigwood deliberately withheld Cream, on the spurious grounds that they could make more impact by breaking into America independently), his superiority was established beyond question.

Any pre-Christmas anxiety possibly harboured by Hendrix and Chas Chandler about the marketability of "Hey Joe" was rapidly dispelled when it broke into the Top 30 in January and moved on up into the Top 10, to No.7, by 11th February. It was to be followed in March by the release of "Purple Haze", the first single to come out on Lambert and Stamp's Track Records label and the first Hendrix A-side to feature one of his own compositions. Originally recorded in January at De Lane Lea Studios on a shoestring, while Chandler was still struggling on his own to pay for session time, it had been considerably finessed after moving to Olympic Studios in February and opening up a productive new working partnership with in-house engineer Eddie Kramer (the time pressures now overcome after Chandler had persuaded Polydor to meet the recording costs of his rising star). Lyrically inspired by Jimi's passion for science fiction (the "purple haze" of the title transmuted from a purple death ray), the enhancement of his thunderous guitar work by fuzz-box and other technical trickery was so far removed from the likes of Bert Weedon's modest plucking or Hank Marvin's mastery of the tremolo, the rightful envy of the previous generation of would-be pop stars, as to be unbelievable in its full-on impact. Playing the record over and over again, I must have driven my mother and father to distraction. It spent three weeks at No.5 from 29th April onwards, in the shadow of other hits already flagged up in this chapter ("Ha! Ha! Said The Clown", "A Little Bit Me, A Little Bit You", "Dedicated To The One I Love", "Silence Is Golden"); the diverse company it kept in the charts reflecting that kept by the Experience on their first major UK tour for most of April, on the road with the Walker Brothers, Cat Stevens and Engelbert Humperdinck. At least in the short term the tour meant exposure, with which Hendrix was pragmatically content for now:

> Those who come to hear Engelbert sing *Release Me* may not dig me, but that's not tragic. You can only plan so far in these things. We'll play for ourselves. We've done it before, where the audience stands about with their mouths open, and you wait ten minutes before they clap.[182]

While "Purple Haze" was still high in the charts, on 5th May Track released the third Hendrix single, "The Wind Cries Mary". As an understated, blues-tinged ballad, it represented a stark shift from its predecessor but afforded Hendrix the earliest opportunity to delineate to listeners the breadth of his scope both as lyricist and performer. Taking its origins, according to his then girlfriend Kathy Etchingham, from a tempestuous argument culminating in hurled crockery and her walking out on him, the song could simply be taken at one level as a touchingly poetic apology. Speaking for himself, he modestly dismissed it as: "nothing but a story about a breakup, just a girl and a boy breaking up, that's all … There's no hidden meaning. It's just a slow song, that's what I call it. Slow, quiet."[183]

It transcends such a mundane explanation, however, in the universality of its wider depiction of sadness, isolation and remorse, as Hendrix adopts imagery worthy of his acknowledged hero Dylan:

> After all the jacks are in their boxes,
> And the clowns have all gone to bed,
> You can hear happiness staggering on down the street,
> Footprints dressed in red,
> And the wind whispers Mary.

A broom is drearily sweeping
Up the broken pieces of yesterday's life.
Somewhere a queen is weeping,
Somewhere a king has no wife,
And the wind, it cries Mary.[184]

The guitar playing throughout is subtle and delicate, deceptive in its simplicity and sustained all the way to the gently receding finale, tripping in slow motion to the end against the repeated three-note theme as a backdrop.

In the chart for 13th May, in the third week of "Purple Haze" standing proud at No.5, "The Wind Cries Mary" entered at No.24, a fortnight later reaching its peak of No.7; where above it at No.6 sat the single disowned by the Beach Boys, "Then I Kissed Her", and higher still at No.2, the Kinks' "Waterloo Sunset". And still more new material kept on coming, to amaze, delight and surprise. Even before the new single's chart entry had been published, the first LP on the Track label was released on 12th May, Hendrix's debut album *Are You Experienced*, this event more than any other conclusively demonstrating to Clapton the Experience's superiority over Cream:

> I will never forget returning to London after recording *Disraeli Gears*, with all of us excited by the fact that we had made what we considered to be a groundbreaking album, which was a magical combination of blues, rock and jazz. Unfortunately for us, Jimi had just released *Are You Experienced* and that was all anyone wanted to listen to. He kicked everybody into touch really, and he was the flavour, not just of the month, but of the year. Everywhere you went, it was wall-to-wall Jimi, and I felt really down. I thought we had made our definitive album, only to come home and find nobody was interested. It was the beginning of a disenchantment with England, where it seemed there wasn't really room for more than one person to be popular at a time.[185]

Hitting the high street three weeks before *Sgt.Pepper*, the album sold strongly from the outset and would eventually reach No.2 in the LP charts: the copy I finally tracked down was the last one in Boots' record department in Solihull's Mell Square and even then I had to be content with a sleeve thoughtlessly creased in one corner from having been put out on display rather than housed in the record racks. Hendrix said of it himself that he didn't "want people to get the idea it's a collection of 'freak-out' material": he saw it as "a very personal album", almost "an ad lib album because we did so much of it on the spot".[186] And he was absurdly modest about the technical achievement it represented to any listener on first acquaintance:

> We have all these different sounds, but all of them are made from just nothing but a guitar, bass and drums, and slowed-down voices.

The feedback you hear is from a straight amp and a little fuzz thing
I had built … It was mostly Chas Chandler and Eddie Kramer who
worked on that stuff. Eddie was the engineer and Chas as producer
mainly kept things together. Maybe some of the stuff is far ahead, I
don't know. I'm very happy with it, but already I can hardly wait for
something else.[187]

Picking out his own highlights, he called "Foxy Lady" "the only happy
song I've written", "Manic Depression" "ugly times music" and "Red
House" "American soul"; dedicated "I Don't Live Today" "to the American Indian and all minority repressed groups"; thought "Can You See Me"
typical of "songs for teenyboppers"; and cited "Third Stone From The
Sun" as an opportunity to "write your own mythology".[188] And that selection still reckoned without at least two more of my favourites; the ethereal
"May This Be Love" and the sharp staccato of "Fire". Charles Shaar Murray
has offered possibly the most succinct summary of its contents as follows:
"Inexpensively recorded in four-track studios, *Are You Experienced* brings you
hard rock, deep blues, thermonuclear soul, psychedelic landscapes, pretty
songs and science-fiction guitar-2-die-4."[189] No wonder, then, that Clapton
should have felt totally blown away by the competition: there had never been
anything like it on the market before.

On 18th June, Hendrix resoundingly broke America with his performance
at the Monterey Pop Festival (to which the Experience had been invited on
the recommendation of Paul McCartney, a Festival board member). Introduced to an estimated audience of 90,000 by Brian Jones, seeking temporary
refuge from the judiciary's hostility towards the Rolling Stones in England,
the trio went through a nine-song set that concluded memorably, during
"Wild Thing", with Hendrix's melodramatic flourish of setting fire to his
guitar, dropping to his knees on stage to fan the flames.[190] The group then
spent the next two months on tour around the USA as well as intermittently
attempting some new recording, a stint that included the week immediately
after Monterey playing at the Fillmore Auditorium in San Francisco and,
strangest of all, a week from 8th July onwards on the road as opening act for
the Monkees.

Micky Dolenz and Peter Tork had both been at Monterey, seen Hendrix's
performance and Dolenz in particular was an immediate convert to his cause:
"The Monkees was very theatrical in my eyes and so was the Jimi Hendrix
Experience. It would make the perfect union."[191] Much to Chas Chandler's
annoyance at not being consulted, Mike Jeffrey had negotiated the deal on
Hendrix's behalf; but the Experience pulled out after eight days, under cover
of a face-saving press release to the effect that serious objections to the
group's unsuitable stage act had been raised: "We hadn't really played to that
kind of kids' audience before, and you have to realise that though the parents

of the kids in England don't interfere too much, the parents in the States are something else."[192] Individually, the Monkees were in awe of Hendrix's talent and were glad to have had the chance to be associated with him; but in hindsight the episode merely went to prove, for both groups concerned, the old adage that there's no such thing as bad publicity.

Immediately preceding their return to England, on 18th August came the release of their next single, "Burning Of The Midnight Lamp". The fourth hit in a row in the space of eight months, nevertheless it proved to be the most disappointing so far, not managing to climb higher than No.15 during its seven weeks in the Top 30. (The very opposite of "The Wind Cries Mary", it suffered from over-production, with a harpsichord and a female backing chorus thrown in for added effect, and in the muddy mix of the foreground Hendrix's vocal was indistinct.) Concert dates then alternated with intensive work on recording a second LP, *Axis: Bold As Love*, which occupied most of October – although a near-disaster at the end of that month, after the master tapes of Side 1 were lost by Hendrix when he left them in a taxi, required urgent action on 1st November to remix half the album. Then, beginning at the Royal Albert Hall on 14th November (where the concert was billed as the 'Alchemical Wedding') and ending in Glasgow on 5th December, the Experience undertook their second – and, as it was to be, final – UK tour, but now as the headline act, in the far better matched company of Pink Floyd, the Move, the Nice and Amen Corner.

This was – with the exception of the Nice – a hitmakers' package tour. The Move, as detailed earlier, were already a well-established and popular act, thereby entitled to second billing below the Experience. Pink Floyd were still on the rise in 1967, although by now well known as regular contributors to 'underground' events in and around London, where their music was complemented by a light show. Signed to EMI's Columbia label, they had two chart hits to their name: their debut single "Arnold Layne" (No.24 in April) and the far more successful "See Emily Play", which had taken them to No.8 in July. (A third single, issued to coincide with the tour, "Apples And Oranges", failed to chart.) They had also recorded and released their first album in August, *The Piper At The Gates Of Dawn*, which climbed the LP charts to No.6.

Album tracks like "Astronomy Domine" or "Interstellar Overdrive" were far more representative of their preferred style of music than any of their singles, a bone of contention with many of their original concert audiences:

> Both 'Arnold Layne' and its June follow-up, 'See Emily Play', were as far removed from their stage act as they could possibly be. Their quaint pop songs were ignored completely in favour of high-volume mind-bending workouts lasting in some cases well over ten minutes. While these were acceptable on their home turf of London, provincial audiences were nonplussed, fully expecting to

hear their chart hits. Pink Floyd literally hit the audience with a wall of sound verging on 'white noise'.[193]

At this juncture, the group's line-up was: Syd Barrett (lead guitar & vocals), Roger Waters (bass guitar & vocals), Rick Wright (keyboards) and Nick Mason (drums). Barrett, however, hitherto the group's principal source of inspiration and composer, had become increasingly unpredictable in his behaviour both on and off stage, by virtue of being a hardened user of LSD and thus edging perilously ever closer to a nervous breakdown. His days with Pink Floyd were therefore numbered and for many of the dates on the Hendrix tour his place was taken at short notice by Davey O'List of the Nice.

This leaves the Cardiff-based Amen Corner, erstwhile stablemates of the Move on the Deram label, fronted by Andy Fairweather-Low, whose "vision was to create a Welsh band which offered its own twist on American soul and R&B"[194]; a traditional foursome of vocalist, two guitars and drums in this instance being augmented by two saxophones and keyboards. Very much still an up-and-coming act, their debut single, "Gin House" (a reworking of the old standard "Gin House Blues"), was released in July, meandering around the lower reaches of the Top 30 at much the same time as both "Burning Of The Midnight Lamp" and "See Emily Play" until achieving its highest placing of No.17 at the end of August; but the September follow-up, "The World Of Broken Hearts", had missed the *NME* charts altogether.

As the tour drew to its close, *Axis: Bold As Love* was released on 1st December, making it a pre-Christmas competitor with *Disraeli Gears* (which by then had been out for three weeks). In terms of staying power in the LP charts, the latter won hands down (42 weeks to 16) but there was nothing to choose between them in respect of their highest chart placing, as both reached No.5. On tracks like the concluding "Bold As Love", Hendrix was able to take advantage of George Chiantz's breakthrough with phasing (as originally devised for "Itchycoo Park") to enhance the extended guitar solo that makes up the second half of the piece. Elsewhere, he appeared equally content to keep things far simpler, confining his ideas to "one very, very small little matchbox"[195] as with "Little Wing", arguably one of the LP's most popular and enduring songs; and even allowed bass player Noel Redding space to perform his own composition "She's So Fine". But, as ever with Hendrix, as soon as the album had been completed and released, he was itching to move on: "As soon as you finish you get a hundred completely new ideas."[196] So it was that on 20th December the Experience were hard at work again back at Olympic Studios, recording "Crosstown Traffic" as the first track of a third album – Hendrix's crowning glory, *Electric Ladyland*.

Olympic Studios had earlier been home to the recording of the most celebrated single of the year and its performers could boast of at least one other passing connection with Hendrix, in that Procol Harum made their live debut at his historic Saville Theatre concert on 4th June. A week later, "A Whiter Shade Of Pale" had taken the No.1 slot, where it would hold fast for another month and forever be associated with that summer. Procol Harum had risen from the ashes of the Paramounts, who had failed to live up to the expectations of an EMI recording contract and had latterly been employed as Sandie Shaw's backing group before folding in 1966. Founded in early 1967 by pianist and vocalist Gary Brooker and non-performing poet and lyricist Keith Reid, its other instrumentalists were: Matthew Fisher (Hammond organ), Ray Royer (guitar), Dave Knights (bass guitar) and Bobby Harrison (drums). In common with the Move, they were signed to Deram initially, for which label Denny Cordell produced "A Whiter Shade Of Pale", before they too subsequently switched to Regal Zonophone.

Through skilful use of a motif on the organ taken from Bach's "Air On A G-String", the song renders itself instantly memorable before it has hardly begun, even though the sublime poetry of Reid's lyric defies interpretation. The narration of events has all the lucid inconsequentiality of a dream. Utterly mystifying in its imagery, lent further gravity by the desperate edge in Brooker's voice, it achieves the startling and unsettling effect of a vignette from the Theatre of the Absurd set to music. Being enabled to visualise the unfolding story in snatches – if, indeed, it is a story – only serves to offer more hindrance than help:

> We skipped the light fandango,
> Turned cartwheels 'cross the floor.
> I was feeling kinda seasick
> But the crowd called out for more.
> The room was humming harder
> As the ceiling flew away.
> When we called out for another drink,
> The waiter brought a tray.[197]

Where exactly are we? Who are the protagonists of these actions? And what is their relationship to the spectral girl who now appears before us in the chorus, with its sly hint of Chaucerian ribaldry in the second line?

> And so it was that later,
> As the Miller told his Tale,
> That her face, at first just ghostly,
> Turned a whiter shade of pale.[198]

At whose hands, then, is the fate of this phantasmagorical apparition to be determined? Is her future well-being dependent on a favourable reading of the cards – of the Tarot, possibly?

> She said, 'There is no reason

And the truth is plain to see.'
But I wandered through my playing cards
And would not let her be
One of sixteen vestal virgins
Who were leaving for the coast.
And although my eyes were open,
They might have just as well've been closed.[199]

We are truly none the wiser at the end than we were at the beginning, still struggling to make sense of these tantalising visions as they abruptly disappear from view, exactly as we might find ourselves frustrated in the familiar experience of half-waking, half-dreaming.

Yet this perplexing experience was one with which so many felt an intangible empathy, as demonstrated by *NME* readers ultimately voting it the best single of the year. Anything that followed was bound to be a disappointment. Although a No.5 placing in October for "Homburg", Procol Harum's first release on Regal Zonophone, was possibly better than they had reason to expect, they would never regain the heights of acclaim to which "A Whiter Shade Of Pale" had taken them. And in the longer term there was a protracted sting in the tail when, in 2005, organist Matthew Fisher brought a law suit against Gary Brooker and the song's publishers, Onward Music, claiming a joint composing credit for himself and thereby an entitlement to a share of the royalties. A finding in Fisher's favour in 2006 was partly overturned on appeal in 2008, withdrawing his newly granted right to royalty payments on the grounds that he had been unduly tardy in submitting his original claim to the courts; but having won the right to appeal that judgement, he was vindicated by a second, definitive ruling in his favour in 2009 and the case was at last settled.

Seeking to move beyond hit singles to establish a name for themselves as well in the increasingly lucrative market for LPs, Deram next devised its 'Deramic Sound System' as an advertising ploy, much as its parent company Decca before it had used 'ffrr' to attest to the superior sound quality of their records[200], and cast round for a suitable project to launch it. Decca had on their books the Moody Blues, who had re-formed in 1966 – with Justin Hayward (guitar & vocals) and John Lodge (bass guitar) replacing Denny Laine and Clint Warwick respectively – but whose few new singles as yet had failed to take them back into the Top 30. By the spring of 1967, they had decided to turn their back on rhythm and blues in favour of writing and performing original compositions in an altogether different style, which attracted favourable responses from previously untapped audiences when they acquired a new agent and were booked to play what Hayward described as "festival and psychedelic club dates"[201] ranging from the West Country to France and Belgium. Hayward further attributed their change in musical direction to three specific factors:

> Firstly, there was an American album on Elektra, "The Zodiac" by
> Cosmic Sounds, an early concept album ... Secondly, we found that
> when the four of us – me, John [Lodge], Ray [Thomas] and Mike
> [Pinder] – sang together, we had a unique vocal sound. And thirdly,
> we bought a Mellotron. It was a turning point, really.[202]

The mellotron, fittingly, had been built and developed in Birmingham
in 1963 to an original American specification, by a company specialising in
tape recording technology called Bradmatic Ltd., for whom Mike Pinder had
once worked.[203] In the very simplest of terms, it extended the limited scope
of an existing instrument like the electronic organ by linking a keyboard to
a tape sampling device, thus offering the player a far wider range of artificial
orchestral and other sound effects. Early UK models, designed to be played
at home by niche-market enthusiasts as an alternative to the organ, were not
cheap, retailing for up to £3,000 each, and were not built to be portable:
Pinder bought the one for his intended use with the Moody Blues for £300
secondhand from the social club at Fort Dunlop (the iconic Birmingham tyre
factory), where no-one apparently had been able to play it. Building upon
the additional versatility the mellotron had now given them, the Moodies
then devised their own stage show, "a psychedelic story loosely based around
the idea of a day-in-the-life of one guy".[204] Their employment of this new
'instrument' on a regular basis, as part of their stage act, was, of course, in
total contrast to the way groups like the Beatles or the Rolling Stones initially
embraced it as a novelty, confining it to the environs of the recording studio;
but even so it was, according to Ray Thomas, "a right pig to travel with"[205],
being highly sensitive to atmospheric conditions and fluctuations in power
supply.

With their Decca contract soon to expire, the Moody Blues were
approached to contribute to a demonstration LP that would combine pop and
classical music as a showcase for the 'Deramic Sound System', in exchange
for which they would not be required to pay back the advances they had
received from the record company for their hitherto unsuccessful singles. It
was envisaged as a collaboration with conductor and musical director Peter
Knight and the 'London Festival Orchestra' (in reality, Decca's in-house
studio orchestra) but, as Ray Thomas explains, the Moody Blues soon turned
the project to their own advantage:

> [Decca] wanted us to play rock'n'roll and Peter Knight to do
> Dvorak to play to their reps to give them an idea of the scope of
> this new Deramic wall-to-wall sound. But we thought it would
> be very bitty, so we asked Peter to stick his neck out, because we
> wanted to record our stage act. We never actually worked with the

orchestra. All we did was ship each track to Peter, who wrote and scored the orchestral bridges.[206]

They even went so far as to insist on the lifting of constraints on recording time. John Lodge:

> … we went to Decca and said, can we have lockout time? – i.e.,
> we wanted the studio 24 hours a day so we could set up all our
> equipment and just record. In those days you could only record in
> strict morning sessions. They agreed and then we said instead of
> using the melodies from Dvorak, we would use our own songs.[207]

The resulting LP, produced by Tony Clarke, was *Days Of Future Passed*. It went so far beyond Decca's original expectations of a demonstration disc that the company was obliged, albeit uncertainly, to release it on the Deram label on 11th November 1967, in the hope of being able to recoup at least some of their costs. The original sleevenotes (by executive producer Hugh Mendl) show just how far the emphasis of the project had shifted from its conception to completion:

> In *Days Of Future Passed* the Moody Blues have at last done what
> many others have dreamed of and talked about: they have extended
> the range of pop music, and found the point where it becomes one
> with the world of the classics.
>
> Here, where emotion and creativity blend – where poetry,
> the beat group and the symphony orchestra feed on each other's
> inspiration – the Moodys have chosen to paint their picture of
> everyman's day, which takes nothing from the nostalgia for the past
> – and adds nothing to the probabilities of the future.
>
> For such a fusion of pop composition and classical writing,
> it seemed obvious that the *Deramic Sound System* would be the ideal
> recording technique. And here in DSS's deep, wide spectrum of
> 'all-round-sound' it has, we believe, become more possible than
> in any other way to be totally submerged – and hence totally
> committed to such a deeply emotional statement of the human
> condition today.[208]

The Deramic Sound System *per se* may have turned out to be a nine days' wonder of marketing but it has to be remembered that even as late as 1967 the overwhelming majority of records were still being engineered and sold in mono. Stereophonic sound for the masses remained some way off, so any effort to enhance the quality of mono reproduction, be it ever so marginal, potentially had popular appeal and, if nothing else, the admittedly light classical component of the album offered sonic enrichment to the discerning ear. For the Moody Blues, more importantly, it marked a watershed in their flagging career and assured their future as album makers rather than singles artists. More than *Sgt.Pepper* ever seriously attempted to be, *Days Of Future Passed* was a concept album, sustaining a clearly unifying theme from beginning to end, and as such represents a landmark in pop history. Sales were modest: ultimately, it only reached No.27 in the LP charts. But the blend of musical styles it represented, together with the group's inventive approach to their own instrumentation, firmly laid the foundations of a new genre –progressive rock. The album is best remembered today as the source, in its concluding track, of Justin Hayward's breath-taking love song "Nights In White Satin", so far removed in the sensitive arrangement here of its full version from the relative coarseness of the Moody Blues' first – and possibly still greatest – hit, "Go Now", as to beggar belief.

But it could all have been so different, if Hayward's original intentions had been realised; for his was one of a batch of applications forwarded to Mike Pinder by Eric Burdon in 1966, having been received by him in the preliminary stages of his auditions for membership of the New Animals. Had he been taken on by Burdon, his life in the spotlight would not only have been far less ordered but also far shorter. By 1967 the UK charts had little room for the New Animals and it would be the last year in which they would have any British Top 30 hits. Another change of record label (from Decca now to MGM), a new producer (in the person of Tom Wilson) and a new songwriting team (of Eric Burdon and John Weider) should all have boded well for establishing the group's desired credentials as the "English West Coast psychedelic band", but their first offering in May served only to highlight the credibility gap between Burdon's LSD-fired imagination and the strained loyalties of his British fans.

"When I Was Young" was brilliant and exciting, prominently featuring the pop debut of the electric violin on record (as played by Weider), but was a miss. They would have to wait until their next release in August, "Good Times", for a hit, yet even this was modest by comparison with former glories. Entering the Top 30 for 16th September at No.24, in the same week that the Move's "Flowers In The Rain" entered at No.18, it stalled – and peaked – for the next two weeks at No.21. Greatest interest was reserved to the last. "San Franciscan Nights" – Burdon's blinkered tribute to the hippie lifestyle, adorned by melodic acoustic guitar runs from Vic Briggs – was released in October, having already been a US No.9 hit (their highest there since "House Of The Rising Sun"), and reached No.11 in November. Deeper and deeper immersion in American counter-culture prompted the recording of two more singles with little or no resonance in the UK: "Monterey" (a hymn to the pop festival) and "Sky Pilot" (a lengthy anti-Vietnam War diatribe). Then, as noted by biographer Sean Egan: "In January 1968, the New Animals left Britain … They did not – except for gigs and promotional obligations

– come back."[209] And by the end of that year they had fallen into disarray and disbanded.

Where Burdon's wilful attempts to mould music and audiences to his own tastes ultimately failed, others who opted for a more subtle approach succeeded. On the less well-explored borders of pop and folk, for example, there was the potential at least for greater receptivity to new ideas and different styles of performance, and transatlantic influences were by no means shunned. Donovan was certainly one artist to take advantage of such opportunities, now that his contractual differences with Pye in the UK had been resolved, and 1967 brought him back into the limelight. After his belated British success with "Sunshine Superman", his next single release was "Mellow Yellow", which took him back to No.9 in March. Written "as a sing-along at private parties, nothing else, a throwaway"[210] and recorded in London the previous August (at a session where Paul McCartney can be heard boisterously joining in the chorus), it had already been a million-seller and No.2 hit in America at the tail-end of 1966, and was yet another of those few in-joke singles of dubious sentiment that somehow managed to get under the BBC censors' radar: "… what I really meant by the phrase 'Mellow Yellow' was that I was a laid-back kind of dude, smoking the safe little green herb. The electric banana in my song was a reference to the 'vibrators' which had become available through mail-order ads in the back pages of certain types of periodical."[211]

June then saw, at long last, the UK release of the LP *Sunshine Superman*; although unbeknown to British purchasers this was an amalgam of tracks compiled by Ashley Kozak from two LPs previously issued by Epic in America: *Sunshine Superman* and *Mellow Yellow* – seven (including the title track) from the former, five from the latter.[212] Nevertheless, the overall impact of its musical diversity remained stunning, a superb collection of songs all inspired in some way or other by events of particular significance in Donovan's own recent past and further enriched by a combination of Mickie Most at the top of his game as producer and John Cameron's lavish arrangements; and it came in a striking sleeve designed by Mick Taylor and Sheena McCall, the front cover bearing the outline of a sweeping capital S, populated by characters from the songs and from children's literature, set against a plain white ground.

"Legend Of A Girl Child Linda" (a contemporary nursery rhyme), "Celeste", "Young Girl Blues" (a forthright dramatisation of separation and solitude) and "Three Kingfishers" were all intended to illuminate diverse aspects of Donovan's ongoing unrequited yearning for Linda Lawrence. "The Observation" was the jazzy successor to *Fairytale*'s "Sunny Goodge Street". "Guinevere" was a romantic evocation of mediaevalism, while "Writer In

The Sun" and "Sand And Foam" recalled time spent abroad in Greece and Mexico respectively with Gypsy Dave and others. "Bert's Blues" was Donovan's homage to his personal guitar hero, Bert Jansch.

There remain two outstanding tracks, however. The first of these, "Season Of The Witch", was recorded before the event but was later interpreted by Donovan as prophetic of the drugs raid on his flat mounted by Detective Sgt. Pilcher: precisely enunciated over a backing of electric guitar, swirling organ and an over-amplified bass line (that Most had to force the engineers at CBS's Hollywood studios to record), it harbours a deep-seated sense of unease. The second – and finest of all – is "Hampstead Incident", a stylish piece of baroque to which John Cameron brought harpsichord and a string quartet for dramatic effect. Donovan termed it a "Gothic ballad"[213], a composition informed by a liberal mix of thoughts and emotions:

> I was standing by the Everyman cinema in Hampstead, in the
> soft misty rain, on mescalin; melancholic over the continued
> estrangement from Linda; philosophical comments on Zen and the
> everlasting 'now' of the teachings. These are the main inspirations.
> The musical form is from the work of Nina Simone and the chord
> progression of Davy Graham's seminal folk-blues, 'Anji'.[214]

It was, in my opinion, wrongly located as the second track on Side 2: it should have been held back to the very last as a fitting conclusion to the album, closing as it does with a final, rocking flourish on the harpsichord to leave the listener gasping for more. Nevertheless, the whole LP, for all the randomness of its re-ordering for UK consumption, remains for me unrivalled as a collection of the finest examples of Donovan's work. Given, after the long wait, that it only went to a disappointing No.25 in the LP charts, he may well have suffered, like the Kinks before him, from lukewarm promotion on his behalf by Pye; and again like them, his best efforts were swiftly undercut by the issue in the autumn of a cheap Marble Arch compilation, *Universal Soldier*, that spent more than twice as long in the charts and reached No.5. His next single, "There Is A Mountain", a blend in his own words of "Zen and Caribbean music"[215], seemed almost to be revisiting the good-time frivolity of "Mellow Yellow" but still brought him a Top 10 hit at No.8 in November – in the near company, amongst others, of "Autumn Almanac", "I Can See For Miles" and "San Franciscan Nights".

Donovan had thus taken full advantage of every opportunity in 1967 to reinvent himself, to the point of near-self-parody, pretentiously referring to his songs as 'sonnets' and to the influence he was exerting on the UK music scene from which he had been a lengthy absentee, claiming through his admittedly well-received concert appearances throughout the year as well as through his records to have now emerged as the foremost exponent of a "folk-classical-blues-pop-jazz-poetical-ethnic"[216] synthesis. The next steps he would take, in the auspicious company of the Beatles and other like-minded celebrities, would be on the road to enlightenment under the tutelage of the Maharishi Mahesh Yogi.

In fact, Donovan was not, of course, alone in pursuit of a fusion of musical styles and was, indeed, roundly trounced in this regard by the Incredible String Band with their second celebrated LP, *The 5000 Spirits Or The Layers Of The Onion*, a truly eclectic assemblage of inspired – but also inspirational – oddities. It was jointly created by Scottish folk musicians Robin Williamson and Mike Heron, in conjunction with up-and-coming American-born record producer Joe Boyd, whose other affiliations were with the London underground music scene in general and Pink Floyd in particular. In 1966, Boyd had also become the UK representative of Elektra Records and signed the band (then a trio, with banjoist Clive Palmer) on encountering them in Edinburgh, playing "completely original [songs] influenced by American folk and Scottish ballads, but full of flavours from the Balkans, ragtime, North Africa, music hall and William Blake".[217] After recording an eponymous first album with Boyd, the trio went their separate ways: while Palmer was content to say his farewells and hitch-hike off into the sunset to India and beyond, after spending four months away in Morocco Williamson returned to Scotland and was reunited with Heron, sharing a cottage with him on the edge of the Campsie Fells, to the north of Glasgow, where together they composed a batch of new songs.

With Boyd's assistance at Sound Techniques Studio in London, in the spring of 1967 they recorded thirteen of their songs to create *The 5000 Spirits*; the title, according to Williamson, alluding to "a symbol of consciousness. You know, you either think of it as layers and layers and layers of onion or thousands of voices."[218] Both band members were accomplished acoustic multi-instrumentalists, but to their own ensemble they added the peculiar skills of Williamson's girlfriend Licorice (*aka* Christina McKechnie) on finger cymbals and vocals, while Boyd brought in respected double bass player Danny Thompson, John 'Hoppy' Hopkins on piano and Soma (*aka* Nazir Jarazbhoy) on sitar and tamboura. What it lacked in sophistication – it sounded home-made – it more than made up for in vocal and lyrical dexterity.

The album was so off the wall that it almost totally bypassed any considerations of commerciality. It was, however, imbued with an obvious love of poetry and music for their own sake, combined with the positive nurturing of a sense of the absurd. In "Little Cloud", for example, Heron imagines a conversation with a juvenile cloud too happy to have yet acquired the skill of dispensing rain; and in "The Hedgehog's Song", he readily accepts, as if in Wonderland, the wise counsel of a hedgehog as to his inability to find true love:

Sitting one day by myself,
And I'm thinking, "What could be wrong?"
When this funny little hedgehog comes running up to me
And it starts up to sing me this song.
"Oh, you know all the words, and you sung all the notes,
But you never quite learned the song she sang.
I can tell by the sadness in your eyes
That you never quite learned the song."[219]

Williamson, for his part, tackles love from another direction, speculating in "First Girl I Loved" on the changes in relationships wrought by time: "And you're probably married now, kids and all/And you've turned into a grown-up female stranger"[220]; offers, in "Way Back In The 1960s", a teasing post-apocalyptic retrospective on the decade; and in "Blues For The Muse", he definitively nails the seductive allure of making music:

Well, she sings like the seashore,
Tonight I'm going to ride on your seesaw.
I will call up the angels if they have a little word to say,
And I think I'll try cloud-walking.
It's just my face you see here talking,
And it's just the guitar singing
And I have to let her have her way.[221]

Brought to market in July in a multi-coloured psychedelic sleeve designed by Simon & Marijke, it was an alternative masterpiece. Although not destined for huge sales here (like *Sunshine Superman*, it only made No.25), it exhibited a mystical affinity with other disparate elements of the British folk revival and its reputation slowly spread; whilst astonishingly in America, where Jac Holzman, Elektra's founder, intuitively knew it would appeal to young hippies, it was the Incredible String Band's entry pass to the 1967 Newport Folk Festival.

Moving in the opposite direction, the Elektra label also brought to Britain from the USA the work of Washington-born singer/songwriter Tim Buckley, on whom, for want of airplay, you could, like me, take a punt in response to minimal advertising in the *NME*. Now posthumously revered for his later more improvisational works, his earliest albums tend to be overlooked; but *Tim Buckley* (available here from December 1966) and its successor a year later, *Goodbye And Hello*, were both productions of high quality, captivating and melodic collections of intelligent songs, exquisitely arranged and beautifully sung, to be listened to intently in a darkened room. From the latter comes the paradoxical "Pleasant Street", the ultimate song of dislocation:

You don't remember what to say
You don't remember what to do

You don't remember where to go
You don't remember what to choose
You wheel, you steal, you feel, you kneel down.[222]

As do the faltering explorations of doomed relationships such as "Hallucinations", "I Never Asked To Be Your Mountain" and "Phantasmagoria In
Two". In the title track, "Goodbye And Hello", that runs to more than eight
minutes long, Buckley blends folk, rock and opera in an almost Brechtian
denunciation of contemporary America:

The vaudeville generals cavort on the stage
And shatter their audience with submachine guns
And Freedom and Violence the acrobat clowns
Do a balancing act on the graves of our sons
While the tapdancing Emperor sings "War is peace"
And Love the magician disappears in the fun
And I wave goodbye to murder
And smile hello to the rain.[223]

After which the hysteria is dissipated by the album's last track, "Morn-
ing-Glory", in which Buckley himself stands exposed to the vagaries of criticism, condemning those who refuse to engage with him:

I lit my purest candle close to my
Window, hoping it would catch the eye
Of any vagabond who passed it by,
And I waited in my fleeting house.[224]

Although Buckley was never widely known or appreciated here, such a
consummate piece of work as *Goodbye And Hello* was in its day deserving of
a far wider audience and certainly should have been, with the right exposure,
a worthy chart contender.

A clear distinction was thus emerging between the popularity and the
quality of music, with more and more hits sadly reverting to becoming a
measure of the former rather than the latter, as in the pre-Beatles era. In
the wake of that trend, several of the acts to which I have drawn attention
in earlier chapters were now members of an unrewarding underclass. At the
end of the day, Dave Dee, Dozy, Beaky, Mick and Tich were no more than
hired hands of the Howard and Blaikley hit factory, with "Zabadak!" their
crowning glory at No.2 in November after earlier successes with "Touch Me,
Touch Me" (No.18 in April) and "Okay!" (No.5 in July). The Troggs, who
had originally promised so much more, could only offer "Give It To Me"
(No.15 in March) and "Night Of The Long Grass" (No.21 in June) before
plumbing new depths with "Love Is All Around" (No.4 in November, the

so-called 'highlight' of their dismal autumn LP *Cellophane*). The Tremeloes veered from good-time with "Here Comes My Baby" (No.4 in March) to the tear-jerking harmonies of "Silence Is Golden" (No.1, as mentioned earlier, from May into June) and back again to an approximation of good-time with "Even The Bad Times Are Good" (No.5 from August into September), only to fall at the last hurdle with "Be Mine" (No.29 in November). Herman's Hermits took "There's A Kind Of Hush (All Over The World)" to No.6 in March ... and so the mostly dreary catalogue went on.

How much more difficult, then, for the female voice to make itself heard. You might strike lucky with a film theme if it caught the public's imagination; as was the case for Judith Durham and the Seekers with "Georgy Girl" (at No.8 in March), or Nancy Sinatra with "You Only Live Twice" (No.15 in August). Alternatively, like Nancy again, you might be fortunate enough to have an indulgent father to invite you to record with him – hence the stultifying April No.1 for Frank and Nancy Sinatra with "Somethin' Stupid". But in any review of 1967, Sandie Shaw can hardly escape being credited as the year's most acclaimed female artist for the achievement alone of winning the Eurovision Song Contest with "Puppet On A String", her No.1 hit for four weeks in late April and early May. It has, however, been a burden to her for most of the rest of her life, to which she has only relatively recently become reconciled, re-recording it in 2007 with the assistance of Howard Jones as a much slower electro-synth ballad, "Puppet (No Strings)"[225], and conceding in a 2012 radio interview that the original song "was OK, it was just the bloody arrangement".[226]

In her autobiography, she recounts how, as a nineteen-year-old, her initial resistance to taking part was unforgivingly ground down by her ruthless manager Eve Taylor:

> "This will really help your career. You'll get a TV series. You can't go on making records for ever."
>
> "Why not? There's nothing else I want to do – anyway I'm good at it," I slammed back.
>
> "But you've got to show you have *real* talent," she thumped. Then her killer hook, "Anyone can make hit records," (she must be joking), "but you have to be an ALL ROUND ENTERTAINER!"[227]

Even as she reluctantly submitted to the song selection process on prime-time Saturday night TV (as featured on *The Rolf Harris Show*), she harboured a specifically feminist grudge against the last of the six potential UK entries, Phil Coulter & Bill Martin's "Puppet On A String":

> I hated it from the very first oompah to the final bang on the big bass drum.

Even in those days, before the phrase 'chauvinist pig' had been coined, I was instinctively repelled by its sexist drivel and cuckoo-clock tune. The writers were men, the panel of judges were men, all white faced and stiff collared. Was this how they wanted women to behave – like stupid puppets? I dismissed the song as a joke. It had no chance of being selected, it was so awful.[228]

With her expectations completely overturned by the viewers' votes in its favour, in the end she "determined philosophically to lie back, grit my teeth, close my eyes and think of le Royaume-Uni".[229] On the night of the contest itself in Vienna, as she prepared to go on stage, she was weighed down "by the heavy feeling that if I lost, no one would ever speak to me again" but, as she put on her detested "pink chiffon sequined dress", she decided she "would win like no one had ever won before", and was subsequently suit-ably amazed at her reception: "… I was staggered at the number of points I received. I had so many they ran off the scoreboard."[230] Nevertheless, as she reflected later, she felt her victory to be decidedly bitter-sweet:

I have since seen a film of my performance. I seem so full of youthful confidence and joy, I positively shine. It looks like I must have known I had something special that no number of stupid songs or silly frocks could disguise. It was all mine and nobody could take it away from me. I can also see a hint of something else – inside I was crushed by the hard facts of life I was learning at such a delicate age.[231]

In an all too obvious piece of manipulation, Sandie recorded another Coulter & Martin song, "Tonight In Tokyo", as the follow-up but it was a sorry misjudgement, for no-one much wanted to buy into its stereotypical Oriental kitsch and its feeble premise of two lovers separated by thousands of miles. Compared to the patriotic fervour dancing attendance on "Puppet On A String", it flopped spectacularly, scraping a high spot of No.25 on entry before dropping out of the charts and re-entering just once more, two weeks later, at No.29. Her fortunes were only partially restored by falling back on her old partnership with Chris Andrews, when "You've Not Changed" made a sluggish climb to No.14 in mid-November.

The charts were indifferent to other big-hitters as well, it seemed. Cilla Black surfaced only once, at the end of June, with "What Good Am I", peaking at No.18, and the follow-up, "I Only Live To Love You", released in time for the Christmas market, failed to chart. For much of the first half of 1967, she continued to appear in revue with Frankie Howerd but was also given a part in the offbeat comedy film *Work Is A Four-Letter Word* (starring David Warner and directed by Peter Hall), thus necessitating regular trips from London to Birmingham for shooting on location. Trying her best to take it in her stride, she was nevertheless overcome with embarrassment in character:

> I had to be made up to look like a plain Jane for that part, and I felt very self-conscious and uncomfortable. Being on stage and looking fabulous I loved, but this was different. Also, I've never liked people gawping at me, but I had to get used to all the technicians staring at me when we were on location. In the film studio there was a crew of ninety.[232]

Probably the most devastated of all Brian Epstein's artists on receiving the news of his death in August, one of his last acts on her behalf had been to conclude negotiations with the BBC over a showcase television series for her, although she had baulked at the suggestion that it should feature her as Sandie Shaw's successor in the selection of 1968's Song for Europe. After Epstein's death, she turned to her husband Bobby Willis to be her personal manager and together they prepared the ground for "the beginning of a new phase in my professional life … as an all-round television entertainer".[233]

Dusty Springfield had already, of course, crossed that threshold into a television show of her own and a year on from Series 1, she would return in August as host and star of Series 2 (which she began recording in June). Otherwise, she lived a nomadic existence, her UK performing commitments in concert and now in cabaret too (with a season in May at London's Talk of the Town) interspersed with trips to America, Japan and Australia. Although still retaining the loyalty of her British fans to the extent of once more topping the *NME* poll as Best International Female Singer of the year, by now this was generous for she was by no means a constant presence in the Top 30. Of her three single releases (in February, May and September), only the first two were hits, neither of them made the Top 10 and together they gave her a minimal chart presence of nine weeks. Both "I'll Try Anything" and "Give Me Time" reached No.17, in March and June respectively, whereas "What's It Gonna Be?" was a complete flop. (Ironically, one of her best-known recordings of this period, Bacharach & David's "The Look Of Love" – written for the original spoof James Bond film *Casino Royale* – was only issued here as a B-side, coupled with "Give Me Time": as an A-side in America, it reached No.22 in the *Billboard* Top 40.) In a September interview with Penny Valentine, she openly acknowledged that she had reached a cross-roads in her career:

> What upsets me most at the moment in this business is that I'm moving into a cabaret bag. It's nice, but the cabaret league isn't for me. What direction can I go in? I always wanted to be an actress but it's pretty unlucrative unless you can break into films. I'm just groping and wandering. All I know is that I have a distinctive voice

I don't particularly like listening to.[234]

Dusty lost her crown in the 1967 polls as Best UK Female Singer to Lulu, by a mere 421 votes and on the strength of a marginally stronger chart presence of fifteen weeks. Lulu's singing career was in the process of being revitalised by her new producer Mickie Most but he remained steadfastly unimpressed by her desire to record a theme song for *To Sir, With Love* and gave it scant attention, relegating it in Britain to the B-side of "The Boat That I Row", composed by Neil Diamond and her first single for the Columbia label. When the film had its US premiere in June, Lulu's theme song was released in America as an A-side and eventually spent five weeks at No.1, selling more than two million copies and turning her there overnight into a celebrity much in demand on TV chatshows. By comparison, back home "The Boat That I Row" reached No.6 for two weeks (and Lulu would later be bitterly disappointed to find that the film aroused little interest at its London premiere in September). Her follow-up, "Let's Pretend", went to No.12 in July, but by November precious few could muster interest in the desperate miss that was "Love Loves To Love Love". She too therefore found herself being steered firmly in the direction of television by manager Marian Massey, as a means of alleviating the constant "struggle to find the right songs and to stay in the charts"[235] in the face of changing musical tastes; although her initial break was not as a singer but more of a 'straight' foil to comedian Ray Fell and impressionist Mike Yarwood in the BBC's *Three Of A Kind*.[236]

Eurovision and *NME* polls notwithstanding, the consistently strongest female performer of the year was Petula Clark, racking up a total of twenty-one weeks in the charts. This was all the more remarkable a tally considering that she was a non-UK resident and had spent more than three months in Hollywood, filming her part in the musical film *Finian's Rainbow* (directed by Francis Ford Coppola), in which she starred with Fred Astaire and Tommy Steele. She had an almost instantaneous hit in February with "This Is My Song", which entered the Top 30 at No.3 and next week was No.1, and even today it remains one of the songs for which she is most renowned. When it was first pitched to her, however, she was less than convinced that it would be right for her; certainly not for an English-speaking market, because of the outdated phrasing of the lyric. It had been composed by Charlie Chaplin as the theme song to the last film he wrote and directed, *A Countess From Hong Kong*, starring Marlon Brando and Sophia Loren, and he was determined that Petula should record it. Her husband Claude Wolff commissioned more modern rewritten lyrics for both English and French consumption but when Chaplin found out, he insisted that the song remain as he had written it; backing this up with a threat to Warner Brothers that without the song in its original form, he would withhold the film from distribution.

Petula, still dubious of its lyrical content in English but amenable to the melody, played for time by recording alternative versions in French and German. Her first public performance of it in English came virtually by default, when she was asked to include a new song for airing on the US TV show *Hollywood Palace* and was taken aback by the enthusiastic response of the studio audience. Hence she was finally persuaded to record it, in the form in which Chaplin had written it, in English, and it became a world-wide best-seller; fighting off simultaneous competition in Britain from Harry Secombe (whose rival version extraordinarily reached No.2 in April).

For all her earlier disagreements with Tony Hatch and Jackie Trent over their relationship, Petula was concerned that she should not be seen as disloyal to them by opting to record Chaplin's song, so in the spring of 1967 they were commissioned by Claude to write a more upbeat follow-up for her. [237] They came up with "Don't Sleep In The Subway", much more in keeping with the idiom to which Petula had grown accustomed since "Downtown", based on the theme of reconciliation after a lovers' tiff. With chart entry on 3rd June, it eventually climbed to No.11 on 8th July, the unlikeliest of meat in a sandwich between "Here Comes The Nice" above it and "Strange Brew" below. After a season in Las Vegas at Caesar's Palace, Petula returned to London in November, to appear in a new TV series of *This Is Petula Clark*, and capitalised on the opportunity to record again in England – another Hatch & Trent song, "The Other Man's Grass (Is Always Greener)", being her next single. In the charts for the last two weeks of December onwards, it would peak at No.17 the following January.

Historically, 1967 has left us a strange legacy, the demise of old-fashioned values for their own sake juxtaposed with the emergence of new environ-mental and technological preoccupations. That passing of the old order was signified in a variety of ways. On 4th January, for example, Donald Campbell was killed on Coniston Water in his jet-powered boat *Bluebird*, attempting to break the world speed record on water. A fortnight later, the *Boys' Own Paper*, the magazine traditionally priding itself on its diet of manly adventure tales, announced it was closing down after eighty five years of publication. And on 7th July, in a public ceremony at Greenwich the Queen knighted Sir Francis Chichester in honour of his solo circumnavigation of the globe, dubbing him with the self-same sword used by Elizabeth I to knight Sir Francis Drake.

Other links with the swiftly receding past were broken by the deaths of J. Robert Oppenheimer, the American scientist both feted and reviled as director of the Manhattan Project in World War II to create and deploy the first atomic bomb; Siegfried Sassoon, the famous First World War poet and author; Clement Attlee, who succeeded Winston Churchill as Prime Minister in 1945 and whose post-war Labour administration established the Welfare State; and Pu-yi, the last Emperor of China who abdicated in 1924 and died in Beijing as a 'rehabilitated' commoner. Equally notable was the action taken by Bolivian forces on 9th October to preclude further upheaval in Latin America, when they tracked down and killed Ernesto 'Che' Guevara, the Cuban revolutionary who thereafter acquired untarnished iconic status around the world as a left-wing martyr and whose image became synonymous with protests against all manner of perceived wrongdoings.

On 19th March, the oil tanker *Torrey Canyon* ran aground off Land's End and broke in two, prompting urgent government action to contain what contemporary reports described as "the greatest peacetime threat to Britain".[238] The resultant spillage from the wreck's cargo of 100,000 tons of oil, estimated to have polluted at least 100 miles of the Cornish coastline, was dealt with in spectacular fashion by a bombing raid on 30th March, ordered by Prime Minister Harold Wilson "as it rapidly became clear bombing and setting fire to the oil was the only way to halt its spread":

> Sea Vixens, Buccaneers and Hunters dropped 48 incendiary bombs and 1,200 gallons of napalm on what remains of the 61,263-ton tanker … After he returned from watching the bombing, Air Vice-Marshal John Lapsley said today: "We are satisfied beyond reasonable doubt that the source of the oil on the ship is now destroyed." Divers will check the wreck over tomorrow to make sure no more oil is trapped in its tanks.[239]

(Two days before the RAF flew in, the *Daily Express* published an uncharacteristically satirical cartoon by its resident artist Carl Giles, showing hordes of sightseeing donkeys disembarking from a 'Happy Tours Unlimited' coach – showing as its destinations 'Aberfan and Cornish Coast' – to gawp at the oil spills coming on shore. On the cliff top stands a telescope, with a sign offering 'Grand view of the oil 2/6d'.) More benignly, a major advance in aeronautics was heralded on 11th December with the roll-out at Toulouse of Concorde 001, the prototype of the Anglo-French supersonic airliner.

For those willing on the progress of the space race, however – not least US President Johnson and USSR President Brezhnev for their own respective political advantages – 1967 brought disastrous setbacks. The continuation of American manned space missions was abruptly halted on 27th January by an uncontrolled fire that engulfed the Apollo 1 spacecraft during pre-launch testing at Cape Canaveral, instantly killing its crew of three astronauts: Gus Grissom, Ed White and Roger Chaffee. It was the grimmest of conclusions to a chapter of accidents about which flight commander Grissom had been complaining vociferously for months, as NASA and manufacturers North American Aviation struggled to eradicate fault after fault with Apollo's initial construction.

On the day in question, with Apollo 1 (still designated technically as

Spacecraft 012) mounted on a Saturn 1B rocket and now located on the launch pad, various tests had been scheduled:

> One test considered essential for a thorough review of the ship's operating systems involved pressurising the unmanned ship with 100 percent oxygen. When the test had been completed to everyone's satisfaction, a final test would be run with the three-man crew aboard the craft, suited up and with all electrical and communications live. Under the pressure of time, however, NASA decided to skip the unmanned test and go directly to the "full dress rehearsal" with 100 percent oxygen, the crew in position, and the spacecraft hatch sealed just as tightly as it would be for a launch.[240]

Critical to maintaining this pressurisation was the construction of the entry and exit hatch, that had been re-engineered after the failure of the hatch on an earlier Mercury capsule, piloted by Grissom, had almost led to his drowning on splashdown:

> The command module's side hatch was one of the inevitable design compromises. It was a two-piece affair, with an outer hatch and an inner hatch that opened inward, into the cabin ... even under the best conditions it was very difficult to open. The inner hatch was a heavy, cumbersome metal plate secured by a set of bolts. The man in the centre couch had to reach back over his head, undo the bolts using a special tool, and then lower it out of the way.[241]

It had been calculated that it would normally take the astronauts somewhere between ninety seconds and two minutes to open it.

With the crew aboard and strapped in horizontally on their couches, in their spacesuits as if ready for lift-off, the pressurisation test proceeded, the capsule being flooded with pure oxygen which was then raised to a pressure of 16.7 pounds per square inch, two pounds higher than normal atmospheric pressure. Under these conditions, the astronauts were immersed for more than five hours in a highly inflammable and volatile gas, which was then ignited without warning by a spark arcing off a wire with worn insulation beneath Grissom's couch. All three made futile attempts to go through their emergency drills, Grissom even managing to call out to ground control "I've got a fire in the cockpit!", but within less than nine seconds they were dead, asphyxiated by the fireball that had overwhelmed them.

The savage irony of this tragedy was that it occurred on the very day when President Johnson and the Soviet Ambassador to the United States, Anatoly Dobrynin, met in the White House, in the midst of the Cold War, to put their signatures to a symbolic tripartite treaty "signed simultaneously in Washington, London, and Moscow and still in effect today [outlawing] the militarisation of space".[242] The occasion, witnessed by a delegation of astronauts that included Neil Armstrong and Jim Lovell, understandably gave the President an ideal opportunity to wax lyrical about America's progress towards a moon landing; but that evening's diplomatic reception in honour of the agreement, hosted by Vice President Hubert Humphrey, was disrupted by the arrival of news of the disaster. A board of inquiry, publishing its findings in April in a report that ran to well over 3,000 pages, although not conclusive, identified some ten possible sources of faulty electrical wiring that might have started the fire inside the capsule; with blame squarely placed on the long-standing lack of attention to detail amounting to negligence on the parts of both NASA and North American Aviation. In the aftermath of redesigning and rebuilding the Apollo spacecraft to ever-more exacting spec-ifications, it would take until October 1968 before America would resume its programme of manned spaceflights.

Even at the very moment of putting his signature to the space treaty, Dobrynin had been quietly confident that in any event Russia would be stealing a march on America by the end of April with a spectacular Soyuz mission. This had been planned to include the rendezvous and docking of two Russian spacecraft, after which cosmonauts would exchange places via a spacewalk and pilot each other's capsule back to Earth. Like Apollo, the Soyuz testing programme was beset with design faults and critical failures of equipment: even as close to the intended April launch date as 7th February, an unmanned Soyuz craft sent up into orbit developed serious problems with its power supply and thruster engines. Nevertheless, on 23rd April, Soyuz 1 was launched from Russia's Baikonur cosmodrome, piloted by Vladimir Komarov, veteran of the 1964 three-man Voskhod spaceflight; with the intention that next day he would be joined in orbit by the three-man crew of Soyuz 2.

Unluckily for Komarov, who had had a premonition that he might not survive his mission, he was confronted with major difficulties as soon as he had completed his first orbit of Earth. Whereas Apollo's systems were battery-powered, once launched Soyuz – in a visionary piece of engineering – was supposed to collect energy from the sun by deploying a huge pair of solar panels. One opened, the other jammed shut and Komarov was unable to rectify the fault, leaving his craft seriously starved of electricity. Then radio communications with the ground failed, causing him to switch to a back-up. After that, he found that Soyuz 1 was not automatically being held in stable flight and took over manual control, yet still could not stop it from pitching, tossing and tumbling through space. In the face of such calamity, the launch of Soyuz 2 was cancelled, Komarov was ordered to attempt re-entry on his seventeenth orbit; and, in a rare show of Soviet compassion, his wife was brought urgently to mission control for them to say their farewells to each other. Suffering all the while from terrible motion sickness, Komarov never-theless found the strength to guide his erratic spacecraft into the correct alignment for re-entry to the Earth's atmosphere. This achieved against all the odds, he was doomed in the final moments of his descent to Earth, when both the main and reserve braking parachutes failed to open. Crash-landing uncontrollably at four hundred miles per hour, Soyuz's malfunctioning retro-rockets exploded on impact, instantly killing the heroic Komarov and thus forcing the Russians too to impose an extended moratorium on manned spaceflights.

The tragic loss of Apollo 1 did not deter American efforts to continue launching an increasingly sophisticated series of unmanned satellites and probes to carry out photographic and geological surveys of the Moon. Launched in February and May respectively, Lunar Orbiters 3 and 4 between them would spend a total of 426 days mapping the Moon in the quest for possible landing sites; while between April and November, three out of four Surveyor probes launched were successfully landed at different locations on the Moon's surface, transmitting a huge amount of data and a staggering combined total of 55,000 photographs back to Earth. The most significant breakthrough of all, however, came on 9th November – only three days after the launch of Surveyor 6 – with the successful launch of Apollo 4, the first unmanned test flight of a Saturn V rocket, constructed to Wernher von Braun's latest design and carrying a prototype Command and Service Module into orbit, from which an automated camera then took over 700 photographs of Earth. Much-needed public and political confidence in NASA's ability to carry the Apollo programme forward was restored at last.

Meanwhile the Vietnam War careered on its merciless way through a third year, fuelling the frustration of war correspondents like John Laurence:

> There was no end in sight; a stalemate seemed more likely. Yet, day after day, TV news reports told a familiar story: allied troops were engaging enemy forces everywhere they could find them, were grinding them down relentlessly, bombing them senseless in the North, killing them by the thousands in the South – *just look at that body count!* – measuring progress, like the establishment, by the number of people killed. The official organs of the US government claimed that the allied war effort was rooting out the V[iet] C[ong] infrastructure, pacifying more and more villages, helping to train more aggressive South Vietnamese fighting forces, and building more democratic institutions of government. [Keith] Kay [Laurence's cameraman] and I didn't believe it. We thought what was happening on the battlefields of Vietnam was more urgent, more dramatic, more terrible than the news reports being broadcast on American television. We wanted to capture on film and sound the *horror* of the war.[243]

In April, President Johnson's National Security Adviser, Walt Whitman Rostow, had not only advocated stepping up the bombing campaign to deny the Ho Chi Minh Trail to the Viet Cong but also going further on the offensive by attacking and capturing the North Vietnamese city of Vinh, which could then be used as a bargaining tool: "We could have taken it by an amphibious attack from the coast. Then we'd tell Ho Chi Minh, 'Get the hell out of Cambodia and South Vietnam or we're going to stay in Vinh until you do'."[244]

But as on similar occasions in the past, the President rejected such blatantly hawkish advice, for fear of further disturbing the perilously delicate balance of interests between the world's superpowers:

> He felt the rules of engagement should remain: that no Americans should cross the South Vietnamese border on the ground. He and Secretary of State Rusk were much influenced by the entrance of the Chinese into the Korean War. They were afraid that sending ground troops into North Vietnam or Laos would draw China directly into the war … Johnson figured he was up against two nuclear powers – China and the Soviet Union. He said over and over again that the alternative to what he was doing was a larger war and quite possibly a nuclear war. He felt for America and the human race he had no right to start such a war and that accounted for his rules of engagement being what they were.[245]

So the war of attrition continued, prolonging in effect a military stale-mate that to John Laurence grew ever more reminiscent of the First World War. Reporting in the autumn from a US Marine stronghold on the northern border of South Vietnam, he noted solemnly that on "September 25, Con Thien was struck by twelve hundred rounds of incoming fire. There had been nothing like it in the war. It *was* like Verdun."[246] And as the casualties mounted, and the wounded survivors were repatriated, back home in the United States feelings about the war began to intensify and polarise:

> The anti-war demonstrations grew in 1967 as the wounded veterans came home in sizeable, highly visible numbers, often leading the demonstrations … But, duty done, the veterans increasingly found themselves alienated, arousing guilt among their elders and anger among their own generation who often shunned them, and damned them, as killers. There was never … any 'homecoming', no official welcome back as in other wars, no special thankfulness beyond family and friends, no great understanding that a war unwon exacted the same blood as a victory. There was no sense, no dignity in their sacrifice, so many came to feel.[247]

The most highly organised of the protests forged a new, counter-intuitive coalition between the anti-war and civil rights movements, a strange alliance of "student and teacher associations, women's groups, war veterans, movie stars, major authors and intellectuals, civil rights pacifists and black militants, family doctors and anarchists".[248] Holding firm to his refusal to present himself for military service, Casius Clay (*aka* Muhammad Ali) was stripped of his heavyweight championship title in January. Amongst other prominent speakers drawn to the cause was Martin Luther King, who addressed a gathering of no less than 400,000 people in New York on 15th April, at the end of a march from Central Park to the United Nations building; whilst on the same day, his wife Coretta led a march of 100,000 in San Francisco. On 21st October, another 100,000 took part in a demonstration at the Lincoln Memorial in Washington, where they were addressed by, amongst others, Dr. Benjamin Spock, well-respected guru of baby rearing. This was followed by a further rally and night-long vigil at the Pentagon, in the course of which many arrests were made (including that of author Norman Mailer), yet undeterred protesters symbolically placed flowers for peace in the rifle barrels of troops guarding the building. The week before, Joan Baez had been arrested in California for her part in demonstrations against the draft at the Oaklands military induction centre.

Tensions probably ran at their highest, however, in race riots in Detroit in the summer, when on 23rd July:

> ... police raided an after-hours social club where about eighty people were celebrating the return of two servicemen from Vietnam. The raid triggered a week of looting and burning that destroyed thirteen hundred buildings and left five thousand homeless. The resultant crackdown, by five thousand National Guardsmen and an almost equal number of army paratroopers, resulted in forty-three deaths and more than seven thousand arrests.[249]

Playing in Detroit soon afterwards, on 15th August, Jimi Hendrix was moved to make a direct appeal for mutual racial tolerance:

> There is no such thing as a colour problem. It is a weapon for the negative forces who are trying to destroy the country. They make black and white fight each other so they can take over at each end. That is what the establishment is waiting for. They let you fight, they let you go out into the streets and riot. But they'll still put you in jail.[250]

And subsequently he would embody an emotive artistic response to the riots in his composition "House Burning Down":

> Well, someone stepped from the crowd, he was nineteen miles high.

He shouts, "We're tired and disgusted so we paint red through the sky."
I say, "The truth is straight ahead, so don't burn yourself instead.
Try to learn instead of burn, hear what I say." [251]

While the Johnson administration outwardly showed no sign of appeasing their multitude of critics, in September the President did make secret overtures to the North Vietnamese regime in Hanoi, offering peace talks in return for the cessation of US bombing and the Viet Cong's agreement to draw up a timetable for negotiations, which he then publicly disclosed in a speech he delivered in San Antonio, Texas. The North Vietnamese, however, were already well advanced in their plans for a major offensive against the South in the New Year and the US offer was rejected out of hand. Despairing of ever being able to win the war despite his years of support for and investment in advanced military technology, and shamed by press reports of the scale of destruction now being visited on the civilian population, Robert McNamara, much-vilified US Secretary of State for Defence, was finally moved to tender his resignation in November and he would step down the following March.

This is not to say, of course, that America had the monopoly on war. 1967 will also be remembered for the bloody civil war in Nigeria, following the declaration in May of the breakaway state of Biafra in the south-eastern corner of the country; and for the so-called 'Six-Day War' in June in the Middle East, when Israel launched pre-emptive strikes against its Arab neighbours of Egypt, Jordan and Syria, occupying significant tracts of new territory by the time a ceasefire took effect. But the conscience of the Western world could not fail to be most deeply troubled by the inescapable statistics of Vietnam, a war apparently without end, in a year that saw US troop levels rise by over 100,000 to 486,000 and US fatal military casualties rise by over 5,000 to 11,363. "Is it any wonder," mused Donovan, "a generation sang of Peace and Love?" [252]

NOTES

1   G. Clark/J. McGuinn/D. Crosby, © 1966 by Essex Music.

2   The Monterey Pop Festival was funded by a "core group of five artists and producers – Lou Adler, the Mamas and the Papas, Terry Melcher, Johnny Rivers, and Simon and Garfunkel [who] each put up ten thousand dollars to finance the idea". [See Pete Fornatale, "Back to the Garden: The Story of Woodstock" (Touchstone, 2009), p.70.]

3   Derek Taylor, op. cit., pp.13-14. Taylor's naïve wonderment is eerily reminiscent of Wordsworth's intellectual rapture in the face of the French Revolution: "Bliss was it in that dawn to be alive,/But to be young was very heaven …" [from the 1805 text of *The Prelude*, Bk. X, lines 693-694].

4   Rob Young, op. cit., p.366.

5   Mick Houghton, op. cit., p.201.

6   Rob Young, op. cit., p.350.

7   See Ian MacDonald, op. cit., pp.191-192.

8   Lennon/McCartney, © 1967 by Northern Songs.

9   Quoted in Barry Miles, op. cit., p.308.

10   Ian MacDonald, op. cit., p.196.

11   Lennon/McCartney, © 1967 by Northern Songs.

12   In America, where the sales of either side were reckoned separately on the *Billboard* chart, "Penny Lane" did reach No.1, whereas "Strawberry Fields Forever" only reached No.8.

13   Quoted in Barry Miles, op. cit., pp.303-304.

14   "Sgt. Pepper's Lonely Hearts Club Band", composed by Lennon/McCartney, © 1967 by Northern Songs.

15   Quoted in "The Beatles Anthology" (Cassell, 2000), p.241.

16   George Martin with William Pearson, op. cit., pp.64-65.

17   It was, inevitably, the source of further conflict with EMI, for fear of actions of breach of copyright over the unauthorised use of photographic images, and its realisation was delayed by company chairman Sir Joseph Lockwood insisting that Brian Epstein obtain prior consent from those still alive (or from the executors of those deceased) to the publication of their pictures. Lockwood personally vetoed the inclusion of Mahatma Gandhi, as being seen potentially as disrespectful and thus prejudicial to EMI's future trade with India.

18   It was specially painted by fairground artist Joseph Ephgrave. [See Brian Southall, "Drive My Car: 100 Objects That Made The Beatles **The Beatles**" (SevenOaks, 2013), pp.212-213.]

19   Simon & Marijke had originally come up with their own artistic representation of the Beatles for the centre of the gatefold, which was rejected in favour of Michael Cooper's photograph, but they did famously go on to design the psychedelic sleeve of the Incredible String Band's *The 5000 Spirits Or The Layers Of The Onion.*

20   Lennon/McCartney, © 1967 by Northern Songs.

21   George Martin with William Pearson, op. cit., p.151. On its UK release, it also made it into the Top 30 singles' chart, peaking at No.21 in the week ending 10th June.

22   Quoted in Barry Miles, op. cit., p.347. It was not quite the instantaneous response McCartney imagined, however, for Hendrix had had access for several days to an advance copy of the LP given to his manager, Chas Chandler.

23   In the composite *Record Retailer* chart for 19th July, the Young Idea are credited with a highest position of No.10 and Joe Brown a No.32 placing.

24   Quoted in Barry Miles, op. cit., p.320.

25   Lennon/McCartney, © 1967 by Northern Songs.

26   Ian MacDonald, op. cit., p.215.

27   George Martin with William Pearson, op. cit., p.129.

28   Harrison, © 1967 by Northern Songs. It was eventually used a year later, on the *Yellow Submarine* soundtrack.

29   Quoted in Barry Miles, op. cit., p.332. It was immediately preceded, at John's suggestion, by the sound of a whistle at a pitch beyond the reach of human hearing, specifically for the entertainment of any dog listening.

30   From letter of 23rd May 1967 from Frank Gillard to Sir Joseph Lockwood, reproduced in facsimile as an accompanying document to Kevin Howlett, "The Beatles: The BBC Archives 1962-1970" (BBC, 2013).

31   Barry Miles, op. cit., p.352.

32   From letter of 28th February 1967 from David Filkin (BBC) to Brian Epstein, reproduced in Kevin Howlett, op. cit., p.221.

33   Quoted in "The Beatles Anthology" (Cassell, 2000), p.257.

34   George Martin with William Pearson, op. cit., p.159.

35   Ian MacDonald, op. cit., p.230.

36   Quoted in "The Beatles Anthology" (Cassell, 2000), p.259.

37   Ibid.

38   Quoted in "The Beatles Anthology" (Cassell, 2000), p.264.

39   Tony Barrow, op. cit., p.238.

40   Ibid.

41   George Martin, quoted in "The Beatles Anthology" (Cassell, 2000), p.268.

42   Neil Aspinall, quoted in Peter Doggett, "You Never Give Me Your Money: The Battle For The Soul Of The Beatles" (Bodley Head, 2009), p.30.

43   Quoted in "The Beatles Anthology" (Cassell, 2000), p.272.

44   Ibid.

45   Quoted in "The Beatles Anthology" (Cassell, 2000), p.273.

46   Even so, it still left further work to do on the sequence, because, as Paul said, "I just ad-libbed the whole thing", meaning that: "Later, when we came to try to edit it all, it was very difficult because I hadn't sung it to synch." (Quoted in Barry Miles, op. cit., p.365.)

47   Barry Miles, op. cit., p.366.

48   Given that he apparently raised no objection to the later strip-club scene, it has to be said that this was a totally bewildering request from Fox for such an innocuous sequence to be cut – in which, to the accompaniment of an orchestral version of "All My Loving", the two characters walk together and embrace each other on the beach and then kiss whilst standing within a heart drawn on the sand!

49   Quoted in Barry Miles, op. cit., p.367.

50   Kevin Howlett, op. cit., p.230.

51   From report of BBC Audience Research Department of 9th February 1968, reproduced in facsimile as an accompanying document to Kevin Howlett, "The Beatles: The BBC Archives 1962-1970" (BBC, 2013).

52   Ibid.

53   Reproduced in facsimile in Kevin Howlett, op. cit., p.228.

54   Lennon/McCartney, © 1967 by Northern Songs.

55   For which role Warren Mitchell had already been named as the best TV actor in 1966.

56   Ian MacDonald, op. cit., p.236.

57   Ian MacDonald, op. cit., p.234.

58   "Flying" was the first Beatles' instrumental since "Cry For A Shadow" to be available on record. In the film, it plays over aerial out-take shots from *Dr. Strangelove* … that have some visual subtlety in colour but were incomprehensible when originally transmitted in black and white.

59   John's film narration and the text of the EP storybook both refer, in an unnecessarily sloppy way, to there being "4 or 5 magicians" – 4 obviously being the Beatles themselves, while the fifth on screen, hiding in the far corner of their laboratory in the clouds, was Mal Evans, who had no speaking part.

60   The Beatles, *Magical Mystery Tour* [Apple Films, remastered DVD edition, 2012.]

61   Martin Elliott, "The Rolling Stones Complete Recording Sessions 1962-2012: 50th Anniversary Edition" (Cherry Red, 2012), p.80.

62   When they played "Ruby Tuesday", "Let's Spend The Night Together" and "Connection".

63   Christopher Sandford, op. cit., p.125.

64   Bill Wyman with Richard Havers, op. cit., p.259.

65   Quoted in Simon Wells, "Butterfly On A Wheel: The Great Rolling Stones Drugs Bust" (Omnibus, 2011), p.112.

66   That afternoon, everyone had gone down to frolic on the beach at West Wittering. In the ensuing horseplay, Marianne's clothes had become sandy and dirty, so she had taken a bath on their return to the house. Not having brought a change of clothes with her, however, she opted afterwards to utilise a sizeable rug she had found in service as a bedspread.

67   Marianne Faithfull with David Dalton, op. cit., pp.142-143.

68   Andrew Loog Oldham, "2Stoned" (Vintage, 2003), p.352.

69   Andrew Loog Oldham, op. cit., p.353.

70   Quoted in Bill Wyman with Richard Havers, op. cit., p.268.

71   Ibid.

72   He and his wife Diane had separated in January.

73   Whom Marianne Faithfull credits with inspiring John Lennon's reference to "semolina pilchard" in "I Am The Walrus".

74   Keith Richards with James Fox, op. cit., p.225.

75   It is widely held that the *News Of The World* conspired with the police against the Stones to raid Redlands, to forestall a libel action Mick Jagger had taken out against the paper for false reporting. On 5ᵗʰ February, it had published an article in which, in error, Brian Jones had been mistaken for Jagger by ill-informed reporters who had allegedly witnessed his drug-taking in London: at the time of the reported events, Mick was still in Italy with Marianne Faithfull.

76   Quoted in Simon Wells, op. cit., p.180.

77   Ibid.

78   In the *Evening News* and *Daily Express* respectively. [See Simon Wells, op. cit., pp.181-182.]

79   Marianne Faithfull with David Dalton, op. cit., p.156.

80   Quoted in Simon Wells, op. cit., p.189.

81   Quoted in Simon Wells, op. cit., p.196.

82   Keith Richards with James Fox, op. cit., p.227.

83   Ibid.

84   Quoted in Andy Neill & Matt Kent, op. cit., p.170.

85   The title being a quotation from Pope's *Epistle to Dr. Arbuthnot*.

86   Quoted in Simon Wells, op. cit., p.212.

87   Quoted in Simon Wells, op. cit., p.213.

88   Assisted by Lord Justice Winn and Justice Cusack; who that same day also heard an appeal on behalf of Robert Fraser. Compared to his friends, his luck continued to be bad and his appeal was dismissed, the court upholding the view that in his case possession of heroin was too grave a matter to be condoned.

89   Quoted in Simon Wells, op. cit., p.238.

90   Dominic Sandbrook, op. cit., p.556.

91   Jagger & Richards, © 1967 by Essex Music International Ltd.

92   "Shades of the prison-house begin to close/Upon the growing boy ..." [from the 1807 text of *Ode: Intimations of Immortality from Recollections of Early Childhood*, Stanza V, lines 67-68].

93   Quoted in Andrew Loog Oldham, op. cit., p.364.

94   Quoted in Andrew Loog Oldham, op. cit., p.365.

95   Andrew Loog Oldham, op. cit., p.366.

96   Ibid.

97   Quoted in Simon Wells, op. cit., pp.254-255.

98   Quoted in Simon Wells, op. cit., p.264.

99   Quoted in Simon Wells, op. cit., p.265.

100   In Decca's press release, the total cost of all the art work for the LP's original gatefold sleeve was estimated at $25,000. [See Bill Wyman with Richard Havers, op. cit., p.296.]

Christopher Sandford converts this figure to £17,000 sterling. [Op. cit., p.151.]

101 Viz.: "Her Britannic Majesty's Secretary of State Requests and requires in the Name of Her Majesty all those whom it may concern to allow the bearer to pass freely without let or hindrance, and to afford the bearer such assistance and protection as may be necessary."

102 Keith Richards with James Fox, op. cit., p.235.

103 Quoted in Bill Wyman with Richard Havers, op. cit., p.297.

104 For which Jagger and Richards were reputedly indebted to Love's song "She Comes In Colours" on their *Da Capo* album.

105 Keith Richards with James Fox, op. cit., p.233.

106 Jimi Hendrix (ed. by Alan Douglas & Peter Neal), "Starting at Zero" (Bloomsbury, 2013), p.75.

107 Quoted in Clinton Heylin, "Bob Dylan: Behind The Shades" (Faber & Faber, 20th anniversary edn., 2011), pp.278-279.

108 On their 1968 debut album, *Music From Big Pink*, the Band would feature "Tears Of Rage" (co-written by Richard Manuel), "This Wheel's On Fire" (co-written by Rick Danko) and "I Shall Be Released".

109 Michael Gray, "The Bob Dylan Encyclopedia" (Continuum, 2006), p.349.

110 Michael Gray, "The Bob Dylan Encyclopedia" (Continuum, 2006), pp.349-350.

111 Quoted in Keith Badman, op. cit., p.179.

112 Quoted in Keith Badman, op. cit., p.183.

113 Quoted in Keith Badman, op. cit., p.184.

114 Quoted in Keith Badman, op. cit., p.185.

115 Ibid.

116 Ibid.

117 However, although a free man, when he subsequently refused to undertake the alternative duties he was assigned at a hospital for war veterans, he entered into a running dispute with the authorities that dragged on until 1969.

118 Quoted in Keith Badman, op. cit., p.207.

119 At Christmas 1971, in my first teaching post, much to the consternation of my Head of Department (who was then fast approaching retirement), I used "I Had Too Much To Dream Last Night" as the backing track to his staging of Lady Macbeth's sleepwalking scene. He saw the music and the drama as a clash of cultures, but still allowed me to get away with it: I saw them – and still do – as perfectly complementing one another.

120 Micky Dolenz & Mark Bego, "I'm A Believer: My Life of Monkees, Music and Madness" (Cooper Square, 2004), p.64.

121 Micky Dolenz & Mark Bego, op. cit., p.61.

122 Dolenz, © 1967 by Screen Gems/Columbia Music.

123 Johnny Rogan, op. cit., p.314.

124   McGuinn/Hillman, © 1967 by Essex Music.

125   Ibid.

126   Ibid.

127   Johnny Rogan, op. cit., p.318.

128   Quoted in Christopher Hjort, "So You Want To Be A Rock'n'Roll Star: The Byrds Day-by-Day 1965-1973" (Jawbone, 2008), p.119.

129   Quoted in Johnny Rogan, op. cit., p.339.

130   Quoted in Christopher Hjort, op. cit., p.136.

131   The name-change symbolically signified his involvement with the Subud religio-philosophical movement, based in Indonesia, who indicated to him that a first name beginning with 'R' would be most propitious.

132   Quoted in Johnny Rogan, op. cit., p.376.

133   Johnny Rogan, op. cit., p.396.

134   Quoted in Matthew Greenwald, op. cit., pp.212 & 213 respectively.

135   Phillips/Gilliam, © 1967 by Dick James Music.

136   Eddi Fiegel, op. cit., p.247.

137   Pete Townshend, op .cit., p.110.

138   Quoted in Nick Hasted, op. cit., p.95.

139   Ray Davies, op. cit., p.338.

140   Ray Davies, op. cit., pp.338-339.

141   Ray Davies, op. cit., p.345. The court's decision on 5th June that the contract between Denmark Productions and Boscobel Productions had been frustrated, thus rendering it void, was contested by the former party on appeal and this aspect of the case was therefore not concluded until June 1968. As noted before in Ch.7, the related but separate dispute between Ray and Kassner Music remained unsettled until October 1970, meaning the prolongation of the freezing of his royalty payments.

142   Ray Davies, op. cit., p.339.

143   Ray Davies, © 1967 by Davray Music/Carlin Music Corp.

144   Dave Davies, op. cit., p.102.

145   Ray Davies, op. cit., p.353.

146   Ray Davies, © 1967 by Davray Music/Carlin Music Corp.

147   Pete Townshend, op. cit., p.93.

148   Pete Townshend, op. cit., p.107.

149   Townshend, © 1967 by Fabulous Music Ltd.

150   Ibid.

151   Pete Townshend, op. cit., p.133.

152   Quoted in Andy Neill & Matt Kent, op. cit., p.149.

153 As reproduced for the remastered deluxe edition of *Something Else By The Kinks* (Sanctuary, 2011).

154 Tony Blackburn, "Poptastic: My Life in Radio" (Cassell, 2007), p.89.

155 Tony Blackburn, op. cit., pp.89-90.

156 Tony Blackburn, op. cit., p.91.

157 Pete Townshend, op. cit., p.136.

158 Pete Townshend, op. cit., p.144.

159 Quoted in Simon Spence, "Immediate Records: Labels Unlimited" (Black Dog, 2008), p.71.

160 With Keith Emerson on keyboards, the Nice became one of the earliest groups to perform progressive rock music. They had a No.24 hit in September 1968 with their version of Leonard Bernstein's "America" from *West Side Story*, notorious in concert for Emerson's enhancement of his playing by sticking ornamental daggers between the keys.

161 Marriott/Lane, © 1967 by Immediate (London) Music Ltd./EMI United Partnership Ltd.

162 Tony Calder, quoted in Paolo Hewitt & John Hellier, "Steve Marriott: All Too Beautiful" (Helter Skelter, 2004), p.154.

163 Quoted in Paolo Hewitt, "The Small Faces: The Young Mods' Forgotten Story" (Acid Jazz, 2010), p.123.

164 Marriott/Lane, © 1967 by Immediate (London) Music Ltd./EMI United Partnership Ltd.

165 Paolo Hewitt, "The Small Faces: The Young Mods' Forgotten Story" (Acid Jazz, 2010), p.123.

166 Graham Nash, "Wild Tales: A Rock & Roll Life" (Viking, 2013), p.109.

167 Mark Paytress, CD liner notes to *The Move: Move* (Salvo, remastered edition, 2007).

168 Quoted by Mark Paytress, op. cit.

169 Wood, © 1967 by Onward Music Ltd.

170 With the airwaves now rid of the pirate radio stations by law, the BBC reorganised its radio broadcasting by splitting the old Light Programme in two: Radio 1 for 'pop' and Radio 2 for 'easy listening', although initially many daytime programmes were broadcast simultaneously on both wavelengths. The Third Programme became Radio 3 and the Home Service Radio 4.

171 Tony Blackburn, op. cit., p.116.

172 Terry Rawlings, "British Beat 1960-1969: Then, Now and Rare" (Omnibus, 2002), p.139. There were persistent rumours for many years that Wilson was having an affair with his private secretary Marcia Williams (later Lady Falkender).

173 Bruce/Brown, © 1966 by Dratleaf Ltd./Chappell & Co. (ASCAP).

174 On 17th April 1983, Collins shot Pappalardi in their New York apartment and was subsequently convicted of his murder.

175 Eric Clapton with Christopher Simon Sykes, op. cit., pp.90-91. Ginger Baker was equally impressed by Pappalardi's skill but Jack Bruce was less happy about the outcome, because the new mix retained his playing a different bass line on the original recording of the day before.

176 Clapton/Collins/Pappalardi, © 1967 by Unichappell Music Inc. (BMI) & Careers-BMG Music Publishing Inc. (BMI).

177 Quoted in Christopher Hjort, "Strange Brew: Eric Clapton and the British Blues Boom 1965-1970" (Jawbone, 2007), p.143.

178 Ibid. A Christmas release for the next album was pure wishful thinking: it would not see the light of day until August 1968. (See Ch.10.)

179 Quoted in John Platt, op. cit., p.75.

180 Quoted in John Platt, op. cit., p.79.

181 Quoted in "1960s Swinging London" (*NME* Originals Vol.1 Issue 11), p.109.

182 Jimi Hendrix (ed. by Alan Douglas & Peter Neal), op. cit., p.71.

183 Jimi Hendrix (ed. by Alan Douglas & Peter Neal), op. cit., p.77.

184 Hendrix, © 1967 renewed 1995 by Experience Hendrix LLC (ASCAP).

185 Eric Clapton with Christopher Simon Sykes, op. cit., p.91.

186 Jimi Hendrix (ed. by Alan Douglas & Peter Neal), op. cit., p.79.

187 Jimi Hendrix (ed. by Alan Douglas & Peter Neal), op. cit., p.82.

188 Jimi Hendrix (ed. by Alan Douglas & Peter Neal), op. cit., pp.80-81.

189 Charles Shaar Murray, "Crosstown Traffic: Jimi Hendrix and Post-War Pop" (Canongate, 2012), p.267.

190 It was a deliberate gimmick to attract attention, rather than a display of philosophical commitment to auto-destruction as an art form (as embraced by Pete Townshend), but he had already attempted it once before, allegedly at the suggestion of the *NME*'s Keith Altham, when the Experience played London's Astoria Theatre on 31st March.

191 Micky Dolenz & Mark Bego, op. cit., p.132.

192 Jimi Hendrix (ed. by Alan Douglas & Peter Neal), op. cit., p.93.

193 Glenn Povey, "Echoes: The Complete History of Pink Floyd" (3C, 2008), p.40.

194 John Reed, CD liner notes to *Amen Corner: Round Amen Corner – The Complete Deram Recordings* [RPM, 2012], p.5.

195 Jimi Hendrix (ed. by Alan Douglas & Peter Neal), op. cit., p.117.

196 Jimi Hendrix (ed. by Alan Douglas & Peter Neal), op. cit., p.116.

197 Reid/Brooker, © 1967 by Essex Music (later renewed by Onward Music and subsequently additionally credited to Fisher).

198 Ibid.

199 Ibid.

200 See Ch.5.

201 In conversation with John Reed, CD liner notes to *The Very Best Of The Moody Blues* [Polygram, 1996].

202 Ibid. *The Zodiac Cosmic Sounds*, subtitled 'Celestial Counterpoint With Words And Music', was released by Elektra in the summer of 1967, soon after the Doors' first album and immediately before the Incredible String Band's *The 5000 Spirits Or The Layers Of The Onion*. Deemed "arguably to be the first time the pioneering Moog keyboard synthesiser was used on a pop record", its twelve tracks "were each inspired by the 12 astrological signs, smoothly narrated by Cyrus Faryar and with a soundtrack using sitars and exotic percussion, flutes, harpsichord, psychedelic guitar licks and the Moog. It was a collaboration between composer and arranger Mort Garson, poet Jacques Wilson, and co-producer (with [Jac] Holzman) Alex Hassilev, formerly with the Limeliters. Holzman says that many people bought the album for the electronics as much as the concept." [See Mick Houghton, op. cit., p.168.]

203 They were marketed by Mellotronics, a company founded in collaboration with the Bradley brothers of Bradmatic Ltd. by popular bandleader Eric Robinson (part-owner of IBC Studios) and TV magician David Nixon.

204 In conversation with John Reed, CD liner notes to *The Very Best Of The Moody Blues* (Polygram, 1996).

205 In conversation with John Reed, CD liner notes to *Days Of Future Passed* (Deram, remastered edition, 1997).

206 Ibid.

207 Ibid.

208 Original sleevenotes to *Days Of Future Passed* (Deram, 1967).

209 Sean Egan, op. cit., p.207.

210 Donovan Leitch, op. cit., p.188.

211 Donovan Leitch, op. cit., pp.188-189.

212 They became directly available on CD in Britain as separate albums in 2005, when, beginning with *Sunshine Superman*, EMI launched remastered editions of Donovan's back catalogue.

213 Donovan Leitch, op. cit., p.194.

214 Quoted in Lorne Murdoch, CD liner notes to *Mellow Yellow* (EMI, remastered edition, 2005), p.13.

215 Donovan Leitch, op. cit., p.205.

216 Donovan Leitch, op. cit., p.194.

217 Joe Boyd, "White Bicycles: Making Music In The 1960s" (Serpent's Tail. 2005), p.121.

218 Quoted in Rob Young, op. cit., p.357.

219 Heron, © 1967 by Paradox Music Ltd. (later renewed by Warner/Chappell Music Ltd.).

220 Williamson, © 1967 by Paradox Music Ltd. (later renewed by Warner/Chappell Music Ltd.).

221 Williamson, © 1967 by Paradox Music Ltd. (later renewed by Warner/Chappell Music Ltd.).

222   Buckley, © 1967 by Third Story Music.

223   Beckett/Buckley, © 1967 by Third Story Music.

224   Beckett/Buckley, © 1967 by Third Story Music.

225   Included on *Sandie Shaw: Long Live Love* (Salvo, 2013), her self-chosen compilation of her 'very best' songs.

226   Talking to Sue McGregor on *The Reunion: 60s Girl Singers*, BBC Radio 4, 19th August 2012.

227   Sandie Shaw, op. cit., pp.36-37.

228   Sandie Shaw, op. cit., p.38.

229   Sandie Shaw, op. cit., p.39.

230   Sandie Shaw, op. cit., pp.40-41.

231   Sandie Shaw, op. cit., p.41.

232   Cilla Black, op. cit., p.143.

233   Cilla Black, op. cit., p.159.

234   Quoted in Lucy O'Brien, op. cit., p.107.

235   Lulu, op. cit., p.94.

236   Not to be confused with the later series of the same title from the 1980s, starring Tracey Ullman, Lenny Henry and David Copperfield.

237   She was not totally averse to recording compositions by Chaplin, however, and went on to include a cover of his song "Eternally" on her 1967 LP *These Are My Songs*.

238   Derrik Mercer (ed.), op. cit., p.960.

239   Ibid.

240   Alan Shepard & Deke Slayton, op. cit., pp.194-195.

241   Andrew Chaikin, "A Man On The Moon: The Voyages of the Apollo Astronauts" (Michael Joseph, 1994), p.24.

242   James R. Hansen, "First Man: The Life of Neil Armstrong" (Simon & Schuster, 2005), p.305. In full, the treaty's title was the "Treaty on Principles Governing the Activities of States in the Exploration and Use of Outer Space". Not only did it preclude "land claims on the Moon, Mars or any heavenly body", but it also "assured the safe and cordial return of any astronauts (or cosmonauts) making an unexpected landing within the legal domain of another country." [Ibid.]

243   John Laurence, op. cit., pp.441-442.

244   Quoted in Christian G. Appy, op. cit., p.125.

245   Quoted in Christian G. Appy, op. cit., p.126.

246   John Laurence, op. cit., p.444.

247   Michael Maclear, op. cit., p.316.

248   Michael Maclear, op. cit., p.317.

249 Christian G. Appy, op. cit., p.148.

250 Jimi Hendrix (ed. by Alan Douglas & Peter Neal), op. cit., p.100.

251 Jimi Hendrix (ed. by Janie L. Hendrix), "The Ultimate Lyric Book" (Backbeat, 2012), p.93. The track saw the light of day in 1968, on Side 4 of *Electric Ladyland*.

252 Donovan Leitch, op. cit., p.222.

Chapter 10

1968

FIRST NO.1 OF THE YEAR –
"Hello, Goodbye" by The Beatles

LAST NO.1 OF THE YEAR –
"Lily The Pink" by The Scaffold

There is little comfort to be found in the bare fact that in the course of a year there was a transition at No.1 from possibly one of the scrappiest Beatles' A-sides ever in January to a novelty number by the Scaffold in December – the first comedy record to make No.1 since Mike Sarne serenaded Wendy Richard with "Come Outside" in June 1962. Despite the tenuous links between these two records (the Scaffold being Liverpudlian and one of their members being Paul McCartney's younger brother Mike[1]), it's impossible to conceal the downward cultural slide they represent, the retrograde turning of almost a full circle back to the jumbled transatlantic discord of the charts of the late Fifties and early Sixties, before pop music in Britain was reinvented and reinvigorated. Curious, too, that this marked decline in 1968 should coincide with, at the beginning, the first-time-round proclamation of an "I'm Backing Britain" campaign and, at the end, the celebration by Cliff Richard and the Shadows of their tenth anniversary in show business (immediately after which the Shadows felt compelled to disband).

In the opening paragraph of the opening chapter to this book, I made no bones about this being a very personal and highly selective musical history of the decade; but it still came as something of a shock to me to remind myself, in reviewing 1968 at the outset by comparing my record collection to the Top 30 charts week by week, that by this point I was struggling to find many hit singles of interest and the critical mass of my record-buying had firmly shifted over to albums. This is, of course, in part simply a reflection of the passage of time. As I had grown older, many of the artists I had previously favoured had either come to grief or passed their sell-by date (I'm sure I was not alone in harbouring unrealistic assumptions of some acts' staying-power); and of those still left, the randomness of the directions they were now taking all too often left me indifferent or just plain cold. In addition, pursuing my researches for this book in depth has repeatedly alerted me to those fatal flaws in relationships between artists themselves, and/or between artists and their public, which were, in general, kept carefully concealed at the time from fans' prying eyes.

For want of anything better to fill the vacuum, US record companies imposed bubblegum music on us, throwing earlier arguments about whether the Monkees were or were not a real group clean out of the window with vapid studio-only creations like "Simon Says" by the 1910 Fruitgum Company, or "Yummy Yummy Yummy" by Ohio Express. Suddenly, too, the Beatles were fair game for parody, as in "Judy In Disguise (With Glasses)" by John Fred and his Playboy Band; and even rock'n'roll classics could survive an opportune temporary facelift, as Tommy James and the Shondells turned Larry Williams' "Bony Moronie" into "Mony Mony". All of these were UK Top 10 hits in 1968, with "Mony Mony" a No.1 for four weeks from July into August.

Far more galling, however, were the significant lapses of taste that countenanced surrendering the No.1 slot to "Cinderella Rockefella" by Esther and Abi Ofarim for four weeks in March, to "What A Wonderful World" by Louis Armstrong for four weeks from April into May, and then allowed the latter to be succeeded for the next *five* weeks by the most suspect song of all – in view of its lyrical content – "Young Girl" by Gary Puckett and the Union Gap. To complete that total retro experience, there was even an *orchestral* No.1 – the first since Acker Bilk or, to stretch the point, Kenny Ball, in early 1962 – the theme to the spaghetti western *The Good, The Bad And The Ugly*, played by Hugo Montenegro and his Orchestra.

Hidden amongst the variety show debris of the charts there were still, mercifully as ever, rare moments of unforeseen excitement to be savoured, although by 1968 the intervals between them were lengthening at an alarming rate. One such was the foolhardy spectacle of Arthur Brown, turned out in what we would recognise today as Gothic robes and make-up, topped off by a precariously perched flaming head-dress, performing his No.2 hit of August, "Fire". Another was the revival of the guitar instrumental with a vengeance by Love Sculpture (a power-trio led by Dave Edmunds), whose lightning-fast, resonating interpretation of Khatchaturian's "Sabre Dance" reached No.6 in December.[2]

But the capacity of others to excite seemed suddenly diminished. Both the Kinks and the Who, for example, had the leanest of years for hit potential. The Kinks put out two singles and two LPs, none of which attracted any detectable groundswell of interest at the time. Weeks after its release in April, "Wonderboy" made its one and only showing in the Top 30, at No.28, its final sales figures equal to just over a tenth of those achieved by either "Waterloo Sunset" or "Autumn Almanac". "Days", released at the end of June, similarly got off to a slow start, although by mid-August it did reach a more respectable No.14. As for their LPs, neither of them reached the charts. The first, *Live At Kelvin Hall* (recorded in concert in Glasgow in April 1967), which came out in January, had already been released months before in America and the Kinks took no interest whatsoever in its promotion. The second, released in November, is now recognised as probably their finest achievement, Ray Davies's nostalgic song-cycle about "the decline of a certain innocence in England"[3] that constitutes *The Kinks Are The Village Green Preservation Society*. If "Days" had been for Ray a record "telling the world that it was the end of the group", he regarded *The Village Green Preservation Society* as one final "farewell gesture".[4] It was no surprise to him when "the album was a commercial flop and received almost no airplay in Britain":

> When it came out in 1968, there were hardly any pirate stations left to act as alternative radio. The illustrious government had outlawed them, those stations that were the last of the truly independent outlets. Now the BBC monopolised the airwaves, and for many of the emerging DJs, the Kinks sounded too English. While everybody else thought that the hip thing to do was to drop acid, do as many drugs as possible and listen to music in a coma, the Kinks were singing songs about lost friends, draught beer, motorbike riders, wicked witches and flying cats.[5]

Dave Davies, although he thought it was "a very beautiful record", similarly thought that it isolated the Kinks "like voices calling out of the darkness".[6]

The Who, likewise, released two relatively unsuccessful singles and a non-charting compilation LP as a stopgap after *The Who Sell Out*, more or less abandoning recording in favour of spending most of the year playing live gigs around the world. A January tour of Australasia with the Small Faces was succeeded in February by a six-week-long tour of the USA and Canada, returning there again at the end of June for another nine-week stint; and from mid-October through to the end of December, they played a series of concert venues at home. As Pete Townshend had already acknowledged in May, "I think we're losing out both in America and England, because we're not spending enough concentrated time in each country."[7] Which was a polite way of saying that they had spread themselves far too thinly.

Their first single to come out since "I Can See For Miles" was released in June. An idiosyncratic choice of follow-up, "Dogs", a song in celebration of greyhound racing at the White City in London, might almost have come from the nostalgic pen of a Ray Davies; and in common with "Wonderboy", its sole chart appearance, at the end of the month, was at No.28. After that, in October, came "Magic Bus", a more obvious rock contender and a regular feature of the Who's stage act but, for all that, an early song (contemporaneous with "My Generation") drafted in to fill a gap:

It was recorded at a time when we had just returned from our first
[sic] trip to America, having been conned left, right and centre, and
no one really wanted to make a single except Kit Lambert, whose
job was to see that we did. We all got absolutely paralytic drunk one
lunch time and by the time we arrived at the studio, no one cared
what we did.[8]

In its four weeks in the Top 30, it peaked at No.22 in November. It was
not a track featured on the *Direct Hits* LP, that had been released a week later,
although "Dogs" was included as one of the hastily put together assortment
of mostly former A- and B-sides from their collective Reaction and Track
recordings. Apart from being invited in early December to contribute to an
'entertainment' dreamed up by the Rolling Stones (more of which later),
Townshend and the Who would otherwise focus their attention on finishing
a new masterwork of their own, to be unveiled in 1969.

After gaining themselves, together with the Who, a reputation as trou-
blemakers and rabble-rousers on their joint tour of Australasia (given the
propensity of both Keith Moon and Steve Marriott for outlandish behaviour
wherever they went), the Small Faces had returned to England intent on
completing the recording of a new LP. With some songs already in the can,
they were still searching for a unifying theme when Ronnie Lane drew inspiration from gazing up one night at the moon:

The story is a kind of mystical journey. There's this kid, who kind
of falls in love with the moon, and all of a sudden he observes the
moon being eaten away by time. You know the way they go, they
wax and wane, don't they? And of course when it's gone, he's all
down and then the thing is that all of a sudden – boosh! – it comes
back again, like life itself. And I thought that was something to pick
up on really, because you can often get brought down by something,
and you're just being stupidly impatient usually.[9]

The group eventually decided against stretching what became the story of
Happiness Stan to fill both sides of an album but adopted its framework for
Side 2 of their most celebrated LP, *Ogden's Nut Gone Flake*, bringing in comic
actor 'Professor' Stanley Unwin to act as narrator with his trademark blend
of plain and nonsensical English.

By now Steve Marriott was particularly anxious to distance the Small
Faces from the fanbase their singles had attracted to date and to re-establish
their credentials as a group worthy of more serious consideration. Bearing
this in mind, he had hoped to persuade Andrew Loog Oldham that a new
heavy composition, "Song Of A Baker", should be the follow-up to "Itchycoo Park", but found him resistant to the idea and it was hived off to become

a track on Side 1 of the LP. Instead, Oldham prevailed upon Marriott that another, more throwaway song he had written, "Lazy Sunday", had much stronger commercial potential as the next single – even to the extent that it included a parody of the riff from the Rolling Stones' "(I Can't Get No) Satisfaction".

"Lazy Sunday" was, as it stated up front in the lyric, an irreverent putdown by Marriott of his neighbours in his Chiswick terraced house and their incessant complaints about the noise he made, sung in the style of a Cockney knees-up. His girlfriend and future wife, Jenny Rylance, vouched for the mutual antagonism explored in the song:

> [Steve] was having a lot of hassle with his neighbours … and ended up writing 'Lazy Sunday' about his time there. Mind you I didn't blame them. It must have been hard living next door to him. They complained continuously about the noise and rightly so. Steve had installed Wharfedale speakers from Olympic Studios in the living room which measured approximately fourteen feet by twelve feet.[10]

Ian McLagan remembers hearing Marriott first playing it through to the rest of the group as a straight ballad and it not coming to life until they treated it more as, in Marriott's own words, a "funny, jokey, novelty thing".[11] (It was further enhanced in the studio by Loog Oldham, who added dream-sequence sound effects of seagulls and gently lapping waves to the instrumental breaks, as well as the church bells of Barnes to the fade-out – making the latter highly reminiscent of the London soundscape that concludes the Kinks' "Big Black Smoke".)

Released on 5th April, it was, as Loog Oldham had rightly predicted, an instant hit and for two weeks in May it was stuck at No.3, its further progress to No.1 blocked by the unspeakable combination of Louis Armstrong and the 1910 Fruitgum Company. It also came to be included on Side 1 of *Ogden's Nut Gone Flake*, as was the B-side, "Rollin' Over", and "Afterglow". The LP was released on 24th May, beautifully and uniquely packaged in a multi-lay-ered circular sleeve resembling a tobacco tin; and was initially promoted in the music press by a controversial full-page advertisement aping the Lord's Prayer:

> Small Faces
> Which were in the studios
> Hallowed be thy name
> Thy music come
> Thy songs be sung
> On this album as they came from your heads
> We give you this day our daily bread
> Give us thy album in a round cover

As we give thee 37/9d
Lead us into the record stores
And deliver us Ogden's Nut Gone Flake
For nice is the music, the sleeve and the story
For ever and ever.[12]

Selling 20,000 copies on the day of issue alone, it instantly became Immediate's best-selling album and went on to top the LP charts for six consecutive weeks.

For all its fame, it was to be the last album Marriott and the Small Faces would complete together; just as the next single release in June, "The Universal", (which peaked at No.16 in August), was to be their last recording for that format. As recalled by Kenney Jones:

> Steve was incredibly fed up at that point. He hated us still being labelled as a pop band, especially after the success of *Ogden's*. It was almost as if he didn't want to follow it up, like he was frightened we couldn't top it, and I think it shows he'd had a taste of other things by then and he wanted to go off and play with the big boys, if you like. But we didn't know that at the time of 'The Universal'. With hindsight, we should have seen something was definitely on the cards.[13]

In truth, it was even more self-indulgent than "Lazy Sunday", with little hint of the whole group's participation and boasting sloppy embellishments by way of sleazy clarinet and trombone, plus a short country-style guitar break. Through the remainder of the year, Marriott's restlessness and discontent with the Small Faces' achievements showed more and more. Depressed at the failure of "The Universal" to be a bigger hit – and equally blind, it has to be said, to its shortcomings – he was all for shaking the group up by adding a new guitarist, Peter Frampton of the Herd, to the line-up, an idea to which the other members were not receptive; and in September, he had taken time out with Alexis Korner on a short concert tour of Scotland.

The crunch finally came on New Year's Eve, at a gala concert at the Alexandra Palace when, after inviting Korner on stage to play, Marriott walked out on them, leaving Kenney Jones and the others stunned: "Steve went on stage that night in a very bad mood and we knew something was up. He had been throwing real wobblers all week and then, halfway through the set, he just threw his guitar down and walked off, leaving us like three lemons."[14] After honouring outstanding live commitments in Germany and the UK, the Small Faces officially broke up in March 1969; and that November Immediate issued a valedictory double LP of their remaining unreleased studio recordings together with a miscellany of live tracks, entitled *The Autumn Stone*.

Staying with the themes of disillusionment and break-up, if Eric Clapton is to be believed, it was success, perversely, that killed off Cream in 1968. Making it big in America, according to him, ultimately did the supergroup no favours:

> Whistle-stop touring America was the beginning of the end for Cream, because once we started constantly working in such an intense way, it became impossible to keep the music afloat and we began to drown … When you are playing night after night of a punishing schedule, often not because you want to but because you are contractually obliged to, it is only too easy to forget the ideals which once brought you together. There were times too when, playing to audiences who were only too happy to worship us, complacency set in. I began to be quite ashamed of being in Cream, because I thought it was a con. It wasn't really developing from where we were. As we made our voyage across America, we were being exposed to extremely strong and powerful influences, with jazz and rock'n'roll music that was growing up around us, and it seemed that we weren't learning from it.[15]

Physically, Cream were strangers to Britain for much of the year (their concert at Manchester University on 10th February was their last here until what became their two farewell appearances at the Royal Albert Hall on 26th November) and their pattern of UK record releases increasingly bore little resemblance to either their current stage material or the changing demands of the marketplace. Although they had declared that they were not a singles band, Polydor (in succession to Reaction) released two, seemingly at random, neither of which left any indelible impression on the charts. First, in May, came "Anyone For Tennis", spending a straight three weeks stuck at No.25 in June. This was inexplicably followed in September by "Sunshine Of Your Love", again only gaining a three-week foothold in the Top 30 with a highest placing of No.26 in October, by then long past its sell-by date as last year's stand-out track from *Disraeli Gears*: when it had been released as a single in the US, seven months earlier, it had gone to No.5 in the *Billboard* Top 40. This left the August release of the much-vaunted double-album *Wheels Of Fire* (the first disc of new studio recordings, the second live recordings from San Francisco's Fillmore and Winterland Auditoria) to bring Cream properly back to the attention of British record-buyers; yet even though it reached No.3 in the LP charts – and went both gold and platinum on the strength of international sales – the length of time it spent in those charts overall was still considerably less than *Disraeli Gears* (26 weeks as opposed to 42).

During a brief ten-day break back in England in mid-April, Clapton was already hinting to *Melody Maker*'s Chris Welch that "the group isn't going to last for ever".[16] What he didn't allow him to print at that time was that they had already decided to split up, exclusive news that Welch was finally allowed to report on 13th July, when Clapton signalled his intention to get off "that virtuoso kick" by performing "contemporary blues" with a new group comprised of "piano, bass, guitar and drums".[17] For his part, Jack Bruce was more phlegmatic:

> I'm glad Cream lasted as long as it did. Eric was already well known in America, and now Ginger and myself have a bit of a name. I didn't expect Cream to last as long as it did. We got a lot of fun out of it. I'm sorry if English fans are disappointed but we did seem to be most popular in the States, which is why we had to be there so long.[18]

So, after coasting downhill to the inevitable end of a final tour of America, on 4th November at Rhode Island, they went out on the unexpected high of their two Albert Hall concerts three weeks later, where they were overwhelmed by the audiences' enthusiasm and repeated demands for encores. After the event, Clapton seemed to have been completely taken aback by such positive reactions: "…I had no idea we were so popular; I was amazed we played to such full houses. I didn't think anybody would remember us."[19] And in his last contemporary word on the subject, in an interview for the *NME* in December, his assessment of what Cream had or hadn't been able to achieve still remained disingenuously self-effacing:

> The Cream never really played that much blues. I think we aimed to start a revolution in musical thought. We set out to change the world, to upset people and to shock them. At the start we were going to play Elvis Presley numbers – but what happened was that we fell into these long instrumental pieces. Really The Cream was just an instrumental group … The public appreciation always surprised me because I never thought we really got it together to deserve that much acclaim.[20]

As a consequence, by the time Cream enjoyed belated success in the UK with two last singles and an LP in 1969 the group was defunct. Released as a single in January, "White Room" (the opening track of *Wheels Of Fire*) only made it into the Top 30 for two weeks, going no higher than No.29. "Badge", on the other hand – with its celebrated contributions from 'L'Angelo Misterioso' (*aka* George Harrison) as co-writer and rhythm guitarist – lasted seven weeks in the charts, peaking at No.19 in May. And ironically it was with their final album, *Goodbye* (released in February and from which "Badge" was taken), that Cream's true place in the affection of British fans was affirmed once and for all, when domestic sales pushed it to the top of the LP charts for four weeks in a row. The best, it seemed, had been saved till last.

One of the specific factors contributing to Clapton's ultimate loss of confidence in Cream and his own self-doubt was hearing the Band's *Music From Big Pink* for the first time, an experience of which he said:

> It stopped me in my tracks, and it also highlighted all of the problems that I thought we had. Here was a band that was really doing it right, incorporating influences from country music, blues, jazz and rock, and writing great songs. I couldn't help but compare them to us, which was stupid and futile, but I was frantically looking for a yardstick, and here it was. Listening to that album, great as it was, just made me feel that we were stuck, and I wanted out.[21]

Although its artistic roots self-evidently lay in the homely, restorative recording sessions with Bob Dylan in 1967 and he contributed a naïve painting for its cover, its title referenced the Band's own hideaway near Woodstock during that period and three of the tracks reworked prominent songs from the motley collection of 'Basement Tapes' ("Tears Of Rage", "This Wheel's On Fire" and "I Shall Be Released"), the album nevertheless marked the first professional recording of the Band in its own right after they had signed up with Albert Grossman as their manager and he had secured them a contract with Capitol. (It also proved to be the catalyst for recalling drummer Levon Helm to the fold after his flight in terror from Dylan's 'World Tour' back in 1966.) Originally released in America in July 1968, it was not – nor ever has been – a hit album, but has consistently been regarded as a seminal work, marking a turning-point intellectually in the development of American rock music through its 'back to the roots' fusion with modern instrumentation.

Aside from the Dylan covers, arguably its most memorable track remains "The Weight", which was stripped out as a single and did briefly penetrate the UK charts at No.25 in September. The song's narrator finds himself increasingly weighed down by the responsibility, willingly enough assumed at the outset, of doing right by other people. Doing a favour for one person locks him into an unstoppable sequence, verse on verse, of being put upon in turn by others, that burden encapsulated and multiplied in each repetition of the memorably simplistic chorus:

> Take a load off Fanny;
> Take a load for free.
> Take a load off Fanny,
> And you put the load right on me.[22]

As its composer, Robbie Robertson, explained, the premise of the song was simple: "I've only come here to say 'Hello' for somebody and I've got myself in this incredible predicament."[23]

The Band were subsequently thwarted in capitalising on *Music From Big*

Pink by Rick Danko being injured in a car accident and thus denying them the opportunity to perform in public until the spring of 1969. They had, however, already made a triumphant return to the stage, in the company of Bob Dylan, on 20th January 1968 for two houses at the Carnegie Hall in New York – their first appearance together again since playing the Royal Albert Hall in May 1966. Dylan had finally been enticed out of seclusion to take part in a tribute concert to Woody Guthrie, who had died the preceding October, and with the Band (calling themselves the Crackers for this sole occasion) effectively stole the show from traditionalists like Pete Seeger.[24] But it signified neither a more permanent reunion nor a possible return to touring, which Dylan categorically ruled out immediately after the shows: "I won't be giving any concerts for a while. I'm not compelled to do it now. I went around the world a couple of times. But I didn't have anything else to do then."[25] And later in the year he would add that "I did it enough to know that there must be something else to do."[26]

Despite the time they had spent together making the 'Basement Tapes', the Band had not even been the musicians of choice when Dylan had returned to the studio to record *John Wesley Harding* (as previously noted in Ch.9). Following its release in January (preceding Dylan's re-emergence at the Guthrie tribute), "the album's sparse music," as Robert Shelton observed, "startled everyone".[27] Having been long awaited since *Blonde On Blonde*, it sold well – some quarter of a million copies in the first week of issue – but all those who had treasured and venerated the old barnstorming iconoclasm were to be in for a surprise: "Buyers were looking for 'the word' and 'the way', and many were shocked by how he enunciated them. They were geared for excitement, anger, wit and frenzy and found in *Harding* a startling reversal by a man who'd learned the value of silence, meditation and self-knowledge."[28]

There was the usual forlorn attempt to nail down the relevance and meaning of this latest set of songs from an artist whose thought processes hitherto had been deemed to be profound; but even more so than ever before, Dylan was having none of it and refused to be drawn – albeit more politely now than in the past – into any detailed discussion of the underlying intent of his music. He did nevertheless go so far as to reiterate patiently for interviewers the point that what he chose to record was solely a matter for him, unfettered by any consideration of what potential audiences might or might not make of the eventual outcome. Asked if he still felt able to retain the following of young people who had thus far constituted the majority of his record-buyers, he replied:

> That's a vague notion, that one must keep contact with a certain illusion of people which are sort of undefinable. The most you can do is satisfy yourself. If you satisfy yourself then you don't have to worry about remembering anything. If you don't satisfy yourself,

and you don't know why you're doing what you do, you begin to lose contact. If you're doing it for *them* instead of you, you're likely not in contact with them. You can't pretend you're in contact with something you're not. I don't really know who I'm in contact with, but I don't think it's important.[29]

And he was equally resistant to any suggestion that he bore a responsibility for writing to the mood of the times, given that through his songs in the past (like "Masters Of War", for example) it seemed he had been willing to set his face against social and/or political injustice:

That was an easy thing to do. There were thousands and thousands of people just wanting that song, so I wrote it up. What I'm doing now isn't more difficult, but I no longer have the capacity to feed this force which is needing all these songs. I know the force exists but my insight has turned into something else. I might meet one person now, and the same thing can happen between that one person (and myself) that used to happen between thousands.[30]

The problems – if they ever existed – of readjustment or reinterpretation ultimately proved to be illusory, for *John Wesley Harding* became (and remains) the most popular of all his albums in the UK, spending no less than thirteen weeks at No.1 in the LP charts. Yet despite the new image that it projected of him – pictorially (on the front cover of the sleeve, short-haired and bearded) and vocally (his familiar rasping sneer now traded for mellowness) – Dylan himself remained self-effacing about it:

I asked Columbia to release it with no publicity and no hype because this was the season of hype. And my feeling was that if they put it out with no hype, there was enough interest in the album anyway, people would go out and get it. And if you hyped it, there was always that possibility it would piss people off. They didn't spend any money advertising the album and the album just really took off. People have made a lot out of it, as if it was some sort of ink blot test or something. But it never was intended to be anything else but just a bunch of songs, really, maybe it was better'n I thought.[31]

Ten of its twelve tracks collectively represent a new intellectual intensity in Dylan's writing, their titles and leading characters alone sufficient to offer a unifying theme in the isolation of the oppressed individual, such as: "Drifter's Escape", "I Am A Lonesome Hobo", "I Pity The Poor Immigrant", the hapless petitioner of "Dear Landlord" and even the outlawed "John Wesley Harding" himself. Biblical or other allusions abound, in Dylan's quest for peace of mind. Is he, for example, aiming the barbs of "Dear Landlord" at

Albert Grossman, the manager from whom he had lately grown estranged ("And if you don't underestimate me/I won't underestimate you"[32])? Does he really see himself through others' eyes as "The Wicked Messenger" ("If ye cannot bring good news, then don't bring any"[33])? He dreams he "saw St. Augustine/Alive with fiery breath"[34], and tells the cautionary tale of "Frankie Lee And Judas Priest". But at the end of Side 2 the final two songs ensure a more restful conclusion to this long and difficult journey, as "Down Along The Cove" and "I'll Be Your Baby Tonight" both hold out the promise of a consummation devoutly to be wished for in a lover's arms.

The truly outstanding track, however, remains "All Along The Watchtower"; a song of weary foreboding, the tower itself a symbolically beleaguered fortification, offering by no means certain protection from the hostile elements beyond. While the joker struggles, in desperate conversation with the thief, to make sense of his predicament, from which he "can't get no relief", the thief in return tries to exert a calming influence over his companion:

"No reason to get excited," the thief, he kindly spoke.
"There are many here among us who feel that life is but a joke ..."[35]

And, as "the hour is getting late", the song concludes with a cinematic construct, an aerial panning shot, if you will, pulling back from the intense activity in and around the tower to focus on the desolation of the middle distance, hinting at an unfolding story that will never be told in its entirety:

All along the watchtower, princes kept a view
While all the women came and went, barefoot servants too.

Outside in the distance a wildcat did growl
Two riders were approaching, the wind began to howl.[36]

In Dylan's hands, the bleakness of the lyric is perfectly matched by the bare insistence of his strumming on acoustic guitar and the high pitch of his harmonica playing; but it was, of course, in another altogether unimagined guise that this song would soon become famous. When Jimi Hendrix recorded it, his arrangement lent it a sonic grandeur that totally transformed it, using the manifold dimensions of the electric guitar as his palette to re-create a haunting vision of the tower and its inmates beset by the fury of an endless storm.

In so doing, Hendrix had intuitively tapped into one of the sources of Dylan's inspiration; for Dylan would later say that the song "probably came to me during a thunder and lightning storm. I'm sure it did."[37] Nine months after the session at Olympic Studios in which Hendrix had originally grappled with some twenty-four takes of the song, it finally saw its UK release as a single on 18th October and spent eight weeks in the Top 30, its highest placing being No.6 in the chart for 23rd November[38] (although, of course, it lived a separate life as one of the outstanding tracks – together with "Crosstown Traffic" and "Voodoo Chile" – of Hendrix's third LP and double-album, *Electric Ladyland*, released a week later). Dylan was so obviously touched and flattered by Hendrix's cover version that he would subsequently acknowledge its rebounding and lasting impact on his own interpretation of the song:

> I liked Jimi Hendrix's record of this and ever since he died I've been doing it that way. Funny though, his way and my way of doing it weren't that dissimilar. I mean the meaning of the song doesn't change like when some artists do other artists' songs. Strange though how when I sing it I always feel like it's a tribute to him in some kind of way.[39]

Dylan's return to the spotlight with the release of *John Wesley Harding* was purely metaphorical. Through his long period of recuperation and withdrawal from the public gaze, he had found new contentment in exchanging the pressures of fame for something approximating to what so many other ordinary people enjoyed as normal family life. Fully restored to physical and mental health by 1968, he and Sara were now the proud parents of two children and he was obviously fulfilled in spending the majority of his time with them: other than through an understandable desire to pay due tribute to his departed hero Woody Guthrie, getting back on stage held no immediate attraction for him.

For others, however, finding inner peace and self-knowledge was proving more elusive. Driven by the unappeased curiosity of George and John, in a flurry of publicity in mid-February all four Beatles and their partners reconnected with the Maharishi Mahesh Yogi at his retreat near the northern Indian city of Rishikesh, situated in the Himalayan foothills; their avowed intention to acquire sufficient knowledge of transcendental meditation to become instructors of others in its contemplative techniques. Ready as ever to court celebrities in the cause of smoothing his path towards world supremacy, the Maharishi also played host at the same time to Jenny Boyd (Pattie's sister), Donovan and Gypsy Dave, Mike Love of the Beach Boys, actress Mia Farrow and her sister Prudence.

The experience brought the Western contingent varying degrees of temporary serenity but by April it was all over, collapsing amid challenges to the Maharishi's integrity in an atmosphere of recrimination. Donovan, motivated as much by lust for Jenny Boyd (to whom his song "Jennifer Juniper" is directed) as by his further quest for enlightenment, seemed to find nothing amiss and had, in effect, already happily dedicated his double-LP *A Gift From A Flower To A Garden* to 'His Holiness' by attaching a photograph of them together to the back of the box in which it was marketed.[40] His memories of what he termed "a strange and momentous period in all our lives"[41] are divided between time spent with the Beatles, teaching them an unaccustomed finger-picking style of acoustic guitar playing, and immersion in the Maharishi's teachings; although on taking his leave of him, he did not turn out to be quite the expected disciple: "I would not go on to build a University of Transcendental Meditation in Edinburgh as the Maharishi asked me to. But I went on to found an Invisible School of Self-Awareness in the hearts and minds of those gentle souls who love my song."[42]

John Lennon, incensed by suggestions that the Maharishi had behaved improperly towards a female 'student', has left us in total contrast the embittered legacy of "Sexy Sadie":

> We gave her everything we owned just to
> sit at her table.
> Just a smile would lighten everything.
> Sexy Sadie, she's the latest and the greatest of
> them all.
> She made a fool of everyone,
> Sexy Sadie.
> However big you think you are,
> Sexy Sadie.[43]

In fact, the Beatles' presence – and levels of commitment – evaporated by slow degrees. First to leave, after barely two weeks, were Ringo and Maureen Starr. Three weeks later, Paul and Jane Asher had decamped too. Finally, after two months, John, claiming support for his action from George (on his own admission, the least sceptical disciple of all), confronted the Maharishi over his alleged misbehaviour:

> I said, 'We're leaving.' – 'Why?' – 'Well, if you're so cosmic, you'll know why.' Because all his right-hand men were always intimating that he did miracles. And I was saying, 'You know why.' He said, 'I don't know why, you must tell me.' And I just kept saying, 'You ought to know.' And he gave me a look like 'I'll kill you, you bastard.' He gave me *such* a look. And I knew then when he looked at me, because I'd called his bluff.[44]

Although John and George and the rest of their party then left forthwith as threatened, George was the one member of the group who, having invested and gained most spiritually from the experience, was the least disillusioned. Totally absorbed in a very personal quest for something of deeper significance beyond the here and now, on one occasion he had specifically chided Paul for allowing his thoughts to stray from meditation to ideas for new songs, hardly an unexpected lapse of concentration for a Beatle and one to which Paul freely admitted: "The difficulty, of course, is keeping your mind clear, because the minute you clear it, a thought comes in and says, 'What are we gonna do about our next record?'"[45]

George's intellectual and spiritual love affair with Indian mysticism was further reinforced, of course, by the complementary development of his own personal musical interests. In a line of natural progression from his naïve sitar playing on "Norwegian Wood", through his own compositions "Love You To" and "Within You Without You", before travelling to Rishikesh he had already spent time in Bombay (now Mumbai) working with Indian musicians to record the score he had been commissioned to write for the film *Wonderwall*; and from one of those sessions in January, he brought back to Abbey Road, for further work in early February, an initial recording of a new song for the Beatles, "The Inner Light". Unusually it found favour with John and Paul, to the extent that they encouraged him to refine it and endorsed it as the B-side of their next single.

The A-side was to be Paul's composition "Lady Madonna", an altogether more workmanlike production than "Hello, Goodbye", infused stylistically with the jazz influences of Humphrey Lyttleton and Ronnie Scott and the barrel-house piano-playing of Fats Domino. Released on 15th March, while three-quarters of the group were still in India (leaving any initial promotional comments to the recently-returned Ringo), it entered the Top 30 at No.6 before spending two weeks in April at No.1; thankfully displacing "Cinderella Rockefella" but then succumbing to Cliff Richard's Eurovision runner-up "Congratulations". It represented a milestone in being the last of their seventeen singles to be issued on the Parlophone label over the previous five-and-a-half years; for while Parlophone/EMI remained the distributor, all subsequent Beatles' releases were to be credited to their own Apple label.

However angry it might have made George at the time, there was no escaping the fact that both John and Paul had used the duration of their stay with the Maharishi most productively by composing between them an unprecedentedly large portfolio of new material, which would form the bedrock of *The Beatles* (aka *The White Album* – so called after its plain white sleeve, designed by Richard Hamilton), to be laid down in studio sessions stretching interminably over almost five months from 30th May to 14th October. Overall, it would be a long, fractious, unenjoyable experience, in the course of which the participants would often lose any rightful sense of objectivity or critical faculty. As Ian MacDonald pithily summed it up:

> Despite the panning administered to *Magical Mystery Tour*, they
> still seemed to believe that everything they did, however casual,
> would somehow turn to gold if they persisted along intuitive
> lines, regardless of time and cost. In business terms, this attitude
> quickly led to the tax-manoeuvre-cum-investment-disaster of Apple
> Corps, a semi-philanthropic enterprise which, within a year, had

all but emptied The Beatles' coffers in the pursuit of witless follies and gargantuan expense-accounts. At the level of working detail, it led to a creative embrace of coincidence and a willingness to see accidents as meaningful, from which it was a perilous step to regarding meaning as accidental.[46]

And it pushed their relationship with George Martin as producer to the limits of his patience and diplomacy:

> There were a lot of influences at that time. The Beatles were getting further and further apart, anyway. They were writing and recording their own songs. I was recording not a band of four, but three fellows who had three accompanists each time. George would do his own thing and the others would join in, a little more reluctantly than they used to. And Paul would do his own thing and sometimes John wouldn't turn up.[47]

Having suffered enough for his art by the beginning of September, Martin took himself away on holiday for a month, asking recording engineer Chris Thomas to deputise in his absence. It appeared to be a shrewd move, on a number of levels, as an initially overawed Thomas testified: "The Beatles had done 10 songs in the previous three months and we did 10 songs in those next three weeks. So, when George came back, he was quite pleased that things were moving along."[48]

Given that *The White Album* was not to be released until November, the earliest public hint that Beatles' music on the Apple imprint was going to be different came at the end of August, with the release of "Hey Jude" (b/w "Revolution"). Composed by Paul as a veiled exhortation to John's son Julian to rise above the immediate disappointment of the collapse of his parents' marriage[49], it came as a shock to many, not for all the right reasons and not necessarily helped by its original TV exposure as a singalong jamboree on London Weekend's *Frost On Sunday* on 8th September.[50] For me, it marked the end of my contemporary Beatle purchases: it was never a song I liked on first hearing and one I have only slowly grown to tolerate by dint of frequent exposure over the years. At seven minutes eleven seconds long, with four minutes taken up by its mindless coda, in creating the first original pop anthem it irrevocably defines that form as the most simplistic idea imaginable stretched to inordinate excess. Although it may have spent three weeks at No.1 in September, and been voted Best Single of 1968 in the *NME* poll, its appeal to those who bought it was light years removed from that distinguishing their records in the now closed and rapidly receding era of Beatlemania: the new generation of Beatles fans obviously had very different tastes indeed from their predecessors.

"Revolution", on the other hand, I did like. It had guts, still maintaining in the latter-day ferocity of its distorted guitars tenuous links to John's earlier predilection for rock'n'roll workouts (such as "Rock And Roll Music" or "Dizzy Miss Lizzy"). Lyrically and conceptually, however, it ran into some awkwardnesses. Was it simply a bandwagon song to chime with the mood of the climactic year of protest, or was it a statement of commitment? Where did John stand on the issue? Was he for or against revolution? As a political *ingénue*, his answers to these questions, like the words of his song, eventually turned out to be fuzzy and equivocal:

> The statement in 'Revolution' was mine. The lyrics stand today. They're still my feelings about politics. I want to see the *plan*. That's what I used to say to Jerry Rubin and Abbie Hoffman [contemporary US political activists].[51] Count me out if it's for violence. Don't expect me on the barricades unless it's with flowers. As far as overthrowing something in the name of Marxism or Christianity, I want to know what you're going to do *after* you've knocked it down. I mean, can't we use *some* of it? What's the point of bombing Wall Street? If you want to change the system, change the system. It's no good shooting people.[52]

The version put out as the B-side was a considerably heavier reworking of the slower, original "Revolution 1" that, before Paul came up with "Hey Jude", John had favoured as an A-side but had been rejected as such by the others for being too overtly political. (The core of "Revolution 1" was nevertheless salvaged for posterity as the first track on Side 4 of *The White Album*, paradoxically retaining a link to the primeval pre-Beatles era in its employment of Don Lang, erstwhile leader of *Six-Five Special*'s Frantic Five, as a session trombonist. A concluding experimental section, devised by John and Yoko, was hived off to become the execrable "Revolution 9", the senseless penultimate track on Side 4.) The association of the Beatles with a song entitled "Revolution" could never have been anything but sensationalist and one thing is certain: if Brian Epstein had been alive to get wind of it, he would have moved heaven and earth to talk them out of it.

The problem with *The White Album* was that it was, after all, just a collection of songs and not, like *Sgt. Pepper*, a coherent artistic entity in its own right, despite John and Paul being closeted with George Martin for twenty-four hours (from 5.00 p.m. on 16th October to 5.00 pm. on 17th October) to thrash out a running order for the agreed thirty final tracks, the outcome of which was purely pragmatic. Objectivity was in short supply in this exercise, for as Sean Egan observes: "By now, The Beatles were too powerful and too sure of their own talents to heed George Martin's advice to trim the fat and put out a single album of uniformly high quality."[53] "In the end," as Mark Lewisohn tells us, "there was an *approximate* structure":

… the heavier rock songs ('Birthday', 'Yer Blues', 'Everybody's Got Something To Hide Except Me And My Monkey', 'Helter Skelter') mostly ended up on side C [3], three songs with an animal in the title ('Blackbird', 'Piggies', 'Rocky Raccoon') were placed together, in succession on side B [2], George's four songs were spread out one per side, no composer had more than two songs in succession and each side lasted between 20 and 25 minutes.[54]

Less charitably, Sean Egan, in his critique of the album, suggests four major categories into which the songs can be grouped:

1) EPHEMERA, DOODLES, SKETCHES AND RUBBISH.

2) FAILED EXPERIMENTS.

3) MATERIAL THAT IS QUITE ENJOYABLE BUT WHICH IN YOUR HEART OF HEARTS YOU KNOW IS NOT QUITE GOOD ENOUGH TO MERIT SPACE ON A BEATLES ALBUM IN NORMAL CIRCUMSTANCES.

4) THE VERY GOOD-TO-CLASSIC.[55]

And in this spurious but well-intentioned cataloguing lies the difficulty at the heart of it all, that uneasy sensation that everybody else who has ever listened to *The White Album* has probably thought the same about it and mentally edited it down to their own far shorter set of preferences. When, furthermore, you know that recording engineer Geoff Emerick walked out less than two months into the project (during a session given over to "Cry Baby Cry"), in despair at the disunity and backbiting in the studio; or that the recording of even an apparently faultless track like "Back In The USSR" led to Ringo temporarily leaving the group for twelve days, after Paul had criticised his drumming; or that George turned to Eric Clapton in preference to one of his fellow Beatles to help him out with the guitar solo on "While My Guitar Gently Weeps"; then you are already accumulating sufficient circumstantial evidence to question the rationale behind it all.

Apart from being insulted for his musicianship, Ringo was bound to come off worst as the non-composing Beatle caught in the crossfire of the other three's egos – or perhaps on reflection that should be the other *four's*, since whenever John was in attendance he was always closely shadowed by Yoko. This time round, however, he did buck the trend of having a song written for him to perform by bringing his own to the table, the country-and-western-tinged "Don't Pass Me By"[56] (on which he was accompanied only by Paul and session violinist Jack Fallon); and after the unapologetically alienating effect of "Revolution 9", he was gainfully employed in gently crooning "Good Night" (John's lullaby to his son Julian) to bring the album to a soothing close, in a pseudo-cinematic arrangement by George Martin incorporating the Mike Sammes Singers as a heavenly choir.

George's contributions, as befitting his complex character, ranged from the austere spirituality of "While My Guitar Gently Weeps" and "Long Long Long" to the Swiftian misanthropy of "Piggies" ("Everywhere there's lots of piggies/Living piggy lives/You can see them out for dinner with their piggy wives"[57]) and, lastly, the ridicule of "Savoy Truffle" (a song, listing the contents of a box of chocolates, aimed at Eric Clapton, known for both his sweet tooth and his correspondingly bad teeth: "yes you know it's good news/But you'll have to have them all pulled out/After the Savoy truffle"[58]).

Slugging it out in the main arena were John and Paul, the former clearly intent on not allowing the latter to dictate the framework within which they both should work, as had happened with *Sgt. Pepper*. For melody and lightness of touch, for sheer *joie de vivre*, all the prizes must go to Paul (consider, for example, "Ob-La-Di, Ob-La-Da", "Martha My Dear", "Rocky Raccoon", "I Will", or "Honey Pie"); and there is little to surpass the poetic sensitivities of either his "Blackbird" or "Mother Nature's Son". But where he overlaps with John, he is equally capable of turning out aggressive rock'n'roll; as in "Birthday", "Why Don't We Do It In The Road?" and not least the infamous "Helter Skelter" (the one song above all others on the album, after "Piggies", that 'spoke' directly to the Hollywood murderer Charles Manson, feeding his psychopathic delusions).

John, meanwhile, egged on by heroin and Yoko, is even more unpredictable and edgy than ever, his songs mapping out distinct spikes and troughs in his moods. Few of them, almost as if by design, make comfortable listening, and "Glass Onion" is less a tease than a slap in the face for the faithful who have hung on in there and come so far on the journey with him:

> I told you about strawberry fields
> You know the place where nothing is real
> Well here's another place you can go
> Where everything flows.
> Looking through the bent backed tulips
> To see how the other half live
> Looking through a glass onion.[59]

"Dear Prudence" and "The Continuing Story Of Bungalow Bill" are both intensely Rishikesh-specific; the former written to encourage Prudence Farrow, Mia's sister, out of her shell and relate to the rest of the impromptu community, the latter to satirise another 'student' whose pursuits alternated between big-game hunting and meditation. Nothing else from his pen on the album – barring "Good Night", which he doesn't sing – is anywhere near as light in tone: "I'm So Tired" may be funny but delights at the same time in its crudity, especially in the last verse's reference to Sir Walter Raleigh being "such a stupid git"[60] for having discovered tobacco.

Elsewhere he uses music as the dark pathway to psychoanalysis; as in "Happiness Is A Warm Gun", for example (a song ominously inspired by his recognition of the sheer insanity of the phrase, a line of 'found poetry' from an American gun magazine), or the eerie "Julia", his tribute to his late mother and to Yoko as her substitute for his affections that Ian MacDonald found "almost too personal for public consumption".[61] He plumbs the ultimate depths of despair, however, in the jarring "Yer Blues":

> Black cloud crossed my mind.
> Blue mist round my soul.
> Feel so suicidal
> Even hate my rock and roll.[62]

For all its rough edges, *The White Album* predictably became the No.1 LP (for eight weeks) but of all the Beatles' albums so far it spent, at twenty-two weeks, the shortest overall time yet in the charts. In retrospect, Paul had this final verdict to offer on it:

> I think it was a very good album. It stood up, but it wasn't a
> pleasant one to make. Then again, sometimes those things work
> for your art. The fact that it's got so much on it is one of the things
> that's cool about it. The songs are very varied. I think it's a fine
> album … I assume we hoped that people would like it. We just put
> it out and got on with life.[63]

Equally unpredictable in their recorded output for 1968, but with far less in quantity to offer than the Beatles, were the Rolling Stones, who managed, after the disasters – personal and musical – of 1967, to release one single and one LP in the UK. Both endeavours marked a turning-away from the previous unrestrained excesses of *Their Satanic Majesties Request* in a revisiting of their surer blues roots; and although by now Brian Jones had become more and more a passenger, they had been bailed out in the studio by the acquisition of an incisive new producer, the expatriate New Yorker Jimmy Miller. Also well respected as an accomplished drummer, Miller quickly gained the confidence of the Stones when they returned to Olympic Studios in March to flesh out new material they had been working up since January.

First to emerge from these sessions was a long-overdue single as a follow-up to the previous August's "We Love You"; and with the release of "Jumpin' Jack Flash" on 24th May, the Stones clearly signalled that they were back to their old form. With a riff as, if not more, memorable than that of "Satisfaction" (originally knocked out on an electronic keyboard at Olympic by Bill Wyman), and a Gothic lyric depicting the improbable upbringing of a darkling child "born in a crossfire hurricane" and "raised by a toothless bearded hag"[64], "Jumpin' Jack Flash" returned the Stones to No.1 in June, a position they had last occupied more than two years ago with "Paint It, Black". (They previewed it on 12th May, in a surprise guest appearance at the *NME* Poll Winners' Concert, their last ever live performance as the original line-up with Brian Jones.) It brought them back, in Keith's words, from the brink of a period when they had "run out of gas" and "could have foundered"[65] and he was thrilled to have imbued it with a distinctive instrumental feel:

> … I'd discovered a new sound I could get out of an acoustic guitar. That grinding, dirty sound came out of these crummy little motels where the only thing you had to record with was this new invention called the cassette recorder. And it didn't disturb anybody. Suddenly you had a very mini studio. Playing an acoustic, you'd overload the Philips cassette player to the point of distortion so that when it played back it was effectively an electric guitar. You were using the cassette player as a pickup and an amplifier at the same time. You were forcing acoustic guitars through a cassette player, and what came out the other end was electric as hell.[66]

From Keith's perspective, it was this simplistic approach that also informed the recording of *Beggars Banquet*, released in December exactly a year on from *Their Satanic Majesties Request*. In his typically loose way of classifying any of their songs, he deemed the two most energised tracks of this set, "Sympathy For The Devil" and "Street Fighting Man", to be rock'n'roll but saw the remainder as being derivations of country, blues or folk; and taken as a whole, the album wears its predominantly American influences on its sleeve.

Although its inspiration was literary (taken from Marianne Faithfull's interest in Bulgakov's Russian satirical novel *The Master and Margarita*), there can be no denying that "Sympathy For The Devil" was deliberately conceived as sensationalist, affording Mick a golden opportunity to revel in posing as Lucifer – the very antithesis, as it turns out, of Dylan bemoaning the lessons of history in "With God On Our Side". As for "Street Fighting Man", for all its swagger and bravado, it is a rabble-rousing song without the courage of its apparent convictions, and as such it poses far more questions about sincerity and commitment than John Lennon's "Revolution" ever did:

> Ev'rywhere I hear the sound of marching, charging
> feet, oh boy
> 'Cause summer's here and the time is right
> for fighting in the street, oh boy
> But what can a poor boy do
> Except to sing for a rock'n'roll band
> 'Cause in sleepy London town

There's just no place for street fighting man
No.[67]

The album's final track, "The Salt Of The Earth", illustrates even more clearly, however, through a winsome anthem of supposed solidarity, the shallowness of Jagger and Richards' political understanding:

Raise your glass to the hard working people
Let's drink to the uncounted heads
Let's think of the wavering millions
Who need leaders but get gamblers instead.[68]

Pre-release, *Beggars Banquet* ran into trouble with Decca, when the company refused to countenance the Stones' suggested front cover shot of a graffiti-daubed toilet cubicle (a belated doff of the cap, perhaps, to Loog Oldham's penchant for never fighting shy of questionable publicity): it was eventually replaced by a plain white cover in the form of an invitation, bearing in three lines of copperplate script the legend "Rolling Stones/ Beggars Banquet/RSVP".[69] Although nowadays rated highly amongst their LPs of the Sixties, originally it was no more successful than *Their Satanic Majesties Request*, similarly peaking at No.3 in the charts despite its superior quality overall.

For a group that had hitherto outstripped all others in its capacity for touring, a second year of comparative idleness did not sit entirely well with the Stones. With the drugs trials of 1967 still casting a long shadow, on 21st May Brian Jones was subjected out of the blue to another police raid and charged with possessing cannabis, found hidden within a ball of wool in the drawer of a bureau in the furnished flat to which he had only recently moved. At his eventual trial at the Inner London Court of Sessions on 26th September, overseen as before by Reginald Seaton but with Michael Havers QC as his defence counsel this time, Brian pleaded 'not guilty' and denied all knowledge of the mysterious ball of wool or its contents (which bore all the signs of planted evidence). Furthermore, he firmly refuted the line taken by the prosecution; namely, that he had been reluctant to admit the police to his flat because he was playing for time while he disposed of incriminating evidence. Yet after deliberating for forty-five minutes, the jury found him 'guilty', leaving him once again at Seaton's mercy as to sentencing. He had no right to think so but he was in luck, for Seaton was obviously displeased at the verdict and thus showed him leniency:

Mr. Jones, you have been found guilty. I am going to treat you as I would any other young man before this court. I am going to fine you and I will fine you relatively according to your means: £50 with 100 guineas' costs. You will have one week to get up the money [sic]. Your probation order will not be changed. But you must really

watch your step and stay clear of this stuff. For goodness sake
do not get into trouble again. If you do there will be some real
trouble.[70]

By way of distraction before his trial, Brian had taken himself off to
Morocco, to explore and record its ethnic music. With it now behind him, his
thoughts turned seriously to removing himself from London and the ever-
present threat of police harassment[71]; to which end in November he bought
himself a country retreat, Cotchford Farm at Hartfield in East Sussex,
formerly the home of A.A. Milne, creator of Winnie the Pooh. One of its
particularly appealing features was that to the rear of the house it boasted its
own swimming pool.

Mick, meanwhile, had occupied himself for much of the summer with
acting in *Performance* (the malevolent *film noir* also starring James Fox, directed
by Donald Cammell and Nicholas Roeg, that did not go on general release
until 1970), playing the part of Turner, "a retired rock and roll singer holed
up with a couple of sexually ambiguous girlfriends and a large stash of magic
mushrooms".[72] The episode posed a potential threat to Keith's equilibrium,
in that his girlfriend Anita Pallenberg was cast in the role of Turner's principal
lover, a conflict of interests that he resolved by seducing Marianne Faithfull
in Mick's absence and being inspired to compose "Gimme Shelter".

The Stones reunited as a group in mid-November, leaking to the tabloid
press their plans to make a television spectacular for Christmas (an idea Bill
Wyman credits to Mick). Entitled *The Rock And Roll Circus*, it smacked of an
attempt to upstage the Beatles' *Magical Mystery Tour*; but, according to Stones'
archivist Martin Elliott, it salvaged the last vestiges of an idea tentatively
hatched earlier between Mick, Pete Townshend and Ronnie Lane to take a
travelling music show on the road. A bizarre coalescence of circus acts and
rock stars, with Mick as ringmaster, this colourful extravaganza was filmed
over two days (10th and 11th December) on a set resembling the Big Top at
the Intertel Studios in London. Amongst the invited musicians appearing
were Taj Mahal, Jethro Tull, the Who (who performed "A Quick One While
He's Away" in its entirety) and 'Dirty Mac' – a scratch band made up of
John Lennon, Eric Clapton, Keith Richards and Mitch Mitchell, who gave a
surprisingly good performance of John's "Yer Blues". Sprawled in the centre
of the circus ring in a very posh frock, Marianne Faithfull sang "Something
Better"; and Yoko Ono murdered sleep by screeching atonally in the false
name of art as her contribution to a second instrumental by 'Dirty Mac' and
violinist Ivry Gitlis. The Stones themselves closed the show with a set that
included "Jumpin' Jack Flash", "You Can't Always Get What You Want",
"Sympathy For The Devil" and three other tracks from the newly-released
Beggars Banquet.

As Bill recalled, however, the considerable effort the Stones put into it was not to be rewarded:

> On the second day we finally began filming our piece around 1
> a.m. Everyone had been in the studio for nearly 14 hours so it was
> a tough situation. You could immediately feel the energy once we
> started playing, the only problem was that we kept on and on and
> on playing. We did endless takes. We did 'Jumpin' Jack Flash' at
> least three times, had six goes at 'Sympathy For The Devil' and lost
> count on most of the rest. We finished around 4 a.m. and all we
> could do was head back to the hotel, totally knackered. When Mick
> saw the rushes, he insisted our segment would have to be re-shot.
> Budgets were drawn up for the shoot, but nothing was done. It was
> not our finest hour.[73]

The folly was therefore abandoned in its unfinished state and, never broadcast, remained unseen until its release by ABKCO on video in 1996.

After the implosion of *Smile*, the painfully long – and ultimately anti-climactic – gestation of "Heroes And Villains" and the critical panning they had
subsequently received for the quality of their live performances, the Beach
Boys faced a new year with some trepidation. To remain credible as America's top group, if that still remained within their grasp, then they urgently
needed to halt and reverse the downward spiral into which they had fallen
during 1967. Doing that would, however, prove far more difficult than they
might have envisaged, for the "sunny little world they continued to imagine
in song"[74] was completely out of phase with the paranoid mood of the USA
in 1968. Even though Dennis Wilson made a spectacularly bad call in April
by opening his Hollywood home to a wild drifter called Charles Manson
and his harem of followers known as the 'Family', and was then forced by
August to flee them to find some peace of mind, it seemed to have eluded the
Beach Boys that the nature of the competition they now faced had changed
dramatically, to the extent that even "the Beatles' eyes [had] darkened as the
year went on, moving from the psychedelic ecstasies of *Sgt. Pepper* to the
monochromatic gloom of *The White Album* and its vaguely ominous songs
that skirted the edge of sex, hard drugs, suicide and violent revolution".[75]

For a while, Mike Love (who, with Carl Wilson, had wrested production
responsibilities for their records from Brian, rendered increasingly incapable
by drug dependency and deteriorating mental health) thought the answer lay
with the Maharishi. Keeping the faith after returning from his own two-week
stint in Rishikesh, Love dreamed up the idea of touring America with the
guru: a "brilliant method", so he thought, "to both spread the word about
T[ranscendental] M[editation] via [the Beach Boys'] own mainstream popularity and simultaneously enhance their coolness factor thanks to their public

association with the world's most prominent Indian mystic".[76] It was a fool-hardy miscalculation of popular appeal that cost them dearly. With a joint tour planned from 3rd to 21st May, it had to be abandoned after only three days and seven performances; one problem being that "the Beach Boys' fans were not only dwindling in number but also uniquely impatient when it came to sitting through long, generally unintelligible lectures on Eastern spirituality"[77], and the other being the Maharishi's own apparent lack of commitment to the enterprise (when, without warning on Day 3, he left the country). With an earlier tour scheduled for April having already been partly abandoned in the aftermath of the assassination of Martin Luther King, it was estimated that the Beach Boys' losses across both tours were in the order of half a million dollars.

And the criticisms just kept mounting, at home and here in the UK, where Penny Valentine threw down the gauntlet in a trenchant piece for *Disc & Music Echo* on 11th June:

> Today, the Beach Boys are floundering pathetically in a mire of stodgy apathy. It is now time for them to stand still and take stock of themselves and the situation they are in today. They have been given too much freedom. Like greedy schoolboys in a sweetshop their sense has not prevailed – their control has snapped. They are no longer the brilliant Beach Boys. They are grey and they are making sad little grey records.[78]

When she wrote that halfway through the year, out of obvious frustration, the UK market had by then only been exposed to two new Beach Boys singles: "Darlin'" (released in January, which had peaked at No.11) and "Friends" (released in May, which failed to make the *NME* chart at all [79]). The best was yet to come, for 19th July saw the release of "Do It Again", an unashamed revival of something approximating to their old surfing sound with a nostalgic lyric to match:

> Well, I've been thinking 'bout
> All the places we've surfed and danced and
> All the faces we've missed, so let's get
> Back together and do it again.[80]

Penny Valentine, for one, was smitten, likening it to "bees humming on a summer breeze" and applauding them for recapturing their "competent, commercial sound".[81] And it was generally very well received, enjoying twelve weeks in the Top 30 from August through to October, with a highest placing of No.2 in the chart for 7th September (compared to No.20 in the *Billboard* Top 40). But it did not denote a return to consistency. The follow-up, "Blue-birds Over The Mountain", co-produced by Carl Wilson and Bruce Johnston but not an original composition (it had been written and recorded by one

Ersel Hickey ten years earlier), was released at the end of November, to coincide with the beginning of a short tour of the UK and Europe in December. Whilst apparently popular in their stage show, it was another non-chart entry and a sure sign that the contemporary love affair with the Beach Boys had nearly run its course.

In May, then again in July, the Byrds were also stopping off in London, to play a few gigs before moving on elsewhere, but on both occasions reconstituted as a group with distinctly new country leanings; which sat oddly with the belated success in the spring of their fifth album *The Notorious Byrd Brothers*. Released here in April and reaching No.12 in the LP charts, it very much represented a moment frozen in time. The famous 'stable doors' cover showed – from left to right – Chris Hillman, Roger McGuinn and Michael Clarke, but Clarke, of course, was now gone. Three of the song credits were to David Crosby but he had left them even before Clarke and his presence on the record had been reduced to one in spirit rather than in person. The content was mixed but still recognisably an extension of the varied repertoire that had previously informed *Fifth Dimension* and *Younger Than Yesterday*, with psychedelic influences still strong in tracks such as "Draft Morning", "Change Is Now" and "Dolphin's Smile" and with McGuinn's continuing love of 'space music' evident in the closing track "Space Odyssey". But it was their treatment of the Goffin & King song "Wasn't Born To Follow" that would become the best-known of all from the album, when it was later included in the soundtrack to *Easy Rider*. On its original January release in the US, the considerable achievement it represented against all the odds was duly noted:

> Logically, a group which decays from a quintet through two quartet permutations then down to a trio, a duo, and another trio has to pay for the process with vitality, retaining only a crippled imitation of the old sound. But Roger McGuinn … guitarist-singer; and Chris Hillman, bassist, the only survivors of what was once the first bright new-wave American group, still have something to give … winging their way through 11 good songs spiked with electronic music, strings, bass, natural and supernatural voices, and the familiar thick texture of McGuinn's guitar playing.[82]

After Clarke's departure, McGuinn and Hillman had recruited Kevin Kelley as their new drummer, and added Gram Parsons to the line-up in February. Parsons, who was hired primarily as a keyboard player, could also sing and play guitar; and was highly influential in prevailing upon the others to cut new tracks in Nashville with a country-and-western flavour. The first song they attempted in this vein was one drawn from the limited circulation by Albert Grossman of selections from the 'Basement Tapes', Dylan's "You Ain't Goin' Nowhere", and this was to be their next single, released in the UK on 3rd May[83], a week before their arrival as a group now further augmented temporarily by the inclusion of banjo-player Doug Dillard. Patronised by Mick Jagger and Keith Richards (who not only enjoyed their two live appearances in London but also mounted an *extempore* sightseeing trip to Stonehenge for them), their varied set of old hits and country music went down well.

When they returned in early July to play at two concerts (held at the Roundhouse and the Royal Albert Hall), they were back to a quartet without Dillard but, on 9th July, Parsons unexpectedly pulled out of the group prior to their onward departure for a tour of South Africa, having developed strong misgivings about it in private conversation with Jagger and Richards. They had no option but to leave without him (he returned to Los Angeles several days later, after spending time with Richards at Redlands), while he in turn bequeathed to them the country legacy of their next album, *Sweetheart Of The Rodeo*[84]; and it is at this point, given this extreme change of musical direction, that, regrettably, the Byrds must now pass out of the scope of this book.

If the Byrds were *passé*, then neither was there much hope for the Monkees, whose luck finally ran out in the autumn of 1968 when, after a second series, their TV show was cancelled. In retrospect, Micky Dolenz freely acknowledges the arrogance that he then believed would pull them through:

> You might think that we would have been devastated. Especially me, who knew the power that the tube could wield. But I had been as deluded by the grandeur as had everyone else … We didn't need the networks, we didn't need television, we didn't need the record companies, or the radio stations, the fan magazines, food, water, or oxygen. We could go on forever just feeding off of ourselves. The Monster Monkee Music and Madness Machine was indestructible![85]

The quality of their final UK hits ("Valleri", No.13 in April, and "D.W. Washburn", No.20 in July) was decidedly inferior to that of their major successes throughout 1967; and, as an already disillusioned Mike Nesmith commented: "The minute the television show went off the air, the Monkees records meant nothing."[86] Other projects into which they misguidedly diverted their energies (making the film *Head*, written by Jack Nicholson and directed by Bob Rafelson, and a TV special directed by Jack Good, *33 1/3 Revolutions Per Monkee*) ultimately failed to spare them the negative reactions of a largely uncomprehending and disaffected US fanbase and at the end of the year Peter Tork left the group. Dolenz, Nesmith and Jones struggled on as a trio, to give their last performance together on 30th November 1969;

after which Nesmith bought out his contract, leaving Dolenz and Jones to "quickly [discover] they were showbiz non-entities".[87]

Having shown its impatience with past heroes, there was nevertheless a limited UK market for more robust American rock music across the board: for example, Sly & The Family Stone's "Dance To The Music" (a No.10 hit in August), Canned Heat's classic "On The Road Again" (No.9 in September), or the Doors' "Hello I Love You" (No.17 in October). And, thanks to the improved distribution of US records in the UK, there were always hidden gems awaiting discovery away from the mainstream charts. One such for me was Love's third LP and masterpiece, *Forever Changes*, recorded in 1967 but not available here until early 1968 and preceded by the single release of its striking opening track, the Spanish-influenced "Alone Again Or". An album that was both beautifully put together and packaged, it still remains enigmatic and mystifying all these years later, even to professional music critics:

> You've got song structures that are not like any other songs. They're not verse-chorus songs, they've got stream-of-consciousness lyrics, orchestral interludes that are more like Herb Alpert and the Tijuana Brass than the heavier ones on *Sgt. Pepper* and *Pet Sounds*. It took me forever to understand the album. The songs were not hummable, but they were so melodic. It took so long to sink in, because it's so confusing.[88]

Group leader Arthur Lee, an idiosyncratic musician prone to outlandish exaggeration, conceived it as his musical epitaph:

> At the time … I thought this might be the last album I'll ever make. The words on *Forever Changes* represented the last words I would say about this planet. The album was made after I thought there was no hope left in the world. I thought I was going to die. I used to sit there in my house on the hillside [in the fashionable Hollywood district of Laurel Canyon] and think of all the things that had happened, or were happening all around, in my life, as well as to others. I would write them the way I saw them. I like to think that I write things about the way life really is, because if these things were happening to me, chances are they were happening to others, too. That was the key. I never was an, 'I love you, I want you, I need you, ooh baby,' kind of writer.[89]

Produced for Elektra by Bruce Botnick and sensitively orchestrated by David Angel, some of Lee's song titles alone are more abstruse than those of Dylan in his prime, loaded as they are with intensely personal nuances and references specific to Los Angeles as well as to wider American culture. "A House Is Not A Motel", for example, opens with a dismissive statement about the grandeur of his own lifestyle before descending into a prophetic reflection on the relentless reporting of the onslaught in Vietnam:

> By the time that I'm through singing
> The bells from the schools of war will be ringing
> More confusions, blood transfusions
> The news today will be the movies for tomorrow.[90]

He wrote "Maybe The People Would Be The Times Or Between Clark And Hilldale" about "the experiences that I went through, on a daily basis, at the junction of those streets, where the Whisky A Go Go is ... the gimmick in that song [being] to start the next verse with the last word from the previous line"; while "The Good Humor Man He Sees Everything Like This" originated in an early morning trip to "my old school, Dorsey High, to watch the kids going to and fro"[91], in which he adopts the perspective of the 'good humor man' – or, in our parlance, the ice-cream man.

At first glance, you might assume "The Daily Planet" to be some fantasy woven around the Metropolis newspaper for which Clark Kent and Lois Lane are reporters; but it turns out to be Lee's punning take on the Earth's rotation that governs all our lives:

> In the morning we arise and
> Start the day the same old way
> As yesterday the day before and
> All in all it's just a day like
> All the rest so do your best with
> Chewing gum and it is oh so
> Repetitious
> Waiting on the sun.[92]

But if, in the light of Lee's commentary on the rationale behind the whole album, you are expecting somewhere to come across a premonition of his death, then look no further than "The Red Telephone", composed in the sure and certain knowledge of the existence of the nuclear war hotline between the Presidents of the USA and USSR: "The lyric to the song ... goes: 'Sitting on a hillside/Watching all the people die/I'll feel much better on the other side.' By which I meant leaving this life for the next."[93]

Even more so than Love's previous two albums, *Forever Changes*, as a masterwork with attitude, did not fall easily into any one identifiable musical genre, thereby confusing its original American audience: in much the same way as the Beach Boys' *Pet Sounds*, it was far better received in the UK, eventually creeping into the lower reaches of the LP charts at No.24. Thereafter, it has always rewarded further study, as gratifyingly rediscovered afresh by successive generations, and it regularly features prominently in polls of the best albums ever recorded, praise indeed that, nearly forty years on, Lee himself would live to receive before his death in 2006.[94]

UK record buyers, myself included, also proved receptive once more, after their notable absence from the charts, to the music of Simon & Garfunkel. "Mrs. Robinson", closely associated with but actually hardly featured in *The Graduate* – the tragi-comedy directed by Mike Nichols in which Anne Bancroft (Mrs. Robinson) seduces Dustin Hoffman (Benjamin Braddock) – quickly became their keynote song of the year, surviving its recirculation in a number of guises. First released as a single in the summer, in August it climbed to No.4 in the Top 30; but it was to come round again twice more as an LP track, initially on *Bookends* and then on *The Graduate* soundtrack album, both of which were big sellers, and would have a fourth and final reincarnation in early 1969 as the title track of a hit EP (another *Graduate* spinoff) that made No.19 that February.

Much enamoured with Simon & Garfunkel's earlier work, to the extent that he had already provisionally blocked out several scenes in the film using existing songs from their first two albums as accompaniment, in the course of 1967 Mike Nichols was drawn into enthusiastic discussions with the head of CBS Records, Clive Davis, about the compilation of a soundtrack album. Paul Simon, however, was harder to win over to the idea, seeing it as a sell-out, but was eventually persuaded to submit possible new additional songs to Nichols for his consideration. The first two having failed to impress (but later finding their way onto *Bookends*), Nichols was completely taken by surprise when, at a subsequent meeting with both Simon & Garfunkel, they sprang a work-in-progress on him, as recalled here by Art Garfunkel:

> Paul had been working on what is now "Mrs. Robinson". But there was no name in it and we'd just fill in with any three-syllable name. And because of the character in the picture we just began using the name 'Mrs. Robinson' to fit ... and one day we were sitting around with Mike talking about ideas for another song. And I said 'What about "Mrs. Robinson."' Mike shot to his feet. 'You have a song called "Mrs. Robinson" and you haven't even shown it to me?' So we explained the working title ["Mrs. Roosevelt"] and sang it for him. And then Mike froze it for the picture as "Mrs. Robinson".[95]

In fact, it was to be the only new song to be included on the soundtrack album, a compilation otherwise made up of the songs Nichols had already lifted from *Sounds Of Silence* and *Parsley, Sage, Rosemary And Thyme*[96], plus several pieces of incidental music composed for the film by Dave Grusin.

In America, the release of *The Graduate* album preceded that of *Bookends*, whereas the situation was reversed in the UK; but irrespective of chronology or country, it was the combined success of both albums that took Simon & Garfunkel to renewed and unprecedented heights of popularity. Of the two, however, naturally it was *Bookends* to which Simon devoted the most attention.

He had told Garfunkel at the outset: "I'm going to start writing a whole side of an album – a cycle of songs. I want the early ones to be about youth and the last song to be about old age, and I want the feel of each song to fit."[97] And that's exactly how Side 1 of *Bookends* came to be realised; beginning with the instrumental "Bookends Theme" and moving through songs of youth ("Save The Life Of My Child"), the idealism of young love ("America") and its opposite in a depiction of a relationship in decline ("Overs"), to a portrait of old age ("Old Friends") and the concluding vocalisation of "Bookends".

There was no comparable thematic thread pulling Side 2 together, just five varied tracks, of which four had previously been issued as singles in the US: "Fakin' It", "Mrs. Robinson", "A Hazy Shade Of Winter" and "At The Zoo". In these terms alone, therefore, *Bookends* offered far better value to UK rather than US purchasers (although its playing time barely ran to a full half-hour all told), yet it still contrived to be a No.1 album on both sides of the Atlantic and the UK's sixth best-selling album of the year. To its further credit, it did display innovative touches added to the songs by the duo and Roy Halee as co-producers. Side 1 encompasses a Moog synthesiser to flesh out the cityscape of "Save The Life Of My Child", the sound of someone drawing on a post-coital cigarette in "Overs", and a short insert of old people's voices (recorded by Garfunkel in New York and Los Angeles) as the prologue to "Old Friends"; while on Side 2, "Fakin' It" contains a brief historical tableau set in a tailor's shop[98] and "Punky's Dilemma" has the sound effect of "Old Roger draft-dodger"[99] falling down the stairs as he tries to steal out of the building unnoticed.

But there was a sting in the tail, a hidden message woven into the lyric of "Old Friends", to be conveyed, ironically, by Garfunkel's habitually pure tones:

> Can you imagine us
> Years from today,
> Sharing a park bench quietly?
> How terribly strange
> To be seventy.[100]

For what Simon had neglected to tell Garfunkel beforehand was that he had intended *Bookends* – with its austere, black-and-white front-cover portrait of them by Richard Avedon – to be the swansong of their partnership and that he nurtured future ambitions strictly as a solo artist; a grand plan now embarrassingly thwarted by the scale of their success in 1968 and the high expectations that had created of what they might next be capable of achieving together.

Simon & Garfunkel, for all the increasing sophistication of their output, were still classified primarily as folk musicians, occupying a position towards the 'pop/decorative' end of the folk spectrum that ran, in the opposite direction, to the 'intellectual/traditional' category. In this respect, at least, they found themselves in the company of Donovan who, as we have already seen, had strayed from the earlier promise of *Sunshine Superman* to write the mawkish "Jennifer Juniper", which, inexplicably, was still a strong enough single to command a Top 10 placement (No.6 in March). Then in April Pye made pop history by issuing his double-album *A Gift From A Flower To A Garden* as a box-set, the first non-classical release in this format in the UK. A vast disappointment compared to the richness and complexity of *Sunshine Superman*, it was an awkwardly pretentious amalgam of "music for my age group, an age group which is gently entering marriage" (Record 1) and music for the "children of the dawning generation" (Record 2)[101]; yet somehow it managed to sell more than its predecessor without any greater promotional exposure, ending up at No.13 in the LP charts. The songs on Record 1 are, in general, poorly written, insubstantial and jazz-tinged: only "Wear Your Love Like Heaven" truly delivers, although Donovan retains pride in his 'adaptation' of Shakespeare's "Under The Greenwood Tree" from *As You Like It* (as commissioned by Sir Laurence Olivier for the National Theatre). The balance of effort in production (by Mickie Most again), arrangements and lyrical content appeared to have been tipped very much in favour of Record 2, from which tracks like "Isle Of Islay", "Lay Of The Last Tinker" and "Widow With Shawl (A Portrait)" stand out as more mature extensions of his earlier repertoire.

The real shock to the system came, however, with Donovan's next single, "Hurdy Gurdy Man", a composition he brought back from Rishikesh with half a mind to give to Jimi Hendrix – an intention from which he was quickly dissuaded by Mickie Most. Instead, he recorded it himself, supported by an illustrious band of session musicians (Allen Hollsworth, Clem Cattini, Jimmy Page, John Paul Jones, and John Bonham[102]), and turned out an even more striking blend of folk and rock than "Sunshine Superman" had been: in his own words, a "warm acoustic opening led into a blazing rock fuzz-guitar sound with manic drums, my vibrato vocal vibing with the tempo".[103] Climbing to No.3 in June, in tandem with "Jumpin' Jack Flash" reaching No.1, not only was it his last Top 10 hit of the Sixties but also, as fate would decree, the last of his greatest hits.[104]

At the opposite end of the continuum, the traditional folk label Transatlantic was making concerted efforts to arouse interest in the newest recorded work (produced by the ubiquitous Shel Talmy, in stark contrast to his earlier undertakings with the Kinks and the Who) of a gifted, if hitherto uncommercial, quintet of artists who had first pooled their talents in 1967:

Combining the pure, folk-orientated vocals of Jacqui McShee with the immense talents of Bert Jansch and jazzateer John Renbourn on guitars, and an innovative rhythm section of Danny Thompson and Terry Cox on upright bass and drums respectively, Pentangle heralded the emergence of a fusion built around jazz and folk.[105]

With the acquisition of a new manager, Jo Lustig, in February 1968, Pentangle were "transformed from a cult folk-club act to a bona fide concert act with an extraordinary appeal across the social spectrum and massive, sustained media coverage".[106] Lustig had already proved his promotional abilities in his management of Julie Felix, making her a late Sixties' TV celebrity, and now he was equally unstinting in the Pentangle's cause:

> In 1968 alone Lustig secured for his group at least eleven Radio 1 sessions and at least eight television appearances. The potential appeal of an act that was pigeon-holeable nowhere but could squeeze in pretty much anywhere made them at once more saleable and simultaneously more exotic as a 'product'. They could move seamlessly from college gigs and Edinburgh Fringe residencies to folk festivals, jazz festivals, the biggest and most unforgiving rock festivals of the day, stylised set-ups in country churches, cathedrals and casinos, and major auditoriums such as Carnegie Hall or the Paris Olympia. If coverage on the airwaves was impressive, in print it was relentless: this was a group, like the Beatles, whose members were all distinct individuals and all capable of providing good copy.[107]

Lest that last remark be thought hyperbole, it is worth remembering that Bert Jansch already held the distinction of sharing a bill with Jimi Hendrix as his equal at the Royal Festival Hall in September 1967, in a one-off concert of guitar virtuosi across the entire breadth of musical disciplines from classical to rock.

·The release of an initial single, "Travelling Song" (a Jansch composition on which he took the vocal lead and to which Talmy had added strings), coincided with that of "Jumpin' Jack Flash" at the end of May. One of my favourite non-charting singles of the year, its true purpose was to blaze a trail for the release a week later of their eponymous debut LP; on which, "for the first time in history", as Rob Young points out, "a rock drum kit can be heard backing English traditional songs"[108] (on the outstanding opening track, the warning to fair maidens, "Let No Man Steal Your Thyme"; and on the murder ballad, "Bruton Town"). It also contains three impressive examples of acoustic improvisation in "Bells", "Pentangling" and "Waltz". Although Lustig's vigorous management strategy for the Pentangle hinged critically on a major concert performance at the Royal Festival Hall in June (which was recorded for the live segment of a second, double-album, *Sweet Child* – with cover design by Peter Blake, no less), *The Pentangle* did its job more than well enough, taking them into the LP charts for nine weeks with a highest placing of No.21: *Sweet Child*, in contrast, failed to chart.

Moving even further out than the Pentangle to the extreme edge of folk, and beyond the visions they had previously realised in *The 5000 Spirits*, under Joe Boyd's tutelage the Incredible String Band extended their New Age mysticism to wider audiences still with *The Hangman's Beautiful Daughter*, one of the first LPs to benefit from the new eight-track recording technology and a No.5 hit album in the charts following its release in March. Indeed, just as he had praised *The 5000 Spirits* before it, Paul McCartney would now be equally generous in nominating this as the best album of 1968. In places it retains the whimsy of its predecessor; as, for example, in Robin Williamson's "The Minotaur's Song" ("I'm the original discriminating buffalo man/ And I'll do what's wrong as long as I can"[109]) or "Witches Hat" ("If I was a witches hat/Sitting on her head like a paraffin stove/I'd fly away and be a bat/Across the air I would rove"[110]). Elsewhere, it articulates early environmental concerns, as in Mike Heron's "Mercy I Cry City":

> But where's your quiet pastures
> Where there's time for me to be?
> Nothing else but what I am,
> That's what you seem scared to see.
> You cover up your emptiness
> With brick and noise and rush.
> Oh I can see and touch you
> But you don't owe reality much.[111]

And there are other preoccupations with the natural world and its relationship to spirituality; as in "A Very Cellular Song" or "The Water Song". Side 2 closes with the juxtaposition of "Swift As The Wind" and "Nightfall". In the former, Mike Heron brilliantly captures, just as I remember it myself, the essence of the conflict between a child's overactive imagination at night, deployed to combat fear of the dark, and its parents' uncomprehending response:

> There is no land.
> The night is all around, my child.
> You must stop imagining all this,
> You must stop imagining all this
> For your own good.
> Why don't you go with the rest
> And play downstairs?[112]

In the latter, however, Robin Williamson portrays surrender to the night as soothingly transformed from terror to tranquillity:

> Nightfall
> O river of night flow through me
> Washing thoughts of the day
> On your waters away
> For the morrow that dawns
> Never knew me.[113]

A short tour of the UK's most prestigious concert halls to promote the album was a sell-out, with audiences delighted to discover the scale of their shared appreciation of this esoteric music; or, as Joe Boyd would have it, "freaks in the provinces didn't realise they were so numerous".[114] From here, unbelievably, it was but a short step away for the Incredible String Band to follow in the footsteps of Cream, to play Bill Graham's Fillmore Auditoria in both San Francisco and New York.

As well as folk in all its varied guises, the blues too were on a roll in 1968, thanks largely to a healthy injection of interest in the genre from Mike Vernon's newly established record label, Blue Horizon, and his premier signing, the increasingly popular Peter Green's Fleetwood Mac. For those raised only on the adult-oriented soft rock of this band in its various post-Sixties' incarnations, it may come as something of a revelation to appreciate that as originally assembled by Peter Green (after leaving John Mayall's Bluesbreakers at the end of May 1967) it was a dyed-in-the-wool blues outfit, that took its musical mission as – if not more – seriously than Eric Clapton and Cream; although Green himself, very much a musician's musician, was the most unassuming of guitar heroes.

For the group's debut in August at the 1967 Windsor Festival (in the company, amongst others, of Cream, Donovan and the Pentangle), the line-up in addition to Green (guitar & vocals) was: Jeremy Spencer (guitar & vocals), Bob Brunning (bass guitar) and Mick Fleetwood (drums). In a matter of weeks, however, Brunning was replaced on bass by John McVie (who had taken far longer than Green to make up his mind to leave John Mayall's Bluesbreakers, despite Green's repeated overtures to him). Spending much of the autumn on the road touring pubs and clubs around the UK, their live act provided the foundations for working with Mike Vernon on recording their first album. Released on 16th February 1968, *Peter Green's Fleetwood Mac* found a ready audience and sales estimated conservatively at 1,000 per day rapidly projected it into the higher echelons of the LP charts, all the way up to No.4 – in the company of the Small Faces' *Ogden's Nut Gone Flake* and Dylan's *John Wesley Harding*.

Green's abilities as a composer were reflected in the choice of "Black

Magic Woman" as a single for release in March. Now recognised as a classic in both Green's hands and those of Carlos Santana, on this first outing, however, it bypassed the Top 30 altogether; yet the reinterpretation of Little Willie John's "Need Your Love So Bad"[115], issued as a follow-up in July, did manage a week at No.28 by mid-September. A second LP, *Mr. Wonderful*, followed in August (packaged in a sleeve famously sporting a horizontally-rotated cover photo of a naked Mick Fleetwood, his modesty barely preserved by foliage) – not so well-received as the first album but nevertheless still reaching No.10[116] and utilising the additional talents of Chicken Shack's Christine Perfect on piano – and in that same month, Green added Danny Kirwan to the line-up as a third guitarist, partly out of frustration at Jeremy Spencer's unpredictability and apparent lack of commitment.

Green's true masterstroke came, however, in the autumn when he composed "Albatross", a piece he predicted himself would be "a real classic in the instrumental field, along with 'Apache' and 'FBI', etc."[117] Recorded at a lengthy session in early October (from which Spencer was absent) and released on 22nd November, it broke into the Top 30 a fortnight before Christmas and went on steadily rising – keeping pace for a while with, but then overtaking, Love Sculpture's "Sabre Dance" – eventually to become the third No.1 of 1969 (and the first guitar instrumental No.1 since the Shadows' "Foot Tapper" in March 1963). Its significance as a breakthrough into the mainstream market not just for Blue Horizon as a record label but, more especially, for Fleetwood Mac as a truly commercial commodity can hardly be underestimated; whereas its contribution to the shaping of Green's personal future would soon have unsuspected dire consequences for him.

Syd Barrett of Pink Floyd, however, had already fallen victim to a devastating combination of unregulated drug use and mental instability, to the extent that he had rendered his position with that group untenable. His departure and full-time replacement by David Gilmour was formally announced in April, after which they moved on to complete their next album, *A Saucerful Of Secrets*; which, as Nick Mason said, nevertheless still contained "the final guttering flame of Syd's contributions"[118] and would, after a June release, in due course reach No.9 in the LP charts. Another departure from a group with a higher profile came in December, when Graham Nash parted company with the Hollies, opting instead to move to Los Angeles and join David Crosby and Stephen Stills in a new venture (to be replaced by Terry Sylvester, formerly of the Escorts and the Swinging Blue Jeans.) In his autobiography, Nash claims the Hollies' hit "Jennifer Eccles" (an April No.5, the commercial antidote to "King Midas In Reverse") was "the straw that broke the camel's back"[119], a song he co-wrote but felt too embarrassed to perform or promote compared to those he was now composing on his own with the active encouragement of his new-found West Coast soulmates (like

"Marrakesh Express" or "Teach Your Children"); although the last Hollies' single on which he sang was the later "Listen To Me" (No.7 in October). A supreme irony therefore lies in the fact that *Hollies' Greatest*, a welcome compilation of their singles' hits spanning Nash's years with the group and released that August, should become a No.1 LP, the best-selling album of all in their lengthy career.

Inevitably any effort to conserve the complex tapestry that represents to me the finest of the music of the Sixties is typically beset by fundamental problems; such as restoring lack of detail in some areas due to decomposition of the fabric, drawing attention away from those brilliant slashes of vivid colour still preserved elsewhere, or locating and repairing any number of broken or loose threads. So it is at this point, at the risk of this narrative suddenly becoming disjointed, that I must make do and mend as best I can, by briefly detailing a few remaining matters otherwise in danger of being overlooked.

What, for instance, became of the principal Brumbeat survivors in 1968? After the Moody Blues' remarkable achievement with *Days Of Future Passed*, they turned to recording a series of albums that utilised to the full their own considerable resources as composers and musicians; the next being *In Search Of The Lost Chord*, a No.5 hit LP in the summer. Always a personal favourite of mine, it's the prime example, above all others, in my collection of deferred gratification: when it was released and I bought it, from Boots' record department in Oxford, I was doing voluntary work at a nearby campsite as a vacation job, so I had to stow it in its carrier bag under my bed and wait for weeks until I could finally play it when I got home. A gem of topicality, its theme was the quest by various routes for personal fulfilment, taking the listener on a journey from traditional exploration ("Dr. Livingstone, I Presume"), through the LSD-induced hallucinations of Timothy Leary ("Legend Of A Mind"), to finding inner strength ("The Actor") and spiritual enlightenment ("Om").[120] As well as having absorbed the contemporary influences of Asian instrumentation, their increasing mastery of the mellotron (now played by both Justin Hayward and Mike Pinder) to create depth and atmosphere was equally highlighted by the skill of Tony Clarke's production. As for the Move, however, they had reached something of a plateau after their initially scandalous rise to fame, with only "Fire Brigade" to their name as a No.3 hit in March, followed by a miss in September with "Wild Tiger Woman" (both of these Roy Wood compositions). A debut album, *Move*, reaching No.15 in the LP charts, included both "Flowers In The Rain" and "Fire Brigade" as well as a cover of Moby Grape's "Hey Grandma"; but its release in April coincided with the departure of 'Ace' Kefford, his replacement by Richard Tandy (on keyboards) and Trevor Burton thus switching to bass guitar.

For those prominent female artists whose progress has been followed through earlier chapters, the inescapable slide into television light entertainment continued; so that Dusty Springfield, Cilla Black, Sandie Shaw and Lulu were all by now becalmed in this backwater and, compared to past glories, the hits were drying up. This said, Dusty fared the best out of all of them. After taking the dramatic "I Close My Eyes And Count To Ten" to No.6 in August, she was back in the Top 30 in December with "Son Of A Preacher Man". Probably *the* song for which she is best remembered today by all her admirers and would-be impersonators alike (even though it was destined to go no higher than No.10 by January 1969), its fame specifically relates to being one of the first tracks she recorded in Memphis in September, under a new US deal with Atlantic. Originally written for, but turned down by, Aretha Franklin, it formed part of the collection of songs making up the acclaimed *Dusty In Memphis* album, the outcome of which she self-deprecatingly described at the time as "rough":

> I got destroyed when someone said 'stand there, that's where
> Aretha stood' or 'stand there, that's where Percy Sledge sang "When
> A Man Loves A Woman"'. I became paralysed by the ghosts of
> the studio. I knew that I could sing the songs well enough, but it
> brought pangs of insecurity, that I didn't deserve to be there.[121]

Even allowing for her pronounced inferiority complex, there is still no rational explanation for the fact that in the 1968 *NME* poll Dusty was runner-up to Lulu in both the Best World and Best UK Female Singer categories[122]; for the quality of Lulu's output in this period was far from impressive, saddled as she was by Mickie Most with lightweight songs like "Me, The Peaceful Heart" (No.9 in March), "Boy" (No.15 in June) or "I'm A Tiger" (No.7 in December). Meanwhile, Sandie Shaw had lost her mojo, her sole hit of the year being the plodding formulaic "Today" from the pen of Chris Andrews, No.21 in February. The only one to seriously enhance her chart potential by television exposure was Cilla Black, for whom Paul McCartney came to the rescue by belatedly writing "Step Inside Love" as the theme song for her new series. Released as the series drew to a close, it went to No.7 in April. McCartney was also responsible for signing to and producing on the Apple label the only female artist with a solo No.1 in 1968, Mary Hopkin, who was 'discovered' as a contestant on the TV talent show *Opportunity Knocks* and whose "Those Were The Days" succeeded "Hey Jude" at the top of the charts for five consecutive weeks.[123]

1968 was the year in which the paths of politics, current affairs and popular music converged ever more closely, a meeting of cross-currents influenced by a potent combination of concerns emanating from America and general unrest amongst the student populations of Europe.

Still haunted by the death of President Kennedy, America now witnessed further senseless assassinations of prominent public figures; of civil rights leader Martin Luther King in Memphis on 4th April (to be followed almost immediately by "rioting in 120 American cities and on military bases at home and in Vietnam, resulting in at least forty-six deaths"[124]), and of Senator Robert Kennedy, the late President's younger brother, in Los Angeles on 5th June.

Opposition to the Vietnam War intensified in the wake of the so-called 'Tet Offensive', coinciding with the Vietnamese celebration of the lunar New Year and hitherto respected as a period of truce:

> On January 31, more than eighty thousand Viet Cong and North Vietnamese troops launched a massive, coordinated surprise attack on hundreds of targets all across South Vietnam. They struck five of the six largest cities, thirty-six out of forty-four provincial capitals, and dozens of airfields, military bases, and government installations. It was a shocking and unprecedented attack. Never before had Communist troops entered major urban centres in force to wage open warfare. Nor had they attempted a synchronised offensive throughout the country. It inaugurated the war's bloodiest, most widespread fighting, greatly escalated public debate about the value and efficacy of US actions in Vietnam, and pushed American officials to think seriously about changing their policy in Vietnam.[125]

The scale and ferocity of the assault, extending as it did to infiltration of the South Vietnamese capital Saigon and a direct, sustained attack on the American Embassy in the heart of the city, took senior US politicians and military commanders totally by surprise. It had been prefaced earlier in the month by diversionary engagements elsewhere, most notably from 20th January onwards in the laying of a siege against the US Marine base at Khe Sanh, in the northwest of South Vietnam close to the border with Laos, where 6,000 US troops were surrounded by close to 40,000 North Vietnamese combatants. For the siege's duration – of 77 days – the base was only accessible and supplied by air, until it was relieved at last, in 'Operation Pegasus', "by a force of US Marines and Army Air Cavalry troops that reached Khe Sanh by ground on 8 April 1968. Two hundred and five Americans died defending the base and an estimated 10,000 NVA [North Vietnamese Army] soldiers were killed attacking the base".[126]

Looked at in its entirety, however, "American media coverage of the Tet Offensive was unprecedented":

> The print media and the television crews brought the fighting of Tet home into the living rooms of America where individuals

could watch the shocking and deadly events unfold on television. This coverage made the war seem more real to the viewers and more controversial to those who opposed the war. Watching the US Embassy in Saigon be overrun by VC [Viet Cong] sappers or mortar rounds dropping in on Khe Sanh or graphic images from the urban warfare of Hue on one's television was unsettling to say the least. The American public had never experienced a war like this before, unsanitised and in living colour. The effects of this coverage were vast.[127]

Although US forces eventually prevailed, regaining their supremacy by the end of February, the strategic importance of this victory was lost in the rising clamour for answers to difficult questions, such as: "how had such a massive country-wide attack been possible; who was responsible; what was the plan now?"[128] Robert McNamara's successor as US Defence Secretary, Clark Clifford, charged by President Johnson with making an urgent assessment of future options and thus obliged to ask "the ultimate question … 'What is the plan for the United States to win the war?'", would be taken aback "to find out that we had no military plan to win the war. The answer was that the enemy will ultimately be worn down so severely by attrition that the enemy will eventually capitulate. And that was our policy in the war".[129]

Had he ventured into the field, of course, he would instantly have seen for himself that this was the case; as had war correspondent Michael Herr, for example, who had gained first-hand experience of its realisation at Khe Sanh:

> We never announced a scorched-earth policy; we never announced any policy at all, apart from finding and destroying the enemy, and we proceeded in the most obvious way. We used what was at hand, dropping the greatest volume of explosives in the history of warfare over all the terrain within the thirty-mile sector which fanned out from Khe Sanh. Employing saturation bombing techniques, we delivered more than 110,000 tons of bombs to those hills during the eleven-week containment of Khe Sanh. The smaller foothills were often quite literally turned inside out, the steeper of them were made faceless and drawless, and the bigger hills were left with scars and craters of such proportions that an observer from some remote culture might see in them the obsessiveness and ritual regularity of religious symbols …[130]

Clearly recent setbacks were increasingly rendering such a stance untenable; and after receiving Clifford's recommendations and consulting further with a trusted inner circle of military and political advisers, Johnson reached the inescapable conclusion that "there was not a military solution that was possible within the political capacity of the United States and the American public to carry it through".[131] Having first decided to recall and replace General Westmoreland as Commander-in-the-Field, on 31st March the President made an historic television address to the nation, announcing a freeze on troop levels, limitations on the bombing of North Vietnam and his intention to proceed with negotiations for peace. He then concluded his speech with an unforeseen announcement as to his own future:

> With America's sons in the fields far away, and with America's
> future under challenge here at home; with our hopes and the
> world's hopes for peace in the balance every day, I do not believe
> that I should devote an hour or a day of my time to any personal
> partisan causes, or to any duties other than the awesome duties of
> this office – the presidency of your country. Accordingly, I shall not
> seek, and I will not accept, the nomination of my party for another
> term as your President.[132]

Unfortunately, his decisions neither hastened the end of the war nor appeased the protesters. Even before his broadcast, discontent had spread further afield, to London, where on 17th March, following a prior gathering of an estimated 80,000 people in Trafalgar Square at an anti-war rally addressed by actress Vanessa Redgrave, a massive crowd of demonstrators clashed with police – some mounted on horseback – outside the US Embassy in Grosvenor Square. An old school friend of mine was in the thick of it and later wrote me a letter in which he admitted that in his haste to escape the police he had abandoned the placard he had been carrying, for fear of arrest for possessing an offensive weapon, a not unreasonable expectation in the circumstances:

> ... the scene was a battlefield as police and protesters traded
> punches in the worst scenes of violence in the capital for years.
>   Three hundred arrests were made and 90 policemen were hurt,
> many seriously, in the trouble. For one and a half hours they held a
> cordon in front of the embassy, despite repeated charges by youths
> using banners as battering rams. Skirmishes broke out across the
> square's gardens and lawns, with officers bringing down the fleeing
> protesters with rugby-tackles amid the daffodils and shrubs.[133]

A far uglier confrontation was to come in the parks and on the streets of Chicago, on 28th and 29th August, in the widely televised suppression of anti-war demonstrations aimed at influencing the outcomes of the Democratic Party Convention being held there in preparation for the forthcoming Presidential election. The Mayor of Chicago, Richard Daley, "more monarch than mayor, called out 26,000 police and National Guardsmen"[134] to contain what materialised as no more than an estimated five or six thousand protesters and they did so with intimidating brutality (likened by Democratic Senator Ribicoff to "Gestapo tactics"[135]), as this participant later recalled:

> For all our bravado, I certainly didn't feel we could fight the police. They were armed to the teeth. They had layers and layers of jackets and shields and sometimes wore gas masks. They had clubs and used them freely and many had removed their badges so they couldn't be identified. And the national guardsmen were there with bayonets drawn. We had nothing to protect ourselves with. It was a scary scene and it didn't make me want to become a violent revolutionary.[136]

As for the police officers involved, it forced some of them, at least, to reflect on why they should now find themselves at the forefront of hostility:

> I'm thinking to myself, they're against the war in Vietnam. Why are those people taking it out on us? What are they really trying to get at? I realised later that we are the only entity of government that people can get to. They can't get to the mayor or the political establishments.[137]

But the Chicago unrest ultimately proved counter-productive to the greater cause, despite the naïve belief of many of those taking part in the persuasive power of chants such as "'US Out of Vietnam', 'End the War' and 'The Whole World Is Watching'":

> We thought that the last one was especially effective until we saw the public opinion polls afterwards and realised that the whole world may have been watching but the American public, at least, wasn't sympathising with us. There was much more sympathy for the police than for the victims of the police. That was quite a sobering realisation for many of us. We thought that unarmed demonstrators fighting to end an unpopular war would be received more sympathetically by the public than policemen who were trampling on civil liberties.[138]

In a last-ditch attempt to kick-start serious negotiations for peace (which had been bogged down in acrimony between the American and North Vietnamese delegates ever since their inauguration in Paris in May) and to boost the chances at the polls of his Vice-President, Hubert Humphrey, on 1st November President Johnson ordered "an immediate cessation of all air and naval bombardment of the North except for contingency 'protective strikes' in support of reconnaissance flights".[139] While it may have marginally smoothed the path of peace, it failed to assist Humphrey, who lost the Presidential election four days later to Republican candidate Richard Nixon; and for all his apparent good intentions, as Johnson prepared to leave office the two critical indicators of 'progress' in Vietnam reached their peaks for the campaign as a whole, with troop numbers for the year having risen to 536,000 and fatalities to 16,899.

Albeit belatedly, Johnson would find more of significance to celebrate in the latest spectacular American achievements in space as his Presidency drew to its close. The manned Apollo programme got back on track on 11th October with the launch of Apollo 7 (crewed by Wally Schirra, Donn Eisele and Walt Cunningham), the first major test of the technology pains-takingly reconfigured in the aftermath of the inquiry into the Apollo 1 fire. In the course of an eleven-day flight in Earth orbit (marked particularly by the irascibility of Schirra as the flight commander – on his last space flight before retirement – and his impatience with the mission controllers back on the ground), the astronauts "tested the spacecraft's systems, conducted experiments, beamed the first extensive live television scenes from a manned orbiting vehicle to fascinated audiences around the world and flew their ship longer than would be required for a trip to the moon and back".[140] Apollo 7's success then paved the way for the next bold step, personally approved in secret by the President, to round off the year by launching a mission into lunar orbit.

On the day before lift-off, 20th December, the crew of Frank Borman, Jim Lovell and Bill Anders received a courtesy visit from aviation pioneer Charles Lindbergh (who in May 1927 had made the first solo non-stop flight across the Atlantic):

> The great flier asked … about the navigation system that would take them to the moon. Then he told the astronauts how before his own trip, he and a friend had gone to the library, found a globe, and measured, with a piece of string, the distance from New York to Paris; from that he had figured out how much fuel he would need for the flight. Lindbergh asked how much fuel the Saturn V rocket would consume during its climb into space; one of the astronauts did a quick calculation: 20 tons per second. Lindbergh smiled. "In the first second of your flight tomorrow," he said, "you'll burn ten times more fuel than I did all the way to Paris."[141]

The next day, Apollo 8 made history as the first manned space mission to leave terrestrial orbit and on 23rd December provided an expectant world with live television pictures of the Earth from the furthest distance yet seen ("so far away now that Jim Lovell could hide it behind his outstretched thumb"[142]), the black-and-white images thoughtfully interpreted by Lovell for the ever-receding audience:

For colours, the waters are all sort of a royal blue; clouds of course are bright white. The reflection off the earth appears to be much greater than the moon. The land areas are generally a sort of dark brownish to light brown in texture ... [143]

Paradoxically, in their direction of travel the astronauts were unable to see the moon, hidden as it was from them by the sun's glare, and were therefore dependent for critical course corrections on monitoring and commands from Mission Control. With almost perfect symbolic timing, the spacecraft entered lunar orbit on Christmas Eve; and as it did so:

> ... suddenly the spacecraft was enveloped by darkness. Anders realised they were deep in the shadow of the moon. As his eyes adapted, he saw that the sky was full of stars, so many he could not recognise constellations. He craned toward the flat glass to look back over his shoulder, where they were headed, and he noticed a distinct arc beyond which there were no stars at all, only blackness. All at once he was hit with the eerie realisation that this hole in the stars was the moon. The hair on the back of his neck stood up. [144]

On their fourth orbit, Anders, clearly the one member of the trio most in awe of their historic experiences, famously deviated from the flight plan by taking the first-ever colour photographs of Earth rising above the curve of the moon. As for the moon itself, from a height of sixty miles above its surface all three had been struck by its lack of colour, likened by Lovell to a grey "plaster of paris ... or sort of greyish beach sand"[145]; and even the incurably romantic Anders was disappointed to find it "a place of such unrelenting sameness – crater upon crater, hill upon battered hill".[146]

The crew crowned Christmas Eve with another live television broadcast, transmitting views of both Earth and the moon before, at the onset of lunar sunrise, reading in turn the account of Creation from the opening verses of the Book of Genesis, then signing off with Christmas wishes to "all of you on the *good earth*".[147] Beginning on Christmas Day, their planned return journey to Earth took two-and-a-half days and they splashed down safely in the Pacific, 1,000 miles SSW of Hawaii, on 27th December. Whilst their unique place in world history is secure as the first-ever human beings to venture into outer space, for some Americans, it seemed, the specific timing and success of their mission held another, deeper meaning: Frank Borman afterwards received a telegram of thanks from a well-wisher, stating simply "You saved 1968".

What that person had no way of appreciating was the cold pragmatism that lay behind the Apollo 8 mission, to see off the threat of the USSR stealing a march on America in the race to the moon; for the Russians had every intention of being equally active in space again after overcoming the loss of Vladimir Komarov and Soyuz 1. But they sustained a further tragedy on 27th March, when the jet aircraft in which the figurehead of their corps of cosmonauts, Yuri Gagarin, was flying on a training mission crashed in bad weather, killing both him and his co-pilot. Nevertheless, an accumulation of data from a series of unmanned spacecraft (two of which – Luna 14 and Zond 5 – successfully completed lunar orbits), launched between March and September, gave rise to intense speculation that a manned Russian flight to the moon might be achievable before the year was out.

On 26th October, fifteen days after Apollo 7 had been launched, the Soyuz programme of manned flights was re-instigated; the intention being that Georgi Beregovoi, piloting Soyuz 3, would rendezvous in orbit with the unmanned Soyuz 2. Although automated systems brought the two space-craft close to each other, Beregovoi was unable to complete the manoeuvre manually and had to abandon it after failing at the second attempt, for lack of remaining fuel to power Soyuz 3's directional thrusters: but at least he was able to return safely to Earth after a total of four days in space. One further setback would, however, put paid to Russian chances of upstaging the Americans for the time being, when the unmanned lunar orbiter Zond 6 crash-landed on its return to Earth on 17th November, having suffered depressurisation on re-entry that destroyed all the biological specimens it had been carrying on board.

In directions other than space, as a hostile superpower the USSR had very clearly signalled its political will to shore up Communist values wher-ever a perceived threat to the status quo might erupt. As student discontent fuelled the spread of pro-revolutionary activity across Europe in the spring of 1968, temporarily threatening the stability of France and West Germany in particular, an equally worrying development from President Brezhnev's perspective was the emergence, from January onwards, of a more liberal regime in Czechoslovakia, headed by the newly-elected Communist Party leader Alexander Dubcek. After the failure of talks in July between Dubcek and other Eastern Bloc leaders to stem the tide of his proposed reforms, on 21st August Russian and allied Warsaw Pact forces invaded Czechoslovakia. A day later, their tanks rolled into the streets of the capital, Prague:

> Russian officers entered the HQ of the Czechoslovak Communist Party, brought out Alexander Dubcek and other liberal Communist leaders, and took them away in an armoured troop carrier. The National Assembly has been occupied, and the Czech news agency, which gave the world the first news of the invasion, has been shut … The Russians now say the invasion was necessary to prevent Dubcek restoring capitalism in the country. Something like a "Brezhnev Doctrine" is being invoked to give Moscow the right to use force to stop any East European country slipping away.

> Tass, the official Soviet news agency, says the Czechs are showing gratitude for the timely arrival of Soviet troops.[148]

By mid-September, when the tanks were withdrawn, the Russian occupation of Czechoslovakia was as secure and unforgiving as feared:

> Strict censorship of press, radio and television has been imposed.
> All meetings and processions that "endanger socialism" are banned.
> Vasiliy Kuznetsov, of the Soviet Politburo, is in Prague as Moscow's viceroy, giving orders to Czech party leaders.[149]

The main – and, it has to said, ineffectual – focus of British foreign policy nevertheless remained the resolution of the Rhodesian crisis. With sanctions against the declared illegal regime still in force three years later but by now manifestly failing to bring it down, in October Harold Wilson met Ian Smith for another five days of seaborne talks, held off Gibraltar on HMS *Fearless*. Predictably, they proved futile; "probably just as well", according to Dominic Sandbrook, "because during the negotiations Wilson had made many concessions on the question of majority rule that would have horrified many of his Cabinet colleagues", and when Smith "returned home he once again made it clear that there was no common ground".[150]

There was already heightened sensitivity to the vexed interconnected issues of Britain's post-colonial responsibilities, immigration policy and the state of race relations, following the passing of legislation in March to impose a quota on the number of Asians with British passports allowed to enter the UK after their displacement from Kenya. What many came to see as an uncomfortable and unwelcome debate of such matters was further provoked on 20th April by Enoch Powell, Shadow Minister for Defence, who delivered a speech in Birmingham to a regional gathering of Conservatives that he intended as a warning but was widely construed as being inflammatory. Set against the broad context of the then current Parliamentary debate of a Race Relations Bill (to outlaw racial discrimination in housing, employment and the provision of commercial services), Powell spoke unashamedly of his sense of foreboding at uncontrolled immigration and the prospect of growing civil unrest comparable with that seen in America: "Like the Roman, I seem to see 'the River Tiber foaming with much blood'."[151] The outcry to which it gave rise was sufficient, in my case, to be presented as an English student with the text for linguistic analysis, in order to try and identify those grammatical and syntactical features that made it so contentious.

Now universally vilified, at the time, as Dominic Sandbrook reminds us, despite being sacked almost immediately from the Shadow Cabinet, "away from the Commons and the liberal press, Powell's words met with firm approval ... At the end of April a Gallup poll found that 74 per cent agreed with what he had said, with only 15 per cent disagreeing."[152] By October, however, he had weathered political ostracism as a back-bencher and had even more radical proposals to put to a largely uncomprehending Tory party conference in the guise of a free-marketeer, fleshing out "much of the ideology that would later be called Thatcherism", to include "dismantling the post-war welfare state, selling off the major state-owned corporations and reorganising industry and commerce on unashamedly 'capitalist' lines".[153]

In the realms of the arts in Britain, the subject matter of the most popular films of the year ranged from the reinterpretation of history, such as Tony Richardson's *The Charge Of The Light Brigade* or Anthony Harvey's *The Lion In Winter*, to the stunningly orchestrated futurism of Stanley Kubrick's *2001: A Space Odyssey* and the overthrow of the Establishment in Lindsay Anderson's satire *If …* Further afield, the world of comedy sustained the loss of Tony Hancock, who committed suicide in his hotel room in Sydney on 24th June. Long since a spent force at home, after forsaking the type-casting of his lugubrious bedsit character in Railway Cuttings, East Cheam, he had gone to Australia to record a new television series for Channel 7, yet remained in agonies of self-doubt, as revealed by the content of one of the notes he left behind him: "This is quite rational. Please give my love to my mother but there was nothing left to do. Things seemed to go wrong too many times."[154] And in the field of literature, prolific children's author Enid Blyton died, on 28th November.

Possibly the most significant cultural event of the year, if not of the decade, was the decision taken by Parliament to relieve the Lord Chamberlain's Office of its responsibilities for censorship in the theatre, which had been in place for more than two centuries, after being introduced in 1737 as a curb on political satire. Under the Theatres Act 1968, this was implemented as from 26th September; and the following night saw the London premiere of:

> "Hair", the "Tribal-Love-Rock" musical from America in which the cast, having divested themselves of their clothes under blankets, stand up and face the audience naked just before the lights go down.
>
> The lights did not have far to go – it was dim enough already, but the first-night audience went wild with enthusiasm at this new "breakthrough" in Sixties permissiveness. Stage nudity is now with us, along with "Hair's" deafening beat, psychedelic light effects, showers of confetti, and barrages of "the" four-letter word in chorus. The show is a celebration of the Hippie values – sexual free-for-all, hashish and hatred (of authority and of the Vietnam war). There is a song extolling long hair.[155]

Which brings us inescapably back once more to the association between pop music and its relation to events in the wider world. On 3rd November, the

BBC arts programme *Omnibus* was devoted to *All My Loving*, a film directed by Tony Palmer in which the juxtaposition of these two spheres of influence was graphically illustrated, thus exploring the hypothesis that the dynamism of pop carried with it the potential to enact change. Specially commissioned to 'explain' pop music (since even by this date BBC senior executives still patronisingly thought of it as a phenomenon rather than a discrete art form), the documentary particularly outraged clean-up-TV crusader Mary White-house by its inclusion of performances by Jimi Hendrix. Describing his behaviour as the "most obscene thing"[156] she had ever seen on television, she further complained that he "used his guitar as the body of a woman, and he masturbated on the neck".[157] Needless to say, others took a less blinkered view of the film in the round.

Vicki Wickham, reviewing it for *Disc & Music Echo*, had this to say:

All the horror, sickness and violence of war and death was expressed in the music and lyrics of today's music.

Suddenly, the so-called glamorous, commercial money-making world of pop stars was stripped bare and they became the mouthpiece for their generation ... The music reflected the expectations and hopes, the frustration and despair, the disillusionment and disgust of all of us.[158]

James Thomas, writing in the *Daily Express*, was similarly moved by Palmer's skilfully-edited depiction of "this mad, mad world of despair which forces its way through the changing face of pop music", acknowledging the right of pop musicians "to bid for a place in society which must now accept their curious sense of protest".[159]

Foremost amongst the images chosen by Palmer were those drawn from Vietnam, notably that of the summary execution, in full view of the cameras, of a suspected Viet Cong sympathiser in the streets of Saigon by South Viet-namese General Loan; ramming home to a British audience detached in its complacency the notion of guilt by association, although by setting images worthy of Hieronymus Bosch to contemporary music he was courting the risk of showing how pop could only heighten the agony of the present day rather than relieve it. War correspondent Michael Herr had testified to the power of pop music to ameliorate the tension of war, writing of "sounds [that] were as precious as water"[160]; yet Palmer now turned that notion on its head and played the juke box louder as the jagged accompaniment to the Apocalypse. And it was not so far-fetched, for had not the youth of South Vietnam already begun to ask of America: "how can a country that produced hippies and such cool people also fight a war and kill people and act cruelly?"[161] Suddenly it was time to hold the dilettante revolutionaries and the tunesmiths-cum-libertarians to account.

NOTES

1   The other two being Mersey poet Roger McGough and comedian John Gorman.

2   The single, released on Parlophone in November, was itself an edited version of the closing track on their 1969 LP *Forms And Feelings* (reissued on CD by Esoteric Recordings in 2008).

3   Ray Davies, op. cit., p.363.

4   Ray Davies, op. cit., p.360.

5   Ray Davies, op. cit., p.361.

6   Dave Davies, op. cit., p.107.

7   Quoted in Andy Neill & Matt Kent, op. cit., p.203.

8   Pete Townshend, quoted in Andy Neill & Matt Kent, op. cit., p.192.

9   Quoted in Paolo Hewitt, "The Small Faces: The Young Mods' Forgotten Story" (Acid Jazz, 2010), p.141.

10 Quoted in Paolo Hewitt & John Hellier, op. cit., p.166.

11 Quoted in Paolo Hewitt & John Hellier, op. cit., p.168.

12 Reproduced in Simon Spence, op. cit., p.101.

13 Quoted in Paolo Hewitt, op. cit., p.149.

14 Quoted in Paolo Hewitt, op. cit., p.154.

15 Eric Clapton with Christopher Simon Sykes, op. cit., pp.100-101.

16 Quoted in Christopher Hjort, "Strange Brew: Eric Clapton and the British Blues Boom 1965-1970" (Jawbone, 2007), p.171.

17 Quoted in Christopher Hjort, op. cit., pp.186-187.

18 Quoted in Christopher Hjort, op. cit., p.187.

19 Quoted in Christopher Hjort, op. cit., p.206.

20 Quoted in Christopher Hjort, op. cit., p.209.

21 Eric Clapton with Christopher Simon Sykes, op. cit., p.101.

22 Robertson, © 1968 by ASCAP, later renewed by Warner/Chappell Music Ltd.

23 Quoted in Rob Bowman, "Life Is A Carnival", article for *Goldmine* magazine, July 1991, as republished on www.thebandhiof.no.

24 As befitted a memorial concert, Dylan and the Band performed three of Guthrie's songs: "I Ain't Got No Home", "Dear Mrs. Roosevelt" and "Grand Coulee Dam". They also joined in ensemble performances of "This Land Is Your Land" and "This Train Is Bound For Glory".

25 Quoted in Howard Sounes, op. cit., p.273.

26 From interview with John Cohen & Happy Traum for *Sing Out!* (October/November 1968), as reprinted in Jonathan Cott (ed.), "Dylan On Dylan: The Essential Interviews" (Hodder & Stoughton, 2007), p.124.

27   Robert Shelton, op. cit., p.267.

28   Robert Shelton, op. cit., p.266.

29   From interview with John Cohen & Happy Traum for *Sing Out!* (October/November 1968), as reprinted in Jonathan Cott (ed.), "Dylan On Dylan: The Essential Interviews" (Hodder & Stoughton, 2007), p.130.

30   From interview with John Cohen & Happy Traum for *Sing Out!* (October/November 1968), as reprinted in Jonathan Cott (ed.), "Dylan On Dylan: The Essential Interviews" (Hodder & Stoughton, 2007), p.137.

31   Quoted in Cameron Crowe, liner notes to *Biograph* (Columbia/Legacy, remastered edition, 2011), p.10.

32   Bob Dylan, © 1968 by Dwarf Music, renewed 1996 by Dwarf Music.

33   Bob Dylan, © 1968 by Dwarf Music, renewed 1996 by Dwarf Music.

34   Bob Dylan, © 1968 by Dwarf Music, renewed 1996 by Dwarf Music.

35   Bob Dylan, © 1968 by Dwarf Music, renewed 1996 by Dwarf Music.

36   Ibid.

37   From Dylan's own liner notes to *Biograph* (Columbia/Legacy, remastered edition, 2011), p.38.

38   It was one of the earliest singles to be released in the new 'stereo playable mono' format, that lent it extra power on a traditional turntable.

39   From Dylan's own CD liner notes to *Biograph* (Columbia/Legacy, remastered edition, 2011), p.38.

40   The box-set's UK release post-dated Donovan's trip to Rishikesh but the songs had all been recorded in 1967 and the picture was of an earlier meeting with the Maharishi in Los Angeles that autumn.

41   Donovan Leitch, op. cit., p.232.

42   Donovan Leitch, op. cit., p.246.

43   Lennon/McCartney, ©1968 by Northern Songs Ltd.

44   John Lennon, "The Beatles Anthology" (Cassell, 2000), p.285.

45   Quoted in Barry Miles, op. cit., p.414.

46   Ian MacDonald, op. cit., pp.245-246.

47   Quoted in David Pritchard & Alan Lysaght, op. cit., p.263.

48   Quoted in David Pritchard & Alan Lysaght, op. cit., p.264.

49   On 19th May, John Lennon was unfaithful to his wife Cynthia with Yoko Ono, as the culmination that day of supposedly artistic endeavours in the cause of making experimental tapes for what became the ironically-titled album *Unfinished Music No.1:Two Virgins*. Cynthia returned to the Lennon house at Kenwood a week later from a short holiday in Greece, to be "confronted by my husband and his lover – wearing my dressing-gown – behaving as though I was an intruder." [See Cynthia Lennon, op. cit., p.284.] The decree nisi for their divorce was granted on 8th November 1968.

50   Although Frost introduced the Beatles as "the greatest tea-room orchestra in the

world" and went on to cue in "their first live appearance for goodness knows how long in front of an audience", the performance of "Hey Jude" on the programme was a pre-recorded insert, filmed at Twickenham Film Studios four days earlier. [See Mark Lewisohn, op. cit., pp.296-297.]

51 Rubin and Hoffman were figureheads of the anarchistic Yippie (*aka* Youth International Party) movement in America. "The Yippie recipe for revolution was effortless and simple: having fun, dressing up and getting high would somehow create a better world." [See Gerard DeGroot, "The Sixties Unplugged: A Kaleidoscopic History of a Disorderly Decade" (Pan, 2009), p.264.]

52 John Lennon, "The Beatles Anthology" (Cassell, 2000), p.299.

53 Sean Egan (ed.), "The Mammoth Book of The Beatles" (Robinson, 2009), p.174.

54 Mark Lewisohn, op. cit., p.303.

55 See Sean Egan (ed.), op. cit., pp.170-183.

56 It was not an impulsive contribution but marked the completion of a composition allegedly knocking around in rudimentary form since 1963.

57 Harrison, © 1968 by Harrisongs Ltd.

58 Harrison, © 1968 by Harrisongs Ltd.

59 Lennon/McCartney, © 1968 by Northern Songs Ltd.

60 Lennon/McCartney, © 1968 by Northern Songs Ltd.

61 Ian MacDonald, op. cit., p.286.

62 Lennon/McCartney, © 1968 by Northern Songs Ltd.

63 Paul McCartney, "The Beatles Anthology" (Cassell, 2000), p.310.

64 Jagger/Richards, © 1968 by ABKCO Music Inc./Essex Music International Ltd.

65 Keith Richards with James Fox, op. cit., p.235.

66 Keith Richards with James Fox, op. cit., p.239.

67 Jagger/Richards, © 1968 by ABKCO Music Inc./Essex Music International Ltd.

68 Jagger/Richards, © 1968 by ABKCO Music Inc./Essex Music International Ltd.

69 For the purposes of ABKCO's CD reissue of the remastered album in 2002, the original cover was restored.

70 Quoted in Simon Wells, op. cit., pp.281-282.

71 The Metropolitan Police did now seem to have declared open season on the pop fraternity. On 18th October, John Lennon and Yoko Ono, then living together in a flat rented from Ringo, were raided by D/Sgt. Pilcher and charged with possessing cannabis and obstructing the police. When the case came to court on 28th November, Lennon pleaded 'guilty' to possession and was fined £159 plus 20 guineas' costs.

72 Christopher Sandford, op. cit., p.168.

73 Bill Wyman with Richard Havers, op. cit., p.317.

74 Peter Ames Carlin, op. cit., p.137.

75   Ibid.

76   Peter Ames Carlin, op. cit., p.136.

77   Ibid.

78   Quoted in Keith Badman, op. cit., p.220.

79   Although it was credited with reaching No.25 in the composite *Record Retailer* chart.

80   B. Wilson/M. Love, © 1968 by Immediate Music.

81   Quoted in Keith Badman, op. cit., p.223.

82   Pete Johnson, quoted in Christopher Hjort, "So You Want To Be A Rock'n'Roll Star: The Byrds Day-By-Day 1965-1973" (Jawbone, 2008), p.157.

83   Despite regular airplay for a while, there was never any real chance of "You Ain't Going Nowhere" being a hit in the UK – and it wasn't.

84   An album topped and tailed by songs from *The Basement Tapes:* "You Ain't Going Nowhere" and "Nothing Was Delivered".

85   Micky Dolenz & Mark Bego, op. cit., p.142.

86   Quoted in Eric Lefcowitz, "Monkee Business: The Revolutionary Made-For-TV Band" (Retrofuture, 2013), p.161.

87   Eric Lefcowitz, op. cit., p.186.

88   Andrew Sandoval, quoted in Andrew Hultkrans, "*Forever Changes*" (Continuum '33 1/3' series, 2003), p.51.

89   Quoted in John Einarson, "Forever Changes: Arthur Lee and the Book of Love" (Jawbone, 2010), p.159. While the majority of the tracks are Lee's compositions, "Alone Again Or" and "Old Man" are by fellow group member Bryan MacLean.

90   Lee, © 1968 by Trio Music Company Inc. (BMI) & Grass Roots Productions (BMI).

91   Quoted in John Einarson, op. cit., p.160.

92   Lee, © 1968 by Trio Music Company Inc. (BMI) & Grass Roots Productions (BMI).

93   Quoted in John Einarson, op. cit., p.159.

94   In 2003 he toured the UK with a band amazingly capable of a note-for-note perfect re-creation of *Forever Changes*, a tour de force captured on DVD.

95   Quoted in Marc Eliot, op. cit., pp.90-91.

96   Namely: "The Sound Of Silence", "April Come She Will", "Scarborough Fair/ Canticle" and "The Big Bright Green Pleasure Machine".

97   Quoted in Marc Eliot, op. cit., p.94.

98   Which Donovan claims in his autobiography – probably spuriously – was a nod to him: "Good morning, Mr. Leitch. Have you had a busy day?" [Simon, © 1967 by Lorna Music.]

99   Simon, © 1968 by Lorna Music.

100   Simon, © 1968 by Lorna Music.

101   Donovan, sleeve notes to *A Gift From A Flower To A Garden* (Pye box-set, 1968). It

brought together two albums first released separately in the US in December 1967, *Wear Your Love Like Heaven* and *For Little Ones*, before being reissued in a box-set there in January 1968.

102   The latter three, of course, constituting three-quarters of Led Zeppelin who, with the addition of Robert Plant, would make their live debut in October 1968.

103   Donovan, op. cit., pp.249-250.

104   Although he attempted a similar blend of 'cool' and 'heavy' rock again in 1969, this time with the Jeff Beck Group, the resulting "Barabajagal (Love Is Hot)" only reached No.14 that August.

105   Martin C. Strong, "The Great Folk Discography Vol.1: Pioneers and Early Legends" (Polygon, 2010), p.515.

106   Colin Harper, "Dazzling Stranger: Bert Jansch and the British Folk and Blues Revival" (Bloomsbury, 3rd edition, 2011), p.216.

107   Colin Harper, op. cit., pp.219-220.

108   Rob Young, op. cit., p.223.

109   Williamson, © 1968 by Paradox Music.

110   Williamson, © 1968 by Paradox Music.

111   Heron, © 1968 by Paradox Music.

112   Heron, © 1968 by Paradox Music.

113   Williamson, © 1968 by Paradox Music.

114   Joe Boyd, op. cit., p.185.

115   To be strictly accurate, this was "Peter Green's version of B.B. King's version of a 1950s more uptempo R&B hit, written and recorded by Little Willie John." [See Martin Celmins, "Peter Green: The Authorised Biography" (Sanctuary, 3rd edition, 2003), p.88.]

116   "It still did very good business though – better than many might have thought possible. You have to remember that there were many non-believers who were just waiting for the so-called 'blues boom' bubble to burst." Mike Vernon, CD liner notes to *Mr. Wonderful* (CBS 'Rewind', 1996).

117   Quoted in Christopher Hjort, "Strange Brew: Eric Clapton & The British Blues Boom 1965-1970" (Jawbone, 2007), p.198.

118   Nick Mason, "Inside Out: A Personal History of Pink Floyd" (Phoenix, 2005), p.123.

119   Graham Nash, op. cit., p.118.

120   "Voices In The Sky", lifted from the album as a single, went to No.23 in September.

121   Quoted in Sharon Davis, op. cit., pp.120-121.

122   Lulu won the titles from Dusty of Best World Female Singer and Best UK Female Singer by margins of 997 and 1485 votes respectively.

123   After seeing her appearance on television, Twiggy had commended her to McCartney.

124   Christian G. Appy, op. cit., p.308.

125   Christian G. Appy, op. cit., p.285.

126 Richard Burks Verrone & Laura M. Calkins, op. cit., p.219.

127 Richard Burks Verrone & Laura M. Calkins, op. cit., pp.221-222.

128 Michael Maclear, op. cit., p.277.

129 Quoted in Michael Maclear, op. cit., p.289.

130 Michael Herr, "Dispatches" (Picador, 1978), p.125.

131 William Bundy, US Deputy Secretary of State, quoted in Michael Maclear, op. cit., p.294.

132 Quoted in Michael Maclear, op. cit., p.297.

133 Derrik Mercer (ed.), op. cit., p.977.

134 Michael Maclear, op. cit., p.303.

135 Quoted in Derrik Mercer (ed.), op. cit., p.986.

136 Peter Kuznick, quoted in Christian G. Appy, op. cit., p.315.

137 J. Shaeffer, quoted in Christian G. Appy, op. cit., p.318.

138 Peter Kuznick, quoted in Christian G. Appy, op. cit., p.315.

139 Michael Maclear, op. cit., p.325.

140 Alan Shepard & Deke Slayton, op. cit., p.221.

141 Andrew Chaikin, op. cit., pp.79-80.

142 Andrew Chaikin, op. cit., p.101.

143 Andrew Chaikin, op. cit., p.102.

144 Andrew Chaikin, op. cit., p.107.

145 Andrew Chaikin, op. cit., p.110.

146 Andrew Chaikin, op. cit., p.111.

147 Andrew Chaikin, op. cit., p.122.

148 Derrik Mercer (ed.), op. cit., p.985.

149 Derrik Mercer (ed.), op. cit., p.986.

150 Dominic Sandbrook, "White Heat: A History of Britain in the Swinging Sixties" (Abacus, 2008), p.379.

151 Quoted in Dominic Sandbrook, op. cit., p.679.

152 Quoted in Dominic Sandbrook, op. cit., p.681.

153 Quoted in Dominic Sandbrook, op. cit., p.684.

154 Freddie Hancock & David Nathan, "Hancock" (BBC Ariel, 1986), p.191.

155 Derrik Mercer (ed.), op. cit., p.991.

156 Letter to Sir Hugh Greene, 5th November 1968, reprinted in Ben Thompson (ed.), "Ban This Filth! Letters from the Mary Whitehouse Archive" (Faber, 2012), p.93.

157 Letter to Quintin Hogg MP, 5th November 1968, reprinted in Ben Thompson (ed.), op.

cit., p.94.

158   *Disc & Music Echo*, 9th November 1968.

159   *Daily Express*, 4th November 1968.

160   Michael Herr, op. cit., p.187.

161   Nguyen Qui Duc, quoted in Christian G. Appy, op. cit., p.297

Chapter 11

> ### FIRST NO.1 OF THE YEAR –
> "Lily The Pink" by The Scaffold
>
> ### LAST NO.1 OF THE DECADE –
> "Two Little Boys" by Rolf Harris

A year that began with the police bringing the Beatles' last-ever live performance together to a halt on the grounds that it was disturbing the peace was bound to be full of bad omens for the British record industry; and if the two No.1 hits that book-ended 1969 proved anything, it was that by the end of the decade that industry had all but lost its way, mired in mediocrity and misplaced sentimentality.

As pop hesitantly approached the threshold of the Seventies, it would be seriously lacking in examples of homegrown British originality to carry it forward with confidence into the future. Instead, the radio waves were seemingly awash with a whole host of other sounds, mostly American but also increasingly Afro-Caribbean. Looking back over the charts of '69 today, it is astonishing to see how many of these songs now firmly regarded as Sixties' classics nearly didn't make the decade at all, and impossible to write about them all without it degenerating into a glorified catalogue.

It was undeniably a golden year for Motown in the UK. For example, the very first chart of 4th January included: "Love Child", by Diana Ross & the Supremes (No.15), "Stop Her On Sight (SOS)", by Edwin Starr (No.21), "For Once In My Life", by Stevie Wonder (No.23) and "This Old Heart Of Mine", by the Isley Brothers (No.26). And the hits just kept on coming for these and other artists on the same label, as you can see from the following selective highlights (which read like a ready-made track-listing from any 'Who's Who of Motown' compilation you care to pick up).

Diana Ross & the Supremes joined with the Temptations for "I'm Gonna Make You Love Me" (No.3 in March), before the Temptations had their own No.10 hit in April with "Get Ready". Marvin Gaye was at No.1 for three weeks in March with "I Heard It Through The Grapevine"; and would return in September to No.3 with "Too Busy Thinking About My Baby". Junior Walker & the All Stars took "(I'm A) Road Runner" to No.10

in May, swiftly overtaken by the Isley Brothers' "Behind A Painted Smile" that reached No.6 at the end of that month and the Temptations' "Tracks Of My Tears", that went to No.11 in June. Stevie Wonder returned with a No.3 hit in August, with "My Cherie Amour"; and by December was back at No.3 with "Yester-Me, Yester-You, Yesterday". The Isley Brothers struck again in October with "Put Yourself In My Place" (No.14); and Marvin Gaye duetted with Tammi Terrell on "The Onion Song", a No.8 in December. The market was riding so high that the label even gambled on a reissue of "Dancing In The Street" by Martha & the Vandellas that, second time around, made it to No.4 in March (as opposed to a disappointing No.27 on its original outing in 1964).

The Stax label too had its share of success, notably with "Private Number", by William Bell & Judy Clay (a February No.6) and classic soul instrumentals from Booker T & the MGs, like "Soul Limbo" (No.23 in January) and "Time Is Tight" (No.4 in June). But there were many more diverse external influences for British artists to contend with, such as: gospel (the Edwin Hawkins Singers), bubblegum (the Archies: No.1 for much of November with "Sugar Sugar"), country and western (Jeannie C. Riley, Glen Campbell, Kenny Rogers, Johnny Cash), music from the Bayou (Joe South, Creedence Clearwater Revival), ska and reggae (Desmond Dekker & The Aces – No.1 in April with "The Israelites", Max Romeo, the Equals, the Upsetters, the Harry J. Allstars, the Pioneers, Jimmy Cliff). Even Elvis had been welcomed back with open arms, returning in grand style with "If I Can Dream" (No.13 in March) before recapturing the No.1 spot in July with "In The Ghetto"[1] and concluding with "Suspicious Minds" standing at No.6 in the very last chart of the year. As the title of Thunderclap Newman's mid-summer No.1 rightly proclaimed, there was indeed something in the air in this shifting of the critical mass of popular appeal away from hitherto bankable British artists; and as for the two greatest acts of all, they both faced the prospect of having to endure bad karma.

Although the Beatles were now stuck in the groove of endlessly rehearsing their eventual break-up by way of rancorous factionalism (at its simplest, Paul v John; at its rawest and most fundamental, Paul & Linda v John & Yoko, plus George v The World), it was the Rolling Stones who would be most cursed by the legacy of 1969, since it visited death on one of their number and brought violent death almost within reach of the stage on which they were obliviously performing.

Although Brian Jones was nominally party to some of the Stones' recording sessions at Olympic Studios in the first half of the year, when they laid down tracks for their next album *Let It Bleed*, by this time he was, to all intents and purposes, *persona non grata* with Mick Jagger and Keith

Richards, the controlling duo of the group. In their minds his drugs convictions (the most recent of which he had appealed against unsuccessfully in January) constituted a major obstacle to the granting of visas that would permit the Stones to re-enter America and resume playing profitable concerts there; and therefore provided them with a compelling reason to sack him, over and above their growing contempt for his rapidly declining standards of musicianship. Apparently unmindful of the potential extra difficulties for the group's future plans posed by Jagger's own latest arrest – together with Marianne Faithfull – on 28th May for possession of cannabis, at Ian Stewart's suggestion they invited Mick Taylor (Peter Green's replacement as guitarist with John Mayall's Bluesbreakers) to stand in for Brian, without his knowledge, at a session on 31st May when they recorded "Honky Tonk Women".

Having then decided to make Taylor a permanent band member, thus fuelling speculation about Brian's future, on 8th June Mick and Keith, accompanied by Charlie Watts, drove down to see Brian at Cotchford Farm to tell him he was ditched and to buy him out of the group with a generous financial settlement.[2] Understandably, there are no reliable accounts of that meeting; and in his extended memoir, Bill Wyman holds to the disingenuous party line that what ensued was a "friendly, but very difficult, half-hour talk": "Mick, Keith and Charlie agreed that Brian should make a statement and that we should all stick to the story. Later in the evening, it was announced that Brian had left the Stones."[3] In framing his statement for release to the press, Brian was assisted in honourable corporate fashion by the Stones' publicist, Les Perrin, as follows:

> I no longer see eye to eye with the others over the discs we are cutting. We no longer communicate musically. The Stones' music is not to my taste any more. I have a desire to play my own brand of music rather than that of others, no matter how much I appreciate their musical concepts. The only solution is to go our separate ways, but we shall still remain friends. I love those fellows.[4]

Just over three weeks later, Brian was dead, after drowning in the apparent course of taking a late-night swim on 2nd July in his own pool at Cotchford Farm, in circumstances that have never been satisfactorily explained. The coroner's verdict was one of 'death by misadventure', in light of evidence to the effect that Brian had been drinking steadily throughout the evening, as well as taking drugs, compounded by post-mortem findings of "'liver dysfunction due to extensive fatty degeneration', as well as a dangerously enlarged heart, incipient pleurisy and asthma".[5] But, as his biographer Laura Jackson, for one, has examined in some depth, there are many inconsistencies in the accounts of those others who were also present that night – namely, Brian's last girlfriend, Anna Wohlin, builder Frank Thorogood (with whose continuing live-in presence at Cotchford Brian was known to be unhappy) and his girlfriend Janet Lawson – leaving to this day unresolved issues of possible foul play.[6]

The Stones had already announced that on 5th July in Hyde Park they would be headlining a free concert at which Mick Taylor would be making his live debut with them. Ironically, Brian's death provided them with the perfect focus of attention for their performance, as later admitted by Keith Richards:

> The all-important thing for us was it was our first appearance for a long time and with a change of personnel. It was Mick Taylor's first gig. We were going to do it anyway. Obviously a statement had to be made of one kind or another, so we turned it into a memorial for Brian.[7]

As the *NME* thus duly reported: "The concert in Hyde Park last Saturday, with 250,000 fans attending, was the greatest tribute any pop star could ever have … and the Stones dedicated it to Brian Jones."[8]

Mick Jagger stumblingly delivered a brief eulogy for Brian, including a reading from Shelley's poem *Adonais*, followed by the symbolic release of 3,500 butterflies from cardboard boxes on either side of the stage; after which, as the Stones began to play their first number of a 75-minute set, he was seen by Nick Logan of the *NME* to rapidly cast his grief aside: "Ten feet above Mick Jagger pouted, blew kisses, looked debauched, happy and sad, leapt skywards, sat down, sung [sic], talked and generally entertained in the manner we haven't seen for 14 months but immediately recognised and loved."[9] Chris Welch of *Melody Maker* was less easily satisfied, however: "Mick Taylor played very little lead guitar and I could barely hear Charlie or Bill, but it was a nostalgic, out-of-tune ritual that summed up a decade of pop." [10]

By the time of Brian's funeral in his home town of Cheltenham on 10th July, Mick (accompanied by Marianne Faithfull) would be in Australia to commence filming in the title role of the nineteenth-century bushwhacker *Ned Kelly*: free to travel abroad for the time being on bail, pending the hearing of their cases in December[11], they paid their respects from afar with a wreath. Keith Richards too was conspicuous by his absence, allegedly unable to free himself for the day from unspecified studio commitments. The Stones, who had paid for a tasteful "eight-foot arrangement of red and yellow roses"[12], were therefore represented in person by the lesser lights of Bill Wyman, Charlie Watts and Ian Stewart. It was, all told, a shabby leavetaking of the man who brought the Stones together in the first place, on which Bill has subsequently reflected: "Brian was weak, had hang-ups and at times was a pain in the arse. But he named us, we were his idea and he chose what we first played. We were Brian's band and without him our little blues outfit wouldn't have become the greatest rock'n'roll band in the world."[13] "Honky

Tonk Women", the first Stones' single 'officially' recorded in Brian's absence, was released the day before the Hyde Park concert and spent five weeks at No.1 from 26th July onwards: *NME* readers would later go on to vote it Best Single of the year. Brian's musical epitaph would follow in September, with the release of the Stones' second hits compilation, *Through The Past, Darkly (Big Hits Vol.2)*.

Brian's death and Mick Jagger's bail both now having afforded the Stones greater ease of movement, plans were swiftly laid for a resumption of touring America, where they had last played concerts three years ago. Running from 7th to 30th November, the tour was virtually sold out as soon as tickets went on sale. At the end, after twenty-three shows at seventeen venues, Bill estimated that their audiences had totalled some 335,000 and that the gross income generated was $1.9 million. He also quotes the *New York Daily News* as saying: "The Rolling Stones took the fans by storm, preaching male chauvinism, sex, drugs, freedom and violent revolution."[14] It was, however, a stance that they would find hard to reconcile with the turbulent undercurrent of menace they encountered on their next engagement, on 6th December at the Altamont Speedway in California, some eighty miles east of San Francisco.

In a year noted for its rock festivals, the free concert at Altamont has gone down in history deservedly as the most notorious of them all, the absolute antithesis to Mick Jagger's altruistic aspirations (as expressed to a New York press conference less than two weeks earlier) for a free festival in California; that would allow those who couldn't afford tickets for the official US tour to see them play, and create "a sort of microcosmic society which sets an example to the rest of America as to how one can behave in large gatherings".[15] The reality was a "full-scale disaster": "Three hundred thousand descended on a bald hillside in California's Central Valley, lured by the communal promise of peace, love and music … What they got was bad vibes, bad drugs, Hells Angels and the murder of a black teenager."[16]

The Stones were not present for most of the chaotic proceedings, being flown in by helicopter immediately before their appearance in the late afternoon, so were blissfully unaware of the prevailing mayhem that had already resulted in members of a preceding act, Jefferson Airplane, being viciously assaulted on stage in mid-performance by Hells Angels. The Angels, nominally led by one Sonny Barger, had descended on Altamont and set themselves up as *de facto* crowd marshals, parking their motorcycles across the front of the stage as a barricade and using their fists and sharpened pool cues as the most primitive means of enforcing crowd control: many, such as the ones responsible for the incursions on stage, were literally fighting drunk, or high as kites, or both. According to Stones' chronicler Stanley Booth, there was "nothing imaginary about the danger. There were hundreds of Hells Angels … they were in a particularly bloody mood and it was horrifying".[17]

Having once arrived, the Stones felt compelled to perform, although they were increasingly unnerved by reports of what had already happened and current disturbances that were, in Keith's words, turning the atmosphere "very lurid and hairy".[18] Taking the stage shortly after 4.30 p.m., as darkness descended, they had little idea of what they would face: "Such a big crowd, we could only see in front of our immediate circle, with lights, which are already in your eyes, because stage lights always are. So you're virtually half-blinded; you can't see and judge everything that's going on. You just keep your fingers crossed."[19]

Fresh trouble broke out almost immediately, when a crowd surge towards the stage toppled some of the motorcycles cordoning it off and the Hells Angels retaliated. Four or five numbers into their set (of which "Sympathy For The Devil" had been the second), partway through "Under My Thumb" the Stones stopped playing and Mick appealed for calm; but almost as soon as they restarted the song, a "young black man, who'd been standing in front of the stage with his girlfriend, was stabbed and killed by one of the Angels"[20]; several others then joining in by brutally kicking and beating him once he had fallen to the ground. The victim was Meredith Hunter, who was seen by eye-witnesses to have been under the influence of drugs and to have brandished a gun; and in the absence of anything resembling organised medical facilities on site, he died then and there at the scene of the crime.

The music stopped again: the Stones knew something serious had just occurred but apparently didn't know how bad it was. After more frightened entreaties from Mick for everyone to "just give ourselves another half a minute before we get our breath back [and] just cool down"[21], the band played on, "actually ... for another hour after this calamity had taken place".[22] (As Keith would later recall, matter-of-factly: "Wrong place, wrong time. When it happened, nobody knew he'd been stabbed to death. The show went on."[23]) The remainder of the set was noteworthy for the debut performance of "Brown Sugar" (recorded only three days earlier at the Muscle Shoals Studios in Alabama), whilst also including the infinitely more provocative "Midnight Rambler" and "Street Fighting Man". Then they were spirited away again up into the sky by helicopter, relinquishing any vestige of responsibility for the events of the day. Keith has since maintained that "if it hadn't been for the murder, we'd have thought it a very smooth gig"[24], but, on mature reflection Bill "can only say that it was naïvety that got us into the whole bloody mess and it was luck, and little else, that got us out of it."[25]; to which he would add, in all due humility: "We believed we could do anything and we had something to prove, when we should have just said no, we're not doing it."[26]

The day before Altamont had seen the UK release of *Let It Bleed* (following its US release the previous Saturday), the last Stones' album of the Sixties, with its iconic cover shot of a stack of 'records' on an autochanger spindle topped off by a cake specially baked and decorated by a then unknown Delia Smith. Its most unrestrained and salacious content lay in the songs "Gimme Shelter" (with its gratuitous references to war, rape and murder) and "Midnight Rambler" (an extended characterisation of a murderer and rapist, mirroring the attendant publicity on the real-life 'Boston Strangler'); although neither "Live With Me" nor the title track were far behind in the extent of their provocatively explicit sexual imagery. (And how was it, incidentally, that after his earlier scandalised response to the lyric of "Let's Spend The Night Together", Ed Sullivan now let his guard down so much as not to challenge the televising of the Stones' performances of "Gimme Shelter" and "Honky Tonk Women" when they appeared on his show for the last time on 23rd November?) Following *Through The Past, Darkly* into the LP charts - where that album had reached No.2 - *Let It Bleed* climbed all the way to No.1, a feat the Stones had last achieved with the far superior *Aftermath* back in 1966. "No set of songs," says Christopher Sandford, "has ever been more topical when it came to capturing, if not defining, a sense of end-of-an-era dissolution and moral decay."[27]

By not performing at all, the Beatles, of course, spared themselves much of the moral dilemma of squaring their musical content with preserving a sense of social responsibility; but even this stance still left them vulnerable to wilful misinterpretations of their 'message' by the likes of homicidal maniac Charles Manson. The rooftop fiasco of their live 'concert' on 30th January served to illustrate, however, that for them the real issues of concern had been reduced to: what were they doing, why were they doing it, and who were they doing it for? Their difficulties arose from them all having different answers to those fundamental questions: the Beatles no longer shared a unity of purpose.

1969 had begun for them with fractious recording sessions at Twickenham Studios as the basis for a barely conceived television special. Paul had thought of the idea, "that you'd see the Beatles rehearsing, jamming, getting their act together and then finally performing somewhere in a big end-of-show concert"[28]; but they were quickly overwhelmed by the practicalities of finding a suitable venue to bring this proposed venture to life and had been unable to agree on anything beyond at least rehearsing at Twickenham. George Martin despaired of this latest project coming to fruition, on the grounds that he could all too plainly see "there was a lot of dissension and lack of steering": "Really, they were rudderless at this time. They didn't like each other too much and were fighting amongst themselves."[29]

The first casualty of the in-fighting was George Harrison. With a working title of *Get Back*, the majority of the songs being attempted at this juncture were ultimately destined for the Beatles' final album release in May

1970, *Let It Be*; and whenever John was present at a session, so too was Yoko. By now intellectually semi-independent of the others and liberated by the establishment of Apple to undertake record production in his own right (initially with Jackie Lomax), George had been uncomfortable with this latest project from the start, describing the working atmosphere as "very unhealthy and unhappy"[30], and quickly felt himself to be under unbearable pressures at Twickenham. On 6th January, for example, he brought a significant clash with Paul to an end with the blunt rejoinder: "I'll play what you want me to play. I won't play at all if you don't want me to. Whatever it is that will please you, I'll do it."[31] By 10th January, his patience had reached breaking-point and, after airing "a litany of complaints":

> Harrison coolly announced: "I'm leaving the group." "When?"
> asked Lennon. "Now," he replied. Even then, there was no serious
> discussion. "You can replace me," Harrison offered. "Put an ad in
> the *New Musical Express* and get a few people in." Then he calmly
> strolled out of the studio.[32]

In "The Beatles Anthology", George says he was persuaded to return at a meeting with the others at Ringo's house (on 12th January), but other accounts identify at least one further meeting, on 15th January, to resolve the matter at Apple HQ in which publicist Derek Taylor played a pivotal diplomatic role. Suffice it to say that George used the opportunity with which he was now presented to his advantage, by insisting that the group should resume recording at their own Apple Studios. He was adamant that he would not return to Twickenham and he wanted no part of a live concert-cum-TV-spectacular. For once, his demands were accepted, although the Apple Studios (in the basement of Apple HQ), supposedly built to state-of-the-art specifications by 'Magic Alex', were wholly inadequate to the task and required the importation of mobile recording equipment from EMI by George Martin and Glyn Johns, who between them then spent two days making essential modifications to create a properly functioning working environment.

When recording eventually resumed, on 22nd January, George played a wild card by inviting keyboard player Billy Preston into the session, using an outsider to offset the inevitable tensions between himself, the other Beatles and Yoko, in much the same way as he had drafted Eric Clapton into playing on "While My Guitar Gently Weeps" during the *White Album* sessions. In fact, Preston participated for several days, lending a particularly fine touch on 28th January to the recording of what would be the two sides of the Beatles' next single, "Get Back" and "Don't Let Me Down". He also joined them and Yoko on the roof of Apple HQ for the 'concert' on 30th January, an event that George saw as "a nice little social study": "We went on the roof in order to resolve the live concert idea, because it was much simpler than going anywhere else; also nobody had ever done that, so it would be interesting to see what happened when we started playing up there."[33]

For just over forty minutes, for the benefit of the camera and no more than a handful of neighbouring rooftop gawpers (who included Vicki Wickham), they shattered the lunchtime calm of Savile Row and the surrounding area of the West End with a number of different takes of "Get Back", "Don't Let Me Down", "I've Got A Feeling", "The One After 909" and "Dig A Pony", before the police – reputedly summoned at the behest of a disgruntled bank manager – made their way upstairs and required Mal Evans to turn their amplifiers off. As they resignedly wound down their third rendition of "Get Back", John could not resist quipping: "I'd like to say 'thank you' on behalf of the group and ourselves and I hope we passed the audition."[34] Hence came the end of gigging for the Beatles, not with a bang but a whimper.

"Get Back" would not go on sale as a single until 11th April but it would rapidly move to occupy the No.1 slot for the whole of May, a welcome return to stylish rock'n'roll after the anthemic tedium of "Hey Jude". In the interim between the rooftop concert and its release, however, there had been significant shifts in the interpersonal dynamics of the Beatles, widening the growing cracks between them all still further.

On 12th March Paul had married Linda Eastman (with whom he had been living for several months): his long-term relationship with Jane Asher, despite the announcement of their engagement at Christmas 1967, had foundered in July 1968. No other Beatle attended the ceremony at Marylebone Register Office (Paul's brother Mike was his best man). Ringo was tied up elsewhere in the filming of *The Magic Christian* with co-star Peter Sellers[35], while John and Yoko were at Abbey Road. George and Pattie Harrison were unavailable for other reasons, having been subjected to a police raid on their Surrey home later that same day, led by Detective Sergeant Pilcher, and arrested for possession of cannabis (for which they were subsequently fined £250 each).

Linda's family were not, as often erroneously reported at the time, members of the Eastman-Kodak dynasty. On the contrary, her father Lee and older brother John worked together in the family law firm, which had an impressive existing track record of involvement in the US entertainment industry, and were therefore the obvious lawyers of choice to whom Paul turned when, from February onwards, the Beatles set upon each other to resolve their financial and management issues for the future. John, George and Ringo had opted instead to be represented in these negotiations by the voracious Allen Klein; and thus the battle lines were drawn for a long and protracted war of supremacy.

Meanwhile, on 20th March John and Yoko had flown from Paris to Gibraltar where, at the British Consulate, they too got married (a little over six weeks after Yoko's divorce from her second husband, Tony Cox); and for them the Beatles now took second place to a very public honeymoon, which after five days famously transferred from Paris to the Amsterdam Hilton and a seven-day 'bed-in' to promote the cause of world peace. On their return to England, the saga of their early married life as conceptual art, looking "just like two Gurus in drag", was then commemorated in the recording of "The Ballad Of John And Yoko" – on which, despite all their differences, John and Paul collaborated:

> Drove from Paris to the Amsterdam Hilton,
> Talking in our beds for a week.
> The newspapers said, say what're you doing in bed,
> I said we're only trying to get us some peace.
> Christ! You know it ain't easy,
> You know how hard it can be.
> The way things are going,
> They're going to crucify me.[36]

For its day, with its references to Christ and crucifixion verging on blasphemy, for many the song was too outspoken, attracting an immediate ban from the BBC on its release on 30th May but soon rescinded: there was undoubtedly an element in it of John getting his own back for the way he had been castigated over the 'Jesus' controversy of 1966. Nevertheless, it still enjoyed two weeks at No.1 at the end of June.

Having deliberately turned themselves into a sideshow, John and Yoko thereafter attracted much bemused interest, publicity they gladly courted for their own ends. In May, for example, over the course of two weeks the BBC broadcast excerpts from an interview with them conducted by David Wigg for Radio 1's *Scene And Heard*. Consider here the deftness of John's response when challenged on the point of the 'bed-in':

> *David:* A lot of people also feel that if everyone goes to bed and stays in bed for a week or a few days for peace, as a protest for peace, the whole country will come to a standstill.

> *John:* Well, wouldn't it be better than producing arms and bombs? Imagine if the American army stayed in bed for a week and the Vietnamese army. Or Nixon ... and Kosygin, Chairman Mao. Imagine it, if the whole world stayed in bed. There'd be peace for a week and they might get to feel what it was like. The tension would be released.[37]

Or his surefooted reaction, a few moments later, to the pair's fear of being ridiculed for their beliefs:

> *David:* But the only thing that disturbs me a little is that a lot of

people are jeering, aren't they? And making fun, not taking you seriously.

John: But that is good. That's part of our policy – not to be taken seriously, because I think our opposition, whoever they may be in all their manifest forms, don't know how to handle humour. And we are humourists. We are Laurel and Hardy, that's John and Yoko. And we stand a better chance under that guise, because all the serious people like Martin Luther King and Kennedy and Gandhi got shot.[38]

Exchanges such as these, in turn, served the purpose of softening the media up for their next trick, the release on 4th July of the Plastic Ono Band's "Give Peace A Chance", written by John and Yoko – although officially credited to Lennon & McCartney – and recorded at the Hotel Reine-Elizabeth in Montreal during a second 'bed-in' there at the end of May. ("It was taped," so Mark Lewisohn tells us, "on borrowed professional equipment and featured John on acoustic guitar/vocal and a suite chock-full of friends and visitors singing along in the choruses."[39]) This simplistic yet instantly memorable anti-war chant broke into the chart for 12th July, while Thunderclap Newman's "Something In The Air" was at No.1, and by 2nd August had lodged at No.2, beneath the Stones' "Honky Tonk Women". Whatever it may have lacked in profundity, it made up for in its raw enthusiasm and would be followed in October by a second Plastic Ono Band single, "Cold Turkey", John's harrowing musical account of drug dependency and withdrawal that bore only a sole composing credit to 'Lennon' and by late November peaked at No.13. The band's line-up showed some discontinuity between recording and live performance but the core remained: John (guitar/vocals) and Yoko (vocals), plus Eric Clapton (lead guitar) and Klaus Voorman (bass guitar). In their two concerts (one in Toronto in September, another in London's Lyceum Ballroom in December), Alan White played drums but in the studio John drafted in Ringo.

The next single released by the Beatles, a week after "Cold Turkey", did, however, constitute a first, in that one of its double-A-sides was a composition by George, "Something", taken (as was its pairing, "Come Together") from the *Abbey Road* LP. Reaching No.5 for three weeks from November into December, it served to illustrate George's growing versatility at this time; for, like John, he too had turned to performing with others, joining Eric Clapton on stage in support of American duo Delaney & Bonnie for five out of six nights from 2nd December onwards[40], as well as having already produced the Radha Krishna Temple's "Hare Krishna Mantra" on the Apple label, the unlikeliest No.11 hit of October. Ringo had also branched out musically, setting about, from the end of October, the recording of a solo album of standards with George Martin's assistance (that would eventually see the light of day, in March 1970, as *Sentimental Journey*).

This left, after a shambolic year of fitful recording from January through to August, *Abbey Road* as the crowning glory of the Beatles' last year together, confusingly their last album to be completed though not their last to be released.[41] With its iconic cover photograph shot on the zebra crossing outside the Abbey Road studios by Ian Macmillan on 8th August, *Abbey Road* was released on 26th September, was No.1 in the LP charts for seventeen weeks and became the Beatles' third best-selling album of the decade, after *Sgt. Pepper's Lonely Hearts Club Band* and *With The Beatles*. "The romantic in you," says Sean Egan, "… likes to think of *Abbey Road* as a statement of where they had taken the music that had inspired them and brought them together in the first instance, and as a public acknowledgement of the fact that they could do no more for it: having taken it as far as it could go, the Beatles bowed out."[42]

Whilst this may be so, it still remains an annoyingly uneven record. There are two outstanding contributions from George, in "Something" and "Here Comes The Sun". There is a reprise of the good-time spirit of "Yellow Submarine" in Ringo's song "Octopus's Garden" (which he had written in Sardinia in August 1968, after taking his voluntary leave of absence from the *White Album* sessions). But there is also a particularly ugly and uncomfortable contribution to the set from John, in the form of "I Want You (She's So Heavy)", a classic example of the genre peculiar to the late Sixties of 'songs that go on interminably because mindless repetition has to be preferable to thinking of a half-decent ending': Ian MacDonald called it "the most emotionally extreme statement on any Beatles record".[43]

The LP is saved and uplifted, as 'twas ever thus, by the collaboration between George Martin and the Beatles in what they termed the 'Long Medley' that takes up most of Side 2 and arguably represents their finest collective work. Ringo certainly thought so: "After the *Let It Be* nightmare, *Abbey Road* turned out fine. The second side is brilliant. Out of the ashes of all that madness, that last section is for me one of the finest pieces we put together."[44]

Nowhere else, I would suggest, can you find a better example of their singing in harmony than in "Because"; although receptivity to its beauty comes with a health warning:

Many have admired this song's mood of visionary detachment without taking account of the heroin then flowing coldly around its composer's [i.e., John Lennon's] body. Fifty days after finishing "Because", he was back in the studio howling his addiction in "Cold Turkey".[45]

And you would be equally hard-pushed to find another smooth-rolling rock number comparable to Paul's "She Came In Through The Bathroom Window", or another song of such compelling contextual poignancy as his "You Never Give Me Your Money". Side 2 is rounded off with a joke, of course, for "The End" is not the end, that honour falling twenty seconds later to the final irreverent snippet of "Her Majesty". (John, of course, was famously less in awe of the Queen than Paul, very publicly returning his MBE via his chauffeur to Buckingham Palace on 25th November and writing to Harold Wilson that the gesture was "in protest against Britain's involvement in the Nigeria-Biafra thing, against our support of America in Vietnam and against 'Cold Turkey' slipping down the charts".[46])

Yet it is to "The End", given its timing in the irreversible progress of the Beatles' demise (as seen, that is, through the eyes of the album's purchasers in the autumn of 1969), that everyone turns in hope for insight into and understanding of their predicament. Many years later, Paul confirmed that it had been a specially contrived piece, imbued for them with symbolism:

> In "The End" there were three guitar solos where John, George and I took a line each, which was something we'd never done before. And we finally persuaded Ringo to play a drum solo, which he'd never wanted to do. And it climaxed with, 'And in the end, the love you make is equal to the love you take …' [47]

Which, in John's considered opinion, was a "very cosmic, philosophical line".[48]

If asked to predict the whereabouts of Bob Dylan's international comeback in 1969, the Isle of Wight would in all likelihood not even have been remotely considered for a place on the shortlist. Indeed, as the summer wore on, many American fans were hoping and praying that by their sheer numbers alone they could exert a sufficient gravitational pull to oblige him to materialise at the giant music festival planned for his own backyard in Woodstock, New York State; but it was that very proximity to his home and family life, that presumption of intrusion upon his privacy, that not just kept him away but drove him away. He chose instead to succumb to the gentler approaches of Ronnie and Ray Foulk, who wanted him to appear as the headline act at their second Isle of Wight Festival for a modest fee of $50,000 (equivalent then to approximately £20,000) and played on his new-found vulnerability as a family man to secure his agreement. At their expense, they offered him a fortnight's holiday with his wife and son "in a farmhouse at Bembridge with a swimming pool and a recently converted barn, suitable for rehearsing in"[49], together with berths on the *QE2* for their passage from New York to Southampton and the services of a dedicated car and driver for the duration of their stay.

Their plan nearly came to grief on embarkation day, 13th August, however, when Dylan's four-year-old son Jesse injured himself prior to sailing with a blow to the head and fell unconscious, causing the family to leave the liner and accompany the boy to hospital ashore in New York. Thankfully, he made a rapid recovery but it meant that the transatlantic cruise had to be traded for a later transatlantic flight on 25th August. On his arrival, Dylan described his English fans as "the most loyal fans I have and that was one of the reasons to … come to England to make my comeback", further claiming that he was less motivated by the money he had been offered than "just [wanting] to play music".[50]

By the evening of 31st August, therefore, when Dylan was due to take to the stage, expectations all round were very high. Since his last UK appearances in 1966, his output in terms of new recordings had been sparse: the overall intensity of 1968's *John Wesley Harding* had been succeeded in the spring of 1969 by the seemingly more frivolous – if not lightweight – *Nashville Skyline*, which had entered the UK LP charts in May and spent four weeks at No.1, despite its total running time of barely twenty-seven minutes. (The release as a single of one of the stronger tracks from the new album, "I Threw It All Away", had offered a further appetiser, peaking at No.21 in the Top 30 chart for 31st May.)

With hindsight, *Nashville Skyline* was another enigmatic stepping-stone en route to Dylan's new-chosen future, picking up where the closing track of *John Wesley Harding*, "I'll Be Your Baby Tonight", had left off in its reinvention of country music. It was a mellow, unconcerned album, decidedly a mixed bag, full of hints of almost mundane preoccupations that the previous angry incarnation of Dylan had kept well hidden. The instrumental "Nashville Skyline Rag", for instance, would not have been out of place four years hence in his soundtrack to *Pat Garrett & Billy The Kid*, as a companion piece, say, to "Turkey Chase". He had always admired Hank Williams, so why not emulate him in "One More Night"? And why not regress to his beginnings in a slightly sloppy reprise of "Girl From The North Country" as a duet with friend and rival Johnny Cash? There was nothing to disturb or excite on offer here, though the strongest song of all, "Lay Lady Lay"[51], was impressively executed, beating "Tonight I'll Be Staying Here With You" into close second place. If, alternatively, you wanted throwaway novelty value, then look no further than "Peggy Day" or "Country Pie".

It meant that all bets were off as to the contents of Dylan's set list for the Isle of Wight and he was not well served on the day by the deficiencies of the festival's organisation. Having been led to expect he would be playing at 7.30 p.m., he didn't actually start his act until shortly after 11.00 p.m., by which time many of the 100,000-plus audience were decidedly restless, some lobbing empty drinks cans at the stage in their frustration. Although he had brought the Band over to back him, he was actually scheduled to appear after their own discrete live set, which itself had started hours late and was then followed by a further forty minutes' delay; the critical issue in all this seeming to be not so much any necessary adjustments to the equipment on stage between acts as the belaboured attention directed to corralling a myriad of press and celebrities into their special enclosures.

Whilst this was to be their first official performance together since the Woody Guthrie memorial concert in January 1968, Dylan had publicly reunited with the Band on 14th July – incognito as 'Elmer Johnson' – to sing three non-original songs with them as they took their encore at the Mississippi River Festival in Edwardsville, Illinois.[52] A subsequent report in *Rolling Stone* had described Dylan on this occasion as a "guitar-toting, cowboyish figure in brown shirt, pants and boots", "relaxed" to the point of his voice still being "*Nashville-Skylined*".[53] Seven weeks on, the voice may have been the same but when at last he stepped out in front of the Isle of Wight crowd he looked cool, in an all-white suit.

History has, however, been unkind to this performance, blaming Dylan for the late start and then complaining about the length of his set (fractionally over an hour) but making very little reference to what he actually sang. He was understandably bemused by this savaging at the hands of the English press. Typical of the criticism levelled at him was the front-page story of the following week's *Disc & Music Echo*, reporting that "most fans were too stunned by the shortness of his act *after what they had been led to expect* [my italics] either to cheer or leave the arena", so instead they "ripped down the arena's surrounding fences and lit bonfires of protest".[54]

Trouble was, the key to understanding this reaction lay in appreciating the full impact of what had been circulating beforehand as ridiculously optimistic pre-festival hype, credited by the same report to the event's promoters, the Foulk Brothers and Rikki Farr:

> … who had announced their anticipation of an act of anything up to three hours followed by a jam session on stage with such stars as the Beatles and Rolling Stones [and] admitted they were "very disappointed" by the brevity of Dylan's act.
>
> "We expected him to be on stage a good bit longer than an hour," said Peter Harrigan, a festival official. "I don't know whether we would want to re-book him after this."[55]

While members of the rock aristocracy, some of whom had visited him privately in the days beforehand, were certainly in the audience (including George Harrison, John Lennon and Ringo Starr; Keith Richards, Charlie Watts and Bill Wyman; and Eric Clapton), they were there essentially to pay homage to him, none of them intent on upstaging him at his first full live concert in years.

The set that Dylan and the Band actually played that night was an eclectic mix of older, newer and unknown songs.[56] It should have had something for everyone, even though it did noticeably lack the unforgiving bite and ferocity of their 1966 UK concerts; and it trailed the intriguing approach that Dylan would take to live performances in the future, reserving the right to edit his songs and/or play and sing them in an infinite variety of arrangements according to his changing moods. Given his long absence from a stage anywhere, it is also worth remembering that he was singing almost half of the seventeen numbers live for the first time, and all of them in his new "*Nashville-Skylined*" voice.

Opening with "She Belongs To Me", there was a liberal helping of other past firm favourites, like "It Ain't Me Babe", a cut-down "Mr. Tambourine Man" and even a revisiting of "To Ramona"; but the rockier numbers of old ("Maggie's Farm", "Highway 61 Revisited" and "Like A Rolling Stone") were admittedly delivered as paler shadows of their former selves. Coming more up to date, he sampled both *John Wesley Harding* ("I Dreamed I Saw St. Augustine", "I Pity The Poor Immigrant" and "I'll Be Your Baby Tonight") and *Nashville Skyline* ("I Threw It All Away" and "Lay Lady Lay"), as well as raiding *The Basement Tapes* for "(Quinn The Eskimo) The Mighty Quinn" – occasioning a favourable name-check for Manfred Mann's hit version – and "Minstrel Boy". There was a rare throwback to much earlier folk days in the company of Joan Baez with a rendition of the traditional ballad "Wild Mountain Thyme"; and a brave attempt to lift the crowd's spirits at the end with "Rainy Day Women Nos.12 & 35" as the closing number.

It was hardly fair, therefore, to accuse Dylan of short-changing the audience, unless you had been expecting to see more fire in his belly as if the trials and tribulations of his past three years had simply evaporated. For his part, he was totally disenchanted with the lukewarm response he had drawn from his supposedly most loyal fanbase, especially since it marked his last concert of the decade, and he would not play live again for another two years (when he accepted George Harrison's invitation to take part in the legendary Concert for Bangladesh, staged at Madison Square Garden on 1st August 1971). Yet it had served its purpose well as the starting-point for a new alchemy that he and first the Band and then others would perfect between them when he resumed serious touring in the mid-Seventies; the undeniable next signs of which you can find in his more confident reworking of songs like "It Ain't Me Babe" or "Highway 61 Revisited", for instance, on the 1974 album *Before The Flood*, or his translation of "I Threw It All Away" into the rock idiom as captured on 1975's *Hard Rain*.

As it happened, Dylan was not the only prominent American artist in 1969 to dare to entrust British audiences with the ability to revive their fortunes. The same was sadly true of the Beach Boys, although Brian Wilson's candour about it could not have been worse timed. With the live band all set to embark on a major UK and European tour for a month from 30th May, three days earlier Brian had convened an impromptu press conference at his house, at which he declared that the Beach Boys were on the verge of bankruptcy and desperately needed the tour to succeed to ensure the group's future. But even this was a smokescreen, up to a point, for the hidden object of the European leg of the tour was to enable them to secure a new recording contract with German label Deutsche Grammophon, as their current contract with Capitol rapidly approached its expiry on 30th June and they remained locked in a legal dispute, initiated in April, to recover close to $2 million in unpaid royalties and production fees owed to Brian.

Despite a disappointing response to "Bluebirds Over The Mountain" before Christmas, the Beach Boys had somehow managed to retain the residual interest of British record-buyers in sufficient numbers to boost sales of their February release, "I Can Hear Music" (like "Then I Kissed Her", a cover version of an earlier classic production by Phil Spector and now rearranged and produced for them by their own Carl Wilson). Entering the Top 30 at No.27 in March, it peaked in mid-April at No.11. The next single, however, marked a return to an original composition – with a twist: "Break Away", a collaboration between Brian and father Murry. Released in June to coincide with their tour, the Beach Boys featured it as a song in their live set but by the time it was a UK hit, eventually spending two weeks at No.6 in July, they were long gone. Its success was at least testimony to the hard work they had put in while they were here, which had gained them some much-needed commendation:

> If the Beach Boys are really in Britain just to make some quick
> money and get themselves in the black again … they're certainly
> making sure they earned it! At the sedate Hammersmith Odeon on
> Saturday [31st May] the world's most popular active group turned
> an uncommonly apathetic first-house audience into rousing cheers
> with 50 non-stop minutes taking in no less than 18 hits.[57]

At the same time, it was noted that Mike Love was still clinging on to his belief in the power of transcendental meditation long after most other celebrities had passed on it, to the extent that he now cut a strange dash on stage; having "grown his beard, grown his hair (on those parts of his head where it still grows, that is)", and having "acquired an incredible white tunic/mini-habit" to create the "overall effect [of] a cross between the Maharishi's younger brother and the original hermit from the hills."[58]

Gratifying to the Beach Boys' egos as the adulation they received may have been, neither record nor ticket sales would rescue them financially on this occasion, and the prospective deal with Deutsche Grammophon fell through too, when Mike Love prevaricated over the offer made to them in a face-to-face meeting at the company's headquarters in Berlin. By the time the group had returned home and Love had overcome his misgivings, it was too late to retrieve the situation and the offer was withdrawn. It would not be until November that they finally managed to strike a new deal with Warner/Reprise and set back out on the long, long road to recovery. At the same time, they were to suffer the unexpected loss of an important and symbolic income stream without warning, when Murry Wilson, believing that by now the Beach Boys were finished, relinquished control of the rights to their back catalogue, selling their music publishing company – of which he had been sole owner since 1965 – for $700,000. Notwithstanding Murry's criminal lack of foresight, the decline in their standing at home was all too evident in the poor attendances of the concerts on their annual Thanksgiving Tour, funded on credit cards and now "turned into a miserable, low-key operation with audience numbers struggling to reach even a couple of hundred at some shows ... a dismal farewell to an otherwise memorable decade for the group".[59] Who could possibly have imagined that by the end of the Sixties America's greatest-ever band would be all washed up?

In contradictory fashion, Jimi Hendrix showed every sign of tiring of Britain, the country that had kick-started his solo career, and looked west for his salvation. By 1969, he had become a virtual stranger to the British charts anyway: his only hit single of the year was in April, with a sole week at No.30 for "Crosstown Traffic", one of the more commercial tracks lifted from his last LP. Having already parted company with Chas Chandler in 1968 during the making of *Electric Ladyland*[60], after wanting more of a personal say in its production, he was now more than ambivalent towards sustaining the illusion of the Experience as the unit to carry him into the future and his working relationship with bassist Noel Redding in particular was at a low ebb.

One of the trio's last UK television appearances typified Hendrix's increasing restlessness and has gone down, for good or ill, as a defining moment in pop history. This was on 4th January, when the Experience were Lulu's guests on her Saturday-night show for the BBC, *A Happening For Lulu*. As the end of the programme rapidly approached, they had played "Voodoo Child", after which, according to the protocol of such variety shows of the period, Jimi and Lulu were allegedly pencilled in to sing a duet together – a bizarre thought, if ever there was one. It never happened, as Charles R. Cross's account explains:

> ... Lulu finished her introduction: "They're gonna sing for you right now the song that absolutely made them in this country, "Hey Joe", and I love to hear them sing it." They played about two minutes

of "Hey Joe" before Jimi paused: "We'd like to stop playing this rubbish and dedicate a song to the Cream, regardless of what kind of group they may be in. We dedicate this to Eric Clapton, Ginger Baker, and Jack Bruce." With that, the band broke into "Sunshine Of Your Love". As the Experience played a lengthy version of the song in honour of the Cream's recent breakup, off camera the stage director was signalling at Jimi to stop. Hendrix's response, which only the director could see, was to gesture with his middle finger. The Experience kept playing, eventually using up all the remaining time on the live show.[61]

As I well remember from viewing it at the time, the programme thus came to a disorderly end, having over-run, with Hendrix protesting gratuitously at being taken off the air. He said of the incident afterwards: "It was the same old thing with people telling us what to do … so I caught Noel's and Mitch's attention, and we went into "Sunshine Of Your Love". If you play live, nobody can stop you or dictate what you play, beyond setting a time limit."[62]

In a matter of weeks, the Experience would be playing their last-ever UK concert, at the Royal Albert Hall on 24th February, and Hendrix would again be further articulating his desire to move on: "A couple of years ago all I wanted out of life was to be heard. Now I'm trying to figure out the wisest way to be heard. I don't want to be a clown anymore. I don't want to be a rock and roll star. I'm just a musician."[63] Redding too was expressing his frustration at how, with the loss of Chas Chandler not just as manager and producer but, more importantly, a critical friend, the Experience was reaching the end of its natural span: "The pressure from the public to create something even more brilliant each time, while basically expecting us to stay the same, was crushing."[64]

At the beginning of March, the group took off for America, months on tour being interspersed with recording sessions in which Hendrix turned to a variety of other musicians, notably his old friend from his US Army days, Billy Cox, who slowly but surely supplanted Redding on bass guitar in the studio. The Experience's final concert was on 29th June, at the Denver Pop Festival, a gig that ended in a riot after Hendrix had ill-advisedly announced to the crowd: "This is the last time we're playing in the States, and like, it's been really a lot of fun."[65] They were forced to vacate the stage, amid clouds of tear gas as police struggled to regain control, and take refuge in a truck that was then besieged by rampaging fans. Although Hendrix was content to retain Mitch Mitchell's services as drummer in his future musical configurations, Redding, now effectively excluded, flew back to England the very next day, leaving Hendrix to deliver his own ambiguous eulogy for the group:

> Noel Redding is into more harmonic things, when you sing and so forth, and he went to England to get his own group together[66] …

Noel and I are still friends, but he has his own ideas, and musically
I want to go somewhere else … Maybe we could have gone on,
but what would have been the point of that, what would it have
been good for? It's a ghost now, it's dead, like back pages in a diary.
I'm into new things, and I want to think about tomorrow, not
yesterday.[67]

In a slight return a little later in this chapter, we shall see what in fact he made
of what tomorrow looked like.

While some were going under and some were keen to start afresh,
others kept going in the belief that their latest enterprises would capture their
public's imagination; and it goes without saying that even in that belief some
were more successful than others. To illustrate the point, let us consider for
a moment the parallel fortunes of the Kinks and the Who, whose respective
major works of the year were based on the same broad concept – namely,
telling a story through music – yet suffered markedly different fates.

First, then, to the Kinks. You won't find *Arthur Or The Decline And Fall
Of The British Empire* in any LP chart listings, for the simple fact that it wasn't
a hit, although you will surely know the album's opening track, "Victoria"
(which, more surprisingly, was hardly a hit either and not within this book's
specific time-frame: it crawled to No.30 for one week only in January 1970).
And one of the fundamental reasons why *Arthur* wasn't a hit was that the
TV drama for which it had been composed was consigned to the dustbin of
history, leaving it high and dry, as Peter Doggett explains, as:

… the soundtrack album for a film that was never made – not
a conceptual art project or an imaginary movie, but the musical
accompaniment for a script that was written, approved, cast,
budgeted, and then cancelled, after a squabble between producer
and production company escalated into a complete breakdown in
relations.[68]

The Kinks had a lot riding on *Arthur*. Once the project had been
agreed in principle with Granada Television in early January, Ray Davies had
been tasked with working up the storyline in association with author Julian
Mitchell. It looked at the world through the eyes of Arthur Morgan, in the
course of one Sunday, the last day spent in England by his son Derek and
daughter-in-law Liz before emigrating to Australia with their two children,
Terry and Marilyn; and Frank Finlay had been cast in the title role. Although
it bore close resemblance to the Davies' own family history, with the emigra-
tion of Ray and Dave's elder sister Rose and her husband Arthur Anning, Ray
was careful to draw a distinction between art and life: "People sometimes still
find it hard to remember that I write from character, not necessarily from an

autobiographical perspective. So the feelings in the songs aren't necessarily mine, or those of anyone else in my family: they belong to my characters."[69]

Recording had commenced at Pye Studios in May, the first sessions attempted by a new line-up of the group. The single "Plastic Man", released on 28th March and barely troubling the Top 30 at No.28 by the end of April, was the last record on which Pete Quaife had played as bass guitarist. (A lively, upbeat song, in many ways a satiric reprise of "A Well Respected Man", it might have been a bigger hit had the straight-laced BBC not taken against it for its nowadays innocuous reference to Plastic Man's "plastic legs that reach up to his plastic bum".[70]) Quaife, who had, of course, all but left once before in 1966, now officially and determinedly left the Kinks as from 3rd April, having reached a low point at which he "felt like a second-rate, hired musician … having nothing to say about my musical abilities, my career or life"[71]; and on his departure, John Dalton was again approached (by Mick Avory on the group's behalf) to be his replacement. After his earlier experience with them as a hired hand, Dalton was initially reluctant to rejoin the Kinks: "I think they expected me to drop everything and jump at it."[72] Nevertheless, he did allow himself to be persuaded to come back on board, timing it perfectly to participate in the studio sessions for *Arthur*.

Apart from its crucial contribution to UK record sales and the forthcoming drama, Ray saw the song cycle he had created for *Arthur* as being of equal significance in recapturing the imagination of the Kinks' long-lost US audiences. For during a visit to Los Angeles in mid-April to produce a new album by the Turtles, Ray had found that, as if by sleight of hand, the Federation of Musicians were at last willing to lift the unofficial ban imposed in 1965 on the Kinks performing in America, thus opening the way again for a US concert tour. Welcome as this was, the tour, scheduled from 17th October to 8th December, was, after four years' absence, an instant culture shock: "The American musical scene had certainly changed, and we were taken aback by our own almost naïve attempts to conform to the new rock industry that had evolved since our previous American tour."[73] Opening at New York's Fillmore East Auditorium, things got off to a shaky start:

> It was the "prodigals'" return, the second coming, but our performance was below par. Unused to the sophisticated stage equipment, we must have sounded like a bunch of skiffle players in the back room of a pub … We were promoting our new album *Arthur* … and the Fillmore was to be a taster event that would set the tone for the rest of the US dates. But anyone who witnessed the Kinks' concerts at that time was astounded by the contradictions in our performance. Foppish, almost effeminate behaviour in some songs and brutal, brute force in some of the harder rock songs.[74]

A reporter covering the Fillmore gig for the music paper *Cashbox* described the Kinks as not seeming "excited about what they were doing" and their music as "lukewarm"[75]; but the pace picked up as they went along and when the tour ended, with a final date at a New York club called Ungano's, Ray thankfully noted that "the show did more to enhance our reputation in America than any of the other dates on the tour"[76], as borne out by this enthusiastic contemporary reviewer:

> At the beginning [at the Fillmore] the group had been friendly and good but unspectacular as it adjusted to the country. Then reports spread of great concerts. They came back again for [this] one show before they split. They were great. The Kinks are simply one of the best, most distinctive rock groups in the world ... The evening was an event. The Kinks, as never before, are exciting and relevant rock artists. Bravo! [77]

Alas, the Kinks' US record company, Reprise, were underwhelmed by the tour's inability to boost sales of *Arthur* (which had been released simultaneously in the UK and US on 10th October): when it ended, a senior executive advised Ray that they should "do the whole tour again, but this time with a worldwide hit, like the ones we had in the old days".[78] Further disappointment greeted them on their return to England, when a spat between producer Jo Derden-Smith and Granada caused the company to cancel the making of *Arthur* as a film for television. The project was never to be resurrected, leaving the album as its only legacy and "Victoria" as the nearest any of the tracks came to being a hit within a year of its making (after unsuccessful single releases of two others, "Drivin'" and "Shangri La", in June and September respectively).

In one of the last coincidences to litter the pages of this book, in the course of the Kinks' revival tour of America, their paths crossed with the Who for a double-billing on 31st October in Chicago. Just as the Kinks turned the spotlight on *Arthur* in their set, the centrepiece of the Who's act was their own highly contentious musical drama, *Tommy* (released as a double album in the UK on 23rd May, reaching No.2 in the LP charts and heralded by the preceding release of "Pinball Wizard" as a single on 7th March – their only UK single of the year and a No.4 hit in May, in the same week as the Beatles' "Get Back" went to No.1).

For all the impenetrability of the concept, *Tommy* proved to be the Who's salvation in 1969, bringing about radical change in the nature of the hitherto fraught relationships within the group as well as in others' perceptions of their musical orientation. As Ray Davies had done in developing a storyline for *Arthur*, so Pete Townshend drew heavily – and, in places, painfully – on personal experience to inform the extraordinary saga of *Tommy*;

but their paths diverged in the ways they related their separate works to a post-war context. Whereas Davies focused much of his attention on articulating the specific impact on his characters of post-imperialism, Townshend ambitiously cast his net far wider:

> … as a young man, when the war was only 25 years old and I was writing *Tommy*, we had this spiritual new wave, this turn to psychedelic drugs, Vietnam, peace campaigns, but people having no sense of belonging to the world. I thought, 'Why does our music have to be so violent, what's it about? What's the anger to do with?' All of this stuff seemed to me to be about the post-war geography of the UK. So I wanted to write this thing about how spirituality had come from street anger that had come from suppressed teenage disaffection that had come from post-war denial. In other words, people who had been in wars who had seen something quite diabolical pretending that it hadn't happened for the benefit of their children who then grew up in a lie, that lie being that everything was OK now, when it wasn't. Because what has to be dealt with is the healing process and it wasn't being dealt with.[79]

High-minded ideals indeed. How precisely they relate to the work conceived over time through a piecemeal process of composition (driven by Townshend taking inspiration from both his spiritual guide, the Indian mystic Meher Baba, and the Who's classically grounded co-manager Kit Lambert, who helped him flesh out the plot) remains unclear even today:

> Germinating from "Amazing Journey", the first Townshend lyric to specify its deaf, dumb and blind protagonist, the Who's opus began to take shape. Eventually a basic plotline emerged involving a war baby who, after witnessing a violent act, is shocked into losing all sensory perception, is then abused by family members, later becomes a media celebrity, rediscovers his senses, is hailed as a messiah but is finally rejected by his followers for failing to deliver them to the same state of spiritual enlightenment.
>
> As the sessions progressed … so the fine details were coloured in. Murder, infidelity, pervy uncles, bullying cousins, drugs, holiday camps, pinball, revolution and the christening of the deaf, dumb and blind hero as Tommy Walker. It was a mind-boggling if illogical yarn featuring several scenes that could easily be misinterpreted as morally offensive.[80]

With recording completed in March and a release date in May, the Who went public with *Tommy* almost before the Kinks had started working seriously on the very different *Arthur*. A precedent for an obscure and dark concept album had already been set, however, by the Pretty Things, who in

1967 had switched labels from Fontana to EMI's Columbia and, forsaking heavy R&B for psychedelia, had come up with *S. F. Sorrow*. The inescapably miserable story of a man called Sorrow, beset with tragedy and whose life is therefore prophetically spent in almost perpetual misery, with the last track appropriately titled "Loneliest Person" ("You might be the loneliest person in the world/You'll never be as lonely as me"[81]), it was released in November 1968, at the same time as the Beatles' *White Album* and the Kinks' *Village Green Preservation Society*, but would receive little or no critical recognition until years later.

"Pinball Wizard" becoming a hit single had, of course, blazed a trail for the completed LP – even if it was the flashiest and most commercial of all the tracks on *Tommy* – and had already drawn the sting of adverse reaction to a hero with multi-sensory deprivation when Tony Blackburn had condemned the song as 'sick'. What happened next was that, as a consciously collective decision, the Who reconstructed their live performances around *Tommy*, a remarkable act of faith on the part of the others in Townshend's creative drive; and Townshend himself would later say that "the 'pretentiousness' of *Tommy* was necessary. Without its audacity and cheek to attract both attention and opprobrium, I believe the Who would have eventually disappeared or become irrelevant".[82]

It was, in particular, the making of Roger Daltrey, who grew in stature by changing his image from that of "a rocker trying to compete in a Mod's uniform"[83] and was at last taken seriously as a vocalist as a result of assuming the title role of Tommy Walker. Townshend's own immediate fear now became "getting a hit single after *Tommy* ... something I thought might never happen again".[84] However, with so little remaining of the Sixties, he would have to be content in the short term with achieving that by proxy, which he did as producer of Thunderclap Newman's "Something In The Air" (on which he also played bass guitar, under the pseudonym 'Bijou Drains'), a song insistently boasting of revolution that gave them a No.1 hit in July.

In a year of festivals, one stood out above all others – Woodstock – and it was here in August, at the first 'Aquarian Exposition', that both the Who and Jimi Hendrix turned in legendary performances. An event from which myths of hyperbolic proportions can still not be detached almost fifty years later, the Woodstock Music and Art Fair took its name from the town in the New York State countryside where famously Bob Dylan had settled with his family but was actually held elsewhere in the State, some sixty-odd miles away on Max Yasgur's farm at White Lake, near the town of Bethel.

On the site today, to paraphrase Joni Mitchell, paradise has been paved and they have put up a parking lot, to accommodate the Bethel Woods Centre for the Arts, where "Hippy T-shirts, music posters and even a piece of the original fence that surrounded the concert are displayed with the reverence of Roman marbles at the British Museum"; while down "a hard-to-find muddy lane in the hills outside town lies another museum that has kept the 1960s spirit firmly alive, rather than putting it inside a display case or selling it as slogans on T-shirts", running on "donations, goodwill and solar power".[85] On the Bethel Woods website, if you're of an age, you're invited to add your name to the registry of Woodstock alumni, donate a reminiscence of the festival or submit artefacts for possible approval as exhibits – always remembering that ultimately "only those items of historical significance that support the museum's mission" will be accepted.[86] On the website for the alternative Woodstock Museum, founded by Nathan Koenig and Shelli Lipton, you're encouraged to make a visit there so you can learn "the truth about organics, solar energy, marijuana and questioning authority".[87]

Back in the day, the fact that Woodstock took place at all was by no means by design but rather thanks to a chapter of happy accidents. In the planning, it had always been envisaged by the organisers as a hard-nosed commercial venture: "We hadn't intended it to be a free festival, we sold tickets and had concessions and intended to exploit the festival in whatever ways we could to make a profit."[88] But a month away from the opening day, consent to use of the original site at a place called Wallkill (geographically much closer to Woodstock) was withdrawn and a new venue had to be found in a hurry. Johnny Roberts, one of the festival's co-founding financial backers, and Michael Lang, the festival's executive producer, lighted upon Max Yasgur's dairy farm, "looking", as Max's son Sam recalled, "to rent a field for three days" and deeming one particularly suitable because of its "bowl-shaped topography".[89]

Although Max was willing to help, he was far more driven by a shrewd business sense than by altruism and struck a deal of $75,000 for the use of his land. Once word got out, though, that a hippie invasion was imminent, it brought him grief from his neighbours, which he was quick to counter with gusto:

> I can remember him saying to one of them, "Look, the reason you
> don't want them here is because you don't like what they look like.
> And I don't particularly like what they look like either. But that's
> not the point. They may be protesting the war, but thousands of
> American soldiers have died so they can do exactly what they're
> doing. That's what the essence of the country is all about." And,
> from that point on, he became a champion.[90]

Aged 49 and Republican by political persuasion, Max apparently had nothing in common with the so-called 'Woodstock nation', and yet on the third day of the festival he was persuaded to take to the stage and address the huge gathering on his land, which he did, with equal measures of trepidation and dignity:

> I'm a farmer. I don't know – I don't know how to speak to twenty people at one time, let alone a crowd like this. But I think you people have proven something to the world … This is the largest group of people ever assembled in one place … the important thing that you've proven to the world is that half a million kids – an' I call yuh kids because I have children that are older than you are – a half a million young people can get together and have three days of fun and music and have nothing but fun and music. An' God bless yuh for it! [91]

It was the unprecedented scale of interest in the festival that caught the organisers off guard, as the inadequate infrastructure of the event collapsed under the sheer weight of numbers from the very beginning of Day 1, Friday 15th August. Estimates of those attending vary wildly, climbing upwards from a baseline of at least 450,000 and most commonly rounded to half a million. Any last vestige of thought of checking who were and who weren't ticket-holders on entry to the site had to be abandoned as totally impracticable, given the press of people and the breaking-through or breaking-down of boundary fences by the vast majority, though not everyone was necessarily set on being lawless: "I, being the good Catholic schoolboy, was looking for an entrance gate and someone to give my ticket to. I looked to the left and the right of the stage, there were no fences, no gate, just all these kids walking up the hill coming and going from all directions."[92]

Production manager John Morris, rapidly reconciled to the impossibility of collecting money from such a multitude of non-payers, was thus forced to bow to the inevitable and make a famous public announcement early in the proceedings: "It's a free concert from now on. That doesn't mean that anything goes. What that means is we're going to put the music up here for free. What it means is … that your welfare is a hell of a lot more important, and that the music is, than the dollar …"[93] Bearing in mind the number of acts booked and the fees paid to each one, in addition to the staging costs and the rental fee for the venue paid to Max Yasgur, the scale of the hit the backers took on this occasion was, like every other aspect of this historic event, monumental.

The continuing ingress of festival-goers on foot and in cars blocked the roads for miles around the site, meaning that many of the intended first-day performers were stranded in their hotels and motels far away and alternative arrangements to fly them in by helicopter had to be hurriedly made. As a consequence, no live music was actually played until late on Friday afternoon, when Richie Havens was thrust on stage with an acoustic guitar and minimal accompaniment, well out of programme sequence, not just to kick off proceedings but to keep the crowds entertained and quiescent in the process; the twenty minutes he was originally asked to play eventually turning into an improvised set lasting for the best part of three hours.

Much of the mythology of Woodstock has been sustained ever since by Michael Wadleigh's documentary film and the two soundtrack double-albums that were subsequently released, but both sources remain misleading in that between them they provide only a partial and impressionistic record of what took place, playing fast and loose as they do with the running order as it unfolded in real time. The British performers who appeared were, in chronological order: the Incredible String Band, the Who, Joe Cocker and the Grease Band, Ten Years After and Graham Nash (as one member of the newly-assembled Crosby Stills & Nash – plus, on this occasion, Young). It's tempting to include Jimi Hendrix on the list too, but he was, of course, American and very much embraced that fact when he played the final set of the festival in the early morning of Monday, 18th August. The other American acts constituted an eclectic mix of folk, blues and rock artists, the latter showing an inherent tendency to revel in the exploitation of riffs as the basis for endless jamming and improvisation: check out Santana's "Soul Sacrifice", to name a typical, though marginally less tedious, example.

Another noteworthy aspect of Woodstock, further emphasised by Wadleigh's film, was its celebration of the emergence of the 'rock chick', those rare female artists who could hold their own in the presence of so much drug- and riff-fuelled testosterone. One was the highly photogenic Grace Slick, the *uber*-cool vocalist with Jefferson Airplane, on whom the camera frequently comes to rest even when she is merely standing on the sidelines. The other was the utterly decadent blueswailer Janis Joplin who, according to Pete Fornatale, existed "at the epicentre of a pentangle where five very powerful late-'60s forces converged: booze, drugs, music, sex, and talent"[94], and who merits only one brief slot in even the director's cut of the film with her earthy performance of "Work Me, Lord".

Neither of them was necessarily a role model for others but they were, refreshingly, about as far removed from the British stereotype of a female singer as imaginable (with the possible exception of, perhaps, Julie Driscoll or Christine Perfect). True, Marianne Faithfull had attempted a comeback in February with "Sister Morphine", a song entirely consistent with her latter-day lifestyle, for which she wrote the lyric and which she sang in a voice now audibly ravaged by smoking and drugs, but Decca withdrew the record two days after its release. In any event, she was burnt out, destined in due course to be the spectacular casualty of a broken relationship with Mick Jagger. Conversely, light entertainment was the dead end down which Sandie Shaw, Cilla Black, Lulu and Dusty Springfield had collectively been driven and for all of them the hits were gradually coming to an end; although Lulu followed Sandie on the ignominious trail to the Eurovision Song Contest in Madrid where, in "a pink dress covered with red and white flowers"[95], she sang herself into a four-way tie for first place with "Boom-Bang-A-Bang" (a UK No.3 in April). In so doing, for the third year in a row Lulu secured the top place in the *NME* poll as the Best UK Female Singer.[96] There was nothing new left to look forward to on this front, just more of the same – or worse – in the form of Clodagh Rodgers.[97]

Any overtly political contributions to the proceedings at Woodstock were barely tolerated. When, for instance, on the second night Yippie activist Abbie Hoffman attempted to interrupt the Who by grabbing the microphone to speak during a hiatus in their act, Pete Townshend knocked him out of the way, using the headstock of his guitar as a weapon and giving him a tongue-lashing at the same time. By contrast, on the first night, Joan Baez (whose husband David Harris was then serving time for refusing the military draft) had carefully tempered her political commentary with the messages in songs such as "I Dreamed I Saw Joe Hill Last Night" and "We Shall Overcome". The most memorable contribution touching on topical issues of concern remains, however, that of Country Joe and the Fish, whose "I-Feel-Like-I'm-Fixin'-To-Die-Rag" (*aka* "Vietnam Rag") was given two outings, first as a solo by Joe McDonald (while the organisers were still desperately trying to plug holes in the first-night programme that had gone awry) and then again by the group as a whole in their pre-ordained slot on Sunday.

A US Navy veteran himself, McDonald united the vast audience in mass protest by preceding the song with his trademark "Fish Cheer", which he subverted on the spur of the moment by turning the call-and-answer "Give me an 'F', Give me an 'I', etc." into "Give me an 'F'-'U'-'C'-'K'", seeing the hundreds of thousands of young people all chanting the 'F-word' in unison as the ultimate rebellious act of empowerment. Then it was straight into the song, very much in the satiric tradition of Tom Lehrer, which even today McDonald urges us not to interpret word for word but to accept as "military humour – tongue in cheek"[98]:

> And it's one, two, three,
> What are we fighting for?
> Don't ask me, I don't give a damn,
> Next stop is Vietnam;
> And it's five, six, seven,
> Open up the pearly gates.
> Well, there ain't no time to wonder why,
> Whoopee! we're all gonna die.[99]

The Incredible String Band, originally listed to play on Friday night amongst the other assorted folk acts until it started to rain heavily, were shunted instead into a new slot on Saturday afternoon; "in the baking sun", as Joe Boyd recalled, when everyone was "ready for something heavy and loud and they came on and just – died!" [100] They were universally seen as "simply the wrong group, in the wrong place, at the wrong time".[101] The Who, on the other hand, were the penultimate closing act of Saturday night running on into Sunday morning and for them the timing worked perfectly, despite Pete Townshend's general disenchantment with the chaotic organisation and his demand that the band be paid up front in cash otherwise they wouldn't go on (which was achieved, against all the odds, by rousing a local bank manager from his bed in the middle of the night). Working their way through *Tommy* reached a climax just as the sun was rising on Sunday, to Roger Daltrey's sheer disbelief:

> The sun coming up to "See Me, Feel Me" was the top. I mean, that was an amazing experience. As soon as the – the words "see me" came out of my mouth from the end of *Tommy*, this huge, red, August sun popped its head out of the horizon, over the crowd. And, that light show you can't beat![102]

Townshend too appreciated that on this occasion the Who had far transcended the ordinary, by putting on a performance that "would elevate us into American rock aristocracy":

> By the time we hit 'I'm Free' most of the audience was on its feet. Before I knew it, Roger was singing 'See me, feel me, touch me, heal me' to waves of young people who suddenly realised that *Tommy* was music unwittingly designed for precisely this kind of festival, for this particular moment, for *them*.[103]

Perhaps the greatest impression left on the audience and, through them, on America by a British performer at Woodstock was, however, by the then relatively unknown Joe Cocker and the Grease Band. Back in Britain, Cocker (an ex-gas fitter from Sheffield) had come from nowhere to No.1 in November 1968 with his unique reinterpretation of the Beatles' "With A Little Help From My Friends" as a white soul classic, and he chose it as the finale of the act with which he opened the festival's third day of music on Sunday afternoon. In one of the few genuine highlights of the film *Woodstock*, Cocker is undeniably mesmerising:

> … more than the band, the music, the voice, the songs, the hair, the shirt, the shoes [blue and red, emblazoned with shiny, five-point stars] – there were the stage movements: the body language, the finger ballet, the facial tics, the convulsions. I think it's fair to say that American audiences had never seen anything like it.[104]

It simply couldn't be followed; for just as Cocker had finished, a cloudburst imposed a two-hour-long moratorium on proceedings.

But the ultimate finale fell to Jimi Hendrix to deliver, beginning at 8.30 a.m. on Monday morning, by which time the vast majority of festival-goers were utterly exhausted and had gone home. The audience remaining for Hendrix was thought be approximately 50,000, roughly a tenth of those attending Woodstock at its peak yet numerically still the equivalent of the largest audience the Beatles had commanded at Shea Stadium back in 1965. Incorrectly introduced as the Jimi Hendrix Experience, this was the first (and not altogether successful) live outing of his new band, as he explained to the crowd at the outset:

> Dig, we'd like to get something straight. We got tired of Experience and every once in a while we was blowing our minds too much, so we decided to change the whole thing around and call it Gypsy Sun and Rainbows. For short it's nothing but a Band of Gypsys.[105]

As well as Mitch Mitchell on drums, he was joined by Larry Lee (rhythm guitar), Billy Cox (bass guitar) and – in some respects, superfluously – by additional percussionists Juma Sultan and Jerry Velez, both of them on congas. (Mitchell reputedly said that "it was the only band he had ever played with that did not get better with practice".[106]) Their set, which lasted for more than two hours, spanned Hendrix's whole musical career by mixing old and new numbers, some that retained a clear structure (like "Red House"; or "Foxy Lady", which was particularly well received) and some that were more improvisational (like "Jam Back At The House" or "Woodstock Improvisation"). No place now for guitar-playing with his teeth or the pyrotechnics of Monterey. Towards the end came his psychedelic *piece de resistance*, the US National Anthem, "The Star-Spangled Banner", as it had never been played before:

> It just sounded like the Vietnam War. It sounded like a firefight. It sounded like helicopters. It sounded like machine guns. He took that song and made it of the moment in a way that no one could've predicted you could do that to the national anthem. He made it sound like everything that was going on in that country, in our country, and around the world at the moment.[107]

But he wasn't done yet. After a segue into "Purple Haze", followed by "Woodstock Improvisation", Hendrix came back down to earth again with a mellow instrumental piece, "Villanova Junction", as a closer. And yet still after all that the audience had an appetite for an encore; which turned out, amazingly, to be "Hey Joe", the song that had made it all happen for him but of which he had long appeared to have grown weary. Having inspired others, two weeks later, at a press conference in Harlem, Hendrix would reveal that he too had been inspired, by declaring Woodstock a "complete success" as a festival; because to him it was an important part of the "changes leading up to love, peace and harmony" and had shown that, in contrast to politics, "music must mean something".[108]

If Woodstock demonstrated one specific musical truth above all others, it was that folk, blues and rock could happily co-exist in pandering to the catholic tastes of an enquiring multitude. In Britain, even though the blues boom here had peaked, the success of "Albatross" for Fleetwood Mac, No.1 for three weeks from January into February, proved the point that a willing market still existed for 'crossover' hits of quality, an advantage they could readily have exploited had they not been so dysfunctional and poorly managed as a group. Brilliant musician though he was, Peter Green came to be preoccupied for much of 1969 with an identity crisis that threatened to engulf him completely; while manager Clifford Davis threw away the opportunity to sustain a productive relationship with Mike Vernon and Blue Horizon Records when Fleetwood Mac's initial contract came up for renewal, by negotiating with Tony Calder for them to move to the Immediate label.

The only record to be released as a result of this short-lived deal was "Man Of The World", the plaintively introspective ballad composed by Green that came out in April and reached No.2 at the end of May. A binding contract could not, however, be finalised because the lawyer representing Davis also acted for the music publishing arm of Immediate, thus constituting a conflict of interests. Forced to look elsewhere, Davis then struck an agreement with Reprise but any new releases on this label were pre-empted by spoiling action in the summer from Blue Horizon; who put out a reissue of "Need Your Love So Bad" as a single in July (scraping a No.30 placement in August), to be followed three weeks later by a compilation album, *The Pious Bird Of Good Omen*.[109]

Fleetwood Mac's new material for Reprise was not forthcoming until late September, the release on the 19th of their LP *Then Play On* preceding by a week that of their single "Oh Well (Parts 1 & 2)". Green appeared to have been on the edge when he composed "Man Of The World" ("And there's no-one I'd rather be/But I just wish that I'd never been born"[110]) but in "Oh Well (Part 1)" he could now be heard matter-of-factly conversing with God:

> Now, when I talked to God I knew he'd understand.
> He said, "Stick by me and I'll be your guiding hand
> But don't ask me what I think of you,
> I might not give the answer that you want me to.[111]

Taken altogether, as well as being slightly disturbing lyrically, "Oh Well" was a complex piece, the vocal in Part 1 being balanced by the richness of the instrumental Part 2, prompting Mike Vernon to think that "this was a strange mixture of blues, rock and the classics, courtesy of some Segovia-styled acoustic guitar work from Peter. Once again, the theme hung on Peter's own disillusionment not only of the music business in general but also of his involvement with the band".[112] Yet its musical strengths were universally recognised, to the extent that it climbed to No.1 in mid-November, for one week temporarily breaking the Archies' stranglehold on the top slot with "Sugar Sugar".

Those close to Green were convinced that his messianic tendencies arose in adverse reaction to his exposure to and experimentation with LSD whilst touring in America. Somehow, like Syd Barrett of Pink Floyd before him, he was losing his grip on reality and had already convinced himself that his future lay other than with Fleetwood Mac (although that break would not come until the end of May 1970). It was a lamentable loss of self-awareness, for at this point he was unrivalled in Britain as the blues guitarist *par excellence* and, properly supported by the right management and record producer, could have taken *his* Fleetwood Mac to even greater heights. (They were, after all, voted the Best UK Blues/R&B Group of 1969 by the *NME* readership, hitherto a title monopolised by the Rolling Stones from its inception in 1964.) Instead, he was in danger of creating a widening – and confusing – credibility gap between the group's output on record and their live performances.[113]

Most significantly, Green had nothing to fear for the time being from Eric Clapton, who had effectively taken himself out of contention. After Cream had disbanded, he had quickly tired in a matter of months of his next much-publicised collaboration with Steve Winwood in Blind Faith, an even more volatile mix than Cream, made up of: Clapton (lead guitar), Steve Winwood (keyboards), Rick Grech (bass guitar) and Ginger Baker (drums). (Winwood had left the Spencer Davis Group in 1967 – their No.10 hit of February, "I'm A Man", was the last single on which he appeared with them – to form Traffic, whose best-known hits, also from 1967, were "Paper Sun" (No.4 in July) and "Hole In My Shoe" (No.2 in October).) They recorded little: the front cover of their only album, released in August and briefly a No.1 LP, was untitled but bore a controversial cover image of Baker's pre-pubescent daughter, photographed topless holding a model of a bomber plane. Their live debut was famously in Hyde Park on 7th June but, after devoting most of their short existence to touring North America, Clapton had decided by September that he'd had enough and moved on to join Delaney & Bonnie as one of their backing musicians, as noted earlier in this chapter. While Winwood withdrew to breathe new life into Traffic, Baker formed Ginger Baker's Airforce (to which he recruited Grech, Denny Laine and accomplished jazz musician Harold McNair[114]).

If there was the slightest hint of serious competition to Fleetwood

Mac remaining, then it might have been expected from their former Blue Horizon stablemates Chicken Shack, whose principal assets were Stan Webb, their formidable, if equally eccentric lead guitarist and vocalist, and Christine Perfect, their keyboard player who also shared vocals with Webb. Chicken Shack had been an early signing to the label (even being briefly managed by Mike Vernon and his wife) and, in the interests of promotion, had played at the Windsor Jazz and Blues Festival in August 1967, a booking they shared in common on that occasion with both Cream and Fleetwood Mac. A debut album, *Forty Blue Fingers, Freshly Packed And Ready To Serve*, was a No.12 LP in the summer of 1968 but it was not until May 1969 that they broke into the singles charts with "I'd Rather Go Blind" (a cover of a song originally recorded by Etta James), that went to No.11 at the end of June. It was to be a bittersweet triumph. Although its success was due in large part to the striking phrasing of Christine Perfect's vocals, its release happened to coincide with her decision to leave the group to spend more time with her new husband, John McVie – of Fleetwood Mac – and soon thereafter Chicken Shack were to disappear off the radar.[115]

Folk, on the other hand, was gaining momentum. Largely unknown beforehand despite two earlier LP releases heavily in debt stylistically to contemporary US West Coast bands, Fairport Convention (a group managed and produced by Joe Boyd, that notably included Sandy Denny as lead vocalist and Richard Thompson on guitar) broke into the Top 20 in September with "Si Tu Dois Partir", a jaunty Cajun take on Dylan's "If You Gotta Go, Go Now" that reached No.18. It was a track taken from their third album, *Unhalfbricking*, which, in addition to two other Dylan covers from *The Basement Tapes* ("Percy's Song" and "Million Dollar Bash"), also memorably included Denny's own composition "Who Knows Where The Time Goes", and went to No.12 in the LP charts. *Unhalfbricking* had, in fact, been recorded much earlier, in the spring, but the group (all bar Denny, who was travelling separately) was involved in a serious crash on the M1 early in the morning of 12th May whilst returning from a gig in a Transit van driven by their road manager, in which drummer Martin Lamble and Thompson's girl-friend Jeannie Franklyn were both killed and the others sustained injuries of varying severity. It was a crisis that generated the rebirth of the group under the assertive influence of bassist and traditional folk buff Ashley Hutchings, with Dave Swarbrick brought in on fiddle and Dave Mattacks on drums, and "what happened in the next five months was one of the most remarkable recuperations in British rock":

> By the end of October the group had created *Liege And Lief*,
> a glorious mixture of melancholic Fairport-penned originals,
> turbocharged jigs and reels, and electrified, magical ancient ballads,
> and which asked the question: could traditional folk song be

claimed and owned by the rock generation, and what could rock learn from the process?[116]

Liege and Lief was released in December and, as Joe Boyd observed, making "English folk music fashionable was an extraordinary accomplishment, pushing against the historic diktat that nothing could be less hip".[117] But, as we saw in the last chapter, under Jo Lustig's stewardship Pentangle had already staked their claim to their own part in this movement, and rose to further prominence in 1969 on the back of recording a group composition, "Light Flight", as the theme tune to *Take Three Girls*, a new BBC television drama series set in bedsit-land.[118] Enthusiastically described by Colin Irwin as a "catchily tuneful singalong number [that] seeped into the nation's consciousness and spilled out of the TV and on to Radio 1 and into the lives of the mass populace"[119], it was also the opening track of their best-selling third album *Basket Of Light*, which was released in October and reached No.5 in the course of the twenty-eight weeks it spent in the LP charts. (Alas, the fine preceding single, "Once I Had A Sweetheart", also featured on the album, was strictly for a minority of their followers like me; as was Bert Jansch's solo album, *Birthday Blues*, released earlier in January, on which he was accompanied by the Pentangle's Danny Thompson and Terry Cox, as well as Duffy Power.)

After their extraordinary successes with *Bookends* and *The Graduate* soundtrack, expectations of Simon & Garfunkel at CBS Records were understandably running high, but the recording of a new album fell victim to inordinate delay after Mike Nichols poached Art Garfunkel for an acting role in his next film, an adaptation of Joseph Heller's anti-war classic *Catch-22*. Perhaps in the interests of diplomacy, Nichols had also offered Paul Simon a minor part but this was cut before he even had the chance to get before the cameras, leaving him largely to his own devices in the recording studio while to his annoyance Garfunkel's continuing absence escalated virtually out of control: filming originally intended to last no more than three months ended up consuming a whole year.

Progress on making the album, *Bridge Over Troubled Water*, was therefore far slower than either Simon or CBS would have liked. However, it was possible to snatch a tantalising glimpse of the masterpiece yet to be unveiled from the one Simon & Garfunkel single release of the year, "The Boxer", reaching No.6 in the UK Top 30 for 7th June just as Fleetwood Mac's "Man Of The World" was beginning to slip down the Top 10. Much has been read into its lyric: some have seen echoes in it of Simon's resentment of Bob Dylan, while others go for the easier option of seeing his impatience with the frequently absent Garfunkel holding back his longed-for solo career. All Simon has ever admitted to, however, is that "the song was about me: everybody's beating me up, and I'm telling you now I'm going to go away if you don't stop"[120]:

> In the clearing stands a boxer
> And a fighter by his trade
> And he carries the reminders
> Of every glove that laid him down
> Or cut him till he cried out
> In his anger and his shame
> "I am leaving, I am leaving"
> But the fighter still remains
> Lie-la-lie …[121]

The whole suite of songs that would eventually see the light of day on 1970's *Bridge Over Troubled Water* would rely for their impact on attention to detail, in a combination of carefully crafted lyrics, painstakingly beautiful vocal harmonies and exquisite arrangements. Tim Buckley had already travelled some way in that direction in 1968 with his ambitious *Goodbye And Hello* but with his third album, released in the UK in July 1969, he opted for something altogether looser and more experimental. *Happy Sad* was stripped back to basics with an "intimate acoustic-based group of players – featuring Buckley's own 12-string, Lee Underwood on lead guitar; and Carter C. C. Collins on congas, plus acoustic bass and vibes", to become his "defining album … replacing romanticism with experimentation".[122]

For those of us who had found his previous work appealing for its depth and structure, on first play *Happy Sad* was strange on the ear, if not downright disappointing: even the shot of Buckley on the rear of the sleeve, looking wasted and dishevelled, was a worrying rather than reassuring image. And we were not alone in disquiet. Even the head of Elektra Records, Jac Holzman, "felt that *Happy Sad* had the sense of a humid afternoon in Santa Monica, where *Goodbye And Hello* was dramatic and intense, bypassing the brain".[123] But on closer acquaintance, the mere six songs on offer (with more than a hint of improvisation in the two extended tracks that between them ran for over twenty-three minutes[124]) grew on you, and there was, on reflection, a direct statement in the first verse of the opening track, "Strange Feelin'", of Buckley's avowed new purpose:

> I got this strange strange feelin'
> Deep down in my heart.
> I can't tell what it is
> But it won't let go.
> It happens every time
> I give you more than what I have
> But now all I need is a little time to sing this song
> And I think we're gonna find a way to lose this strange feelin'.[125]

Not all the lyricism was lost. "Buzzin' Fly" and "Sing A Song For You", for example, could just as easily have been much earlier works; and if you prick up your ears today, you can still recognise occasional snatches of the accompaniment to "Buzzin' Fly" as incidental background music on television, which after all this time is a sort of accolade. But just as in the latest work of several other artists described in this chapter, there was genuine loss in Buckley's new beginning. With *Happy Sad*, Elektra saw "the audience he had acquired [begin] to drift away", while his manager deemed it to be "artistic suicide, in a way – [and] certainly commercial suicide".[126] At least it could not be said of him that he fought shy of trying to become master of his own destiny:

> So let me sing a song for you
> Just to help your day along.
> Let me sing a song for you,
> One I've known so very long.
> Oh, please could you find the time?[127]

As a singer/songwriter, Buckley knew he had options not necessarily open to others and a constant theme running through this book has been the relative power conferred on artists capable of writing their own material, as opposed to being subservient to the judgement of others. The growth of the market for albums in the later Sixties further proved that point and, as we have seen, was the making of groups like the Moody Blues who would otherwise undoubtedly not have survived.

Their good fortune continued with the release in April of their third concept album, *On The Threshold Of A Dream*, giving them their first No.1 LP with an incredible run of seventy-three weeks in the charts. Its title and content (which included the spin-off single "Never Comes The Day") reflected, as John Lodge said, the group's sense of having arrived "on the threshold of something which was hopefully going to make the Moody Blues special"[128]; although they held a deeper meaning for Justin Hayward:

> … we could just as easily have said, "On The Doorstep Of
> Nirvana" – because that's what the music meant to us and that's the
> feeling we were trying to translate. We wanted to collect religious
> and psychedelic influences onto an album and turn them into a
> pathway into enlightenment, if you like. I know it sounds terribly
> pretentious now but as young men, that's what we were searching
> for – we'd always seen ourselves as seekers. It really summed up *On
> The Threshold Of A Dream*.[129]

Together with producer Tony Clarke, they particularly demonstrated on this album a mastery of both electronic effects and the mellotron to enhance the listener's experience, not least in Graeme Edge's opening dialogue between

First Man, the computer voice of The Establishment and Inner Man ("In The Beginning") and the concluding segue of "Have You Heard (Pts.1 & 2)" and "The Voyage".

They also stood out against Decca's inbuilt parsimony, insisting that the record be packaged in a high-quality gatefold sleeve, beautifully illustrated with fantasy artwork by Phil Travers and enclosing a full-size fourteen-page booklet of the complete lyrics (with foreword by David Symonds and afterword by Lionel Bart) that utilised copperplate script throughout. With the possible exception of the 'turntable' construction incorporating Delia Smith's cake for the cover of the Rolling Stones' "Let It Bleed", it probably represented the most costly sleeve for a pop LP Decca had yet produced. It was, nonetheless, from the group's point of view a dispute well worth having, from which they eventually emerged triumphant, as Justin Hayward explains: "We had a disagreement with Decca about our sleeves. We believed in a large, intricate, interesting form to hold when you made an album – and that was the start of Threshold. We were still signed to Decca but they gave us our own label and control within it. The real purpose was to get control of our own releases, visuals and publicity."[130] And in following the Beatles' example of setting up Apple as a subsidiary of EMI, the Moody Blues would go on to enjoy further success before the year was out, as we shall see later.

Others, however, failed in varying degrees to make the necessary transition to new ways of working and early casualties were Manfred Mann, who had always been highly dependent on external composers for their A-sides. Having hit the heights in their second incarnation with Mike D'Abo by taking "The Mighty Quinn" to No.1 in February 1968, they had returned to the Top 10 that July with "My Name Is Jack" (No.8); but then a long interval ensued after the November release of "Fox On The Run" until it finally reached No.5 in February 1969, followed last of all by "Ragamuffin Man" (which peaked at No.8 at the end of May).

By this time, while D'Abo (composer of the near-hit "Handbags And Gladrags", recorded by Chris Farlowe in late 1967) was looking to follow Paul Jones's lead by striking out on his own, Mann and Hugg, as ever the creative core of the group, had already diversified into composing music for films (including *Up The Junction* and *The Charge Of The Light Brigade* – the latter commission no doubt satirically prompted by someone's whimsical recollection of "5-4-3-2-1") and commercials (for products such as Hovis, Mannikin cigars and Dulux paint) and were looking for other new avenues to explore. Manfred Mann:

["Ragamuffin Man"] was the last record we had. We decided after that, Mike [Hugg] and I ... that this was not what our musical life was about, and it really was boring. The public was bored with us, but they liked the records and people were buying them, but there

was no sense of excitement any longer. I think that all of us were
more capable in all different ways. Again, we weren't playing live
anymore and we just decided to quit.[131]

Although Manfred Mann did not officially disband until June, Mann and
Hugg had moved on in April to form a new ten-piece jazz-orientated band,
originally called Emanon but transmuting in October into Manfred Mann
Chapter III and then signing up to a record deal with the Vertigo label.

With Roy Wood as the composing ace up their sleeve, the Move should
have been able to look forward to a comfortably long career but, after "Fire
Brigade", had suffered complete indifference to its successor in July 1968,
"Wild Tiger Woman". Virtually a whole year had passed, therefore, by the
time they returned to the charts in January 1969 with "Blackberry Way",
which unseated "Albatross" to become No.1 for one week in mid-February
but precipitated the departure of bass player Trevor Burton, disenchanted
by its commercialism. With Burton replaced by Rick Price, they made it back
into the Top 10 (at No.10) at the end of August with "Curly", after which
came a disastrous American tour in October (although Roy Wood thought
"it was brilliant and I wouldn't have missed it for the world"[132]). As autumn
turned to winter, however, on their return to England they were to be drawn
further into a downward spiral, as noted here by Pete Frame: "Carl Wayne,
who was the dominant personality in the group at the time, steered them into
cabaret work in the Northern clubs. Horror of horrors! The nerve-shred-
ding effects of this resulted in a fracas, following which Wayne made his last
exit."[133] After which the Move drew a line firmly under the Sixties.

Now minus Graham Nash, the Hollies were somehow taken less seri-
ously, despite having a No.3 hit in April with the run-of-the-mill "Sorry
Suzanne" and a November No.2 with the far more memorable "He Ain't
Heavy, He's My Brother"[134] (by American composers Bobby Scott & Bob
Russell, which survives to the present day in many people's minds as their
archetypal contribution to pop music). (Now one third of Crosby Stills &
Nash, Nash himself, of course, scored a modest No.15 hit in September with
his own composition, "Marrakesh Express".) As for their contemporaries
and fellow Mancunians, Herman's Hermits, they too had all but exhausted
the possibilities of endlessly churning out good-time singalong hits, their
January No.4 with the formulaic "Something's Happening" being followed
by the mawkish "My Sentimental Friend" (the clue's in the title), a strange
bedfellow at No.3 in the chart for 24th May with "Man Of The World" at
No.2 and "Get Back" at No.1. Having broken up the Small Faces, Steve
Marriott re-emerged as leader of his new heavy rock group Humble Pie,
formed with Peter Frampton, their debut and only hit single, "Natural Born
Bugie", making it – largely, it must be said, out of loyalty for old times' sake,
for it was highly derivative[135] – to No.9 in October. And the Dave Clark

Five, having for so long spurned the UK market in favour of their far more lucrative US output, tried one last throw with a revival medley for Christmas, "Good Old Rock'N'Roll", that by the last chart of 1969 had climbed to No.16.

If there was one genre that witnessed an upsurge of interest in 1969, it was the film theme, a reflection in itself of the outstanding quality of contemporary film releases and the consequent growth, in that pre-video age, of the cinema in popularity. First, from *The Thomas Crown Affair* (starring Steve McQueen and Faye Dunaway) came "Windmills Of Your Mind", sung by Noel Harrison, son of actor Rex Harrison and best known himself for his role in the TV series *The Girl From UNCLE*, that reached No.9 in April during its eleven weeks in the Top 30 (but nevertheless still probably better remembered as covered by Dusty Springfield on *Dusty In Memphis*). This was quickly followed by "Sanctus", from the Congolese Mass *Missa Luba* as performed by Les Troubadours Du Roi Baudouin, the African choral chant with which Malcolm McDowell's character Mick is obsessed in *If …*, an April No.27. Given its volume of airplay that summer, you might have expected Steppenwolf's "Born To Be Wild" from the soundtrack of *Easy Rider* to have charted next, but it just missed the Top 30 in June.[136]

Then in August, the dramatic classical theme "Thus Spake Zarathrustra" from *2001: A Space Odyssey*, composed by Richard Strauss and performed by the Philharmonia Orchestra, made an appearance at No.30. Finally, for six weeks from mid-October, along came Harry Nilsson with "Everybody's Talkin'", Fred Neil's idiosyncratic theme song from *Midnight Cowboy* (starring Jon Voigt and Dustin Hoffman), that peaked at No.17. And, if I may be forgiven for stretching the point of a cultural crossover a little further, it is worth noting here that the uncensored stage musical *Hair* also spawned two hit singles during the year. Spending six weeks in the charts, Fifth Dimension's medley of "Aquarius/Let The Sunshine In" reached No.13 in June; only to be outshone from mid-August onwards by Oliver's "Good Morning Starshine", which out of a total of thirteen weeks in the Top 30 spent three at No.8 (from September into October).

Speaking of crossovers, it is fitting that in the year in which space exploration came of age there should also have been two outstanding UK hit records on a related theme; a Top 10 single and a best-selling album. (I deliberately exclude from any serious consideration here the appalling "In The Year 2525" by Zager & Evans, best regarded in my view as little more than a novelty record, for all its success as a summertime No.1 on both sides of the Atlantic.) Admittedly, David Bowie's "Space Oddity" was as much inspired by the stunning visual imagery of Stanley Kubrick's *2001: A Space Odyssey* and the drama of David Bowman's battle of wills with the renegade computer Hal en route to Jupiter as by the real experiences of lunar astronauts. Nevertheless, in the characterisation of 'Major Tom', "sitting in a tin can/Far above the world" [137], Bowie, in a shrewd assessment of the mood of the times, had begun to exercise a fertile musical imagination and the song would give him his first Top 10 hit, with two weeks at No.6 in November.

The album, from the Moody Blues, offered a longer, more benign vision of humanity's future in space than Bowie's. *To Our Children's Children's Children* was released (belatedly) in November as the first LP on their new Threshold label, "at the height", in Justin Hayward's words, "of our intricate, self-absorbed period".[138] It was presented in a more modest gatefold sleeve than *On The Threshold Of A Dream*, but one again graced with Phil Travers's artwork (externally depicting the progress of history through cave-painting, internally showing the group in a futuristic cave setting on another planet) and with a complete sheet of lyrics included.

This time the promise of a mysterious yet ultimately rewarding journey – a recurring Moody Blues motif – is instigated by the re-creation of the sound of a Saturn V rocket lifting off, providing a backdrop against which Graeme Edge intones "Higher And Higher":

> Blasting, Billowing, Bursting Forth with the
> power of ten billion butterfly sneezes,
> Man in his finest hour has conquered the
> wayward breezes,
> Climbing to tranquillity far above the cloud,
> Conceiving the heaven clear of misty shroud.[139]

The songs that follow – notably "Gypsy", "Eternity Road", "Candle Of Life" and "Watching And Waiting" – are not necessarily as well known as others within the Moody Blues' canon but are definitely amongst the best they ever recorded; and the album as a whole, these days a forgotten masterpiece, was to reward them with a top placing of No.2 over the forty-four weeks it would spend in the LP charts.

Everyone blithely rushes to cite 1969 as the year of the first moon landing but NASA's achievement in fulfilling President Kennedy's promise before the end of the decade was so much greater, for it is seldom remembered that it was actually the year of four successful Apollo missions in total and *two* moon landings. After Apollo 8's triumph in completing a manned lunar circumnavigation, as 1969 began NASA was seriously planning for a moon landing by that summer, and yet at that point so many critical issues remained unresolved:

> The lunar module, which had passed an unmanned test in earth orbit, had never been flown with a man aboard. The space suit designed for the first moonwalks had never been tested in the

vacuum of space. No Apollo crew had attempted the intricate and crucial rendezvous between the lander and the command module, which would have to be practised not only in earth orbit but around the moon. Remarkably, NASA was planning to soar over those hurdles with just two missions: Apollo 9, an earth-orbit flight crammed to the hilt with tests, and Apollo 10, a full-up "dress rehearsal" of the landing mission in lunar orbit.[140]

Irrespective of these technicalities still to be overcome, an early announcement was made, on 9th January (the same day the crew of Apollo 8 received medals from President Johnson and then attended a meeting of the full US Congress), of the names of the crew of Apollo 11, two of whom were thus provisionally cast in the role of the first men on the moon: Neil Armstrong, Buzz Aldrin and Michael Collins, a teaming described by Collins, the Command Module pilot, as that of "amiable strangers".[141]

With the all-important announcement made to the world, the Russians moved rapidly to steal America's thunder, with the launch into earth orbit on 14th January of Soyuz 4 (piloted by Vladimir Shatalov) and Soyuz 5 the following day (carrying a three-man crew of Boris Volynov, Aleksei Yeli-seyev and Yevgeni Khrunov). After the two spacecraft had docked, Yeliseyev and Khrunov transferred to join Shatalov in Soyuz 4 and they returned to earth together on 17th January without incident. Next day, however, Volynov in Soyuz 5 encountered major difficulties during his re-entry flight. Firstly, the Descent and Service Modules failed to separate on exiting orbit, leaving Volynov powerless to control what was now an oversize craft's descent into the atmosphere. Having somehow survived that and the attached Service Module's eventual disintegration, the parachutes acting as air brakes on the Descent Module opened but at first their lines were tangled, only untwisting moments before landfall. Volynov was lucky to escape from a near crash-landing with broken teeth as his severest injuries, but far more serious technical mishaps lay in store for the Russians on 21st February, when an N1 rocket (the USSR's equivalent of a Saturn V) lost power barely a minute after lift-off on a test flight and brought its seventeen-mile-long trajectory to an abrupt end by exploding. Their last hope of posing a credible threat to American supremacy in space was gone.

The first US space mission of the year was Apollo 9, launched on 3rd March with the prime objective over the next ten days of testing the Lunar Module (LM) in earth orbit, and as such it was an historic flight in its own right, for the LM was "the first true spacecraft", designed to fly "only in the void of space".[142] Concealed and transported initially within the protective third stage of the Saturn V rocket, once up in space it revealed itself as "a huge robotic insect, with two triangular windows for eyes and a square hatchway for a mouth, antennae jutting at all angles, and four foil-clad landing legs".[143]

Flight commander James McDivitt, and LM pilot Russell 'Rusty' Schweickart were charged with the crucial tasks of separating the LM from the Command Module (CM), leaving the latter under the control of its pilot David Scott as they then cast off into solo flight before completing a re-docking manoeuvre. Delayed to allow Schweickart time to recover from a bad bout of motion sickness, on 7th March the LM (irreverently christened *Spider* for this mission) was undocked from Scott in the CM (*Gumdrop*) and flown on its own for six hours, at a maximum distance of over 100 miles from the parent craft. Before *Spider* could return to *Gumdrop*, however, it had to be split into its two main components:

> The bottom half, descent stage, whose engine in the near future would lower its crew to the lunar surface, was jettisoned, leaving a legless, seemingly helpless space creature with two men sailing through orbit. The ascent stage with the crew cabin carried an engine designed to lift this upper portion of the landing vehicle off the moon and carry it all the way to a rendezvous with a waiting command module. On an actual landing mission, the descent stage would serve as a launch pad and would remain on the moon.[144]

With this part of the flight thankfully completed safely, the truncated *Spider* then successfully re-docked with the parent craft and the crew were reunited.

Just over two months later, Apollo 10 was despatched to the moon on 18th May, for a full dress rehearsal of a lunar landing mission – bar the landing itself – and would also be notable for providing the first live TV transmissions in colour from space. Commanded by Thomas Stafford, the pilot of the LM *Snoopy* would be Eugene Cernan and that of the CM *Charlie Brown* John Young. The day after entering lunar orbit on 21st May, Stafford and Cernan took off in 'Snoopy' for a descent to within 47,000 feet of the moon's surface and two independent orbits that enabled them to survey the proposed landing site on the Sea of Tranquillity, that turned out to be a relatively smooth area (resembling, so they thought, wet clay) compared to the vast ruggedness of the lunar mountains and craters over which they had flown on their initial approach. Far from proceeding in a leisurely manner, *Snoopy* "had traded its altitude for speed, until it [neared] 3,700 miles per hour, more than five times the speed of sound"[145], and all this in a spacecraft trimmed of all excess weight to the point at which "the walls of the crew cabin [had been] thinned down until they were nothing more than a taut aluminium balloon, in some places only five-thousandths of an inch thick".[146] After some four hours of separation – and a short, unnerving period of destabilisation immediately following the breaking apart of the LM's ascent and descent stages – Stafford and Cernan finally re-docked with Young circling above them in his higher orbit, from where *Charlie Brown* carried them round the moon one last time before they set course for a homecoming on 26th May.

The way was therefore clear for Apollo 11 to make the American dream of the decade a reality, but the Russians had not totally abandoned their efforts to upstage their rivals and in desperation attempted the launch of a further modified N1 rocket shortly before midnight on 3rd July. It was to be another unmitigated disaster. After rising no more than 600 feet from the launch-pad, it stalled and exploded as it fell back to earth:

> The light of the morning revealed carnage as thousands of
> dead birds and other wildlife littered the blackened launch site at
> Baikonur. The damage was extensive. It would not be possible to
> recover quickly from such a blow. Mishin [Korolev's successor as
> Chief Designer] was in despair. For months there had been no
> break from his unremitting workload. Three days after the disaster,
> he collapsed with chest pains.[147]

Seemingly undeterred but ever aware, of course, of Apollo 11's fast approaching launch date, the USSR launched the unmanned Luna 15 on 13th July, programmed to land on the moon, collect geological samples and bring them back to Earth; its ultimate fate, of crashing into the moon's Sea of Crises on 21st July, overshadowed by then by the worldwide publicity attendant on the Americans' own triumph. For it was on 20th July 1969, four days after the launch of Apollo 11, that Neil Armstrong and Buzz Aldrin had navigated the lunar module *Eagle* to land on the Sea of Tranquillity.

We know now that there had been considerable tension between Armstrong and Aldrin in advance over which one of them was to be the first to leave *Eagle* and step out onto the moon's surface, ultimately resolved by higher authorities in Armstrong's favour. It was also of passing interest that although Aldrin was nominally the LM's pilot, it had, in fact, been Armstrong as commander who had assumed manual control of the module during its descent and brought it to a safe touchdown as far away as possible from hazardous boulders (at a point, as it happened, four miles away from their pre-determined target). But on completion the landing turned into an anticlimax or a cliffhanger, depending on how you felt about it, because it was followed not by immediate exploration but by what was slated as a rest period for the astronauts (which they opted to forego, in their excitement) and replaced instead by an intensive period of preparation lasting seven hours. In that time, they had run through the all-important procedures for lifting off from the moon again, taken a meal break and then, with great care and difficulty in the confines of the LM, assisted each other with the awkward task of donning their space suits and cumbersome backpacks housing their life-support systems.

Ensuring you were on hand to see *the* truly historic moment of the mission needed willpower and forward planning if, like me, you were a television viewer in the UK; for with British Summer Time in force, the BBC's live broadcast of the first-ever moonwalk was scheduled to begin minutes before 4.00 a.m. on the morning of 21st July. I must have set my alarm to get up in time to see it, although in our house it was purely a generational thing: my parents certainly didn't join me when I went down in the dark to the living room to switch the television on and see history, epic history, in the making. I could recall marvelling, as a boy of eight, at the visible transit of Sputnik 1 like a shooting star over Britain in the autumn skies of 1957, as it went on its melancholy pinging way; and now, as a twenty-year-old student, I was, incredibly, about to see a man walking on the moon.

It's impossible to convey today the sense of how breath-taking it was to conceive of seeing those pictures beamed down live from the moon, but perhaps it can be put in some sort of context by recalling that it had only been two years earlier when the Beatles had serenaded us in the first trans-global TV transmission by satellite. And suddenly there they were on the screen, grainy, blurred black-and-white pictures of the poorest quality by today's standards, almost of the appearance of double exposures on your camera when you forgot to wind the film on before taking the next shot; but there was Neil Armstrong climbing down the ladder, lowering his foot onto the moon and saying, immortally, if a little hesitantly: "That's one small step for man, one giant leap for mankind." And then he was telling Mission Control – and us, the countless millions of his secondary audience worldwide – what he was standing on:

> The surface is fine and powdery. I can kick it up loosely with my
> toe. It does adhere in fine layers, like powdered charcoal, to the
> sole and sides of my boots. I only go in a small fraction of an inch,
> maybe an eighth of an inch, but I can see the footprints of my
> boots and the treads in the fine, sandy particles … It's absolutely no
> trouble to walk around.[148]

Twenty minutes later, he was joined by Aldrin, who summed up his first impressions of the lunar landscape in the phrase "magnificent desolation".

Perhaps the most surreal aspect of that broadcast was its interruption by the furthest ever of all long-distance telephone calls, made by the new President of six months' standing, Richard Nixon, directly to the astronauts just as they had, with some difficulty in no more than six inches of lunar topsoil, planted the Stars and Stripes on a special flagstaff that supported it horizontally:

> Hello, Neil and Buzz. I'm talking to you by telephone from the
> Oval Room at the White House, and this certainly has to be the
> most historic telephone call ever made. I just can't tell you how

proud we all are of what you have done. For every American, this has to be the proudest day of our lives. And for all people all over the world, I am sure they, too, join with Americans in recognising what an immense feat this is. Because of what you have done, the heavens have become a part of man's world. And as you talk to us from the Sea of Tranquillity, it inspires us to redouble our efforts to bring peace and tranquillity to Earth. For one priceless moment in the whole history of man, all the people on this Earth are truly one – one in their pride in what you have done, and one in our prayers that you will return safely to Earth.[149]

Nixon was not alone in his concerns for their safe return: after all, the Presidential speechwriters had taken the necessary precaution of drafting an alternative text for him in the event of a tragedy. As for the forgotten man of the mission, Michael Collins, professing himself perfectly content with his own solitude whilst orbiting above them in the CM *Columbia*, was nevertheless petrified at the thought that his companions might come to harm and not survive, his "secret terror for the last six months [having] been leaving them on the moon and returning to earth alone".[150]

Armstrong and Aldrin's moonwalk officially occupied a total of two hours, thirty-one minutes and forty seconds, in the course of which Armstrong collected geological samples weighing altogether almost forty-eight pounds, they set up several scientific experiments, and between them took a great many photographs – none of which, due to an oversight not appreciated until well after the event, included a direct portrait of Armstrong himself as the First Man on the Moon.[151]

By the time they returned to *Eagle*, they had been physically active for virtually twenty-two hours and were therefore required by Mission Control to at least attempt to sleep for the next seven, which they found uncomfortable (for the LM had no seats or couches) and relatively cold (once they had shaded the windows from the external glare). When they awoke, it would take another three hours of preparation before they were ready to lift off from Tranquillity Base back up to Collins in *Columbia*; leaving behind them not only the descent stage of the LM (with a memorial plaque affixed to one leg) as their launch platform but also an accumulation of space 'garbage' that would otherwise have been excess weight, which included their moon boots and life-support backpacks. They noticed, as they took off, that the blast from their ascent engine had caused the precariously erected US flag to topple over. After the rendezvous with *Columbia* and the transfer of men and materials over into the CM, the ascent stage of *Eagle* was set adrift into a slowly degrading lunar orbit, at some future point to collide with the moon and be destroyed.

The crew of Apollo 11 splashed down in the Pacific Ocean on 24th July and were transferred, in biological containment garments to guard against any possible contamination they might have brought back with them, by US Navy frogmen to the USS *Hornet*; where they were then secured within a special quarantine trailer on deck (and remained incarcerated until arrival back at Houston on 27th July, where they would continue their quarantine in the greater comfort of the specially constructed Lunar Receiving Laboratory). For now, there was one further episode of political hokum to endure, as they dutifully sat at the trailer's large rear window to receive a welcoming speech from the President in person:

> Neil, Buzz and Mike. I want you to know that I think I'm the luckiest man in the world. I say this not only because I have the honour of being the president of the United States, but particularly because I have the privilege of speaking for so many in welcoming you back to Earth. I could tell you about all the messages we received in Washington. Over one hundred foreign governments, emperors, and presidents and prime ministers and kings have sent the most warm messages that we have ever received. They represent over two billion people on this Earth – all of them who have had the opportunity through television to see what you have done. And then I also bring you messages from members of the Cabinet and members of the Senate and members of the House, and Space Agency.[152]

After confiding in them that he'd also spoken by telephone to their wives and was inviting them all to a state banquet on 13th August, on their release from quarantine, he concluded, typically incautiously in view of America's strong tradition of Christian fundamentalism, by describing their achievement as "the greatest week in the history of the world since the Creation".[153]

In the wake of Apollo 11, the space mission that had fulfilled Kennedy's promise to the American people by the narrowest of time margins, NASA was seriously engaged in lobbying Nixon's administration for the extension of a US space exploration programme in the longer term. Meanwhile, "the greatest week in history" had at least stimulated the political will, if not the admiration, of the USSR to pull off a space coup of a different kind, the launching of three Soyuz spacecraft (6, 7 & 8[154]) into earth orbit in three successive days, beginning on 11th October, with the aim of Soyuz 7 and 8 docking and exchanging crew. But within five days the mission had eventually to be abandoned after five attempts at rendezvous, under manual as well as automatic control, had all failed. Thus the initiative was handed back by default to America and the somewhat muted publicity attendant upon Apollo 12, the *second* moon landing within four months to round off the space endeavours of the Sixties.

Given the ultimate proving of lunar flight technology by Apollo 11, by comparison the next mission should have been a walk in the park. It did eventually come good, but not until after a massive electrical failure on lift-off had temporarily threatened to cause its abandonment. In the presence of President Nixon at Cape Kennedy, Apollo 12 was launched in heavy rain on 14th November, with potentially catastrophic consequences as the Saturn V rocket was struck twice by lightning within the first minute of the flight, causing a shut-down of the command module and loss of the navigation system. The crew of Commander Charles Conrad, CM pilot Richard Gordon and LM pilot Alan Bean were suddenly presented with the triggering of alarms and a bewildering array of warning lights in response to the critical loss of power which, thankfully for them, they were soon able to overcome by switching to an auxiliary back-up system and reconnecting the CM's fuel cells. Despite the anxieties the crew inevitably shared with those on the ground at Mission Control, it transpired as the flight continued that no permanent damage had been done to the spacecraft's systems and the mission to the moon could therefore proceed as planned.

The crew had taken the precaution of preparing their own in-flight entertainment, in the form of tapes of their favourite music. Conrad's taste was country-and-western, which was not to the others' liking, but Bean had made up a Top 40 compilation "which they all liked well enough ... especially the bubble-gum hit called 'Sugar Sugar'. When it came on during the trip out from earth, the three of them would hold onto the struts in the command module and bounce weightlessly to the beat, dancing their way to the moon".[155] Which simply goes to prove: a) how comfortable these crew members were with one another; and b) that even in the realms of space there's no accounting for musical taste.

Once in lunar orbit, Gordon remained in the CM *Yankee Clipper* whilst Conrad and Bean departed in the LM *Intrepid* for a new landing site on the Ocean of Storms, an area of stark topological contrast to the Sea of Tranquillity, where they touched down on 19th November. It was one region of the moon specifically targeted in the past by unmanned vehicles from both the USSR and USA and *Intrepid*'s landing was particularly impressive for achieving one of the mission's main objectives; namely, to touch down with precision within reach of Surveyor 3, a US probe that had landed there in April 1967, so that parts could be retrieved from it for detailed examination back on earth. When Conrad and Bean ventured outside for the first time, they were delighted to find that they had parked the LM no more than 200 yards away from it.

As the third and fourth men on the moon, they spent a total of thirty-one-and-a-half hours (ten hours longer than Armstrong and Aldrin) exuberantly undertaking two moonwalks of approximately three-and-a-half hours each; during which they collected geological samples, laid out a new set of scientific experiments and traversed across to Surveyor 3 to cut free its camera and some sections of metal tubing.[156] (The pity of it was that, second time around, there was to be no TV transmission of their activities, because Bean had irreparably damaged their colour TV camera when he inadvertently pointed it at the sun in the process of trying to set it up on its tripod.) After safely docking again with *Yankee Clipper* and the crew were reunited for their journey home, *Intrepid*'s ascent stage was then deliberately crashed into the moon to register the first artificial 'moonquake' via the seismic instruments Conrad and Bean had left behind. The Apollo 12 astronauts returned to earth – and, like their predecessors, to quarantine – on 24th November.

It had fallen then in the end to Richard Nixon, political opponent of both John F. Kennedy and Lyndon Johnson, to capitalise on the realisation of American footsteps on the moon; but that came at the price of his also having to manage the bitter inheritance of the Vietnam War. (Indeed, when Nixon greeted the Apollo 11 crew on USS *Hornet*, it was as only one element of a world trip that also included a Presidential visit to Vietnam.) Nixon had at long last won his place in the White House on a presumed peace ticket, apparently reaffirming his stance in his inaugural speech with this grandiloquent statement: "The greatest honour history can bestow is the title of peacemaker. This honour now beckons America – the chance to help lead the world at last out of the valley of turmoil and on to that high ground of peace that man has dreamed of since the dawn of civilisation."[157]

Once in office, however, he and his newly appointed National Security Adviser, Henry Kissinger, embarked in secret upon an audacious scheme to carry the war beyond Vietnam's borders into neighbouring Cambodia; and, by so doing, so the insane logic of their plan went, to bring the war "quickly … to a conclusion that was satisfactory to them".[158] What these two sought to implement was "a policy that would create political stalemate at home and at least military stalemate on the battlefield":

> Their plan involved complementary but contradictory features: domestic opposition must be reduced, but at the same time Hanoi must be convinced that this administration was willing to sustain the war and even widen it beyond anything that Johnson had considered … Both Kissinger and Nixon were convinced that it was the draft, not the long bleeding of Indochina, that was arousing most of the domestic opposition. If American combat troops could be withdrawn as Vietnamese battalions were developed, an appearance of progress towards peace could be created.
>
> But while the American people were being persuaded that the war was being wound down, plausible threats of escalation would have to be made, and the threats would have to be impressive not

only to Hanoi but to Moscow.[159]

On 9th February 1969, General Abrams, General Westmoreland's successor as US Commander in the Field in Vietnam, informed the President that he had proof of the establishment by North Vietnam of a regional military headquarters in Cambodia from which attacks on the South were being co-ordinated. He further requested Nixon's authorisation to carry out a pre-emptive strike to destroy this HQ (known as COSVN – Central Office for South Vietnam), which in his professional opinion would have "a very significant impact on enemy operations throughout South Vietnam".[160]

The decision to agree to Abrams' request was eased in part by the instigation on 22nd February of a major Viet Cong offensive against over a hundred significant centres of population in South Vietnam, replicating the strategy of 1968's Tet Offensive and now leading to the death of 1,140 US troops. The strike by B-52 bombers, sanctioned under the codename 'Operation Breakfast', went ahead on 18th March; but as Abrams then conjectured that other North Vietnamese safe havens were located within Cambodia, so the bombing raids expanded into the full-blown 'Operation Menu'. After 'Breakfast' had been executed, "Washington then paused for Hanoi's reaction before directing the bombers at 'Lunch', 'Snack', 'Dinner', 'Dessert' and 'Supper'. There was never any response".[161]

Altogether, 'Menu' would last fourteen months, during which time 3,650 air raids were carried out, "involving quadruple the tonnage [of bombs] dropped on Japan in World War II".[162] Worthy of a chapter to itself in a latter-day sequel to *Catch-22*, it involved duplicity and deceit of the highest order, all the way down the chain of command from the President to the operational level in the field:

> After a normal briefing on targets in Vietnam, the pilots and navigators of the planes that were to be diverted that night were told privately to expect the ground controllers to direct them to drop their bombs on a set of coordinates that were different from those they had just received. It was not a wide diversion; the South Vietnamese cover targets were usually selected so that the planes could simply fly another few kilometres beyond, until they were over the Cambodian target.[163]

The post-raid reports were then falsified and processed as if the original South Vietnamese targets had been attacked: "The bombing [of Cambodia] was not merely concealed; the official, *secret* records showed that it had never happened."[164]

It was Nixon and Kissinger's hope that by this subterfuge of additional firepower sufficient pressure would be applied to the North Vietnamese regime to render their representatives at the stalled Paris peace talks more compliant. They were, however, to be thwarted by the death of Ho Chi Minh on 3rd September, inevitably followed by a re-assertion by North Vietnam, through the rhetoric of his funeral ceremonies, of its resolve to oust the Americans and reunite Vietnam as a single Communist state. Washington also faced intransigence from South Vietnam in the face of US proposals to balance the progressive withdrawal of US forces by their replacement in the field with more ARVN troops, the so-called policy of 'Vietnamisation' that looked suspiciously like betrayal to President Thieu in Saigon.

None of this stacked up, leaving Nixon exposed to the charge of hypocrisy, claiming that he was seeking an honourable peace yet demoralising his forces on the ground by requiring them to fight on in the absence of any coherent timetable for their eventual withdrawal (as at the bloody battle of Hamburger Hill, for example, on the Vietnamese/Laotian border in May, where in the course of ten days 476 American troops were killed or wounded); and he had to ride out massive anti-war demonstrations first across America on 15th October and then in Washington on 15th November, when an estimated 250,000 protesters converged on the White House singing "Give Peace A Chance".

Although it is true that US casualties in Vietnam had peaked in 1968, and that Nixon announced the preliminary withdrawal of 25,000 troops from July onwards, nevertheless a total of 11,780 US personnel died in the course of 1969. And further serious doubt was to be cast on the morality of the entire war effort on 5th December, when *Life* magazine published a report, accompanied by horrific confirmatory photographs, of the hitherto undisclosed and unprovoked massacre of Vietnamese civilians in cold blood by US troops on 16th March 1968 in the village of My Lai-4. Those responsible for the murder that day of over five hundred people were infantrymen of "Charlie Company, 1st Battalion, 20th Infantry, 11th Light Infantry Brigade of the 23rd Americal Division"[165]. The platoon commander most closely associated with these atrocities – and subsequently arrested in 1969 for the murder of 109 civilians – was Lieutenant William Calley. The matter only came to light through the persistent representations made to the US government by Ronald Ridenhour, a concerned Vietnam veteran who though not directly involved had himself collated eye-witness reports of the killings, and its follow-up by investigative freelance reporter Seymour Hersh which first gained national press coverage in November 1969 – two months after Calley had been charged.

Exposure, however, led neither to a full nor rapid disclosure of the facts and related judiciary procedures continued in one form or another well on into the Seventies:

> Criminal charges were eventually brought against eighteen officers,
> but every one except Lieutenant Calley was acquitted or had his

charges dismissed without a trial. Calley was convicted of killing twenty-two civilians and sentenced to life imprisonment. However, through President Nixon's intervention, he was released after three and a half years under house arrest.[166]

There were other atrocities closer to home, in California, with which the American public also had to come to terms, after Charles Manson and members of his 'Family' went on the rampage in the suburbs of Hollywood, supposedly inspired by 'messages' embedded in the songs of the Beatles' *White Album*; first killing Sharon Tate, wife of film director Roman Polanski, and four of their acquaintances on 9th August, and then supermarket owner Leno Bianca and his wife Rosemary the next day. (Tate and her friends paid the ultimate price for nothing more than living in a house previously rented by record producer Terry Melcher, a mutual acquaintance of the Beach Boys' Dennis Wilson against whom Manson had nurtured a vendetta for some time.) After finally being apprehended in November, the legal process for Manson and his three female co-accused was as protracted as that for Lieutenant Calley, their trial not beginning until June 1970 and, after 'guilty' findings being returned on all four in January 1971, sentence not passed until that April.[167]

A month into his Presidency, Richard Nixon had paid a courtesy visit to Prime Minister Harold Wilson in Downing Street on 24th February, in the interests no doubt of maintaining the 'special relationship' between the USA and Britain. Wilson, however, was destined to spend much of the year grappling with a domestic constitutional crisis rather than international affairs, as 1969 saw the widespread eruption of political discontent and sectarian violence between the Roman Catholic minority and Protestant majority in Northern Ireland, where religious differences were symptomatic of the rising tensions between pro-Irish Republicans and pro-Unionist Ulstermen. Although the province was at the time subject to semi-autonomy from Westminster, with its own elected Parliament and Prime Minister (Capt. Terence O'Neill, succeeded by Major James Chichester-Clarke from 30th April onwards), British troops were deployed there from late April to assist with the protection of key installations (after power and water supplies had been disrupted by a terrorist bombing campaign) and then brought in to assist with peace-keeping from mid-August, beginning in Londonderry and Belfast, both the scenes of major rioting. The prospect of open civil war breaking out "in a part of the United Kingdom where people listened to the Beatles, watched *Coronation Street* and shopped at Sainsbury's"[168] suddenly seemed very real and very imminent. By the end of September, the Royal Engineers were engaged in what the General Officer Commanding Northern Ireland described as a "very temporary" operation[169] in Belfast – the erection of a 'peace wall' to separate the Protestant community of the Shankhill Road from the Catholic community of the Falls Road. A month later, the Northern Ireland garrison was to be strengthened by the arrival of the 1ˢᵗ Parachute Regiment and new rules of engagement would permit soldiers to return fire on snipers and bombers.

In terms of popular culture on mainland Britain, there were signs that 1969, aside from the music scene, marked a turning point. The top film releases of the year, for example, displayed further ambivalence towards our twentieth-century heritage; one of the last of the gung-ho, play-it-straight war films *The Battle Of Britain* being counterbalanced by the translation from stage to film by director Richard Attenborough of Joan Littlewood's *Oh! What A Lovely War* or by the film adaptation of Muriel Spark's novel *The Prime Of Miss Jean Brodie*, in which Maggie Smith as the title character, an intellectual supporter of Fascism in the inter-war years, seeks to indoctrinate her pupils. In the same year as the Kray Twins were sentenced to life imprisonment for their gangland murders, *The Italian Job* enabled Michael Caine and Noel Coward to combine all the tension of the execution of a highly sophisticated robbery with a classic comic celebration of bungling criminality; while George Lazenby, chosen for his good looks in the TV commercials for 'Big Fry' chocolate, took the James Bond franchise post-Sean Connery to a new low with his under-par performance as 007 in *On Her Majesty's Secret Service*.[170]

For sheer irreverence, it was, however, to television that you had to turn, when on the evening of Sunday, 5ᵗʰ October, the BBC broadcast, in a slot previously allotted to a repeat of a religious discussion programme, the first episode of a new and revolutionary comedy series "designed 'to subdue the violence in us all'"[171], *Monty Python's Flying Circus*:

> *A seashore. Some way out to sea a ragged man is struggling his way to shore. Slowly and with difficulty he makes his way up onto the beach, flops down exhausted and announces:*
>
> **Man** (MICHAEL) It's …
>
> **Voice Over** (JOHN) Monty Python's Flying Circus.
>
> *Titles beginning with words 'Monty Python's Flying Circus'. Various bizarre things happen. When the titles end:*
> *Ordinary grey-suited announcer standing by desk. He smiles confidently.*
>
> **Announcer** (GRAHAM) Good evening.
>
> *The announcer confidently moves to a chair and sits down. There is a squeal as of a pig being sat upon.*
>
> *Cut to a blackboard with several lines of pigs drawn on it in colour. A man steps into view and with a piece of chalk crosses out one of the pigs.*

CAPTION: 'IT'S WOLFGANG AMADEUS MOZART'

Mozart sitting at piano tinkling with the keys. He finishes tinkling.

Mozart (JOHN) Hello again, and welcome to the show. Tonight we continue to look at some famous deaths. Tonight we start with the wonderful death of Genghis Khan, conqueror of India. Take it away, Genghis.[172]

And so it started as it meant to go on, absurd, inconsequential, as "something completely different" in fact, although that classic phrase was barely used in Series 1 (twice only – in Episodes 2 and 9 respectively) and would not come regularly into its own until the beginning of Series 2 in September 1970. The show combined the scriptwriting and acting talents of Eric Idle, Terry Jones and Michael Palin, John Cleese and Graham Chapman with the surreal animation skills of Terry Gilliam; who between them had substantial grounding already in television comedy, notably with *At Last The 1948 Show* and *Do Not Adjust Your Set* for ITV. (Chapman also had the rare distinction of having written incidental comic repartee for Petula Clark to 'ad lib' on her television showcases.)[173] Calling upon the services of actress Carol Cleveland when the need arose for what she herself termed a 'glamour dollie bird'[174], they were not averse themselves to getting up in drag as old busybodies the Pepperpots, Hell's Grannies, or as the Batley Townswomen's Guild to re-enact the Battle of Pearl Harbour.

The epithet of 'episode' was, in truth, no more than a courtesy title for each programme, "a pretty loose excuse for linking sketches together" for the comedy "had an inner logic (or illogic) that was not contingent upon generally accepted notions of drama: there was no narrative drive, no three-act structure, and no character development".[175] Yet as can be seen even from the opening minutes of Episode 1 quoted above, the Pythons were alert from the start to the possibilities of parodying the pomposity of the BBC itself, by creating a satiric blend of its chameleon-like pretensions to be at one and the same time the UK's foremost platform for the arts, sport, news coverage and light entertainment with the palpably irritating mannerisms of its regular presenters and continuity staff. In this regard, they were well up to speed by Episode 5:

'Match of the Day' music. We see a couple. They are standing at the foot of a largish bed. She is in bra and pants. He is in Y-fronts. They kiss ecstatically. After a few seconds there is the sound of a car drawing up. The crunch of footsteps on gravel and the sound of a door opening. The newsreader comes into shot.

Newsreader (ERIC) Ah, I'm terribly sorry it's not in fact 'Match of the Day' – it is in fact edited highlights of tonight's romantic movie. Er. Sorry. *(he goes out of shot; the two clinch again; after a second he pops back into shot)* Ooh, I'm sorry, on BBC2 Joan Bakewell will be talking to Michael Dean about what makes exciting television. *(pops out of shot, then pops in again)* Ah, sorry about all that. And now back to the movie. *(he goes)*

The couple continue to neck …[176]

Although it could just as easily have been another Python sketch, the announcement, in the Boxing Day edition of Radio 4's *The World At One*, of the results of a listeners' poll to find the Man of the Decade was, as far as ascertainable, genuine: the winner was Harold Wilson, the runner-up Enoch Powell. In a parallel exercise conducted by Associated Television (ATV) and shown on 30th December, three 'distinguished guests' (who these days would be termed 'media personalities') were invited to make a similar choice and compile their own 20-minute documentary in support of their nominees. The revered broadcaster of his weekly *Letter From America* for radio, Alistair Cooke, chose John F. Kennedy; the American author Mary McCarthy chose Ho Chi Minh; and the socio-anthropologist Dr. Desmond Morris, whose best-selling books *The Naked Ape* and *The Human Zoo* had enlivened debate about human behaviour in the late Sixties, picked John Lennon, thereby thrusting him ever more firmly into the "new arena of high visibility – the politics of peace".[177]

It was a golden opportunity for Lennon. Having already been the *deus ex machina* of Tony Palmer's documentary *All My Loving* the year before, using that as an indirect means of propounding a vestigial political manifesto for pop, he could now openly compile his own selection of archive material for Morris to include in his film for *Man Of The Decade*. Alongside clips of the Beatles at various stages of their career and more recent ones showing the John and Yoko bed-ins, he could not resist including footage of the anti-war protesters singing "Give Peace A Chance" as they marched on the White House on 15th November: "it was a very big moment for me, that's what the song was about … in me secret heart I always wanted to write something that would take over from 'We Shall Overcome'."[178]

He was not, however, to have it all his own way, even now. Filming with Morris happened to overlap with filming by the BBC of *The World Of John And Yoko*, a profile of the couple to be shown on 15th December as part of the late-night current affairs programme *24 Hours*, in which one particular sequence showed that not everyone was as enamoured with his skittish stance on peace as he would like to think. It certainly cut no ice with Gloria Emerson, the hardened London correspondent of the *New York Times*, who accused Lennon to his face on camera of being "a fake", "vulgar and self-ag-grandising": "I can't think of anyone who seems more remote from the ugliness of what's happening than you. I do see you getting up on a Tuesday morning and thinking, 'Let's see what shall we do today? What war is going on?'"[179] It was, therefore, by no means safe to presume that having aspired to pop divinity you could ever dare to equate yourself – or let others equate you – with being a world leader; and that, in the dying days of the decade, was one lesson worth taking with you from the Sixties.

NOTES

1   Soon after which, in August, he returned to live performance for the first time since March 1961 at the Las Vegas International Hilton.

2   Variously reported as a cut of future royalties plus (in Laura Jackson's account) the sum of £100,000 – or alternatively (according to Christopher Sandford), £20,000 per annum "for as long as the Stones lasted". [See Laura Jackson, op. cit., p.233; and Christopher Sandford, op. cit., p.192.] Whereas Sean Egan asserts that Jones was offered both the lump sum and the annual payments. [See Sean Egan, "The Mammoth Book of The Rolling Stones" (Robinson, 2013), p.130.]

3   Bill Wyman with Richard Havers, op. cit., p.326.

4   Quoted in Bill Wyman with Richard Havers, op. cit., p.326.

5   Christopher Sandford, op. cit., p.193.

6   Jackson's contention is that Jones' drink was spiked by Thorogood, who then drowned him. Thorogood died in 1993, after supposedly making a death-bed confession to his murder. [See Laura Jackson, op. cit., Chs.11 & 12.]

7   Keith Richards with James Fox, op. cit., p.272.

8   Andy Gray, *NME*, week ending 12th July 1969; reproduced in "*NME* Originals" Vol.1 Issue 11.

9   Nick Logan, *NME*, week ending 12th July 1969; reproduced in "*NME* Originals" Vol.1 Issue 11.

10   Chris Welch, *Melody Maker* 12th July 1969, quoted in Bill Wyman with Richard Havers, op. cit., p.335.

11   By the time their cases finally came to court to be disposed of, on 26th January 1970, Jagger and Faithfull were fast approaching the end of their relationship, precipitating her downward slide into drug addiction and penury. While Marianne was cleared of the charge of possessing cannabis, Mick was found guilty and fined £200.

12   Bill Wyman with Richard Havers, op. cit., p.340.

13   Bill Wyman with Richard Havers, op. cit., p.330.

14   Quoted in Bill Wyman with Richard Havers, op. cit., p.347.

15   Quoted in Rob Hughes, "The Day The Music Died", *Record Collector* No.369, December 2009, p.53.

16   Ibid.

17   Quoted in Rob Hughes, "The Day The Music Died", *Record Collector* No.369, December 2009, p.58.

18   Keith Richards with James Fox, op. cit., p.281.

19   Ibid.

20   Stanley Booth, quoted in Rob Hughes, "The Day The Music Died", *Record Collector* No.369, December 2009, p.59.

21   Quoted in Bill Wyman with Richard Havers, op. cit., p.353

22   Stanley Booth, quoted in Rob Hughes, "The Day The Music Died", *Record Collector* No.369, December 2009, p.59.

23   Keith Richards with James Fox, op .cit., p.282.

24   Ibid.

25   Bill Wyman with Richard Havers, op. cit., p.355.

26   Bill Wyman with Richard Havers, op. cit., p.360.

27   Christopher Sandford, op. cit., p.211.

28   Paul McCartney, "The Beatles Anthology" (Cassell, 2000), p.315.

29   George Martin, ibid.

30   George Harrison, "The Beatles Anthology" (Cassell, 2000), p.316.

31   Quoted in Peter Doggett, "*Let It Be/Abbey Road*: The Beatles" (Schirmer, 1998), p.23.

32   Quoted in Peter Doggett, op. cit., p.32.

33   George Harrison, "The Beatles Anthology" (Cassell, 2000), p.321.

34   Quoted in Mark Lewisohn, op. cit., p.313.

35   His second solo excursion into films, the first having been in the cameo role of a Mexican gardener in the sexual comedy *Candy*, given its UK premiere in February 1969 although filming had commenced as long ago as December 1967.

36   Lennon/McCartney, © 1969 by Northern Songs Ltd.

37   Quoted in Kevin Howlett, op. cit., p.271.

38   Ibid.

39   Mark Lewisohn, op. cit., p.323. One of John and Yoko's visitors in Montreal was known to be Petula Clark, who at the time was in concert there and who is credited by Spencer Leigh as having been present when "Give Peace A Chance" was recorded. [See Spencer Leigh, "The Beatles In America:The Stories, The Scene, 50 Years On" (Omnibus, 2013), p.205.]

40   The gigs in which he participated included two houses at the Empire Theatre, Liverpool on 6th December. [See Marc Roberty, op. cit., pp.138-139.]

41   The Beatles created a *de facto* demarcation between the majority of the songs they recorded in January and February (for their grandiose *Get Back* project) and those they recorded later, from July onwards, which made up most of *Abbey Road*. At the

beginning of March, Glyn Johns was charged with knocking the earlier material into a semblance of a coherent LP, that eventually morphed from *Get Back* into *Let It Be*. When they resumed recording on 1st July, it was with the express intention of coming up with a completely different new album. Hence by the time *Let It Be* finally saw the light of day, on 8th May 1970, the original recordings of all the songs on it had been made more than a year earlier – and in the case of "Across The Universe", more than two years before.

42   Sean Egan (ed.), "The Mammoth Book of The Beatles" (Robinson, 2009), p.204.

43   Ian MacDonald, op. cit., p.301.

44   Ringo Starr, "The Beatles Anthology" (Cassell, 2000), p.337.

45   Ian MacDonald, op. cit., p.320.

46   Quoted in Kevin Howlett, op. cit., p.288.

47   Paul McCartney, "The Beatles Anthology" (Cassell, 2000), p.337.

48   John Lennon, ibid.

49   Ray Foulk, quoted in Johnny Black, "Eyewitness: Dylan at the Isle of Wight" (*Q Magazine*, October 1995); reprinted in Sean Egan (ed.), "The Mammoth Book of Bob Dylan" (Robinson, 2011), p.163.

50   Quoted in Robert Shelton, op. cit., p.277.

51   Originally proposed as a possible theme tune for John Schlesinger's film *Midnight Cowboy*, it was submitted too late for his consideration and missed the cut. Released as a single hard on the heels of his appearance at the Isle of Wight Festival, it gave Dylan a No.4 UK hit in mid-October.

52   Namely: "I Ain't Got No Home" (Woody Guthrie), "In The Pines" (Leadbelly) and "Slippin' And Slidin'" (Little Richard).

53   *Rolling Stone*, 9th August 1969.

54   *Disc & Music Echo*, 6th September 1969.

55   Ibid.

56   And was finally made available in its entirety on a bonus CD in the expanded deluxe edition of *Bob Dylan: The Bootleg Series Vol.10/ Another Self Portrait (1969-1971)* (Columbia, 2013). Four of the concert recordings ("She Belongs To Me", "Like A Rolling Stone", "(Quinn The Eskimo) The Mighty Quinn" and "Minstrel Boy") had, however, already been released on his 1970 double-album *Self Portrait*.

57   David Hughes, *Disc & Music Echo*, quoted in Keith Badman, op .cit., p.244.

58   Ibid.

59   Keith Badman, op. cit., p.258. In what he called the Beach Boys' "limbo period", running from 1968 to at least 1971/72, their co-manager Fred Vail remembered "several tours where I had to advance the primary money for the tour out of my American Express and Diners Club credit cards ... And as we went along and played the gigs, I would take the money out to pay the bills." [Quoted in Keith Badman, op. cit., p.248.]

60   Although it did reach No.6 in the LP charts, *Electric Ladyland* was the least successful of his albums to date. *Are You Experienced* had reached No.2, *Axis: Bold As Love* No.5

and even the stopgap *Smash Hits* compilation that had preceded it in 1968 had gone to No.4.

61   Charles R. Cross, "Room Full of Mirrors: A Biography of Jimi Hendrix" (Sceptre, 2006), pp.242-243.

62   Jimi Hendrix (ed. by Alan Douglas & Peter Neal), op .cit., p.172.

63   Jimi Hendrix (ed. by Alan Douglas & Peter Neal), op .cit., p.176.

64   Quoted in John McDermott et al., op. cit., p.140.

65   Jimi Hendrix (ed. by Alan Douglas & Peter Neal), op .cit., p.194.

66   Redding had, in fact, already formed his own group, Fat Mattress, in which he played guitar and sang vocals, in 1968; and in 1969 they had been a support act for the Experience both at the Royal Albert Hall on 24th February and at several of the subsequent concerts on the last US tour. Signed to Polydor, Fat Mattress released an eponymous first LP in 1969 but Redding left in 1970, during the making of a second album.

67   Jimi Hendrix (ed. by Alan Douglas & Peter Neal), op. cit., p.195.

68   Peter Doggett, liner notes to *Arthur Or The Decline And Fall Of The British Empire* [Sanctuary, remastered deluxe edition, 2011], p.4.

69   Quoted in Peter Doggett, op. cit., p.8.

70   Ray Davies, © 1969 by Davray Music Ltd.

71   Quoted in Doug Hinman, op. cit., p.128.

72   Quoted in Rob Jovanovic, "God Save The Kinks" (Aurum, 2013), p.157.

73   Ray Davies, "Americana: The Kinks, The Road and The Perfect Riff" (Virgin, 2013), p.53.

74   Ray Davies, op. cit., pp.54-55.

75   Quoted in Doug Hinman, op. cit., p.133.

76   Ray Davies, "Americana: The Kinks, The Road and The Perfect Riff" (Virgin, 2013), p. 64.

77   Danny Goldberg of *Record World*, quoted in Doug Hinman, op. cit., p.136.

78   Ray Davies, "Americana: The Kinks, The Road and The Perfect Riff" (Virgin, 2013), p. 64.

79   Quoted in interview with Simon Goddard, *Uncut* magazine, April 2004, reprinted in "*Uncut* Ultimate Music Guide Issue No.5: The Who" (February 2011), p.127.

80   Simon Goddard, op. cit., pp.126-127.

81   May/Taylor/Waller/Alder, © 1968 by Lupus Music Company Ltd.

82   Pete Townshend, op. cit., p.164.

83   Tim Ewbank & Stafford Hildred, op. cit., p.107.

84   Pete Townshend, op. cit., p.176.

85   Paul Harris, "By the time we got to Woodstock … it had become a museum piece",

The Guardian, 15th August 2009.

86 Go to www.bethelwoodscenter.org/museum for further details.

87 Go to www.woodstockmuseum.org for all this and more!

88 Stan Goldstein, quoted in Pete Fornatale, "Back to the Garden: The Story of Woodstock" (Touchstone, 2009), pp.23-24.

89 Quoted in Pete Fornatale, op. cit., p.218.

90 Sam Yasgur, quoted in Pete Fornatale, op. cit., p.221.

91 Max Yasgur, quoted in Pete Fornatale, op. cit., p.224.

92 Tom Malone, quoted in Pete Fornatale, op. cit., p.24.

93 John Morris, quoted in Pete Fornatale, op. cit., p.23.

94 Op. cit., p.138.

95 Lulu, op. cit., p.130.

96 As in 1968, Lulu beat Dusty into second place, but this time only by the slender margin of 91 votes, although Dusty regained her title as Best World Female Singer.

97 Nominally, Cilla Black was the most successful of them all in 1969, with "Surround Yourself With Sorrow" reaching No.2 in March; followed by "Conversations" (No.8 in August) and "If I Thought You'd Ever Change Your Mind" (entering the last chart of the decade at No.30, before reaching No.21 in January 1970). Sandie Shaw had two hits: "Monsieur Dupont" (No.7 in March) and "Think It All Over" (No.30 in May). Dusty Springfield had only one, "Am I The Same Girl", that reached No.25 in October. Clodagh Rodgers chalked up three hit singles: "Come Back And Shake Me" (No.7 in May), "Goodnight Midnight" (No.5 in August) and "Biljo" (No.16 in November). The only other contender of note was Paul McCartney's protégé Mary Hopkin, who took one of his compositions, "Goodbye", to No.2 from April through into May; after which she followed Sandie and Lulu into the Eurovision Song Contest in 1970.

98 Go to www.countryjoe.com for Country Joe McDonald's own commentary on the song.

99 McDonald, © 1965, renewed 1977 by Alkatraz Corner Music BMI.

100 Quoted in Pete Fornatale, op. cit., p.112.

101 Pete Fornatale, ibid.

102 Quoted in Pete Fornatale, op. cit., p.188.

103 Pete Townshend, op. cit., p.181.

104 Pete Fornatale, op. cit., p.212.

105 Jimi Hendrix (ed. by Alan Douglas & Peter Neal), op. cit., p.199.

106 Charles R. Cross, op. cit., p.268.

107 Billy Altman, quoted in Pete Fornatale, op. cit., p.271.

108 Quoted from press conference at Frank's Restaurant, Harlem, 3rd September 1969, included as special feature in *Jimi Hendrix: Live At Woodstock* [Experience Hendrix/ Universal DVD, 2008].

109 That is to say, the albatross, for the killing of which the Ancient Mariner was cursed in Coleridge's poem *The Rime of The Ancient Mariner*. Coleridge's own marginal commentary on the last stanza of Part I reads: "The ancient Mariner inhospitably killeth the pious bird of good omen." The inference behind the LP's punning title (reinforced by the picture of a nun holding an albatross on the front cover of the sleeve) can therefore be taken to be – forgiving the mixed metaphors – that Fleetwood Mac, by leaving Blue Horizon, had inadvertently killed the goose that laid the golden egg.

110 Green, © 1969 by Rachel Music (Leosong).

111 Green, © 1969 by Rachel Music (Leosong).

112 Mike Vernon, liner notes to *Fleetwood Mac: Greatest Hits* (CBS, 30th anniversary edition, 1998).

113 Fleetwood Mac still hankered after the traditional blues. In January, whilst on tour in America, they had all too happily visited Chess Studios to cut tracks with several renowned blues artists (such as Willie Dixon, Otis Spann and Buddy Guy); and in the spring they toured the UK with B.B. King. But there was a further mismatch between their domestic recording sessions and live performances: Jeremy Spencer was excluded from the sessions for *Then Play On*, whereas in concert he habitually grabbed the spotlight for a cranked-up rock'n'roll medley.

114 McNair's distinctive flute-playing embellished much of Donovan's work from *Fairytale* onwards, in arrangements by John Cameron, as well as being prominently featured in the theme to Ken Loach's 1969 film *Kes*, but for Baker he would play saxophone. He died in 1971, aged 39.

115 The follow-up single and their only other hit, "Tears In The Wind", with vocals by Stan Webb, had just one week at No.25 in September.

116 Rob Young, op. cit., p.250.

117 Joe Boyd, op. cit., pp.226-227.

118 Written by Charlotte Bingham and Terence Brady, starring Liza Goddard as Victoria, Susan Jameson as Kate and Angela Down as Avril.

119 CD liner notes to *Basket Of Light* (Castle/Sanctuary, remastered edition, 2001).

120 Quoted in Marc Eliot, op. cit., p.104.

121 Paul Simon, "Lyrics 1964-2008" (Simon & Schuster, 2008), p.62.

122 Mick Houghton, op. cit., p.219.

123 Mick Houghton, op. cit., p.220.

124 Namely, "Love From Room 109 At The Islander (On Pacific Coast Highway)", at 10 mins. 47 secs., and "Gypsy Woman", at 12 mins. 19 secs.

125 Buckley, © 1969 by Third Story Music, BMI.

126 Mick Houghton, op. cit., p.220.

127 Buckley, © 1969 by Third Story Music, BMI.

128 Buckley, © 1969 by Third Story Music, BMI.

129 Ibid.

130　Quoted in interview with John Reed, liner notes to *The Very Best Of The Moody Blues* (Polygram TV, 1996).

131　Quoted in Greg Russo, op. cit., p.59.

132　Quoted in Chris Welch, liner notes to *The Move: Hits And Rarities – Singles A's & B's* (Repertoire, 1999).

133　Pete Frame, "Rock Family Trees" (Omnibus, 1993), p.13.

134　Reissued almost twenty years later, as a tie-in to both the Miller Lite beer commercial and *Rambo III*, it was No.1 for three weeks in late September/early October of 1988.

135　A direct lift from Chuck Berry's "Little Queenie", plus contemporary Beatles' guitar phrasing as per "Get Back".

136　It is credited with two weeks in mid-June in the *Record Retailer* composite Top 40, entering at No.35 and departing at No.37.

137　Bowie, © 1969 by Tro-Essex Music Int. Inc. – ASCAP.

138　Quoted in interview with John Reed, liner notes to *The Very Best Of The Moody Blues* (Polygram TV, 1996).

139　Edge, © 1969 by Threshold Music.

140　Andrew Chaikin, op. cit., pp.135-136.

141　Quoted in James R. Hansen, op. cit., p.343.

142　Andrew Chaikin, op. cit., p.155.

143　Ibid.

144　Alan Shepard & Deke Slayton, op. cit., p.240.

145　Andrew Chaikin, op. cit., p.159.

146　Andrew Chaikin, op. cit., p.156.

147　Deborah Cadbury, op. cit., p.333. Andrew Smith goes further, claiming that the explosion of the N1 also killed "over a hundred support staff". [See his "Moondust: In Search of The Men Who Fell to Earth" (Bloomsbury, 2005), p.130.]

148　Quoted in James R. Hansen, op. cit., p.496.

149　Quoted in James R. Hansen, op. cit., p.505.

150　Quoted in Andrew Chaikin, op. cit., p.223.

151　"… while Armstrong took dozens of wonderful photographs of Aldrin, Buzz took not a single explicit picture of Neil. The only pictures of Neil were one with a reflection of him in Aldrin's helmet visor in a picture Neil took, or a very few where Neil was standing in the dark shadow of the LM with his back to the camera or only partially shown." (See James R. Hansen, op. cit., p.507.) They did, however, take pictures of each other once they had returned to the LM and climbed out of their space suits.

152　Quoted in James R. Hansen, op. cit., p.556.

153　Quoted in James R. Hansen, op. cit., p.557.

154　The cosmonaut crews were as follows: Soyuz 6 – Georgi Shonin & Valeri Kubasov;

Soyuz 7 – Anatoli Filipchenko, Vladislav Volkov & Viktor Gorbatko; Soyuz 8 – Vladimir Shatalov & Aleksei Yeliseyev.

155   Andrew Chaikin, op. cit., p.254.

156   Surveyor 3's camera is now housed in the Smithsonian Institute, where Apollo 11's Michael Collins became the first director of the National Air and Space Museum when it opened in 1976.

157   Quoted in Michael Maclear, op. cit., p.387.

158   William Shawcross, "Sideshow: Kissinger, Nixon and the Destruction of Cambodia" (Fontana, 1980), p.89.

159   Ibid.

160   Quoted in William Shawcross, op. cit., p.20.

161   Michael Maclear, op. cit., p.338.

162   Michael Maclear, op. cit., p.391.

163   William Shawcross, op. cit., p.30.

164   William Shawcross, op. cit., p.31.

165   Christian G. Appy, op. cit., p.343.

166   Christian G. Appy, op. cit., pp.345-346. Having been charged on 5th September 1969, Calley's trial began on 17th November 1970, lasting until he was found guilty and convicted on 29th March 1971. On 31st March 1971, he was sentenced to life imprisonment and hard labour at Fort Leavenworth, the US Army's maximum security prison, but the next day President Nixon sanctioned his transfer to house arrest at Fort Benning pending an appeal. On 20th August 1971, his sentence was reduced from life to 20 years (and later commuted to 10 years). He was released from Fort Benning on 25th September 1974, after which Nixon granted him a limited Presidential pardon.

167   In an eerie coincidence, Manson, like Calley, was convicted on 29th March 1971. He and his three followers were all sentenced to death on 19th April 1971 (commuted to life imprisonment in 1972 after California State had voted to abolish the death penalty).

168   Dominic Sandbrook, "White Heat: A History of Britain in The Swinging Sixties" (Abacus, 2008), p.754.

169   Quoted in Derrik Mercer (ed.), op. cit., p.1005.

170   The film was also cursed with an unappealing theme song in the form of "We Have All The Time In The World" by Louis Armstrong, which was not a contemporary hit.

171   Quoted from the *Radio Times* in David Morgan, "Monty Python Speaks!" (Fourth Estate, 1999), p.52.

172   Graham Chapman et al., "Monty Python's Flying Circus: Just The Words Vol.1" (Methuen, 1989), p.1.

173   The Pythons included a nostalgic reference to this in Episode 13, the last of Series 1, broadcast on 11th January 1970. In the sketch "Historical Impersonations", Michael Palin (as Cardinal Richelieu) takes off Petula Clark singing "Don't Sleep In The Subway".

174   Quoted in David Morgan, op. cit., p.50.

175   David Morgan, op. cit., p.2. In this respect, the Pythons were indebted to Spike Milligan's anarchic *Q* comedy series.

176   Graham Chapman et al., "Monty Python's Flying Circus: Just The Words Vol.1" (Methuen, 1989), pp.62-63.

177   Albert Goldman, op. cit., p.431.

178   Quoted in Jann Wenner, "Lennon Remembers: The Rolling Stone Interviews" (Penguin, 1972), p.110.

179   Quoted in Kevin Howlett, op .cit., p.289. Emerson, a forthright opponent of America's involvement in Vietnam, went on to report on the war as a foreign correspondent for the New York Times from 1970 to 1972, and in 1976 published her award-winning book "Winners and Losers: Battles, Retreats, Gains, Losses and Ruins from the Vietnam War" (Penguin, 1986).

Chapter 12

... and The Outro

Reaching the end of our guided tour through the many galleries of the Sixties, after pausing countless times en route to pay our respects to and marvel at the myriad changing faces of the decade's masterpieces, it's almost tempting to linger in the basement a while longer in the awesome presence of the reserve collection, all that other stuff for which there simply wasn't the hanging space upstairs or that, even more sadly, somehow never quite made it. But you and I both know that won't do. All that's left now is a little time for reflection and then we really must clear the building, turn out the lights, lock up and go home.

Altogether it's turned out not to be such an orderly conducted tour as I had originally anticipated. By that I mean that at the outset I thought I knew what I wanted this book to be, how the story would unfold neatly from year to year, how it would – here comes that unintended pun from Ch.1 again – set the record straight. What I had not allowed for was how my own preferences, my own tastes as curator of this singular exhibition would still be susceptible to change after all these years. My memories and enjoyment of the music remain largely unimpaired, whereas researching the context in which it came into being in depth has often pulled me up short and led me to re-evaluate its worth. I am nevertheless unshaken in my belief that for those of us who were there, as we left the Sixties behind us we were far more musically enriched than we had been when they started.

That said, the Seventies were definitely not the Sixties continued, as rapidly became clear. (John and Yoko had even put the boot in before 1969 was done, by issuing a New Year's message to the world on 30th December in which they proclaimed: "We believe that the last decade was the end of the old machine crumbling to pieces."[1]) The overwhelming majority of artists whose work I had enjoyed and collected for years had fallen by the wayside long before 1969 turned into 1970, either because they had folded (i.e., most of them) or had opted to go in directions not to my particular taste (like the Rolling Stones or the Who). Out on their own as complete one-offs, the Beatles were on the verge of implosion anyway, while Jimi Hendrix, having turned his back on commercialism, had – did he but know it only months to live. For me, it meant there were precious few current acts left to retain my interest into the next decade, the notable exceptions being: Simon & Garfunkel with *Bridge Over Troubled Water* (February 1970), the Moody Blues with *A Question Of Balance* (August 1970) and Bob Dylan with *New Morning*

(November 1970). By the time Matthews Southern Comfort reached No.1 – also in November 1970 – with Joni Mitchell's "Woodstock", a pure unsullied gem of a one-hit wonder, then the game was well and truly up for anyone still trying to invoke the lost spirit of the dear departed Sixties.

The trouble was that while what we really wanted from the Sixties' survivors was more of the same, they no longer wanted to serve it up, and this mismatch of expectations would, in some instances, threaten to tarnish reputations as time went on. In his excellent biography of George Harrison, Graeme Thomson offers the telling example of adverse audience reaction to his North American tour of 1974 (the year, as it happened, in which Bob Dylan and the Band had also ventured back out on the road). First he quotes one reviewer's account for a Vancouver newspaper of Harrison's performance, as follows: "All I could think about was Dylan a few months ago, *singing all his songs wrong for all the people who wanted to hear them the way they were used to hearing them* [my italics]."[2] And then the exasperated promoter Bill Graham, pondering on a less than jubilant concert in San Francisco:

> I think what the public leaves with is a continuing respect
> and reverence for what he has done, and perhaps a feeling of
> bittersweetness about not having gotten just a bit closer to what
> their expectations were. I don't know. *They didn't get to go back in the
> time machine enough* [my italics].[3]

Part of this problem emanates, of course, from the increasing strain placed on the relationship between artists and their audiences from the mid-Sixties onwards. Once the Beatles led the exodus from the stage by kicking the dust of Candlestick Park off their heels in 1966 and choosing instead to retreat to the sanctuary of the recording studio, the participatory dimension of that relationship was traded in for a wholly auditory experience. The subsequent fertile period of studio experimentation may have taken Sixties' pop forward in bold, hitherto unimaginable strides; but more often than not it simultaneously confined it to the turntable, since ironically it was also the comparatively primitive technology of the day that precluded it from being performed live. Once all you're doing is only selling people records – albeit better, longer, more complex records and more albums than singles, so superficially offering more value for money – then you're inviting replay after replay, so that every listener becomes over-familiar with every nuance of that one studio performance that is forever frozen in time. And thus by default every listener turns into a pseudo-professional armchair critic, growing harder and harder to please.

When highbrow pop and progressive rock eventually caught up with itself, to the extent that sound systems developed to the point of serviceably reproducing records note for note on stage and groups embarked on a reinvigorated stadium circuit, it didn't always result in a new meeting of minds: quite the opposite, in fact, in its more extreme manifestations, where it provoked a corrosive sense of alienation. One of the strongest expressions of this comes from Pink Floyd's Roger Waters, vividly recalling with disbelief a key incident in the late Seventies:

> Some crazed teenage fan, screaming his devotion, began clawing his way up the storm netting that separated the band from the human cattle pen in front of the stage, and the boil of my frustration finally burst. I spat in his face. Immediately afterwards I was shocked by my behaviour. I realised that what had once been a worthwhile and manageable exchange between us (the band) and them (the audience) had been utterly perverted by scale, corporate avarice and ego. All that remained was an arrangement that was essentially sado-masochistic. I had a very vivid image of an audience being bombed – of bombs being lobbed from the stage – and a sense that those people getting blown to bits would go absolutely wild with glee at being at the centre of all the action.[4]

It proved to be a prime catalyst in conceptualising and recording that most disturbing of albums *The Wall* in 1979, about which David Gilmour would have this to say: "*Building a wall between ourselves and the audience was a striking metaphor for the intimacy we had lost* [my italics] as a stadium band. And though I believe we were still delivering to the majority of fans – despite the noise and conditions – the loss of control over our environment often troubled me." [5]

That abiding sense of a loss of intimacy was not, however, solely a by-product of scale, articulated here by Waters and Gilmour as by Lennon and McCartney before them. It also had its origins in the over-intellectual-ising of music criticism from the mid-Sixties onwards, which increasingly poured scorn on the most popular and listenable forms of pop music as 'lowbrow' and attached higher value to less accessible improvisation and experiment – but only, of course, after a decent interval made it safe to do so, once the Beatles had peaked with *Sgt. Pepper* and Brian Wilson had shown with "Heroes And Villains" that he really had lost his marbles.

One of the more depressing aspects of Sixties music that hadn't struck me before but has come through most clearly to me now is the unliberated plight of the female singer, for whom, generally speaking, fame came – if it came at all – at the price of being manipulated and forced into the mould of the stereotypical light entertainer. It's far easier to identify the role models for most British males wanting to make a go of pop music in the early Sixties. If they sang, they copied the Everly Brothers; if they played guitar, they copied Hank Marvin[6]; if they sang *and* played the guitar, then they copied Buddy Holly; and they took it from there. There wasn't any comparative kudos for girls in being the next Brenda Lee or Connie Francis look-alike – unless, that is, you happened to be Susan Maughan. Singers like Cilla Black and Lulu started out as honorary rockers, fronting male groups, before being encouraged to stand on their own two feet and then being tamed. Sandie Shaw cut out the apprentice stage and went straight from talent contest-cum-audition to doing what she was told by an imperious (female) manager. With the benefit of her wider experience in both the Lana Sisters and the Springfields behind her, Dusty Springfield broke free from the most conventional 'showbiz' background of them all when she went solo. Yet sooner or later they all ended up in much the same place, losing whatever edge they had once had in the tradition of another era entirely, subservient to the narrow cabaret format of their own respective TV series or, even worse, being turned into Eurovision fodder.

Even though I wanted to do them justice, they proved more self-effacing and difficult to write about than I imagined, the problem being compounded by the paucity of relevant research material that extended across the piece as far as many of the British acts were concerned. I was by no means dependent on the internet but the predominance of American entries on Wikipedia, for example, very soon became apparent and looking to put more flesh on the bones of British performers of the period often proved frustrating. In addition, several British niche websites that I discovered when I began my research have closed down in the interim. In that regard, at least, the music of the Sixties embodies a high degree of lost, if not now irretrievable, heritage. By way of compensation, I was surprised to find not just how much of a personal research archive I already possessed in my own library and record collection, sub-consciously laying down over fifty years or thereabouts the foundations for this project, but also how much more I could still source by way of other books and audio-visual material to fill in the gaps. (Even so, autobiographical and biographical accounts of the period by musicians and those who worked with them are only helpful up to a point, for their recollections are often highly selective and their memories in some instances notoriously unreliable.) In this regard, the propensity in recent years for record companies to release remastered extended editions of classic Sixties' albums or anthologise the long-unavailable output of lesser known artists, with comprehensive liner notes, has been a godsend, proving that it is still possible by bringing scholarship to bear on it to add substantial value to the music of the period.

None of this music existed in a vacuum and this for me is the key point of dispute with the revisionists. You cannot claim to understand Sixties' pop if you do not or will not appreciate that: a) it was composed and recorded in an historical context specific to the performer and producer, and b) once released, it was bought and heard in an historical context specific to the listener. Throwing it all in the air and letting it land as one agglomerate mass labelled 'The Sixties' (i.e., circa roughly 1967) obscures rather than illuminates. As a straightforward example, to assess the full impact of "Telstar" by the Tornados in 1962, you need to know that Joe Meek was obsessed with space and that the record celebrated the launch of the first communications satellite, an event itself part of a greater whole, five years on into the space race between the USA and USSR. Without that background knowledge, it exists merely as a decorative piece of early electronic experimentation but is otherwise completely meaningless.

The admitted difficulty comes in the persistent non-convergence of music and matters of moment for almost the entire decade; although by the time you get to Woodstock, the dimensions of politics and pop are almost within touching distance of each other. This is where preserving as far as possible the chronology of the period comes into play, recognising the distinction, for example, between the incidental music of the Macmillan years (a panacea for the masses in a time of plenty) and that of the Wilson era (a valuable contribution both to the export industry and tax revenues, as well as a flag-carrier for Britain, an enhancer of domestic political prestige and a popular adjunct to the promised technological revolution). Nor is it possible to discount the all-pervasive influence of US culture. It was a revelation to uncover the persistently high saturation rate of American music in the UK charts, to the extent that so many records thought of for years as quintessentially British hits, especially – but by no means exclusively – at the height of Merseybeat, turned out to be cover versions of US originals; as it was to examine the subjugation of British interests in the American adoption of our headline acts during the 'British Invasion', and the vehemence with which American acts in turn then sought to reassert themselves over here. As for the wider impact of international affairs, the Sixties decisively promoted American concerns above our own, whilst simultaneously making them our concerns too: why else would our news media have been so preoccupied with the space race, the Cold War, the Presidency, political assassinations, the civil rights movement, the Vietnam War …?

Compared to the music of the Fifties, in the fullness of time that of the Sixties brought us a hitherto unimagined embarrassment of riches in its boundless diversity of genre and regionality, of depth and colour; and as we continue on our headlong dash into the future, so the Sixties increasingly seem, in Ian MacDonald's words, "like a golden age to us because, relative to now, they were".[7] Where Cliff Richard and the Shadows could not have carried it off on their own, the release of "Love Me Do" in 1962 and the subsequent promotion of the Beatles effectively marked the rebirth of the British music industry. Without those events, we would never otherwise have witnessed the group phenomenon that specifically characterised the next four years; and on the back of that came the ever-widening exploration of possibilities, melodically and instrumentally, passing well beyond the earlier constrictions of the three-minute single.

While the guitar may have remained the instrument of choice overall and technical proficiency upon it held in high regard by performers and listeners alike, its augmentation by other sounds – some imported from other cultures, some artificially created by the growing sophistication of electronics and embryonic computerisation – grew incrementally from the mid-Sixties onwards. There was also demonstrable innovation lyrically, forsaking at last the meaningless doo-wop drivel of the Fifties, for which the Beatles and Bob Dylan between them must take prime credit as the inaugural architects of pop's transformation into the new poetry of the twentieth century. Love might always be the one constant theme; but as the decade unfolded, it offered unprecedented scope for gaining a multitude of insights into the human condition through the emotive power of song.

Although the ability of Sixties' music to move mountains always remained tantalisingly out of reach, and at its worst it made you cringe, at its best it could take your breath away *and* make you think, be it as entertainment with an agenda or just pure entertainment. "Much have I travell'd in the realms of gold" [8] in the effort to tell its story: I hope that as a result you too have caught a glimpse of the wealth it still has to offer the intrepid explorer.

NOTES

1   Quoted in Phil Sutcliffe, "The Dream Is Over", article in Paul Trynka (ed.), "John Lennon: *Mojo* Special Edition" (Winter 2000), p.46.

2   Jeani Read for the *Vancouver Province*, quoted in Graeme Thomson, "George Harrison: Behind The Locked Door" (Omnibus, 2013), p.275.

3   Quoted in Graeme Thomson, op. cit., p.276.

4   Quoted in liner notes to *Pink Floyd: Is There Anybody Out There? – The Wall Live 1980-81* [EMI, 2000].

5   Ibid.

6   A persistently seminal influence, it seems: check out Hank playing Brian Bennett's composition "Maggie's Samba" on *Established 1958*, the tenth anniversary album of Cliff and the Shadows, and then listen to the title track of Eric Clapton's 2001 album *Reptile*.

7   Ian MacDonald, op. cit., p.33.

8   John Keats, *On First Looking Into Chapman's Homer*.

Acknowledgements

All song lyrics referred to in the text are quoted solely for the purposes of criticism and review. Although every effort has been made to cite the current copyright-holders in the relevant notes accompanying each chapter, the author will be pleased to rectify any omissions from, or undertake corrections to, any attributions as necessary on their being brought to his attention.

Unless otherwise stated, all UK chart positions are taken from the relevant *NME* Top 30 charts as collated in "40 Years of *NME* Charts", by Dafydd Rees, Barry Lazell and Roger Osborne (Boxtree, 1992), since these were not only the ones I followed myself in the Sixties and thus had the strongest influence on my own record purchases, but were also the ones most contemporary artists of the period themselves held in the highest regard.

Alternative placings credited to the composite *Record Retailer* charts are taken from the Official Chart Company's "Virgin Book of Top 40 Charts" (Virgin, 2009). Separate UK EP and LP chart placings are taken from the relevant listings in: a) "The Complete Book of The British Charts: Singles and Albums", by Neil Warwick, Jon Kutner and Tony Brown (Omnibus, 3rd edition, 2004), and b) "The Virgin Book of British Hit Albums", edited by Martin Roach for the Official Chart Company (Virgin, 2009). I am further indebted to Sharon Mawer's "Official Album Chart History" (as published in 2007 on the Official Chart Company website www.theofficialcharts.com) for additional details of the sales of UK LPs within and across years.

All US chart positions are taken from the relevant listings in "The *Billboard* Book of Top 40 Hits" by Joel Whitburn (Billboard, 9th edition, 2010).

I should also record here my thanks to the Brierlow Bar Bookstore, near Buxton in Derbyshire, for its unusually comprehensive collection of remaindered books both past and present on pop music, from which I was repeatedly able to make significant additions of reference works to my own library.

I gratefully acknowledge the specific contribution of my cousin Gaynor Wiltshire, who took the time and trouble to share with me her memories of attending the Beatles' concert at the Birmingham Hippodrome in November 1963, even to the extent of passing on to me her copy of that night's programme for my archives; as well as that of my daughter Claire, whose encouragement as critical friend I truly valued at key stages of this project.

Finally, I wish to express my particular gratitude to M-Y Books, in the persons of managing editor Jonathan Miller and designer/typesetter David Stockman, for their support and assistance in bringing this book's publication to fruition; and conclude in the hope that one day the outcome may entice my granddaughters Sophie and Molly respectively to acquaint themselves with a bygone era through my eyes.

Bibliography

Books

Abbott, Kingsley – 500 Lost Gems of the Sixties [Ovolo, 2008].

Aldrin, Buzz, with Abraham, Ken – Magnificent Desolation: The Long Journey Home from the Moon [Bloomsbury, 2009].

Allen, Frank – Travelling Man: On The Road with The Searchers [Aureus, 1999].

Allen, Frank – The Searchers and Me: A History of the Legendary Sixties Hitmakers [Aureus, 2009].

Appy, Christian G. – Vietnam: The Definitive Oral History Told from All Sides [Ebury Press, 2006].

Attenborough, David – Life on Air: Memoirs of a Broadcaster [BBC, 2003].

Badman, Keith – The Beatles After the Break-Up 1970-2000 [Omnibus, 1999].

Badman, Keith – The Beach Boys [Backbeat, 2004].

Barrow, Tony – John, Paul, George, Ringo & Me [Andre Deutsch, 2nd edition, 2011].

Beatles, The – The Beatles Anthology [Cassell, 2000].

Beatles, The - The Beatles Lyrics [Omega, 1975]

Bell, Ian – Once Upon A Time: The Lives of Bob Dylan [Mainstream, 2013].

Bennett, Alan; Cook, Peter; Miller, Jonathan & Moore, Dudley – The Complete *Beyond The Fringe* [Methuen, 1987].

Black, Cilla – What's It All About? [Ebury Press, 2003].

Blackburn, Tony – Poptastic: My Life in Radio [Cassell Illustrated, 2007].

Blaney, John – Beatles For Sale: How Everything They Touched Turned to Gold [Jawbone, 2008].

Boyd, Joe – White Bicycles: Making Music in the 1960s [Serpent's Tail, 2005].

Braun, Michael – Love Me Do: The Beatles' Progress [Penguin, 1964].

Brocken, Michael – Bacharach: Maestro! The Life of a Pop Genius [Chrome Dreams, 2003].

Brown, Peter & Gaines, Steven – The Love You Make: An Insider's Story of The Beatles [Macmillan, 1983].

Burdon, Eric, with Craig, J. Marshall – Don't Let Me Be Misunderstood [Thunder's Mouth Press, 2001].

Cadbury, Deborah – Space Race [Fourth Estate, 2005].

Caine, Michael – What's It All About? [Century, 1992].

Carlin, Peter Ames – Catch A Wave: The Rise, Fall and Redemption of The Beach Boys' Brian Wilson [Rodale, 2006].

Celmins, Martin – Peter Green: The Authorised Biography [Sanctuary, 3rd edition, 2003].

Chaikin, Andrew – A Man on the Moon: The Voyages of the Apollo Astronauts [Michael Joseph, 1994].

Chapman, Graham et al. – Monty Python's Flying Circus: Just The Words Vol.1 [Methuen, 1989].

Clapton, Eric, with Sykes, Christopher Simon – Eric Clapton: The Autobiography [Century, 2007].

Clayson, Alan – Call Up The Groups! [Blandford, 1985].

Clayson, Alan – Beat Merchants [Blandford, 1995].

Clayson, Alan & Ryan, Jacqueline – Rock's Wild Things: The Troggs Files [Helter Skelter, 2000].

Clayson, Alan – The Yardbirds [Backbeat, 2002].

Clayson, Alan – Keith Moon – Instant Party: Musings, Memories and Minutiae [Chrome Dreams, 2005].

Clayson, Alan – The Rolling Stones: The Origin of the Species [Chrome Dreams, 2007].

Clayton, Ian – Bringing It All Back Home [Route, 2007].

Cohn, Nik – Awopbopaloobop Alopbamboom: Pop from the Beginning [Pimlico, 2004].

Coleman, Ray – Clapton: The Authorised Biography [Pan, 1995].

Cott, Jonathan (ed.) – Dylan on Dylan: The Essential Interviews [Hodder, 2007].

Creasy, Martin – Legends on Tour: The Pop Package Tours of the 1960s [Tempus, 2007].

Creasy, Martin – Beatlemania! The Real Story of the Beatles UK Tours 1963-1965 [Omnibus, 2010].

Cross, Charles R. – Room Full of Mirrors: A Biography of Jimi Hendrix [Sceptre, 2006].

Cross, Colin, with Kendall, Paul & Farren, Mick – Encyclopedia of British Beat Groups & Solo Artists of the Sixties [Omnibus, 1980].

Davies, Dave – Kink: An Autobiography [Boxtree, 1996].

Davies, Hunter – The Beatles: The Authorised Biography [Heinemann, 1968].

Davies, Ray – X-Ray [Penguin Viking, 1994].

Davies, Ray – Americana: The Kinks, The Road and The Perfect Riff [Virgin, 2013].

Davis, Sharon – Dusty: An Intimate Portrait of Dusty Springfield [Sevenoaks, 2008].

DeGroot, Gerard – The Sixties Unplugged: A Kaleidoscopic History of a Disorderly Decade [Pan, 2009].

Delaney, John – The UK 45 rpm Sleeves: A Collector's Guide to 7" Record Company Sleeves [Premium, 2013].

Doggett, Peter – *Abbey Road/Let It Be*: The Beatles [Schirmer, 1998].

Doggett, Peter – You Never Give Me Your Money: The Battle For The Soul Of The Beatles [Bodley Head, 2009].

Dolenz, Micky & Bego, Mark – I'm A Believer: My Life of Monkees, Music, and Madness [Cooper Square, 2004].

Dylan, Bob – Writings and Drawings [Jonathan Cape, 1973].

Dylan, Bob – Lyrics 1962-2001 [Simon & Schuster, 2004].

Dylan, Bob – Chronicles (Volume One) [Pocket Books, 2005].

Egan, Sean – Animal Tracks – The Story of the Animals: Newcastle's Rising Sons [Helter Skelter, 2001].

Egan, Sean – Not Necessarily Stoned, but Beautiful: The Making of *Are You Experienced* [Unanimous, 2002].

Egan, Sean (ed.) – The Mammoth Book of The Beatles [Robinson, 2009].

Egan, Sean (ed.) – The Mammoth Book of Bob Dylan [Robinson, 2011].

Egan, Sean – Animal Tracks – The Story of the Animals: Newcastle's Rising Sons [Askill Publishing, revised edition, 2012].

Egan, Sean (ed.) – The Mammoth Book of The Rolling Stones [Robinson, 2013].

Einarson, John – Forever Changes: Arthur Lee and the Book of Love [Jawbone, 2010].

Eliot, Marc – Paul Simon: A Life [Wiley, 2010].

Elliott, Martin – The Rolling Stones Complete Recording Sessions 1962-2012: 50th Anniversary Edition [Cherry Red Books, 2012].

Emerson, Ken – Always Magic in the Air: The Bomp and Brilliance of the Brill Building Era [Fourth Estate, 2006].

Epstein, Brian – A Cellarful of Noise [Four Square, 1965].

Evans, Mike – Rock & Roll: Facts, Figures & Fun [Facts, Figures & Fun, 2006].

Ewbank, Tim & Hildred, Stafford – Roger Daltrey: The Biography [Piatkus, 2012].

Faith, Adam – Acts of Faith [Bantam, 1996].

Faithfull, Marianne, with Dalton, David – Faithfull [Penguin, 1995].

Faithfull, Marianne, with Dalton, David – Memories, Dreams and Reflections [Harper Perennial, 2008].

Fiegel, Eddi – Dream a Little Dream of Me: The Life of 'Mama' Cass

Elliot [Pan, 2006].

Fornatale, Pete – Back to the Garden: The Story of Woodstock [Touchstone, 2009].

Frame, Pete – Rock Family Trees [Omnibus, 1993].

Frame, Pete – The Beatles and Some Other Guys: Rock Family Trees of the Early Sixties [Omnibus, 1997].

Frost, David – An Autobiography: Part One – From Congregations to Audiences [Harper Collins, 1993].

Gambaccini, Paul; Rice, Tim & Rice, Jonathan – Top 40 Charts [Guinness, 1992].

Geldof, Bob – Is That It? [Penguin, 1986].

Goldman, Albert – The Lives of John Lennon [Bantam, 2nd edition, 1989].

Gould, Jonathan – Can't Buy Me Love: The Beatles, Britain and America [Piatkus, 2008].

Gray, Michael – The Bob Dylan Encyclopedia [Continuum, 2006].

Greenwald, Matthew – Go Where You Wanna Go: The Oral History of The Mamas & The Papas [Cooper Square, 2002].

Hancock, Freddie & Nathan, David – Hancock [BBC Ariel, 1986].

Hansen, James R. – First Man: The Life of Neil Armstrong [Simon & Schuster, 2005].

Harper, Colin – Dazzling Stranger: Bert Jansch and the British Folk and Blues Revival [Bloomsbury, 2nd edition, 2006].

Harrison, Olivia – George Harrison: Living in the Material World [Abrams, 2011].

Hasted, Nick – The Story of The Kinks: You Really Got Me [Omnibus, 2011].

Hastings, Max & Jenkins, Simon – The Battle for The Falklands [Michael Joseph, 1983].

Heller, Joseph – Catch-22 [Corgi reprint, 1967].

Hendrix, Janie L. (ed.) – Jimi Hendrix: The Ultimate Lyric Book

[Backbeat, 2012].

Hendrix, Jimi (ed. by Douglas, Alan & Neal, Peter) – Starting at Zero [Bloomsbury, 2013].

Herr, Michael – Dispatches [Picador, 1978].

Hewitt, Paolo & Hellier, John – Steve Marriott: All Too Beautiful … [Helter Skelter, 2004].

Hewitt, Paolo – The Small Faces: The Young Mods' Forgotten Story. [Acid Jazz, revised edition, 2010].

Heylin, Clinton – Revolution in the Air {The Songs of Bob Dylan Vol.1: 1957-73} [Constable, 2009].

Heylin, Clinton – Bob Dylan: Behind The Shades [Faber, 3rd edition, 2011].

Hill, Tim – The Beatles: Then There Was Music [Transatlantic, 2010].

Hinman, Doug – The Kinks: All Day and All of the Night [Backbeat, 2004].

Hjort, Christopher – Strange Brew: Eric Clapton & The British Blues Boom 1965-1970 [Jawbone, 2007].

Hjort, Christopher – So You Want To Be A Rock'N'Roll Star: The Byrds Day-By-Day 1965-1973 [Jawbone, 2008].

Houghton, Mick – Becoming Elektra: The True Story of Jac Holzman's Visionary Record Label [Jawbone, 2010].

Howes, Paul – The Complete Dusty Springfield [Reynolds & Hearn, 3rd edition, 2010].

Howlett, Kevin – The Beatles: The BBC Archives 1962-1970 [BBC, 2013].

Hultkrans, Andrew – *Forever Changes* [Continuum '33 1/3' series, 2003].

Jackson, Laura – Brian Jones [Piatkus, 2nd edition, 2009].

Jovanovic, Rob – God Save The Kinks: A Biography [Aurum, 2013].

Keeler, Christine, with Thompson, Douglas – Secrets and Lies [John Blake, 2012].

Kelly, Mike – 50 Years of Hits: An International A to Z of Hitmakers

1952-2002 [Southgate, 2002].

Kerr, Gordon – Timeline of the Sixties [Canary Press, 2009].

Knightley, Phillip & Kennedy, Caroline – An Affair of State: The Profumo Case and the Framing of Stephen Ward [Jonathan Cape, 1987].

Kon, Andrea – This Is My Song: A Biography of Petula Clark [Comet, 1984].

Larkin, Colin (ed.) et al. – The Guinness Who's Who of Sixties Music [Guinness, 1992].

Larkin, Colin (ed.) et al. – The Virgin Encyclopedia of Sixties Music [Virgin, 1997].

Larkin, Colin (ed.) et al. – The Encyclopedia of Popular Music [Omnibus, 5th concise edition, 2007].

Laurence, John – The Cat From Hue [Publicaffairs, 2002].

Lawrence, Sharon – Jimi Hendrix: The Man, the Magic, the Truth [Pan, 2006].

Lefcowitz, Eric – Monkee Business: The Revolutionary Made-for-TV Band [Retrofuture, 2013].

Leigh, Spencer – Twist and Shout! Merseybeat, The Cavern, The Star-Club and The Beatles [Nirvana, 2004].

Leigh, Spencer – The Cavern: The Most Famous Club in the World [SAF, 2008].

Leigh, Spencer – It's Love That Really Counts: The Billy Kinsley Story [Cavern City Tours, 2010].

Leigh, Spencer – The Beatles in Hamburg: The Stories, The Scene and How It All Began [Omnibus, 2011].

Leigh, Spencer – The Beatles in Liverpool: The Stories, The Scene, and The Path to Stardom [Omnibus, 2012].

Leigh, Spencer – The Beatles in America: The Stories, The Scene, 50 Years On [Omnibus, 2013].

Leitch, Donovan – The Hurdy Gurdy Man [Century, 2005].

Lennon, Cynthia – John [Hodder & Stoughton, 2005].

Levy, Shawn – *Ready Steady Go!* Swinging London and the Invention of Cool [Fourth Estate, 2002].

Lewisohn, Mark – The Complete Beatles Chronicle [Pyramid, 1992].

Lewisohn, Mark – The Beatles: All These Years – Vol.1: Tune In [Little, Brown, 2013].

Long, Pat – The History of The *NME*: High Times and Low Lives at the World's Most Famous Music Magazine [Portico, 2012].

Loog Oldham, Andrew – Stoned [Vintage, 2001].

Loog Oldham, Andrew – 2Stoned [Vintage, 2003].

Lovell, Jim & Kluger, Jeffrey – Apollo 13 [Mariner, 2006].

Lulu – I Don't Want to Fight [Time Warner, 2003].

McAleer, Dave – Beatboom! Pop Goes The Sixties [Hamlyn, 1994].

McAleer, Dave – The Fab British Rock'n'Roll Invasion of 1964 [St. Martin's, 1994].

McAleer, Dave – Hit Singles: Top 20 Charts from 1954 to The Present Day [Backbeat, 5th edition, 2004].

McAleer, Dave (intro.) – The Virgin Book of Top 40 Charts [Virgin/ Official UK Charts Co., 2009].

McDermott, John, with Kramer, Eddie & Cox, Billy – Ultimate Hendrix: An Illustrated Encyclopedia of Live Concerts and Sessions [Backbeat, 2009].

McLuhan, Marshall & Fiore, Quentin – The Medium is the Massage: An Inventory of Effects [Penguin, 1967].

McNab, David & Younger, James – The Planets [BBC, 1999].

MacDonald, Ian – Revolution in the Head: The Beatles' Records and the Sixties [Fourth Estate, 2nd edition, 1997].

Maclear, Michael – Vietnam: The Ten Thousand Day War [Thames Methuen, 1981].

Marcus, Greil – Invisible Republic: Bob Dylan's Basement Tapes [Picador, 1998].

Marcus, Greil – Like A Rolling Stone: Bob Dylan At The Crossroads

[Public Affairs, 2006].

Martin, George, with Pearson, William – Summer of Love: The Making of Sgt. Pepper [Macmillan, 1994].

Mercer, Derrik (ed.) et al. – Chronicle of the 20th Century [Longman Chronicle, 1988].

Miles, Barry – Paul McCartney: Many Years From Now [Henry Holt, 1997].

Miles, Barry – The British Invasion: The Music, The Times, The Era [Sterling, 2009].

Miles, Barry – Hippie [Bounty, 2nd edition, 2013].

Morgan, David – Monty Python Speaks! [Fourth Estate, 1999].

Murray, Charles Shaar – Crosstown Traffic: Jimi Hendrix and Post-War Pop [Canongate, 3rd edition, 2012].

Nash, Graham – Wild Tales: A Rock & Roll Life [Penguin Viking, 2013].

Neill, Andy & Kent, Matt – Anyway Anyhow Anywhere: The Complete Chronicle of The Who 1958-1978 [Virgin, 2007].

Neill, Andy – The Beatles Across The Universe: John, Paul, George and Ringo On Tour and On Stage [Haynes, 2009].

Norman, Philip – Shout! The True Story of The Beatles [Elm Tree, 1981].

Norman, Philip – The Stones [Elm Tree, 1984].

O'Brien, Lucy – Dusty [Pan, 2000].

Orton, Joe – Loot [Eyre Methuen, 1975 reprint].

Orwell, George – The Road to Wigan Pier [Penguin, 1963 reprint].

Page, Bruce; Leitch, David & Knightley, Phillip – Philby: The Spy Who Betrayed A Generation [Sphere, revised edition, 1977].

Palmer, Robert – Dancing in the Street: A Rock and Roll History [BBC, 1996].

Peel, John & Ravenscroft, Sheila – Margrave of the Marshes [Corgi, 2006].

Pennebaker, D.A. – *Bob Dylan: Dont Look Back* [Transcript, New Video Group Inc., 2006].

Pepper, Terence & Savage, Jon – Beatles to Bowie: The 60s Exposed [National Portrait Gallery, 2009].

Perry, George – The Life Of Python [Pavilion, 1994].

Platt, John – *Disraeli Gears*: Cream [Schirmer, 1998].

Povey, Glenn – Echoes: The Complete History of Pink Floyd [3C, 2008].

Pressley, Alison – The 50s and 60s: The Best of Times [Michael O'Mara, 2003].

Priore, Domenic – Riot on Sunset Strip: Rock'n'Roll's Last Stand in Hollywood [Jawbone, 2007].

Pritchard, David & Lysaght, Alan – The Beatles: An Oral History [Allen & Unwin, 1999].

Quantick, David – Revolution: The Making of the Beatles' White Album [Unanimous, 2002].

Rawlings, Terry – British Beat 1960-1969: Then, Now and Rare [Omnibus, 2002].

Read, Mike – The Story of the Shadows [Elm Tree, 1983].

Read, Piers Paul – The Train Robbers [Coronet, 1979].

Rees, Dafydd; Lazell, Barry & Osborne, Roger – 40 Years of *NME* Charts [Boxtree, 1992].

Repsch, John – The Legendary Joe Meek: The Telstar Man [Cherry Red Books, 2008].

Reynolds, Anthony – The Impossible Dream: The Story of Scott Walker and The Walker Brothers [Jaw Bone, 2009].

Ribowsky, Mark – The Supremes: A Saga of Motown Dreams, Success and Betrayal [Da Capo, 2009].

Richard, Cliff, with Junor, Penny – My Life, My Way [Headline Review, 2009].

Richards, Keith, with Fox, James – Life [Weidenfeld & Nicholson, 2010].

Roberts, David – Rock Atlas [Clarksdale, 2011].

Roberty, Marc – Eric Clapton, Day By Day: The Early Years, 1962-1983 [Backbeat, 2013].

Rodriguez, Robert – Revolver: How The Beatles Reimagined Rock'n'Roll [Backbeat, 2012].

Rogan, Johnny – Timeless Flight: The Definitive Biography of The Byrds [Square One, 3rd edition, 1991].

Rogan, Johnny – The Byrds: Timeless Flight Revisited – The Sequel [Rogan House, 1997].

Rogan, Johnny – Byrds: Requiem For The Timeless Vol.1 [Rogan House, 2012].

Rolling Stones, The - The Rolling Stones Concise [Wise Publications/ EMI Music Publishing Ltd., 1991].

Rotolo, Suze – A Freewheelin' Time: A Memoir of Greenwich Village in the Sixties [Aurum, 2008].

Royle, Trevor – The Best Years of Their Lives: The National Service Experience 1945-63 [Coronet, 1988].

Rushby, Chris – Bob Dylan – The Illustrated Biography [Transatlantic Press, 2009].

Russo, Greg – Mannerisms: The Five Phases of Manfred Mann [Crossfire, 1995].

Sandbrook, Dominic – Never Had It So Good: A History of Britain from Suez to the Beatles [Abacus, 2006].

Sandbrook, Dominic – White Heat: A History of Britain in the Swinging Sixties [Abacus, 2007].

Sandford, Christopher – The Rolling Stones: Fifty Years [Simon & Schuster, 2012].

Santelli, Robert – The Bob Dylan Scrapbook 1956-1966 [Simon & Schuster, 2005].

Scaduto, Anthony – Bob Dylan: An Intimate Biography [W.H. Allen, 1972].

Sculatti, Gene – The 100 Best-Selling Albums of The 60s [Igloo, 2005].

Shaw, Sandie – The World at My Feet: A Personal Adventure [Fontana,

1992].

Shawcross, William – Sideshow: Kissinger, Nixon and the Destruction of Cambodia [Fontana, 1980].

Shelton, Robert – No Direction Home: The Life & Music of Bob Dylan [Omnibus, revised/updated edition, 2011].

Shephard, Alan & Slayton, Deke – Moon Shot: The Inside Story of America's Race to the Moon [Virgin, 1994].

Simon, Paul – Lyrics 1964–2008 [Simon & Schuster, 2008].

Smith, Andrew – Moondust: In Search of The Men Who Fell to Earth [Bloomsbury, 2005].

Sounes, Howard – Down The Highway: The Life of Bob Dylan [Black Swan, 2002].

Sounes, Howard – FAB: An Intimate Life of Paul McCartney [Harper, 2011].

Southall, Brian – The A-Z of Record Labels [Sanctuary, 2nd edition, 2003].

Southall, Brian – Jimi Hendrix: Made In England [Clarksdale, 2012].

Southall, Brian – Drive My Car: 100 Objects That Made The Beatles **The Beatles** [SevenOaks, 2013].

Spence, Simon – Immediate Records: Labels Unlimited [Black Dog, 2008].

Strong, Martin C. (ed.) et al. – The Great Rock Discography [Canongate, 4th edition, 1998].

Strong, Martin C. (ed.) et al. – The Great Folk Discography Vol.1: Pioneers and Early Legends [Polygon, 2010].

Stubbs, David – Jimi Hendrix: The Stories Behind Every Song [Carlton, 2nd edition, 2010].

Summers, Anthony – Conspiracy: Who Killed President Kennedy? [Fontana, 1980].

Summers, Anthony – Goddess: The Secret Lives of Marilyn Monroe [Victor Gollancz, 1985].

Summers, Anthony & Dorril, Stephen – Honeytrap [Coronet, 1988].

Sweeting, Adam – Cover Versions: Singing Other People's Songs [Pimlico, 2004].

Taylor, Derek – It Was Twenty Years Ago Today [Bantam, 1987].

Thompson, Ben (ed.) – Ban This Filth! Letters from the Mary Whitehouse Archive [Faber, 2012].

Thompson, Gordon – Please Please Me: Sixties British Pop, Inside Out [Oxford, 2008].

Thompson, Harry – Peter Cook: A Biography [Hodder & Stoughton, 1997].

Thomson, Graeme – George Harrison: Behind The Locked Door [Omnibus, 2013].

Townshend, Pete – Who I Am [Harper Collins, 2012].

Turner, Alwyn W. – Halfway to Paradise: The Birth of British Rock [V&A, 2008].

Turner, Alwyn W. – My Generation: The Glory Years of British Rock [V&A, 2010].

Turner, Steve – Cliff Richard: The Bachelor Boy [Carlton, 2009].

Upshall, Michael (ed.) et al. – The Sixties [Helicon, 1994].

Vat, Dan van der & Whitby, Michelle – Eel Pie Island [Frances Lincoln, 2009].

Verrone, Richard Burks & Calkins, Laura M. – Voices from Vietnam [David & Charles, 2005].

Walker, John & Gary – The Walker Brothers: No Regrets – Our Story [John Blake, 2009].

Warwick, Neil; Kutner, Jon & Brown, Tony – The Complete Book of The British Charts: Singles and Albums [Omnibus, 3rd edition, 2004].

Wells, Simon – Butterfly On A Wheel: The Great Rolling Stones Drugs Bust [Omnibus, 2011].

Welsh, Bruce – What About Us? A Rocklopaedia of Britain's *Other* Recording Groups 1962-1966 [M-Y Books, 2012].

Wenner, Jann – Lennon Remembers: The *Rolling Stone* Interviews

[Penguin, 1972].

Whitburn, Joel – The *Billboard* Book of Top 40 Hits [Billboard, 9th edition, 2010].

Whitehouse, David – One Small Step: The Inside Story of Space Exploration [Quercus, 2009].

Wolfe, Tom – The Right Stuff [Bantam, 1981].

Wyman, Bill, with Havers, Richard – Rolling with the Stones [Dorling Kindersley, 2002].

Young, Rob – Electric Eden: Unearthing Britain's Visionary Music [Faber, 2010].

Magazine & newspaper articles

Beaumont, Mark – Interview with Paul McCartney, *NME*, 12th September 2009.

Blake, Mark (ed.) – *Psychedelic!: Q/Mojo Special Edition* [February 2005].

Brown, Mark – "Beatles to Bowie", *The Guardian*, 26th June, 2009.

Clarke, Tony – Obituary, *The Times*, 23rd January 2010.

Clayson, Alan – Interview with Billie Davis ("Me And My Shadow"), *Record Collector* No.389, June 2011.

Clayson, Alan – "Life of Pie", *Record Collector* No.423, January 2014.

Cohen, Elliot Stephen – Interview with Carol Kaye ("Ace Of Bass"), *Record Collector* No.386, March 2011.

Egan, Sean – Interview with Bill Harry ("In The Beginning: The Beatles And Me"), *Record Collector* No.368, November 2009.

Egan, Sean – "Highway 61 Revisited: Bob Dylan", *Record Collector* No. 381, November 2010.

Harris, Jet – Obituary, *The Times*, 19th March 2011.

Harris, Paul – "By the time we got to Woodstock … it had become a museum piece", *The Guardian*, 15th August 2009.

Hart, Tim – Obituary, *guardian.co.uk*, 29th December 2009.

Hughes, Rob – "The Day The Music Died", *Record Collector* No.369, December 2009.

Humphries, Patrick – "Sixth Beatles and Other Tales", *Record Collector* No.401, May 2012.

Humphries, Patrick – "When I Was In My Prime", *Record Collector* No.413, April 2013.

James, Nick – "Pop Idle", *Record Collector* No.404, August 2012.

Leigh, Spencer – Interview with Helen Shapiro ("Helen of Joy"), *Record Collector* No.389, June 2011.

McBain, Hamish – Review of *Please Please Me*, *NME*, 12th September 2009.

McCann, Ian – Interview with Kenney Jones ("Afterglow Of Their Love"), *Record Collector* No.402, June 2012.

McCann, Ian – Interview with Jimmy Winston ("Real Crazy Times"), *Record Collector* No.402, June 2012.

Needs, Kris – "Brother From Another Planet", *Record Collector* No.380, October 2010.

Needs, Kris – "Faithfull Forever", *Record Collector* No. 385, February 2011.

Needs, Kris – Obituary: Bert Jansch, *Record Collector* No.395, December 2011.

Needs, Kris – "Axis All Areas", *Record Collector* No.405, September 2012.

Needs, Kris & Monck, Chip – "Back To The Garden", *Record Collector* No.367, October 2009.

Needs, Kris & Wilentz, Sean – "The Making of Bob Dylan", *Mojo*, December 2010.

Perrone, Pierre – "The Clapton Chronicles", *Record Collector* No.378, August 2010.

Quaife, Pete – Obituary, *guardian.co.uk*, 27th June 2010.

Reed, John – "A Is For Apple", *Record Collector* No.379, September 2010.

Sandoval, Andrew – "Face To Face", *Record Collector* No.406, October 2012.

Sandoval, Andrew – "Well Respected Men", *Record Collector* No.407, November 2012.

Sharp, Ken – "Hindsight is 20/20", *Record Collector* No.418, September 2013.

Shirley, Ian – "The Top 200 Rarest Records: The Ultimate UK Collectables", *Record Collector* No.382, December 2010.

Shirley, Ian – "The Record Rich List", *Record Collector* No.420, November 2013.

Solly, Bob – "Absolute Beginnings", *Record Collector* No.399, March 2012.

Solly, Bob – "One Day, All The World Will Hear", *Record Collector* No.409, Christmas 2012.

Stanley, Bob – "Snap judgments on the Sixties", *The Times*, 10th October 2009.

Staunton, Terry – Interview with Tony Hicks & Bobby Elliott ("It's Too Late To Stop Stop Stop Now"), *Record Collector* No. 374, April 2010.

Sutherland, Steve (ed.) – *1960s Swinging London: NME Originals* [Vol.1 Issue 11].

Trynka, Paul (ed.) – *John Lennon: Mojo Special Edition* [Winter 2000].

Unterberger, Richie – "The Making of Tim Buckley", *Record Collector* No.386, March 2011.

Warwick, Clint – Obituary, *independent.co.uk*, 3rd June 2004.

Watkins, Jack – "British Soul Power", *Record Collector* No.376, January 2012.

Welch, Chris – "Clapton: The Stuffed Bear Years", *Record Collector* No.378, August 2010.

Whitworth, Damian – "Sandie Shaw: Proud to be a Dagenham girl", *The Times*, 25th September 2010.

Wingate, Jonathan – Interview with Jurgen Vollmer ("The Beatles in Hamburg, 1961"), *Record Collector* No.387, April 2011.

Websites

www.adiebarrett.co.uk

www.allmusic.com

www.bethelwoodscenter.org

www.bobdylan.com

www.brianepstein.com

www.brumbeat.net

www.countryjoe.com

www.davemcaleer.com

www.discogs.com

www.en.wikipedia.org

www.everyhit.com

www.expectingrain.com

www.gingerbaker.com

www.hollies.co.uk

www.ibcstudio.co.uk

www.independent.co.uk

www.jananddean-janberry.com

www.johnnykidd.co.uk

www.judithdurham.com

www.kenhoward-alanblaikley.com

www.kindakinks.net

www.left-and-to-the-back.blogspot.com

www.mersey-beat.com

www.petulaclark.net

www.procolharum.com

www.radiorewind.co.uk

www.readysteadygirls.eu

www.sandieshaw.com

www.searchingforagem.com

www.sing365.com

www.sixtiescity.com

www.televisionheaven.co.uk

www.theband.hiof.no

www.theofficialcharts.com

www.the-searchers.co.uk

www.theseekers50th.com

www.thewho.com

www.ukrockfestivals.com

www.winwoodfans.com

www.woodstockmuseum.org

LP sleevenotes & CD liner notes

Alfonso, Barry et al. – *Morning Glory: The Tim Buckley Anthology* [Elektra/ Rhino, 2001].

Barnes, Richard – *The Who: Tommy* [Polydor, remastered edition, 1996].

Barrow, Tony – *With The Beatles* [Parlophone, 1963].

Barrow, Tony – *A Hard Day's Night* [Parlophone, 1964].

Barrow, Tony – *The Best Of Cilla Black* [Parlophone, 1968].

Bauldie, John - *Bob Dylan: The Bootleg Series Vols.1-3/(rare and unreleased) 1961-1991* [Columbia/Sony, 1991].

Black, Cilla et al. – *Cilla Black – Completely Cilla: 1963-1973* [EMI, 2012].

Bradford, Rob – *The Shadows At Abbey Road: The Collectors Edition* [EMI, 1997].

Bradford, Rob – *The Shadows Complete Singles As & Bs 1959-1980* [EMI, 2004].

Chacksfield, Tim – *Adam Faith: Complete Faith* [EMI, 2011].

Charlesworth, Chris – *My Generation – The Very Best Of The Who* [Polydor, 1996].

Crowe, Cameron & Dylan, Bob – *Bob Dylan: Biograph* [Columbia Legacy, 1985; remastered 2011].

Diken, Dennis – *The Lovin' Spoonful: Daydream* [Buddha/BMG Heritage, 2002].

Diken, Dennis – *The Lovin' Spoonful: Hums Of The Lovin' Spoonful* [Buddha/BMG Heritage, 2003].

Doggett, Peter – *Something Else By The Kinks* [Sanctuary, remastered deluxe edition, 2011].

Doggett, Peter – *The Kinks: Arthur Or The Decline And Fall Of The British*

Empire [Sanctuary, remastered deluxe edition, 2011].

Dopson, Roger – *Manfred Mann: The EP Collection* [See For Miles, 1989].

Dopson, Roger; Hatch, Tony & Viney, Tim – *The Searchers 30th Anniversary Collection 1962-1992* [Sequel, 1992].

Dopson, Roger – *The Rockin' Berries: They're In Town* [Sequel, 1998].

Dopson, Roger – *Humble Pie: Natural Born Bugie – The Immediate Anthology* [Immediate/Sequel, 2000].

Dopson, Roger – *The Red Bird Story* [Charly, 2011].

Dopson, Roger et al. – *The Searchers: Hearts In Their Eyes* [Universal, 2012].

Eder, Bruce – *The Rolling Stones Singles Collection: The London Years* [ABKCO, 1989].

Edmonds, Ben – *The Lovin' Spoonful: Do You Believe In Magic* [Buddha/BMG Heritage, 2002].

Edmonds, Ben – *Love: Forever Changes* [Rhino/Elektra, remastered edition, 2001].

Elliott, Bobby – *The Hollies At Abbey Road 1963 to 1966* [EMI, 1997].

Elliott, Bobby – *The Hollies At Abbey Road 1966 to 1970* [EMI, 1998].

Escott, Colin – *Bob Dylan: The Bootleg Series Vol.9/The Witmark Demos: 1962-1964* [Columbia Legacy, 2010].

Fielder, Hugh – *Cream: The Very Best Of Cream* [Polydor, remastered edition, 1995].

Fricke, David & Rogan, Johnny – *The Byrds: Mr. Tambourine Man* [Columbia Legacy, 1996].

Fricke, David & Rogan, Johnny – *The Byrds: Turn! Turn! Turn!* [Columbia Legacy, 1996].

Fricke, David & Rogan, Johnny – *The Byrds: Fifth Dimension* [Columbia Legacy, 1996].

Fricke, David & Rogan, Johnny – *The Byrds: Younger Than Yesterday* [Columbia Legacy, 1996].

Fricke, David & Rogan, Johnny – *The Byrds: The Notorious Byrd Brothers* [Columbia Legacy, 1997].

Fricke, David & Rogan, Johnny – *The Byrds: Sweetheart Of The Rodeo* [Columbia Legacy, 1997].

Fricke, David & Rogan, Johnny – *The Byrds: Dr. Byrds & Mr. Hyde* [Columbia Legacy, 1997].

Fricke, David & Rogan, Johnny – *The Byrds: Ballad Of Easy Rider* [Columbia Legacy, 1997].

Fricke, David – *Fleetwood Mac: Then Play On* [Warner/Rhino, remastered edition, 2013].

Frumento, Mark – *The Quiet Five: When The Morning Sun Dries The Dew* [RPM, 2005].

Glover, Tony – *Bob Dylan: The Bootleg Series Vol.4/Bob Dylan Live 1966: The "Royal Albert Hall" Concert* [Columbia Legacy, 1998].

Gorodetsky, Eddie & Kooper, Al – *Bob Dylan: The Bootleg Series Vol.7/No Direction Home: The Soundtrack* [Columbia Legacy, 2005].

Granados, Stefan – *The Mindbenders: A Groovy Kind Of Love – The Complete LP's & Singles 1966-1968* [RPM, 2010].

Greenwald, Matthew – *The Mamas & The Papas: All The Leaves Are Brown – The Golden Era Collection* [MCA, 2001].

Harry, Bill – *The Best Of The Fourmost* [EMI Gold, 2005].

Hewitt, Paolo – *Small Faces: The Decca Anthology 1965-1967* [Deram, 1996].

Hogg, Brian – *Gerry & The Pacemakers At Abbey Road 1963 to 1966* [EMI, 1997].

Hogg, Brian – *Rhythm & Blues At Abbey Road 1963 to 1967* [EMI, 1998].

Hogg, Brian – *Psychedelia At Abbey Road 1965 to 1969* [EMI, 1998].

Houghton, Mick & Nash, Graham – *The Hollies – Clarke, Hicks & Nash Years (The Complete Hollies April 1963-October 1968)* [EMI, 2011].

Howlett, Kevin – *The Beatles: 'Live At The BBC'* [Apple/EMI, 1994].

Howlett, Kevin – *The Beatles: 'On Air – Live At The BBC Volume 2'* [Universal/BBC, 2013].

Irwin, Colin – *The Pentangle: Basket Of Light* [Castle/Sanctuary, remastered edition, 2001].

Leigh, Spencer – *Herman's Hermits & Peter Noone: Into Something Good. The Mickie Most Years 1964-1972* [EMI, 2008].

Leigh, Spencer – *The Swinging Blue Jeans: Good Golly, Miss Molly! The EMI Years 1963-1969* [EMI, 2008].

Leigh, Spencer – *Billy J. Kramer with The Dakotas: Do You Want To Know A Secret? The EMI Years 1963-1983* [EMI, 2009].

Lewisohn, Mark – *The Beatles Anthology Vol.1* [Apple/EMI, 1995].

Lewisohn, Mark – *The Beatles Anthology Vol.2* [Apple/EMI, 1996].

Lewisohn, Mark – *The Beatles Anthology Vol.3* [Apple/EMI, 1996].

Lewry, Peter & Goodall, Nigel – *"The Young Ones" Soundtrack* [EMI, remastered edition, 2005].

Lewry, Peter & Goodall, Nigel – *"Summer Holiday" Soundtrack* [EMI, remastered edition, 2003].

Linett, Mark; Wilson, Brian & Leaf, David – *The Beach Boys: Pet Sounds* [Capitol, remastered edition, 1990].

McGuinness, Tom – *Manfred Mann At Abbey Road 1963 to 1966* [EMI, 1997].

McGuinness, Tom – *Manfred Mann: Down The Road Apiece – Their EMI Recordings 1963-1966* [EMI, 2007].

Marcus, Greil & Simmons, Michael – *Bob Dylan: The Bootleg Series Vol.10/ Another Self Portrait (1969-1971)* [Columbia, 2013].

Marsh, Dave & Neill, Andy – *The Who Sell Out* [Polydor, remastered deluxe edition, 2009].

Murdoch, Lorne – *Donovan: What's Bin Did And What's Bin Hid* [Castle/Sanctuary, remastered edition, 2001].

Murdoch, Lorne – *Donovan: Fairytale* [Castle/Sanctuary, remastered edition, 2001].

Murdoch, Lorne – *Donovan: Sunshine Superman* [EMI, remastered edition, 2005].

Murdoch, Lorne – *Donovan: Mellow Yellow* [EMI, remastered edition, 2005].

Murdoch, Lorne – *Donovan: The Hurdy Gurdy Man* [EMI, remastered edition, 2005].

Patrick, Mick – *Phil Spector Presents The Philles Album Collection* [Sony Legacy, 2011].

Paytress, Mark – *The Move: Move* [Salvo, remastered edition, 2007].

Phillips, John – *The World Of Wayne Fontana And The Mindbenders* [Spectrum, 1996].

Platt, John – *The Yardbirds: Yardbirds (aka Roger The Engineer)* [Diablo, remastered edition, 1998].

Powell, Mark – *The Moody Blues: Days Of Future Passed* [Deram, remastered expanded edition, 2008].

Rachel, Daniel – *The Kinks: Face To Face* [Sanctuary, remastered deluxe edition, 2011].

Reed, John – *The Spencer Davis Group: Eight Gigs A Week – The Steve Winwood Years* [Chronicles/Island, 1996].

Reed, John – *The Very Best Of The Moody Blues* [Polygram, 1996].

Reed, John – *The Moody Blues: Days Of Future Passed* [Deram/Decca, remastered edition, 1997].

Reed, John – *The Applejacks* [Cherry Red, 2009].

Reed, John – *The Big Three: Cavern Stomp – The Complete Recordings* [RPM, 2009].

Reed, John – *Lulu: Shout! The Complete Decca Recordings* [RPM, 2009].

Reed, John – *Dave Berry: This Strange Effect – The Decca Sessions 1963-1966* [RPM, 2009].

Reed, John – *Changes: The Story Of Beryl Marsden* [RPM, 2012].

Reed, John – *Amen Corner: Round Amen Corner – The Complete Deram Recordings* [RPM, 2012].

Ridley, Walter J. & Ennis, Ray – *The Swinging Blue Jeans At Abbey Road 1963 to 1967* [EMI, 1998].

Rounce, Tony – *Del Shannon: The Complete UK Singles (And More) 1961-1966* [Ace, 2013].

Rudland, Dean – *Georgie Fame: Mod Classics: 1964-1966* [BGP, 2010].

Ruhlman, William – *Donovan: Love Is Hot, Truth Is Molten – Original Essential*

Recordings 1965-1973 [Raven, 1998].

Sandoval, Andrew – *The Definitive Everly Brothers* [Warner, 2002].

Sculatti, Gene – *Woodstock: Music From The Original Soundtrack And More* [Cotillion/Rhino, remastered edition, 2009].

Sculatti, Gene – *Woodstock Two* [Cotillion/Rhino, remastered edition, 2009].

Shaw, Mike et al. – *The Who: My Generation* [MCA, remastered deluxe edition, 2002].

Simpson, Graham – *The Seekers: All Bound For Morningtown (Their EMI Recordings 1964-1968)* [EMI, 2009].

Solomon, George & Skurow, Andrew – *Diana Ross & The Supremes: 50th Anniversary – The Singles Collection 1961-1969* [Motown, 2011].

St. John, Mark – *The Pretty Things: S.F. Sorrow* [Snapper, remastered edition, 1998].

Stamp, Chris – *The Who: A Quick One* [Polydor, remastered edition, 1995].

Stanley, Bob – *Kinks* [Sanctuary, remastered deluxe edition, 2011].

Stanley, Bob – *Kinda Kinks* [Sanctuary, remastered deluxe edition, 2011].

Stanley, Bob – *The Kink Kontroversy* [Sanctuary, remastered deluxe edition, 2011].

Taylor, Derek – *Beatles For Sale* [Parlophone, 1964].

Tobler, John – *The Very Best Of The Four Pennies* [Spectrum, 1996].

Tracy, John – *The Very Best Of Marianne Faithful* [London, 1987].

Tracy, John – *Them: Them featuring Van Morrison* [London, 1987].

Tracy, John – *Jet Harris & Tony Meehan: Diamonds And Other Gems* [Deram, 1989].

Tracy, John – *The Zombies: Odessey And Oracle* [Repertoire, remastered edition, 2001].

Tracy, John – *The Moody Blues: The Magnificent Moodies* [Repertoire, remastered edition, 2006].

Trynka, Paul – *John Mayall with Eric Clapton: Blues Breakers (aka The Beano*

Album) [Deram, remastered edition, 1998].

Tyler, Kieron – *A-ha: 25* [Warner Brothers/Rhino, 2010].

Unattributed – *The Zombies: The Singles Collection As & Bs 1964-1969* [Big Beat, 2000].

Unattributed – *Bob Dylan* [Columbia/Sony, remastered edition, 2005].

Vernon, Mike – *Fleetwood Mac: Mr. Wonderful* [CBS 'Rewind', 1996].

Vernon, Mike – *Fleetwood Mac: Greatest Hits* [CBS, 30th anniversary edition, 1998].

Vernon, Mike – *Chicken Shack: The Complete Blue Horizon Sessions* [Blue Horizon, remastered edition, 2005].

Waters, Roger et al. – *Pink Floyd: Is There Anybody Out There? – The Wall Live 1980-81* [EMI, 2000].

Welch, Chris – *The Move: Hits And Rarities – Singles A's & B's* [Repertoire, 1999].

Welch, Chris – *The Nashville Teens: Tobacco Road* [Repertoire, 2000].

Wells, David – *The Small Faces: The Darlings Of Wapping Wharf Launderette – The Immediate Anthology* [Sequel, 1999].

White, Chris – *Goin' Back: The Very Best Of Dusty Springfield* [Philips, 1994].

Wilentz, Sean – *Bob Dylan: The Bootleg Series Vol.6/Bob Dylan Live 1964: Concert at Philharmonic Hall* [Columbia Legacy, 2004].

Williamson, Nigel – *The Rolling Stones: Singles 1963-1965* [ABKCO, 2004].

Wilson, Brian et al. – *The Beach Boys: The SMiLE Sessions* [Capitol, 2011].

Young, Jayne – *The Pentangle* [Wooden Hill/Transatlantic, 1996].

DVDs & DVD liner notes

Beatles, The – *Magical Mystery Tour* [Apple Films, remastered edition, 2012.]

Lerner, Murray – *The Other Side Of The Mirror: Bob Dylan Live At The Newport Folk Festival 1963-1965* [Sony/BMG, 2007], with liner notes by Piazza, Tom.

McDermott, John – *The Jimi Hendrix Experience: At Last ... The Beginning: The Making Of Electric Ladyland* [Experience Hendrix/Universal, 2008].

McDermott, John – *Jimi Hendrix: Live At Woodstock* [Experience Hendrix/Universal, 2008].

Palmer, Tony – *All My Loving* [Isolde, remastered edition, 2007].

Peck, David – *Gerry And The Pacemakers: It's Gonna Be All Right 1963-1965* [British Invasion, Reelin' In The Years, 2009], with liner notes by Harry, Bill.

Peck, David – *Herman's Hermits: Listen People 1964-1969* [British Invasion, Reelin' In The Years, 2009], with liner notes by Bowman, Rob.

Peck, David – *The Hollies: Look Through Any Window 1963-1975* [British Invasion, Reelin' In The Years, 2011], with liner notes by Fong-Torres, Ben.

Peck, David – *Small Faces: All Or Nothing 1965-1968* [British Invasion, Reelin' In The Years, 2009], with liner notes by Sharp, Ken.

Peck, David – *Dusty Springfield: Once Upon A Time 1964-1969* [British Invasion, Reelin' In The Years, 2009], with liner notes by Randall, Annie J.

Pennebaker, D.A. – *Bob Dylan: Dont Look Back* [65 Tour Deluxe Edition, Sony/BMG, 2006].

Rolling Stones, The – *Rock And Roll Circus* [ABKCO, 2004].

Rossacher, Hannes – *Sunshine Superman: The Journey Of Donovan* [SPV, 2008].

Scorsese, Martin – *No Direction Home: Bob Dylan* [Paramount, 2005].

Wadleigh, Michael – *Woodstock: 3 Days Of Peace And Music* [Warner, remastered Director's Cut, 2009].

INDEX

C

E

M

S

About the author

A confirmed audiophile since his early teens, when every week he would eagerly devour the *New Musical Express* from cover to cover, Tony Dunsbee has spent a lifetime listening to, reading about and collecting the popular music of the Sixties. Born and brought up in and around Birmingham, he entered teacher-training as a student of English and art, before spending eleven years teaching English, drama and library skills in secondary schools in Colchester and Warwick; experience on which he drew for his first book, *Mark My Words: A study of teachers as correctors of children's writing* (published in 1980). At the end of 1982, he exchanged teaching for a new career in local government as an education officer, in which capacity he worked as a middle manager in Warwickshire and Leicestershire for eighteen years, followed by a brief spell as a freelance educational consultant and inspector of special schools. In 2002 he became a senior manager in the field of professional regulation, from which position he retired in 2009 and decided the time was ripe to write *Gathered From Coincidence*.

Tony has been married for over forty years and lives in happy retirement with his wife in Leicestershire.